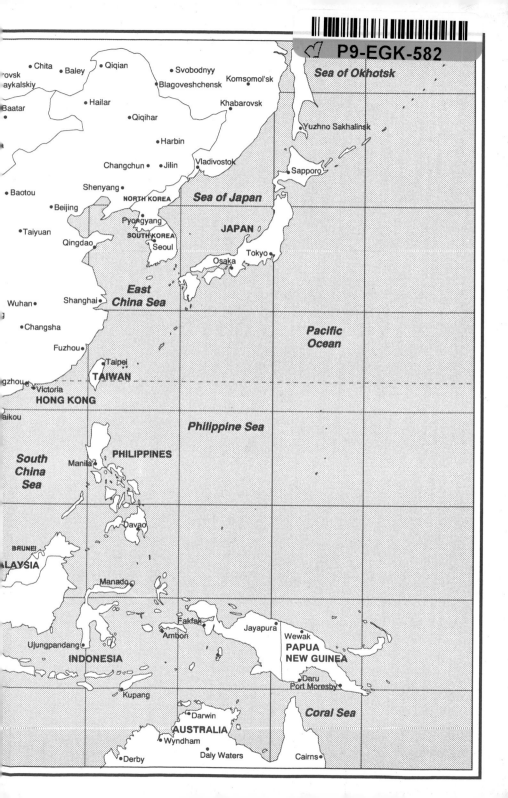

Doing Business in Asia

Doing Business in Asia

THE COMPLETE GUIDE

Sanjyot P. Dunung

LEXINGTON BOOKS
An Imprint of The Free Press
NEW YORK   LONDON   TORONTO   SYDNEY   TOKYO   SINGAPORE

Library of Congress Cataloging-in-Publication Data

Dunung, Sanjyot P.
    Doing business in Asia : the complete guide / Sanjyot P. Dunung.
    p. cm.
    Includes bibliographical reference and index.
    ISBN 0-02-907761-3
    1. Asia—Foreign economic relations. 2. Investments, Foreign—Asia. 3. International business enterprises—Asia. 4. Intercultural communication—Asia. 5. Foreign trade regulation—Asia. 6. Asia—Economic conditions—1945– I. Title.
    HF1583.D86   1995   94-42226
    658.8'48'095—dc20   CIP

Lexington Books
An Imprint of The Free Press
A Division of Simon & Schuster Inc.
1230 Avenue of the Americas
New York, N.Y. 10020

Printed in the United States of America

printing number
1   2   3   4   5   6   7   8   9   10

To my husband, for always believing in me,
and
To my parents, for encouraging me to always reach for the "stars"

Author's Note

The information in the book is true as of January 1995. Readers should note that addresses and telephone numbers can change frequently and therefore should be verified prior to usage. In the interest of improving future editions, I welcome comments, experiences, anecdotes, and general suggestions from readers.

Contents

Acknowledgments

I am grateful to the countless people around the world who in many different ways have touched my life and, directly or indirectly, this book as well. The collective efforts of the wide network of people who have contributed to this project far outweighs anything I have done myself.

The information provided in this book is not the opinion of any single person or source, but instead reflects a combination of written sources and the personal experiences of various individuals, only some of whom are noted below. I could not cover every issue or circumstance, and I extend my apologies up-front for any shortcomings and accept full and sole responsibility for any omissions or errors in this book.

Although it is impossible to note everyone who has shared their insights and experiences, I would like to thank the following people, who took the time to share their experiences, to read drafts of individual chapters, to graciously answer countless questions, and to painstakingly respond to my detailed questionnaires: James R. Aley, Fortune; Anshu Balbir, B & B; Paul Cunnion, Philippine American Chamber of Commerce; Jaspar De Fazio; Arvind R. Doshi, The Premier Automobiles; Michael R. Doyle, KPMG Peat Marwick; Craig Etcheson, Cambodia Campaign; Kenneth D. Felberbaum, Viam Communications Group; Virginia B. Foote, U.S.–Vietnam Trade Council; Wayne J. Forrest, American Indonesian Chamber of Commerce; Stephen Fox; Robert M. Gage, K & G Associates; A. R. Garde, Ahmedabad Textile Industry's Research Association; Linda Graves; Paul D. Griesse, Bry-Air, Inc.; Nobel Gulati, Raymond James; Vijay K. Gupta, Tata Telcom; Tim Gurney, British Information Services; Raj Hajela, Linkages; David C. Jenkins, Baskin-Robbins International Company; Vicente A.

Laza; John Meagher, General Construction Company; Jon Manns, PPG Industries; Ajit Mantagani, Arvind Mills; Radha Muthiah, Council on Foreign Relations; Nguyen Thi Thu Van, Russin & Vecchi; Rupande Padaki, The P & P Group; S. P. Patel, Ahmedabad Textile Industry's Research Association; Ambassador Nicholas Platt, The Asia Society; Kishor M. Pole, The Premier Automobiles; Fritz R. Rigoni, Swiss Bank Corporation; Miriam Marshall Segal, Peregrine Capital Management Ltd-MMAI; Julie Sell, The Chicago Group; H.R.H. Prince Sisowath Sirirath, Ambassador Extraordinary and Plenipotentiary and Permanent Representative of His Majesty the King of Cambodia to the United Nations; Sichan Siv, Commonwealth Associates; Sou Sorath, Permanent Mission of the Kingdom of Cambodia to the United Nations; Phoukhao Soulivong, Embassy of the Lao P.D.R.; Lewis Sperber; Richard S. Tam, Hong Kong Trade Development Council; Sesto E. Vecchi, Russin & Vecchi; and Vincent W. Yeh.

I am also grateful for the assistance of Lexpress International, a translation and interpretation agency, in Norwalk, Connecticut, for their efforts in translating key phrases.

I wish to express my gratitude to my friends and family, who have been supportive and understanding while this Herculean task of researching twenty countries consumed the better part of my time for almost a year. To my editor Beth and her assistant Charles, I extend my appreciation for all their efforts, particularly their patience in sifting through early drafts of this manuscript. I would like to thank Lynne Byrne, a close and treasured friend, for helping with the final editing.

To I. G., who had a greater impact on my life than she will ever know, I extend a special thank-you. By meeting with me years ago and treating me with dignity, not condescension, she taught me that we are all equal human beings, no matter what we may or may not achieve in life.

To my parents, Prafulla and Vaijayanti, I extend my loving gratitude for never questioning the reality of my "dreams" and allowing me to explore the world with no boundaries. They instilled discipline around my creative spirit, and provided emotional and material support through every conceivable and imaginative venture.

I am deeply blessed to have one person as both my best friend and husband—Deepak. His undemanding love and support have provided me with comfort through difficult times and have encouraged me to fulfill my "childhood dreams." Without complaint, he patiently endured months of solitude while I labored endlessly on weekends and nights on this project. His everlasting enthusiasm and optimism renewed my wavering spirit in the many days of frustration and exhaustion. For all that and much more, I return my deepest gratitude and love.

To all the readers of this book, I hope that it is a valuable tool in promoting a long and rewarding relationship, professionally and personally, with Asia.

Introduction

By the year 2000, Asia alone is expected to account for half of the annual growth in world trade. For global companies this means that, if they want to participate in the expansion of trade, they must do business with Asia. Although there are significant differences among Asian countries in terms of their individual economic growth potentials and business prospects, there is no denying that the Asian economies comprise a significant global force today and will be even more significant in the future. Asia has become a huge magnet attracting all types of global businesses, either as a source of cheap labor and raw materials or because of the potential market offered by Asia's enormous population. The twenty Asian countries covered in this book account for approximately three billion people, representing 54 percent of the population of the 185 member countries of the United Nations.

During the past two decades, individual Asian nation economies, often referred to as the "Asian Tigers," have experienced extraordinary rates of growth. Other Asian nations who have been slower in reforming their economies are just beginning to enjoy similar benefits. Regardless of when and how the respective economic expansion began, all of the Asian countries are and will continue to be the focus of global investors for several decades to come.

It is common to find people who are interested in doing business with a country simply because they have read that it is the new, "hot" economy. Yet they know nothing about the country, its history, evolution of thought, people, or how things are generally handled in business and social contexts.

To conduct business with people from other cultures, you must put aside preconceived notions and strive to learn about the culture of your counterpart. Often the greatest challenge is learning not to apply your own value system to people from other cultures. It is important to remember that there is no right and wrong when dealing with other people, just differences. Concepts like morality and time are viewed differently from place to place, and the smart business professional will seek to understand the rationale underlying another culture's concepts.

Cultural issues and understanding will affect your ability to enter a local market, develop and maintain business relationships, negotiate successful deals, conduct sales, marketing and advertising campaigns, and engage in manufacturing and distribution. Too often, people send the wrong signals or receive the wrong messages, and as a result, become tangled in the cultural web. In fact, there are numerous instances where deals would have been successfully completed if finalizing them had been based on business issues alone. Just as you would conduct a technical or market analysis, you should also conduct a cultural analysis.

It is critical to know the history and politics of any country or region in which you work or with which you intend to deal. Particularly in Asia, assuming an American–European ethnocentric attitude will get you nowhere. As a result of its recent economic successes, Asia has a renewed sense of pride in its own culture and mind-set. In the current economic climate, this decade has been touted as the "Asian Decade," leaving most Asians with a somewhat inflated view of their part of the world. As Asia's prosperity increases, Asians' willingness to tolerate condescension or ignorance by Westerners has rapidly diminished. It is important to remember that to each person, his or her "sphere" or "world" is the most important, and hence their center. As a result of decades of global focus on Europe and the United States, Asians have more factual knowledge of American and European history and modern social issues than the reverse. Asians expect Westerners to reciprocate in their knowledge, and often view those having little familiarity with Asia as intellectually inferior.

Many Asians find American and European business styles confrontational and demanding. Americans surprise Asians by being so up-front and quick to give information. Europeans, while somewhat more discreet, still tend to be too matter-of-fact for the Asian professional. Asians, on the other hand, tend to hold back information because they do not like to present negative news, are wary of letting foreigners in, or because by selectively controlling the flow of information they can maintain control of the negotiations. As a result, Westerners believe that it is difficult to conduct business with Asians and that their markets are difficult to penetrate.

In general, when considering doing business in Asia (or anywhere else for that matter) there are a number of steps to follow in order to learn about the region's history, culture, and people as well as determine the cultural suitability and overall business prospects for your product or service. The following is a brief series of development steps. Depending on your industry or product, you may need to undertake additional steps.

- Contact the Asian country's commercial office within its embassy or consulate in your home country. If the country does not have a trade office in your home nation, contact the respective diplomatic offices. Even tourist offices can provide you with general information about a country.
- Contact the chamber of commerce for that country in your home country. In the United States, there are two types of chambers: American Chambers of Commerce (located in numerous countries) and binational Chambers of Commerce offices (located in the United States). The primary difference between the two organizations is their location. Both organizations seek to facilitate business interactions between the United States and the respective country, often collaborating on specific projects. The American Chambers of Commerce (AmCham) are affiliated with the U.S. Chamber of Commerce. A list of overseas AmCham offices can be obtained by calling the United States Chamber of Commerce in Washington D.C. at (202) 659-6000. Both types of offices are noted at the end of each chapter under addresses.

- Contact the U.S. Department of Commerce / International Trade Administration office in your state and in Washington, D.C., or the respective trade office in your home country and speak with the desk officer for the country of interest. In the United States, general trade information can be obtained by calling 1-800-USA-TRAD. General information on Pacific Rim countries can be obtained by fax through the PacRim Hotline (Tel. 202-482-3875), which provides trade and economic statistics as well as summaries of other business-related issues. Press 1000 on your telephone to receive a menu of the different reports. The hotline provides information on Cambodia, China, Hong Kong, Indonesia, South Korea, Laos, Malaysia, the Philippines, Singapore, Taiwan, Thailand, and Vietnam, as well as other Pacific Rim countries.

- Contact export promotion agencies in Washington, D.C., your home state, or home country. In the United States, this could include the Overseas Private Investment Corporation (OPIC) and the Ex-Im Bank.

- Find out if your home state or city has a "sister" state/city relationship with specific places in Asia.

- If possible, conduct a fact-finding trip to your country of interest. Participate in any delegations or trade missions that the U.S. Commerce Department, your local chamber of commerce office, or other trade organizations sponsor.

- Develop a relationship with your home country's embassy and commercial service office in the Asian country. Twice a year, the United States Department of State publishes *Key Officers of Foreign Service Posts: Guide for Business Representatives*. Call (202) 783-3238 for an annual subscription (US$5).

- Contact the your home nation's Chamber of Commerce in the foreign country of interest. Utilize the expatriate community located within that country, as well as those who have recently returned to your home country as sources for valuable information about the country and its business climate and practices.

- Attend trade shows in the country of interest. Most of these shows are organized by industry; schedules are available through the country's trade or diplomatic offices.
- Be creative. Find common connections with companies in the country or with those individuals who have experience doing business in the country or with the specific company with which you are dealing. For example, perhaps a supplier or client company or individual that you interact with also does business in the Asian country. Talk to natives from the Asian country who live in your home nation. Even if there is no direct business application for the information you glean from such sources, you will be able to gather a great deal of cultural and social information that you may be able to put to good use.

Recognize that some embassies, offices, and individual officers are better able to assist you in your efforts. For example, junior-ranking people who have spent more time in the local country are often more insightful and knowledgeable than senior officers with less in-country experience. Over time and through research and references, you will learn which officers have the most experience and knowledge. As a safety measure, double check all information with at least two independent sources. Conversely, the Asian embassies in your home country may differ in their degree of responsiveness to foreign interest. Do not automatically assume that the embassies or trade representatives of the larger and "high-demand" countries are more efficient or helpful. Each chapter in this book includes a section that lists potentially useful contacts.

Building relationships with government officials and private business-people from each country takes time. Do not wait until you are ready to enter a country or are bidding for a contract before you visit the country or join the local chamber of commerce and other trade groups. To promote your long-term interests, develop relationships with as many people as possible and learn as much as you can about local procedures and policies. Be ready to demonstrate how your project and company can benefit the local country. Offers of assistance for local companies and worker training are generally well-received by the governments and private industry.

When researching and selecting partners, exercise caution and make sure that there is mutual business compatibility. Make sure that your potential partner is credible, reputable, financially sound, and technically capable of living up to their side of an agreement. Pay close attention to the local business history, as well as to the political relationships, of your potential partner. In most cases, your local partner will be responsible not only for day-to-day operations, but for the management of your company's reputation. Failure to select carefully may lead to the failure of the venture and a squandering of resources.

Every culture has its share of unscrupulous businesspeople. However, maintain your business sense and listen to your instincts. Posture yourself in a culturally acceptable manner in terms of communications style and verbal and physical gestures. Understand the trigger points or "hot buttons" for that culture. If you are dealing with government officials, take the time to research their political priorities and objectives before you seek a face-to-face meeting. The more you are able to address *their* objectives and concerns verbally or in the terms of a proposal, the easier it will be for you to gain approvals and contracts. Remember to be discreet and tactful in any verbal discussions, particularly with government officials.

Even if you have been invited to bid on a contract, you are still trying to sell your company and youself. Do not be patronizing or assume you are doing the Asian company or its government a favor. They must like and trust you if you are to succeed. Think about your own business encounters with people, regardless of nationality, who were condescending and arrogant. How often have you given business to people who irritated you?

In some countries, it can be almost impossible to get through the right doors without some sort of introduction. Be creative in identifying potential introducers. If you do not know someone who knows the company with which you would like to do business, consider indirect sources. Trade organizations, lawyers, bankers and financiers, common suppliers and buyers, consultants, and advertising agencies are just a few potential introducers.

It is difficult to make generalizations about any culture as there are always exceptions, nevertheless this book tries to provide some overviews of the characteristics of each Asian country. There is a common misconception that all Asian countries share the same *Asian* values, attitudes, and mind-set. To suggest that there is a pan-Asian mind-set is as ludicrous as to suggest a pan-European mind-set. The British and Italians, for example, share certain traits, but also exhibit significant differences resulting from the specific historical, religious, social, and philosophical traditions of their respective countries.

This book is intended to be a historical and cultural information resource. It will provide you with concise, comprehensive information about each country. The more you know about a country, the better. Combine this book with international periodicals and you will be in an excellent position to successfully interact with the people from a specific country. When choosing periodicals, be sure to pick a variety of journals published in different countries. Periodicals should represent American, various European, and also Asian views. For the latter viewpoint, the *Far Eastern Economic Review* is one excellent resource. Most Asian countries have their own news and business periodicals that provide in-depth information about that country's marketplace. Be careful that the local government does not censor or control the publication. Further, understand the local government's unofficial attitudes toward the media. Some publishers may self-censor just to remain in print.

Readers will note that the history section in each chapter is the longest. I hold to the firm belief that the key to understanding people begins with an understanding of "what" created and influenced them. How mind-sets have evolved over history provides the basis for cultural understanding. Westerners, Americans in particular, often view the world from a post–World War II perspective. For Asians these brief fifty-some years since World War II are just a small speck in their long and complex histories. It is also important to remember that for some Asian countries their present borders are relatively new. As a result, this affects Asia's mix of cultural attitudes, for many people in different Asian countries share common cultures, and at times similar rivalries and tensions.

It is also important to understand the major Asian religions, the basis for the area's values and customs. Language is a secondary, but still important, factor. It is impossible to become fluent in any language overnight, and you should not be overly concerned about your language capabilities. While it helps to learn some phrases and to show an interest in your host country's language, you must be careful about pronunciation: some Asian languages are tonal languages and the same word spoken with a different tone can have various meanings. For example, in Mandarin, the sound *ma*, depending on the inflection, can mean "mother," "horse," "hemp," "numb," or "to scold." If you do business in several countries, it is unlikely that you will be conversant in each language. However, if you are focused on one country, it is a significant advantage to try to learn the language.

Verbal language aside, body language and the packaging of information must be treated with sensitivity. People may not understand your words, but they will certainly interpret your body language according to *their* accepted norms. It is *their* perceptions that will count when you are trying to do business with them. Forbidden body interactions include no social kissing, although Western-exposed Asians may attempt to engage in this, and not using the left hand, for it is considered unclean because it is used to clean oneself after defecating. Do not use the left hand alone to greet someone or to pass food or other items. Asians also consider it rude to point at someone. Beckon by using the whole hand, palm facing down and fingers pointing away from you, but moving toward you in a scratching motion.

When negotiating with people from a different culture, try to understand your counterpart's position and objectives. This does not imply that you should compromise easily or be "soft" in your style. Rather, understand how to craft your argument in a manner that will be culturally more effective. For example, in most Asian cultures calm voices are highly valued. Do not distract your counterpart by being loud and overbearing. When negotiating a contract or venture, it is often best to send a more entrepreneurial manager to negotiate the terms, as he or she will usually be more flexible and creative. Each country has different constraints, including the terms of payment and regulations, and you will need to keep an open mind about how to achieve your objectives. Successful international companies of all sizes have found that giving their local manager or partner more authority, flexibility, and responsibility usually leads to more favorable terms in negotiations.

You may meet Asians who will insinuate that the West (in particular, you, the Western businessperson) owes them for centuries of exploitation and profiteering. It is as if the Asian feels that the Westerner has all the money and know-how and it is the Asian's *right* to collect. As might be expected, this attitude is more prevalent in the countries whose economies are lagging. In some countries, this notion that Westerners are wealthy is used as an indirect excuse to extract higher prices and more generous concessions from Western businesses, at times, by unscrupulous methods. There is a double standard throughout much of Asia. Westerners are expected to be prompt, to be efficient, to know everything, and to have unlimited financial resources. This double standard can make interactions difficult, especially for small foreign businesses with limited resources for travel, entertainment, or up-front financial investments in projects. At times, Asians can seem insensitive about other people's time and limitations. However, this results more from value differences, particularly concerning time.

There are several additional points to keep in mind. Understand your final objectives and prioritize your goals in order to avoid being delayed on less important issues. Understand local priorities and sensitivities, particularly if you are dealing with government officials. Do not accept the first offer quickly, for this may cause Asians to perceive you as an amateur. The art of negotiation is highly valued in most Asian countries. Avoid making concessions too quickly. Give yourself ample time to negotiate. Make sure your home office understands local timeframes and is supportive of your negotiation efforts.

Unless you are already transacting business, it is best not to communicate with Asia by fax: the transmissions can be illegible and potentially easy to ignore. Further, in some countries the cost of faxes can be prohibitive and will thus reduce your chances of timely responses. As with all business, plan thoroughly for a worst-case scenario, particularly with legal documents. The Asian preference for loosely crafted contracts may place you in an awkward position later. Many legal professionals recommend that you opt to use the international courts or a third-party arbitration system in case of a dispute. Translate contracts into both languages and have a second independent translator verify the copies for the accuracy of concepts and key terminology. But be warned: no translation can ever be exactly accurate as legal terminology is both culture- and country-specific.

Many foreigners are perplexed by Asian customs regarding gifts, tips, and graft. In many East Asian countries, gift giving is a well-defined and obligatory aspect of business and social interactions. In other Asian countries, gift giving is less structured and the line between it and graft easily becomes blurred.

Graft is a difficult issue to address, as there is no general solution because circumstances differ widely between each country. No doubt, dealing with corrupt officials and business people can be very costly. Nonetheless, it is sometimes a necessary part of doing business in certain countries. Thus each company must address the legal and business issues for itself. Develop a company policy for worldwide operations by being consistent between and within countries. Tolerating graft in one country and not in another will negatively affect your company's reputation for consistency. Keep in mind the legal climate limitations of your home country. The United States Foreign Corrupt Practices Act, which established strict definitions of graft and imposed serious penalties for violations of the act, often places American companies at a disadvantage. Many European, Japanese, and other Asian companies tend to have a more relaxed approach and often view graft as an expensive, but necessary part of doing business. Some European countries and Japan allow bribes made in foreign countries to be tax deductible under certain circumstances. Interestingly enough, these same countries do not legally permit bribes in their own countries.

This book is not intended to be a legal resource on this issue. You should consult with your legal and accounting experts. It is important to remember that graft is often present in developing countries worldwide. Corruption flourished when regimes and public officers in specific countries exercised monopoly power. Today, many of these same countries are undergoing political and economic transitions, and the chaotic conditions and weak governments in some nations have allowed even more opportunities for corruption to emerge. Most of the Asian governments are aware of the economically harmful effects of corruption on their countries and have taken measures to reduce the need for graft. Due to the differences in the stages of each nation's political and economic development, some countries have been more successful than others at curtailing corruption. When encountering graft situations, avoid taking a publicly visible, moral high ground, as your counterparts will consider your attitude to be condescending. Many Asians are often just as frustrated as Westerners by the extent of graft in their countries, but fear that noncompliance with the system may result in the loss of important business. Bribes and kickbacks often remain a critical determinant of how some governments and private businesses allocate their financial resources.

In some countries, tipping is a means of *getting* a particular job done rather than a reward offered for a job that *was* well done. In this context, the distinction between "tipping" and "graft" may become blurry. Giving a sum of money to a local person to ensure a train seat or to speed the installation of a telephone in a local office may be construed differently by individuals. In this book, "tipping" generally refers to monies paid for hotel and travel-related services after the fact. *Baksheesh*, or "grease money" as it is sometimes called, is addressed as part of a culture's expectations concerning the giving of "gifts" or graft.

There are some general guidelines for tipping for services in Asia. A few Asian societies find tipping an insult, for in these countries doing a good job is a matter of pride and duty. However, in most countries tipping is widespread, often because tips constitute the bulk of a person's income or because low salaries encourage people to find ways to supplement their income. Although money, local and foreign, is the most preferred form of a tip, in some countries you can tip by giving a pack of foreign cigarettes or another small gift. It is advisable to carry a lot of American currency in small bills, such as ones and fives, or the equivalent in your own country's currency if it is a widely accepted global currency.

Westerners should be prepared for Eastern values and etiquette. Saving face and maintaining honor and group harmony is important throughout the continent, although the extent varies between countries. In some countries, harmony in the group is more important than all other issues, in others less so. Remember that honest and frank comments must be worded politely in order to avoid offending anyone. On the flip side, Asians are not usually impressed by excessive compliments and may judge the person who offers profuse compliments to be insincere. Tradition and respect for seniority and elders is important, although the extent is changing in some countries. Asians generally tend to value wisdom and experience as well as low-key, nonaggressive approaches.

Handshakes are soft and less vigorous in Asia. Women may barely touch an offered hand. Do not assume your counterpart to be weak-minded just because of a limp handshake. Asians view the handshake as a courtesy made to Westerners, and are often unaware of the importance placed by Westerners on a firm grip. Further, the Asian handshake may linger longer than the traditional Western one, making it almost a handhold, or even may shake with both hands.

Asians tend to escort guests in all business and social situations to the outside door of an office or to the elevator. This indicates respect: how far you escort someone is dependent on their seniority and importance. Be sure to reciprocate the gesture, especially if you are hosting Asians in your home country. This is more common in dealings with East Asians, who tend to come from more structured cultures.

It is important not to judge Asians by American or European etiquette standards. Do not be offended if people do not say "Thank you," "Please," or "You are welcome." Asians express gratitude in different ways other than through verbal "Thank yous." In some countries people may try to return a favor at a later date or may inform others of your acts as a way to show respect for you. Excessive usage of the phrase "Thank you" may even be perceived as insincere or inappropriate by Asians. Depending on the situation, Asian responses can differ, as can Asian expectations. Use the general etiquette that you are accustomed to using in your own culture, combined with common sense and a degree of cultural understanding. In all Asian countries, never place your feet upon a table or chair regardless of how informal you think the setting is. To avoid cultural misunderstandings, refrain from all physical contact such as back-slapping.

In general, all Asian societies have retained their strict hierarchies. Managers do not socialize with junior-level people. Managers are placed on a pedestal and are expected to take care of the junior levels in exchange for their respect and loyalty. The role of women differs from country to country. In general, most Asian societies view women as secondary to men. In some countries, their position is more visibly inferior, in others it is less so. Given today's rapid economic and social changes, it is best not to make any assumptions about a female professional's role.

The importance of listening skills can never be overstated. Sometimes Westerners lose patience with the slow speed of the English language spoken by a non-native speaker. Even if you think you know the information already, *listen first*. You may hear a new perspective or angle. If nothing else, your counterpart will be pleased that you listened attentively.

It is important to make sure that your counterpart is a decision maker and not just someone who was appointed to meet with you because he or she speaks, reads, and writes in English or your native language. If your counterpart does not speak English, you will need to use a translator. Even if you know the language, it is always advisable to hire a translator. In addition to minimizing misunderstandings, a translator provides you with additional time to prepare a response while the discussion is being translated. Here are some tips for using translators:

- Whenever possible, educate your translator beforehand about the intricacies of your product and/or service. The translator's accuracy in translating may depend on the product/service knowledge that you provide him or her with beforehand. If you travel to a country frequently, you may want to hire the same translator so that over time he or she will become more cognizant of the technicalities of your business. In essence, your translator will be your most valuable marketing and presentation tool.

- Always use your own translator. Never rely on the translator of your counterpart, because that translator works for your counterpart and is more likely to protect his or her business interests. It is common and preferable to have a different translator represent each side during negotiations and meetings.

- Always face your business counterpart, not your translator. The translator is only there to facilitate your business interests. Your goal is to develop a business relationship and personal rapport with the local businessperson, despite your language differences.

- Recognize that the audio level in some of the Asian countries is lower than in Western conversations. If your translator is speaking softly, it may be considered normal. Do not ask him or her to speak louder, unless necessary. Similarly, make sure to speak at the same audio level as the others in a discussion. Often people speak very loudly when interacting with people who communicate in another language, subconsciously forgetting that there is a language barrier, and not a hearing one.

- Use short, simple sentences. Avoid use of slang, clichés, analogies, or idiomatic expressions that are specific to your language or culture. Westerners, particularly Americans, should be careful not to use sports analogies, as not all American sports are popular in Asian countries. Even concerning baseball, a popular sport in East Asia, analogies can be misinterpreted by your listeners and should be avoided.

- Pause after each sentence and allow the translator to translate it; otherwise, he or she may try to summarize groups of sentences. Speak about only one concept at a time.

- Avoid buzzwords and explain concepts thoroughly. For example, words like "empowerment" may not have a direct translation, and therefore the translator may translate parts of the word separately and most likely incorrectly. Instead of saying "MBO" or "management by objectives," explain exactly what you mean. This does not imply that your counterpart does not understand terms and concepts, but rather that these concepts may have different names in his or her culture. More importantly, the translator may not understand the intention or concept and may incorrectly translate the words.

- Ask direct questions and avoid double negatives to minimize confusion. It may be valuable to verify the cultural suitability of certain direct questions with your translator before the encounter. You may simply need to reword a question. The key to success is making sure that your translator understands the intention behind your questions.

Finally, there are a few travel-related miscellaneous pointers that many businesspeople have found to be important:

1. Always carry a battery-operated flashlight because power outages remain common in some Asian countries.
2. Carry an adapter for your personal appliances, particularly personal computers.
3. If you golf, take your own golf shoes. You can always rent golf clubs, but the right shoes are difficult to find, as Asian feet tend to be smaller than Western feet.
4. If you are approached by a beggar, never be rude, as that will reflect poorly on you. Politely decline to give anything while maintain a calm and low voice.
5. When placing international telephone calls while in each Asian country, use an international telephone company such as AT&T, MCI or Sprint by dialing the respective access code. The call will usually be cheaper. Each international phone company will supply you with a list of access codes to be used when dialing in that country.

   In general, the key words to dealing with Asia are "patience," "patience," and "patience." Flexibility and creativity are also important. You should focus on the end result and find unique ways to get there. Asians pride themselves on being able to take the long-term view, and you would be well advised to adopt the same approach. Make a long-term commitment to a market or country and then focus on the business specifics.

Doing
Business in
Asia

1 Japan

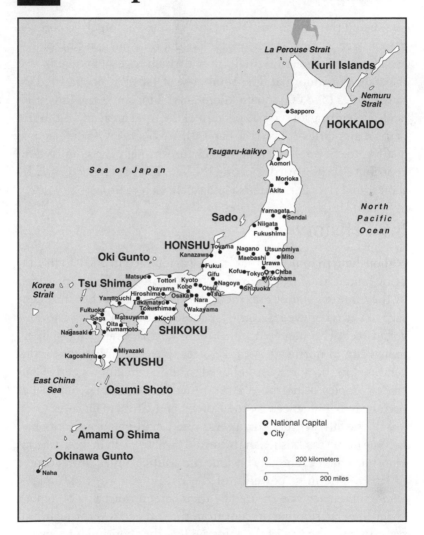

La Perouse Strait

Kuril Islands

Nemuru Strait

●Sapporo

HOKKAIDO

Tsugaru-kaikyo

Sea of Japan

Aomori

Morioka

Akita

Yamagata

Sado

Niigata ●Sendai

Fukushima

North Pacific Ocean

HONSHU Toyama Nagano Utsunomiya

Oki Gunto Kanazawa● Maebashi ●Mito

Urawa

Fukui Kofu ●Tokyo○ ●Chiba

Gifu Nagoya Yokohama

Matsue● Tottori Kyoto

Korea Tsu Shima Okayama Kobe ●Otsu Shizuoka

Strait Hiroshima● Osaka Tsu

Yamaguchi Nara

Fukuoka Takamatsu● Wakayama

Saga Tokushima● ●Kochi

Oita●

Nagasaki ●Kumamoto SHIKOKU

Matsuyama

Kagoshima● Miyazaki

KYUSHU

East China Sea Osumi Shoto

Amami O Shima

Okinawa Gunto

●Naha

○ National Capital
● City

0   200 kilometers

0   200 miles

1

Geography

Located off the east coast of Asia, the Japanese archipelago consists of four large islands—Honshu, Hokkaido, Kyushu, and Shikoku— and about four thousand small islands which together equal in size the state of California. The total area of Japan is about 146,000 square miles (378,000 square kilometers). Honshu is the largest island, accounting for over 60 percent of the total area, and is the site of the major cities Tokyo (the capital), Yokohama, Osaka, Nagoya, and Kyoto. Several volcanic ranges run through the country and contribute to its varied topography. The land is characterized by short, rapid rivers; mountains; and small, rich plains.

Brief History

Although myth indicates that Japan was founded in 660 B.C. by Emperor Jimmu, the first clear records concerning Japan are provided by the Chinese almost one thousand years later, in the third century A.D. It is believed that the Japanese are descendents of a Mongoloid race who migrated from the Asian continent, most likely from a site in northeast Asia or Korea. Japan's Ainu people, concentrated in the north, are believed to be descendants of early Caucasoid peoples of northern Asia. Since its beginnings, Japan has been heavily influenced by the Korean and Chinese cultures.

By the fifth century A.D. a centralized, clan-based authority had become firmly established in the fertile Yamato plain in west-central Honshu, which eventually became the political and cultural center of Japan. The most powerful of the rival clans was the Yamato, whose supremacy was ensured by their careful nurturing of a myth about the clan's divine descent from the sun goddess through Emperor Jimmu, the first of the imperial line that continues today.

During the sixth century A.D. various clans scattered over Honshu island formed a loose confederacy under the central political control of the modern city of Nara, which became the country's capital in 710. In the Nara period, as it is sometimes called, society and architecture were heavily influenced by the Chinese Tang period (A.D. 618–907). Buddhism became entrenched as the faith of the aristocracy, but Shintoism, the indigenous faith of Japan, remained popular at the grass roots level.

In 794 Heian (modern Kyoto) became the capital, marking the beginning of the Heian period, noted for its cultural sophistication in architecture, arts and literature. The well-known *Tale of Genji* (*Genji Monogatari*), written around A.D. 1000 by Lady Shikibu Murasaki, depicted life at the Kyoto court. Also during this period, *kana*, an indigenous phonetic alphabet, was created to supplement the Chinese characters that had been introduced in the fifth century through Korea. Politically, the salient feature of the Heian period was the dominance of the Fujiwara clan, the wealthiest and most influential of the aristocratic court families. Through political manipulation and intermarriage with the Yamamoto line, the Fujiwara clan controlled the imperial court from about 857 to 1160.

In the tenth century Fujiwara control of the central government began to decline and tensions between rival clans mounted. Fighting broke out between two warrior households, the Taira and Minamoto, with the Taira emerging as victors in 1160. However, Yoritomo, the heir of the defeated Minamoto leader, revolted and swept aside the Taira. The formal period of military overlord rule began in 1192, when Yoritomo of Minamoto established a new feudal system that was dominated by local powerful noble families and their samurai warrior retainers. Even today the samurai are known for their allegiance to military virtues, including self-discipline, bravery, and honor. Rather than face the humiliation of defeat, they often took their own lives. Emperors were relegated to a ceremonial role and true power was held by successive families claiming the title of *shogun*, which means "generalissimo of the emperor's army." Accordingly, family lineage, honor, and loyalty to the family holding the shogunate remained a key factor determining rank and prestige in medieval Japanese society.

The Yoritomo shogunate was based in the town of Kamakura and lasted until 1333. During this period the spirit of fighting, *bushi,* became popular and honorable among the samurai, much the same way as chivalry did in the West. This martial code benefited the Japanese during the Mongol invasions in 1274 and 1281, although it is generally believed that the weather was the more forceful deterrent. A severe typhoon in 1281 called the *kamikaze*, or "divine wind," helped to repel the Mongol invaders and further solidified Japanese belief in the divine uniqueness of their land.

Ashikaga, the next great shogunal dynasty, rose to power in 1333 and ruled until 1573. The dynasty's power was limited by disorder and political changes as it attempted to create a three-tier feudal system. Power became concentrated in the hands of regional feudal leaders, known as *daimyos*. The daimyos fought among themselves and in 1467 the Onon War ushered in a new era called "The Age of the Warring States" which lasted for almost a full century. Despite the fighting, the economy expanded as Japanese trade with its neighbors grew.

Prior to the first encounters with Westerners, Japan was primarily an agrarian economy. In about 1542 Portuguese traders reached Japan, bringing with them European missionaries. The Japanese rulers viewed these missionaries with suspicion because the Christian faith demanded allegiance to a foreign source of authority and threatened local loyalty.

In 1603 Tokugawa assumed the title of shogun, ending the country's political instability and beginning a period characterized by strict political control of the daimyos by the shogun. Further, a policy of strict international isolation was implemented to ensure that no foreign influence would undermine the dynasty. By the mid-1600s the potentially threatening foreign missionaries had been expelled and Japan thereafter cut itself off from most of the world for the next two hundred years. This isolation contributed to Japan's internal stability, although in terms of technology the country fell far behind the rest of the world.

The Japanese do not have a long history of experience with democratic principles. For most of its history, Japan was a feudal society that encouraged the inferior members of society to give absolute

obedience and loyalty to their superiors, whose authority stood un-
challenged by the lower levels. This attitude remains deeply imbed-
ded in all aspects of modern Japanese society.

By the mid-1800s Japan began to adopt some elements of the
democratic system. However, this did not result from any strong belief in the principles of democracy, but rather from the recognition
that only a strong and centralized Japan could meet the encroaching military and economic challenges of the West, which had already colonized the Indian subcontinent and taken over parts of
Southeast Asia. The Japanese recognized that they needed to adopt
the superior technology of the West and work to achieve military,
political, and economic equality with it if Japan was to preserve its
independent identity.

In general, democracy has spread smoothly throughout Japan.
Except for a temporary deviation from democracy during the mili-
taristic 1930s, Japan has slowly, but steadily, embraced democracy.
Because of Japan's slow and methodical transformation from a feudal society to a modern one, change in Japan has been evolution-
ary, not revolutionary. As a result, unlike many other countries,
Japan has experienced only gradual change in its political system
and national beliefs over the years.

Japan's political and military isolationist policy ended in the
mid 1850s with the signing of treaties with the United States, Great
Britain, Russia, France, and the Netherlands. In 1868 the Tokugawa
shogunate was overthrown by disaffected provincial lords, who restored a degree of political power to the emperor. The transformation of Japan from a feudal society to a modern state took place
under what is known as the Meiji Restoration, named after the Meiji
"year period" that began in 1868. Meiji also posthumously became
the name of the emperor of the time, who died in 1912. During the
Meiji period, Japanese society was transformed from one in which
status was primarily determined by heredity and family to one in
which the education and achievement of a person also became important factors. A primary goal of the Meiji leaders was to achieve

economic and military parity with the Western powers. In 1912, Meiji's son assumed the throne and took the name Taisho. In 1926 Taisho's son, Crown Prince Hirohito, became emperor.

Japan's modern expansionist strategy began in the 1890s when it tried to win military security from the West. In 1894–1895, the Japanese fought with China over control of Korea. After its victory, Japan asserted its hegemony over Korea and annexed Taiwan. Japan's early effort to annex the southern tip of Manchuria was aborted by Russia, which claimed the area for itself three years later. In 1904–1905 Japan fought Russia for control of Korea. Japan's victory enabled it to also acquire the southern tip of Manchuria, the southern half of the island of Sakhalin, and complete control of Korea, which was quietly annexed to Japan in 1910. By 1931 Japan occupied all of Manchuria.

As a result of these actions, Japan had become a major colonial power and *the* major power in the East. The goal of achieving full modernization in order to meet the West's economic and military challenges had been accomplished. Europe's preoccupation with World War I allowed Japan to continue its expansionist policies, gradually acquiring more of China. During World War II Japan seized Vietnam and other Asian territories. All along, the United States had refused to recognize Japan's conquests, but was unwilling to take any military measures to force Japan out of the occupied countries.

Hitler's threat in Europe combined with Japanese hegemony in East Asia and pacts between Japan, Germany, and Italy compelled the United States to impose limited economic sanctions on Japan in 1940. Japan's sneak attack on Pearl Harbor in 1941 finally forced the United States to go to war with Japan, culminating in the atomic bombings of Hiroshima and Nagasaki in 1945, which resulted in a huge military and psychological defeat for Japan. After the war, the Allied forces stripped Japan of all the territories it had acquired since 1894, including Korea, the Philippines, Vietnam, Singapore, Taiwan, and China.

The American Occupation of Japan following Word War II laid the foundation for today's modern economic and political society. The Occupation was intended to demilitarize Japan, to fully democratize the government, and to reform Japanese society and the economy. The Americans revised the then-existing constitution along the lines of the British parliamentary model. The Japanese adopted the new constitution in 1946 as an amendment to their original 1889 constitution. On the whole, American reforms rebuilt Japanese industry and were welcomed by the Japanese. The American Occupation ended in 1952 when Japan was declared an independent state.

As Japan became an industrial superpower in the 1950s and 1960s, other countries in Asia and the global superpowers began to expect Japan to participate in international aid and defense programs and in regional industrial-development programs. By the late 1960s Japan had the third largest economy in the world. However, Japan was no longer free from foreign influences. In one century, the country had gone from being relatively isolated to being dependent on the rest of the world for its resources with an economy reliant on trade.

Although Japan's international stature changed and expanded, there has been only one reigning family since its early beginnings. However, the emperors lost political power in the ninth century and thereafter became ceremonial symbols. Although little effort has been made to restore political authority to the emperor, most Japanese have some deep, although vague, respect for the imperial family. Since World War II, the emperor's functions have been symbolic, much the same as those of the royal family in the United Kingdom.

In the post–World War II period, Japanese politics has not been characterized by sharp divisions between liberal and conservative elements. The Liberal Democratic party (LDP), created in 1955 as the result of a merger of two of the country's biggest political parties, has been in power for most of the postwar period. The LDP, a major proponent of big business, generally supports the conservative viewpoint. The "Iron Triangle," as it is often called, refers to this tight relationship among politicians, bureaucrats, and big business leaders.

The lack of divergent political opinions as well as the Japanese preference for harmony and nonconfrontation has kept the LDP in power for so long. Until recently, the overwhelming success of the economy overshadowed other policy issues. Opposition parties focused instead on other less tangible issues such as individual rights versus big business and other authorities. The war left many Japanese deeply suspicious of authority and sensitive to acts in which the government showed little regard for the ordinary citizen.

By the 1980s the LDP was plagued by reports of corruption. However, the LDP was able to retain power because the peculiar Japanese political system gave rural voters more political weight than voters in urban areas, where the corruption was worse. In the late 1980s and the first half of the 1990s, Japanese politics were characterized by chaos as accounts of illegal political donations and bribery brought down several prime ministers and a series of scandals rocked the financial sector. In 1989 the LDP briefly lost power to a coalition led by the Social Democratic party (previously the Japanese Socialist party). Later the same year, the LDP regained power, first under Toshiki Kaifu, and then under Kiichi Miyazawa in 1991. The past few years have been marked by political confusion: new political coalitions have been created and prime ministers have changed frequently.

In the early 1990s Japan's political situation was aggravated by the effects of the global recession. Japan's bubble economy, characterized by overinflated values in the Japanese stock market and the Tokyo property market, burst. In contrast to the fast-paced 1980s, Japan, amid economic stagnation and political upheaval, was caught off guard, and business and public confidence decreased dramatically, slowing the country's economic momentum. Companies struggled to emerge from extended periods of losses and were forced to reevaluate certain corporate policies regarding lifetime employment, supplier networks, and decision-making processes. Despite the economic downturn, Japan continued to enjoy large trading surpluses with several nations, including the United States, whose negative trade balance with Japan remains a source of economic and political tension.

In August 1993 the LDP were finally voted out of power in what was considered a highly unusual turn of events for a country that prides itself on harmony at all costs. A coalition of reformists under the banner of the Japan Renewal party, headed by Morihiro Hosokawa, assumed power and were successful in pushing through electoral reform aimed at reducing the power of the farmers and giving more influence to the heavily populated urban areas. By mid-1994 the threat of scandal had ushered in two new prime ministers, Tsutomu Hata, head of a coalition party, and Tomiichi Murayama, leader of the Social Democratic party, whose election was the result of an LDP–Socialist alliance. Today's political system remains dominated by powerful, behind-the-scenes political bosses. The LDP, though out of office, continues to wield enormous power and exercises influence through various coalitions. Nevertheless, talk of political and economic reform dominates the political scene today.

Although Japan is a major international economic power, it is not always equated with the other major powers primarily because it is still prohibited from maintaining a military force. Japan's relations with the United States and the major European powers have been damaged by Japan's huge trade surpluses and what many Western countries claim to be Japan's unfair trading practices. Despite the speed of Japan's economic success over the past fifty years, the evolution of an intellectual revolution has been slow and gradual.

Regionally, Japan has been criticized for giving too little in outright economic and technical aid to neighboring Asian countries who have not prospered. Much of Japan's aid has been linked to obtaining advantages for Japanese business interests. As a result of both long-term and recent history, Japan's relationship with China remains a combination of immense respect with an equal amount of distrust. Other East Asian nations still view Japan with suspicion due to its brutal expansionist policies in the 1930s and during World War II. Nevertheless, Japanese businesses are looking to expand their commercial opportunities with China and other parts of Asia by investing in development.

Political Structure

Japan has been a parliamentary democracy since the 1889 constitution was signed. The government consists of executive, legislative, and judicial branches and functions similar to the system in the United Kingdom. The legislative power resides in the Diet, which consists of the House of Representatives (511 members) and the House of Councillors (252 members), both of which are elected by the citizens of Japan. The emperor, currently Emperor Akihito, is the official head of state, but has no governing authority.

The House of Representatives selects the prime minister from the majority party. The prime minister selects twenty-two members of the Diet from his party to form a cabinet that serves as an executive committee. The lower House of Representatives, elected for up to four years, retains the larger share of power. The House of Councillors, the upper house, is elected for six years with half its numbers up for reelection every three years.

The bulk of legislation is not produced by the Diet, but by the bureaucracy. In Japan, ministers and bureaucrats exert a great deal of power not only in the development of policy but the implementation as well. Cabinet members are usually appointed to head a ministry or agency for a very brief period of time and establish at most only general policy control over their ministries or agencies. Ministries and agencies are primarily made up of an organized corps of bureaucrats, most of whom are recruited from the best universities for lifelong prestigious careers. A vice-minister or vice-chief actually runs the ministry or agency. This situation is similar to the parliamentary systems of Europe and contrasts with the American system in which presidential appointees attempt to exercise much more control over branches of the bureaucracy on behalf of the president.

As a result, Japanese ministries and agencies have substantial identity and political voice. Further, their influence and power over policy often outlives the reign of any one prime minister. This is particularly evident with the powerful Ministry of International Trade and Industry, better known as MITI. For much of Japan's modern history, MITI has been responsible for establishing, coordinating, and regulating specific industry policies and targets as well as having control over foreign trade interests. Two other important ministries are the Ministry for Foreign Affairs and the Ministry for Finance, which is responsible for the nation's budget.

One important aspect of the Japanese political heritage is its long tradition of group rather than personalized leadership. This is also characteristic of Japanese decision making in all areas, including the business world. Even today, groups of elderly statesmen and party chiefs make the decisions, not individual prime ministers. This method of governing stands in stark contrast to the method in the United States and many other countries, where the president or the prime minister is directly responsible for setting the agenda for his or her term.

The Japanese judiciary is an independent branch of the government with powers equal to those of the executive and legislative branches. Japan's postwar constitution created a Supreme Court in which all judicial power resides. The court also has full authority to nominate lower court judges and to determine the constitutionality of all laws, similar to the U.S. system.

It should be noted that culturally the Japanese are not very litigious and generally prefer arbitration and compromise. The courts are used only as a last resort. This fits appropriately with their preference for nonconfrontation. Japanese courts do not have juries. Judges review only the facts and lawyers serve as advisers to the involved parties. In criminal cases, public prosecutors will not bring charges unless they have overwhelming evidence, which gives the courts a very high conviction rate.

It is important to understand, however, that the Japanese have a great deal of respect for laws, rules, and regulations. Private and public entities go to great lengths to observe all rules, even the most minute detail, corresponding directly to the methodical and meticulous nature of the Japanese.

Economy

Japan's post–World War II success has been the result of a well-crafted economic policy closely administered by the government in alliance with large businesses. Prior to World War II, giant corporate holding companies called *zaibatsu* worked in close cooperation with the government to promote specific industries. At one time, the four largest *zaibastu* organizations were Mitsui, Mitsubishi, Sumitomo, and Yasuda. Each of the four had significant holdings in the fields of banking, manufacturing, mining, shipping, and foreign marketing. Policies encouraged life-time employment, employer paternalism, long-term relationships with suppliers, and minimal competition. Today, the influence and control of the *zaibatsu* has greatly diminished, although some of their policies continue to have an effect on Japan. In recent times, the government and businesses, in response to global economic challenges, have recognized the need to restructure and deregulate parts of the economy, particularly in the financial sector.

Extensive international trade has made Japan heavily dependent on outside markets for raw materials and energy resources, as well as for customers from whom to earn the monies to pay for these and other goods. The Japanese are acutely aware of this interdependency. Japan has the second largest gross national product (GNP), the sum of the total goods and services produced including exports, in the world, the United States is first.

Japan has very few mineral and energy resources and relies heavily on imports, bringing in almost all of its oil, iron ore, lead, wool, and cotton. It is the world's largest importer of numerous raw materials including coal, copper, zinc, and lumber. Despite a shortage of arable land, Japan has gone to great lengths to minimize its dependency on imported agricultural products and foodstuffs such as grains and beef. The country's chief crops include rice and other grains, vegetables, and fruits. Japanese political and economic protectionist policies have ensured that the Japanese remain fully self-sufficient in rice, which is their main staple. For brief periods in recent years, the Japanese government has permitted the import of foreign rice to supplement low supplies of Japanese rice. This remains a politically and culturally controversial issue, as the Japanese perceive foreign rice to be inferior to Japanese rice. Only about 8 percent of the labor force is employed in agriculture-related work.

Manufacturing accounts for the greatest part of the country's output. Japan benefits from its highly skilled workforce. However, the high cost of labor combined with the cost of importing raw materials has significantly affected the global competitiveness of its industries. Japan excels in high-tech industries, particularly electronics and computers. Other key industries include automobiles, machinery, and chemicals. The service industry is beginning to expand and to provide high-quality computer-related services, advertising, financial services, and other advanced business services.

People, Values, and Social Customs

The population of Japan is approximately 125 million. Japan's population is homogeneous: 99 percent of its people are ethnic Japanese. The remaining percentage is composed of three minority groups: people of Korean descent; indigenous, but ethically distinct Ainu people; and outcast people (*burakumin*), who are ethnically and culturally Japanese, but who are considered social outcasts because of their historical association with trades involving blood and killing, for example, butchers, tanners, and shoemakers.

Japan's geographic isolation as an island nation has allowed the government to keep out foreign influences and to limit the Japanese people's interactions with other peoples and cultures. This policy has resulted in Japanese ethnocentrism and a high degree of cultural homogeneity. Throughout history the Japanese people have been very careful to maintain a distinction between things foreign and things Japanese. Until recently, their preference has always been for things

Japanese. This attitude is also evident in the way the Japanese treat people who are not ethnically Japanese. Such a person is a *gaijin*, a "foreigner" or "outsider." Even Koreans and members of other ethnic groups who have grown up in Japan are not viewed as "Japanese." Even today there are very strict immigration and citizenship rules intended to keep Japan's population as "Japanese" as possible.

Japan has been a secular nation for over three centuries. Its people are adherents of Shintoism, Buddhism, Christianity, and Confucian philosophy. Shintoism is a native Japanese religion that teaches respect for nature and counsels harmony between man and nature. Shinto gods (*kami*) are worshipped at shrines (*jinja*) which are distinguished by their red wooden archways. All objects and phenomena are considered to possess *kami*, and, as a result, there are many Shinto gods. Shintoism has been influenced by both Confucianism and Buddhism. Shinto was the national religion from the nineteenth century when the emperor was deified, until after World War II when the American Occupation forced the Japanese to desanctify the emperor and separate religion from the state. However, the emperor is still considered the spiritual head of the nation and is responsible for performing a variety of important rituals.

Confucianism, which was introduced in the fifth century A.D., heavily influenced Japanese society. Buddhism, which originated in India, came to Japan in about the sixth century A.D. via China and Korea. Christianity, brought to Japan in 1549 by Portuguese Catholic missionaries, was prohibited during much of the seventeenth and eighteenth centuries, but flourished again in the nineteenth century after Japan established ties with the United States and Europe. Today Christianity is practiced on a relatively small scale compared with the Eastern religions. Nevertheless, due to its importance in the West, the Japanese are curious about Christianity and mark Christmas with commercial decorations and Christmas carols. The Japanese view Christians as people of high morals and are impressed by the firmness of their beliefs. In modern times, the Japanese have adopted Western ethical attitudes, many of which are associated with Christianity.

Most Japanese would not characterize themselves as religious, either by practice or in belief. The Japanese do not usually visit places of worship on a daily or weekly basis. They are more likely to have a small place of worship, such as an altar in their home, where they pay their respects on a more regular basis. They also participate in rituals for special occasions such as births, weddings, and deaths. Many follow the beliefs and practices of different religions for different life events.

Because the Japanese are generally nonconfrontational, they prefer to establish unaminous consensus when making decisions. They believe in maintaining harmony even at the expense of truth and honesty. Moreover, as in many other Asian countries, "saving face" and maintaining dignity is absolutely critical in every situation. Rather than risk becoming a social outcast, a Japanese person will obey those with greater age, seniority, social position, political position, or rank at work. In fact, there is very little room in society for individuality, as people are "rewarded" for blending completely into groups.

The Japanese are methodical and meticulous in their approach to most situations in both social and business situations. They tend to enjoy following procedures and are not known for their flexibility in bending rules. This is one reason the Japanese have excelled in areas such as manufacturing and producing high-quality products. However, throughout history, the Japanese people have also proven to be rather practical and unsentimental about the past. Always resilient, the Japanese have shown a willingness to gradually adapt to new situations and ideas over long periods of time.

In recent years, Japanese society has seen a slight shift toward more individualistic attitudes. Young Japanese seek to take more control of their lives; for example, they are not as likely to agree to an arranged marriage. They also want to enjoy leisure time with their families and are willing to change employers to achieve a better balance between their professional and personal lives. Professionally, the Japanese are no longer willing to give complete, blind loyalty to their employers. Nevertheless, upholding the honor and respect of the family name remains an obligation for all family members.

Japan remains a male-dominated society to this day. The old Confucian adage that a woman should obey her father in youth, her husband in maturity, and her son in old age is still widely followed. Women continue to be the primary, and in most cases, the sole caregiver to children and elderly parents. Generally they are homemakers and managers of the household budget. Young women often work in companies as tea ladies, but then quit once they become engaged or married. This situation is gradually changing as more women continue working after marriage. Most companies continue to delegate menial or "lower" tasks to women. However, Japanese women are gradually becoming more assertive, both politically and socially.

Some college-educated women are pursuing careers, seeking opportunities for advancement through the traditional Japanese rotational system. But due to the widespread discrimination in Japanese firms, many Japanese women are opting to work for foreign firms, particularly American and European ones, which have better reputations for offering greater responsibilities and equal opportunities for advancement .

Work Schedule

Most businesses and government offices are open from 9:00 A.M. to 5:00 or 6:00 P.M. on weekdays. Some companies still operate for a half day on Saturdays. Banks are open from 9:00 A.M. to 3:00 P.M., Monday through Friday. Shops are open daily from 10:00 A.M. to 8:00 P.M., although department stores usually close at 6:00 or 7:00 P.M.

The workday for white-collar professionals (salarymen) usually begins at 9:00 A.M., and may extend late into the evening, often until 11:00 or 12:00 P.M. It is important to understand that people are not necessarily working in their offices all that time. They will usually leave the office for a few hours in the evening to dine and drink with customers and/or colleagues within the firm or the industry at large. This form of social interchange is considered to be a vital part of the professional workday. White-collar professionals are especially likely to engage in these types of practices.

Some employees return home after the business socializing. Others may go back to the office to finish tasks or simply to put in "face time." Junior employees feel distinct pressure to be "seen" at the office for longer hours than more senior professionals. This "face time" gives the impression that a person is hard-working, diligent, and conscientious. A junior person rarely leaves the office before his superiors. It should be noted that the Japanese do not expect a foreigner to work as late as themselves. However, a foreigner may gain the respect of the Japanese by staying at the office as long as his or her Japanese counterpart.

Many foreign executives will, in fact, work longer hours than their Japanese counterparts. If assigned to a company's foreign offices in Japan, a senior foreign employee should make it clear that the junior employees may leave when they desire, even before the senior employees. It would be appropriate, and perhaps even desirable, to indicate a concern for the junior person's well-being, and to indicate that he or she should go home if it is late or if there is no need for him or her to remain in the office.

Making Contacts

The Japanese place a very high importance on personal interactions and spend a great deal of their time building relationships and developing trust. Throughout Japanese history and into modern times, the family name, one's social relationships, and prestigious and honorable associations have been very important in both the social and business worlds.

Accordingly, there is very little cold calling in Japan. All new contacts are developed via introductions by third parties. In order to make a new contact, the foreigner must find some person or organization to make the introduction. Your country's trade and diplomatic offices are often good resources. In addition to personal contacts and references, trade organizations, bank and invest- ment banks, consulates and embassies, and country chambers of commerce can provide a formal introduction. Foreigners should also consider using mutual suppliers/buyers of goods and services as potential references. If you do not know of any mutual acquain- tances, you can also contact law, accounting, and consulting firms with offices in Japan, who will provide you with an introduc- tion, often for a fee. Whenever possible, it is helpful to have a local agent, representative, or distributor manage local issues for you.

You will find that having a strong personal connection with a highly respected third party who acts as your introducer, will give you a better chance of achieving business success, especially if the person you want to meet has a sense of obligation to your introducer. The introducer (*shokaisha*) can also function as a trusted and re- spected go-between and may be called upon later to advise both sides or act as a mediator during difficult negotiations.

But foreigners should be careful not to ask too much of the in- troducer and thereby place him in an awkward position with the person to whom you have been introduced. Further, you should take care to respect this introduction and not jeopardize the relationship and trust of your introducer. In other words, you should ensure that you continue to be "worthy" of your introduction.

JETRO, the Japan External Trade Organization, can help for- eign businesses enter Japan by hosting trade shows in Japan and by facilitating meetings between specific companies and industries. Accordingly, private businesses looking to win favor for public pro- jects and/or on trade-related issues should focus their attentions on the ministries and agencies that promote business.

The *Keidanren*, the Federation of Economic Organizations, is Japan's powerful association of businesses, which periodically produces reviews of Japanese business sentiment in the country. In addition to providing information on the overall economy as well as on specific industries, Keidanren operates as a network for Japan's business leaders to forge relationships with one another and with those government officials participating in the development of business policies. You, too, may want to consider joining a trade association in Japan. In addition to providing information from ministries that regulate specific industries, trade associations can provide extensive market research information. Be careful not to limit your memberships to foreigner-dominated associations, as they often lack the native bureaucratic and political networks that can be so valuable to the foreigner seeking to do business in Japan.

Be aware of the existence of the *Keiretsu* network. *Keiretsu* refers to the intricate web of financial and nonfinancial relationships between companies that virtually links together in a pattern of formal and informal cross-ownership and mutual obligation. The *keiretsu* nature of Japanese business has made it difficult for foreign companies to penetrate the commercial sector.

It is not necessary to interact only with the top people in a company. The Japanese are very conscious of titles and will seek to match you with a person of similar stature after the initial introduction. The mechanics of most business transactions in large companies are analyzed, structured, and even negotiated by lower level professionals. Be sure to pay attention to all members of your counterpart's team or office. However, when dealing with small companies, direct your initial communications toward the senior people.

Meeting People

Avoid scheduling meetings during the three main holiday periods and adjacent weekends: year's end and the New Year, from December 27 to January 4; Golden Week, from April 29 to May 5; and the Obon Festival at mid-August. Because punctuality is critical in Japan, be sure to take Japan's heavy traffic into account when scheduling appointments.

There are several key things to keep in mind for the first meeting with a Japanese businessperson, including saying the appropriate phrases, presenting your business card, bowing, and discussing the appropriate topics.

When referring to another person, the Japanese add the suffix -*san* to the end of a person's family name as an honorific title. It is the English equivalent of "Mr." or "Mrs." and should be used in place of these titles. However, be sure to never place -*san* at the end of your own name when you refer to yourself. You may also refer to a person using the English "Mr." or "Mrs." The Japanese also refer to each other by using their professional titles. If you are familiar with a person's title, you may use either that title or his or her family name with the -*san* suffix; never use both the title and the family name together. For example, "Mr. John Smith" would be called "Smithsan" (pronounced Sumisusan) by his Japanese colleagues. First names are only used within a family and with very close friends, and should *never* be used in business. Many Japanese have worked together for many years but do not know each other's first names.

The Japanese will be impressed if you have taken the time to learn a couple of Japanese phrases. In the Japanese language, every syllable is pronounced exactly as it is written. A good first greeting is: "*Hajimemashite. Watakushi no namae wa Smith desu. Dozo yoroshiku,*" which means "This is my first time to have the pleasure of meeing you. My name is Mr. Smith. Please feel kindly toward me." (Additional suitable expressions are presented later in this chapter.) The verbal introduction should be simultaneously accompanied by a bow and presentation of your business card. People should be introduced in order of seniority.

The presentation of the business card (*meishi*) is actually an acknowledgment of a person's identity. Business cards are very important. It is wise to have cards printed in Japanese on one side and English on the other. Many hotels in Tokyo and other major cities can assist you in obtaining such cards. In Japan, business cards are *presented* and received using both hands. The words should face the receiver. When you present cards written in *kanji,* Chinese characters, make sure the cards are facing in the correct direction. Traditional Japanese text is written from right to left and read downward. Accordingly, some Japanese business cards may be written vertically. Ask your hotel or a colleague for assistance prior to a meeting. The recipient of a business card should read it slowly and carefully to demonstrate full respect for the other person. Once you have read it, place the card on the table in front of you to refer to during the meeting. Do not put it in your pocket immediately.

The Japanese view bowing as an art form. Care and attention is given to the correct angle and style of bow. A bow is accomplished by placing your arms straight along the sides of your body, with your trunk and head bowing together and your eyes always facing the floor beneath you. Your hands should never be in your pockets, but instead always at your side. The more junior person always bows first and with a greater depth and angle. If you are meeting a professional at the same level as yourself, you may bow at the same angle, although if your Japanese counterpart is older than you are, you should bow slightly lower than he does. It can be very difficult for non-Japanese to master the art of bowing without extensive study. The Japanese recognize this truth, and do not expect foreigners to bow. It is best not to try and imitate Japanese bows unless you have studied the art thoroughly, for your good intentions may result in an improper bow that offends someone. For foreign men or women, a respectful slight nod of the head and shoulders will be considered appropriate in most situations. On some occasions, the Japanese may exchange handshakes after the bow out of deference to western customs. Be careful to keep your handshake light, and do not judge a person by the strength of his or her grip.

The Japanese smile often. They are not avid joke tellers, but in group situations they will sometimes do humorous imitations of friends and colleagues. Such imitations are not considered rude; as indeed, they are often performed in front of the person being imitated. It is considered rude to display an open mouth. Accordingly, most Japanese women will cover their mouths when laughing or expressing shock or disbelief. In general, a straight posture is very important for women and men. When you are seated, both your feet should be placed firmly on the floor and your arms should rest in your lap or on the armrests. Traditionally, junior people are more likely to sit with their hands in their laps, and also with a slight forward tilt of the head and shoulders, out of deference to the senior people present. Senior people are more likely to sit with both arms resting on the sides of a chair or table. Hands should never be placed inside your pockets while standing or seated. Never rest your foot on your knee.

Most Japanese are not accustomed to dealing with women in business situations. As international business has increased, the frequency of business interactions involving Japanese men and non-Japanese women has also increased, but not significantly. If you are a foreign woman, the Japanese may find it difficult to socialize with you on a business level. Do not take it personally. Try to avoid any situation or confrontation that may cause embarrassment to your counterparts. With patience and gentle persistence, you will be able to gradually win their respect and business, but do not expect to be able to develop close relationships with them. As with all cultures, there are differences among the Japanese. Some, particularly the younger Japanese, will be able to deal with you better than their older colleagues.

Wherever possible, present written information on your company as well as your proposal at the beginning of a meeting or prior to it. The Japanese are technically-oriented and are impressed by clear, colorful professional presentations and graphics. If your information is written in English, it will give an English-speaking Japanese person an opportunity to fully review your information at a later date at his or her own speed. The Japanese tend to understand written English better than spoken English. But you should consider having your marketing literature translated into Japanese as a way of ensuring that you get your message across.

A first meeting is used primarily to establish a relationship. It is not uncommon for your Japanese counterpart to bring several associates to a meeting. Begin the encounter with light pleasantries, such as remarks about the weather, your plane trip, and your experiences since arriving in the city. Ask your counterparts about their experiences with other countries. General questions regarding place of residence, city/country attractions, children's schooling and activities, sports, world travel, and arts/culture are always appropriate. Neutral topics like these work best during initial meetings. Gradually, as you get to know an individual, you will be able to use your own judgment about introducing other topics. It is best to avoid controversial subjects. The Japanese do not usually discuss personal topics, nor do they issue compliments very often. Thus you should avoid excessive statements of praise. It is acceptable to gradually shift the conversation to the purpose of the meeting. If you are pressed for time and want to discuss business issues sooner, make a brief apology and gently shift to your business purpose.

Avoid appearing rash and hard in your attitude, speech, or mannerisms. The Japanese do not respond well to aggressive manners. You may notice that your counterpart is actually soft-spoken and quiet mannered. This is not because he is a weak professional, but because the Japanese value these characteristics because they are identified with wisdom, experience, and age. You may also notice that some Japanese, particularly those of the older generation, may close their eyes during a meeting. This does not mean that they are sleepy or bored, but rather that they are reflecting on the topic of discussion.

If you are meeting with your counterparts for the first time or are revisiting clients after overseas travel, you may want to present a small gift, souvenir, or sample product. Generally, these are not expected at first meetings. If you choose to present gifts, they should be presented toward the end of a meeting or visit. Always have enough gifts for everyone present in a meeting. Senior people should not receive the same items as junior people. It is advisable to carry a variety of tasteful items with you just in case you need them. If you have a gift for only one person, present it privately after your meeting. If you have a group gift, make its group nature known prior to presenting the gift.

The Japanese always formally escort visitors upon departure, usually to a door or elevator. In turn, if Japanese business people are visiting your offices, be sure to escort them to the door or elevator. It is important to bid a formal and polite good-bye, which again is accompanied by a bow. The Japanese are very formal in their body language. They usually stand about two to three feet apart in the business setting.

Corporate Structure

Japanese businesses have a well-defined corporate structure with specific management roles and titles. Most foreigners are familiar with the image of the Japanese white-collar professional, commonly referred to as "the salaryman." Salarymen join a company directly after leaving college, with the understanding that they and the company are making a lifetime commitment. The most prestigious companies recruit from the best schools, using interpersonal skills and academic performance as the key criteria for selection. It is important that the potential employee shows a strong ability to fit in smoothly with the new "group" (i.e., the company). The Japanese find their personal identities by belonging to various group units, of which the company and the family unit are the most important. In order to ensure harmony and common loyalty, many companies recruit from the same one or two universities or from the same geographic region. Loyalty and allegiance to the company is very important. A young employee is expected to sacrifice time and energy to help the company prosper in exchange for this lifetime employment. In time, through promotions, he will be rewarded for this loyalty regardless of his ability.

Since the turn of the century, Japanese companies have had a very paternalistic attitude toward their employees and their families. The close-knit conformist attitudes of the historical feudal village were transferred to the corporation, which helped to foster Japan's well-known teamwork concept. Companies became the "feudal lord" requiring loyalty and providing security. The concept of lifetime employment grew out of the employer's fear of labor shortages. Employers offered their workers special privileges, including job security, in order to retain trained and skilled labor. Further, the companies installed a wage system in which financial rewards were delayed until a worker's senior years to encourage people to stay with one company. Gradually, as a result of global economic challenges, this relationship is beginning to shift. Today, employers and employees are both beginning to question their lifetime loyalty and commitment to one another.

Many Japanese consider the traditional salarymen "bootlickers" because their unwavering loyalty makes them possessions of the company. With recent changes in the economy and corporate restructurings, some corporations are questioning the value of lifetime employment. As a result, more Japanese professionals are considering switching companies at mid-career. The system is beginning to shift from a traditional, seniority-based promotion system to one based more on performance and ability, as companies restructure to meet the changing economic environment. Efficiency and effectiveness are becoming valued characteristics.

It is important to recognize that there are significant generational differences emerging in Japanese society. Many of the country's younger professionals have been exposed to Western value systems and are more willing to display their individuality in their mindset, their actions, and their appearance. However, at the core, these individuals usually retain their Japanese character.

In the Japanese company or *kaisha*, junior employees are expected to perform any and all duties, including menial tasks, their superiors demand. The manager/senior person functions much like a mentor. In Japanese society, there are various traditional vertical relationships, of which this role between younger and older employees is one. In the Japanese language there are several words to describe the variations on this concept. Translated, they mean dependence (*amae*), master–apprentice (*oyabun–kobun*), and senior–junior (*senpai–kohai*). Further, to ensure that status and seniority are respected, the Japanese have specific words and employ varying degrees of formality. The Japanese always use respectful language when speaking to their seniors. However, a Japanese refers to himself or herself with humility. Although hierarchy remains important, Japanese businesses are beginning to realize that they will need to soften their traditional belief in hierarchy in order for young, bright, creative, and capable professionals to succeed.

The Japanese system requires that people to gain experience in different areas of the company through a structured rotation program, each usually lasting about two to three years. A person advances primarily by age and personal stability. In Japanese business, a man's marital status may influence his career path. Traditionally, while it is acceptable for a man to remain a bachelor until his late twenties, he faces distinct social and professional pressure to find a wife soon after turning thirty. An unmarried man over thirty may be bypassed for promotion and suffer poor postings or assignments, because the Japanese view marriage and family as symbols of stability and maturity.

Traditionally, image has been considered more important than substance in Japan. For example, appearing to work hard is more important than actually accomplishing something substantial. This is gradually beginning to change as Japanese companies place more emphasis on efficiency and effectiveness rather than mere appearance. Typically, junior employees work harder and longer than senior executives. As a result, there are occasions when senior managers know less about their department than their subordinates, especially if they have just been rotated into the department. In that case, junior employees are expected to accomplish the work that needs to be done on behalf of the senior person and allow him full credit for it. When dealing with the Japanese, you must take the appropriate time to politely discuss any issues with all interested parties. Give priority to the most senior person, but do not ignore a junior person, particularly if you are roughly the same age. Not only may he be guiding the decisions on the present deal, but it is a very likely, assuming a normal Japanese corporate structure, that he will move into a position with more authority one day. You may need his introduction or business in the future.

Although it can differ slightly by industry, the following list of titles reflects the typical ranking system in a *kaisha*. (Note that the *-choo* suffix is used to form words with meaning "head of. . . .")

Kaichoo	Chairman
Shachoo	President
Fuku-shachoo	Vice-president
Senmu Torishimariyaku	Senior managing director
Joomu Torishimariyaku	Managing director
Torishimariyaku	Director
Buchoo	General manager of a division/ Department head
Fukubuchoo or Bucho dairi	Deputy general manager of a division
Jichoo	Deputy general manager of a section
Kachoo	Manager/Section chief
Kakarichoo or Kacho dairi	Deputy section chief
Buin/Kain (Shain)	Staff (Company employee)
Hirashain	Titleless staff (slang)

The following list describes the typical corporate structure of most Japanese firms:

Torishimariyaku kai	Board of directors
Jigyoohonbu	Division
Bu	Department
Shitsu	Office
Ka	Section

Negotiation

The Japanese place a high degree of importance on developing long-term relationships through which trust grows. Loyalty, honor, and the spoken commitment are highly valued. As a result, many business decisions are agreed to verbally, followed by a written agreement which functions more as a formality. The Japanese frequently build relationships and even conduct business on the golf course and in similar social settings. No matter how hard you work at building your relationship, remember that you, as a non-Japanese, will always be perceived as *gaijin*, a foreigner, to the Japanese. It is very difficult, if not impossible, to become part of a Japanese person's inner circle. Foreigners should not let this reality obstruct business relationships, but simply recognize that the concept of close business relationship will take on a new and more formal dimension in Japan.

One Japanese concept that is particularly difficult for non-Japanese to comprehend is *honne and tatemae*. *Honne* refers to the substance or real or inner truth of an issue, and *tatemae* is the public, diplomatic truth or official position. This important concept helps the Japanese to maintain harmony. The Japanese will avoid voicing their true feelings or *honne* in order to preserve harmony. The best way to counter this problem is to ask more questions to get a better sense of their true opinion on an issue. Remember to keep the questions nonoffensive and somewhat indirect to avoid causing any embarrassment to your Japanese counterpart.

In Japan, age is synonymous with wisdom and experience. Consequently, the Japanese often have a difficult time negotiating or conducting business with foreigners who appear substantially younger and inexperienced. If you are in a situation where you are significantly younger than your counterpart, work on establishing a level of mutual respect and trust. Do not appear aggressive, extroverted, or rude. Be patient, soft-spoken, and gentle, even as you try to be firm in your dealings. Show respect to your counterpart out of deference to his age and seniority with the firm. If appropriate, utilize the assistance of an older colleague and, if possible, use an older person as your introducer. Do not direct all of your attention to the English-speaking member of the Japanese team, for he will probably be younger and be without much influence. If you ignore the senior decision-makers of the team, you will insult them. The best approach is to determine to whom the Japanese defer to when speaking in Japanese. In almost all circumstances, the oldest person is the most important.

The Japanese tend to be very cautious and thorough in their decisionmaking. Their willingness and ability to tolerate risk is relatively low. The Japanese prefer to conduct business by using a group of employees, usually two or three people of various ranks, as the negotiating team. There are, of course, some Japanese firms that do not fit the typical mold and employ aggressive executive managers who are quick decision makers. The Japanese are very process-oriented and the way in which business in conducted is often more important to them than the results.

The Japanese are wary of allowing one person to gain praise. Work must be performed such that the team as a whole receives credit and praise. Similarly, no one person has the authority to make decisions on an individual basis. The Japanese share authority and responsibility through what they call the *ringi seido*, or consensus in decision-making. The *ringi-sho* is a written proposal that is circulated throughout various departments and then upward through the chain of management command. Typically, a junior-level employee will carry out the actual work or analysis and present a detailed proposal or report. Each subsequent colleague and senior person along the way will add a small comment and stamp his approval. If an approval is not received at any level, the proposal will be redirected back to the original group for changes or it will be rejected outright.

Only proposals/reports that have received full approval will be passed on to the next higher level. Eventually, a senior executive will grant the final approval. Depending on the level of commitment required of the company involved, approval by a member of the board or executive committee may be required. For most medium- and major-level issues, final approval rests with the most senior executives.

Used primarily for major decisions, the *ringi* system is very time-consuming because each reviewer may conduct a thorough inquiry and analysis of the terms of the proposal. Usually, there are lengthy informal discussions even before a *ringi* is prepared so that no reviewer is completely unaware of a proposal before it arrives on his desk. Some Japanese companies circulate informal drafts of a *ringi* in order to gradually build consensus. The informal, predecision discussion process is referred to as *nemawashi*.

This drawn-out procedure can be very frustrating to a foreigner, for negotiations can turn into very lengthy processes, particularly in comparison to negotiations in Western timeframes. However, you should try to view it from the Japanese perspective, in which building consensus and group decision making is critical. The *ringi* system ensures that all levels of management approve of a proposal. As a result, once a *ringi* has obtained 100 percent approval, decisions are rarely changed unless certain fundamental underlying conditions have changed.

The Japanese do not bargain over price and other terms as much as many of their Asian neighbors. However, do not make concessions too quickly, for the Japanese may question the sincerity of your original proposal. Whenever possible, wait for the Japanese team to make the first concession. You will notice that they will only make one point at a time, rather than presenting all the issues for debate at one time. While this may appear time-consuming, adopt the same strategy and never show all of your "cards" at once.

When negotiating with the Japanese, keep in mind that they do not always say what they mean. If a Japanese says something like "I work for a small company, and I may not be able to do it," his words may not be literally true. In Japanese tradition, he may be being polite to you and humble about his origin. You should know his and the company's background so that you can interpret his concerns more accurately. He may in fact be telling you that he does not want to do it.

The Japanese often avoid sustained eye contact as it can be considered intimidating. Junior people are less likely to make eye contact and will keep their visual focus low and their heads slightly bowed down out of respect for the speaker. Westerners should not assume that this posture implies a lack of trust, honesty, or sincerity.

Do not try to fill up the silent gaps during a conversation. Silence usually means that the Japanese are seriously contemplating the issue. The Japanese rarely ever say "No" outright. A blunt "No" is considered rude, almost like an opinion on a person rather than on his idea. Other expressions that can mean "No" include the following:

— "It is difficult"
— "We would like to, but . . ."
— "I will think about it"
— "I am not sure"
— "I will try, but . . ."
— "It is an interesting idea, but . . ."

If you need to say "No," do so in a similar roundabout manner to avoid a confrontation and offending your counterpart. Never say "No" outright, as it may cause your counterpart to lose face. Similarly, the Japanese are rarely candid about their opinions, as frankness may cause discomfort and confrontation. Instead, they speak in a roundabout manner utilizing the gentler phrases noted above. Never confront your counterpart directly or place him in an awkward situation.

The Japanese may also say "Yes" and mean something different. *Hai* is the word for "Yes" and is often used during a conversation to mean "Yes, I am listening" or "Yes, I understand." It is best to listen to the full response before deciding what the person is trying to say. The foreigner should be very careful to distinguish between the humorous laugh and the nervous laugh. Usually, the circumstances will be the best determinant. Anytime you hear a laugh that appears inappropriate, it may be hiding some discomfort over an issue or situation.

The Japanese routinely engage in a verbal and physical gesture that is best described as a guttural moan with the tilt of head. This is usually done in a situation in which they feel uncomfortable. This is a typical situation where they will say an indirect "No," as mentioned above. The nervous laugh or smile can also indicate difficulty. The Japanese also indicate "No" by placing their hand perpendicular to their face and waving it rapidly back and forth.

The Japanese often rely more on a verbal commitment than on a written contract. Feeling bound by their word, some Japanese may even be offended by a foreigner's insistence on written contracts. By and large, most large Japanese companies have global business experience and recognize the need to document any terms and agreements. If a Japanese person or company expresses reluctance or is slow to draw up a contract, politely explain the policy of your company. Explain that it is standard procedure for your company to detail specific terms, and it in no way reflects on the trustworthiness of the Japanese company. It is always best to point out how written contracts can also protect the Japanese company.

Conducting Business in a Social Setting

Dining and Drinking

Business entertaining is where the Japanese relax a bit with their colleagues and clients. Foreigners should use these opportunities to get to know their Japanese counterparts. Avoid overly personal questions about a person's background or family. Let them offer such information voluntarily. Also avoid disclosing intimate information about yourself because it is liable to make the Japanese uncomfortable. Business lunches and dinners are common, but the Japanese rarely meet for business breakfasts.

In traditional restaurants, the Japanese sit on the floor on tatami mats. Men sit cross-legged and the women sit with their legs tucked neatly to one side. Remove your shoes before entering a tatami room. Never leave your chopsticks standing in your rice: this is part of a funeral ritual. Always lay your chopsticks across your rice bowl or the corner of your plate.

Drinking before and at dinner is expected and encouraged. Moderate drinking, usually of beer, may be acceptable for lunch meetings. It is best to follow your counterpart's lead. This is the only setting in which the Japanese allow themselves some freedom. For the foreigner, it can be an ideal opportunity to become accepted. It is probably best that you do not drink too much, as you may make errors in judgment. On the other hand, it is important that you participate in the socializing, particularly by taking part in the conversation and drinking if your companions expect it.

The drinking and dining is often done in karaoke bars (sing-along bars). An excellent way to show that you are a team member is by participating enthusiastically and singing when it is your turn. You should not be concerned about your singing ability: participation is more important than talent. That is not to say that a good voice or stage "ham" would not be appreciated. The Japanese enjoy a good performer. The same attitude colors the company sports team. Although the star player will always be the office hero, those who do not play at all are the "outcasts" as compared to those who play poorly. Participation is key.

Visiting a Home

The Japanese do not entertain at home very often because their homes are usually small and modest compared to Western homes. Furthermore, the businessman is less likely to want to mix his business group with his personal group. If invited to someone's home, be sure to take a gift. Most fine department stores in Japan will assist you in selecting an appropriate gift. Flowers are not usually given as gifts when visiting friends. Shoes should always be removed before entering a home. A few days after you visit a home, you should send a thank-you letter or make a phone call much the same as you would in Western countries.

Gift Giving

Gift giving is taken seriously in Japan. There are specific guidelines for the type and price of gifts, their packaging, and their timing for various occasions. The Japanese give gifts out of a sense of obligation and duty as well as to convey feelings such as gratitude and regret. Therefore care is given to the appropriateness of the gift as well as to its aesthetic beauty. Gift giving has always been widespread in Japan. While many Westerners may view it as a form of corruption, it is really just part of the system. This is one of those occasions, however, when the foreigner should be wary of inserting his or her own value system. Money is given to children on certain holidays, to sick people, or to families at funerals. Overall, it is best for foreigners to refrain from making a monetary gift. There are alternative gifts that are equally suitable for the above mentioned occasions. Elaborate food gifts tend to be the most reliable and should be purchased at a fine department store in Tokyo or another international city.

Gifts given for first-time business encounters should be tasteful, moderate-to-low in price, never gaudy or overly expensive. Suitable gifts include items from your native country or specific region, special products from your company, leather goods, fine products from prestigious stores, and wines and liquors. If you give expensive pens, make sure that they have fine points which are more suited to writing in *kanji*. It is advisable to carry extra gifts when you travel. Further, refrain from giving gifts emblazoned with blatant advertising of your company. Golf shirts or baseball caps can be exceptions. Gifts must always be wrapped in tasteful paper, but never in white because it is the funeral color. Wrapped gifts are often kept in the shopping bag (usually from a prestigious store) during a meeting to avoid calling excessive attention to the gift.

During successive rounds of gift giving, be certain to present gifts of equal or slightly greater value than the previous round. This is why you should take care not to upset the balance or to begin with expensive gifts that will create a burdensome obligation for your Japanese counterpart and yourself. For future gifts, keep an eye on the likes and dislikes of your counterpart. Adding items keyed to a hobby or a collection of interest is a valued way to communicate respect and friendship. Giving copies of photographs of groups including each other is typical of the Japanese culture.

As with business cards, gifts are given and received with both hands and accompanied with a slight bow. Usually, gifts should not be opened in the presence of the giver. However, sometimes for birthdays and in situations involving foreigners, gifts are opened in public. Regardless of its value, a gift is always presented humbly by the giver. As you give a gift, to show modesty, you should say something to the effect of, "Please accept this small trifling thing," which is *Tsumaranai mono desu ga,* in Japanese.

In Japan, there are specific business gift giving occasions, specifically *oseibo* (year's end) and *ochugen* (midsummer). These are must-give occasions for Japanese businesses. *Oseibo* gifts are presented in the first half of December as a token of gratitude for earlier favors and loyalty. This is a good opportunity to thank clients for their business. *Ochugen* usually occurs in mid-July in Tokyo and mid-August in some other regions. Originally an occasion to provide consolation to the families of those who had died in the first half of the year, *ochugen* falls two weeks before *obon,* which is a holiday for honoring the dead.

If you find yourself in Japan at these times, it is appropriate to exchange *oseibo* and *ochugen* gifts. There is an established price level that one should pay for each corporate level. For help in choosing such gifts, shop at a prestigious store in Japan. Such stores have displays of appropriate gifts, and will wrap the gifts in the store's trademark paper. Elaborate packages of cooking oil, whiskey, other liquors, condiments, specialty fish and meats, and other food treats make good gifts. The Japanese are very materialistic and brand-conscious. Make sure to buy top-of-the-line products from internationally renowned producers.

At the most senior levels, it is not uncommon for people to exchange gifts worth $300 or $400. However, you should note that you are not obligated to exchange gifts for *oseibo* and *ochugen*. You may simply present a first-time gift or the appropriate subsequent-visit gift instead.

Care should be taken when giving gifts that consist of a number of items fewer than ten. In these circumstances, the items should be given in odd number quantities, or in pairs, which represent good luck. Avoid packages with either nine and four items, for those numbers have homonyms relating to death. Further, flowers are only given when courting or in the event of a death or illness. When sending cards or gifts for sickness or death, do not use red ink or paper because they are reminders of blood. However, red is considered auspicious on other occasions and is used for wrapping paper and ribbon, particularly at Christmas. The Japanese also often wear red kimonos for various occasions.

The following department stores in Tokyo have an English-speaking staff that can assist you in selecting the most appropriate gifts for any occasion:

Isetan Shinjuku: Tel.—3352-1111
Takashimaya: Tel.—3211-4111
Tokyu Nihonbashi: Tel.—3211-0511
Mitsukoshi Nihonbashi: Tel.—3241-3311

Dress Code

The dress code in urban business and social settings is formal and conservative—generally the same as in most western societies. Suits and ties for men and suits or conservative dresses for women are expected in all business situations, including business social settings. In leisure social settings or for business golf outings, slacks and sports shirts are acceptable for men and slacks or casual skirts and dresses for women. At all times, the Japanese take care to appear neat and well groomed. Clothes should be clean and ironed, and shirts should always be worn tucked in.

Useful Phrases

The standard dialect of Japanese is spoken throughout the country with some regional differences in accents. English is taught in many schools and is the most common foreign language. However, until recently, many instructors were not orally fluent in English, so despite their years of English language instruction, most Japanese have difficulty understanding and conversing in the language and are more likely to understand written English. Now that language instruction has improved, many young people speak English with more ease and fluency. In most business situations, it is advisable to utilize an interpreter.

Since the sixth century, the Japanese have used Chinese characters, *kanji*, although in recent times the Japanese pronunciation of these characters differs significantly from the Chinese pronunciation. The Chinese and the Japanese can read each other's *kanji* texts. *Kana* is a Japanese writing style that was developed to allow the phonetic pronunciation of specific syllables. There are two types of *kana*, *hiragana* and *katakana*. Today, *katakana* is used for the phonetic pronunciation of all foreign words and *hiragana* is used for all other phonetic pronunciations. The following list is the romanization of Japanese words, commonly known as *romanji*. The words are pronounced exactly as they are written.

Hello	*Konnichiwa*
Good morning	*Ohayoo gozaimasu*
Good afternoon	*Konnichiwa*
Good evening	*Konnichiwa*
Goodnight	*Oyasumi nasai*
How are you?	*Ogenki desu ka?*
Please	*Onegai shimasu*
Please (come in or go ahead)	*Dozo*
Thank you	*Domo arigatoo gozaimasu*
You are welcome	*Doo itashimashite*
Excuse me	*Sumimasen desu ga*
I am sorry	*Gomen nasai*

My name is ———	*Watakushi no namae wa* ———
I (We) work for ———	——— *kaisha ni tsutomete imasu*
I am Mr. X (last name) of Company Y	*Y no X desu*
Here is my business card	*Kore wa watakushi no meshi desu*
I am very pleased to meet you	*Hajimemashite*
Please accept this small gift	*Tsumaranai mono desu ga*
I hope to have continued friendship with you	*Yoroshiku onegai shimasu* (literal— used when meeting someone or at the end of a negotiating session)
I understand	*Hai wakarimasu*
No, I do not understand	*Iie, wakarimasen*
Please wait a minute	*Chotto matte kudasai*
Please repeat that	*Mo ichido itte kudasai*
Where is the restroom?	*Ote arai wa doko desu ka*
I humbly receive	*Itadakimasu* (said before starting a meal)
I humbly thank you for the meal	*Gochisosama deshita* (said only after eating a meal)
Good-bye	*Sayoonara*
Cheers	*Kampai*

Major Holidays

January 1	New Year's Day
January 15	Adulthood Day
February 11	National Foundation Day
March 20/21	Vernal Equinox Day
April 29	Emperor's Birthday (Greenery Day)
May 3	Constitution Memorial Day
May 5	Children's Day
mid-August	Obon Festival (held in July in some cities)
September 15	Respect for the Aged Day
September 23/24	Autumnal Equinox Day
October 10	Health and Sports Day
November 3	Culture Day
November 23	Labor Thanksgiving Day

General Facts

Climate: There are four distinct seasons with temperatures varying by area. In Tokyo, the temperature averages between 30F (-1C) and 50F (10C) in the winter, and between 80F (26C) and 95F (35C) in the summer. The rainy season is from mid-June to mid-July.

Currency: The main unit of currency is the yen (abbreviated as Y).

Dates: In business, the standard Western calendar is used and dates are abbreviated month, day, and year. For example, August 21, 1965, would be written as 8/21/65. In contrast the Japanese calendar is measured in terms of eras and is used only in official documents, with dates shown as year, month, and day.

Earthquakes: Japan is an earthquake-prone country. It is important that visitors and residents be aware of the procedures to observe during an earthquake, including the following:

1. Move under a solid desk or table to protect yourself from falling objects.
2. Extinguish all sources of fire, including cigarettes.
3. Do not rush outdoors. You may be hit by falling objects, including window panes. Know where the exits are in the event you need to evacuate. Do not use an elevator and refrain from using a car.
4. If you are driving, immediately curb your car on the left side of the road.

Electricity: The voltage is 100 volts, 50 or 60 cycles.

Entry Requirements: American, Canadian, British, French, and German citizens need a valid passport for entry. United States, French, and Canadian citizens need a visa for stays longer than ninety days; British and German citizens for visits exceeding one hundred and eighty days.

Time: Japan has one time zone, which is nine hours ahead of Green-wich Mean Time and fourteen hours ahead of U.S. Eastern Standard Time (thirteen hours during Daylight Savings Time).

Tipping: There is no tipping in Japan as workers take pride in their duty to do a good job. The Japanese may even feel insulted if you tip them. If you feel particularly grateful to someone such as a secretary or maid, a small gift is appropriate. Porters charge a set fee that is usually posted. A service charge of 10–15 percent is added in some international hotels and restaurants, but no further gratuity is expected.

Transportation: Transportation in Japan is highly advanced. Within cities, buses, subway trains and taxis are used extensively. Between cities, high-speed railways provide relatively easy and fast service. There is also an extensive network of domestic airlines. In major cities, taxis, buses, and trains provide transportation between the airports and city centers. Ask for assistance, as taxis can become very expensive, and trains and buses may be more efficient. When using a taxi stand, be sure to enter the first taxi in line and not one in the middle.

It is not advisable to rent cars in Tokyo because its streets can be congested and confusing. Driving is on the left and an International Driver's License is required. Public transportation is more convenient and efficient.

Helpful Telephone Numbers

Most public telephones are painted green and gray. There are, however, some red, yellow, blue, and pink telephones, which also accept coins for domestic calls. Local calls require a minimum of a Y10 coin, which is good for three-minutes. Use telephones that accept both Y10 and Y100 coins for long-distance calls. No change is returned when a Y100 coin is used. Telephone cards are accepted at gray and some green telephones, and are the most convenient for international calls. To call for an ambulance or the police, push the red emergency button on the telephone. No coin is necessary. The country code is (81) and the city codes are Tokyo (03), Nagoya (052), and Osaka (06). Omit the zero when calling from outside the country.

The following list of Japanese words will help you to understand addresses:

ku	ward
shi	city
machi	town
mura	village

Hospitals:

Emergency Medical Information Service A twenty-four-hour English-language hotline, that can provide you with the telephone number and address of the medical facility nearest your location. This service is located in Nagoya, and its number is (052) 264-1155 / 263-1145. The following Japanese hospitals all have English-speaking staff:

Tokyo Metropolitan Hospital
10-41 Fujimi 2-chome
Chiyoda-ku, Tokyo 102
Tel.: (3) 3263-1371

St. Luke's International Hospital
1-10 Akashi-cho
Chuo-ku, Tokyo
Tel.: (3) 3541-5151

International Catholic Hospital
2-5-1 Naka-Ochiai
Shinjuku-ku, Tokyo 161
Tel.: (3) 3951-1111

Tokyo Medical and Surgical Center
Mori Building No. 32
3-4-30 Shiba Koen
Minato-ku, Tokyo 105
Tel.: (3) 3436-3028

Nagoya University Hospital
1 Kawasumi
Mizuho-cho, Mizuho-ku
Nagoya
Tel.: (52) 851-5511

Osaka Teishin Hospital
2-6-40 Karasugatsuji
Tennojiku
Osaka
Tel.: (6) 773-7111

Doctors and Dentists:

International Clinic
1-5-9 Azabudai
Minato-ku, Tokyo
Tel.: (3) 3583-7831

Yanagisawa Dental Clinic
Capitol Tokyu Hotel
2-10-3 Nagata-cho
Chiyoda-ku, Tokyo
Tel.: (3) 3581-4511

Yamauchi Dental Clinic
3-16-10 Shiroganedai
Minato-ku, Tokyo
Tel.: (3) 3441-8377

All-Night Emergency Clinic
4-38 Aoi 1-chome
Higashi-ku, Nagoya
Tel.: (52) 937-7821

Umeda Dentists
2-1-15 Umeda
Kita-ku, Osaka
Tel.: (6) 346-5321

Ambulance: Dial 119 anywhere in Japan

Police: 110 anywhere in Japan. The number for the Tokyo Metropolitan Police is (3) 3581-4321

Operator/Information: You may speak in English when calling any of the following telephone numbers. Speak slowly and clearly.

- Overseas telephone calls (operator-assisted): 0051
- Directory assistance: 104
- Tokyo English Life Line: (3) 264-4347
- Teletourist information (recorded information on current cultural events in English): (3) 3503-2911
- Nagoya Information Hotline: (52) 741-4343 (prerecorded) / 581-5678

When dialing from the United States, the major long distance telephone carriers provide 1-800 numbers for operator assistance in Japan to identify telephone numbers. The operators can speak English, although they may answer in Japanese.

Useful Addresses

In Japan:

American Chamber of Commerce in Japan
Fukide Building, No. 2
4-1-21 Toranomon
Minato-ku, Tokyo 105
Tel.: (3) 3433-5381

P.O. Box 235
Okinawa City 904
Tel.: (9) 889-8935 / 2684

British Chamber of Commerce in Japan
No. 16 Kowa Building
9-20 Akasaka 1-chome
Minato-ku, Tokyo 107
Tel.: (3) 3505-1734

Canadian Chamber of Commerce in Japan
No. 16-1, Nishi-azabu 2-chome
Minato-ku, Tokyo 106
Tel.: (3) 3498-9745

Chubu Trade Ministry
5-2 Sannomaru 2-chome
Naka-ku, Nagoya
Tel.: (52) 951-2551

French–Japanese Chamber of Commerce
Groupe Schneider
DF Building
Miami-Aoyama 2-2-8
Minato-ku, Tokyo 107
Tel.: (3) 3402-6623

Fukuoka Chamber of Commerce and Industry, International Division
9-28, Hakataekimae 2-chome
Hakata-ku, Fukuoka 812
Tel.: (92) 441-1111

German Chamber of Commerce in Japan
Akasaka Tokyu Building
7th Floor
Central P.O. Box 588
14-3 Nagata-cho 2-chome
Chiyoda-ku, Tokyo 100
Tel.: (3) 3581-9881/3

Japan Chamber of Commerce and Industry, International Division
2-2 Marunouchi, 3-chome
Chiyoda-ku, Tokyo 100
Tel.: (3) 3283-7875

Japan External Trade Organization (JETRO)
The main functions of JETRO are to collect information on the world's economies, and to promote trade, industrial cooperation, and technology exchange.

2-2-5 Toranomon
Minato-ku, Tokyo
Tel.: (3) 3582-5521

4-7 Marunouchi 2-chome
Naka-ku, Nagoya
Tel.: (52) 211-4517

1-51 Bingomachi
Higashi-ku, Osaka
Tel.: (6) 203-3601

Japan Junior Chamber of Commerce
2-14-3 Irakawa-cho
Chiyoda-ku, Tokyo
Tel.: (3) 3234-5601

Ministry of International Trade and Industry (MITI)
1-3-1 Kasumigaseki
Chiyoda-ku, Tokyo
Tel.: (3) 3501-1551 / 0645

Nagoya Chamber of Commerce
and Industry, International
Division
10-19 Sakae 2-chome
Naka-ku, Nagoya 460
Tel.: (52) 221-7211

Nagoya International Center
(Japan National Tourist Office)
1-47-1 Nagano
Nakamura-ku, Nagoya
Tel.: (52) 581-5678

Osaka Chamber of Commerce
and Industry, International
Division
2-8 Honmachibashi
Chuo-ku, Osaka 540
Tel.: (6) 944-6412

Tourist Information Center
(Japan National Tourist
Office)
Kotani Building
1-6-6 Yurakucho
Chiyoda-ku, Tokyo
Tel.: (3) 3503-1461

U.S. Trade Center
World Import Market, 7th Floor
1-3 Higashi Ikebukuro 3-chome
Toshima-ku, Tokyo 107
Tel.: (3) 3987-2441

Embassies and Consulates:

American Embassy
10-5 Akasaka 1-chome
Minato-ku, Tokyo 107
Tel: (3) 3224-5000

American Consulates
2564 Nishihara
Urasoe City
Okinawa 90121
Tel.: (98) 876-4211

11-5 Nishitenma 2-chome
Kita-ku, Osaka 530
Tel.: (6) 315-5900

Kita 1-Jo Nishi 28-chome
Chuo-ku, Sapporo 064
Tel.: (11) 641-1115 / 7

5-26 Ohori 2-chome
Chuo-ku, Fukuoka 810
Tel.: (92) 751-9331 / 4

Nishiki SIS Building, 6th Floor
10-33 Nishiki 3-chome
Naka-ku, Nagoya 460
Tel.: (52) 203-4011

British Embassy
1 Ichiban-cho
Chiyoda-ku, Tokyo 102
Tel.: (3) 3265-5511 / 6340

British Consulate
Sieko Osaka Building, 19F
3-5-1 Bakuro-machi
Chuo-ku, Osaka 541
Tel.: (6) 281-1616

Canadian Embassy
3-38 Akasaka, 7-chome
Minato-ku, Tokyo 107
Tel.: (3) 3408-2101

Canadian Consulates
FT Building, 9th Floor

4-8-28 Watanabe-Dori
Chuo-ku, Fukuoka 810
Tel.: (92) 752-6055

Nakato Marunouchi Building,
6th Floor
3-17-6 Marunouchi
Naka-ku, Nagoya
Tel.: (52) 972-0450 / 3

Daisan Shoho Building, 12th
Floor
2-2-3 Nishi Shinsaibashi
Chuo-ku, Osaka 542
Tel.: (6) 212-4910

French Embassy
Tameike Tokyu Building
1-1-14 Akasaka
Minato-ku, Tokyo 107
Tel.: (3) 5570-3333

French Consulate
Obayashi Building, 21st
Floor
4-33 Kitahama-Higashi
Chuo-ku, Osaka 540
Tel.: (6) 941-4111

German Embassy
5-10 Minami Azubu,
4-chrome
Minato-ku, Tokyo 106
Tel.: (03) 3473-0151

German Consulate
Kobe International House
Chuo-ku, Goko-dori 8
chome, 1-5
Kokusai Kaikan, Kobe 651
Tel.: (78) 232-1212-14

In Canada:

Japanese Embassy
255 Sussex Drive
Ottawa, Ontario K1N9E6
Tel.: (613) 241-8541

Japanese Consulates
600, Rue de la
Gauchetiereeouest, Suite 1785
Montreal, Quebec H3B 4L8
Tel.: (514) 866-3429

Toronto-Dominion Centre,
Suite 2702
Toronto, Ontario M5K 1A1
Tel.: (416) 363-7038

900 Board of Trade Tower
1177 West Hastings Street
Vancouver, B.C. V6E 2K9
Tel.: (604) 684-5868

2480 ManuLife Place
10180 101st Street
Edmonton, Alberta T5J 3S4
Tel.: (403) 422-3752

Canada–Japan Trade Council
75 Albert Street, Suite 903
Ottawa, Ontario K1P 5E7
Tel.: (613) 233-4047

**Japan External Trade
Organization (JETRO)**
181 University Avenue
Suite 1600
Toronto, Ontario M5H 3M7
Tel.: (416) 861-0000

Place Montreal Trust Tower-
Suite 2902

1800 McGill College Avenue
Montreal, Quebec H3A 3J6
Tel.: (514) 849-5911

World Trade Center, Suite 660
999 Canada Place
Vancouver, B.C. V6C 3E1
Tel.: (604) 684-4174

**Japan National Tourist Office
(JNTO)**
165 University Avenue
Toronto, Ontario M5H 3B8
Tel.: (416) 366-7140

**Toronto Japanese Association
of Commerce and Industry**
141 Adelaide Street West
Suite 1801
Toronto, Ontario M5H 3L5
Tel.: (416) 360-0235

In France:

Japanese Embassy
7 Avenue Hoche
75008 Paris
Tel.: (1) 4766-0222

Japanese Consulate
70 Avenue de Hambourg
13008 Marseille
Tel.: (91) 734555

**Japanese Chamber of
Commerce in France**
1 Avenue de Friedland
75008 Paris
Tel.: (1) 4563-4333

**Japan External Trade Organi-
zation (JETRO)**
151 bis, Rue Saint-Honore
75001 Paris
Tel.: (1) 4261-2727

**Japan National Tourist Office
(JNTO)**
4–8 Rue Sainte-Anne
75001 Paris
Tel.: (1) 4296-2029

In Germany:

Japanese Embassy
Godesberger Alle 102-104
5300 Bonn 2
Tel.: (228) 81910

Japanese Consulates
Wachtelstrasse 8
1000 Berlin 33
Tel.: (30) 832-7026

Rathausmarkt 5
2000 Hamburg 1
Tel.: (40) 333017

Immermannstrasse 45
4000 Dusseldorf, 1
c/o Deutsch-Japanisches
Center
Tel.: (211) 353311

Prinzregentenplatz 10
8000 Minchen 80
Tel.: (89) 471043

Hamburger Allee 2-10
6000 Frankfurt am Main 90
Tel.: (69) 770351

Japanese Chamber of Commerce in Germany
Immermannstrasse 45
Deutsch-Japanisches Center
4000 Dusseldorf
Tel.: (211) 369001

Japan External Trade Organization (JETRO)
Colonnaden 72
20354 Hamburg
Tel.: (40) 356-0080

Internationales Handelszentrum, 12th Floor
Friedrichstrasse 95
10117 Berlin
Tel.: (30) 2643-3162 / 3163

Konigsallee 58
40212 Dusseldorf
Tel.: (211) 136020

Rossmarkt 17
60311 Frankfurt am Main
Tel.: (69) 283215

Promenadeplatz 12
80333 Munchen
Tel.: (89) 290-8420

Japan National Tourist Office (JNTO)
Kaiserstrasse 11
60311 Frankfurt am Main
Tel.: (69) 731-8140

In the United Kingdom:

Japanese Embassy
101–194 Piccadilly
London W1V 9FN
Tel.: (71) 465-6500

Japanese Chamber of Commerce
Salisbury House, 2nd Floor
29 Finsbury Circle
London EC2M 5QQ
Tel.: (71) 628-0069

Japan External Trade Organization (JETRO)
Leconfield House, 6th Floor
Curzon Street
London W1Y 7FB
Tel.: (71) 493-7226

Japan National Tourist Office (JNTO)
167 Regent Street
London W1R 7FD
Tel.: (71) 734-9638

In the United States:

Embassy of Japan
2520 Massachusetts Avenue, N.W.
Washington, DC 20008-2869
Tel.: (202) 328-2187

Japanese Consulates
Olympia Center, Suite 1100
737 North Michigan Avenue
Chicago, IL 60611
Tel.: (312) 280-0400

1742 Nuuanu Avenue
Honolulu, HI 96817
Tel.: (808) 536-2226

250 East First Street
Suite 1507
Los Angeles, CA 90012
Tel.: (213) 624-8305

299 Park Avenue
New York, NY 10171
Tel.: (212) 371-8222

50 Fremont Street, Suite 2300
San Francisco, CA 94105
Tel.: (415) 777-3533

601 Union Street,
Suite 500
Seattle, WA 98101
Tel.: (206) 682-9107

One Poydras Plaza
Suite 2050
639 Loyola Avenue
New Orleans, LA 70113
Tel.: (504) 529-2101

First Interstate Bank Plaza
Suite 5300
1000 Louisiana Street
Houston, TX 77002
Tel.: (713) 652-2977

2519 Commerce Tower
911 Main Street
Kansas City, MO 64105
Tel.: (816) 471-0111

2400 First Interstate Tower
1300 S.W. 5th Avenue

Portland, OR 97201
Tel.: (503) 221-1811

400 Colony Square Building
Suite 1501
1201 Peachtree Street, N.E.
Atlanta, GA 30361
Tel.: (404) 892-2700

Guam International Trade
Center Building, Suite 604
590 South Marine Drive
Tamuning
Guam 96911
Tel.: (671) 646-1290

Federal Reserve Plaza
14th Floor
600 Atlantic Avenue
Boston, MA 02210
Tel.: (617) 973-9772

550 West Seventh Avenue
Suite 701
Anchorage, AL 99501
Tel.: (907) 279-8428

Horiguchi Building, 5th Floor
Broadway Street
Garapan Saipan
Mariana Islands 96950
Tel.: (670) 234-7202

**Japan External Trade
Organization (JETRO)**
McGraw-Hill Building
44th Floor
1221 Avenue of the Americas
New York, NY 10020
Tel.: (212) 997-0400

401 North Michigan Avenue
Suite 660
Chicago, IL 60611
Tel.: (312) 527-9000

235 Pine Street, Suite 1700
San Francisco, CA 94104
Tel.: (415) 392-1333

725 South Figueroa Street
Suite 1890
Los Angeles, CA 90017
Tel.: (213) 624-8855

One Houston Center
Suite 2360
1221 McKinney Street
Houston, TX 77010
Tel.: (713) 759-9595

World Trade Center, Suite 152-1
2050 Stemmons Freeway
Dallas, TX 75258
Tel.: (214) 651-0839

Marquis One Tower, Suite 2012
245 Peachtree Center Avenue
Atlanta, GA 30303
Tel.: (404) 681-0600

1200 Seventeenth Street
Suite 1410
Denver, CO 80202
Tel.: (303) 629-0404

**Japan National Tourist Office
(JNTO)**
1 Rockefeller Plaza
Suite 1250
New York, NY 10020
Tel.: (212) 757-5640

401 N. Michigan Avenue
Chicago, IL 60601
Tel.: (312) 222-0874

2121 San Jacinto Street
Suite 980
Dallas, TX 75201
Tel.: (214) 754-1820

360 Post Street, Suite 601
San Francisco, CA 94108
Tel.: (415) 989-7140

624 S. Grand Avenue
Suite 2460
Los Angeles, CA 90017
Tel.: (213) 623-1952

**Kansas City Office of the
Japan Chamber of Commerce
and Industry**
Commerce Tower,
Suite 2628
911 Main Street
Kansas City, MO 64105
Tel.: (816) 221-6140

**Japanese Chamber of
Commerce**
115 West 57th Street
New York, NY 10022
Tel.: (212) 935-0303

2454 South Beretania Street
Honolulu, HI 96826
Tel.: (808) 949-5531

685 Market Street, Suite 820
San Francisco, CA 94105
Tel.: (415) 543-8522

345 South Figueroa Street
Los Angeles, CA 90071
Tel.: (213) 485-0160

244 South San Pedro Street
Suite 504
Los Angeles, CA 90012
Tel.: (213) 626-3067

401 North Michigan Avenue
Suite 602
Chicago, IL 60611
Tel.: (312) 332-6199

14133 Memorial Drive, Suite 3
Houston, TX 77079
Tel.: (713) 493-1512

(Shokookai of Portland)
10700 S.W. Beaverton-Hillsdale
Highway
Beaverton, OR 97005
Tel.: (503) 644-9579

c/o Pentax Corp.
35 Inverness Drive East
Englewood, CO 80112
Tel.: (303) 799-8000

U.S. Department of Commerce
International Trade
Administration
Japan Desk, Room 2318
14th & Constitution Avenues,
N.W.
Washington, DC 20230
Tel.: (202) 482-2425

U.S.–Japan Business Council
1020 19th Street, N.W.
Suite 130
Washington, DC 20036
Tel.: (202) 728-0068

2 South Korea

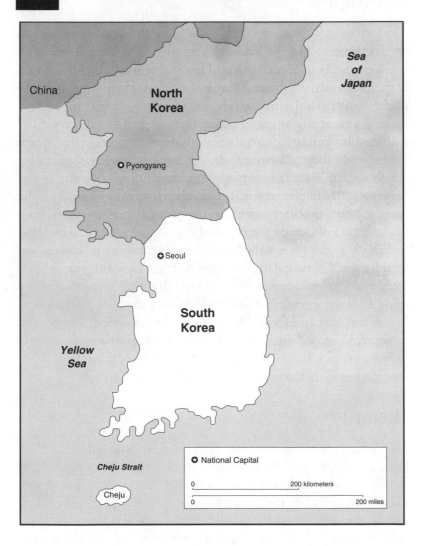

Geography

The Republic of Korea, better known as South Korea, is located on the southern half of the Korean Peninsula; North Korea occupies the northern half. Manchuria and Russia border the northern part of the peninsula. To the east across the Sea of Japan lies Japan and to the west across the Yellow Sea is the Chinese mainland. The total land area of the Korean Peninsula, including islands, is 85,269 square miles (220,847 square kilometers). Communist-run North Korea, with about 55 percent of the land, is slightly larger than South Korea, which occupies the remaining 45 percent of the peninsula. About 70 percent of the terrain is mountainous, with the highest mountains in the north. Only about 20 percent of the land is arable and is located mainly in the west. After the Korean War in 1953, a buffer zone, called the Demilitarized Zone (DMZ), was established as a boundary between North and South Korea. The DMZ is a 4-kilometer-wide strip of land that runs along the line of cease-fire (also known as the Demarcation Line or the 38th parallel) for a distance of about 150 miles (243 kilometers). The capital of South Korea is Seoul and is located in the northern portion of the country just 35 miles (56 kilometers) south of the DMZ. Other major cities include Pusan, Taegu, Inchon, and Kwangju.

History

The earliest known inhabitants of the Korean Peninsula were Neolithic descendants of the Paleo-Asiatic peoples. They established settlements all over Korea in the period 5000–1000 B.C. These people were absorbed by the Yemaek Tungus, an Altaic people, during the Bronze Age, around 1000–300 B.C. According to myth, "Tangun," who was half-human and half-divine, founded the Korean nation in 2333 B.C.

By 57 B.C. three kingdoms had emerged to control the entire peninsula: Koguryo in the north, Paekche in the southwest, and Silla in the southeast. In A.D. 668, Silla conquered the other two and created a state whose boundaries matched those of Modern Korea. Silla's power began to weaken in the eighth century and was finally overthrown by the rival state of Koryo in 935. During the Koryo period, the Koreans clashed with the Mongols several times. The Mongols finally conquered Korea in 1259 and thereafter dominated the peninsula for almost one hundred years. In 1392 General Yi Song-gye seized the Korean throne and established the Yi dynasty. The Yi, also known as the Choson Dynasty, ruled Korea until 1910.

The Japanese invaded Korea in 1593, but were driven off by a combined Korean and Chinese force. Western views and concepts, including Christianity, came to Korea in the early seventeenth century. Suspicious of the Roman Catholic missionaries, the Choson government quickly banned all forms of Western views and religions. Korea closed itself off to foreigners. Although Korea maintained relations with China and Japan, it was isolated from the rest of the world even longer than Japan, earning itself the nickname of "the Hermit Kingdom." Korea finally opened itself to trade with the Western world in the 1860s, but continued to foster an "us versus them" mentality based on feelings of cultural superiority to Western "barbarians."

In the nineteenth century both Japan and China vied for control of the Korean Peninsula. As a counterbalance, the Korean king turned to the Russians for assistance. But his plan backfired, for the Russians had a strategic interest in seizing control of one or more of Korea's warm water ports. Koreans then launched a campaign to achieve independence from all foreign powers. Under the leadership of So Chae-p'il, Korean citizens staged protests, while their government requested Chinese assistance. These actions triggered Japanese involvement in the Korean sphere, providing the basis for the first Sino-Japanese War of 1894–1895. The victorious Japanese assumed indirect control of Korea and dictated policy to the government. Japanese hold over Korea was reaffirmed in 1905 after a year-long war between Japan and Russia, which Japan won.

In 1910 the Japanese abolished the Korean monarchy and took

direct control of the country. The Japanese treated Korea as a colonial possession to be utilized for Japan's benefit. The Japanese seized
land and businesses from the Koreans, exploited the country's natural
resources, and ruled ruthlessly. Meanwhile, Korea was being transformed into a base for the Japanese military, who intended to add to
Japan's colonial empire by seizing Manchuria and parts of northern
China from the politically and militarily weak Chinese.

When Japan and China went to war for the second time from
1937 to 1945, Japan decided to mobilize Korea for the war effort.
They took control of all Korean industries and totally reorganized
the economy. The Japanese also forced Koreans to adopt Japanese
names, the Japanese language, and Japanese beliefs in Shintoism
and the divinity of the Japanese emperor. Many Koreans still have
vivid memories of Japan's brutal rule of their country and the Japanese attempt to eradicate Korean national identity.

When World War II ended, Soviet forces assumed control of
Korea north of the 38th parallel and American forces occupied the
south. The Soviets withdrew in 1948, after creating a communist
state in their zone. The Democratic People's Republic of Korea
(DPRK, or North Korea) was proclaimed on September 3, 1948.
The following year U.S. forces withdrew from the South, leaving
behind the Republic of Korea (ROK, or South Korea), which had
been proclaimed on August 15, 1948.

The newly created United Nations tried to work out a scheme by
which the north and south could be reunited. But no plan would satisfy both the Soviets, who hoped to see a reunited *Communist* Korea,
and the Americans, who intended the reunited country to be *democratic* and *capitalistic*. When negotiations bogged down, North Korea
used force to achieve its goal of reunification under a communist
regime. On June 25, 1950, North Korea invaded South Korea, initiating the Korean War. A United Nations' army, led by a U.S. general
and composed primarily of U.S. troops, went to the aid of South Korea. United Nations troops successfully pushed back North Korea's
army and carried the war into North Korea. At this point Communist
China came to the aid of North Korea. The war settled into stalemate

and an armistice was signed on July 27, 1953. The armistice restored the status quo and created the Demilitarized Zone, which still exists today. Technically, North Korea and South Korea are not at peace, but merely in a state of suspended hostilities. To this day, neither country accepts the legitimacy of the other nor do they have diplomatic relations.

Syngman Rhee was elected the first president of South Korea in 1948 and served until 1960. Politics during his tenure revolved around his struggle to remain in power. Under the Rhee regime, educational opportunities were greatly enhanced, providing many Koreans with upward mobility. Democratic ideas and principles were taught in the schools and presented in the mass media. Nevertheless, the economy was mismanaged and corruption was widespread. Rhee utilized martial law and fraudulent tactics to remain in power after his first four-year term was over in 1952. He was finally forced to resign in 1960 after students protested the rigged elections of that year.

After Rhee's resignation and exile to Hawaii in 1960, the government became even more disorganized. Two weak leaders were appointed as president and premier. The political and economic chaos continued. In 1961 the army carried out a coup d'etat. A military junta led by Park Chung Hee quickly consolidated its power by removing those it considered corrupt or unqualified and disbanding all political parties. In 1962 the junta, under the military leadership's Democratic Republican party (DRP), wrote a new constitution that received widespread public support and provided for a president to be elected directly by popular vote. Park officially became president in 1963 and kept the position until his death in 1979. Park was committed to bringing Korea in line with other economically developed countries. Despite widespread opposition to his authoritarian regime, Park was successful in promoting South Korea's general economic growth, encouraging private entrepreneurs, increasing exports, and laying the foundation for the country's economic success today.

In 1969 Park amended the constitution in order to ensure his reelection in 1971. In 1971 Park proclaimed a national emergency and forced a bill through the National Assembly that granted him dictatorial powers. In 1972 Park proclaimed martial law, dissolved the National Assembly, censored the press, and suspended all political activities. Students protested these actions and called for the restoration of democracy. After the oil shocks of 1973 and 1978, the Korean economy, which had been strong, fell into recession and became inflationary. The New Democratic party (NDP) won a plurality in the National Assembly in 1978 and its leader, Kim Young Sam, began to challenge the Park government in 1979. However, he was ousted from the National Assembly by Park for criticizing him. In 1979 Park's chief of military intelligence, Kim Chae-kyu, assassinated Park and his bodyguards as the result of a conflict over the management of the student protests.

After Park's assassination, South Korea experienced a power struggle, increased student unrest, and the emergence of a new military order. Ch'oe Kyu-ha, who had been the premier under Park, was elected interim president in 1979, but General Chun Doo Hwan was the real head of state. He controlled the military and effectively the government. In May 1980 almost 2,000 people were killed in the city of Kwangju by army units loyal to General Chun. Since the South Korean Army was (and still is) under the joint command of the United States, many Koreans held the United States indirectly accountable for the incident. The American position was that the Korean military informed them of the massacre only after it had occurred. Nonetheless, anti-American sentiments began to spread and were further aggravated by U.S. support for General Chun after he assumed the presidency in August 1980.

Chun, now the leader of the Democratic Justice party (DJP), purged elements of the government that he perceived as threatening to his rule or corrupt. The economy began to improve gradually by 1983, due to Chun's anti-inflationary policies and the general upturn in the global economy. Nevertheless, the Chun government failed to win public support and the regime became increasingly unpopular. In 1987 student unrest led to the downfall of the government. Kim Dae-Jung, the leader of the opposition NDP, succeeded in gaining control of the National Assembly.

In 1988 Roh Tae-Woo, another army officer and the new leader of DJP, became the first democratically elected president. He announced a new democratic constitution embodying many of the opposition's demands. In 1990 the DJP and the Reunification Democratic party merged to form the Democratic Liberal party (DLP). However Roh's program for economic and social change failed to meet the demands and expectations of the people.

South Korea's current president is Kim Young Sam, who was elected in 1993 and represents the DLP. He is the first civilian president in over thirty years. To stimulate the economy, Kim has promoted a liberalization program that includes deregulation of certain industries, a reduced bureaucracy, and an end to corruption. Today, South Korea is in a state of transition from a controlled and centralized society and economy to a more open and democratic one.

Mutual trade has helped to normalize South Korea's relations with Japan, but many Koreans continue to harbor ill feelings for the Japanese. Japan's history of invading and exploiting Korea, as well as poor treatment of Koreans living in Japan, remains a sore spot for many Koreans. Further, Japan's refusal to acknowledge and apologize for its aggression against and occupation of Korea along with the harsh treatment of "comfort women," Korean women forced into prostitution for the Japanese troops, continues to fuel anti-Japanese feelings. Nevertheless, the two countries' cultural and linguistic similarities, their shared histories, and their close physical proximity have resulted in a strong economic relationship between Japan and Korea.

Anxiety about North Korea has remained a constant aspect of the South Korean psyche since 1950. The two Koreas have held numerous talks, but most of these focused only on sideshow issues, such as complaints of alleged or real military provocations across the narrow DMZ. Over the decades, differences among the two Koreas have widened, as South Korea has modernized and enjoyed an expansive economy. In contrast, North Korea's self-imposed isolation and communist policies have led it to the brink of economic collapse. Over the decades, trade between the two Koreas has been limited to basic goods and commodities, carried on through indirect channels in China. In the second half of 1994, the government of Kim Young Sam began to consider lifting his country's ban on trade with North Korea, primarily as a consequence of a potential breakthrough in relations between the United States and North Korea.

In 1994 anxiety over North Korea's nuclear program generated concern in South Korea and throughout the rest of the world. With the July 1994 death of Kim Il Sung, the dictatorial leader of North Korea for forty-nine years, the two Koreas have entered a new period of uncertainty. The new leader of North Korea, Kim Jong Il, the son of Kim Il Sung, remains an enigma to foreigners as well as South Koreans. Nevertheless, in light of such events as the reunification of Germany and the collapse of the Soviet Union, South Koreans continue to believe that reunification of the two Koreas is eventually inevitable. They worry, however, about the financial costs of unifying the two economies, which have a gap greater than that of West and East Germany at the time of reunification.

Political Structure

The most recent constitution became effective in 1988. The president is both the chief of state and the head of the government and, therefore, has a great deal of power. He is elected to one five-year term directly by the people. The State Council, or cabinet, is headed by the president and consists of the prime minister and various ministry heads. The president has the power to appoint and dismiss the prime minister, who oversees the coordination of the ministries and agencies. Legislative authority rests with the unicameral National Assembly, which has three hundred members. Two-thirds of the members are elected by popular vote for a term of four years: parties who win five or more seats in the direct election split the remaining one-third of the seats among themselves proportionately. The National Assembly has the technical right to impeach the president.

The Republic of Korea is divided into nine provinces and has six main cities: Seoul, Pusan, Kwangju, Taejon, Taegu, and Inchon. The Supreme Court and the Constitutional Court share judicial authority, each with specific functions. The civil code has been influenced primarily by European law and the political and commercial codes have been influenced by both American and European laws.

Economy

Since the end of the Korean War in the 1950s, the country has achieved substantial economic growth, due in large part to extensive government planning, cooperative government and business efforts, and the hard work of South Korean people. The South Korean government has developed a well-educated and highly skilled work force and has implemented five-year plans since 1962 that have established the framework for development, focusing on an export-led industrialization strategy. Since 1970, the gross national product (GNP) has increased 35-fold in nominal terms. Almost 45 percent of the current GNP comes from industrial and manufacturing activity due to South Korea's focus on becoming a manufacturer and an exporter of finished products, not just an exporter of raw materials. The country ranks as one of the world's largest trading nations. The government actively participates in several sectors, including public services, utilities, mining, and other industries requiring heavy capital investment. Modern expressways and other transportation systems connect the major cities and industrial sites and efficient telecommunications systems exist throughout the country.

Korea has no known petroleum resources and its mineral resources are limited. Natural resources consist of iron ore, coal, tungsten, and nonmetallic minerals. At one time Korea was heavily dependent on petroleum imports. In the 1970s the country embarked on an energy diversification policy to promote use of nuclear energy, natural gas, and hydroelectric power.

Since the early 1990s, the South Korean economy has slowed

down considerably. The economy is highly dependent on foreign trade, as most industries are export-oriented. In recent years, many of South Korea's Asian neighbors have become more competitive due to lower labor and other costs and favorable exchange rates. South Korea has also been affected by slower growth in productivity. As a result, South Korea has found itself shifting to high-tech and higher value products.

Korea's major industries include electronics, automobiles and automotive parts, armaments, textiles, clothing, and leather. The country also earns foreign exchange from construction services. The major crops include rice, barley, millet, corn, sorghum, buckwheat, soybeans, and potatoes. Tourism is also a growing industry in Korea. The government has enacted various laws designed to encourage continuing foreign interest in Korea, both economically and socially.

People, Values, and Social Customs

With a population of about forty-four million, South Korea is one of the most densely populated countries in the world. Almost 50 percent of the people live in one of the six largest cities. Due to South Korea's economic success, the standard of living for its citizens is relatively higher than that of most of its Asian neighbors. Korea is a relatively homogeneous society in which the people share a common language, culture, and history. Despite their country's physical proximity to China and Japan, Koreans do not trace their origins to either country. The ancestors of modern Koreans most likely migrated from Siberia, Inner Mongolia, and Manchuria to eventually form a homogenous ethnic group. There are no significant linguistic minorities.

The national identity is relatively strong and, at times, xenophobic. Similar to the Japanese, Koreans perceive citizenship or nationality as being the equivalent of membership in a race or homogeneous ethnic group. They are unable to comprehend the idea of multi-racial and multi-ethnic societies such as the United States. This consciousness of homogeneity is one reason that Koreans in both the north and south perceive the division of the peninsula as unnatural and wrong. Although the two nations have pursued different political and economic policies, the people of both nations share a common heritage and culture. While they cannot agree about reunification, most Koreans view themselves as a common race with a common destiny.

Korea's geography, as well as its historical military and economic ties with China, created a natural role as a cultural bridge between the Japanese archipelago and mainland Asia. Nevertheless, Koreans have always had a general hostility toward any foreign control or influences. South Koreans have a love–hate relationship with the United States and Western culture in general. While they enjoy aspects of Western pop culture, many of the younger generation believe that the United States and the former Soviet Union are responsible for the division of Korea. Further, this same group believes that South Korea's ties to the United States are one reason why reunification has not progressed. The American troops still stationed in South Korea have become the focus of a small segment of South Koreans fostering anti-American sentiment. Koreans are also very suspicious of Japan, having suffered greatly under Japanese control before World War II. However, mixed with the feelings of hostility is admiration for Japanese economic advancements, as well as some jealousy. Despite historical setbacks, Koreans tend to be resilient and tough, which has led to their post-war economic success.

Koreans tend to be more conservative than many of their Asian neighbors. Some Koreans may feel threatened rather than flattered if a foreigner displays too much knowledge of their society and language. Foreigners who know the culture well are sometimes perceived to be "invading" the Korean world. Like the Japanese, the Koreans feel that their culture is truly unique and superior to other cultures and, as a result, well beyond the comprehension of a foreigner.

Buddhism had an early influence on the Korean culture and remains the traditional religion. But today Korea is also heavily influenced by Confucianism and Christianity. About 43 percent of the population is Christian, predominantly Protestant. Other religions that have influenced Korea include Shamanism, Taoism, and Islam. Neo-Confucianism, which combines the social ethics of classical Confucianism with Taoism and Buddhist metaphysics, has also been very important in shaping modern society. One of the key principles is that social relations are not based on individual happiness or satisfaction, but on the harmony of the collective group. Traditionally, individuals' rights are less important than community obligations, although the influx of Western ideas concerning democracy, equality, and respect for the individual have affected South Korean society. Shamanism, Korea's oldest religion, originated in Siberia and was brought to the peninsula by Neolithic tribes. The religion is based on the premise that the world is inhabited by various spirits. The Shaman priest, can communicate with the spiritual world and placate the spirits through rituals involving incantation, music and dance. The Shaman mixes practical advice with ritual lore. The influence of Shamanism, although much less in modern Korea, contrasts sharply with the self control of Confucianism as is reflected in the Korean tendencies to be self-controlled and meticulous and yet, on occasion, be volatile and emotional.

Throughout history, two enduring principles of Korean society have been the importance of authoritarian centralized control and the significance of a social system that makes a clear distinction between the rulers and the masses. The Confucian belief that scholar-officials should lead society has always been strong in Korea. As a result, education has always been viewed as *the* tool for advancement. However, historically, only the rich and well-educated were able to provide their children with the benefit of education, thereby making upward mobility in Korean society difficult. During the Yi dynasty, which embraced Confucian values, family lineage and social status became important, and a class called the *yangban* emerged as dominant. The *yangban* became the ruling scholar-official class of traditional Korea and was noted for its knowledge of Confucianism and its monopoly of government positions.

Confucianism declined as a religion and political philosophy once Japan conquered Korea in 1910. However, today it continues to influence social relations. The relationship between father and son is still stressed and the traditional rituals are conducted to show respect for ancestors and family obligations. However, contemporary Koreans are moving away from some of the traditional culture and practices. For instance, complex extended families are being replaced by the nuclear family structure. Further, there is more equality among family members, including women. Nevertheless, Koreans continue to place the family above all other concerns. As in many Asian societies, sons are expected to financially support the family and to carry on the family name by marrying and having sons of their own. Koreans are often preoccupied with family honor and with maintaining dignity at all times.

Korean women enjoy a relatively positive position in comparison with their Asian counterparts. Some women hold middle-management jobs and many are receiving higher education. Most women manage the family finances and, as in most other Asian cultures, are responsible for the well-being of their family and the education of their children. In public, women may appear quiet and submissive, although they may exert power behind the scenes. Public display of a woman's power is socially unacceptable, even if she holds a management-level position.

The influence of Confucianism is also evident in Korean's appreciation of knowledge and education. The literacy rate is one of the highest in the world at over 90 percent. Historically, Koreans have always felt that what separated them from the West was not racial inferiority, but lack of knowledge. As a result, young people are pushed to absorb extensive amounts of knowledge in the hope that it will improve their position in life. Social classes in South Korea are now based on one's education, profession, and wealth. Accordingly, personal improvement is an important cornerstone of

Korean culture. Intensely competitive, Koreans perceive wealth as a positive sign of success. After the end of World War II, most Koreans living in the south were poor peasants. The Korean War deepened the poverty. Education, then, became the only tangible key for betterment. As modernization transformed Korea into a dynamic and industrial society, people became even more convinced of education's value as the means to achieve professional and social success. While Koreans value knowledge and achievement, they also value age and seniority. At times, people are promoted based on merit alone, but age is usually the primary determinant.

The school system in Korea is similar to that in the United States. There are six years of primary school, six years of secondary school, and four years of higher education. The high school years are the hardest and most important part of a Korean student's education. An extremely rigorous curriculum prepares students for a difficult exam that must be passed in order to move on to a university. It is common for most students to attend evening cram sessions to master subjects, particularly if they want to gain admission into the elite universities. This grueling high school experience builds important lifelong bonds. As a result, attending the "right" high school is an integral part of developing the right network and connections, which in turn serve to open doors later in life. At one time, students used to travel great distances or bribe officials to attend the "right" high school, but the government is working to eliminate such situations. Admittance into high schools is based on academic excellence. Many Koreans attend university in the United States, particularly for postgraduate work. However, "old school ties" remain critical for advancement and professional success. The elite universities in South Korea are the Seoul National University, Yonsei University, Koryo University, and Ehwa Women's University.

Since the early 1900s many South Koreans have sought to move overseas to better their situation. During the Japanese colonial period, many Koreans emigrated to Manchuria, other parts of China, the Soviet Union, and the United States. During World War II almost two million Koreans lived in Japan while serving in the army or in labor battalions. Koreans who remained in Japan after the war were denied Japanese citizenship and often had a lower standard of living as the Japanese continued to discriminate against them. Therefore, most modern Koreans often prefer the United States for relocation because it contains established Korean communities. Europe, which has fewer Koreans, is less familiar and offers less support.

Work Schedule

Most businesses and government offices operate from 8:30 or 9:00 A.M. to 6:00 P.M. on weekdays and from 9:00 A.M. to 1:00 P.M. on Saturdays. It is common to find employees in the office after 6:00 P.M. From November to February government offices close daily at 5:00 P.M. Banks are open from 9:30 A.M. to 4:30 P.M. on weekdays and from 9:30 A.M. to 1:30 P.M. on Saturdays. Shop hours vary, but most are open from 8:00 A.M. to 9:00 P.M. everyday. Department stores are open from 10:30 a.m. to 7:30 p.m. everyday.

Making Contacts

Koreans value good introductions and referrals. Thus, you should try to obtain a formal introduction. Use common acquaintances, suppliers, accountants, lawyers or consultants. If you are seeking an introduction to a large Korean firm, check to see if it has a subsidiary in a country where your company also has an office. If you can develop a relationship with the Korean subsidiary, it can serve as your introducer. In most business circumstances it is very helpful to have a local partner. If you need an agent, use one who is approved by the Korean government. Cold calls or letters usually do not work. Prior to going to Korea, you should have made contact with the firms that interest you and scheduled meetings. Do not expect to arrive in Korea, make calls to those companies, and then be able to meet with them.

Before selecting a local partner, research the market very care-fully. It is not uncommon for Korean companies to enter into part-nerships with foreign firms in order to learn about their products and technology and then seek to withdraw from those partnerships once they have learned as much as possible. It is advisable to establish relations with several firms, so that if one partnership breaks down, you will have other business relationships. Korean businesspeople can be opportunistic and well might drop you if a better deal comes along. It is also advisable to assign someone from your firm to represent you on a permanent basis or at least visit the country regularly to supervise the implementation of a venture. In many cases, this person will need to discreetly verify that work has been properly completed. Frequent visits will also assure your Ko-rean associates that you are committed to them and to the market.

The Korea Trade Promotion Corporation (KOTRA) publishes a guide, *How to Trade with Korea*, that provides a good overview of business information. In the United States, general information on doing business in Korea can be obtained by fax through the PacRim Hotline (Tel. 202-482-3875), which provides trade and economic statistics as well as summaries of other issues, and is updated every three months. The Association of Foreign Trading Agents of Korea, in cooperation with the American embassy, publishes an annual guide, *American Business in Korea*. This guide includes a list of registered agents in Korea as well as other valuable information. There are several other books and directories of Korean firms oper-ating overseas. Check with the local Korean trade office in your home country for these and other resources.

Meeting People

Many South Korean professionals are accustomed to Western val-ues and customs because they have studied or worked overseas. You can expect almost all South Korean businesspeople to have some familiarity with Western culture. Government officials, however, tend to be more traditional and conservative and may have had less exposure to Western culture.

Most South Koreans prefer to hold a first meeting in their office, but some may prefer to meet with you initially in a restaurant. Punctuality is very important. It is common to shake hands with both men and women upon greeting; this is often accompanied with a slight nod of the head or a slight bow. Unless you have experience with other Eastern cultures, you may be surprised by some common Korean customs. For instance, men have priority and Korean men will go through a door first rather than holding it for a woman.

Business cards are always exchanged at the first meeting. They should be presented and received with both hands, with the writing facing the receiver. To show respect, read the business card slowly and carefully before placing it on the table in front of you. Koreans feel more at ease once they are familiar with the company and the position of the person with whom they are meeting. If you can, have the message on your business card translated into Korean and printed on its back side. If you are representing a small or less-well-known firm, be sure to give your counterpart some descriptive corporate literature as an introduction.

In most business situations Koreans will seek to match you up with someone of similar rank, as determined by their interpretation of your title. Koreans tend to base a person's status on his or her age, level of education, current rank in a company, and previous professional associations. Keep this in mind when selecting a representative to work for you in South Korea, for these factors are often more important than familiarity with the country and its language.

Most Koreans have three names: two given names and a surname. When written in Chinese or Korean script, the surname always appears first. When written in English, various combinations are possible, although most Koreans will write the surname last to ensure that foreigners will not call them by their given name. You should feel comfortable asking a person how he or she would like to be addressed. The majority of Koreans use just a half-dozen surnames: 22 percent use the surname "Kim," about 15 percent use "Lee" or "Yi," about 9 percent use "Park" or "Pak," 5 percent use "Ch'oe," and 4 percent use "Chong." When addressing a new acquaintance, use formal titles such as "Mr.," "Mrs.," "Miss," "Dr.," and "President." First or given names are considered personal and are rarely used in business. You should wait to be invited to use first names. Most Korean wives retain their maiden names. It is best to learn each person's entire name. If you are meeting a woman, ask her secretary if she prefers to be addressed as "Mrs." or "Miss." The Western "Ms." is not common in most of Asia.

It is important that you speak clearly and slowly; your hosts may have some familiarity with English, but not be fluent. Do not assume that everything spoken in English is understood. Most Koreans can understand written English better than spoken English. It is important to reiterate your key points and, wherever possible, use written materials and graphics. It is a good idea to have your written materials translated into Korean. Hotels can assist you with this task. If your negotiations are technical or you are unsure of your counterpart's English ability, it is best to hire an interpreter to accompany you.

It is important to remember that although South Korea and its people appear to be Westernized in terms of business values and living standards, they do not necessarily adhere to all the common Western values. Rather, they hold Asian and, more specifically, Korean values. For example, the concept of *kibun*, which relates to a person's mood or current state of mind, affects all interpersonal relationships. To hurt someone's *kibun* is to cause a loss of dignity. Maintaining harmony is more important than absolute truth.

The Korean sense of humor tends to be direct. Koreans smile in a variety of situations including when they are happy, sad, or nervous. Koreans will often laugh when embarrassed or when they feel uncomfortable. Look for other signs to determine the emotion that is being expressed.

Begin a first meeting with casual conversation about your trip.

Your Korean counterpart will probably try to find out who else you are meeting with during your visit. Usually, Korean businesspeople will become more interested in you and your proposal if they feel other Koreans are also interested in your company and its products or services. Of course, it is best to be a bit vague and not to provide too much information to your counterpart. Do not try to accomplish too much at the first meeting. Koreans need to feel you out and get a sense of your trustworthiness and objectives. If you appear too pushy, Koreans will assume that you are desperate. Public perception and image matters a great deal to Koreans. How they appear to you and how you appear to them is an integral aspect of your business interaction. Thus, representatives of well-known multinationals will usually receive a better initial reception from Koreans.

Gifts are not required for the early meetings. If you have developed a relationship with your Korean counterpart by letter or telephone prior to your visit, you may want to bring him or her a small token such as pen or a gift with your company logo. A gift of liquor is also appropriate. If you meet with a group, you should have a gift for the senior person as well as other gifts for all subordinates attending the meeting. The senior person's gift should be different and more expensive than the others. For example, you could give the senior person an expensive bottle of liquor and give everyone else small gifts with the company logo. If you receive a gift, refrain from opening it in front of the giver.

Corporate Structure

The Korean economy continues to be dominated by *chaebols*, which are large business conglomerates, many of which are still family-owned and family-operated. During the period of Japanese rule, Japanese business interests established family-owned firms that were the precursors to the *chaebols*. The relationship between the government and the chaebols remains very close, for the government has traditionally turned to these large companies to promote national development goals. In the past, the government has officially supported the *chaebols* by offering them special privileges and lending rates. As a result small businesses have fared poorly.

In general, Korean management practices and the country's business structure have been heavily influenced by the Japanese. The typical corporate structure has a chairman of the board at the very top. In large, family-run *chaebols*, the chairman is usually the most senior family member. Below the senior level in descending order are division chiefs, section chiefs, managers, and employees. The division chiefs and the section chiefs usually have enough authority to make a deal, but their authority often depends on the type and amount of the deal. The highest person has the ultimate decision-making responsibility. As in Japan, senior people are expected to take the blame for corporate misdeeds or poor performance by resigning, thereby protecting the company's reputation. Koreans do not often move between firms, although they are not as firmly entrenched as Japanese employees.

Politics continues to have a major influence on Korean businesses, although less so than in the past. Most foreigners will have to interact with the Economic Planning Board as well as the Ministry of Finance for approvals regarding investments and transactions. Your Korean representative should be able to manage this process for you. Your country's embassy and chamber of commerce should also be able to assist you in navigating the system.

Negotiation

To be productive in Korea, you must develop a trusting personal relationship with business partners. Koreans have a local saying, "Make a friend first and a client second." A person's character is just as important as the strength of the contract or deal. As part of the process of developing a personal relationship, Koreans spend time on business socializing. It is important to accept social invitations and to reciprocate. However, it is important to remember that just because your Korean counterpart entertains you, it does not automatically imply that a deal has been agreed upon. Further, be careful not to let your business judgment slip by allowing the pleasantries to affect your negotiations.

In terms of decision-making, Koreans prefer group consensus, with the senior person issuing the final verdict. At each stage of a negotiation, all senior people are kept abreast of developments and related issues. In general, Koreans are very conservative, are risk-averse, and have a very strong work ethic.

Koreans do not appreciate aggressive and adversarial negotiators. Out of preference for nonconfrontation, Koreans may appear to agree just to keep negotiations harmonious. It is important to allow your Korean counterparts ample time to reach an agreement; otherwise, your hoped-for deal will never be consummated. Koreans may appear to be stubborn, rigid, and difficult negotiators. Their competitive spirit combined with their ambition can make them unyielding. Your best strategy is to be firm and clear about your own position. Koreans may become emotional and might express anger and frustration. It is best if you, as the foreigner, do not raise your voice or become visibly angry or frustrated, unless absolutely necessary in the latter stages of a negotiation. Always present your arguments calmly, clearly, and in a dignified manner. When making a decision, Koreans take personal relationships and character into account in addition to standard business issues.

Often in order to preserve harmony, Koreans will report good news, even if it is unwarranted. Koreans have a desire to keep an optimistic and hopeful attitude that "things will get done". As a result, there are times when Koreans will say that action has been taken when in fact nothing has been done. Avoid appearing condescending and politely follow up to make sure that all parties are following though on their commitments. In other situations, Koreans may withhold information because they believe that knowledge is power and that if you and your firm knew everything, you would find a better deal and no longer need the Korean entity.

Koreans do not like to say "No" directly. Instead, they may say something like: "I will consider it," "I am not sure," "I would like to, but . . ." You may need to ask several indirect questions in order to understand the true response. Koreans often perceive themselves as "giving" a contract to someone rather than the person or company "winning" the contract. Try to use similar terminology, stating "You would be pleased if they awarded or gave you the contract", instead of saying "We would like to win your contract." Using the word "win" implies a one-sided benefit in favor of the foreigner. The goal is to always keep harmony and allow everyone to "maintain face." However, it should be noted that Koreans view negotiations as a win–lose situation where one side must lose and the other side must win. Accordingly, they will seek to gain as many concessions as possible from you.

You may be asked the same question repeatedly. The intent is to ensure consistency in information and responses so that mistakes and misunderstandings do not occur. Culturally, Koreans will publicly assume responsibility if they make a mistake. It is not uncommon for superiors to loudly berate junior staff if errors occur. Koreans take their power and authority very seriously and may frequently display it. However, this would rarely be done in the presence of a foreigner. You should, of course, refrain from doing the same. Koreans accept the hierarchical system of their own culture, but can become defensive and insulted if they are made to feel inferior to a foreigner.

Most Koreans tend to be concerned more with price than with cost-efficiency or effectiveness. In the public sector, bidding for smaller items is evaluated first on a technical basis and second on a financial review. Usually, only the top three proposals are invited to the financial review. The winning bid is usually the lowest priced proposal that passed the technical phase. Larger projects are opened for bidding to a select list of about fifteen Korean companies. Only if the government believes that the technology does not exist in Korea will they invite foreign firms to bid on a contract. Historically, foreign firms have fared the best when they worked in collaboration with a Korean company. Foreign firms that wish to bid directly from their home base need certification by the local Korean diplomatic or commercial office in their home country.

Written contracts should be used in all business interactions, but Koreans tend to view contracts loosely. They believe that contracts summarize a deal that has been negotiated, but allow for flexibility and adjustment as circumstances change. It is not uncommon for Koreans to change the "rules" as the situation changes. Often, issues that have already been agreed upon are subject to future negotiations by the Koreans in order to extract additional advantages. Be sure to specify responsibilities and roles clearly.

Conducting Business in a Social Setting

Dining and Drinking

Koreans enjoy meeting for business over any meal. Business meals are used more to strengthen and enhance business relationships and less for conducting actual business. Power lunches, business dinners, and drinking are very common. Ask your hotel or local counterpart for suggestions about appropriate locations to host a meal. When dining out, Koreans do not split the bill. You will always be the host or the guest. Among Koreans, the younger person usually pays. Foreign businesswomen should indicate their willingness to participate in business entertaining, as some Koreans may hesitate to invite a woman out for a "business" meal.

Business entertaining occurs in two main venues aside from restaurants: the traditional *kisaeng* house and the more modern room salon. You will likely be seated in a private room or section. Wait until your host indicates where you should sit. If you are the host, be sure to direct your guest to a seat of honor. When drinking, be aware that tradition dictates that no glass should remain empty. If you do not want to drink excessively, leave some alcohol in your glass. The local alcohol, *soju*, is very strong. If you do not drink alcohol, simply inform your host and you will be served a soft drink or juice. Your host will pour for you and you should reciprocate by pouring for him. Toasts are made by raising your glass with your right hand and saying *gun-bei*. Food and drinks are passed using the right hand, with the left hand supporting the right forearm.

Group sing-alongs are common, with each guest taking a turn to sing a song. Skill is less important than good-natured participation: the emphasis is on taking part and having fun. Most parties will end around midnight when the government's curfew on entertainment establishments begins.

Visiting a Home

After you establish a personal relationship, your Korean counterpart may invite you to his home. Shoes are removed before entering homes (or religious places). Appropriate gifts are fruits, cakes, expensive cognacs, liquors, wines, or champagne.

Gift Giving

Corruption or bribery, although existent, is less widespread in South Korea than in other neighboring countries. However, gift giving is very important. New Year's is a common time in Korea to exchange gifts, particularly with business associates in other firms. The government recognizes the first three days of January as the New Year; however, most Koreans celebrate the New Year according to the lunar calendar. Appropriate gifts include silk ties and scarves, leather goods, quality pens, and items with corporate logos. Korean businesspeople will also appreciate an invitation for a fine meal and drinks. Never give money as a business gift. However, money is the common gift for weddings, funerals, and the first and sixtieth birthdays. Money should always be placed in a nice envelope.

When giving a gift, Koreans will often say something humble to the effect that "It is a small worthless gesture." When receiving a gift, they may show hesitation. You should react similarly when receiving a gift. It is considered very rude to open a gift in the presence of the giver.

Dress Code

Conservative, formal dress is best for both men and women. Men should wear suits and ties. Women should wear suits or dresses. Slacks are only appropriate for informal social occasions. Flashy colors and heavy perfumes are inappropriate.

Useful Phrases

Korean is the official language and English is a common second language throughout the country. Chinese and Japanese are spoken in some areas. The Korean language is said to have once belonged to the Ural-Altaic group and has been influenced by both China and Japan. Early on, Chinese characters were used; however, in the fifteenth century scholars in the Yi dynasty invented the *Han'gul* writing system, which is based on phonetics and contains few characters. In modern times, either *Han'gul* combined with Chinese characters or just *Han'gul* are used. The Korean language uses polite and honorific speech. The following list includes some useful Korean phrases and a guide to their pronunciation.

Hello. — Yo-bo-say-yo (use only when on the telephone; otherwise say in English)

Good morning / Good afternoon / Good Evening — Say in English
How are you? — *Ahn-yung hah-seem-yee-kah*
Please — *Cheh-song hap-nee-da*
Thank you — *Kahm-sah hahm-nee-dah*
You are welcome — *Chun-mahn-ay-yoh*
Excuse me — *Chil-song hahm-nee-dah*

I am sorry	Mee-ahn hahm-nee-dah
My name is———	Cheh ee-rum en———ip-nee-da
I work for———	Cheh hoi-sa ee-rum en———ip-nee-da
Here is my business card	Chey myung ham ip-nee-da
I am pleased to meet you	Mahn-nah-soh pan-gap-sum-nee-dah
Please accept this small gift	Yakso ha-jee-man bah-da joo-sip si yo
I look forward to developing a good relationship with you / your firm	Kwi-sah-wha cho-un-sa-up quan-kay rool met-kee-rool kee-teh ham-nee-da
I understand	Ee-heh ham-nee-da
No, I do not understand	Chahl modara toot-ket-sum-nee-da
Please wait a minute	Cham-kahn-mahn kee-ta-ree-ship-shee-yo
Where is the bathroom?	Whua-chang-shill-ee oh-dee eet-sum-ni-ka?
Good-bye	Ahn-nyung-hee kay-ship-shee-yo
Cheers	Gun-bei

Major Holidays

January 1–3	New Year's
January / February*	Lunar New Year's Day
March 1	Independence Movement Day
May*	Buddha's Birthday
May 5	Children's Day
June 6	Memorial Day
July 17	Constitution Day
August 15	Liberation Day
September / October*	Chusok (Korean Thanksgiving)
October 3	National Foundation Day
December 25	Christmas Day

*These holidays are based on the lunar calendar and can vary widely from year to year.

General Facts

Climate: Korea has four distinct seasons. Spring is mild and breezy with temperatures averaging between 50F (10C) and 55F (13C). The monsoon season begins in mid-June and lasts until mid-July. The typhoon season begins in August. Temperatures during the summer are hot and can reach 95F (35C). Autumn is generally pleasant with warm days and cool nights. Fall temperatures average between 32F (0C) and 66F (19C). Winters are long and cold with relatively small amounts of snowfall. Temperatures average between 16F (-9C) and 37F (3C).

Currency: The currency is the *won* and is (abbreviated as W). Each won consists of 100 *chon*.

Dates: Dates are written year, month, and day. For example, March 15, 1995, would be abbreviated 95/3/15.

Electricity: Both the 110-volt (60 cycle) and 220-volt (50 cycle) systems are found in Korea. However, the 110-volt system is being gradually phased out and the 220-volt system is becoming more widespread. Hotels tend to have both levels of power. Be sure to check an outlet before usage.

Entry Requirements: United States, United Kingdom, Canadian, French, and German citizens need only a valid passport. A visa is required for stays longer than fifteen days (sixty days for EEC citizens) and must be obtained prior to entering Korea. Business visas are valid for up to two months and require a letter from the foreign company stating the purpose and length of visit. No letter is required from the Korean company.

Time: Korea has one time zone, which is nine hours ahead of Greenwich Mean Time and fourteen hours ahead of U.S. Eastern Standard Time (thirteen hours in Daylight Savings Time).

Tipping: Tipping is not widespread in Korea. Usually a 10 percent service charge and a 10 percent tax are added to hotel and restaurant bills. If the service was exceptional, up to an additional 10 percent may be left if you choose. Taxi drivers do not expect to be tipped, but appreciate the gesture. It is always acceptable to leave the change. It is customary to tip about 10 percent if the driver assists you with your luggage.

Transportation: Taxis are convenient, plentiful, and easy to use. In city areas, taxis can be hailed on streets as well as at taxi stands and in front of hotels. An increasing number of taxi drivers speak some English. You may need to remind your driver to turn on the meter, and you may want to negotiate your fare in advance. It is also advisable to have your destination written in Han'gul. Korean addresses do not use street and building numbers in the manner of Western addresses. Landmarks are often used to give and receive directions. In Seoul, there are two types of taxis: regular and deluxe (88 taxi), which are more spacious and also more expensive. The deluxe taxis are black with gold trim and provide receipts for fares. Roads are very congested during rush hours in the morning and evening; at these times taxis are not always the best means of transportation. Korean taxi drivers commonly pick up more than one set of passengers who are going in the same direction: each passenger must pay the metered fare when he or she is dropped off.

There are several modes of transportation to travel to and from the airport including free hotel airport shuttles, taxis, airport limousine buses, and airport express buses. The free hotel shuttles are listed by hotel near the curb outside of the baggage claim area. Taxis are the most convenient. Be sure to take into account the usual heavy traffic when traveling to and from the airport.

If you are located in the city center the most convenient method for getting around is walking. Caution should be exercised when crossing the street: cars do not always yeild the right of way to pedestrians. Most street crossings are underground.

Rental cars are readily available in the cities; however, this is not advisable because traffic is dense and street signs are not in English. You can rent a car and driver for the day for moderate prices. Car rental information is available at the airport or through hotels. An international drivers license is required

Buses and subways are modern, reliable, and cheap, but often crowded. Subway stations in Seoul and Pusan have station names, ticket windows, and transfer signs posted in English and Korean. A subway ticket is used to enter and exit the subway system and should be retained until you reach your destination. The bus system differs slightly from city to city. There are two types of buses—local and express—in Seoul. Because the route numbers are written in Korean, have a local person write the number down for you and also indicate the correct stop. Local buses in Seoul are very crowded, but run extensively throughout the city. The green city express buses called *chwasok* (seat) buses will only accept enough passengers to fill available seats and are often air-conditioned in the summer. Subway and bus maps are usually available at hotels, subway stations, and small booths near bus stops.

There is also an extensive train and bus system connecting the various cities and towns. It is best to check with your hotel for maps, routes, and fares, as the schedules are only written in Korean.

Helpful Telephone Numbers

There are four types of public telephones: gray, orange, blue, and card-operated. The orange telephones are only for local calls, and have a maximum time limit of three minutes. A warning beep will sound and the connection will be cut automatically. You will then have to place the call again. Additional money will not continue the call. Gray and blue telephones can be used for domestic and international calls, as well as for calls longer than three minutes. International calls can also be made from hotels as hotel operators usually speak English. In addition to the card-operated pay phones, some gray telephones accept phone cards which can be purchased from small shops close to the telephone boxes. The country code is (82). The area codes for major cities include: (02) for Seoul; (051) for Pusan; (0652) for Chonbuk; (062) for Kwangju; (0431) for Chungbuk; (032) for Inchon; (0361) for Kangwon; (0331) for Kyonggi; (0551) for Kyongnam; (053) for Taegu; and (042) for Taejon. Omit the first zero when dialing from outside of the country.

Hospitals and Doctors:

Asian Medical Center
388-1 Pung Nap-dong
Song Pa-ku, Seoul
Tel.: (2) 480-3026

Asia Emergency Assistance
S-12 Bldg., 1st Floor
274-14, UN Village
Hannam-dong
Yongsan-gu, Seoul
Tel.: (2) 790-7561

Seoul Adventist Hospital
29-1, Hwikyong-dong
Tongdaemoon-ku, Seoul
Tel.: (2) 244-0191

Severance Hospital
134 Shinch'on-dong
Sodaemun-gu, Seoul
Tel.: (2) 361-5114

Ambulance in Seoul: Dial 129.

Police in Seoul: Dial 112 /
313-0842 (English).

Operator Assistance: Dial 007 /
114; 0077 / 004 for International
calls.

Information Hotlines:
Korea Tourist Information:
(2) 757-9986
Korea National Tourism
Corporation: (2) 665-0088 (at
Kimpo International Airport in
Seoul)
International Information: 1035
/ 1037

Useful Addresses

In Korea

**American Chamber of
Commerce**
Westin Chosun Hotel,
Room 307
87 Sokong-dong
Chung-ku, Seoul 100
Tel.: (2) 753-6471

**Association of Foreign Trading
Agents of Korea**
Dongjin Building
218 Hangang-ro
2-ga Yongsan-gu, Seoul
Tel.: (2) 792-1581 / 780-3377

**British Chamber of Commerce
in Korea**
Naewoi Building, 13th Floor
9-1 Ulchiro 2-ga
Chung-gu, Seoul
Tel.: (2) 757-5143

Economic Planning Board
1-Chungang-dong
Kwacheon-shi
Kyunggi-do, Seoul
Tel.: (2) 500-9144 (Bilateral
Trade) / 503-9016 (Fair Trade
Commission)

**French Chamber of Commerce
and Industry in Korea**
Kyong-hyangshinmun
Building 22
Annex, 6th Floor
Chong-dong
Chung-gu, Seoul
Tel.: (2) 720-7547

Immigration Bureau
Ministry of Justice
2nd Government Complex
Building 1
Chung-ang-dong
Kwachon, Kyonggi-do
Tel.: (2) 503-7097 / 655-2103
(push #3 for information in
English)

**Korean-American Business
Institute**
Paik Nam Building, Room 808
188-3 Ulchiro 1-ka
Chung-gu, Seoul 100-191
Tel.: (2) 753-7750

Korean Chamber of Commerce
Namdaemunno 4-ga
Chung-ga, Seoul
Tel.: (2) 757-0757

Korea Exhibition Center
159 Samsundong
Kangnam-ku, Seoul
Tel: (2) 551-0114

**Korea Foreign Trade
Association**
159-1 Samsundong
Kangnam-ku, Seoul
Tel.: (2) 551-4181

**Korean–German Chamber of
Commerce and Industry**
KCCI Building, 10th Floor
45 Namdaemun-ro 4-ka
Chung-ku, Seoul 100 094
Tel.: (2) 776-1546

**Korea National Tourism
Corporation (KNTC)**
10 Ta-dong

Chung-ku, Seoul
Tel.: (2) 757-0086

Kimpo Airport
Tel.: (2) 665-0086

Korea Trade Network
159 Samsong-dong
Kangnam-gu, Seoul
Tel.: (2) 551-8500

**Korea Trade Promotion
Corporation (KOTRA)**
Kimpo International Airport,
Room 162
272 Gwahae-dong, Kangsu-ku
Seoul
Tel.: (2) 663-3026 / 3328 or
662-2204

Trade Center Building,
6th Floor
Pusan, 87-7, Choongang-dong
4-ka, Choong-ku
Pusan
Tel.: (51) 463-3691 / 2 or
463-3631

Kimhae International Airport,
lst Floor, Room 112
2347 Daejeo-2-dong
Kangseo-ku, Pusan
Tel.: (51) 971-6665

**Korea–U.S. Economic
Council, Inc.**
Trade Tower #159, Suite 4304
Samsung-dong
Kangnam-ku, Seoul
Tel.: (2) 551-3366

Ministry of Finance
1-Chungang-dong

Kwacheon-shi
Kyunggi-do, Seoul
Tel.: (2) 503-9259 / 9260

**Ministry of Trade, Industry
and Energy**
1-Chungang-dong
Kwacheon-shi
Kyunggi-do, Seoul
Tel.: (2) 504-0105

Seoul Immigration Office
319-2, Shinjong 6-dong
Yangchon-gu, Seoul
Tel.: (2) 653-3041/8

**Seoul City Tourist
Information Center**
(behind City Hall)
Tel.: (2) 731-6337

U.S Trade Center
82, Sejong-ro
Chongro-ku, Seoul 110-050
Tel.: (2) 397-4114

Embassies and Consulates:

American Embassy
82 Sejong-ro
Chongro-ku, Seoul
Tel.: (2) 397-4114

American Consulate
24 2-ka, Daechung-dong
Chung-ku, Pusan
Tel.: (51) 246-7791 / 2

British Embassy
4 Chong-dong
Chung-gu, Seoul
Tel.: (2) 735-7341 / 3

Canadian Embassy
Kolon Building, 10th Floor
45 Mugyo-dong
Chung-gu, Seoul 100 170
Tel.: (2) 753-2605 / 8

French Embassy
30 Hap-dong
Seodaemun-ku, Seoul
Tel.: (2) 312-3272

French Commercial Office
Samheung Building, 705-9,
8th Floor
Yoksam-dong, Kangnam-ku
Seoul
Tel.: (2) 564-9032

German Embassy
Daehan Fire & Marine
Insurance Building, 4th Floor
51-1 Namchang-dong,
Chung-ku, Seoul 100
Tel.: (2) 726-7114

In Canada:

Korean Embassy
151 Slater Street, 5th Floor
Ottawa, Ontario K1P 5H3
Tel.: (613) 232-1715 / 7

Korean Consulate General
1000 Sherbrooke Street West
Suite 1710
Montreal, Quebec H3A 3G4
Tel.: (514) 845-3243 / 3244

555 Avenue Road
Toronto, Ontario M4V 2J7
Tel.: (416) 920-3809

830–1066 West Hastings Street
Vancouver, B.C. V6E 3X1
Tel.: (604) 681-9581

**Korean Trade Promotion
Corporation (KOTRA)**
Thompson Building, Suite 600
65 Queen Street West
Toronto, Ontario M5H 2M5
Tel.: (416) 368-3399

One Bentall Center, Suite 1710
505 Burrard Street
Vancouver, B.C. V7X 1M6
Tel.: (604) 683-1820 / 687-7322

Korea National Tourism Corporation (KNTC)
480 University Avenue
Suite 406
Toronto, Ontario M5G 1V2
Tel.: (416) 348-9056

In France:

Korean Embassy
125 Rue de Grenelle
75007 Paris
Tel.: (1) 47-53-01-01

**Korea Trade Promotion
Corporation (KOTRA)**
25–27 Rue d'Astorg
75008 Paris
Tel.: (1) 47-42-00-17

In Germany:

Korean Embassy
Adenauerallee 124
5300 Bonn 1
Tel.: (228) 267960

**Consulate General of
Korea**
Kurfuers Tendamm 180
10707 Berlin 33
Tel.: (30) 885-9550

Eschersheimer Landstrasse 327
6000 Frankfurt / M.1
Tel.: (69) 563051 / 3

Hagedornstrasse 53
20149 Hamburg 13
Tel.: (40) 4102031 / 2

**Korea Trade Promotion
Corporation (KOTRA)**
Im Internationlen Handels-
zentrum, 4th Floor
Zi-Nr.405 (Box Nr. 11)
Friedrichstrasse 95 D-10117
Berlin
Tel.: (30) 2643-2637 / 2638 /
2640

Mainzer Landstrasse 27-31
6000 Frankfurt am Main-1
Tel.: (69) 236895 / 7

Heidenkampsweg 66
20097 Hamburg
Tel.: (40) 232235

In the United Kingdom:

Korean Embassy
4 Palace Gate
London W8 5NF
Tel.: (71) 581-0247/9

**Korean Trade Promotion
Corporation (KOTRA)**
Vincent House, Ground Floor

Vincent Square
London SW1P 2NB
Tel.: (71) 834-5082 / 828-4275

**Korea National Tourism
Corporation (KNTC)**
Vogue House, 2d Floor
1 Hanover Square
London W1R 9RD
Tel.: (71) 409-2100

In the United States:

Korean Embassy
2450 Massachusetts Avenue, N.W.
Washington, DC 20008
Tel.: (202) 939-5600

Korean Consulates
305 GCIC Building
Agana, GU 96910
Tel.: (671) 472-6488

101 Benson Blvd., Suite 304
Anchorage, AK 99503
Tel.: (907) 561-5488

Cain Tower, Suite 500
229 Peachtree Street
Atlanta, GA 30303
Tel.: (404) 522-1611 / 3

1 Financial Center, 15th Floor
Boston, MA 02111
Tel.: (617) 348-3660

NBC Tower, 27th Floor
455 North Cityfront Plaza Drive
Chicago, IL 60611
Tel.: (312) 822-9485 / 8

2756 Pali Highway
Honolulu, HI 96817
Tel.: (808) 595-6109

1990 Post Oak Blvd., Suite 745
Houston, TX 77056
Tel.: (713) 961-0186

3243 Wilshire Blvd.
Los Angeles, CA 90010
Tel.: (213) 385-9300

Miami Center 201, Suite 800
South Biscayne Blvd.
Miami, FL 33131
Tel.: (305) 372-1555

460 Park Avenue, 5th Floor
New York, NY 10022
Tel.: (212) 752-1700

3500 Clay Street
San Francisco, CA 94118
Tel.: (415) 921-2251

2033 Sixth Avenue, Suite 1125
Seattle, WA 98121
Tel.: (206) 441-1011

**Korean Trade Promotion
Corporation (KOTRA)**
460 Park Avenue, Suite 402
New York, NY 10022
Tel.: (212) 826-0900

111 E. Wacker Drive, Suite 519
Chicago, IL 60601
Tel.: (312) 644-4323

4801 Wilshire Blvd., Suite 230
Los Angeles. CA 90010
Tel.: (213) 954-9500

12720 Hillcrest Road, Suite 390
Dallas, TX 75230
Tel.: (214) 934-8644

Two South Biscayne Blvd.,
Suite 1620
Miami, FL 33131
Tel.: (305) 374-4648

California Street, Suite 1905
San Francisco, CA 94111
Tel.: (415) 434-8400

1129 20th Street, N.W.
Suite 410
Washington, DC 20036
Tel.: (202) 857-7919

**Korean Foreign Trade
Association**
460 Park Avenue, Suite 555
New York, NY 10022
Tel.: (212) 421-9904

1800 K St., N.W., Suite 700
Washington, DC 20006
Tel.: (202) 686-1560

U.S. Department of Commerce
International Trade Adminis-
tration
Korea Desk, Room 2325
14th and Constitution Avenues,
N.W.
Washington, DC 20230
Tel.: (202) 482-4390

**U.S. Department of State,
Office of Korea Affairs**
Room 5313
2201 C Street, N.W.
Washington, DC 20520
Tel.: (202) 647-7717

U.S.-Korea Business Council
1023 15th Street, N.W.
7th Floor
Washington, DC 20005
Tel.: (202) 842-1381

3 China ────────────

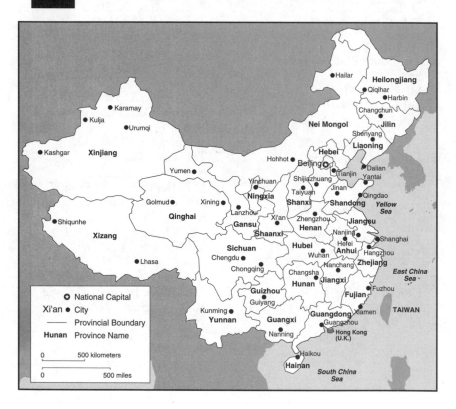

Geography

Located below Russia on the western seaboard of the Pacific Ocean, China is about as large as the continent of Europe and slightly larger than the United States. It is the third largest country in the world after Russia and Canada, with a total land area of 3.7 million square miles (9.6 million square kilometers). The country is dominated by mountain ranges, broad plains, and expansive deserts which have created different climate zones as well as regional and cultural boundaries. Of the country's numerous rivers, the Huang He (Yellow River) in the north, the Yangtze River in central China, and the Xijiang (West River) in the south are the three longest and most important rivers. Most of the country's people live in the east where agricultural prospects are better than in the western and northern inland areas, which are covered by mountains and deserts. The major cities include Shanghai, Beijing (the capital), Tianjin, and Guangzhou (also known as Canton).

Brief History

China's known history begins with the Age of Five Rulers, which occurred roughly between 2852 B.C. and 2205 B.C. However, Chinese legend states that the first ancient ruler was Fu Xi who reigned in the thirty-fourth century B.C. Fu Xi is said to have inspired the sacred book, the *I Ching*, which promotes the theory that the universe is subject to alternating yin and yang. The theory states that history is cyclical: dark periods precede periods of enlightenment, which are followed by periods of darkness and repression, and so on. This theory of history has greatly impacted the Chinese mind-set.

The following list chronicles the successive recorded dynasties in China:

Xia (Hsia)	2205 B.C.–1766 B.C.
Shang	1766 B.C.–1122 B.C.
Zhou (Chou)	
(Spring and Autumn Period)	1122 B.C.–476 B.C
(Period of the Warring States)	476 B.C.–221 B.C.
Qin (Ch'in)	221 B.C.–206 B.C.
Western Han	206 B.C.–A.D. 23
Eastern Han	A.D. 25–220
Three Kingdoms	A.D. 220–280
Western Jin (Chin)	A.D. 265–316
Eastern Jin	A.D. 317–420
Southern and Northern Dynasties	A.D. 420–581
Sui	A.D. 581–5

Tang	A.D. 618–907
Five Dynasties and Ten	A.D. 907–960
Kingdoms	
Northern Song (Sung)	A.D. 960–1127
Southern Song	A.D. 1127–1279
Yuan (Mongol)	A.D. 1279–1368
Ming	A.D. 1368–1644
Qing (Manchu)	A.D. 1644–1912

The Zhou dynasty was the first to establish the capital at XiAn, present-day Luoyang. During the Zhou dynasty, the philosophy of the "mandate of heaven," the notion that a ruler governed by divine right, became widespread and provided legitimacy for existing and future rulers. During the Zhou period numerous philosophies developed, including Confucianism, so the period is also known as the "Era of a Hundred Schools of Thought."

The Qin dynasty was established by the emperor Qin Shi Huang Di, who was the first to establish a unified Chinese empire and is credited with building the Great Wall. (Rather than one continuous wall built in one period, the Great Wall is actually four large walls rebuilt or extended during the Western Han, Jin, Sui, and Ming dynasties.) Qin made his greatest impact on Chinese society by creating an administrative system that provided the basis for the present system. He divided the country into thirty-six provinces, and appointed civil and military governors to administer them, collect the taxes, and maintain the peace. These governors were made directly accountable to the emperor.

The Han dynasty is best known for its prosperity, which led to a flowering of the arts and literature. During this period Buddhism was introduced into the country from India. The collapse of the Han dynasty was followed by nearly four centuries of civil wars and disunity, except for a brief period during the Western Jin when unity was restored. Despite its political fragmentation during these centuries, China witnessed great technological advances in medicine, astronomy, and cartography.

During the Tang dynasty China became a powerful regional and global force. Its advanced civilization was characterized by further developments in science, philosophy and religion. Commerce was active, and China conducted trade with most of the known world. Arts and literature flourished and magnificent ceramics and porcelain were created. During this period many Muslims entered China from the northwest.

The first foreign conquerors of China were the Mongols, who under Genghis Khan invaded China in the thirteenth century and won control of the north. Kublai Khan continued the Mongol conquest and took over all of China, establishing the Yuan dynasty in 1279, thereby placing China under foreign rule for the first time. China became part of the large Mongol Empire that stretched from Europe and Persia in the west, to Russian and Siberia in the north, and to China in the east. Rivalry among Mongol imperial heirs, natural disasters, and peasant uprisings led to the collapse of the Yuan dynasty in 1368.

The Ming dynasty was founded by a rebel army leader who was a Han Chinese peasant and former Buddhist monk. The Mings are credited with rebuilding the Great Wall, although there were active periods of wall construction in earlier dynasties. The Great Wall was intended to keep out the northern barbarian nomads.

The Manchus, originally known as Jurchen, were not Han Chinese, but descendants of Tungus tribes who had founded the Chin (Ta-ch'ing) Empire (1115–1234) in the northeastern territories of China, now known as Manchuria. Prior to the twentieth century, Manchuria was the private domain of the Manchu conquerors of China. In 1644 the Manchus conquered Beijing and became the second foreign culture to control China and the last dynasty to rule China. The Manchus adopted Chinese ways very quickly. However, they also sought to preserve their own cultural identity by various means. One such method was to mandate a physical distinction between themselves and the Chinese by requiring Chinese males to wear a long braid and shave the rest of their head, thereby creating the stereotypical image of the Chinese in the eyes of later visitors to China, primarily Westerners. The Manchus successfully absorbed Outer Mongolia, Tibet (Xizang), and Taiwan into their empire.

The first Westerners to visit China were the Portuguese, who eventually established a foothold at Macao, and who were followed by the Spanish, British, and French. From 1839 to 1842 the Chinese fought against the British in the First Opium War, after which China ceded control of Hong Kong to the British and opened five ports to trade with the West. The Second Opium War took place from 1856 to 1860. The Opium Wars fostered Chinese fears that Westerners intended to take advantage of China. In 1851, as a result of economic tensions, military defeats, and anti-Manchu sentiments, Hong Xiuquan, a village teacher, led the Taiping Rebellion. He advocated a new order based on the ancient Chinese state where peasants owned and tilled the land, and slavery and the degradation of women would be banned. Almost thirty million people were killed before the movement was finally suppressed fourteen years later.

Beginning in 1860, when the Russians seized Manchuria, the Western nations and Japan gradually encroached on Chinese territory and forced China to relinquish land through treaties. China lost part of Taiwan and conceded influence over Vietnam to France as a result of the Sino-French War (1884–1885). From 1894 to 1895, China fought with Japan and lost Korea, Taiwan, and the Pescadores Islands. In 1898 the British secured a ninety-nine-year lease on Hong Kong, Kowloon, and the Outlying Territories.

China's weak state spurred the development of secret societies to protect the country against foreign influence. The Yi He Tuan (Society of Righteous Fists), or Boxers as they were more commonly known, led an attack, often referred to as the Boxer Rebellion, in 1900 on the foreign quarters in Beijing. A force of seven Western powers and Japan responded, put down the rebellion, and occupied the imperial palace as the empress fled. Revolutionary movements began to spread throughout China. The Qing (Manchu) dynasty lost the "mandate of heaven" and finally fell in 1912.

As the Qing dynasty began to collapse in 1911, the revolutionaries established a provisional government at Nanjing. In early 1912 Sun Yat-sen was declared the first provisional president. However, the actual overthrow of the Manchu throne occurred later in 1912. This was accomplished by Yuan Shikai, who declared the death of the empire and the birth of the Chinese republic. He became president and Beijing was restored as the capital of the country. In the same year Sun Yat-sen formed the Kuomintang (also spelled Guomindang), a nationalist, republican party. In 1913 Yuan Shikai outlawed the Kuomintang and tried unsuccessfully to establish himself as the emperor. Upon Yuan Shikai's death in 1916, Sun Yat-sen returned to China from exile. Yuan's supporters continued to maintain a nominal government in Beijing. Sun Yat-sen set up a rival government in Guangzhou (Canton). In the same period regional warlords assumed control of other parts of China and vied for power. During the warlord period China's economy collapsed as the result of widespread banditry and an expansion of opium production, which was a major source of revenues for the warlords.

In 1915 Japan took advantage of China's internal turmoil and occupied Shandong province, which had previously been occupied by Germany. In 1915 the Japanese issued a list of "Twenty-one Demands," which were aimed at making China a protectorate of Japan. The Beijing government rejected the demands, but recognized Japan's authority over Shandong, southern Manchuria, and eastern Inner Mongolia. Japan's occupation of parts of China and its political influence during this period humiliated the Chinese and continues to fuel anti-Japanese feeling in China today. In 1917 China entered World War I with the hope of regaining control of the lost province, a hope that was dashed at the Versailles Peace Conference. This denial sparked anger in China, leading to the 1919 demonstrations now called the "Fourth of May Movement." By 1921, with revolutionary passions high, the Chinese Communist party was formed in Shanghai with Mao Zedong (former spelling Tse-tung) as one of the founding members.

In 1921 Sun Yat-sen reorganized the Kuomintang and formed

a nationalist government in Canton despite a lack of support from the Western democracies. With guidance from the newly established government of Russia, the Kuomintang attracted members from the Chinese Communist party and formed a revolutionary army. When Sun Yat-sen died in 1925, his brother-in-law, Chiang Kai-shek, assumed control of the Kuomintang and the Guangzhou national government. Chiang Kai-shek pursued a strategy to conquer the north. Nationalist forces captured one province after another, finally reaching Shanghai in 1927. Then the right wing of the Kuomintang led by Chiang Kai-shek broke with the Communist party and purged the Kuomintang of all left-wing members. In April 1927 Chiang Kai-shek set up a provisional nationalist government at Nanjing. The government was recognized in 1928 by the Western powers. The Kuomintang became dominant throughout the country and Chiang Kai-shek was appointed president. The communists were forced to retreat underground where they regrouped to form a revolutionary base.

Chiang Kai-shek tried to reestablish political unity throughout the country, but was unsuccessful because throughout the 1930s his energies were focused on routing the communists. During this same period, the Japanese further encroached on Chinese territory. In 1931 the Japanese took the rest of Manchuria and by the mid-1930s had advanced to the outskirts of Beijing. Despite Chiang Kai-shek's attempts to eliminate the communists, they maintained a steady presence under Mao Zedong, who by 1935 was their undisputed leader. Chiang Kai-shek's focus on the communists rather than on the Japanese advances made him very unpopular with the people. On December 1, 1937, a Japanese attack on the city of Nanjing resulted in the deaths of more than one hundred thousand soldiers and civilians; this outrage is commonly called the Nanjing Massacre. In the resulting chaos the Japanese army raped numerous Chinese women and pillaged Chinese property. Japan's unwillingness for decades to publicly admit to the brutality of the situation fueled widespread resentment of the Japanese among the Chinese. By

1938, the Japanese army controlled the northern provinces, a significant portion of the Yangtze Valley, and all of the major towns in the eastern provinces from Manchuria to Guangdong.

In 1945 Japanese forces were defeated by Allied forces. World War II, which the Chinese refer to as the War of Resistance (with Japan), was over. Although the Chinese communists tried to hold all the provinces they occupied at war's end, Chiang Kai-shek's nationalist armies, with U.S. aid, seized control of the strategic points in formerly Japanese-occupied territory. Despite American attempts to reconcile the two Chinese factions, civil war broke out 1946. The communists, skilled in guerrilla tactics, gained control of most of the north by 1948; in 1949 they took control of Beijing and the rest of China. Chiang Kai-shek and his followers fled to Taiwan.

On October 1, 1949, Mao Zedong proclaimed the establishment of the People's Republic of China. The Communist party was led by Chairman Mao and the government was headed by Zhou Enlai (formerly spelled Chou En-lai), who served as premier. One year later, China entered the Korean War to aid communist North Korea in its war with South Korea and United States–led United Nations forces.

After creating a pact with the Soviet Union in 1950, the new communist government directed its efforts to restoring the economy and creating a socialist infrastructure and institutions. It promoted land reform, which was accompanied by widespread executions of members of the landlord and rich peasant classes. The First Five-Year Plan, based on Soviet economic models, reorganized the land into cooperative farms. The cooperatives created a cradle-to-grave welfare system in which workers were assigned and guaranteed jobs in a work unit. All of an individual's or family's needs were met by the unit. However, people were not allowed to leave their unit, thereby making mobility impossible. This system was referred to as the "iron rice bowl." Political dissent was not tolerated and critics of the new system were eliminated.

In 1958 the Second Five-Year Plan was introduced, organizing industrial and rural sectors into communes. The "Great Leap Forward" program tried to promote huge increases in production in industry and agriculture, but failed when quality was sacrificed in favor of quantity and bad harvest seasons resulted in a two-year famine. Dissension within the party weakened Mao's political power, although he retained his prestige and honor. Liu Shaoqi became chairman of the republic in April 1959.

By 1960 the China–Soviet Union relationship had seriously deteriorated and the Soviet Union canceled aid and assistance to China. Relations continued to worsen throughout the decade. In 1962 border clashes with India erupted into a small war. In 1964 China tested a nuclear bomb for the first time.

In 1965 Mao Zedong and his supporters criticized President Liu Shaoqi and his supporters, as well as certain writers and teachers. This attack was the first battle in what is now called the "Great Proletarian Cultural Revolution." The Cultural Revolution was Mao's attempt to destroy China's "Four Olds": old thoughts, old culture, old customs, and old habits. Mao hoped to pit political factions against one another, regain control of the Communist party and the government, and promote a radical transformation of the society. In 1966 students, in response to an appeal by Mao, formed themselves into the Red Guards. Entrusted with the fate of the revolution throughout China, they sought to destroy counterrevolutionary forces and individuals suspected of lacking sympathy with Mao's designs. They stormed homes and offices, destroying books, artworks, historic buildings and other manifestations of China's prerevolutionary culture. Universities were seized and teachers were attacked. Officials and intellectuals were subjected to public humiliation, exile to rural areas, forced work as laborers, trials, imprisonment, and execution. One of the major goals of the revolution was to create a completely equal society in which all educational, class, and labor distinctions were abolished.

However, by the end of 1966 it became apparent that the Red Guards had gone too far. Anarchy and chaos were spreading throughout China. Attacks by the Red Guards often forced local party leaders to abandon their posts. As a result, in some places, it was unclear who wielded power. Some people, frustrated by the Red Guards, formed rival groups that also pledged their allegiance to Mao Zedong, and confrontations between the groups increased.

The army remained the only institution not affected by the Red Guards and the general social disintegration. In 1968 the army put down the Red Guard movement. Mao held control, and Lin Biao was chosen to be his successor. In addition to its effort to create an equal society, the Cultural Revolution is also noted for creating the cult of Mao Zedong. Mao's wife, Jiang Qing (also spelled Chiang Ch'ing), was rapidly elevated within party ranks and became a powerful force in the revolution.

In 1971 Lin Biao was killed in a mysterious plane crash after it was announced that he had tried to seize control of the government. In 1972 the American president Richard Nixon made his historic visit to China. Later in 1972 Japan established diplomatic relations with China. Meanwhile, Chinese relations with the Soviet Union continued to deteriorate.

In 1976 both the Premier Zhou Enlai and Mao Zedong died. Before Mao's death in September, the radicals in the Communist party, including Mao's wife, launched a campaign against Zhou Enlai's successor, Deng Xiaoping, forcing him out of power. Hua Guofeng, an unknown, was selected as acting premier. After Mao's death, leading party radicals, including Mao's wife, now branded "the Gang of Four," were arrested and sentenced to long jail terms. In 1977 Deng Xiaoping returned to power as the choice of all moderates and pragmatists interested in promoting economic development and reform in industry, agriculture, science and technology.

On January 1, 1979, China and the United States established full diplomatic relations. One month later China invaded Vietnam due to Vietnam's poor treatment of ethnic Chinese and Vietnam's attacks on the Khmer Rouge in Cambodia, who were allies of China. Having demonstrated its power, China withdrew after seventeen days. By 1980 it was evident that China's economy was in trouble. Severe droughts plagued the north and floods hit the south. In response, Deng Xiaoping restructured the political leadership while maintaining his own place at the top. Throughout the 1980s, his government focused somewhat successfully on China's economic problems and he is credited with the economic modernization of China. The economic reforms included dismantling the collectives and the gradual introduction of market forces into the economy in order to force companies to operate with a profit motive. These economic reforms also permitted foreign companies to enter China's markets. In 1984 China signed an agreement with Britain providing for the return of Hong Kong to Chinese rule in 1997.

By the mid-1980s the political situation became tense as student demonstrations protesting against political corruption and advocating democratic reforms spread across the country. In 1987 the secretary general of the Communist party, Hu Yaobang, was forced to resign because he was viewed as too sympathetic to the student demonstrations. He was replaced by Zhao Ziyang. A conservative backlash swept the party and "liberal" members were purged. Fear of bourgeois liberalism or more accurately, Western ideas and influence, swept through the conservative elements of the party. In April 1989 Hu Yaobang died, prompting a renewed call from China's students for more political freedom, democratic reforms, and the elimination of government corruption and nepotism. As student demonstrations spread, martial law was imposed. On the night of June 3, 1989, the Chinese military cracked down on the student demonstrations in Tian An Men Square. While the world watched the melee on television, hundreds of students were killed; thousands more were eventually arrested.

By 1990, when martial law was lifted, the economy was already responding well to the reforms. As more and more members of the international community reestablished ties with China, the economic situation continued to improve. By the mid-1990's, China's economy was booming as foreign business interests eagerly sought to enter the Chinese market. Despite the economic advances and reforms, the political system remains closed. Deng Xiaoping continues to lead the country, although as of late 1994 his health was fragile and there was growing speculation about his successor. China's human rights abuses have been a source of contention in relations with the United States. Despite disagreements with China, the United States, primarily as a result of the extensive U.S. commercial interests in China, renewed China's "Most Favored Nation" status in 1994, thereby ensuring that Chinese products will continue to enjoy cheap and easy access to the American marketplace.

Political Structure

The government of China is communist in structure. Although the Chinese constitution provides for three separate branches of government—executive, legislative, and judicial—in reality there is no such separation. The political power rests with three organizations: the Chinese Communist party (CCP), the state, and the army. Generally, the CCP dictates policy and the state implements that policy. The army is controlled by the CCP. The party constitution, adopted in 1982, abolished the post of party chairman to reduce the possibility of any future personality cults like the one that grew around Mao. The current president and party general secretary is Jiang Zemin.

Party members hold key positions in the government, thereby ensuring the CCP's complete control of the country. The CCP is headed by a general secretary who is elected by the CCP Central Committee and who manages all aspects of the party and government. Within the Central Committee, power resides with the Political Bureau and its Standing Committees, which are the chief policymaking bodies. The Central Committee is elected by the National Party Congress, theoretically the highest body in the CCP (not to be confused with the National People's Congress, discussed below), which meets once every five years. The CCP exercises authority over the military through the General Political Department of the People's Liberation Army (PLA). At the bottom of the party hierarchy are three types of organizations, general party branches, primary party committees, and party branches, all of which operate in factories, shops, schools, offices, neighborhoods, PLA companies, and other party-approved places.

The State Council is the highest body of state administration and is the executive body of the National People's Congress (NPC), the highest legislative body. Headed by a premier (currently Li Peng), vice premiers, and ministers, the State Council coordinates the work of numerous ministries, commissions, and various other government offices. The State Council is responsible for implementing economic policy. The members of the State Council are technically appointed by the NPC but in fact the CCP Secretariat and Central Committee make all of the "recommendations." Often senior members of the State Council are concurrently influential party leaders. Therefore, the NPC has very little power or control over the State Council. Like almost everything else in China, it is under the leadership of the CCP. Even the People's Courts are actually controlled by the CCP. However, local ministries and bureaus are beginning to exert more power.

Administratively, China is divided into 23 provinces, 3 municipalities (Beijing, Shanghai, and Tianjin), 5 autonomous regions, 174 prefectures, and about 2,200 counties.

The People's Procuratorates are the state organs responsible for supervising the administration of justice. China has a four-level court system with the Supreme People's Court in Beijing being the highest level. There are special courts to handle matters relating to the military, rail and water transportation, and forestry.

Economy

For the past fifty years China has had a centrally planned economy in which the state controls most of the commercial activity. Since the late 1980s the Chinese economy has been in transition away from central planning and toward a market-driven economy. The economy has been caught between two opposing forces: a burgeoning market sector that is outgrowing government control and the inability of that market to function efficiently due to continued influence by the state on production and prices.

There are four main economic sectors: state-run organizations; state-run and family-run farms; urban and rural, collectively owned industrial enterprises, which operate under the watchful eye of the state; and small private and individual businesses. State ownership dominates every sector of the economy except agriculture. Various ministries manage the regulatory and planning issues for specific industries including aeronautics, astronautics, chemicals, coal, electronics, metals, petroleum, textiles, railways, water resources, and the power sector. Many of the state-owned companies have become publicly held corporations and more privatizations are expected.

In 1979 China instituted economic reforms, established "special economic zones," and opened the economy to foreign investments and companies. This change in attitude brought remarkable changes to the formerly socialist economy, resulting in improved living standards and new social attitudes. As local provinces have benefited from foreign investment, particularly in the south, central economic control has weakened. Since 1978 industrial output has increased more than sixfold, in large part due to foreign manufacturers and investors who have established operations in China, usually as joint ventures with corporations owned or influenced by the Chinese government, but also with some private-sector companies. Most industrial companies are owned and managed by the state, either at the national, provincial, or municipal level, and account for the majority of the country's output. One recent negative effect of global attention and increased foreign investment has been soaring inflation.

In many areas China remains a predominantly agricultural society. Major crops include rice, barley, millet, tobacco, sweet potatoes, wheat, soy beans, cotton, tea, raw silk, rape seed, corn, peanuts, watermelon, and sesame seed. Under the 1979 regulations, peasants were permitted to lease land for private farming and were allowed to sell for profit any surplus produce above the quota demanded by the state in the open market. There are still more collectives than family farms, but this is gradually changing.

Besides agriculture, the leading industries include textiles, machinery, chemicals, communications and transportation equipment, building materials, and electronic machinery and equipment. The economic reforms of 1979 also apply to private citizens working in industry, and allows them more opportunity to profit from their own efforts.

Government attention and foreign investment has been focused on further developing the country's inadequate infrastructure, including roads, railways, seaports, communications systems, and power generation. Industrial capability, in both light and heavy industries, has also improved. China is a vast country rich in natural resources, including coal, oil, gas, various metals, ores, and minerals.

People, Values, and Social Customs

The culture varies greatly from region to region. Due to a lack of space, this book only addresses general attitudes and significant characteristics prevalent in major cities and regions. Readers familiar with the recent history of Taiwan might find it useful to know that mainland China is currently addressing many of the same issues Taiwan addressed about thirty years ago.

The population of China is approximately 1.2 billion, making it the most populous country in the world. The primary ethnic group is the Han Chinese, who constitute about 93 percent of the population. This group traces its history in China back to the Han Dynasty (206 B.C.–A.D. 220), but has since assimilated with other non-Chinese cultures. About fifty-five minority groups, collectively referred to as "the National Minorities," make up the remaining 7 percent of the population. These National Minorities are guaranteed special representation in the National People's Congress. These minorities include Mongolian, Hiu, Tibetan, Uygur, Miao, Yi, Zhuang, Bouyei, Korean, Manchu, Dong, Yao, Bai, Tujia, and Hani peoples. As in most countries with diverse populations, there is a tangled web of prejudices, rivalries, and tensions between various ethnic and regional groups. Among the different ethnic groups and between the various regions in China, there are wide differences in physical features, languages and dialects, social customs, and attitudes, so much variation that it is very difficult to generalize about China as a whole. Even among the Han Chinese, there are about eight mutually unintelligible dialects and numerous subdialects as well as wide cultural differences. Generally, southern Chinese are often noted for their emotional and expressive tendencies, which may explain why the modern revolutionary movements have primarily originated in the southern provinces. The Cantonese, from the southern province of Canton (Guangdong), enjoy playing word games and their humor comes from the variations of words. They often give each other nicknames that reflect an individual's personality and traits.

Despite decades of programs requiring family planning, China's population growth, 1.5 percent per year, continues to be a challenge for the country and its government. Eighty percent of the country's population lives modestly in rural areas. Urban dwellers, the majority of whom belong to a work unit, or *danwei*, and are employed in factories and workshops, have benefited most from the economic reforms. Per capita income, purchasing power, and living standards in cities like Guangzhou, Beijing, and Shanghai have increased dramatically.

Over the past decade young people have joined the Communist party not for ideological reasons, but as a way to advance economically. Party membership elevates one to the top of the social hierarchy and helps to ensure financial well-being. Party members in good standing tend to get the best jobs and enjoy rapid promotion. Even in the current reform atmosphere, those in senior party positions in various state-run organizations have financially bene-fited the most.

The four main religions in China are Confucianism, Buddhism, Taoism, and ancestor worship. Christianity, which did not success-fully penetrate China until the nineteenth century, is a minor religion. Most Chinese mix the beliefs and practices of the various re-ligions, resulting in a interwoven religion of Taoism-Confucianism-Buddhism. Confucianism has had a very strong influence on Chinese life, particularly on the role of family obligations, close contact with the extended family, respect for elders, and ancestor worship.

Throughout history, the Chinese have permitted religion to per-meate society provided that the religion's beliefs did not significantly alter the Chinese way of life. Today, religion is not practiced as de-voutly as before the 1949 liberation. (The Chinese refer to the events of 1911 as "the Revolution" and the events of 1949 as "the Libera-tion.") Temples, monasteries, and shrines are preserved more as his-torical artifacts rather than to encourage people to practice a faith.

Under communism, religious organizations have suffered. Their property, their independence from government interference, and their rights have all been curtailed. In recent times, symbolic ges-tures have been offered to suggest that religious tolerance is per-mitted. For example, in 1952 the Chinese Buddhist Organization was formed under communist guidance both to control Buddhism in Tibet and Inner Mongolia and to convey an impression of reli-gious tolerance. In practice, since the 1949 liberation the state re-ligion has been communism and Chinese have only just begun to publicly admit belief in religion.

One religious concept that is central to the Chinese is faith in *feng shui*, which means wind and water. It is based on the idea that man and nature must exist in harmony. Closely related to the yin and yang theory, *feng shui* is a school of environmental and cultural doctrines. The Chinese will consult with a *feng shui* man before building anything new to ensure a propitious site. Basically good spirits must be encouraged and bad spirits placated. When dealing with traditional Chinese, be aware that new ventures or new construction may need to be blessed by a *feng shui* person.

Traditionally, for most Chinese, the world is one entity populated by one great family and ruled by only one sovereign or emperor, who is Chinese of course. Interestingly enough, for centuries the Chinese people have viewed natural disasters such as earthquakes and floods to be the result of a lack of virtue in the emperor. A series of such disasters was considered symbolic of imminent change in dynastic leadership.

The Chinese are ethnocentric and xenophobic. Historically, and even today, the Chinese have been suspicious of outsiders, calling them *yang guai* (or *gwailo*), meaning "foreign devils." That the Chinese have viewed themselves as culturally superior is evident even in the name "China," whose Chinese characters mean "the central nation." For the Chinese, their world is the true center of the universe. Foreigners are to be looked down upon because they were not fortunate enough to be born Chinese. The Chinese, like the Japanese, have tried to adopt Western ideas and technologies slowly so as to maintain the Chinese cultural identity.

Outsiders are welcomed, but are seldom trusted. While the Chinese appreciate foreigners who make attempts to speak the language or participate nominally in the culture, they are very suspicious of those who speak the language well or who appear to have a deep understanding of their culture. The Chinese are concerned that such a "foreign devil" is getting too close to the core of their culture. Among Westerners, Americans are usually the preferred "foreign devil." Northern Europeans are often perceived to be too authoritarian.

The Chinese are not the most helpful people to outsiders. People will rarely go out of their way to assist someone they do not know. A common phrase in China is *mei-you*, which is a negative concept and means "I don't have," "I don't want to deal with you," "It's too much trouble," "Don't bother me," and "Beat it." If a Chinese person is uninterested in helping you or performing his or her job, he or she will utter this phrase.

The work ethic in China is weak, primarily as a result of the communist system, although it differs between regions. Chinese in free market environments, such as Hong Kong, cultivated a very strong work ethic. Until recently, people in China were guaranteed a job for life through the "iron rice bowl" system. This is changing, especially in the south, given the spread of a free market economy. Women are still discriminated against in China although not as much as in many other countries in the region. There are some women in positions of responsibility, although their prominence varies by industry. Chinese women tend to be strong and capable and are often the backbone of their families.

Most Chinese tend to be modest and humble. They are unlikely to respond to a compliment with a "Thank you" or any other acknowledgment of its validity. Usually, people will deny or diminish the importance of their presence or demonstrate humility. For example, if you are a guest at a lavish meal, your host will invite you to join "the simple meal." In contrast, the Chinese always appreciate praise of their children, who are a parents' pride and the focus of their attention.

For the Chinese, their family, including extended family and friends, is the central unit. Confucian values continue to influence family member relationships. Senior family members are obeyed, for they acquire dignity and status as they age. The Chinese take care of each other and the part of the world in which they live. Everything else is irrelevant because it does not affect their family or themselves. For example, the Chinese keep their own homes spotless, but don't think twice about littering the streets or public areas.

A foreigner in China, unlike a foreigner in Japan, can eventually become part of a Chinese person's circle of family and friends. However, a foreigner who enjoys the honor of becoming friends with a Chinese person should understand that he or she is expected to accept the traditional Chinese obligations of being a friend and must be reliable and dependable. Most foreigners find that creating friendships in China are not difficult. However, maintaining friendships at the levels the Chinese expect can be difficult. Chinese expectations of friendship can be burdensome for those foreigners unaccustomed to such a high level of mutual dependency. Friendships are expected to last throughout a person's life. A friend is expected to provide assistance whenever necessary.

Historically, due to the Confucian influence, Chinese culture has stressed individual achievement and advancement through education. The 1949 liberation was successful in reforming education and making it more available. As a result, literacy rates have increased. Until recently, due to the education bureaucracy and the assignment system, slots in higher education and jobs were assigned to young people while they were still in secondary school. Even overseas educational opportunities required government approval. As a result, many students were forced to study subjects or to take jobs in which they had no interest. The Cultural Revolution was in part an attack on the educational system then in place, for it was obvious that those who fared best in the school system and received the better jobs were the children of the bourgeoisie and urban professional groups rather than the children of the workers and the peasants. The Cultural Revolution belittled education and expertise; led to the closing of many schools, to the exile of teachers and students into rural areas, and to their forced labor on farms; and deprived an entire generation of access to higher education.

By the late 1970s this policy was reversed and the government began to encourage education and expertise over political motivation and ideology. By the late 1980s, students were allowed much more flexibility in determining their field of study and profession. Many Chinese students, primarily in technical fields, attend university in foreign countries, providing them with greater exposure to different attitudes and philosophies.

Work Schedule

In most cities in China businesses and government offices are usually open Monday through Friday and every other Saturday from 8 A.M. to noon and from 1:00 or 2:00 P.M. to 5:00 or 6:00 P.M. China officially has a five and a half-day workweek consisting of forty-four hours. Although the two-hour lunch break is becoming less common in Beijing, it is still not the best time to conduct business or go shopping. Banks are open Monday to Saturday from 8:00 A.M. to 5:00 P.M. Shops are open everyday from 8:00 A.M. to 6:00 or 7:00 P.M.

Making Contacts

Whenever possible, obtain an introduction. If you are representing a well-known international company, you can send a letter to the senior-most person in a Chinese company in which you state your purpose for contacting him or her. However, connections and relationships, known as *guanxi*, are very important; the right connections can ensure you an attentive audience for your proposal and subsequent interactions. *Guanxi* also incorporates an element of graft, for those who have the connections will often try to profit from them. *Guanxi* creates an interdependency between the two parties because favors received must be reciprocated at some future time. When sending an initial letter it is a good idea to have the letter translated into Chinese. It is not necessary to translate everything you send to China. Make sure there is sufficient interest on the other end before you translate much of your marketing literature and the like, because translation costs could become expensive.

Once you have decided to visit China, either you, your counterpart, or local representatives should schedule meetings for you at least one to two weeks in advance of your arrival. Before your arrival, make your desires regarding accommodations and the like known to your business contact. This can be particularly important if you represent a small firm with a limited budget. The Chinese tend to believe that all foreigners, particularly Westerners, are wealthy and can therefore afford to pay for all services. Arrangements may be made without consulting you and you may be overwhelmed with hospitality. You may find a car and driver waiting for you at the airport. You may be booked into a luxurious guest house, where you are the guest of honor at a banquet. Be warned: you will probably have to pay for everything and subsequently be presented with the bill on your final day. You should feel comfortable in politely declining any service that you do not want, such as a car. Further, foreign visitors can be surprised to discover that their Chinese business contact will make an effort to keep them entertained at all times. In China, a host's responsibility includes fulfilling needs and ensuring the comfort, care, and protection of their guests. If you wish to spend some time alone, indicate so very politely, perhaps by saying that your counterpart should meet you later in the day and at the place of business rather than at your hotel room.

You should hire a local representative or consultant to monitor deals and relationships in your absence and to maintain a constant presence for your company in China. This is particularly important if you are sourcing from or selling to China. You can use a regionally based person from Hong Kong, but be warned: mainland Chinese from the north are often wary of Hong Kong Chinese, who have a reputation for devious practices. Chinese in the south are usually more comfortable conducting business with Hong Kong Chinese due to similarities in language and cultural preferences. When hiring a local representative, be sure to carefully check references and to obtain a list of his or her former and current clients. With the increased interest in China, there are numerous people and individuals in China who claim to be able to work "magic" in addition to having "high-level" contacts. Check with local embassies and consulates as well as with the chamber of commerce. Directories are available at the Chinese commercial and trade offices in foreign countries. If you are ready to make a long-term commitment to the country, you should consider joining a trade group such as the U.S. China Business Council in Washington, D.C.

Meeting People

Most of China's business world slows down considerably during the spring festival in late January and early February. Business visitors would be wise to avoid this two to three week holiday period. Avoid scheduling meetings between noon and 2:30 or 3:00 P.M., during which most people take a one-hour lunch which is sometimes followed by a *wushui*, an afternoon nap. Although the Chinese are not always on time, punctuality is viewed as a positive asset in others. In fact, arriving early indicates respect for the host.

The Chinese pride themselves on holding their feelings inside; thus they may not smile at a first greeting or as often as people do in some other Asian countries. The Chinese usually greet one another with a slight bow or nod of the head. In business and with foreigners, a handshake is common upon greeting and departure. The Chinese are informal, but also traditional in all interactions. Various greetings are used. One common greeting is *Ni hao*, which means "Hello." Another is *Ni hao ma*, which means "How do you do?" Many Chinese appreciate foreign use of these greetings. The Chinese may greet you at subsequent interactions with questions like "Have you eaten" or "Where are you going?" These questions are not intended to elicit specific information, but are similar to the casual general Western greeting, "How are you?" Appropriate responses include, "I have eaten," "I am going to eat soon," or "I am going there," with no specific information about the destination.

There are about one hundred widely used family names. The five most common surnames are "Chang" ("Chan" in Cantonese), "Wang," "Li," "Chao," and "Liu." Although many of the surnames may be pronounced the same, the Chinese characters can be different. In China, the family name precedes the given name, which is occasionally followed by the second name or the western equivalent of a first name. For example, "Huang Hua" would be called "Mr. Huang" and "Hua" would be his given name. However, some Chinese will switch the order of their names when they are dealing with foreigners. Further, many Chinese adopt given names early in their life, many of which are Western names. These Western given names are listed first with the surname last. If you are unsure about which is the family and which is the given name, it is advisable to ask how to address someone. It is useful to know that the majority of Chinese family names have one syllable and most given names have two syllables. A given name is not usually an indication of a person's gender. Businesspeople should be addressed with the appropriate title—"Mr.," "Mrs." or "Miss,"—along with their family name. Official and occupation-related titles, such as "Dr.," "Mayor," "Ambassador," are used wherever appropriate. Chinese formal titles, *xiansheng* (Mr.), *nushi* (Madam), or *xiaojie* (Miss), follow a person's family name. However, foreigners do not need to use the Chinese titles and should use the Western equivalents. The word *nushi* is used as a formal title for an adult woman and does not necessarily connote marriage. Keep in mind that married women rarely take their husband's family name.

Business cards, called name cards (*ming pian*) by the Chinese, are presented when everyone first meets. They should be given and received with both hands. If possible, your business card should state your firm's kind of business, your functional responsibility, and your title. It is advisable to have this information translated into Chinese and printed on the reverse side of your business cards. Most hotels in China, Taiwan, and Hong Kong can assist you in this. It is also advisable to hire a translator, particularly if you know that you and your counterpart do not share a common language.

The Chinese have a high regard for rank and seniority. As in most Eastern countries, senior members of an organization are introduced first. The Chinese will be impressed by and are usually more attentive to senior representatives of foreign firms. Company name is also important, as the Chinese believe that they are dealing primarily with the company and secondly with you as its representative. Ranking your company can help to impress the Chinese, especially if you are the "biggest" or the "oldest."

Do not pat others on the back and in general refrain from physically touching a Chinese person; most Chinese do not physically touch one another, especially in public. Beckoning is done with your palm facing down, fingers pointing away from you, but waving toward you in a scratching motion. The Chinese are sensitive to issues of yielding at doors, when getting into cars, and when choosing seats. It is advisable to yield to your Chinese counterpart. Personal space is less important than in Western countries and the Chinese will generally stand closer to you than Westerners do.

You will probably be served some tea. Meetings often begin with small talk, and appropriate topics include the weather and your recent travels. It is important to establish a smooth business relationship and friendship. Trust and cooperation are key. Regardless of the circumstances, it is important to be patient. Your Chinese counterpart may make a brief introduction, particularly if she or he works for a state-owned entity. The introduction will usually state the history and statistics of the local area as well as general information on the company. Avoid discussing political and human rights issues. These topics can be very sensitive and they may place your Chinese counterpart in an awkward position because Chinese people are not allowed to publicly criticize the government. The Chinese feel comfortable asking blunt personal questions about financial matters and do not always understand Westerners' hesitance in answering such queries.

The Chinese tend to maintain a level of formality in the early stages of a relationship. This fosters respect for each side and ensures that contacts will proceed harmoniously. To become informal too quickly would upset the balance the Chinese require to develop a meaningful business and personal relationship. The Chinese often interpret Western informality, for example, the early use of first names and disclosure of too much information, as a willingness to bypass the usual formal preliminaries so as to forge a close, durable relationship without delay. As this is not necessarily the Westerner's intent, misunderstandings damaging to business can occur. So do not be in a rush to establish what your Chinese opposite might well consider a false sense of intimacy.

Gifts are not required or expected at initial meetings. You may present a small sample of your company's product or an item with a corporate logo. However, anything more elaborate or expensive will be inappropriate.

Corporate Structure

One of the most frustrating aspects of doing business in China is determining who has authority for decision making, particularly in the public sector. It is critically important to understand the business structure in both the public and the private sectors. Today, as authority becomes more decentralized in China, identifying the correct trade organization and level of authority is crucial if you want to be efficient. Most traditional companies are state-run and have a hierarchy in which party officials parallel management people. All import–export companies are state-owned enterprises. There are also numerous companies owned and operated by the People's Liberation Army, the military arm of the CCP. At one time, ministries were involved in both setting policy and in commercial and industrial management. Since the recent economic reforms, most ministry officials are not allowed to participate in both areas of responsibility, and many of the commercial and industrial operations have been turned into semi-independent enterprises.

In the public sector, most businesspeople will have to interact with members of the State Council, which is the highest government body and the one in charge of the ministries, bureaus, and other state organizations. The headquarters of the State Council are located at Zhongnanhai in Beijing. Under the State Council is the State Planning Commission, which is one of the key economic policymaking organizations. Under the State Planning Commission are four key divisions: the Ministry of Foreign Economic Relations and Trade (MOFERT), the Industrial Ministries, the Ministry for Provinces and Cities, and the Ministry of Finance. The State Planning Commission authorizes large purchases of foreign products by Chinese companies. MOFERT, often considered the single-most important agency in China, reviews most large joint ventures.

The People's Bank of China, which is the Chinese equivalent of the U.S. Federal Reserve, and the People's Insurance Agency are under the supervision of the Ministry of Finance, which is responsible for monetary policy.

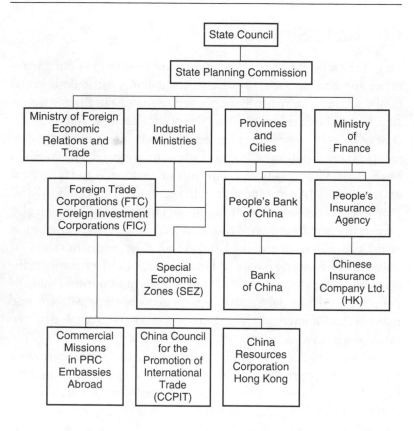

The China International Trust and Investment Corporation (CITIC) is a national organization headquartered in Beijing with local and overseas offices. CITIC is theoretically an independent company, not a government agency. However, it does enjoy government status. The primary roles of the CITIC are to facilitate foreign investment in the country and to approve technology acquisitions ensuring that all terms of a deal are consistent with China's overall policy on technology acquisition. Through its subsidiary merchant bank, China Investment and Finance Corporation (CIFC), CITIC issues bonds and manages China's overseas financial investments. The Hong Kong office of CITIC operates with a high degree of independence.

Most of China's foreign trade is carried out by the Foreign Trade Corporations (FTCs), which are supervised by MOFERT. Recently, the Industrial Ministries, provinces and cities, and private individuals have begun to establish FTCs and Foreign Investment Corporations (FICs). Most of the FTCs under MOFERT supervision are organized by commodity or product. Those FTCs under the Industrial Ministries focus on products in targeted areas such as petrochemicals, transportation, infrastructure, shipbuilding, and agriculture. FTCs and FICs under the supervision of local provinces and cities focus on attracting investment and trade in specific industries and securing financing for joint ventures in their area. All of the FTCs are permitted to initiate and develop contacts, coordinate technology transfers, and conduct negotiations with foreign companies. However, final approval for large transactions, the definition of which varies, must come from the appropriate ministry.

To complicate the situation further, three municipalities—Beijing, Shanghai, and Tianjin—and several provinces have been permitted total autonomy in pursuing economic ventures with foreign companies. Accordingly, these local governments have established local Foreign Trade Corporations, which often oversee the local branches of the national FTCs.

As is the case in many developing countries, China has created special economic zones (SEZs) that fall under the jurisdiction of the Ministry for Provinces and Cities. The primary purpose of the SEZs is to facilitate foreign investment and encourage the inflow of technology, information, and capital. There are five SEZs: Shenzhen, Zhuhai, Shantou, Xiamen, and Hainan Island. There are also fourteen coastal cities that have been granted special economic privileges. These cities are Dalian, Quinhuangdao, Tianji, Yantao, Qingdao, Lianyungang, Nantong, Shanghai, Ningbo, Wenzhou, Fuzhou, Guangzhou, Zhanjiang, and Beihai. The economic development of these provinces and cities has not been consistent, and so the plans for some of them have been modified to reflect local differences. Major growth has occurred in Shanghai, Guangzhou, Tianjin, and Dalian; these four coastal cities are expected to become even more economically powerful. Due to wide economic disparity between the inland and coastal areas, the government is offering more incentives to help develop industry in inland cities.

The various SEZs were created without an overall national strategy and, as a result, they essentially compete against one another. Nevertheless, it is important to remember that China's underlying goal is to attract foreign investment into the country. Foreign companies should utilize government resources to monitor changes in policy, priorities, and investment incentives. While the local trust and investment corporations work closely with CITIC, they are able to act independently.

The following missions and councils fall under the FTCs and the FICs: Commercial Missions in PRC embassies abroad; the China Council for the Promotion of International Trade; and the China Resources Corporation (HK). Under the China Council for the Promotion of International Trade (CCPIT) are the Trade Promotion Commission, the Foreign Trade Arbitration Commission, and the Maritime Arbitration Commission.

Many FTCs have offices in Hong Kong and in other countries around the world. You should first consult the local Commercial Mission at the Chinese embassy in your home country to find the whereabouts of industry-specific FTCs and FICs. In some countries, the FTCs will conduct activities in conjunction with the Chinese embassy; in others, the FTC office is listed as a separate business entity. Initiating contacts through an FTC in your home country will enable you to develop business contacts prior to a visit to China.

Another useful starting point is the CCPIT, which publishes a handbook titled *China's Foreign Trade Corporations and Organizations* that lists all major corporations and organizations engaged in business with foreign firms. The CCPIT works closely with MOFERT, other ministries, the FTCs, and Chinese financial institutions. The CCPIT also has a unit that will distribute literature and occasionally samples of foreign products to Chinese end-users.

It is often difficult to identify the right authorities with whom to negotiate. There have been instances where Chinese government offices failed to inform foreign businesspeople that they are not the appropriate decision makers. Verify with your local embassy or consulate or chamber of commerce that the government agency with which you are dealing is the appropriate one. The infrastructure is continuing to evolve and the confusion created by the evolution of numerous entities can be overwhelming. A good Chinese representative should be able to navigate the system for you. You should consider a regional or local representative(s) if your business interests are focused in specific provinces or cities.

In summary, a foreign firm interested in doing business in China is advised to go through the following general steps:

- Research the Chinese market and learn about the country.
- Contact your country's commerce department for China (e.g., the U.S. Department of Commerce, China Desk).
- Identify the correct Foreign Trade Corporation (use the CCPIT handbook noted above).
- Communicate with the Chinese embassy or consulate in your home country, as well as with any appropriate FTC offices in your own country.
- Contact the appropriate FTC in China by letter. Also contact your country's commercial office or embassy in China to obtain advice and guidance.
- Attend or participate in trade shows in China.
- Visit China with a business delegation from your country. Check with your commerce department or trade offices.
- Invite a delegation to visit your offices. Check with the Chinese embassy or consulate for scheduling. (Be clear about financial obligations.)

In the private sector, the family head, usually a male, is the senior decision maker. The hierarchy can differ based upon the size
of the company. However, these types of companies are closely held
and operate under very centralized control. Generally, Chinese
companies are adopting the American corporate hierarchy of president and vice-president. This is in contrast to Hong Kong, where
a managing director or general manager is the senior person.

Negotiation

The Chinese do not always respond favorably to the direct approach. It is best to allow your counterparts to set the tone and level
for frankness and to follow their lead. Usually, the Chinese do not
like surprises. Keep them informed of details as much as possible.
Further, negotiations and interactions should be conducted in a
low-key manner with little or no publicity. This will help to keep
possible political pressures away from the negotiating table.

Most of your negotiations will involve the FTCs because foreign
trade is channeled primarily through these "party" organizations. It
is important that you interact as much as possible with the potential
end-user company because this input is very valuable in any transaction. In the negotiation process, it might appear to you that the
Chinese are deliberately attempting to drag out the discussions to
gradually wear down your patience. In truth, the Chinese pace for
decision-making is slower than the Western style. Achieving consensus is very important in China and may require input from national, provincial, and local levels. As a result, it may appear that
negotiations have stalled because talks are stopped for one or two
days. But these delays often occur because contract terms are being
passed from one agency to another for advice or approval. Be patient
and never indicate your frustration, for the Chinese will attempt to
use your impatience to extract more concessions from you.

Further, the Chinese pay a great deal of attention to details, often ones that may seem trivial to outsiders. Most negotiations are
divided into two phases: technical and commercial or business is-

sues. The Chinese will utilize their technical experts to focus on the technical phase until they are satisfied with basic issues of quality and usefulness. Often the strongest decision makers are those in the middle who conduct all the research. Accordingly, make sure to include at least one technical expert in your negotiation team along with those who are authorized to legally and financially commit the firm. Be clear about how much technical information you are willing to disclose. The Chinese will push you as far as you will permit. The commercial phase will usually proceed relatively quickly.

However, it should be noted that the Chinese often hesitate to provide information out of concern that someone will use it against them. Use mutual contacts to assist if you are concerned about establishing trust and credibility with your Chinese counterpart, if negotiations stall, or you encounter disagreements.

Often, government officials who are responsible for negotiating deals do not have the authority to commit financial resources. They may be unable to make or authorize an up-front, good-faith payment. Be flexible and creative in your approach, but do not lose sight of your business interests. Above all, be patient. Depending on the size of the deal, most transactions must be approved by senior officials. In many instances, even small changes to existing agreements cannot be made without the approval of senior officials. This is one reason why it helps to develop relationships with both senior and lower-level people.

The Chinese do not like to say "No" or to be the bearers of negative news. They will hint indirectly by saying something like "It is inconvenient." Similarly, you will hear a "Yes" response to almost everything. However, this could be an "empty" yes and you should be careful not to draw positive conclusions from "Yes" responses. Verify what has been said to you. Do not place your counterparts in an awkward position by asking them direct questions or by raising issues that will make them uncomfortable. It is important that all parties maintain "face." If you think the answer to an issue is really "No," verify your feeling by asking questions that can be answered positively.

The Chinese use several key tactics in negotiations. It is not uncommon for the Chinese to switch negotiators and to change the terms of a deal even after a long period of discussion. This may result from a change in officials and management or it may be part of a negotiation strategy to encourage you to make concessions. In such situations, foreigners should be slow to concede to these new demands in the hopes of expediency. Instead, explain the progress and status of the negotiation terms to your new counterparts and reiterate your commitment to completing a good transaction regardless of the time required. The Chinese also often use the "friendly" banquet as a way to put you to the test. Exotic and unusual specialties might be served to you in order to test you. Every business book that discusses eating in China will recommend that you eat a little of whatever is served to you. But everyone has their limits and no doubt so do you. For example, if you are a committed vegetarian, you do not need to violate your principles in order to be accepted by the Chinese. Be adventurous to the best of your ability. After that, just be very polite, discreet, and nonjudgmental.

Another common tactic is to ask you, upon arrival, the date and time of your departure flight. This tactic is used by the Chinese to delay decision-making and possible concessions until the last possible minute before you must leave, so as to force you to accept a less favorable deal. An appropriate response if you are not comfortable lying is "I will stay here as long as it takes to finish a deal." Your company president or other superiors should also publicly support the negotiation process and not indicate any rush to close a deal. Chinese negotiators who sense that their counterpart is more concerned with deadlines than negotiations will definitely seek to use that fact for their own advantage.

Be prepared for tough negotiations. Adhere to your principles and objectives. Maintain a quiet and dignified manner. If problems develop, you should be firm about your limits and your willingness to work with your counterparts to find a mutually agreeable solution. Fiery outbursts will not earn you any respect. Patience, flexibility, and creativity are the keys to negotiating successfully in China. You should recognize that most Chinese view the negotiation as a win-lose situation. This attitude stands in contrast to the attitude in many other Asian countries where people strive for a win-win situation for both sides. Extracting as many concessions from you as possible is a critical part of the Chinese negotiating strategy.

Most Chinese are under the impression that Westerners have ample financial resources. Accordingly, there is an implicit belief, fostered by government officials, that it is acceptable to charge Westerners higher prices on all products and services.

Due to the vastness of China, different Chinese have varying business styles. The Cantonese tend to be more Westernized due to the influences of Hong Kong and constant contact with Western traders for the past four hundred years. They are more accustomed to doing business with foreigners and are more efficient. However, Cantonese businesspeople can often be more adamant about having things their own way and so foreigners should be firm about their position in a negotiation. Throughout the country, there is still very little accountability as incentives to perform well are not common. In general the Chinese will not easily admit to mistakes or errors.

The counting system in China differs from the system used in the West. The number system includes the following denominations: 1; 10; 100; 1000; 10,000; 100,000,000. The Chinese refer to numbers higher than 10,000 and below 100,000,000 as multiples of 10,000. For example, 1,000,000 is the equivalent of one hundred 10,000s. It is advisable to verify all numbers in any transaction or negotiation by checking the number of zeros.

The Chinese will interpret contracts strictly when it is to their advantage, particularly when they are purchasing products and the product specifications differ from those in the contract agreements. Problems for foreigners arise because the Chinese version of a contract governs in a dispute and because interpretations can differ due to the tonal quality of the language. Chinese officials have been known to disregard contracts signed by their predecessors. Recognize that most Chinese believe that the primary purpose of contracts is to establish a positive relationship that focuses on shared interests and is expected to continue and change indefinitely. Accordingly, many contracts are drafted in terms of principles rather than specifics. The underlying belief among the Chinese is that deals are done based on relationships. Attempts to document potential problems may be viewed as a lack of faith in the relationship. However, as a precaution, you should use your business sense, be as thorough as possible in drafting contracts, and address all contingencies to the best of your ability, without offending anyone. When disputes do occur, the Chinese usually make attempts to resolve them amicably and outside of the legal system through negotiations. The Foreign Trade Arbitration Commission in Beijing settles legal disputes. If you prefer, you can demand as part of your contract that disputes will be settled in a specific foreign jurisdiction. It is also advisable to structure payments up-front or at closing, for Chinese firms have been known to delay or ignore payments.

Conducting Business in a Social Setting

Dining and Drinking

Chinese do not usually conduct business over breakfast. Informal business discussions may be conducted over lunch and dinner, and deals are often concluded over a meal. Entertaining is a critical part of Chinese business culture.

The banquet is a old and important custom for the Chinese, both in business and social settings. When you first arrive at a banquet, your host will invite you to sit and exchange polite conversation over tea. After about ten minutes you will be taken to the dining table. Generally guests do not bring gifts. However, if you are simply visiting China, it is appropriate to present a gift to the host during the speeches. Gifts can be presented to all attendees, but they are not required. At these formal dinners, the host presents the guest with a lavish spread to signify the friendly nature of their relationship. Seating is done by title and seniority. The host will begin by serving you food with long chopsticks or his own chopsticks held in reverse and using the handles. If you are the host, make sure you serve your guests. Wait until you have been invited to eat and drink. Similarly, when you are the host, be sure to invite your guests to eat and drink.

It is not necessary to finish everything you are served, but it is polite to sample each dish. Soup is usually served toward the end of a meal. Sometimes the second-to-last course is plain boiled rice. Leave some food on your plate after you have finished eating, for this gesture signals that your host has provided you with more than enough food. The Chinese will be pleased if you use chopsticks. Never leave your chopsticks standing upright in your rice: this is a gesture done only at funerals and is synonymous with death.

Your host will make a short speech. In turn, you will be called upon, as the guest, to make a toast of general goodwill and friendship. Keep the toast simple and speak slowly, especially if it is being translated. Banquets are meant to be warm, friendly, and filled with good humor. Throughout the dinner, several toasts will be made by individuals at your table. You can toast with a nonalcoholic beverage. If you host a dinner or banquet, be sure to arrive at least fifteen minutes early because most Chinese guests will arrive a few minutes early. The guests always leave before the hosts. You will know that the meal is near its end when fruit is served and hot towels are distributed. Coffee or after-dinner cocktails are not served and should not be requested. It is polite to leave about ten to fifteen minutes after the hot towels are brought to the table and the last cups of tea have been served. Banquets end abruptly and after-dinner talk is rare. Typically, evening banquets begin around 6:30 or 7:00 P.M. and end around 8:30 or 9:00 P.M. This can differ between regions and for different purposes.

It is sometimes acceptable for foreign businesspeople to stage a banquet in return if business is proceeding well. It is best to check with your Chinese counterparts and associates first. Most hotels and restaurants will assist you in planning a banquet. Invitations to a banquet may be given verbally. There is no need to send written invitations unless the occasion has been planned well in advance. However, government officials should receive written as well as verbal invitations. Be sure that the rank and status of the Chinese attendees is similar. Someone who is too senior or too junior may feel awkward or make the other guests feel uncomfortable and constrained. When constructing your seating plan, be conscious of the pecking order. If you are the only host, be sure to place the highest ranking guest on your right, for that seat has the highest honor; the second highest ranking guest should be on your left. Cohosts should sit directly across from one another. The two highest ranking guests should be seated to the right of each cohost.

Chinese businesspeople drink considerably less liquor on average than their Western counterparts. However, heavy drinking of toasts is common at banquets, and can sometimes develop into a contest. Women are often encouraged to participate in the toasts. But it is acceptable for men and women to politely refuse alcoholic drinks and to request orange juice or some other nonalcoholic beverage instead. However, all guests must participate in the toasts by drinking some beverage. The proper toast when drinking *moa tais*, a traditional sorghum liquor served at special occasions and banquets, is *Kai pay*, which means "Empty your glass."

Karaoke, or singalong, bars are becoming quite popular throughout China. As is the case in other Asian countries, your participation is more important than your skill.

Visiting a Home

The Chinese will rarely invite foreigners to their home unless they know them very well. Most Chinese are embarrassed by the small size of their homes. If you are invited to a home, suitable gifts for your hosts include sweets, chocolates, or a small token from your home country. It is advisable to leave shortly after the meal, unless you know your hosts very well. Unlike most Western cultures, which rely on the guest to determine the time of his or her departure, in China, the guests wait for the host to tactfully indicate that it is time to leave because doing otherwise would be considered disrespectful.

Gift Giving

Gift giving has reached the level of graft in some situations as international companies compete for access to the Chinese marketplace. As more business interests crowd into China, corruption has become a serious problem for the government. Prior to doing business in China or any other foreign country, you and your company should establish company guidelines for dealing with the issues of gift giving, low-level bribery, and demands for graft. If you are an American company, the guidelines are already established by law and generally prohibit graft. Some companies view the system in China of paying something "to get permission" as a cost of doing business. During negotiations involving large transactions, you may be asked to finance a "working trip" to your home country via "Disney World," technically to visit the company, but more likely for leisure purposes. Your local partner or representative should manage such issues.

Gifts of reasonable value are a normal part of business interactions and are not considered to be graft in China. In general, gifts are exchanged to mark the establishment of a relationship. Accordingly, you should wait until the business interaction or negotiation is mature or finished before presenting a gift. Red is a very auspicious color in China and is used on happy occasions, such as weddings. Accordingly, wrap your present in red paper. However, do not write in red ink as that implies severing a relationship. Like business cards, gifts should be given and received using both hands. Gifts should be presented to everyone involved in a transaction or present at an event, with the value of each gift based on the rank of the person. Suitable items include pens, books, calculators, imported whiskey, brandy, chocolates, and company logo gifts. It is common for the Chinese to decline a gift several times out of a sense of courtesy. You should keep insisting several times until he or she takes it. Similarly, decline a gift several times before accepting it. Once people get to know you, they will often tell you what they want as a "gift" on the next visit.

Repeat visitors may want to consider giving gifts to the children of their Chinese business associates. Never give cash. The government is wary of cameras, so a camera is not a good gift choice at this time. However, it is appropriate to take a photograph of the group and send each person a print as a gift. Avoid gifts of watches, clocks, handkerchiefs, white flowers, scissors, and knives—all these things have negative or morbid connotations. Do not give gifts involving amounts of the number 4. The number 4 in Cantonese sounds like death and is considered to have a negative connotation for the Chinese. Gifts are often given in groups of 2; gifts in sets of 2, 6, and 8 are appropriate, with 8 being the lucky or most auspicious number. Be humble in giving the gift and indicate that it is a small token of gratitude for their assistance. Be wary of accepting expensive gifts for acceptance will create significant future obligations that you may not be able to fulfill.

Dress Code

The dress code is conservative, but generally informal. Suits and ties are not required even in the best restaurants. For men, suits and ties are the best option at early meetings. After that, you should allow your counterparts and associates to set the tone. After the first meeting, it may be appropriate to dress less formally, particularly in warmer weather. Often a shirt and tie is sufficient. For women, conservative, nonflashy suits and dresses are acceptable. Many Chinese women wear slacks, but these are not advisable for first meetings.

Useful Phrases

Mandarin is the national dialect for mainland China. Other dialects throughout the country can be as different as two European languages. The other main Chinese dialect is Cantonese and is spoken primarily in the south and in Hong Kong. Since 1949 the government has tried to promote a national language called Putonghua (literally, "ordinary language") as the unifying language throughout the country. Putonghua is based on the northern language of Mandarin and is taught in Chinese schools, although students may speak different languages at home. Each of the fifty-five minorities has its own dialect. The common element throughout the country is the use of Chinese characters. While the pronunciation of any character differs between dialects, a character will mean the same thing in each dialect or language. There are approximately fifty thousand characters, although less than eight thousand are commonly used. On a daily basis, only about fifteen hundred to two thousand are used. These are the same Chinese characters that are used in Japan, Korea, and throughout various parts of Asia.

Pinyin is the official Chinese system for simulating the sound of the English language and translating the Chinese characters into understandable Latin letters. In 1958 China announced that Pinyin was the official transcription system. Due to the tonal differences in the spoken language, ask your Chinese counterpart for assistance with the correct pronunciation, otherwise you may say something unintended or perhaps even negative. The following list includes some useful Mandarin phrases and a guide to their pronunciation. (Please refer to Chapter 4, on Hong Kong, for Cantonese phrases.) Pinyin is not noted below.

Hello	*Nee how*
Good morning	*Tsow or Tsow an*
Good afternoon	*Woo an*
Good evening	*Wan shang how*
How are you?	*Nee how mah?*
Please	*Ching*
Thank you	*Sheh-sheh*
You are welcome	*Boo yong kuh chee*
Excuse me	*Duway boo chee*
I am sorry	*Doway boo chee*
My name is ———.	*Wo da ming tsi jow* ———.

I work for ———.	*Wo tsai ——— gong tsuo*
Here is my business card	*Wo da ming pee-an*
I am pleased to meet you	*Wo hung gow shing lung shi nee*
Please accept this small gift	*Chin so shia jay gu shiao lee woo.*
I look forward to developing a good relationship with you /your firm	*Shee wong wo men her draw yiu kuai.*
I understand	*Wo ming bye*
No, I do not understand	*Wo boo ming bye*
Please wait a minute	*Chin done yee shia*
Where is the bathroom?	*Tser shuo jai nar lee?*
Good-bye.	*Tsai Jee-in*
Cheers	*Gan bei*

Major Holidays

January 1–2	New Year
Late January/early February*	Spring Festival and Chinese NewYear (3 days)
March 8	International Working Women's Day
May 1	Labor Day
May 4	Youth Day
June 1	Children's Day
July 1	Anniversary of the Founding of the Communist Party of China
August 1	People's Liberation Army Day
October 1–2	National Day

*These holidays are based on the lunar calendar and accordingly the date changes annually.

General Facts

Climate: Due to the vastness of the country, temperatures and weather conditions can vary greatly. Check with a consulate or tourist office for temperatures and conditions for the region(s) that you plan to visit.

Northern China experiences cold winters with little to moderate snow or rain. Beijing has very cold winters from November to February and hot summers from June to September. In the spring, the city often experiences blinding dust storms. Temperatures average between 20F (-7C) and 42F (6C) in the winters and between 65F (18C) and 89F (32C) in the summers.

Southern China has short winters with rain. Summers are hot and humid with frequent rains. Guangzhou (Canton) has warmer and subtropical weather. The summers are hot and humid with heavy rainfall. The months of August and September are the typhoon season. The winters are generally mild, but autumn is the most pleasant time of year. Temperatures average between 48F (9C) and 70F (21C) in the winters and between 75F (24C) and 91F (33C) in the summers.

Shanghai has very cold winters and very hot summers. Temperatures average between 33F (1C) and 53F (12C) in the winter and between 66F (19C) and 89F (32C) in the summers.

Currency: The Chinese currency, *reminbi*, is denominated by the *yuan* which is the unit of currency and is also called *kuai*. The *yuan* is composed of 100 *fen*. Units of ten *fen* are called *jiao*, or more commonly *mao*. Until 1993, FEC (foreign exchange certificates) were used by foreigners and were the only currency accepted by most hotels, shops, restaurants, and taxis. When the government shifted to the single exchange rate system, FECs were no longer printed and were eventually withdrawn from circulation. Do not exchange currency at unofficial sites or with people on the street.

Dates: Dates are written day, month, year. For example, June 16, 1995, would be abbreviated as 16/6/95.

Electricity: Both the 220 volt (50 cycle) and the 380 volt (three-phase) systems are used in China. It is advisable to bring a transformer as well as three-prong plugs (flat, not round, prong). Some hotels will supply them or you can purchase them locally at a Friendship Store in the large cities.

Entry Requirements: For American, British, Canadian, French, and German citizens, valid passports and visas are required. The length of stay can usually be extended in China, but verify this when obtaining a visa. Officially all people doing business in China must enter with a business visa; however, some business travelers use only a tourist visa. In order to obtain a business visa, foreigners must have a written invitation from a Chinese agency, organization, or company. Most of the invitations actually come from one of China's Foreign Trade Corporations (FTC). A visa can be obtained in person or by mail from an embassy or consulate office.

If you are pressed for time, visas can also be obtained in Hong Kong or upon arrival at either the Beijing or Shanghai airports; however, there is no guarantee that a visa will be issued, so this method is not recommended. In Hong Kong, foreigners should apply at a branch of the China Travel Service (CTS). Tourist visas can be issued overnight, but business visas may take three days.

Time: China has one time zone, which is eight hours ahead of Greenwich Mean Time and thirteen hours ahead of U.S. Eastern Standard Time (twelve hours in Daylight Savings Time).

Tipping: The official government policy discourages tipping for services. Nevertheless, foreigners do occasionally tip hotel staff and taxi drivers when the service warrants it. Most of the new hotels and some restaurants include a 15 percent service charge on the bill. With the increase in the number of foreigner visitors, this custom is becoming more widespread.

Transportation: In most cities, walking is the easiest form of transportation. Taxis are a convenient, inexpensive mode of transportation. In most major cities, hotel limousines and shuttle buses can provide transportation to and from the airport. There are counters to assist with transportation to the city at the Beijing airport.

Taxis can be flagged down in front of hotels and major office buildings and on the streets. Make sure the meter is turned on when entering a taxi, otherwise you will have to haggle with the driver at the end of the ride. You should keep small denominations of *yuan* (1, 5, 10) to pay for taxis; tipping is not necessary. Have your hotel write out your destination in Chinese because most drivers do not speak English. Also keep a hotel card with the hotel's name and address written in Chinese with you at all times in case you get lost. Be sure that your taxi driver knows how to get to your destination, otherwise he will simply drop you at the wrong place. If you will be at your destination for only a brief time, it is advisable to have the taxi wait for you because it may take thirty minutes to get another cab. Waiting charges are relatively inexpensive, although you should confirm this with each taxicab driver as some are prone to inflating the charges. On average, fares are inflated by at least 50–100 percent. Always offer to pay half of the asking amount. If you feel the fare is too unreasonable, ask for assistance from a tourist official.

Driving a car is not advisable, particularly in Beijing and other major cities with heavy bicycle and car traffic. There are no car rental agencies at the airports. Hiring a car and driver is relatively inexpensive and is an advisable form of transportation. Cars can be booked at most hotels.

Throughout China, buses are also abundant and cheap, although very crowded and sometimes less convenient depending on your destination. Beijing has a clean and relatively easy-to-use subway system. Stops are noted in both Chinese characters and roman letters. Subway and bus maps can be purchased at most major hotels.

Helpful Telephone Numbers

In the major cities, public telephone booths are becoming more common on the streets and can be operated with phone cards that can be purchased at hotels, post offices, and some shops. Public telephones are also located in shops, marked by a picture of a telephone, and are inexpensive. The country code for China is (86). The area code for major regions are: Beijing (01); Guangzhou (Canton) (020); and Shanghai (021). When calling from outside China, omit the (0) from the area code. Collect calls from China to international locations can often be cheaper as the receiving rates in many countries are less than the rates in China.

Hospitals, Doctors, and Dentists:

While the hospitals in the major Chinese cities are adequate, it is probably best to go to Hong Kong or Japan for medical treatment. The standards of medical facilities vary greatly within China, as do sanitary conditions. In Beijing, any foreigner who needs medical assistance can dial (1)505-3521 for a referral to the closest and best Chinese clinic or hospital. The following list includes reliable medical/dental facilities:

Australian Consulate Doctor
Shanghai
Tel.: (21) 433-4604

Beijing Union Medical College Hospital
1 Dong Shai Fuyuan Hutong (near the Beijing Hotel)
Beijing
Tel.: (1) 513-0920 / 512-7733 (217 for emergencies) (clinic for foreigners, ext. 251)

Foreign Guest Medical Center
Dong Fang Hotel
120 Liuhua
Guangzhou
Tel.: (20) 669-900

Guangzhou No. 1 Hospital
602 Renmin Bei Lu
Guangzhou
Tel.: (20) 333-090

Huashan Hospital
Shanghai
Tel.: (21) 248-9999

International Medical Center
Beijing Lufthansa Center
50 Liangmaqiao Road
Beijing 100016
Tel.: (1) 465-1561 / 3

International SOS Assistance
Beijing Representative Office
Kunlun Hotel, Suite 433
P.O. Box 4710
Beijing 100004
Tel.: (1) 500-3388 (ext. 433)

Shanghai Representative Office
Hua Shan Hotel, Suite 324
Shanghai International Business Center

2004 Nanjing Xi Road
Shanghai 200040

Sun Yat Sen Memorial Hospital
Guangzhou
Tel.: (20) 888-2012

Ambulance: In Beijing, dial 120;
in Guangzhou, dial (20)882-012

Fire: In Beijing, dial 09.

Police:
85 Beichizi Dajie
Beijing
Tel.: (1) 55-3102
Emergencies: Dial 110.

863 Jiefang Bei Lu
Guangzhou
Tel.: (20) 331-326 or 331-060
Emergencies: Dial 110.

Information Hotline (in English)
Dial (1) 513-0828 in Beijing; dial
(20) 439-0630 in Guangzhou.

Useful Addresses

In China:

**American Chamber of
Commerce**
Great Wall Sheraton
Room 301
North Donghuan Avenue
Beijing 100026
Tel.: (1) 500-5566, ext. 2271

Shanghai Centre, Room 435
1376 Nanjing Road, West
Shanghai 200040
Tel.: (21) 279-7119 / 8056

**Beijing Foreign Enterprises
Services**
Beijing
Tel.: (1) 512-1167

**Center for Introducing Litera-
ture and Samples of New Products (unit of CCPIT)**
CCPIT, Box 1420
Beijing

**China Council for Promotion
of International Trade
(CCPIT)**
4 Fuxingmenwai Street
Beijing
Tel.: (1) 867229

**China International Travel
Service (CITS)**
Fuxingmenwai Road
Beijing
Tel.: (1) 601-1122

179 Huanshi Road
Canton
Tel.: (20) 661-369 or 662-948

**China International Trust and
Investment Corporation**
CITIC Building
19 Jianguomenwai
Beijing 100004
Tel.: (1) 500-2255

China National Tourist Office
Chong Wen Men Hotel
2 Chong Wen Men XI Daijia
Beijing
Tel.: (1) 512-2521

66 Nanjing Dong Lu
Shanghai
Tel.: (21) 432-4960

China Resources Corporation
(CRC) (responsible for some
of China's FTC's offices in
Hong Kong)
China Resources Building
18th Floor
26 Harbour Road
Wanchai, Hong Kong
Tel.: (852) 831-7111

French Chamber of Commerce
Landmark Building, Unit U9-05
8 North Dongsanhuan Road
Chaoyang District
Beijing 100004
Tel.: (1) 501-6688 (ext. 20905)

Tianjin
Tel.: (22) 528611 / 4

Delegation of German
Industry and Commerce
Haus 2
Sanlitun Don Si Jie 3
Beijing 100600
Tel.: (1) 532-2161-65/
532-5556-61

Shanghai Bund Center
555 Zhongshan Dong (E) Road

Shanghai 210010
Shanghai
Tel.: (21) 326-9204/3

Guangdong Travel and
Tourism Bureau
185 Huanshi Lu
Guangzhou
Tel.: (20) 661-093

Ministry of Foreign Economic
Relations and Trade
(MOFERT)
2 Changan Dong Lu
Beijing
Tel.: (1) 512-8319

Shantou SEZ Administrative
Office
4/F Foreign Trade Building
Yingchun Lu
Shantou, Guangdong Province

Shekou Development
Company
Nanshan, Shekou Industrial Area
Shenzhen SEZ, Guangdong
Province
PRC

Shenzen Economic Zone
Development Co.
2/F Luohu Building
Jianshe Road
Shenzen

United States–China Business
Council
19 Jian Guo Men Wai
Beijing 100004
Tel.: (1) 500-2255 (ext.2263)

Xiamen SEZ Development Corporation
105 Xian Jie
Fujian Province

Zhuhai Development Co.
Zhuhai SEZ
Shuiwantou,
Guangdong Province

Embassies and Consulates:

American Embassy
3 Xiu Shui Bei Jie
Beijing 100600
Tel.: (1) 532-3831

U.S. Consulates
1469 Huai Hai Zhong (Middle) Road
Shanghai 200031
Tel.: (21) 433-6880

1 South Shamian Street
Shamian Island
Guangzhou 510133
Tel.: (20) 888-8911

52, 14th Wei Road
Heping District
Shenyang 110003
Tel.: (24) 282-0068

4 Lingshiquan Lu
Renmin Nan Lu Si Duan
Chengdu 610041
Tel.: (28) 558-3992

British Embassy
11 Guanghua Lu
Jian Guo Men Wai

Beijing 100600
Tel.: (1) 532-1961

Canadian Embassy
19 Dong Zhi Men Wai Street
Chaoyang District
Beijing 100600
Tel.: (1) 532-3536

Canadian Consulate
American International
Center at Shanghai Center
West Tower, Suite 604
1376 Nanjing Xi Lu
Shanghai
Tel.: (21) 279-8400

French Embassy
Jing Guang Center,
37th Floor
Hu Jia Lou - Choa Yang Qu
Beijing 100020
Tel.: (1) 501-4866

French Consulate
Rui Jin Building 2008, 205
Maoming Nan Lu
Shanghai 200020
Tel.: (21) 433-6273/ 78

German Embassy
5 Dong Zhi Men Wai Dajie
Bejing 100060
Tel.: (1) 532-2161

German Consulate
Yong Fu Lu 151 and 181
Shanghai
Tel.: (21) 433-6951/ 3

In Canada:

Chinese Embassy
411–415 St. Andrew
Ottawa, Ontario K1N 5H3
Tel.: (613) 234-2718

Consulates
240 St. George Street
Toronto, Ontario N5R 2P4
Tel.: (416) 964-7260

3380 Granville Street
Vancouver, BC V68 3K3
Tel.: (604) 736-3910

In France:

Chinese Embassy
11 Avenue George V
75008 Paris
Tel.: (1) 723-3445 / 3843 / 3677

In Germany:

Chinese Embassy
Kurfurstenalee 12
5300 Bonn 2
Tel.: (228) 345051

In the United Kingdom:

Chinese Embassy
49 Portland Place
London W1N 3AH
Tel.: (71) 636-8845 / 636-5637

Chinese Chamber of Commerce
19 Frith Street
London W1V 5TS
Tel.: (71) 734-8135

In the United States:

Embassy of the People's Republic of China
2300 Connecticut Ave., N. W.
Washington DC 20008
Tel.: (202) 328-2500

Consulates of the People's Republic of China
520 12th Avenue
New York, NY 10036
Tel.: (212) 868-7752 / 330-7400 / 502-0271

104 N. Michigan Avenue
Suite 1200
Chicago, IL 60603
Tel.: (312) 346-0287

3417 Montrose Blvd.
Houston, TX 77006
Tel.: (713) 524-0780 / 0778

501 Shatto Place, Suite 300
Los Angeles, CA 90020
Tel.: (213) 380-3104 / 2507

1450 Laguna Street
San Francisco, CA 94115
Tel.: (415) 563-4858 / 1708

China National Tourist Office
354 Fifth Avenue,
Suite 6413
New York, NY 10108
Tel.: (212) 760-9700 / 8218

333 West Broadway, Suite 201
Glendale, CA 91204
Tel.: (818) 545-7505

U.S. Department of Commerce
International Trade
Administration
China Desk, Room 2317

14th and Constitution Avenues,
N.W.
Washington, DC 20030
Tel.: (202) 377-3583 / 4681

U.S.–China Business Council
1818 N. Street, N. W.
Washington, DC 20036
Tel.: (202) 429-0340

Hong Kong ──────

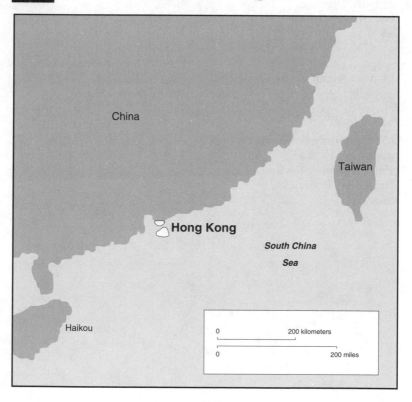

China

Taiwan

Hong Kong

South China

Sea

Haikou

| 0 | 200 kilometers |
| 0 | 200 miles |

Geography

Located on the southeast coast of China, Hong Kong is divided into three main parts: Hong Kong Island, Kowloon, and the New Territories. Hong Kong Island is located on the southern side of the harbor and is the business and political center of Hong Kong. Kowloon is located just across the harbor on the mainland. The New Territories, located north of Kowloon and south of the Chinese border, occupy almost 91 percent of Hong Kong's land area, which totals 413 square miles (1,070 square kilometers), including 235 so-called

Outlying Islands, many of which are uninhabited. Almost one-third of Hong Kong's residents live in the New Territories. The name Hong Kong is used interchangeably to refer to Hong Kong Island and the entire area.

Brief History

Archaeological evidence shows that the earliest settlers of the islands were seagoing people of Malaysian-Oceanic origin who arrived more than five thousand years ago. Modern Hong Kong's history began in 1513 when the first Portuguese traders arrived in the city of Guangzhou (also known as Canton), which was located across the harbor from Hong Kong. Canton was officially opened to foreign trade in 1685. By 1699, the British were regularly conducting trade with the Chinese there. Disdainful and suspicious of foreigners, China opened Canton to foreign trade with the Western "barbarians" primarily because of the city's distance from the power centers of Beijing and Nanjing. By the late eighteenth century the British, French, Dutch, Danes, Swedes, and Americans were all trading through Canton.

In 1757 Cantonese merchants, fearful of outside influence, attempted to impose restrictions on foreign merchants. These restrictions included one proviso that foreigners could reside in Canton for only half the year and another forbidding foreigners to learn Chinese. In order to shift the balance of trade in favor of themselves, the British began to import opium from India into Hong Kong in the early 1770s. Alarmed by the growing number of opium addicts, China tried unsuccessfully to ban the drug trade in 1799. By 1839 opium was the key to British trade and the number of Chinese addicts had increased dramatically. From 1839 to 1842 the Chinese and British fought over the drug trade in the first Opium War. Both sides tried to negotiate a settlement, but were unable to reach an agreement. On January 26, 1841, the British seized the island of Hong Kong and claimed it for themselves. Over the next eighteen months, the British also seized the Pearl River, Canton,

Xiamen, Dinghai, Ningbo, Wusong, Shanghai, and Jingjiang. When Nanjing (Nanking) came under threat in 1842, the Chinese were forced to accept the Treaty of Nanking which, among its various terms, formally ceded the island of Hong Kong to the British.

The second Opium War broke out between the British and the Chinese in 1856. The British were joined this time by French, Russian, and American troops. The Treaty of Tientsin in 1858 ended the conflict, opened ten new ports to foreign trade, and allowed the British to establish a diplomatic outpost in China for the first time. When Chinese resistance flared and the treaty was violated, the British—supported by the French—invaded China, reaching the capital city of Beijing. This resulted in the signing of the Convention of Beijing in 1860, which gave the British the Kowloon Peninsula (now Kowloon and the New Territories). In 1898 China was forced to accept the Second Convention of Beijing, which gave the British a ninety-nine-year lease on Hong Kong, Kowloon, and the outlying islands beginning on July 1, 1898, and ending on June 30, 1997.

For most of its history Hong Kong was an undeveloped land mass that had no value. However over the past century it has flourished as a transshipment center between the West and China. Prior to World War II, Hong Kong was considered economically and commercially insignificant compared to other regional Asian centers such as Shanghai and Singapore. During the period of civil wars and political turmoil in China in the 1920s and 1930s, large numbers of Chinese capitalists fled to Hong Kong. In 1938 the Japanese occupation of Canton prompted more Chinese refugees to move to Hong Kong.

In December 1941 Hong Kong was seized by the Japanese, and remained under their control for almost four years. During this period trade dried up and many residents moved to nearby Macau, the Portuguese province. The British regained control of Hong Kong in 1945. The 1948–1949 civil war in China resulted in another influx of Chinese capitalists. Unlike the traders who had immigrated to Hong Kong in the century before, these new Chinese capitalists were financiers and industrialists. As a result, they became instrumental in transforming Hong Kong into an international arena of finance and industry. Hong Kong also benefited in the period following World War II and during the Korean War because much of the commerce to and from China had to be rerouted through Hong Kong. Over the past fifty years communist China has periodically expressed interest in reclaiming Hong Kong by force. One of the more significant events occurred in 1967 during the Cultural Revolution in China when Red Guards instigated riots in Hong Kong and a small Red Chinese military unit crossed the Chinese border into Hong Kong. In Hong Kong, curfews were established and commerce came to a halt. The Hong Kong economy was temporarily paralyzed and property values plummeted. Many families, fearing for their safety, sent their children overseas to study and transferred their assets out of the country. The 1967 scare has had a deep impact on the way many Hong Kong residents view Hong Kong's future after its return to China in 1997.

However, Hong Kong recovered quickly from its panic and has since enjoyed phenomenal economic success as a major international manufacturing, trading, and financial center. The colony's economic success has enabled the government to transform Hong Kong into a modern city with a well-developed, efficient infrastructure and excellent education, housing, and health and social welfare systems.

According to the Sino-British Joint Declaration signed in 1984, Hong Kong will become a Special Administrative Region (SAR) of China on July 1, 1997. Theoretically it will be allowed to retain its present legal, economic, and social systems for at least fifty years.

The initial reaction to the transfer of Hong Kong back to Chinese rule was capital flight out of the country. Speculators sought to profit from the resulting decrease in land prices and other investments. But by the early 1990s, as China instituted reforms and its economy began to boom, many Chinese and foreigners sought to utilize Hong Kong as a regional base in an effort to capitalize on the burgeoning opportunities in China. Many overseas Chinese in other Asian countries, particularly Taiwan (which is prohibited from direct commercial interactions with China for political reasons) as well as those living in the West, now invest in China through Hong Kong channels. By 1994 Hong Kong was the largest investor in China and the source of about 30 percent of China's foreign exchange. Nevertheless, as a precautionary measure, many citizens have moved at least some of their personal assets out of Hong Kong.

In 1988 China issued the "Basic Law for Hong Kong," which resembles a constitution. Hong Kong will retain its legal system based on British common law, with guaranteed freedom of speech, freedom of association, and freedom to travel. Publicly, the Chinese government asserts that after 1997, there will be "one-country, two-systems." But, despite extensive talks between the Chinese and British, it is still uncertain as to what China will ultimately permit after 1997. Fearful about their future, many Hong Kong residents have emigrated. Until the area reverts to Chinese control, Hong Kong remains a visible symbol to the Chinese of humiliation at the hands of foreign imperialism. Hong Kong's political future remains uncertain as the 1997 transfer date approaches, although many feel that China, as the largest beneficiary of Hong Kong's change of status, will do little to jeopardize the stability, strength, and independence of Hong Kong's economy. Neighboring Macau, which is still controlled by the Portuguese, will revert to Chinese authority in 1999.

Political Structure

The government of Hong Kong is similar to that of other former British colonial governments. The government is headed by a governor appointed by the British Crown. There are two constitutional bodies, the Executive Council (EXCO) and the Legislative Council (LEGCO). The governor presides over the EXCO, the highest policymaking body, which also functions as his cabinet. All of EXCO's members are either appointed by or are accountable to the

British government. LEGCO enacts legislation and controls the expenditures.

Both EXCO and LEGCO include three ex-officio members: the chief secretary, the finance secretary, and the attorney general. EXCO consists of an unspecified number of other members appointed by the governor. LEGCO includes fifty-seven nonofficial members, eighteen of whom are appointed by the governor, twenty-one of whom are elected by functional constituencies (representing occupational or professional groups such as commerce, finance, labor, or medicine), and eighteen of whom are elected by geographical constituencies in Hong Kong. LEGCO elects a president from among its members. The term for all LEGCO members is four years.

It should be noted that despite the fact that *some* LEGCO members are elected, the present system of government is not fully democratic. The governor, with whom most authority rests, is appointed by and is accountable to the British Crown, not to the people of Hong Kong. After the Tian An Men Square Massacre in China in 1989, Hong Kong residents have become more politically active. Many people demonstrated in Hong Kong as a sign of solidarity with the students. Subsequent elections have received more attention and more candidates have sought to obtain office in LEGCO. However, in September 1994, the Chinese government declared that it would disband any Hong Kong government in effect at the time of the transition in 1997. This attitude is in response to the attempts of the current governor Chris Patten to further democratize Hong Kong prior to transfer to Chinese rule.

Lower councils are responsible for day-to-day operations of services in Hong Kong, Kowloon, and the New Territories. Traditionally a small percentage of civil servants from the United Kingdom have occupied nearly all of the senior policymaking positions. This situation is gradually changing as more Chinese are being promoted to top administrative posts in anticipation of 1997. Although Hong Kong is adamantly capitalist in nature, it has had a Communist party, the Hong Kong Macau Work Committee (HMWC), since

1949. About fifty Hong Kong delegates attend the National People's Congress, the powerless, rubber-stamp parliament in Beijing, providing China with a public image of a united front of support for the Chinese takeover in 1997.

Hong Kong has a well-established and stable legal structure based on British common law. The Supreme Court is the highest court. The judiciary is independent of the executive and legislative branches of government. Technically, this system is expected to continue after 1997.

Economy

Hong Kong is one of the world's six richest countries. It has the world's tenth largest trading economy, is one of the world's largest and busiest container ports, and is a global financial center. Major industries include textiles, clothing, footwear, tourism, electronics, plastics, toys, and watches and clocks. Approximately 40 percent of the population is employed in textile and clothing manufacturing. In recent years, however, many manufacturing facilities have moved to southern China due to cheap labor and land.

There are almost no trade barriers or capital controls within Hong Kong, as the government has traditionally believed in little or no intervention. Hong Kong is shifting toward a service economy, particularly in the areas of financial and business services. As the mainland Chinese market opens, Hong Kong has become the ideal regional base for doing business with China and Taiwan. In fact, Hong Kong and China have become each other's primary trading partners: bilateral trade accounts for about 35 percent of China's total international trade and about 33 percent of Hong Kong's total global trade. The Chinese province of Guangdong has become heavily dependent on Hong Kong trade and investment and, as a result of its Hong Kong connection, was the fastest growing province in China throughout the 1980s. Hong Kong is also a major investor in other Asian economies, including those of Taiwan, Indonesia, Malaysia, Thailand, and the Philippines. Re-exports, which are goods transshipped through Hong Kong, account for about 75 percent of all of Hong Kong's exports throughout the world.

The growth of Hong Kong's economy slowed in the early 1990s as concerns over the Chinese takeover mounted and the colony was impacted by the global recession. Today, despite rising inflation and the continuing exodus of capital and skilled labor, the business and trade outlook in Hong Kong remains positive. Hong Kong has an educated and industrious workforce, a sophisticated commercial structure, and an advanced communications network.

People, Values, and Social Customs

The population of Hong Kong is about six million, making it one of the most densely populated places in the world. About 98 percent of the population is ethnic Chinese. The largest group are migrants or descendants of migrants from the Guangdong (Canton) province in mainland China. But the Tankas, nomadic boat people, and the Hakkas, a distinct group of Chinese who fled persecution in northern China, have an established presence there as well. Only about 2 percent of Hong Kong's population are foreigners—Westerners, Australians, Canadians, and non-Chinese Asians—of which the largest groups are Filipinos and Indians. In the late 1970s and early 1980s Hong Kong was flooded by thousands of boat people from Vietnam. After initially accepting all of the boat people, Hong Kong attempted to differentiate between political refugees and economic migrants, giving preference to the former.

The major religions in Hong Kong are Buddhism, Taoism, and Confucianism. Christianity, Hinduism, Sikhism, and Judaism are also practiced in various communities. Traditional beliefs involving ancestor worship, animism, and *feng shui* ("wind water"), which is based on the notion that man and nature must exist in harmony and involves manipulating the environment, coexist with these religions. Before any house or structure may be built or grave site designated, rituals must be performed to drive away the bad spirits. Today the Chinese in Hong Kong are much less religious and more focused on material wealth and gain. Nevertheless, rituals must be performed to keep the spirits happy and belief in the *joss*, luck or a blessing, stick ritual is common.

Families are an integral part of life in Hong Kong and family members are committed to upholding family honor through loyalty, respect, and obligation. Hong Kong Chinese are also very conscious of a person's social and economic status. Education is highly valued, for it provides one of the best means for social and economic mobility. Schools and universities provide forums for developing relationships and connections. To increase their prestige, many Chinese have pursued higher education in the United States or Europe. In recent years, due to concerns about 1997, many educated Hong Kong Chinese have emigrated to more stable countries, resulting in a "brain drain."

The Hong Kong Chinese may be cautious at first in dealing with Westerners, for the Chinese as a people generally tend to distrust foreigners. Historically, the British discriminated against the Chinese, who in turn discriminated against each other. However, as a result of the upcoming change of power, Hong Kong residents now are upfront and pragmatic, and take very little for granted no matter with whom they are dealing.

The pace of life in Hong Kong is frenetic. Its residents are entrepreneurial, hard-working, highly competitive, and have strong commercial instincts. Hong Kong residents can also be somewhat brusque and less willing to help than people in other Asian nations, but they are also among the most expressive and emotional of all Chinese. Hong Kong residents smile only when they are happy and tend to express their emotions more frequently, in contrast to their northern Chinese counterparts. They also have a healthy sense of humor. Without a doubt, money is the biggest and often the only motivator in Hong Kong.

Women in Hong Kong are more respected and achieve greater opportunity outside of the home than their counterparts in many other parts of Asia. While they are still responsible for maintaining the home and childrearing, many women have received higher education and are employed in positions of responsibility in a wide variety of fields.

Work Schedule

Businesses and government offices are usually open from 9:00 A.M. to 5:00 P.M., Monday to Friday, and Saturdays from 9:00 A.M. to 1:00 P.M. The lunch hour is usually from 1:00 P.M. to 2:00 P.M.; most government offices close during this period. Although it varies by branch and location, banks are generally open from 9:00 or 9:30 A.M. to 4:00 or 4:30 P.M., Monday to Friday, and Saturdays from 9:00 or 9:30 A.M. to 12:00 or 12:30 P.M. Stores are open everyday from 10:00 A.M. to 6:00 P.M. in Central and until about 9:00 P.M. in Wanchai, Causeway Bay, and Tsim Sha Tsui, all of which are different areas on the island and in Kowloon.

Making Contacts

Foreign businesspeople can write directly to Hong Kong companies. While introductions and connections, *guanxi*, always help to establish credibility, they are not essential. Hong Kong professionals are focused on money-making opportunities and profits and are receptive to making contact with new companies and hearing new ideas. When sending a letter of interest, direct it to the senior-most person. Your query will then be directed to the appropriate level. Generally, businesspeople are well received and well treated, particularly if locals perceive your presence or company as a benefit to them.

While it is not necessary to have a local representative to develop initial business, it is advisable to establish a local office if you are committed to doing business in Hong Kong or using it as a regional base. It is best to hire a local Chinese professional to supervise your office, for they are best suited to managing local employees. Establishing a local office is relatively straightforward. All incorporated companies must be recorded by the Registrar of Companies. The Hong Kong commercial office, the chamber of commerce from your home country, and the Hong Kong government commerce offices can all assist you.

The Hong Kong Tourist Association (HKTA) publishes a guide of associations and societies in Hong Kong with addresses and telephone numbers for all commercial, trade, and social organizations. There are numerous offices in Hong Kong representing major countries, particularly the United States and European nations, that can also help you facilitate trade and investment. The American Chamber of Commerce in Hong Kong publishes various resource guides including *PRC Business Firms in Hong Kong and Macau, Living in Hong Kong, Hong Kong Connection—Doing Business in Guangdong Province,* and *Establishing an Office in Hong Kong,* all of which can be obtained through its office in Hong Kong.

Meeting People

If possible, do not schedule meetings during or near the Chinese New Year, which occurs in January or February, and is the most elaborate Chinese holiday. Many Chinese treat this holiday as an annual vacation period much the same as Westerners treat Christmas. It is advisable to schedule meetings prior to your arrival in Hong Kong. It is very important to be punctual. Meetings may be scheduled by fax and telephone, and may be changed or canceled. It is best to confirm appointments in Hong Kong near or on the scheduled day. The pace of business is fast and hectic, and business is conducted largely as it would be in the United States or Europe. Early interactions should be formal and professional. *Guanxi* can be more important with Chinese family-owned businesses: family ties and friendships are a common part of Hong Kong business. Accordingly, seek to develop your network by socializing and dining with associates and other contacts.

When interacting with Hong Kong Chinese, you should follow the lead of your host or colleagues. Businesspeople greet one another with a handshake. Business cards are exchanged liberally in all types of encounters, for this exchange is perceived as a way to expand networks. Business cards are exchanged at the beginning of a meeting using both hands, often accompanied by a slight nod of the head. Study the card before putting it away to indicate respect. To create a positive impression on your Chinese counterparts, have your business cards printed in Chinese on the reverse side. Most hotels can assist you with this.

Chinese names are listed with the family (surname) first, followed by a given name and then the second name (usually the Western equivalent of the first name). Some Chinese also adopt Western first names. In that case, the given (Western) name is listed first. The Hong Kong business culture is formal, so be sure to use formal titles such as—"Mr.," "Mrs.," "Dr.," and surnames unless invited to use first names. The title "Ms." is not commonly used in Hong Kong. It is appropriate to ask someone how they would like to be addressed. There are numerous women holding positions of responsibility, so do not dismiss a female staff member as inconsequential.

Refrain from winking or excessive blinking; both are considered rude because they may imply boredom. Beckoning should be done using the whole hand, with the palm down and the fingers pointing away, but moving toward you in a scratching motion. Always use your entire hand, rather than just one finger, to point. Never write in red ink, for it is considered a sign of unfriendliness. Refrain from touching anyone. When you are seated, your posture should be upright and you should not fidget or shake your legs. The Chinese will often stand closer to one another than most Westerners.

Begin your first meeting with some casual conversation about your trip, the general business climate, or your host's overseas experiences. Refrain from mentioning any political topics. If you are pressed to reveal personal information, be polite and vague if you are uncomfortable divulging too much information. Hong Kong professionals are much more business-oriented and are much more conscious of time (theirs and yours) than other Asians and will seek to discuss business issues within a few minutes. Although English is a common business language, be sensitive to your counterpart's knowledge of the language and speak clearly and slowly if necessary. Gifts are not traditionally exchanged in the initial meetings. If you wish, you may present a small sample product from your company, but only if it is appropriate in the business context.

Corporate Structure

Many of the largest and oldest businesses in Hong Kong started out as large British trading firms, also known as "hongs," which have since passed into Chinese hands. Most Chinese businesses in Hong Kong are family-owned and family-operated. The key decision-makers are the senior family members, usually men and on occasion women. Hong Kong companies follow strict hierarchies. The most senior person in a business is usually the chairman or the senior managing director, with managing directors, directors, and managers ranking below him or her. Titles can be misleading because nonfamily members may have higher sounding titles than their true responsibility level. It is advisable to maintain relationships with both the family members and their subordinates.

In Hong Kong business and government work together in partnership, although not as closely as in Japan. Government tends to be relatively efficient and prompt when addressing business-related issues, though this may change after 1997. Government enterprises from mainland China, the Chinese Foreign Trade Corporations (FTCs), are investing heavily in companies in Hong Kong and are developing close relations with Chinese business families there. To better understand the decision-making process and relevant issues that might affect your company, research the "true" ownership of a company with which you intend to do business *before* you start negotiations.

Negotiation

In negotiations, Hong Kong Chinese are extremely conscious of time and value efficiency. Decisions can be made very quickly, depending on the issue. For family-owned and family-operated businesses, senior family members are usually the final decision makers. Their decisions are often based on intuition. However, in large firms, decisions may be made based on the research and groundwork conducted by subordinates. The Hong Kong Chinese are results-oriented and usually able to focus on relevant details and discard unnecessary information. Patience, perseverance, and flexibility are valuable characteristics for foreigners.

A common negotiating strategy for Hong Kong Chinese is to find out when you intend to leave Hong Kong, to delay discussions and decisions in the hopes of forcing you to make concessions as your departure date approaches. Either do not disclose the real date you intend to leave or say that you will stay until the deal is completed. Further, Hong Kong Chinese may try to monopolize your time with meetings and social events. The Hong Kong Chinese are tough, adamant, and shrewd negotiators. Be firm in your position and do not waiver easily. Generally, concessions are made at latter stages in a negotiation.

Do not assume that Western-dressed and Western-educated Chinese are Western in attitude. More often than not, they have developed a balance between their Asian culture and modern Western capitalist attitudes. Most Chinese do not like to say "No," and may merely hint at a negative response because they believe in maintaining public harmony despite the situation. A common avoidance technique is to tell you that they do not have time for you because they are too busy.

Feng Shui, or geomancy rituals, can influence business decisions, particularly in determining the suitability of locations of offices or other sites, as well as doors and windows. Foreign businesses may wish to consult geomancers in order to appease their Chinese staff.

Preserving dignity and maintaining family honor is important for Hong Kong Chinese. Refrain from putting your counterpart in a publicly awkward position. Never directly criticize anyone. It is much better to calmly explain the problem or situation without making any references to blame. It is best not to exhibit any loud and negative behavior even if your counterpart does.

While personal relationships are important, most business interactions are conducted formally. Verbal agreements are always supported with written contracts. Detailed contracts are always used and are adhered to closely.

Conducting Business in a Social Setting

Dining and Drinking

Business entertaining is important in Hong Kong. The better restaurants serving either Chinese or other ethnic cuisine are very suitable for business meals. Business lunches and dinners are more common than business breakfasts. Business dinners include many courses and are expected to be impressive as they are considered primarily social rather than business occasions. Hong Kong restaurants can be expensive, so check with your hotel concierge for appropriate recommendations.

If you have been invited to dinner, you should bring a small, tasteful gift for your host, unless you intend to reciprocate the dinner. If you intend to reciprocate, do so quickly or your degree of interest in doing business may be questioned. The objective is to take care of the obligation. After a meal you may offer to pay the bill, an offer that is usually refused, but never offer to split the bill, for this would cause your host to lose face. "Fighting for the bill" is a common sight in Hong Kong restaurants.

The Chinese banquet is an integral part of business. In Chinese family-owned businesses, the entire family often attends these banquets. Never leave your chopsticks standing vertically in your rice, for this reminds the Chinese of a death ritual: use the chopstick rests. For further information on dining and the traditional Chinese banquet, please refer to Chapter 3, on China.

Many Chinese businesspeople enjoy going to the racetrack as a form of business entertainment. Further, karaoke, or singalong, clubs are becoming popular in Hong Kong. Participation is more important than skill. The Hong Kong Chinese are also are avid gamblers and enthusiastically partake in mahjong, a tile game, and other related activities.

Visiting a Home

If you are invited to a home, take a gift of fine chocolates or liquor (cognac is particularly appreciated) or a crystal object. During the Chinese New Year, it is appropriate to take gifts of money, about HK $100, for each child. Be sure to place the money inside a crisp, new, red envelope designated especially for this purpose and available in most shops. Due to extensive British influence in Hong Kong, European manners and etiquette are observed in many homes.

Gift Giving

Corruption and bribery exist in Hong Kong, but are less prevalent than in neighboring China. Cronyism has always been a common aspect of business in Hong Kong. The government, through its Independent Commission Against Corruption, has made significant progress in curtailing corruption, which is usually linked to winning contracts or gaining a business or financial advantage. Therefore it is possible to avoid engaging in questionable practices and still be successful in Hong Kong.

As noted earlier, gifts are not normally exchanged in Hong Kong during early encounters. Your counterparts may appreciate small gifts, such as gourmet chocolates, flowers, or handicrafts, after initial contacts have been made. More expensive items, such as crystal, are appropriate later in the relationship. The Hong Kong Chinese have very discriminating tastes and prefer tasteful and expensive gifts. When giving flowers, only present them in even number quantities. Never give clocks or knives, or anything white or black, because these things have negative connotations. Do not give (or wear) green hats as it implies that the wearer's wife or girlfriend has been unfaithful. Gifts should be wrapped in red and gold paper. Usually, Chinese people do not open gifts in front of the giver so as not to embarrass them. Verbal thank-yous are exchanged on the spot and follow-up cards are not expected, though they are appreciated. Do not be too effusive in your thank-yous, for that might make you appear insincere to your counterparts.

It is important to give gifts at the Chinese New Year to all employees and other professional and domestic staff. The professional staff should receive gifts; subordinate office workers and drivers, particularly young people, should be presented a *laisee*, red envelopes containing money. The color red symbolizes happiness and is considered a lucky color.

When giving gifts that contain more than a single piece, remember that certain numbers are associated with luck and beneficial qualities. The "good" numbers include 2, which sounds like the word for "easy"; 3, which sounds like "living" or "giving birth"; 6, which sounds like the word for continuous; 8, which also sounds like the word for "prosperity"; and 9, which sounds like the word for "eternity." The number 8 is the most auspicious number. Chinese seek to have this number on as many of their personal items as possible, including license plates, telephone numbers, and street addresses. In fact license plates with "8888" are considered very lucky, and Hong Kong residents bid several hundred thousand US dollars in an effort to obtain such license plates at government auctions.

Unlucky numbers include 1 (the lonely number) and 4, both of which sound like the word for "death."

Dress Code

Business attire is formal and conservative, although it can be fashionable within reason. For men, suits and ties should always be worn. Women should wear suits, dresses, or skirts and jackets. Hong Kong businesspeople often judge others by their appearance, so be sure to dress tastefully and elegantly. Do not dress casually for business purposes, unless you know your counterpart well and the occasion warrants it, such as a factory visit or a golf outing.

Useful Phrases

Hong Kong has two official languages: English and Cantonese, a dialect from southern China. English is the primary language of business, law, and international trade. Some Hong Kong residents also speak other Chinese dialects, including Mandarin and Shanghainese, particularly in light of the increasing trade with the mainland. Hong Kong uses Chinese characters for written script. Pinyin, which is a romanization system used on the mainland, is for Mandarin and is not applicable to Cantonese. The following list includes some useful Cantonese phrases as they should be pronounced.

Hello	*Nay ho*
Good morning	*Jo-sun*
Good afternoon	*Mo an*
Good evening	*Mine shong ho*
How are you?	*Neh ho mah?*
Please	*Cheng nay* (not used alone)
Thank you	*Dor-ts-yeh* (for a gift); *mm-goy* (for a service rendered)
You are welcome	*Mm'sai mm-goy*
Excuse me	*Doy ing choo*
I am sorry	*Dui mm geeyu*

My name is ———	*Ngau gau men hi* ———
I work for ———	*Ngau-hi* ——— *jo gong*
Here is my business card	*Nee goy hi ngauga ming peen ka*
I am pleased to meet you	*Ngau ho go hing seh da nay*
Please accept this small gift	*Tsian sohar neegaw shiu lie ma*
I look forward to developing a	*Haymong ngau day hup tsaw yiu fi*
good relationship with you /	
your firm	
I understand	*Ngau ming buk*
No, I do not understand	*Ngau mm ming buk*
Please wait a minute	*Tsian done ye-done*
Where is the bathroom?	*Sai sau g-an hi been doe*
Good-bye	*Joy geen*
Cheers	*Yum-sing* or *Gone boo-i*

Major Holidays

January 1	New Year's Day
January/February*	Chinese Lunar New Year
Early April	Easter
April 5	Ching Ming Festival
May/June*	Dragon Boat Festival
June 11	Queen's Birthday
Last Monday in August	Liberation Day
September/October*	Mid-Autumn Festival
December 25	Christmas Day
December 26	Boxing Day

*These holidays are based on the lunar calendar and change every year.

General Facts

Climate: Hong Kong has a tropical climate. The cool season is dry with temperatures averaging between 56F (13C) to 66F (19C). Summers are hot and humid, with average temperatures ranging from 77F (25C) to 91F (33C), and experience monsoon rains. Autumn is mild and pleasant, with temperatures averaging between 59F (15C) and 80F (27C). Typhoons can occasionally occur in October, but are more common during the summer months. Spring can be mixed in terms of weather and has temperatures averaging between 66F (19C) to 84F (29C).

Currency: The *Hong Kong dollar* (abbreviated as HK$), which is divided into 100 cents.

Dates: Dates are written day, month, year. For example, March 15, 1995, would be abbreviated as 15/3/95.

Electricity: The voltage is 220 volts (50 Hz). Many outlets use three-prong, round plugs. Adapters are available at hotels and in most stores, but it is easier to carry one with you. Common personal appliances, such as hair dryers and shavers, with variable power selections, are widely available in Hong Kong.

Entry Requirements: American, British, Canadian, French, and German citizens need only a passport and a roundtrip ticket. A visa is required for stays longer than: thirty days for U.S. citizens; ninety days for Canadian, French, and German citizens; and one year for citizens of the United Kingdom.

Time: Hong Kong has one time zone, which is eight hours ahead of Greenwich Mean Time and thirteen hours ahead of U.S Eastern Standard Time (twelve hours in Daylight Savings Time).

Tipping: At hotels, doormen and porters should be tipped about HK $5 per item, with a minimum of about HK $10. Concierges are usually tipped at least HK $10. Waiters, whether in a restaurant or for delivering hotel room service, are tipped about 5–10 percent in addition to the standard service charge. There is rarely a tip for housekeeping. Many restaurants and hotels include a 10 percent service charge. In such cases, waiters should be tipped an additional amount only if you feel the service is exceptional. Taxi drivers are tipped about 10 percent of the fare.

Transportation: It is easy to get around in Hong Kong. Taxis are the most convenient and inexpensive mode of transportation.

Taxis serving Hong Kong Island, Kowloon, and the New Territories are usually red with a "Taxi" sign on the roof that lights up when the taxi is available. Taxis serving only the New Territories are painted bright green. All taxis can be hailed on streets, in front of hotels, and at the numerous taxi stands around the city. If you have difficulty finding a taxi, go into a major restaurant or hotel and ask them to telephone a cab company for you. Most drivers speak some English, but it can help to have your destination written in Chinese.

The subway (Mass Transit Railway [MTR], Tel. 2750-0710) runs from Hong Kong Island through Kowloon and is easy to use and relatively convenient. Maps are available at hotels, the airport, and at bookstores. Eating, drinking, and smoking are not permitted on the subway and offenders are fined. Buses, minibuses, and trams are slower and more crowded, but offer extensive routes. There are two types of minibuses: beige buses with a green stripe follow a predetermined route as noted above the windshield and beige buses with a red stripe follow flexible routes to any unrestricted location. Be sure to carry change, as buses and subways require an exact fare. The easiest and most inexpensive way to cross the harbor is the Star Ferry (Tel. 2366-2576), which operates daily from 6:30 a.m. to 11:30 p.m. Frequently, due to the traffic in the Cross Harbor Tunnel, it is advisable to take the MTR across the harbor and then shift to a taxi to reach your destination.

For transportation to and from the airport, in addition to taxis, the Airbuses travel to fifteen hotels in Kowloon and on Hong Kong Island and are relatively inexpensive and efficient. Some hotels will meet you at the airport for a fee. Inform them when you make your reservation that you desire this service.

Driving is not recommended. Parking is very difficult, traffic very congested, and the roads difficult to navigate. If you prefer driving your own car, driving is on the left side of the street and an international driver's license is required. There are no car rentals at the airport, but cars may be rented at offices and hotels on Hong

Kong Island or in Kowloon, and drivers can be provided upon request.

Helpful Telephone Numbers

Public telephones are available. Local calls cost HK $1. English instructions are written on the telephone. Phonecards are also available in many shops or at the Hong Kong Telecom Office, from which you can also make international calls. Most hotels and shops have public telephones. The country code is (852) and all telephone numbers have eight digits.

Hospitals:

Baptist Hospital (Private)
222 Waterloo Road
Kowloon Tong
Tel.: (852) 2337-4141

Hong Kong Adventist Hospital (Private)
40 Stubbs Road
Wanchai
Hong Kong
Tel.: (852) 2574-6211

Hong Kong Central Hospital (Private)
1B Lower Albert Road
Central, Hong Kong
Tel.: (852) 2522-3141

Queen Elizabeth Hospital (Public)
Wylie Road
Yaumati, Kowloon
Tel.: (852)2710-2111

Queen Mary Hospital (Public)
Pokufulam Road

Hong Kong
Tel.: (852) 2819-2111

St. Teresa's Hospital (Private)
327 Prince Edward Road
Kowloon
Tel.: (852) 2711-9111

International SOS Center
Kai Tak Commercial Building
Room 904-908, 9/F
317-321 Des Voeux Road
Central, Hong Kong

Medical, Fire, or Police Emergency: Dial 999.

Police: Dial 2527-7177 (non-emergency) (English-speaking police wear a red flash under their shoulder badge).

Ambulance: Dial 2576-6555.

Operator Assistance: Dial 108; overseas, 010, 011, 012; international direct dial information, 013.

Information Hotlines: Hong Kong Tourist Association Tel. 2801-7177 Shopping advice Tel. 2801-7278.

Helpful Addresses

In Hong Kong:

American Chamber of Commerce
1030 Swire House
Chater Road
Central, Hong Kong
Tel.: (852) 2526-0165

British Chamber of Commerce
1712 Shui On Centre
8 Harbour Road
Wanchai, Hong Kong
Tel.: (852) 2824-2211

Canadian Chamber of Commerce
14/F One Exchange Square
8 Connaught Place
Central, Hong Kong
Tel.: (852) 2526-3207

French Business Association, French Chamber of Commerce and Industry
Far East Exchange Building
Room 1202
8 Wyndham Street
Central, Hong Kong
Tel.: (852) 2523-6818

German Business Association of Hong Kong
2207–2210 World Wide House

19 Des Voeux Road
Central, Hong Kong
Tel.: (852) 2526-5481

Hong Kong General Chamber of Commerce
United Centre 22F
95 Queensway
Hong Kong
Tel.: (852) 2529-9229

Hong Kong Government Publications
GPO Building, Ground Floor
Connaught Place
Hong Kong
Tel.: (852) 2523-5377

Hong Kong Information Services Department
Beaconsfield House
4 Queen's Road
Central, Hong Kong
Tel.: (852) 2842-8777

Hong Kong Tourist Association (HKTA)
Jardine House, 35th Floor
1 Connaught Road
Central, Hong Kong
Tel.: (852) 2524-4191
(Hotline) 2801-7177

Hong Kong Trade Development Council
Convention Plaza,
36–39th Floor
1 Harbour Road.
Wanchai, Hong Kong
Tel.: (852) 2584-4333

Immigration Department
Wanchai Tower Two,
2d Floor
7 Gloucester Road
Wanchai, Hong Kong
Tel.: (852) 2824-6111

Registrar of Companies
Queensway Government
Offices, 13th Floor
66 Queensway
Hong Kong
Tel.: (852) 2862-2448

Foreign Diplomatic Offices:

American Consulate
26 Garden Road
Central, Hong Kong
Tel.: (852) 2523-9011

British Trade Commission
Bank of America Tower
9th Floor
12 Harcourt Road
Central, Hong Kong
Tel.: (852) 2523-0176

Canadian Consulate, Canadian Commission
One Exchange Square
11th–12th Floor
8 Connaught Place
Central, Hong Kong
Tel.: (852) 2810-4321

French Consulate
Admiralty Centre, Tower Two
25th Floor
18 Harcourt Road
Central, Hong Kong
Tel.: (852) 2529-4316

German Consulate
United Centre, 21st Floor
95 Queensway
Central, Hong Kong
Tel.: (852) 2529-8855

In Canada:

Hong Kong Economic and Trade Office
174 St. George Street
Toronto, Ontario M5R 2M7
Tel.: (416) 924-5544

Hong Kong Trade Development Council
National Building, Suite 1100
347 Bay Street
Toronto, Ontario M5H 2R7
Tel.: (416) 366-3594

Hong Kong Tourist Association (HKTA)
347 Bay Street, Suite 909
Toronto, Ontario M5H 2R7
Tel.: (416) 366-2389

In France:

Hong Kong Trade Development Council
18 Rue d'Aguesseau
75008 Paris
Tel.: (1) 4742-4150

Hong Kong Tourist Association (HKTA)
Escalier C-8 eme Etage
53, Rue Francois ler
75008 Paris
Tel.: (1) 4720-3954

In Germany:

Hong Kong Trade Development Council
Bockenheimer Landstrasse 93
W-6000 Frankfurt am Main 1
Tel.: (69) 740161

Hong Kong Tourist Association (HKTA)
Weisenau 1
D-6000 Frankfurt am Main 1
Tel.: (69) 722841

In the United Kingdom

Hong Kong Government Office
6 Grafton Street
London W1X3LB
Tel.: (71) 499-9821

Hong Kong Tourist Association (HKTA)
125 Pall Mall, 5th Floor
London SW1Y 5EA
Tel.: (71) 930-4775

Hong Kong Trade Development Council
Swire House
59 Buckingham Gate
London SW1Y 5EA
Tel.: (71) 930-4775

In the United States:

Hong Kong Economic and Trade Office
680 Fifth Avenue, 22d Floor
New York, NY 10019
Tel.: (212) 265-8888

1233 20th St., N. W., Suite 504
Washington, DC 20036
Tel.: (202) 331-8947

222 Kearny Street, Suite 402
San Francisco, CA 94108
Tel.: (415) 397-2215

Hong Kong Trade Development Council (HKTDC)
219 East 46th Street
New York, NY 10017
Tel.: (212) 838-8688

333 North Michigan Avenue
Suite 2028
Chicago, IL 60601
Tel.: (312) 726-4515

World Trade Center, Suite 120
2050 Stemmons Freeway
Dallas, TX 75207
Tel.: (214) 748-8162

Los Angeles World Trade
Center, Suite 282
350 S. Figueroa Street
Los Angeles, CA 90071
Tel.: (213) 622-3194

Courvoisier Center, Suite 509
601 Brickell Key Drive
Miami, FL 33131
Tel.: (305) 577-0414

Hong Kong Tourist Association (HKTA)
590 Fifth Avenue, 5th Floor
New York, NY 10036
Tel.: (212) 869-5008

333 N. Michigan Avenue
Suite 2400

Chicago, IL 60601
Tel.: (312) 782-3872

10940 Wilshire Blvd.
Suite 1220
Los Angeles, CA 90024
Tel.: (213) 208-4582

U.S. Department of Commerce
International Trade Administration
Hong Kong Desk, Room 2317
14th and Constitution Avenues, N. W.
Washington, DC 20230
Tel.: (202) 482-3932

5 Taiwan

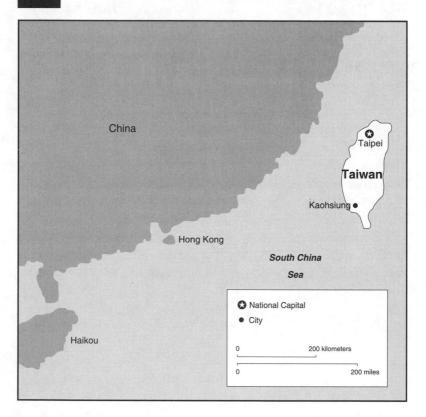

China

Taipei ✪

Taiwan

Kaohsiung ●

Hong Kong

South China
Sea

✪ National Capital
● City

Haikou

0   200 kilometers

0   200 miles

Geography

Shaped like a tobacco leaf, the island of Taiwan (once known as Formosa) is located about 100 miles (160 km) east off the coast of mainland China in the western Pacific Ocean. It lies about 700 miles (1,120 km) south of Japan and 200 miles (320 km) north of the Philippines. Taiwan, officially called the Republic of China on Taiwan, claims jurisdiction over surrounding islands. These islands are also claimed by China, which considers Taiwan its province. The important islands are the Pescadores, Kinmen, Matsu, and Orchid. The total land area of Taiwan is about 13,803 square miles (35,751 square kilometers). Approximately two-thirds of the terrain is mountainous and hilly, and half of the island is covered by dense forests. The five largest cities are Taipei, Kaohsiung, Taichung, Tainan, and Keelung. Taipei is the political, financial, and commercial center, and Kaohsiung is the major industrial center.

History

Relatively little is known about Taiwan's early history. It is believed that the earliest inhabitants settled on the island as much as ten thousand years ago. They are believed to have been of Indonesian or Malaysian origin. They were followed by the Hakkas, meaning "guest people," a persecuted minority who were driven out of the Henan province in China almost fifteen hundred years ago and slowly moved to southern China. Gradually they migrated to the Pescadores (P'eng-hu Islands) and eventually to Taiwan from A.D. 500–1000.

The Chinese from the Sui dynasty to the Ming dynasty referred to the island of Taiwan as Little Liu Chiu, but did not know its exact location. The Chinese finally located the island during the Ming dynasty (1368–1644). During the fourteenth century, the Taiwanese (Han Chinese), mainly from China's present-day, southern province of Fujian, sailed to the island to escape the encroaching Mongols and to establish trading posts.

In 1517 Portuguese ships on their way to Japan sighted the island and called it *Ilha Formosa*, "beautiful island." In 1624 the Dutch East India Company laid claim to the island. The Spanish established a stronghold in the north of the island in 1626, but were driven out in 1641 by the Dutch, who became the sole rulers of the island conquering the local Taiwanese. Gradually, the island became a wealthy entrepôt.

In 1661 Cheng Cheng-kung (also known as Koxinga), the son of a Ming dynasty loyalist and opponent of the invading Manchus

(Qing), conquered Taiwan, forced the Dutch off the island within a year, and used it as a base to defend the Ming dynasty from the Manchus. But the Manchus overpowered mainland China and eventually took over Taiwan in 1683, ending its independence and making it a strong base to protect China from foreigners. Manchu rule over the island was marked by corruption and social and political instability.

The 1858 treaties of Tientsin allowed the British and the French to establish trading posts on Taiwan. Christian missionaries quickly followed Western traders. In 1885, after the first Sino-French War, France partially occupied Taiwan. As a result of its defeat in the Sino-Japanese War in 1894–95, China was forced to relinquish Taiwan to Japan. France turned its ambitions towards southwest China and the newly created Indochinese Union. The Japanese were instrumental in improving the island's agricultural productivity, infrastructure, and the general economic and social structure, while also promoting Japanese language and culture. However, the Japanese benefited the most from these improvements, often at the expense of the Taiwanese, who were never treated as equals. By World War II, Taiwan's ties to China had been drastically reduced. Indeed, many Taiwanese served in the Japanese army and supported Japan's war effort. After Japan's defeat, however, Taiwan was returned to Chinese rule. However, the Japanese influence remains evident in many aspects of the social and commercial culture even today.

General Chiang Kai-shek's troops took control of the island at war's end. Members of his Kuomingtang party, the KMT, established a government and filled all major posts with their own people. This left the Taiwanese without a voice in decision-making. Corruption was widespread and many Taiwanese suffered the confiscation of their property. As a result, Taiwan's economy deteriorated. (See Chapter 3, on China, for a discussion of Chiang Kai-shek and the KMT.)

On February 27, 1947, local Taiwanese citizens came to the aid of a woman being attacked by KMT officials. The attack prompted riots by the Taiwanese against the mainland Chinese in Taiwan.

Governor Chen I retaliated by launching an island-wide massacre, in which eighteen to twenty-eight thousand people were killed; this massacre is known as the "February 28th Incident." Despite Chiang Kai-shek's efforts to make amends for this brutal action, the incident remains one of the underlying causes of Taiwanese suspicion and bitterness toward the mainland followers of Chiang Kai-shek and their descendants.

When the communists took over China in 1949, Chiang Kai-shek and his followers fled to Taiwan. Almost two million mainland Chinese, the majority of whom were soldiers and government officials and their families, migrated from the coastal provinces to Taiwan in the same year. The KMT made Taipei the temporary capital of the Republic of China (R.O.C.). Chiang Kai-shek assumed the post of president on March 1, 1950, with the intention of using the island as a base until the eventual recovery of the mainland.

The threat of an invasion by communist China haunted the KMT on Taiwan during its first few years, but became less likely when communist North Korea invaded South Korea in 1950 and China was drawn into that war. In 1954 the United States formally pledged its support for the R.O.C. on Taiwan, and refused to recognize the legitimacy of the Communist government on mainland China. This early U.S. support provided much of the initial foreign investment for Taiwan.

Although the KMT claimed that its government was a constitutional democracy, it offered one-party rule under the leadership of strongman Chiang Kai-shek. Although native Taiwanese accounted for the majority of the population, they had no voice in government. The KMT continued to assert its goal of one China under KMT rule and maintained control over the political system and government by successfully discouraging the formation of credible opposition in the interests of national security. Chiang Kai-shek served five consecutive terms as president and finally died in office.

In the early 1970s moderate elements in China sought to reestablish relations with the United States and the West, primarily in an effort to counter the perceived expansionist aims of the Soviet Union. In 1972 Taiwan, which had represented China in the United Nations General Assembly, was denied the right to represent China and was removed from the United Nations. The People's Republic of China (PRC) was finally recognized by the United Nations as the "real" China.

In 1975 Chiang Kai-shek died and was succeeded by C. K. Yen. Chiang Kai-shek's son, Chiang Ching-kuo, was elected president in 1978. He continued to support the KMT's claim over all of China, rejecting an independence movement and disregarding attempts by China to hold talks to introduce a "one country, two systems" policy. Chiang Ching-kuo maintained the "Three No's Policy": no contact, no compromise, and no negotiations. Further, he sought to politically incorporate more Taiwanese into the KMT.

Taiwan suffered another blow in 1978 when the United States, at the urging of the PRC, pulled its troops out of Taiwan, allowing the 1954 mutual defense treaty to expire. In 1979 the United States formally recognized the PRC. This meant that the United States had to withdraw its recognition of the Taiwanese government. In an effort to minimize the diplomatic damage, the United States quickly passed the Taiwan Relations Act restoring relations with Taiwan to almost normal. The American Institute in Taiwan (AIT) was established to replace the embassy, staffed by U.S. State Department officials who are on "a leave of absence" from their government jobs. But American and Taiwanese diplomats were not allowed to visit one another at official locations. Taiwan's former embassy in the United States was not permitted to use Taiwan or Taipei in its name and was reduced in status to a kind of trade organization called the Coordination Council for North American Affairs. As more and more nations granted official recognition to the PRC, Taiwan entered a period of diplomatic isolation.

The 1980s were a time of economic growth and political liberalization for Taiwan. Its economy was rapidly industrializing. Its middle class was becoming more prosperous and more numerous. The Democratic Progressive party (DPP) was permitted to organize in

1986, providing the Taiwanese with their first opposition party. After thirty-eight years, martial law was finally lifted in July 1987. In 1988, after Chiang Ching-kuo died, Lee Teng-hui became president, becoming the first native Taiwanese president and chairman of the KMT. He accelerated the economic liberalization plan and established contacts with the PRC, eliminating the "No Contact" part of his predecessor's policy. Lee Teng-hui was reelected in 1990 for a six-year term.

In 1991 the National Assembly voted to repeal a 1949 decree calling for the end of communist rule on the mainland, which ended the hostility between the two Chinas—although the current relationship is far from being friendly. Also in 1991, real elections were held for the National Assembly. The aging KMT bureaucrats and politicians who had crossed over from the mainland in 1949 were forced to step down due to rising support for democratic processes. However, the KMT has retained much of its political control as a result of the victories of its younger members in the election.

Taiwan has developed from an authoritarian system into a relatively democratic one. Today it has fourteen opposition parties. The DPP, the main opposition party, has advocated independence as the Republic of Taiwan. Internationally this plan has received little support out of fear of upsetting China, which has declared that it would invade Taiwan if it tried to claim independence. The KMT continues to be against independence; most observers feel that this policy is intended to preserve the status quo against any threats from a currently unpredictable China. Taiwan has been a major investor in mainland in China, but because of political tensions, there are still no direct communication links, air flights, or other transportation connections between Taiwan and mainland China. All contact is conducted through a third country, usually Hong Kong.

Despite concerns over the repercussions, Taiwan has been creeping closer toward declaring nationhood. The KMT and the DPP have come closer to each other's position in recent years: both parties now assert that China and Taiwan are two sovereign states. Foreign countries are trying to balance Taiwan's desire for independence with their concerns about China's reactions. As of September 1994, only twenty-nine countries, most of whom are eager for Taiwanese aid, forgo relations with China in order to maintain ties with Taiwan. Further, the U.S. has relaxed its policy to allow the Taiwanese representative office in the U.S. to officially use the word Taipei.

Political Structure

Taiwan is a constitutional democracy. The 1947 constitution provides for a president, a National Assembly, and five Yuan (independent branches). The five Yuan are the Executive Yuan (effectively the cabinet), the Legislative Yuan (equal to a parliament), the Judicial Yuan, the Control Yuan, and the Examination Yuan.

The president, elected for a six-year term, is the head of state and commander-in-chief. The Executive Yuan, the highest administrative body, is headed by the premier, who is appointed by the president, and includes various ministers, all of whom are nominated by the premier and appointed by the president. The National Assembly, elected directly by popular vote, selects the president and vice-president and has the authority to revise the constitution; however, it has few other functions. The Legislative Yuan is popularly elected and reviews the administrative policies of the Executive Yuan, enacts laws, and passes budgetary bills. The Judicial Yuan controls the judicial system. The Control Yuan monitors and audits government accounts and investigates or impeaches government officials. The Examination Yuan examines and selects government officials and has jurisdiction over pay scales, public-sector insurance, and retirement and pension issues.

Taiwan has a strong system of local government, at both the provincial and the county levels. The Provincial Assembly has seventy-seven popularly elected members who serve four-year terms. The overall policymaking body of the provincial government is the Taiwan Provisional Government Council. County and city governments are below the Provincial Assembly, and have an extensive role.

Economy

Taiwan's economy is heavily dependent on foreign trade and the import of most of its basic raw materials and natural resources. The country has accumulated a huge surplus of foreign exchange reserves, totaling about U.S. $90 billion. Although Taiwan has a predominantly free-enterprise economy, the government has invested in key strategic areas such as petroleum refining, electricity generation, steel, banking, fertilizers, shipbuilding, railroads, sugar, tobacco, and alcohol. Taiwan has a very strong manufacturing base which is primarily export-oriented. The major industries include textiles, clothing, electronics, chemicals, machinery and equipment, and basic metals. In recent years, Taiwan's high-tech industries and service sector have grown. Due to the rising value of the "new Taiwan dollar" (NT), Taiwan's wealth has enabled it to become a major regional investor as labor-intensive industries are being shifted to mainland China and southeast Asia. Taiwan has a well-educated and skilled labor force.

The country's major resources include coal, timber, natural gas, limestone, and dolomite. Agriculturally, Taiwan's major crops include rice, sugar, fruits and vegetables, tea, pork, and poultry. Only about 12.3 percent of the population is employed in agriculture-related areas.

Due to its economic successes, the country has built a strong infrastructure to support its export-oriented trade. Taiwan is on a major air route from Hong Kong to Tokyo and has an extensive highway and railway network providing easy access to all parts of the island. Further, the country has five international seaports: Keelung, Kaohsiung, Hualien, Suao, and Taichung. The government has targeted additional investment to further develop the country's infrastructure.

People, Values, and Social Customs

The population of Taiwan is about twenty-one million. There are four main ethnic groups: Taiwanese (70 percent), Hakkas (10–15 percent), recent mainland Chinese (14 percent), and aborigines (1.5 percent). The issues of ethnic origin continue to plague Taiwanese society. Most of the older generation of mainland Chinese identify with China, as many were born there and migrated to Taiwan for political and economic reasons. However, the younger generation, increasingly aware of the social, economic, and political gap between the two countries, identify themselves as Taiwanese and speak the local dialect.

The major religions are Buddhism and Taoism. Confucianism provides a code for ethics. Christianity and Islam are also practiced. Belief in folk religion and ancestor worship is widespread.

In general, maintaining public harmony is more important than telling factual truth, another example of Japanese influence. However, unlike the Japanese, the Taiwanese are prone to emotional outbursts and allow their feelings to show. Despite the Japanese influence, the Taiwanese are generally suspicious of the Japanese. The Taiwanese are somewhat suspicious of all foreigners and become uncomfortable if you know the country, culture, or language too well. However, in time, the Taiwanese will accept outsiders. Taiwanese do not initially trust each other and tend to be vindictive.

Most of the younger generation is less willing to tolerate authoritative government policies. They have had a more comfortable life than their elders and are less concerned about basic daily survival. Modern Taiwan is becoming more materialistic, but due to the poverty it experienced in the decade after World War II, the older generation tends to be more industrious and competitive. Although family ties have weakened and obligations are becoming more ceremonial, family connections remain very important in business. Education, which traditionally has been viewed as the key to social and economic mobility, is important to both individuals and to the government, which wants to ensure a well-educated labor force.

The Taiwanese tend to dominate business and identify more closely with the island than with mainland China. Throughout Taiwan, the work ethic is adequate, but not exceptional. There is a general attitude, particularly in the government, that one can only get ahead by stepping on someone else. As a result, the Taiwanese do not work well in teams and tend to be very individualistic. This is believed to be one reason why the Taiwanese have demonsrated an entrepreneurial flair. The Taiwanese are not service-oriented and are not always helpful to outsiders. A common phrase is *mei-you* (pronounced may yo) which is the equivalent of "I don't want to deal with this" or "Don't bother me."

Taiwan remains a male-dominated society in which women are considered socially inferior. Nevertheless, women are gradually moving into positions of authority and have achieved success in some professions, such as medicine and academia. Women tend to run the household finances and in some instances even the finances of a family business.

Work Schedule

Most businesses are open on weekdays from 8:30 or 9:00 A.M. to 5:00 or 5:30 P.M., with a one to one and a half hour break for lunch, and on Saturdays from 8:30 A.M. to 12:30 P.M. Banks are open on weekdays from 9:00 A.M. to 3:30 P.M., and on Saturdays from 9:00 A.M. to noon. Government offices are open on weekdays from 8:30 A.M. to noon and from 1:30 P.M. to 5:30 P.M., and on Saturdays from 8:30 A.M. to noon. Shops are open everyday from 9:00 or 10:00 A.M. to 10:00 P.M.

Making Contacts

Taiwan will disappoint many foreigners if they enter the market expecting quick results. Businesspeople need to learn about the culture, develop relationships, and understand the local intricacies of doing business to be successful. You can write to a company without an introduction, especially if you can indicate how the Taiwanese company will benefit. But generally, connections (*guanxi*) and political ties are very important. Therefore, foreigners should establish a local presence either by hiring a local agent, consultant, or representative; by setting up a branch, representative, or liaison office; or by entering into a joint venture. When selecting an agent or representative, check his or her references and financial condition thoroughly. Generally, friends of the ruling party tend to receive special treatment, as government work is usually awarded to political allies or in deference to long-standing relationships. Even the hiring of subcontractors and individual workers can be politically based. Foreigners based in Taiwan with strong relationships may be suitable local representatives.

A helpful resource, *Doing Business with Taiwan, R.O.C.*, is published by the China External Trade Development Council (CETRA) annually. Any Taiwanese diplomatic or commercial office should be able to assist you in obtaining a copy. CETRA is the premier trade-promotion agency and is supported by domestic business associations and exporters. Although their chief focus is on export opportunities for Taiwan, CETRA remains a valuable resource. Through its Taiwan Industrial Products Services (TIPS) and Trade Opportunities Project (TOP), CETRA maintains an extensive database of trade information.

The Far East Trade Service (FETS), a sister organization, assists CETRA in the promotion of Taiwanese products. Other related organizations are the Taipei World Trade Center and the World Trade Center Taichung, which are members of the New York-based World Trade Centers Association and offer various avenues for foreign manufacturers to display their products.

Companies interested in Taiwan should also consider participating in the Taipei International Fair (TIF), which is held once every two years. It is organized by CETRA and offers foreign manufacturers an opportunity to display their products. Specific foreign cities and states have trade organizations already operating in Taiwan. Check the address section or call your local government commercial offices to see if a city or state from your home country has representation in Taiwan. Contact them either in your home country or directly in Taiwan.

If you are investing in Taiwan, you must submit an application to the Investment Commission of the Ministry of Economic Affairs. General questions about investing should be directed to the Industrial Development and Investment Center at the Ministry of Economic Affairs, which also produces a brochure titled, *Q&A on Investment by Foreigners in Taiwan, R.O.C.* This guide addresses various issues, but most importantly, has a flow chart in the appendix, which outlines the specific steps and agencies with which foreigners must deal.

Meeting People

Punctuality is very important in Taiwan. You should take Taiwan's heavy traffic into account when planning your schedule. If you are going to be more than five minutes late, call your counterpart and explain your situation. Local Taiwanese usually meet in their office or over lunch or dinner. If you are hosting the meeting, a hotel room, coffee shop, or business center is appropriate.

Upon meeting, shake hands and exchange business cards. A slight nod of the head, a smile, and a greeting are appropriate. A common Chinese greeting is *Ni hao ma*, which means "How are you?" Out of respect for older people, you should greet them first and always stand when they enter or depart the room. Cards should be extended in the right hand or with both hands and the writing should face the recipient. Study the card before storing it to indicate respect. Your business card should state your title and department, as status is very important to the Taiwanese. It is advisable to have your cards printed in English or your native language with a Chinese translation on the reverse side. Hotels can help you find printers to produce these cards.

Most Chinese have three names and list the family name first, followed by the given name and, on occasion, a second name. Use formal titles, "Mr.," "Mrs.," "Miss" (not "Ms.") or "Dr.," plus the family name. Due to the influence of Western business practices, many Taiwanese businesspeople place their surname last on the business card, but others continue to place it first. Ask a colleague or your host which is the appropriate surname and the suitable way to address someone. The Taiwanese do not use first names in formal settings. Many Taiwanese choose Western names or words as names, some of which may seem odd to a Westerner. Exercise judgment and diplomacy when discussing a name.

Many women still occupy the lowest level position of "office lady" and serve tea to the other, mostly male, office employees, illustrating the influence of the Japanese. However, there are an increasing number of women in professional and managerial positions, primarily in middle management. Accordingly, refrain from making assumptions about a woman's level in her firm.

The Taiwanese will smile often, even when they are nervous or in negative situations. The Taiwanese tell few jokes; their humor is associated with wordplay because in their language words that sound the same have many different meanings depending on the tone. It is considered impolite to wink or blink at someone. Do not touch someone's head, for the head is considered the spiritual part of a person. Never point at someone: a raised and slightly curved index finger implies death. Beckoning should be done with your palm facing down and your fingers pointing away from you, but waving toward you in a scratching motion. Do not touch or push anything with your feet because they are considered dirty.

The Taiwanese consider rude, loud, or boisterous behavior offensive. Further, they value good posture, so refrain from slouching. Most men sit with both feet on the floor; women cross their legs at the ankles or knees. Similar to the Japanese, the Taiwanese indicate "no" by gesturing with their hand perpendicular to the face, but not touching it, and waving it back and forth. On rare occasion, people will show special respect to very elderly people by covering their left fist with their right hand and holding it close to their heart.

Always begin a meeting with pleasant general conversation. Avoid political topics. It is appropriate to talk about your country, your travels, or the weather, or to offer general praise for Taiwan. To avoid offending your Taiwanese counterpart, refer to China as the "mainland." Do not discuss politics or communism. The Taiwanese are more direct and businesslike than the mainland Chinese, although slower than people from Hong Kong. They will seek to discuss business within a few minutes.

Gifts are not required, but are always appreciated and usually win you some goodwill. Suitable gifts for a first meeting are inexpensive items with a company logo, nice pens, calendars, golf balls, and baseball caps. One note of caution about an obscure tradition: do not give caps that have any green on them, for green hats imply that the wearer's wife or girlfriend has been unfaithful.

Corporate Structure

Most Taiwanese companies are small businesses and are closely held by the controlling family. There are a few large companies, which also tend to be family-owned, but these are not the driving force behind the economy in the manner of the large conglomerates in Korea and Japan. Usually a senior family member, most often a male, is the central decision maker. Generally, promotions are based on a combination of both connections and ability, with the latter counting for more in private sector and the former counting more in the public sector.

Most companies have a president or managing director at the top, with vice-presidents, directors, managers, and supervisors below. The director title has become commonplace, so assess your counterpart's actual authority and responsibilities before you make any assumptions. Many Taiwanese enjoy displaying their power.

The government controls certain key industries. To encourage the development of specific industries, promote exports, and facilitate the transfer of technology, the government has established three export processing zones (EPZs): Kaohsiung EPZ, Nantze EPZ, and Taichung EPZ. For firms that qualify to establish operations in one of the EPZs, the government offers numerous benefits including special investment incentives and exemption from certain duties and taxes. There are also eighty-seven privately or publicly managed special industrial parks, which offer all of the facilities necessary for most industrial operations, including transportation, sewage, and utilities

Negotiation

Decision-making in both the private and public sectors is frequently dependent on the intuition of one or two key senior people, who may not even be present at the negotiation. Usually the decision-maker is a senior person who may rarely speak. While the Taiwanese will make attempts to conduct research and ask questions, this is often a mere formality. Decisions can take a long time. Generally the Taiwanese are risk-averse and prefer calculated, limited, or no-risk situations.

The Taiwanese are tough negotiators. Having grown up bargaining for everything, they are comfortable and patient in their bargaining. The Taiwanese will try to get every concession possible from you. Outwardly, they value maintaining a pleasant, friendly, and yet slightly reserved atmosphere throughout the negotiations. Never show your frustration, for they will use it to squeeze more concessions out of you. The Taiwanese do not react well to a hard-sell approach.

Do not assume that a Western-educated or a Western-dressed Taiwanese is Western in attitudes. Taiwanese do not always say "No" directly, for they do not like to give negative news. Further, they hope that if they avoid or ignore an issue it will simply go away. A Taiwanese will rarely admit that he or she has made a mistake and will avoid accepting responsibility for a mistake at all costs. Further, he or she will rarely tell you if there is a problem, regardless of how bad it is. Forcing a Taiwanese to take responsibility for a mistake will only result in a loss of face. Ask questions, but never cause your counterpart to lose face and never get angry.

Efficiency and initiative are not widespread and the Taiwanese are not consistent in meeting deadlines. Account for such lapses when you set your schedules and incorporate mini-deadlines. Often if a Taiwanese does not want to do something, he won't, even if he has already agreed to do it. Keep in close contact with the local office or representative and outline clearly each person's responsibilities. Taiwanese tend to procrastinate; be persistent.

Contracts are viewed as a guide for developing a relationship. The problem with most contracts is that the Chinese version usually governs and interpretations of that version can differ due to the tonal quality of the language. If you have a legal dispute and the contract does not specify how and where to resolve problems, consider using the assistance of the Board of Foreign Trade or third-party arbitration. It is rare for a Taiwanese to agree to foreign arbitration when signing a contract, but it is worth asking for it.

Conducting Business in a Social Setting

Dining and Drinking

The dinner is usually the most important business social event. Lunches are not uncommon, but breakfasts are rare. Many Taiwanese still take short naps after lunch. Refrain from business talk topics during a meal, unless your local counterpart brings them up. Drinking and dining can last for several hours over many courses of food. It is acceptable for foreign businesswomen to entertain local counterparts. (Please see Chapter 3, on China, for more information about dining rules, especially for Chinese banquets.)

Company outings are common, for example, picnics and hiking. It is important to participate in these activities if asked to do so. Organize similar outings for your staff and business acquaintances if you have an office in Taiwan. Your local counterpart should be able to provide suitable guidance in planning appropriate gatherings. As in other Chinese communities, gambling is a favorite pastime.

Visiting a Home

Most business entertaining is done in restaurants. However, if you are invited to a home, you must bring a gift everytime you visit. Suitable gifts include smoked meats and cured hams, expensive fruits (such as apples), expensive liquors, and wines. At the Chinese New Year, take a red envelope with about NT $100 for each child. (Never give money to adults except for weddings, funerals, and sometimes birthdays.) The Taiwanese are hospitable and generous. Remove your shoes before entering most homes (or holy places).

Gift Giving

Graft is widespread. Develop a global policy for your company and stick to it. Nevertheless, if you have a local representative, he will invariably have to engage in some form of gift giving or commissions in order to keep business moving forward, particularly if you are bidding for government contracts. It is advisable to let your local counterpart manage this aspect of doing business in Taiwan.

Gift giving is very important in Taiwan and each occasion warrants slightly different attention. If you meet someone in an office or restaurant, a gift is not necessary, but it is always good to give at least a token item for it may earn you some goodwill. Do not present any cutting gifts like knives and scissors, for they symbolize the cutting of a relationship. Handkerchiefs are unacceptable too, for they signify permanent departure. Clocks and watches are also not appropriate: they symbolize termination of time or death. Expensive, foreign-brand liquor is one of the best gift choices. Company logo gifts, like a baseball cap (not green), or tasteful pen and pencil sets are also appropriate. Make sure that your foreign gift was not made in Taiwan.

Gifts are never opened in public so as to avoid embarrassing either the giver or the receiver. The usual gift for weddings (and sometimes for birthdays) is money. Money should be placed in red envelopes (*hung bao*), which are available at stores. Be sure to use new or clean, crisp bills. Although the amount you give will differ based on your relationship with the recipient, never give less than NT $600. Usually NT $2000 to NT $3000 is appropriate. Part of the intention of the wedding gift is to help defray the cost of the meal, so take the location of the reception into account. For wedding money gifts, do not give odd-numbered amounts. Odd versus even amounts are based solely on the digit before the zeros. For example, NT $680, NT $1200 would be appropriate, but NT $670 or NT $1000 would not be appropriate. Avoid the number 4 in all circumstances, as it sounds like the word for "death." If your recipient is Taiwanese, it is also best to avoid 5, as it sounds like the word for "mistake." Never wear black to a wedding.

For funerals, money is given as well, but in smaller amounts. Use white envelopes for funerals, for white is the mourning and death color. Send the envelope to the home of the deceased. Use amounts in odd numbers (the opposite of weddings). For example, appropriate sums would be about NT $1000 or NT $1100. Never wear red to a funeral.

For the Chinese New Year, suitable gifts include sweets and cookies. At New Year's, it is customary (and very important) to give bonuses to factory and blue-collar workers, secretaries, and household help. A bonus equal to one or two months' salary is appropriate for those who have worked for you or the company for more than one year. A bonus of half a month's to one month's salary is fine for employees who have worked for you less than a year. Check with you local counterpart to find out who else should receive gifts.

Dress Code

Business dress codes in Taiwan are similar to those in Western countries for both men and women. Conservative suits and ties are best. In the summer months, more informal attire, such as a short-sleeve shirt and tie, are acceptable after your first meeting. For women, conservative suits or dresses are appropriate. It is best to avoid slacks because they can appear too casual. For banquets, more formal attire, such as suits and dresses, are appropriate for both men and women.

Useful Phrases

The official language is Mandarin, called *gwoyu* (national language) locally, although Taiwanese, a southern Fujian dialect, is also widely spoken. English is widely understood as it is taught in schools beginning in the junior middle school (seventh grade). Taiwanese are sometimes reluctant to speak English with foreigners because they are self-conscious about their abilities. Many older people, especially those educated before World War II, also speak some Japanese. Please refer to Chapter 3 on China for a list of useful Mandarin phrases.

Major Holidays

January 1	National Founding Day of the Republic of China
January/February*	Chinese Lunar New Year
February 6	Lantern Festival
March 29	Youth Day
April 5	Tomb Sweeping Day and Chiang Kai-shek's Memorial Day
June*	Dragon Boat Festival
September*	Mid-Autumn (Moon) Festival
September 28	Confucius's Birthday

October 10   Double Tenth National Day
October 25   Taiwan Restoration Day
October 31   Birthday of President Chiang Kai-shek
November 12   Birthday of Dr. Sun Yat-sen
December 25   Constitution Day

*These holidays are based on the lunar calendar and change yearly.

General Facts

Climate: Intersected by the Tropic of Cancer, Taiwan has a subtropical climate in the north and a tropical climate in the south. The spring has frequent rains and temperatures range from 58F (14C) to 84F (29C). Summer is hot and humid with temperatures ranging between 74F (23C) and 92F (34C). Autumn is usually pleasant with temperatures ranging from 74F (23C) to 89F (31C). Taiwan experiences typhoons between July and September. Winter temperatures range from 54F (12C) to 69F (21C), although it can seem colder because of the damp climate. December can be a rainy month.

Currency: The *New Taiwan dollar* (NT$) which is divided into 100 cents.

Dates: The official way of stating the date is based on the number of years since the establishment of the Chinese republic in 1911. This translates into an official difference of 1911 years from the Western calendar. The official way to write the date is by year, month, and day. For example, a date of August 21, 1995, in the Western calendar would be written as 84/8/21 on official documents in Taiwan. However, most Taiwanese businesspeople would use the western calendar and state the year as 1995, particularly when doing business internationally.

Electricity: The electricity is supplied at 110 volts (60Hz). Most sockets accommodate both the two-pin and flat type of plug.

Entry Requirements: In general, American, British, Canadian, French, and German citizens need a valid passport and visa for entry and for any length of stay. American passport holders can enter Taiwan for up to five days (120 hours) without a visa. However, for most initial business trips, it is advisable to obtain a visa as you may need to extend your trip. In the United States, the Taiwan Coordination Council for North American Affairs can issue a visa. In the United Kingdom, visas may be obtained from the Free Chinese Center. In other countries, visas may be obtained from diplomatic and consular offices or nongovernmental organizations such as trade missions, Chinese cultural institutes, and Free Chinese Centers.

Time: Taiwan has one time zone, which is eight hours ahead of Greenwich Mean Time and thirteen hours ahead of U.S. Eastern Standard Time (twelve hours in Daylight Savings Time).

Tipping: At one time, tipping was not generally expected or required. However, this is beginning to change. Hotels and restaurants routinely add a 10 percent service charge to bills. You may leave additional tips for excellent service. Approximately 10 percent is appropriate for room service and other hotel staff. Taxi drivers may be tipped small change or about NT $20 to NT $30 per bag if you have luggage. Porters receive about NT $50–NT $100 per bag. At the very least, leave the change when a bill is paid.

Transportation: Although traffic congestion can be extensive, Taipei's streets are relatively easy to navigate. The longest streets run across the city and are divided into a maximum of five sections, each of which contains ten to twenty blocks. The sections are identified on the street signs as well as on all local maps. Shorter streets are not divided into sections.

Taxis are the most convenient method of transportation. Taxis can be hailed from any street; however, it can take up to thirty minutes to hail a cab in poor weather or at rush hour. Some hotels can assist you in calling for taxi service. Most taxi drivers do not speak English. Your hotel can assist you in writing down addresses in Chinese to be shown to drivers. Make sure to carry a hotel card with the hotel's name in Chinese in case you get lost. The bus system is efficient, but signs are not in English and drivers do not speak English. The *Taipei Bus Guide* is an English compilation of relevant bus information and is available at kiosks near bus stops.

Car rentals are available at the airport but require an international driver's license. A credit card is also advisable, as you will be required to leave a large deposit if you do not use a credit card. However, the traffic congestion makes this an inadvisable option. Hotels can arrange for a private driver and car, which is a better option.

Transportation from the Chiang Kai-shek International Airport into Taipei or from the Kaohsiung International Airport into Kaohsiung includes taxis, buses, airport shuttles, and hotel bus service for the larger hotels. Taxi fares are based on a combination of time and distance, so fares can increase dramatically during rush hours. Further, taxis can charge up to 50 percent more than the meter when traveling to the airport. You will probably have to negotiate with the driver. Rush hours are typically between 7:30–9:30 a.m. and between 5–7 p.m. The public bus service can take about fifteen to twenty minutes longer than a taxi, but is relatively inexpensive. Hotel buses only run during certain time periods. It is best to check with the hotel when making your reservation. (Airport bus service: Tel. 383-4004 or 715-1339 in Taipei.)

Helpful Telephone Numbers

There are two types of public telephones, blue and card-operated, both of which can be used for local and domestic long-distance calls. To operate the blue telephone, dial after you insert a coin and hear the dialtone sound. When you hear your party, press the release button located on the telephone. This button will release your coin into the collection box and your party will be able to hear you. If you do not wish for the call to proceed (e.g., wrong party or a fax machine), do not push the release button and hang up to retrieve your coin. The blue telephone will sound a warning signal about five seconds before the end of the first three minutes. To continue talking, you must deposit another coin. International calls can be made from private phones or at public facilities at the International Telecommunications Administration (ITA) offices.

The code for Taiwan is (886). The city code for major cities are: Taipei (2); Kaohsiung (7); Keelung (32); Taichung (4); and Tainan (6).

Hospitals and Medical Services:

Most Taiwanese doctors have studied abroad and are conversant in English.

Cathay General Hospital
280 Jen Ai Road, Section 4
Taipei
Tel.: (2) 708-2121

Kaohsiung Veterans General Hospital
386 Tachung 1st Road, Tsoying
Kaohsiung
Tel.: (7) 342-2121

Mackay Memorial Hospital
92 Chung Shan N. Road, Section 2
Taipei
Tel.: (2) 543-3535

National Taiwan University Hospital
7 Chungshan S. Road
Taipei
Tel.: (2) 397-0800

Taichung Veterans General Hospital
160 Chungkang Road, Section 3
Taichung
Tel.: (4) 359-2525

Taiwan Adventist Hospital
424 Pa Teh Road, Section 2
Taipei
Tel.: (2) 771-8151
(Dentists are also available.)

Today Dental Clinic
6F, 72 Heng Yang Street
Taipei
Tel.: (2) 371-4396

Ambulance: Dial 110.

Police: Dial 110 or (3) 398-2242 (airport police).

Operator: Dial 100 (overseas operator).

Information Hotline: Tourist Hotline, (2) 717-3737; English-Language Directory Service, (2) 311-6796.

Useful Addresses

When mailing to any addresses in Taiwan, be sure to add Taiwan, R.O.C., after the city name.

In Taiwan:

China External Trade Development Council (CETRA)
333 Kee Lung Road, Section 1
7th Floor
Taipei
Tel.: (2) 757-6297

Confederation of Asia-Pacific Chambers of Commerce and Industry
122 Tun Hua N. Road
10th Floor
Taipei
Tel.: (2) 716-3016

Foreigners' Service Center, Taipei Municipal Police Headquarters
96 Yen Ping S. Road
Taipei
Tel.: (2) 381-8341

Government Information Office, Executive Yuan
2 Tien Chin Street
Taipei
Tel.: (2) 322-8888

Ministry of Economic Affairs
15 Fu Chou Street
Taipei
Tel.: (2) 321-2200

Board of Foreign Trade Ministry of Economic Affairs
1 Hu Kou Street
Taipei
Tel.: (2) 351-0271 / 0286

Industrial Development and Investment Center, Ministry of Economic Affairs
No. 4, Chung Hsiao West Road, Section 1
19th Floor, Room B
Taipei
Tel.: (2) 389-2111

International Cooperation Department, Ministry of Economic Affairs
15 Fu Chou Street
Taipei
Tel.: (2) 391-8198

Investment Commission, Ministry of Economic Affairs
7 Roosevelt Road, Section 1
8th Floor
Taipei
Tel.: (2) 351-3151

Ministry of Finance
2 Ai Kuo W. Road
Taipei
Tel.: (2) 322-8000

Securities and Exchange Commission, Ministry of Finance
3 Nan Hai Road, 12th Floor
Taipei
Tel.: (2) 392-8572

Ministry of Foreign Affairs
2 Chieh Shou Road
Taipei
Tel.: (2) 311-9292

Ministry of the Interior
5 Hsu Chou Road, 5th Floor
Taipei
Tel.: (2) 356-5000

Ministry of Transportation and Communications
2 Changsha Street, Section 1
Taipei
Tel.: (2) 349-2900

Taiwan Chamber of Commerce
158 Sung Chiang Road
4th Floor
Taipei
Tel.: (2) 536-5455

Tourism Bureau, Ministry of Transportation and Communications
280 Chung Hsiao E. Road
Section 4, 9th Floor
Taipei
Tel.: (2) 349-1500 / 721-8541

American Trade Offices in Taiwan:

American Chamber of Commerce
Chia Hsin Building, Room 1012
Annex 96
Chung Shan N. Road, Section 2
Taipei
Tel.: (2) 581-7089

American Institute in Taiwan (AIT)
7, Lane 134
Hsin Yi Road, Section 3
Taipei
Tel.: (2) 709-2000 / 720-1550

American Institute in Taiwan (AIT), Commercial Unit
Room 3207
333 Keelung Road, Section 1
Taipei
Tel.: (2) 720-1550

American Trade Center
32d Floor
333 Keelung Road, Section 1
Taipei
Tel.: (2) 720-1550 / 725-2853

Guam U.S.A. Office in Taipei
Room 7B-17
5 Hsin Yi Road, Section 5
Taipei
Tel.: (2) 723-2734

Indiana Department of Commerce, Taipei Office
Room 7D-16
5 Hsin Yi Road, Section 5
Taipei
Tel.: (2) 725-2060

Oregon Trade and Information Center
Room 7C-14/15
5 Hsin Yi Road, Section 5
Taipei
Tel.: (2) 723-2310 / 11

State of Alaska, Taiwan Trade
Office
Room 7B-16
5 Hsin Yi Road, Section 5
Taipei
Tel.: (2) 723-1882

State of Arizona, Asian-Pacific
Trade Office
Room 7E-01, 7D-17/18
5 Hsin Yi Road, Section 5
Taipei
Tel.: (2) 725-1134 / 5

State of Arkansas,
Taipei Office
Room 7D-12
5 Hsin Yi Road, Section 5
Taipei
Tel.: (2) 723-2660

State of Florida, Taipei Office
Room 7B-16
5 Hsin Yi Road, Section 5
Taipei
Tel.: (2) 758-5181 / 2

State of Idaho, Asia Trade
Office
Room 7D-15
5 Hsin Yi Road, Section 5
Taipei
Tel.: (2) 725-2922

State of Louisiana, Taipei
Office
Room 7D-13
5 Hsin Yi Road, Section 5
Taipei
Tel.: (2) 723-1921

State of Maryland,
Taipei Office
Room 7C-03
5 Hsin Yi Road, Section 5
Taipei
Tel.: (2) 725-1553 / 4

State of Mississippi,
Taipei Office
Room 7C-12/13
5 Hsin Yi Road, Section 5
Taipei
Tel.: (2) 723-1856/7

State of Missouri,
International Business
Development Office
Room 7D-09
5 Hsin Yi Road, Section 5
Taipei
Tel.: (2) 725-1622

State of Montana,
Taipei Office
Room 7D-21
5 Hsin Yi Road, Section 5
Taipei
Tel.: (2) 723-1762

The Oregon Trade and
Information Center
Room 7C-14 / 15
5 Hsin Yi Road, Section 5
Taipei
Tel.: (2) 723-2310 / 1

State of Rhode Island,
Taipei Office
Room 6F-09
5 Hsin Yi Road, Section 5
Taipei
Tel.: (2) 725-1945

State of Texas, Taipei Office
Room 7D-07/08
5 Hsin Yi Road, Section 5
Taipei
Tel.: (2) 723-1914/5

**State of Utah, Taiwan Trade
Office**
Room 7C-16
5 Hsin Yi Road, Section 5
Taipei
Tel.: (2) 725-2522

**State of Wyoming, Taiwan
Trade Office**
Room 7D-20
5 Hsin Yi Road, Section 5
Taipei
Tel.: (2) 725-1711

**Washington State, Trade
Development Office**
Room 7G-01
5 Hsin Yi Road, Section 5
Taipei
Tel.: (2) 725-2499

Select Foreign Trade Offices in Taiwan:

**Canadian Trade Office in
Taipei (This is the highest
representation of Canada.)**
13th Floor
365 Fu Hsing N. Road
Taipei
Tel.: (2) 713-7268 (trade)
514-0056 (travel)

**Representative Office of
British Columbia, Canada**
Room 2202
333 Keelung Road, Section 1
Taipei
Tel.: (2) 722-0805

**Trade and Investment Office
for Ontario in Taipei**
Room 2102, 21st Floor
333 Keelung Road, Section 1
Taipei
Tel.: (2) 757-6597

**Anglo-Taiwan Trade
Committee (This is the highest
representation of the United
Kingdom.)**
9th Floor
99 Jen Ai Road, Section 2
Tel.: (2) 322-4242

**Chinese–French Industrial,
Commercial, and Services
Cooperation (OCIFA)**
10th Floor
7 Roosevelt Road, Section 1
Taipei
Tel.: (2) 312-3258

**French Trade Commission
(France–Asia Trade Promotion
Association)**
Room 1401, 14th Floor
205 Tun Hwa N. Road
Taipei
Tel.: (2) 713-3552

**French Chamber of Commerce
and Industry in Taipei**
Room 7B-01

5 Hsin Yi Road
Section 5
Taipei
Tel.: (2) 723-2740 / 2

French Institute in Taipei
Room 1003, 10th Floor
205 Tun Hwa N. Road
Taipei
Tel.: (2) 545-6061

**German Trade Office,
Taipei (Deutsches Wirtschafts-
buro Taipei)**
4th Floor
4 Min Sheng E. Road
Section 3
Taipei
Tel.: (2) 506-9028

**State Capital of Hanover,
Germany**
7C-04
Room 5 Hsin Yi Road
Section 5
Taipei
Tel.: (2) 725-1187

In Canada:

There are no official diplomatic
offices in Canada.

**Taipei Economic and Cultural
Office, Economic Division**
2 Bloor Street East, Suite 3315
Toronto, Ontario M4W 1A8
Tel.: (416) 922-2412 / 3

**Far East Trade Services, Inc.,
Montreal Branch**
1800 McGill College Avenue
Suite 2108
Montreal, Quebec H3A 3J6
Tel.: (514) 844-8909

#650-409 Granville Street
Vancouver, B.C. V6C 1T2
Tel.: (604) 682-9501

In France:

There are no official diplomatic
offices in France.

**Centre Asiatique de Promotion
Economique et Commerciale**
3, Avenue Bertie Albrecht,
5E Etage
75008 Paris
Tel.: (1) 4563-3354 / 7900

**Far East Trade Service, Inc.
Succursale a Paris**
25–27 Rue d'Astorg
75008 Paris
Tel.: (1) 4266-0512 / 0562

In Germany:

There are no official diplomatic
offices in Germany.

Taiwan Trade Center, Berlin
Kaiser-Friedrich-Str-62
10627 Berlin
Tel.: (30) 324-3040 / 8900

**Taiwan Design Center,
Dusseldorf Gmbh (CETRA)**
Rooms 601–602
Willi Becker-Allee 11
40227 Dusseldorf 1
Tel.: (211) 781810

**Taiwan Trade Service,
Dusseldorf**
6th Floor
Willi-Becker-Allee 11
40227 Dusseldorf 1
Tel.: (211) 781810

**Taiwan Trade Center,
Dusseldorf**
5th Floor
Willie-Becker-Allee 11
40227 Dusseldorf 1
Tel.: (211) 781810

Taipei Trade Office
Mainzer Landstrasse 51/3 OG
D-6000 Frankfurt am Main 1
Tel.: (69) 250105 / 250009 /
250046

**Taipei Trade Office, Hamburg
Branch Office**
Grosse Bleichen 12
20354 Hamburg
Tel.: (40) 351627 / 341981

Taipei Trade Office, Stuttgart
Rotebuehlplatz 20C
70173 Stuttgart
Tel.: (711) 226-4085 / 6

In the United Kingdom:

There are no official diplomatic
offices in the United Kingdom.

Free Chinese Centre
Dorland House
Regent Street
London
Tel.: (71) 930-5767

Majestic Trading Co., Ltd.
Bewlay House, 5th Floor
2 Swallow Place
London W1R 7AA
Tel.: (71) 629-1516 / 8

**Taiwan Products Promotion
Co. Ltd. Centric House**
Centric House, 4th Floor
390–391 The Strand
London WC2R 0LT
Tel.: (71) 379-0765 / 8

In the United States:

There are no official diplomatic
offices in the United States.

**Taipei Economic and Cultural
Representative Office**
4201 Wisconsin Avenue
Washington, DC 20016
Tel.: (202) 895-1800

**Taipei Economic and Cultural
Representative Office,
Economic Division**
4301 Connecticut Ave., N.W.
Suite 420

Washington, DC 20008
Tel.: (202) 686-6400

Taipei Economic and Cultural Representative Office
801 Second Avenue, 9th Floor
New York, NY 10017
Tel.: (212) 697-1250

Taipei Economic and Cultural Representative Office, Investment and Trade Office
126 East 56th Street
8th Floor
New York, NY 10022
Tel.: (212) 752-2340

Taipei Economic and Cultural Representative Office, Commercial Division
Two Prudential Plaza
58th Floor, Suite 5802
180 N. Stetson Avenue
Chicago, IL 60601
Tel.: (312) 616-0120

3660 Wilshire Blvd., Suite 918
Los Angeles, CA 90010
Tel.: (213) 380-3644

1360 Post Oak Blvd., Suite 2150
Houston, TX 77056
Tel.: (713) 961-9794 / 6 or 961-9785

801 Brickell Avenue,
Suite 2380
Miami, FL. 33131
Tel.: (305) 371-2860

China External Trade Development Council, Inc. (CETRA)
420 Fifth Avenue, 28th Floor
New York, NY 10018
Tel.: (212) 730-4466

Far East Trade Service, Inc., Chicago Branch
225 N. Michigan Avenue
Suite 333
Chicago, IL 60601
Tel.: (312) 819-7373

555 Montgomery Street
Suite 603
San Francisco, CA 94111
Tel.: (415) 788-4304

Taiwan Trade Center, Miami
8491 N.W. 17th Street
Suite 107
Miami, FL 33126
Tel.: (305) 477-9696

Tourism Bureau of the Republic of China/Taiwan Visitors Association
1 World Trade Center
Suite 7953
New York, NY 10048
Tel.: (212) 466-0691

333 N. Michigan Avenue
Suite 2329
Chicago, IL 60601
Tel.: (312) 346-1037

166 Geary Street, Suite 1605
San Francisco, CA 94108
Tel.: (415) 898-8677

U.S. Department of Commerce
International Trade
Administration
Taiwan Desk, Room 2327
14th and Constitution Avenues,
N.W.
Washington, DC 20030
Tel.: (202) 482-4390

Brunei Darussalam

6

Legend:
- ⭐ National Capital
- ● City

0 — 500 kilometers
0 — 500 miles

Thailand
Bangkok

South China Sea

Manila

Philippine Sea

Philippines

Iloilo
Cebu

Songkhla

Davao

Andaman Sea

Medan

BRUNEI

Malaysia

Kuala Lumpur
Singapore

Malaysia
Sibu

Manado

Padang

Pontianak
Balikpapan
Banjarmasin

Kaimana

Telukbetung

Majene

Bula

Jakarta

Ujingpandang

Indonesia

Indian Ocean

Ternate

Kupang

Geography

Brunei Darussalam is a tiny country located on the northern coast of the island of Borneo in the South China Sea. Brunei is surrounded by the Malaysian state of Sarawak on all but its northern coast. The total area of Brunei is 2,226 square miles (5,765 square kilometers). The country is divided into four districts: Brunei/Muara, Tutong, Seria/Belait, and Temburong. The capital is Bandar Seri Begawan, which is located in Brunei/Muara. The major industries,

193

oil and natural gas production, are centered in the towns of Seria and Kuala Belait.

History

Records indicate that early settlers were present in Brunei in the sixth and seventh centuries A.D. Brunei was a kingdom of the Srivijaya empire of Sumatra from the tenth to the thirteenth centuries, when the Hindu Majapahit Empire of Java came to power. Islam was established in Brunei in the late fourteenth century and in the early fifteenth century Muslim conquerors invaded the island, displacing the Majapahit Empire. The sultans of Borneo then began their independent rule of the area.

Brunei Darussalam reached its golden age under a powerful Islamic sultanate between the fourteenth and sixteenth centuries, extending throughout the island of Borneo and into the Philippines. The Portuguese were the first Europeans to visit Brunei, arriving in the sixteenth century with the Magellan expedition. The Spanish attempted to take over the area, but were ousted by the middle of the seventeenth century.

Gradually corrupt sultans and chieftains gained more influence within Brunei, setting up piracy flotillas and selling land to foreigners. By the early nineteenth century, Brunei was a much weaker state with considerably less power and territory than in its heyday. In 1840 James Brooke, a British adventurer, was visiting Kuching, which was then part of Brunei's domain, and successfully intervened in a revolt against the sultan of Brunei. In 1841, as a reward for his efforts, the sultan made Brooke rajah of Sarawak. By 1888, the once-powerful sultanate was reduced to just a small trading post and applied for British protection. In 1929 oil was discovered, changing the political fabric of the country permanently.

In 1959 a new constitution introduced self-government, with the United Kingdom retaining responsibility for Brunei's foreign affairs, security and defense. In 1962 Sultan Omar Ali Saifuddin allowed elections. When the opposition party, the Brunei People's party, won a majority, Omar suspended the constitution and refused to hand over power, inciting a rebellion that was put down by British Gurkha (Nepali) troops from Singapore. Almost three hundred political dissidents were imprisoned.

In 1967, after years of turmoil within the country, Omar handed over power to his son, Sultan Hassanal Bolkiah (formally known as "His Majesty the Sultan and Yang Di-Pertuan of Brunei Darussalam, Sultan Haji Hassanal Bolkiah Mu'izzaddin Waddaulah"). He has served as the Sultan Yang Di-Pertuan, which means "he who is selected lord" since then.

In 1979 Brunei and the United Kingdom signed a treaty that granted Brunei full independence at midnight on December 31, 1983. Since independence, Brunei has led a quiet and peaceful existence, amassing great wealth through its oil and gas industries. The sultan maintains tight control over economic development and does not allow criticism of his regime. The press and media continue to be heavily censored.

Political Structure

Brunei is a hereditary, autocratic monarchy ruled by Sultan Hassanal Bolkiah, the twenty-ninth ruler of a dynasty. The sultan is the head of state, the head of the Islamic religion, the prime minister, and the minister of defense. The current sultan has been somewhat progressive by forming a cabinet that is no longer dominated by royal family members. He has also divided ministerial positions among more people and allowed the formation of political parties. As a result, the country has started to shift toward a parliamentary state, although the sultan still retains the true power.

The legal system is based on English common law, provides for an independent judiciary, and uses the English language. The criminal justice system is based on the Indian Penal Code. Brunei has an arrangement with Hong Kong whereby Hong Kong judges are appointed as judicial commissioners of the country by the sultan.

Economy

Enormously wealthy in proportion to its size, Brunei is virtually dependent on oil wealth. Brunei Shell Petroleum is the only real oil company. The country is also one of the world's largest exporters of liquefied natural gas; rubber is a minor export. Brunei imports about 80 percent of its food. Due to the surplus revenue accumulated during the oil-boom decades, Brunei became an exporter of investment capital in the 1980s. The Brunei Investment Agency (BIA) manages the country's international investments.

In recent years, revenues from the petroleum sector have decreased as a result of lower world oil prices and a government policy to conserve its most valuable resource by gradually reducing production. Nevertheless, the petroleum sector and foreign investment earnings have remained the primary revenue components of the economy. The government has started to implement diversification plans to develop other industries, including rice farming, agriculture, forestry, and financial services. As a result of these diversification efforts, the government welcomes foreign investment in key industries such as power generation, aircraft, telecommunications, defense, and hospital and medical equipment.

Brunei has one of the highest per-capita incomes in the world. Citizens pay no taxes and their minimum wage is the highest in the region. Everyone receives pensions, free medical care, free schooling, free sports and leisure centers, and inexpensive loans and subsidies for many big purchases, such as homes, cars, and travel to Mecca for religious pilgrimages. The infrastructure is well developed.

People, Values, and Social Customs

The population of Brunei is about 275,000. The ethnic heritage of the population is divided into Malay (69 percent), Chinese (18 percent), indigenous peoples (5 percent), and Indians, Europeans, and other ethnic groups (8 percent).

Islam was declared the state religion in the 1959 constitution. The sultan serves as the head of the religion. Although Islam is emphasized, religious freedom is tolerated, allowing a small group of citizens and foreign workers to practice Buddhism and Christianity. People tend to be very conservative, but are also warm, friendly, and hospitable. The people tend to smile only when they are happy and are less likely to smile in situations in which they feel nervous.

Brunei has not encouraged a tourist industry and therefore has not been spoiled, architecturally and culturally, in the way that many other countries in the region have been. However, symbols of modern material success—expensive cars, homes, appliances, and other luxuries—are evident everywhere.

Work Schedule

Government offices and businesses are open from 7:30 or 8:00 A.M. to 4:30 P.M., Monday to Thursday and on Saturday, with a daily break from noon to 1:00 or 1:30 P.M. Government offices are closed on Fridays and Sundays. Many commercial offices are closed on Saturday afternoon as well as on Friday and Sunday. Brunei Shell Petroleum is closed on Saturday and Sunday. Banks are open from 9:00 A.M. to noon and from 2:00 P.M. to 3:00 P.M. Monday to Thursday; on Saturday from 9:00 A.M. to 11:00 A.M. Most shops are open from 8:00 or 9:00 A.M. to 9:00 P.M. Monday to Saturday. Many department stores are open seven days a week. The workday is usually shortened during Ramadan due to fasting by Muslims during this period.

Making Contacts

The government of Brunei publishes a booklet, *Brunei Darussalam Business in Perspective*, that offers a detailed overview of the country. The Brunei diplomatic missions can assist you in obtaining a copy or you can request a copy from the Ministry of Finance.

The Ministry of Industry and Primary Resources was created in 1989 as a "one-stop agency" to facilitate the development of all industries in Brunei. Potential foreign investors should contact this ministry first. Introductions can help establish credibility. Here, as elsewhere in Asia, developing the correct contacts in the right ministry is critical. Appearances and early impressions carry a great deal of weight.

Once you have made a commitment to do business in Brunei, you are legally obliged to appoint a local representative or agent or to establish a branch office in Brunei. In order to minimize costs, you can maintain a regional presence by basing your business in Singapore or even Malaysia and appointing a Brunei-based partner or representative.

Meeting People

Bruneians have a high regard for punctuality. If you are behind schedule, make sure to inform the people you are intending to meet.

A handshake accompanied by a slight nod of the head is an appropriate greeting. Brunei women usually do not shake hands, unless they are Christians. It is best to follow the native businessperson's lead and wait until a hand is offered. In general, it is best to refrain from any physical contact with women. Many Muslim men will bring their hands back to touch their chest after a handshake to symbolize that the greeting is from the heart.

Be sure to know people's correct titles and social standing before making introductions. This may be difficult unless you are familiar with the very complicated Malay social hierarchy. The business center at your hotel or the embassy/consulate can help you. It is best not to consult with a Bruneian, who may regard your ignorance of the culture as an insult. Appearing to know the social structure is very important.

Malay Muslims often use their given name as their first name and their father's given name as their last name. For example, if your name was "Tom" and your father's name was "Ed," you would be called "Tom Ed" in Malay. Bruneians often use the respectful prefix *Encik* for men and *Cik* for women before the addressee's given name. Many Muslims also use *bin*, "son of," or *binti*, "daughter of," followed by their father's name. For example, in Malay, "Tom Ed" might be called "Tom bin Ed." Chinese Bruneians have three names, unless they have adopted Western names; the first of the three names is the surname.

When addressing a person, you should use the appropriate title ("Mr.," "Mrs.," "Dr.," and the like) and the surname. Business cards are always exchanged during the first meeting and should be presented with both hands. Read the card before putting it away to show respect. Your business card should indicate your position and department.

On most formal occasions, it is considered rude to cross your legs. Both your feet should remain flat on the floor and the sole of your foot should never face anyone nor should your foot touch anyone. Avoid physically touching a person, particularly their head, for the head is considered the most spiritual part of the body. Beckoning is done by using the whole hand with the palm facing the floor and the fingers pointing away from you, but moving toward you in a scratching motion.

The first few minutes of a meeting should be spent in casual conversation. Suitable topics include your travels, your counterpart's travels, and positive things about the country. Refrain from mentioning or discussing the wealth of the sultan and/or the nation. It is not expected or appropriate to present a gift on the first or even subsequent meetings; this could be considered a bribe. After your meeting, a follow-up letter should be sent to demonstrate your appreciation and interest.

Corporate Culture

The Brunei Shell Petroleum Company is jointly owned by the Brunei government and Shell. There are also other private oil companies in Brunei, but none is as significant as Brunei Shell.

Bruneians adhere to a rigid and respected social and corporate pecking order. In general, the corporate structure is headed by the president or managing director followed by vice-presidents and managers. Given the dominance of the government in the economy, the government of Brunei is a major purchaser of foreign goods and services, and thus relationships with the government are very important.

Negotiation

It is very important to establish contact with the appropriate ministry for government-related issues and with the right level of bureaucrat, for only the senior-most people have decision-making authority. The foreign businessperson must take the time to develop trust and to establish a good relationship with potential partners. Bruneians often take a long time to make decisions due to the layers of the country's bureaucracy. Therefore, do not expect a decision on your first trip.

Bruneians are very conservative. It is important to maintain a calm, nonconfrontational and polite composure throughout the negotiation process. Always try to preserve harmony. Allow all parties the opportunity to save face in the event of difficult decisions. Angry outbursts are frowned upon, as is public criticism. Bruneians may not say "No" directly, so you will need to ask indirect questions to assess a situation.

Legal contracts are written out in detailed form. Once a decision has been made and a contract written and signed by both parties, that contract will be honored and rarely changed.

Conducting Business in a Social Setting
Dining and Drinking

Bruneian food is similar to Malaysian, Thai, and Indonesian food. There are few Malay restaurants; Muslim Bruneians tend to eat at home or at private clubs. Because the Chinese enjoy eating out there are numerous Chinese restaurants.

The Bruneians do not consider it appropriate to discuss business over a meal. They do, however, see social meetings at lunch or dinner as a part of the process of doing business. Bruneians view lunch and dinner meetings as an opportunity to get to know one another. Breakfast meetings are very rare.

Be sensitive to religious practices. For example, do not eat in public in the daytime during the Ramadan holidays. Muslims do not eat pork and do not drink alcoholic beverages. However, the Chinese do both. Liquor is served only at Western hotels and some Chinese restaurants. Beer is the more common alcoholic beverage. Muslim Bruneians eat only with their right hand. You will be given Western-style utensils and it is appropriate to use them. But when eating Chinese food you will be expected to eat with chopsticks.

Visiting a Home

It is very unlikely that you will be invited to a Bruneian's home early on. Gifts are not required when visiting a home. If you wish to give a gift, remember that it is inappropriate to give Muslims anything containing pork, gelatins from unspecified fats, or alcohol. Suitable items include souvenirs from your home country, decorative items, expensive chocolates, and sweets. For the Chinese, refrain from giving clocks, knives, or white flowers, for these all have negative connotations. A follow-up thank-you letter after a visit is usually appropriate.

Gift Giving

There is very little corruption in Brunei. Bruneians do not exchange gifts as rigidly and methodically as do people in some other Asian cultures. Sometimes a gift may be considered a bribe. For normal gift-giving situations, tasteful and elegant gifts are appreciated, although not expected.

Dress Code

The dress code for business is conservative. Women should wear dresses or suits and expose as little skin as possible. The appropriate attire for men is a suit and tie. Jackets may be removed during meetings, but ties should not be loosened. Clothes should appear neat and ironed. Shoes should be shined.

Useful Phrases

The official language is Bahasa Melayu (Malay). Please refer to Chapter 8 on Malaysia for useful Malay phrases. English is widely used, particularly in business, and Chinese is also spoken.

Major Holidays

January 1	New Year's Day
January/February*	Chinese New Year
February 23	National Day and Israk Mekraj
February/March*	Ramadan
April**	Good Friday
April*	Hari Raya Puasa
May 31	Armed Forces Day
June*	Hari Raya Haji
July*	Muslim New Year (First Day of Hijrah)
July 15	Birthday of His Majesty
September*	Prophet Muhammad's Birthday
December 25	Christmas Day
December 26	Boxing Day

* These holidays are based on the lunar calendar and accordingly the date changes every year.
** This holiday is observed on the First Friday after the Paschal full moon and changes from year to year.

General Facts

Climate: The weather in Brunei is usually hot and humid, with temperatures ranging between 73F (23C) and 95F (35C). The monsoon season begins in November and ends in February. Average temperatures during this season are lower, averaging about 82F (28C).

Currency: The official currency is the *Brunei dollar* (abbreviated B$), but Singapore dollars are widely accepted. There are 100 cents to the dollar.

Dates: Dates are written day, month, year. For example, October 20, 1995, would be abbreviated as 20/10/95.

Electricity: The voltage is 220.

Entry Requirements: Citizens of France, Germany, and Canada need visas for visits of more than fourteen days. British citizens need visas for stays longer than thirty days. American citizens need visas for visits longer than ninety days. All visitors need valid passports and should carry proof of an onward ticket and sufficient funds.

Time: Brunei is eight hours ahead of Greenwich Mean Time and thirteen hours ahead of U.S. Eastern Standard Time (twelve hours in Daylight Savings Time).

Tipping: There is a 10 percent service charge at hotels. Porters expect at least 1 B$ per bag. The businessperson should note that Brunei does not encourage tourism and as a result has few hotels catering to international visitors. At better restaurants, it is appropriate to leave a 10 percent tip. Taxi drivers are generally not tipped, but hired drivers appreciate a tip of 10 percent of the cost of the daily car rental fee.

Transportation: Driving is on the left. Bruneians are slow and cautious drivers. A valid international driver's license is usually required, although a British driver's license is occasionally acceptable.

Seat belts are required and failure to wear them is punishable by a fine. Taxis are usually the most convenient method of transportation, although you will usually have to call one. In Bandar Seri Begawan, the telephone number for taxis is (2) 26853.

Helpful Telephone Numbers

There are very few public telephones in Brunei. Businesspeople will find telephones in offices, hotels, and private residences. The country code is (673) and the city code for Bandar Seri Bergawan is (2).

Doctors and Dentists:

RIPAS Hospital
Jalan Putera
Bandar Seri Begawan
Tel.: (2) 242424

Katong Clinic
3/4 Jalan Katong 4, 1st Floor
Bangar Dowi Jaya
Bandar Seri Begawan
Tel.: (2) 228715

Tan Dental Clinic
Block B2, 1st Floor
PAP Hajjah Noram Blvd.
Bandar Seri Begawan
Tel.: (2) 220604

Police: Dial 222333.

Ambulance: Dial 222366.

Useful Addresses

In Brunei:

Brunei Investment Agency (BIA)
Finance Building

Jalan James Pearce
Bandar Seri Begawan
Tel.: (2) 240591

Economic Development Board (Ministry of Finance)
State Secretariat Office
P.O. Box 2318
Bandar Seri Begawan
Tel.: (2) 220243

Economic Development Board (Tourism)
State Secretariat Office
Bandar Seri Begawan
Tel.: (2) 231794

Ministry of Finance
Jalan Elizabeth II
Bandar Seri Begawan 1130
Tel.: (2) 242406 / 241991

Ministry of Industry and Primary Resources
Bandar Seri Begawan 1220
Tel.: (2) 244882

National Chamber of
Commerce and Industry
3d Floor, Suite 411
Bangunan Guru Guru
Bandar Seri Begawan
Tel.: (2) 227297

PITO Brunei
c/o KEMUDA Resource Agency
Abdul Razak Complex
1st Floor, Unit 3, Block C
Gadong 3180
Bandar Seri Begawan 1918
Tel.: (2) 448679

Embassies:

American Embassy
Teck Guan Plaza, 3d Floor
Jalan Sultan
(P.O. Box 2197)
Bandar Seri Begawan 1929
Tel.: (2) 229670

British High Commission
Hong Kong Bank Chambers
3rd Floor
Jalan Pemancha / Sultan
Bandar Seri Begawan
Tel.: (2) 222231 / 223121

Canadian High Commission
c/o Canadian High Commission
to Singapore
Robinson Road
P.O. Box 845
Singapore 9016
Tel.: (65) 225-6363

French Embassy
Teck Guan Plaza, 5th Floor
56–60 Jalan Sultan
Bandar Seri Begawan
Tel.: (2) 240924

German Embassy
Lot 49–50, 6th Floor
Jalan Sultan
Bandar Seri Begawan
Tel.: (2) 225547

In Canada:

There are no diplomatic offices in Canada. The New York Consulate serves Canada.

In France:

Embassy of Brunei Darussalam
4 Rue Logelbach
75017 Paris
Tel.: (1) 4267-4947

In Germany:

Embassy of Brunei Darussalam
Kaiser Karl Ring No. 18
5300 Bonn 1
Tel.: (228) 672-044

In the United Kingdom:

Brunei Darussalam High
Commission
19/20 Belgrave Square
London SW1X 8PG
Tel.: (71) 581-0521

Brunei Investment Office
10 Sussex Square
London W2 2SL
Tel.: (71) 724-0834

In the United States:

Embassy of Brunei Darussalam
Watergate, Suite 300
2600 Virginia Avenue, N.W.
Washington, DC 20037
Tel.: (202) 342-0159

Brunei Darussalam Consulate
866 U.N. Plaza, Suite 248
New York, NY 10017
Tel.: (212) 838-1600

U.S. Department of Commerce
International Trade
Administration
Brunei Desk, Room 2036
14th & Constitution Avenues,
N.W.
Washington, DC 20230
Tel.: (202) 482-4958

7 Indonesia _____

Map Legend:
- ⭐ National Capital
- ● City

0 — 500 kilometers
0 — 500 miles

Thailand
Bangkok
South China Sea
Manila
Philippine Sea
Philippines
Songkhla
Iloilo
Cebu
Andaman Sea
Davao
Medan
Malaysia
Brunei
Kuala Lumpur
Malaysia
Singapore
Sibu
Manado
Padang
Pontianak
Balikpapan
Banjarmasin
Telukbetung
Majene
Bula
Kaimana
Jakarta
Ujingpandang
I N D O N E S I A
Indian Ocean
Ternate
Merauke
Kupang
Australia

Geography

The Republic of Indonesia is the world's largest archipelago, consisting of 13,667 islands, of which about 6,000 are inhabited. The main islands are Java, Sumatra, Sulawesi, Kalimantan (western Borneo), and Irian Jaya (western New Guinea). Although it differs by region, the terrain of the country is primarily mountainous and includes four hundred volcano peaks. Two-thirds of the country is covered by forest and jungle. The total land and sea area is 1.85 million square miles (4.8 million square kilometers), although only 741,000 square miles (1.92 million square kilometers) is land. Stretching from east to west, Indonesia covers a distance of 3,174 miles (5,120 kilometers), making it wider than the United States. Indonesia is usually divided into four main groups of islands. The first is the Great Sunda complex consisting of the large islands of Sumatra, Java, Borneo, and Sulawesi. The second group, known as the Lesser Sunda Islands, consists of the islands east of Java from Bali to Timor. The third group is the Maluku Islands between Sulawesi and the Lesser Sunda Islands. The fourth group is Irian Jaya. Indonesia forms a natural barrier separating the Indian Ocean from the South China Sea and the Pacific Ocean. The country shares land borders with Malaysia on the island of Borneo and with Papua New Guinea on the island of New Guinea. The capital is Jakarta, which is located on the island of Java. Other major cities include Surabaya and Bandung on Java, and Medan on Sumatra.

History

The earliest records date back almost 250,000 years to Java Man, whose remains were found on the island of Java. The indigenous Indonesians are Negritos, dark-skinned people of short stature. But the Indonesian population, language, culture and genetics have all been influenced by migrants. Neolithic Malay and Indian people from Polynesia and Asia settled in Indonesia beginning some five thousand years ago.

Around two thousand years ago, small Hindu kingdoms flourished around the sites that were frequented by Indian seamen and traders. As a result, India's culture, languages, and religions have had a significant impact on Indonesian life. Buddhism was brought by Indian Buddhists between A.D. 100 and 200. Over the next six centuries, Buddhism spread over most of the Indian-influenced kingdoms of Indonesia and permeated most aspects of daily life, religion, commerce, art, and education. The Sumatran-based Srivijaya kingdom flourished in the seventh century A.D. and lasted until the thirteenth century, when the Java-based kingdom of Majapahit rose to power and was preeminent for the next two centuries. Both kingdoms were heavily influenced by Indian civilization.

Islam appeared in the region as early as the seventh century A.D., but did not gain any popularity until around the twelfth century, when it was reintroduced by Persian and Indian traders from the west coast of India. The religion spread rapidly throughout the region and took firm hold in the Melaka kingdom on the Malay Peninsula. Hindus who resisted Islam fled to Bali, which remains the only major Indonesian island where a majority of the people still practice Hinduism.

The Portuguese were the first Europeans to colonize the area, arriving in the fifteenth century in search of spices. Toward the end of the sixteenth century the first Dutch traders arrived in Indonesia. In 1602 the Dutch East India Company was established to manage the area's spice trade. Over the next 300 years the various islands of modern-day Indonesia were brought increasingly under Dutch control as the Netherlands East Indies. However, the Dutch were unsuccessful in dislodging the Portuguese from the eastern part of the island of Timor in the Lesser Sunda Islands and they remained there until 1975. The Dutch government took over control of the islands in 1799 and ruled until the Japanese invasion in 1942.

Unlike the British colonial rulers in India, the Dutch did little to develop Indonesia's infrastructure, civil service, or educational system. The Dutch did not allow Indonesians to assume responsible roles in government or in business. Rather than promote political or social transformation, the Dutch believed that control of the region was dependent on winning the loyalty of the Indonesian elites and sought to utilize the traditional native political structure to achieve their economic goals. The upper levels of administration consisted of European civil service members. The lower levels were occupied by native Indonesians, usually from the *priyayi* class, which was an aristocracy defined by descent from ancient Javanese royal families. The general economy was characterized by three layers: the Europeans owned all the large-scale enterprises and banks; the Chinese were middlemen and provided much of the private credit;

and the Indonesians farmed and ran shops and other small businesses. The latter two tiers have remained even in modern times
and have been the source of tension between the Indonesians and
Chinese.

The Dutch exploited the land, resources, and people of Indonesia. Despite their efforts, though, the early Dutch were frustrated in their attempts to achieve massive profits. One serious
problem was the extensive corruption in the civil service; government agents commonly engaged in illegal trade and did not advance
the commercial interests of the Dutch East India Company. The
Dutch focused much of their attention on Java and in the trade of
such commodities as coffee, sugar, indigo, tea, cinnamon, pepper,
tobacco, cotton, silk, and cochineal. By the late 1800s and the early
1900s lucrative rubber plantations were established and other islands surpassed Java in economic importance. Petroleum, originally
used as lamp oil, also became a major commodity in the late nineteenth century. The industry was eventually controlled by the Royal
Dutch Shell Company, which was a dominant global producer of
oil in the pre–World War II period.

For a brief period from 1811 to 1816, during the French occupation of the Netherlands, the British took over Indonesia with the understanding that they would return Indonesia to the Dutch after
Napoleon was defeated. The British, under Thomas Stanford Raffles, attempted to introduce agrarian and social reforms, including
the abolition of forced labor, although this was not successful until
1860. The 1824 Treaty of London reconfirmed Dutch control over
Sumatra and British control over the Malay Peninsula. As part of
this treaty, the northern Sumatran sultanate of Aceh was allowed to
remain independent. The Dutch, however, sought to control Aceh,
for its pepper trade was very lucrative. In 1873, during talks between
the American consul in Singapore and Acehnese representatives,
the Dutch bombarded the capital of Aceh. The Aceh War was one
of the longest and bloodiest of the wars fought by the Dutch in Indonesia. Although the Dutch captured Banda Aceh in 1874, fierce
guerrilla resistance against the Dutch continued until 1904.

Throughout the period of Dutch rule, there were pockets of anti-colonial resistance in specific villages or on certain islands, but there was no widespread movement until the 1900s. The concept of an Indonesian nation defined by political centralization and cultural homogenization was slow to develop due to the geographic separation of the islands and the many differences in language, religion, and culture of the region's peoples. In the early part of the twentieth century, nationalist independence movements formed throughout Asia, including parts of Indonesia, whose leaders urged educational and social reform. In addition to improving the quality and accessibility of education, leaders asserted the importance of retaining indigenous cultural values rather than imitating Europeans. To encourage more social equality, they urged the elimination of the honorific Javanese speech and encouraged everyone to use the type of language that was reserved for superiors when speaking with inferiors. However, concerns about the Javanese language were overshadowed by the rise of Malay as a pan-Indonesian language. In 1928, Bahasa Melayu, which was widely used in the archipelago, was adopted as the unifying language and called Bahasa Indonesia.

In the late 1920s Sukarno became the country's first truly national leader and eventually its first president. In 1927 he founded the Indonesian Nationalist Association which later became the Indonesian Nationalist party (PNI). The party stressed mass organization and noncooperation with the Dutch as the way to eventually win independence. Sukarno was more concerned with his role as a leader and less with the need to develop political institutions and infrastructure. He had a socialist belief in the benefits of a classless society, although he did not believe in communism. He had a romantic concept of his mission and regarded himself as involved in a struggle against the forces of evil. For him, politics was based on conflict between good (us) and evil (the Dutch), providing the foundation for his political movement between Indonesians (us) and Western imperialism (them). This political philosophy netted Sukarno a widespread following. Additionally, he created an image of a united and free Indonesia that appealed to all significant national groups rather than to narrow class or religious interests.

The image of Dutch invincibility was shattered in 1942 when the Japanese easily captured Indonesia. The Japanese oversaw the creation of political and military institutions that later provided the framework for independence. For instance, the Japanese mobilized the country for the war effort by establishing the first genuine Indonesian armed forces, which would eventually become one of the nation's more important political players. Sukarno and some other leaders cooperated with the Japanese, for they believed that such cooperation would help them to to secure independence for the archipelago. Nonetheless, the Japanese ruled harshly and to this day many Indonesians continue to resent Japan.

On September 7, 1944, Japan granted independence to the archipelago, effective at the end of the war, thereby vindicating Sukarno and the other leaders who had been increasingly criticized by other Indonesians as lackeys of the Japanese. A republican constitution providing for a president and elected Congress was drafted. In June 1945 Sukarno outlined *pancasila* (the five principles of God, humanitarianism, national unity, democracy, and social justice) and *Nasakom* (nationalism, religion, and communism) in an effort to create a common ground after independence for the diverse social, economic, and religious groupings throughout the islands. The Indonesian armed forces played a major role in the unification process. On August 17, 1945, following Japan's surrender, independence was formally declared. The Dutch tried to reimpose their colonial rule, but after several years of intermittent fighting and feeling increasing pressure from the international community, the Dutch accepted Indonesia's independence in 1949. The greatest pressure came from the United States, which threatened to cut off all Marshall Plan aid to the Netherlands if the republican Indonesian government was not reinstated. The Dutch did, however, continue to hold on to western New Guinea.

After achieving independence, the Indonesians had to turn

their attention to developing the basic institutional framework for their new society. In 1949 Indonesia was a very poor country with low levels of education and a tradition of authoritarian government. Under a constitution that created a parliamentary political system, the country initially attempted a European-style democracy with multiple political parties. This system proved to be ill-suited to ruling the archipelago with its three hundred ethnic groups and almost as many distinct languages. Initially, the outlying islands had considerable freedom. However, the new nation's leaders were intent on establishing a Java-based, centralized authority.

From 1950 to 1957 there were six different cabinets as numerous political parties vied for power. Political confusion and economic chaos ruled the day. In 1957 under the banner of "Guided Democracy," Sukarno, who had been president since 1945, declared martial law and assumed dictatorial power. He created an authoritarian political system that promoted a unique mix of nationalism, Marxism, and Islam. His brand of Marxism caused the Western nations to turn against him, so he isolated the country from international organizations and sought closer ties with China and the Soviet bloc.

In 1963 Indonesia took over the Dutch-controlled western portion of the island of New Guinea, now known as Irian Jaya, and made it the twenty-sixth province of the republic. The takeover angered the Dutch and the Australians, and there was also local opposition to Indonesia's move. But the United States, which had pushed the Dutch to grant Indonesia's independence, supported the annexation, arguing that Indonesia should control the entire area.

During Sukarno's rule the army became the dominant force in Indonesia. Radical political and religious groups were allowed great freedom. Anti-Chinese sentiments led to the repatriation of more than 119,000 Chinese to China; those remaining in Indonesia were forbidden from trading in rural areas so that native Indonesians could become merchants and entrepreneurs. Sukarno's regime gradually lost power as social and political pressures mounted. On September 30, 1965, an unsuccessful coup against Sukarno regime resulted in the deaths of six army generals and great confusion, and eventually led to a radical transformation of Indonesian government. The Indonesian Communist party (PKI) was blamed for the coup attempt. Retaliation by the army resulted in the deaths of about 500,000 Indonesians, many of whom were members of the PKI or were Chinese. However, Sukarno himself did not blame the communists. International political observers have since debated who was responsible for the coup attempt. As political and economic conditions in the country worsened, Sukarno, although still popular with the people, was obliged to transfer power in 1966 to his chief of staff, General Suharto, who became president in 1967. Suharto was the leader of Golkar, a political party created in 1964 by the military to counter the rising influence of the PKI. It was designed to coopt different social groups into harmonious cooperation. Elections were held for the first time in sixteen years in 1971 and Golkar received a majority of the vote.

By this point, as a result of heavy foreign debt and spiraling inflation, the economy was devastated. This was the new government's primary problem. Suharto completely reversed foreign policy and focused domestic and foreign policy on rejuvenating the economy. Indonesia rejoined the United Nations and in 1967 was a cofounder, along with Thailand, Singapore, Malaysia, and the Philippines, of the Association of South East Asian Nations (ASEAN).

By abolishing the anti-business policies of the previous government and enacting new laws and policies to encourage investment and promote new business development, Suharto formed a "New Order," but one that was still based on authoritarian rather than democratic principles. Much of Indonesia's economic development stemmed from the emergence of a political patronage system in which powerful public officials gained control of lucrative contracts, particularly in key economic sectors such as mining, power, communications, and shipping, and used them to create fiefdoms and state enterprises as well as to advance their own political careers. As a result, the line between public and private was blurred. Resentment of the foreign domination of the economy spread as Chinese and other businesspeople profited at what appeared to be the expense of native Indonesians. In reaction to this animosity the government embarked on a policy of promoting the *pribumi*, native Indonesians, by granting them special privileges, by demanding that foreign enterprises organize joint ventures with *pribumi* entrepreneurs, and by providing favorable credit terms to *pribumi* businessmen. However, many native Indonesians sought to profit from these special privileges by obtaining government licenses and then selling them for huge profits to Chinese businesspeople, who would manage the operations of the businesses.

Indonesia has sizable oil reserves and is a member of OPEC. As an OPEC country, Indonesia profited greatly during the 1970s and used these profits to invest in infrastructure. Although the army dominated the government, economic policymaking was conducted by a group of U.S.-educated economists who became known as the "Berkeley Mafia," because they had received degrees from the University of California at Berkeley. These technocrats have managed economic policy since 1969. With their guidance, Suharto succeeded in turning the economy around; inflation decreased dramatically and foreign lending institutions provided the aid for recovery and building infrastructure.

Following the 1974 revolution in Portugal, the Portuguese government ordered a withdrawal from all of the country's colonies, including East Timor. The island was briefly ruled by Fretilin, the local political party that had worked to win East Timor's independence. Indonesia, threatened by the left-wing nature of Fretilin, occupied East Timor, set up a provisional government, and then annexed the island as its twenty-seventh province in 1976. During the late 1970s and 1980s Fretilin waged sporadic guerrilla warfare against the Indonesian government. However, by the 1990s, armed resistance had decreased dramatically, although many people in East Timor still hoped to eventually win independence. The Indonesian government continues to be criticized by the international community for human rights violations in East Timor, although today it is working to find a compromise solution to the problem of local Timorese demands for more autonomy.

The government's stability depends in large part on the military, which dominates the government at all levels. A system of corruption, nepotism, and cronyism is widespread and gaining the approval of army officers remains necessary for obtaining business licenses, concessions, and contracts. The military's dominant role in Indonesia since 1966 has been justified as part of a dual function that gives it both military and social-political duties, in contrast to other countries where the army is often an apolitical organization. Golkar is the country's main political party. It consists of a coalition of groups supported by Suharto. The military's dominant role has affected the development of other political parties. In addition to Golkar, the two other legally permitted political opposition parties are the Muslim-dominated United Development party (PPP), a loose coalition of Muslim-influenced parties, and the Indonesian Democratic party (PDI), which is an amalgam of several parties, many of which hold Christian ideals. Legally, no Indonesian political party can be organized on religious terms. In general, political dissent has not been tolerated under Suharto and media censorship is common, although this is beginning to change.

With memories of the 1965 coup attempt, the resulting bloodbath, chaotic government changes, and food shortages still fresh in everyone's mind, much of the population today has little appetite for political dissent. When it does occur, the communists are usually blamed. Public resentment of the military and the Chinese continues to exist because these two groups are the primary beneficiaries of the government's policies. Today, Indonesians prefer to focus on maintaining stability and achieving economic growth rather than gaining widespread political freedoms. Accordingly, parliamentary debate over legislation is conducted primarily behind closed doors to preserve the appearance of harmony. Therefore, despite the dictatorial nature of the Suharto government, the military's de facto political party, Golkar, has won all the elections since

1971 (most recently in 1993). It should be noted, however, that opposition parties have been receiving an increasing number of votes. There has also been an increase in some political freedoms, for example, parliamentary dissent, and limited tolerance for criticism by the press.

Political Structure

Although Indonesia is predominantly Muslim, it is not officially an Islamic state. The Indonesian state promotes a policy called *Pancasila*, which advocates five principles: one supreme God, humanitarism, national unity, democracy, and social justice.

The three branches of government, the executive, the legislative and the judicial, share powers as outlined by the 1945 constitution. The president is indirectly elected to a five-year term by the People's Consultative Assembly (MPR - *Majelis Permusyawaratan Rakyat*). The president has great power, including the power to appoint and dismiss cabinet ministers.

The MPR is theoretically the highest policymaking authority. Its powers include electing the president and vice-president; establishing the broad outlines of State Policy; and amending the constitution. But the MPR meets only once every five years, making its role largely ceremonial. The MPR has one thousand members, five hundred of whom are members of the House of People's Representatives (DPR, *Dewan Perwakilan Rakyat*), the Indonesian parliament, and five hundred of whom are appointed by the government and represent the military and various regional groups. The DPR drafts legislation and approves presidential budgets and decrees. The DPR meets four times per year for two-month sessions. DPR members serve five-year terms; four hundred of its members are elected directly by the people and the remaining one hundred members, the majority of whom represent the military, are appointed.

The Repelita, the country's five-year business plan, is drafted by Bappenas, the National Development Planning Council, which is charged with economic planning, coordination, and implementation and is accountable to the president. The Sixth Five-Year Plan began in 1994–95 and will end in 1998–1999. Indonesia is one of the few countries that has also developed twenty-five-year business plans. The first one began in 1968 and ended in 1993. The Second Twenty-Five-Year Plan has just begun.

Indonesia's legal structure is based on Dutch laws. However, laws related to foreign investment companies, specialized industries, and taxation are new. Due to differences in law, practical application can be difficult, time-consuming, and sometimes unpredictable. There are four court systems: the general court handles criminal and civic cases; the religious court handles Muslim civil cases including marriage and divorce; the military court manages disputes between military personnel and civilians and within the military; and the administrative court handles cases between civilians and government officials. Among legal professionals, the notary public manages the incorporation of limited liability companies, other entities that must have official documentation, the transfer of real property, and civil cases such as marriage. The advocate provides advice on administrative, civil, commercial, and criminal issues. A counselor-at-law advises on civil, commercial, corporate, and tax matters, but does not provide litigation services.

In addition to the laws, presidential and ministerial decrees are an important part of the country's legal system. Much of Indonesia's regulatory system is a set of decrees that have the force of a law, but have not yet passed through parliament. The highest level are presidential decrees, followed by presidential directives, and then by ministerial decrees and directives. Although more laws are being drafted and passed through the parliament, decrees and proclamations remain an integral part of the legal structure that governs much of society, including politics, business, and finance. According to the Decree of the National Assembly No. 20 of 1966, Indonesian laws and regulations have the following hierarchy: (1) the 1945 Indonesian Constitution; (2) decrees of the National Assembly; (3) government regulations replacing laws—the president announces such regulations with the understanding that the parliament must subsequently approve it; (4) government regulations declared by the president to implement laws; (5) presidential decrees; (6) ministerial decrees; and (7) ministerial instructions. Given the overwhelming authority of the president's office, presidential decrees carry far more weight than this hierarchy might suggest.

Economy

The Indonesian economy has been transformed during the past twenty years. Prior to 1966, the economy suffered from hyperinflation and foreign exchange reserves were almost depleted. Suharto brought inflation under control and economic growth has been steady ever since. Much of this growth is it due to foreign aid and investment combined with the rising revenues from oil and gas exports in the 1970s. The fall in oil prices in the early 1980s negatively affected the Indonesian economy. As a result, many of the economic policies of the 1980s were aimed at reducing Indonesia's dependency on oil products. Despite its economic successes, Indonesia remains a relatively poor country. Income is not equally distributed throughout the islands and the different ethnic groups, although the incidence of poverty is decreasing.

Indonesia has abundant natural resources, most of which remain undeveloped. The major industries are petroleum, textiles, and mining. Indonesia's main exports include timber, petroleum products, textiles, and rubber. Petroleum products account for about 40 percent of foreign revenues, as compared with 80 percent prior to the drop in oil prices in 1982. Agriculture remains a major sector of the economy and employs about half of the population. Major crops include rice, soybeans, copra, tea, cassava, and peanuts. The manufacturing sector continues to grow as the government encourages more private investment, industrialization, and economic diversification.

A sensitive economic issue concerns the delicate balance between the government and the Chinese minority that controls most of Indonesia's big business. Many Indonesians fear that economic liberalization and privatization will lead to the Chinese minority's assumption of even greater economic control. Nevertheless, the government has focused on market reforms including the deregulation and liberalization of both the industrial and financial sectors of the economy and the development of the country's inadequate infrastructure.

Indonesia's major trading partners include Japan, the United States, and Singapore. Indonesia and Japan have enjoyed close relationships because Japan imports almost 60 percent of Indonesia's oil exports. Japan has also been a major foreign aid lender and direct investor in the country. Indonesia enjoys strong and favorable relationships with the IMF and the World Bank. Although external debt has been relatively high, the country adheres strictly to its repayment schedule. The government's approach to its debt has been conservative and focuses solely on long-term debt.

People, Values, and Social Customs

The population of Indonesia is approximately 187 million, making it the fourth largest country in the world. Two-thirds of the population lives on the island of Java. The major cities in Indonesia are: Jakarta, the capital (pop. 8 million) located in West Java; Surabaya (pop. 3 million), Medan (pop. 1.8 million), and Bandung (pop. 1.6 million). Approximately 70 percent of the people live in rural areas.

The people of Indonesia are primarily Malay except in Irian Jaya, where they are mainly Papuan. Chinese descendants make up about 3 percent of the population. There are also small groups of Arabs and Indians in the main cities. Despite the Malay predominance, there are a wide variety of different cultures, languages, and ethnic groups, known locally as *suku*. The major ethnic groups are Javanese (45 percent), Sundanese (14 percent), Madurese (8 percent), and coastal Malays (7.5 percent). *Pribumi*, the Indonesian equivalent of the Malaysian *bumiputra*, refers to indigenous Indonesians of Malay descent, in contrast to nonindigenous Chinese and Dutch. There are at least three hundred ethnic groups throughout Indonesia, each with different customs, languages, and social structure. All Indonesians learn Bahasa Indonesia, the national language, in primary school. Yet ethnic identity is usually as important as national identity and is the primary basis for building and maintaining relationships. Geographic and economic distinctions among the rural, coastal, tribal, and urban Indonesians further the country's heterogeneity.

Approximately 90 percent of Indonesians are Sunni Muslims, making Indonesia one of the most populous Muslim nations. The remaining population follows Christianity (6 percent), Buddhism (2 percent), Hinduism (1 percent), or Confucianism (1 percent). Religious freedom is guaranteed and tolerance is highly valued by Indonesians. Nevertheless, recently there has been a shift toward Islamic fundamentalism as some people feel threatened and ambivalent about modernization. Most offices and buildings are required to have a prayer room. Despite this recent shift, most Indonesians are not very orthodox in their beliefs.

The colonial experience has had a lasting impact on the older generation and on the nation's leadership. Indonesia's recollection of the resistance struggle and independence is usually slanted in its favor, as is evident through the Indonesian history books used in schools. The government has propagated a reinterpretation of history primarily for the benefit of nation-building. Indonesians continue to resent the Japanese, although this is now turning into a love–hate relationship due to Japan's profitable trade and generous aid. Attitudes toward Americans, in contrast, are generally favorable, although that can differ by area.

The Chinese in Indonesia have experienced discrimination and resentment over the years due primarily to their business success. The Dutch first isolated the Chinese community by using them as local business partners. When Chinese businesses flourished, the concentration of wealth in the hands of this small ethnic and religious minority fed discrimination.

Among Indonesians, individuality is secondary to community concerns. They are very loyal to family, friends, and members of the same ethnic group. Traditionally, Indonesians have valued large families; extended families often live together, assuming responsibility for one another. However, this interdependence on extended families is gradually changing in the urban areas. All efforts are made to prevent disturbances that might affect the smooth harmony of communities. By and large, Indonesia still remains a hierarchical and honor-oriented society.

Due to the Hindu influence, the Balinese have a very fatalistic attitude. Other parts of Indonesia also display this fatalistic attitude, although less intensely. Further, the Balinese are less concerned with conquering bad or evil influences as they believe that good and evil coexist and it is impossible to get rid of either.

Indonesians, like most modern societies, have become materialistic. A person's status can be dependent on his or her family position, as well as on personal and family wealth. Modern Indonesians have generally been motivated by status, which in turn is expected to lead to wealth. Traditionally, university graduates competed to get jobs in the government and military. These jobs brought status and respect, as well as wealth in the form of gifts and bribes from people seeking favors. Today, more graduates are beginning to perceive business and other professions as equally rewarding.

The literacy rate in Indonesia is about 62 percent. Education is still not widespread; about 22 percent of the population has finished elementary school, less than 15 percent have completed high school, and less than 2 percent have graduated from college. Families must often bribe teachers before they will instruct their children and issue grades. In Indonesia, payments are sometimes required in order for children to be promoted or accepted into higher institutions. Admittance to public universities is based on both academic excellence and significant payments.

Under Islamic law, Muslim men may have up to four wives, although this is not a widespread practice. The government actively promotes one-spouse and two-children families. Although Indonesia is a Muslim country, there are some female professionals in Indonesian companies. Indonesian women have more rights than most Muslim women in other parts of the world: they can vote, they can seek divorce, and they can inherit or acquire property. The women do not wear veils.

Work Schedule

Most businesses are open weekdays from 8:00 or 9:00 A.M. to about 4:00 or 5:00 P.M., and some are open on Saturdays from 8:00 or 9:00 A.M. to 12:00 or 1:00 P.M. Some businesses close at midday on Fridays in observance of Muslim worship. Government offices are open from 8:00 A.M. to 3:00 P.M., Monday to Thursday; from 8:00 A.M. to 11:30 A.M. on Fridays; and from 8:00 A.M. to 2:00 P.M. on Saturdays. Banks are open from 8:00 A.M. to noon or 2:00 P.M., Monday to Friday, and some are open on Saturdays. Certain hotel bank branches may stay open later each day. Shops are usually open Monday to Saturday from 8:00 A.M. to about 9:00 P.M. Sunday is a public holiday, but some shops may be open for at least part of the day.

Making Contacts

Introductions are the preferred method for developing business opportunities in Indonesia. Meetings that occur without an introduction will focus first on establishing credentials and developing trust. When contacting the private sector, direct your communications to the senior-most person. Your request will then be directed to the correct person at the appropriate rank.

It is vital that foreign companies find a local partner, representative, or agent to serve as an intermediary. This partner can be an actual business partner or a consulting or trade firm that acts as a formal go-between. Ideally, once you are committed to doing business in Indonesia, it is best to have a dedicated professional, based in Indonesia, operating a representative office. This person should either be Indonesian or have a senior Indonesian on staff who would interface with the government and other ethnic communities.

When researching local partners and consultants, it is important to hire the local firm that has the "correct" political connections. Suharto's family have benefited financially from political access and power. His six children, often referred to as simply "the children," and their commercial interests have permeated all aspects of the economy. Many foreign businesspeople feel that unless one of Suharto's children or other family members is involved, a large project will not be able to obtain the necessary government approvals. Although the Chinese business community, which controls most of the country's largest businesses, has been immensely successful in Indonesia, its relations with indigenous Indonesians are often strained. There is currently a delicate, interdependent balance between the government and the Chinese, although this may change with any future transfers of government leadership. A substantial *pribumi* business class is also emerging.

You should look for politically influential members of the local firm and consider the ethnic, *pribumi*, or Chinese backgrounds of the firm's senior members. Further, be sure to check out the firm's references and its track record. For American companies, the American-Indonesian Chamber of Commerce in the United States or the AmCham office in Indonesia are knowledgeable and reliable and can assist you in identifying appropriate and credible local representation.

It is important to remember that doing business in the private sector is vastly different than doing business with the government. When doing business with the government, it is important to start with the relevant department and work your way to the top. Never start directly at the top. It is important to build relationships. Further, it is advisable to keep your interest and interactions as private and as low-key as possible in order to avoid creating unrealistic public expectations. Marketing to the government can be very time-consuming and frustrating.

Meeting People

The best time of year to schedule business trips is between September and June. Many Indonesians vacation in July and August. Avoid local holidays—particularly Ramadan, which occurs over a period of several weeks—when people's attentions are distracted. Indonesians will often accept visitors without an appointment, but it is best to schedule one in advance if you are traveling from a long distance and are on a tight schedule. In Bali, it is best to schedule a morning meeting as people like to get work done early to avoid the afternoon heat.

Indonesians have great respect for age, status, and position. It is important to recognize the status hierarchy and ethnic backgrounds of people you meet. When arranging meetings, be sensitive to the position level of the people with whom you are meeting. Make sure that a senior person from your group is available to meet with a senior Indonesian. There is a large gap between the president of a firm and its senior executives, and a similar gap between senior and middle management. Middle-level Indonesians may overstate their status and responsibility level, especially in dealings with foreigners.

Indonesians are not always punctual, although they will expect and appreciate your punctuality. Indonesians often use the phrase *jam karet*, which means "rubber time," as an excuse for their tardiness. Early meetings are generally held in hotel lobbies or offices, and on occasion, over a meal.

It is appropriate to greet men and women on a first encounter with a handshake, a slight bow of the head, and a pleasant smile. Indonesians tend to smile often in all types of situations, including when they are happy, sad, and nervous. Foreigners should be wary of automatically interpreting a smile as having a positive meaning. After the first meeting, it is uncommon to shake hands on each greeting. A nod or a small bow is more appropriate. Most Indonesians shake hands lightly, so do not apply Western standards of strength. Due to the Muslim influence, Indonesians will often shake hands and then bring both hands back to the chest as if to symbolize that the greeting is from the heart. Indonesians also shake hands when congratulating someone or when saying good-bye before a long trip.

Indonesians often have just one name. When addressing an Indonesian who is older, socially superior, or politically higher, it is considered courteous to use the titles *bapak* (bah-pak) for men, which means "father," and *ibu* (ee-boo) for females, which means "mother," before his or her name. Both are similar to the English "Mr." or "Mrs." Traditionally, these terms were used only for people in the same ethnic community, but foreigners who become accepted by an Indonesian may use the terms. On the first encounter, it is safest to use the English "Mr." or "Mrs.," or a title. Indonesians may call you *tuan* or *nyonya*, which is a very honorific term used for foreigners in place of "Mr." or "Mrs." and is considered to be very respectful.

Business cards are exchanged upon the first greeting. Indonesians are impressed by credentials and titles, so indicate your advanced degrees or professional certifications on your business cards.

In general, businesswomen will be accepted by Indonesians, especially if they work for internationally well-known firms. Foreign women working in Indonesian firms may find that it is difficult to earn the respect of local Indonesians. Some Indonesian women are employed in business and government; however, most women are employed as factory workers. Most professionals, including doctors and engineers, are men. Secretaries are usually female, although some can be male, depending on the specific role. There are several different types of office workers including drivers, tea servers, and errand runners, most of whom are men, although on occasion women may serve tea.

Indonesians tend to be mild, but not soft. They favor proper, polite, well-mannered, refined, subtle, and respectful behavior. People who are rude, loud, and coarse are not appreciated. Further, Indonesians value foreigners who show an interest in their country, culture, and language. Connections with socially acceptable people will have a significant influence on business interactions. In fact, in some instances, family, friends, and contacts may prove more important in a business relationship than the quality of the product or service being offered.

During the first meeting and at the beginning of all subsequent meetings, it is important to engage in polite social and general conversation. Suitable topics include the weather, your travels, your appreciation of some aspect of Indonesian culture, or common contacts. Avoid questions regarding your counterpart's salary and perks or his material goods, such as his home or car. In terms of casual conversation, Indonesians enjoy speaking about their culture as well as talking about the popular Indonesian sports: badminton, soccer, volleyball, tennis, and bicycling. If someone compliments you, do not simply reply "Thank you." It is important to be humble. A more appropriate response would be along the lines of, "Thank you, but it was very little / not very important / no effort."

It is best to refrain from speaking about politics and Indonesia's internal ethnic divisions, as these can be sensitive topics. Avoid appearing aggressive or pushy. First meetings are often used as an opportunity to get to know one another and business may not even be discussed. At the end of every meeting, it is appropriate to say *Terimah kasi*, which means "Thank you." This helps in building and strengthening a warm business relationship.

Gift giving and graft are a normal part of Indonesian life, in both social and business situations. Senior officials will not indicate their "commission" (i.e., graft) preference to you directly. Rather, junior officers will communicate these "commission requirements" to your local partner, who will then inform you.

Although there are differences between regions and between urban and rural areas, Indonesians observe some general social customs. Crossing your legs is usually inappropriate, particularly in the presence of senior people. However, if you choose to cross your legs, do so only at the knee or ankle. Never prop one foot on the other knee. The sole of your foot should never face another person, for the soles of the feet or of shoes are considered dirty. It is considered rude to sit on a desk or to prop your feet on desks or tables. Indonesians also consider standing with your hands in your pockets or on your hips as a sign of defiance or arrogance.

In general, men go first when walking through doors or when sitting in a formal gathering. The most senior person goes first, with subsequent ranking people following in descending order. Due to Western influences, you may find that this is not always true in larger cities when foreign women are present. Never touch an Indonesian women except for the initial handshake. In major cities, members of the opposite sex may walk hand in hand. Nevertheless, since Muslim law dictates most social rules, public contact between the sexes is minimal. Though you may see people of the same sex holding hands in public, this does not have the same connotations it has in most Western countries.

The left hand should never be used in any situation. You should never point a finger, for this gesture is considered rude and sometimes threatening. If Indonesians need to point to something, they use their thumb. Beckon by using the whole hand, palm facing down and fingers pointing away from you, but moving toward you in a scratching motion. Wherever possible, avoid beckoning anyone except for a taxi, a *becak* (pedicab), or a child. Do not pat anyone on the head, for Indonesians believe that this is where the spirit resides. Backs are considered private as well. Indonesians sometimes show approval by a pat on the shoulder, but it is best for foreigners to refrain from this gesture.

Corporate Structure

Although they are usually profitable, Indonesian businesses are not well-managed in a Western sense. There is very little accountability or delegation of work. In general, the corporate structure includes a chairman at the top, followed by a president, a vice-president, and managers. Indonesian companies are hierarchial and centrally organized, and decision making is controlled by top management. In most Indonesian companies, the firm's founder or one key family member, male or female, has most of the decision-making authority. Indonesians feel that this approach works best in both the public and the private sectors. The concept of professional management was introduced by multinational corporations, primarily American ones. The training of modern Indonesian managers continues to be an important goal for most foreign companies.

Indonesian firms often maintain two sets of accounting books to circumvent tax and other issues.

Traditionally, Indonesians have had a higher regard for a person's social background and ethnic group than his or her ability. Social harmony was valued more than work efficiency. While this is gradually changing, it remains the predominant philosophy.

There are numerous state-owned enterprises, which are accountable to various government departments. For example, Perumtel, the state telecommunications company, is an arm of the Ministry of Tourism, Post, and Telecommunications. Different government agencies exercise influence at different stages of a project. The Coordinating Ministry for Economics, Finance, and Industrial Affairs (EKUIN) reviews prospective projects at the precontract stage. EKUIN consists of five separate branches: monetary affairs, balance of payments, and state finance; international financial relations; agricultural production and distribution; manufacturing industries, mining, and energy; and infrastructure and services. The Agency for Assessment and Application of Technology (BPPT) reviews all technology transfers and imports. The Investment Coordinating Board (BKPM) is a state agency dedicated to promoting the development and expansion of industry in Indonesia. Designed to be a one-stop center, the agency assists foreign companies in establishing businesses, but it does not handle investments in the oil and gas or banking industries.

Negotiation

The informal nature of Indonesian business and the importance of family and friend relationships results in a great deal of business being conducted on the golf course and over lunches and dinners. Chinese businesspeople tend to be more formal due to their exposure to Western business values. For most Chinese professionals, meetings and business meals must have a specific business purpose, something more than general relationship building. Traditionally, Indonesians view time as an abstract concept and a limitless commodity. The giving of one's time freely to one another has always been an important part of society. As such, business is conducted leisurely.

As with any business encounter, when doing business with Indonesians it is best to observe and listen and not rush into any decisions. Indonesians are very patient in their dealings. Like most Asians, Indonesians grow up bargaining in almost every aspect of their daily lives. As a result, bargaining and negotiating for more favorable terms is an almost automatic reponse. Foreigners should not make concessions quickly, but instead should bargain for better terms. Quick concessions will simply be attributed to the foreigner's lack of experience. Business negotiations can be slow and frustrating, so you should plan to make several trips to negotiate a sizable deal or at least plan to stay for several days.

Decision-making is done by informal consensus, although there is usually one senior decision-maker who has the ability to override the group. Most Indonesians will not question the authority of a senior decision-maker. Preserving group harmony and consensus is important because Indonesians strive to have complete agreement without hurting anyone's feelings. This drive for harmony varies in strength according to the ethnic group. The Chinese business community is more motivated by profit and is less intent on maintaining harmony. Native Indonesians tend to be emotional people and not always practical. They tend to rely on intuition and emotion in decision making rather than fact and reason. Westerners should be careful not to assume that this implies poor decision-making on the part of Indonesians. On the contrary, Indonesians need to feel that a business interaction feels "right and is for the greater good." Indonesians also believe in fate, so that "if a deal is meant to be, then it will be."

While there are several factors that can affect their decision-making, Indonesians focus primarily on a combination of product or service quality and personal relationship. The concept of using facilitators or advisers is a well-developed and essential part of business in Indonesia. Price is often less important than the financing terms. Assuming that the appropriate connections are in place, the government will negotiate more on price than on quality, although in high-tech industries such as telecommunications quality will usually take precedence. Follow-up service and training for employees are also important considerations, particularly when doing business with the government. The process can be as important as the end result or product, as Indonesians tend to focus more on hierarchical structures, including everyone's specific titles and roles, rather than the business concepts.

Indonesians rarely disagree in public and seldom say "No." They often use the phrase *belum*, which means "Not yet." It is important to note this when dealing with the government. Within reason, if your product or service is good and you have followed the appropriate steps, there is a strong chance that you will win a contract over time. The key here is patience and persistence. Despite rejections by the government, if you and your company continue to foster relationships and maintain a presence in Indonesia, either through a dedicated company representative or a consultant/ adviser, eventually the government may award you a contract. This is a result of the Indonesian's inability to say no to a "good," credible party. Also, in large transactions the government attempts to maintain a balance by awarding contracts to companies from different countries. For example, one contract may be awarded to Americans, another to Germans, and yet another to the Japanese. The private sector operates differently. While polite persistence is always viewed as a positive sign of commitment, the private sector will not always give in.

Indonesians appreciate a quiet voice and discretion. Displays of temper are frowned upon. Indonesians do not readily admit mistakes or lack of knowledge. Ask questions in an indirect and unassuming manner to confirm a point. Many Indonesians will be hesitant to ask you questions out of fear of being wrong. Be sure to explain your ideas and position clearly. As a result of their society's top-down structure, Indonesians are often reluctant to take action or make changes and may wait for direction from others. Because Indonesians rarely attempt to assign tasks or assume responsibilities, you should suggest that both parties identify responsibilities and outline the steps or actions to be taken and the corresponding time frames. Be careful not to appear commanding or patronizing. Never say anything negative in public. Criticisms should be reserved for private meetings in order to allow your counterpart to "save face." Indonesians tend to understate issues—especially negative ones—and may not inform you of problems.

Local partners should assume much of the negotiating role, for locals will probably win you a better deal than if you did the negotiating. Local partners will also negotiate the appropriate "commission." As this "commission" is a common aspect of doing business in Indonesia, American companies are sometimes able to pay these bribes and still comply with U.S. international trade laws (check with your legal representative). Unlike some other peoples, once a commission is agreed to, Indonesians are highly unlikely to change their minds or ask for additional compensation. The completion of a transaction with the government depends on how financially satisfied the relevant government officers are. Indonesians view the government as a "partner," not as a "servant," as is typical in many Western countries. The Indonesians believe that a commission is appropriate for those in higher offices who are doing you a favor by giving you official approval. Again, who you know is much more important than what you know.

Another important reason to have a local partner, or at least a representative in Indonesia or Singapore, is to keep your transaction and company active in the Indonesian counterpart's mind. If there is no one to keep things moving, it is likely that no action or progress will be made. The cliché, "Out of sight, out of mind," is a valid concept for foreigners in Indonesia. Further, Indonesians tend to prefer doing business in person and may ignore faxes or other long-distance communication efforts.

Indonesians tend to view a legal contract as a starting point for a business interaction or venture. After operations have begun, all involved parties can determine what is in their best interests and change, within reason, the spirit of the original contract. Deviation from the contract is tolerated, for Indonesians believe that fate or bad luck makes certain things happen or not happen. Indonesians tend to favor deliberation (*musyawarah*) and consensus (*mufakat*) rather than opt for litigation. A contract or agreement serves as a reference point and is not always an accurate breakdown of responsibilities. This is why maintaining a close relationship with the Indonesian firm will allow you to monitor the progress of an agreement, identify potential problem areas in a contract, and resolve them informally. Although the Indonesian culture tends to be informal, the signing ritual is considered important and is taken seriously. Senior people who may not have been present during the day-to-day negotiations are brought to the signing.

Conducting Business in a Social Setting

Dining and Drinking

Indonesians often conduct business over breakfast, sometimes as early as 6:30 A.M. before daily temperatures rise. Lunches are less common. Business dinners are common for socializing and developing relationships. If a foreign businesswoman wants to host a dinner, she should indicate so in advance to her Indonesian counterparts by saying the equivalent of "It would give me pleasure to invite you to dinner on behalf of my company." She should inform the waiter or maître d' that she should be given the bill or arrange payment in advance by credit card.

There is very little drinking in restaurants due to the Islamic influence. It is best to completely avoid drinking hard liquor and wine during your stay. However, drinking beer is acceptable. Follow your counterpart's lead. Many Indonesians drink alcohol in their homes and at private parties. Always wait until your host invites you to drink or eat. If you are the host, be sure to invite your guests to begin eating because traditional Indonesians may wait for your invitation. If you finish a drink (alcoholic or nonalcoholic) or food, your host will be inclined to assume you want more. It is polite to leave just a small amount in your glass or plate when you are finished. Similarly, if you are the host, be sure to fill up empty glasses and plates.

At large gatherings, your host may make welcoming speeches and may ask you to make a small speech. It would be appropriate to say that you and your company associates are pleased to be at the event and visiting the country, thank the host, and make general positive remarks.

Women should be careful not to go out at night alone. It is best to travel with a car and driver and to have an escort. Men should feel comfortable about declining invitations to massage parlors.

Visiting a Home

By and large, most businesspeople and their families have some familiarity with Western dining customs. If your host or hostess is not wearing footwear, it is polite for you to remove yours. Shoes are usually removed before entering a carpeted area (also in feasting places and holy places). Although gifts are not required when visiting homes, it is a good idea to take fruits, cakes, or a souvenir from your country. Westernized Indonesians appreciate flower gifts.

Guests should rise when the host or hostess enters the room. A guest should not drink until invited to do so. To be polite, wait until your host invites you to drink a couple of times. If you are visiting a home, you may eat the meal with a spoon and fork or with your fingers. A right-handed person should hold the spoon in the right hand and push the food onto it with the fork in the left hand. It is polite to sample any food or drink offered to you. When you are finished eating, place the fork under the spoon with the fork facing down. When eating with your fingers in the traditional manner, use only your right hand. Foreigners should refrain from eating or drinking in public during the holy month of Ramadan.

Gift Giving

In Indonesia, gift giving and graft share a common gray area, yet are very important aspects of business. In order to win contracts, gifts are presented often, although they are not usually given at a first meeting. Although gift giving is not an official policy or necessarily legal, it is crucial to *concluding* business negotiations. Unless gifts are presented in a timely manner, documents may remain unsigned or pages may disappear. Gifts are presented after a negotiation begins and well before the signing or conclusion of the agreement. Indonesian counterparts will often hint about or even suggest what they would like to receive. If you are unsure about a hint, it is appropriate to ask if there are any "additions" they would like to make to the contract. Foreigners should refrain from directly offering money gifts. Such issues are best left to your local counterpart to handle. If you are requested to provide something as a commission or a "goodwill" gesture, do not express displeasure or moral outrage. This will only serve to alienate your Indonesian counterpart. Be diplomatic, discreet, and nonjudgmental in your response and approach.

Due to the Muslim influence, liquor-related items are not suitable gifts. Gifts can range from ties and athletic shoes, to household appliances, to prestigious gifts from international designers, such as leather bags, silk scarves, and sunglasses. A gift commonly requested by someone negotiating large transactions is an airline ticket to your country, supposedly to enable a visit to your company, which is actually used for the purpose of a holiday.

Any gift should be accepted graciously; it is considered impolite to refuse anything. It is best not to open gifts in the presence of others so as not to embarrass the giver. Be very humble and polite when receiving a gift.

It has been insinuated that just before the end of Ramadan, police officers and other government officials will fine foreigners more often for common, mundane offenses, such as minor speeding or traffic violations. These infractions can be easily resolved with a monetary gesture. Fines become more common at the end of Ramadan because, by Muslim law, people must give family and friends gifts at the end of Ramadan. Fines received at other times throughout the year can be resolved in much the same way. In most instances use an Indonesian to make the bribe. For example, your driver should handle any violations related to your car.

Dress Code

Although the dress code in Indonesia is casual due to the warm weather, care should be given to neatness. A shirt and tie or safari suit is acceptable for men. However, jackets are becoming more common. A full business suit should be worn at formal meetings with government officials. Women should dress modestly out of respect for the Muslim culture. A dress or suit is appropriate. Slacks are considered too casual. Makeup and perfume should be used conservatively. The evening attire for men is often batik shirts and dark pants. The traditional dress for women is a sarong, which is a long wraparound, batik-printed dress. Indonesians are pleased when foreigners wear traditional local clothing.

Useful Phrases

The main language is Bahasa Indonesia, which has common roots with Malay. Throughout the country, there are about 365 languages and dialects spoken. Javanese is the most common language. Dutch, which was the official language until 1942, is occasionally spoken by the older educated generation, although this is decreasing. English has been taught as a third language (after the main ethnic language and Bahasa Indonesia). Most businesspeople speak Indonesian, English, or Chinese. The following list includes some useful Indonesian phrases and a guide to their pronunciation:

Hello	*Hah-loh*
Good morning	*S'lah-maht pah-gee*
Good afternoon	*S'lah-maht see-yahng*
Good evening	*S'lah-maht soh-ray*
How are you?	Same as Good Morning / afternoon / evening
Please	*Mee tah* (request)
Thank you	*T'ree-mah kah-sih*
You are welcome	*T'ree-mah kah-sih come-bah-lee*
Excuse me	*Mah-ahf*
I am sorry	*Sah-yah meen-tah mah-ahf*
My name is ——	*Nah-mah sah-yah* ——
I work for ——	*Sah-yah p'gah why* ——
Here is my business card	*Boh-lay- kah sah-yah b'ree-kahn car-too nah mah*
I am pleased to meet you	*Sah-yah m'rah-sah gum-bee-rah car-nah burr-k'nah-lahn deng-ahn bah-pahk* (male)/*ee-boo* (female)
I look forward to developing a good relationship with you/ your firm	*Sah-yah hah-rahp kee-tah dah-paht b'curr-jah-sah-mah deng-ahn bike.*
I understand	*Sah-yah muhng-urr-tee*
No, I do not understand	*Sah-yah b'loom muhng-urr-tee*
I do not speak Indonesian	*Say-yah tee-dahk dah-paht bee-chah-rah bah-hah-sah in-doh-nay-see yah*
Please wait a minute	*See-lah-kahn toong-goo s'ben-tahr*
Where is the bathroom?	*Meen-tah toh-long, dee-mah-nah-kah kah-mahr k'cheel?*
Good-bye.	*S'lah-maht jah-lahn* (to the one who is leaving) *S'lah-maht teeng-gahl* (*to the one remaining behind*)
Cheers	*S'lah-maht*

Major Holidays

January 1	New Year's Day
January /February*	Mi'raj Nabi Muhammad (the ascension of the Prophet Muhammad)
February/March*	Ramadan
March*	Nyepi (Hindu holiday celebrated nationwide and a day of silence observed in Bali)
March/April**	Good Friday
March/April*	Eid-el-Fitr (holiday to mark the end of Ramadan fasting month)
May 21	Waisak (anniversary of the birth and death of Buddha)
May*	Eid al-Adha
July*	Haji (celebrating Mecca pilgrimages)
August 17	National Independence Day
August*	Maulid Nabi Muhammad (birth of the Prophet Muhammad)
December 25	Christmas Da

*These holidays are based on the lunar calendar and vary widely on an annual basis.
**This holiday is observed on the first Friday after the paschal full moon and changes from year to year.

General Facts

Climate: The climate in Indonesia is tropical and has two main seasons with relatively mild and consistent temperatures. The rainy season is from November to March, with the heaviest rainfall in December and January. During the rainy season temperatures average between 74F (23C) and 85F (30C). The dry season is from April to October, and temperatures range from 74F (23C) to 88F (31C). Temperatures in the mountains are usually slightly lower.

Currency: The currency is the *rupiah* (pronounced rupee, and abbreviated as Rp), divided into 100 *sen*.

Dates: Dates are written in the order of day, month, and year. For example, August 6, 1995, would be abbreviated as 6/8/95.

Electricity: The voltage is 220 (50 cycles), although there are some outlets that are wired for 110 volts.

Entry Requirements: All tourists from the United States, the United Kingdom, Canada, France, and Germany are required to have a visa. However, visitors can obtain a free visa upon arrival in Indonesia, providing they have a passport valid for a minimum of six months from the date of entry along with a departure ticket for air or by sea. These visas are also available for business visits limited to investigating and discussing investment and trade opportunities. Business visitors who are concluding transactions or conducting other services should obtain a visa from an Indonesian embassy or consulate prior to arrival in the country.

Time: Indonesia has three time zones: Western Indonesian Standard Time, which is seven hours ahead of Greenwich Mean Time and twelve hours ahead of U.S. Eastern Standard Time; Central Indonesia Time, which is eight hours ahead of Greenwich Mean Time and thirteen hours ahead of U.S. Eastern Standard Time; and East Indonesian Standard Time, which is nine hours ahead of Greenwich Mean Time and fourteen hours ahead of Eastern Standard Time. (All U.S. times lose one hour in Daylight Savings Time.)

Tipping: Excessive tipping is not expected or required. Most hotels and restaurants automatically add a 10 percent service charge. If this charge is not added, then a 10 percent tip is appropriate. At hotels, small tips of about Rp 2000 are suitable for bellboys and doormen, and slightly more for the concierge. For porters, about Rp 500 per item is appropriate. Give taxi drivers the small change from a bill or a tip of at least Rp 300. Rented car drivers are tipped at least Rp 2000 for the day.

Transportation: Most hotels provide some sort of transfer service to and from the airport. There is a hotel reservations desk at the airport that can assist you with related matters. Taxis are convenient and readily available. The most reliable and safest taxi service is the Blue Bird Taxi company. All taxis do have meters, so make sure the driver turns the meter on. Buses also provide service to and from the airport.

Car rentals are available, but not advisable due to traffic and parking difficulties. An international driver's license is required, and driving is on the left-hand side of the road. The best option for getting around is to rent a car and driver. Ask your hotel concierge for assistance. Buses are convenient, although crowded. People are expected to offer their seats to elderly people. Minibuses (Colts) are slightly more expensive, but less crowded. *Becaks* (pedicabs) are also readily available.

Helpful Telephone Numbers

The telephone system in Indonesia is not very reliable. Patience and persistence is required because you may have to dial a number several times before reaching your party. Public telephones take only coins. The country code is (62). The city codes are: Bali (361); Balikpapan (542); Bandung (22); Banyuwangi (333); Jakarta (21); Manado (431); Medan (61); Padang (751); Palembang (711); Pamekasan (324); Semarang (24); Surabaya (31); Tegal (283); and Tretes (343).

Hospitals:

Rumah Sakit Cipto (Central Hospital)
71 Jalan Diponegoro
Jakarta
Tel.: (21) 330808 / 344003

Rumah Sakit Pondok Indah Hospital
Jalan Metro Duta Kav. UE
Jakarta
Tel.: (21) 767525 or 768347

Pertamina Hospital
Jalan Kyai Maja
Jakarta
Tel.: (21) 707214

Doctors / Dentists:

Doctors-on-Call (Provides English-speaking doctors who make house calls; cash only)
Jakarta
Tel.: (21) 683444 or 681405

Metropolitan Medical Centre
Wisata Office Tower
Jalan Thamarin
Jakarta
Tel.: (21) 320408

SOS Jakarta
Jalan Adityawarman I No. 14
Kebayoran Baru
Jakarta

SOS Medika (a twenty-four-hour clinic and pharmacy with an English-speaking staff)
33-34 Jalan Prapanca Raya
Jakarta
Tel.: (21) 771575 or 774198 or 733094

Operator and Directory Assistance: Dial 104.

Ambulance: Dial 119; Blue Bird Taxi at (21) 325607 also provides emergency transportation.

Police: Dial 110; in Jakarta dial 587771.

Information Hotline:

Visitor Information Center
Jakarta
Tel.: (21) 364093

City Information Center
Jakarta
Tel.: (21) 354094

Useful Addresses

In Indonesia:

American Chamber of Commerce in Indonesia
World Trade Center, 11th Floor
Jalan Jendral Sudirman Kav. 29–31
Jakarta
Tel.: (21) 526-2860

BAPPENAS (National Development Planning Agency)
Jalan Taman Suropati 2
Jakarta Pusat
Tel.: (21) 334643

Chamber of Commerce
Chandra Building, 3d Floor
20 Jalan M.H. Thamrin
Jakarta
Tel.: (21) 310-1885

Department of Agriculture
Jalan Harsono, Room 3
Ragunan, Pasar Minggu
Jakarta Selatan
Tel.: (21) 780-4116

Department of Communication
Jalan Merdeka Barat 8
Jakarta Pusat
Tel.: (21) 382-0694

Department of Industry
Jalan Jend. Gatot Subroto
Kav. 52–53
Jakarta Selatan
Tel.: (21) 510954

Department of Mines and Energy
Jalan Merdeka Selatan 18
Jakarta Pusat 10110
Tel.: (21) 360232

Department of Public Works
Jalan Patimura 20
Kebayoran Baru
Jakarta Selatan
Tel.: (21) 739-5588

Department of Tourism, Post, and Telecommunications
Jalan Kebon Sirih 36
Jakarta Pusat
Tel.: (21) 384-9142 / 0172

EKUIN (Coordinating Ministry for Economics, Finance, Industry, and Development Supervision)

Jalan Lapangan Banteng
Timur 2–4
Jakarta Pusat
Tel.: (21) 373309 / 371028

Forestry Department
Gedung Manggala Wanabakti
Blok 1, Lantai 4
Jalan Gatot Subroto-Senayan
Jakarta Pusat
Tel.: (21) 570-4501

French Commercial Office
Wisma Antara 1201
Jalan Medan Merdeka Selatan 17
Jakarta 10110
Tel.: (21) 384-1270

**Indonesian Chamber of
Commerce and Industry**
Gedung Chandra, 4th Floor
Jalan M.H. Thamrin 20
Jakarta
Tel.: (21) 324000 / 324064

**Indonesian–German Chamber
of Commerce**
Wisma Metropolitan
14th Floor
P.O. Box 3151
Jakarta
Tel.: (21) 511208

**Indonesian Tourist Promotion
Board**
81 Jalan Kramat Raya
Jakarta
Tel.: (21) 310-3063

Indonesia PITO
Bumina E.K. Building, 1st Floor
Jalan Bulungan 1/9
Kebayoran Baru

Jakarta 12130
Tel: (21) 724-7332

**Indonesian Trade Ministry,
Department Perdagangan**
5 Jalan M.I. Ridwan Rais
Jakarta
Tel.: (21) 348667

**Investment Coordinating
Board (BKPM)**
Jalan Jenderal Gatot Subroto 44
Jakarta
Tel.: (21) 512008 / 514429 /
514945 / 514961 / 514981

**Ministry Council on Strategic
Industries, Agency for
Strategic Industries**
Arthloka Building, 3d Floor
Jalan Jenderal Sudirman 2
Jakarta 10220
Tel.: (21) 570-5335

Embassies and Consulates:

American Embassy
Medan Merdeka Selatan 5
Jakarta
Tel.: (21) 360360

American Consulates
Jalan, Imam Bonjol 13
Medan
Tel.: (61) 322200

Jalan Raya Dr. Sutomo 33
Surabaya
Tel.: (31) 582287 / 8

British Embassy
75 Jalan M.H. Thamrin

Jakarta
Tel.: (21) 330904

Canadian Embassy
Metropolitan Building 1
5th Floor
29 Jalan Jendral,
Sudirman Kav. 29
Jakarta
Tel.: (21) 525-0709

French Embassy
World Trade Center, 19th Floor
Jendral Sudirman, Kav. 31
Jakarta 12920
Tel.: (21) 570-1668

German Embassy
Jalan M.H. Thamrin No. 1
Jakarta
Tel.: (21) 323908

In Canada:

Indonesian Embassy
287 MacLaren Street
P.O. Box 430
Terminal A. Kln 8V5
Ottawa, Ontario, K2P OL9
Tel.: (613) 236-7403
(Commercial Attache:
232-0635)

Indonesian Consulates
425 University Avenue
9th Floor
Toronto, Ontario M5G 1T6
Tel.: (416) 591-6461

1455 West Georgia Street
2d Floor
Vancouver, B.C. V6G 2T3
Tel.: (604) 682-8855

In France:

Indonesian Embassy
47–49 Rue Cortambent
75016 Paris
Tel.: (1) 4504-1371
(Commercial Attache:
4503-0760)

Indonesian Consulates
25 Boulevard Carmagnole
13008 Marseille
Tel.: (91) 9171-3435

In Germany:

Indonesian Embassy
2 Bernkasteler Strasse
5300 Bonn 2
Tel.: (228) 382990
(Commercial Attache:
310091)

Indonesian Consulates
Bebelallee 15
22299 Hamburg
Tel.: (40) 512071

Georgspaltz 1
D-3000 Hannover
Tel.: (511) 103-2150

Sophienblatt 33
D-2300 Kiel
Tel.: (431) 603010

**Indonesian Trade Promotion
Centre (ITPC)**
Glockengiesserwall 20
D-2000 Hamburg 1
Tel.: (40) 330639

In the United Kingdom:

Indonesian Embassy
38 Grosvenor Square
London W1X 9AD
Tel.: (71) 499-7661
(Commercial Attache:
629-5924)

**Indonesian Trade Promotion
Centre (ITPC)**
Sherborne House, Ground Floor
13 Saville Row
London WIX 2NE
Tel.: (71) 439-0189

In the United States:

Indonesian Embassy
2020 Massachusetts Avenue, N.W.
Washington, DC 20036
Tel.: (202) 775-5200
(Commercial Attache:
775-5350-3)

Indonesian Consulates
5 East 68th Street
New York, NY 10021
Tel.: (212) 879-0600

233 North Michigan Avenue
Suite 1422
Chicago, IL 60601
Tel.: (312) 938-0101

10900 Richmond Avenue
Houston, TX 77042
Tel.: (713) 785-1691

3457 Wilshire Blvd.
Los Angeles, CA 90010
Tel.: (213) 383-5126

1111 Columbus Avenue
San Francisco, CA 94133
Tel.: (415) 474-9571

**Indonesian Trade Promotion
Center (ITPC)**
4 E. 54th Street, 5th Floor
New York, NY 10022
Tel.: (212) 947-8889

3457 Wilshire Blvd., Suite 101
Los Angeles, CA 90010
Tel.: (213) 738-8955

World Trade Center, Suite 158
2050 Stemmons Freeway
Dallas, TX 75207
Tel.: (214) 651-9060

**Indonesian Tourist Promotion
Board**
3457 Wilshire Blvd.
Los Angeles, CA 90010
Tel.: (213) 387-2078

**American Indonesian Chamber
of Commerce**
711 Third Avenue, Suite 1702
New York, NY 10017
Tel.: (212) 687-4505

U.S. Department of Commerce
International Trade
Administration
Indonesia Desk, Room 2036
14th & Constitution Avenues,
N.W.
Washington, DC 20230
Tel.: (202) 482-3877

8 Malaysia

Geography

The country of Malaysia consists of two parts, Peninsular Malaysia and East Malaysia, with a total land area of 124,569 square miles (332,633 square kilometers). Peninsular Malaysia is a long strip of land extending south below the tip of Thailand. Singapore lies at the southern tip of Peninsular Malaysia across the Strait of Malacca. East Malaysia, consisting of the states of Sarawak and Sabah, is located on the northern portion of the island of Borneo. Indonesia occupies the southern part of the island and Brunei lies in the northern part of Sarawak. Peninsular Malaysia is characterized

245

by dense jungle and high mountains in the north and a fertile plain in the west. East Malaysia is covered by dense jungles with large rivers. The capital is Kuala Lumpur, which is located on Peninsular Malaysia.

History

The earliest known inhabitants of the Malay Peninsula are believed to have lived there as long as 40,000 years ago. Although very little is know about the Stone Age Malaysians, evidence suggests that aboriginal Malays, known as Orang Asli, came to the peninsula from southwest China. About 4,500 years ago they were supplanted by Proto-Malays, who are considered to be the ancestors of modern Malays. Ethnically, the ancestral Malay people were similar to the people of Java, Sumatra, and the Philippines.

For the first six centuries A.D., the Indian-influenced kingdom of Funan, based in modern-day Cambodia, controlled the northern part of the Malay Peninsula. In the seventh century A.D., the Sumatran-based Srivijaya Empire assumed control of the area. In the late thirteenth century, the Java-based, Hindu Majapahit Empire took over the Srivijaya Empire.

Although areas of the Malay Peninsula were on ancient trade routes, the history of Malaysia truly begins with the founding of Malacca in 1402 by a Sumatran prince, Parameswara. Malacca became the most powerful city-state in the region and controlled the peninsula until the arrival of the Dutch. Gradually, Malacca's rule extended over the entire Malay Peninsula, the state of Patani in present-day Thailand, the Riau and Lingga archipelagos, the island of Singapore, and the states along the northern Sumatran coast, including Rokan, Siak, Kampar, and Indragiri. Malacca's influence also extended over the Brunei sultanate on the island of Borneo.

In 1405 the Chinese Ming dynasty emperor Yung-lo reestablished the tribute system and sought close relations with the new kingdom of Malacca. As a result, Malacca's reputation as a port favored by the Chinese attracted traders from all parts of coastal Asia and the city became a flourishing entrepôt for eastern and western goods. Arab and Indian traders brought Islam to the region around the same time. Malacca's rulers took the lead in converting the people of the Malay Peninsula, and ever since the Muslin faith has had a profound influence on Malaysian society.

In 1511 Malacca was captured by the Portuguese, who were unable to capitalize on the wealth and strategic location of the city. In 1641 the Dutch overthrew the Portuguese and began an occupation that lasted for more than 180 years, until the British assumed control in 1795. In 1819 the Dutch reacquired most of the land, but only for a short time. In the same year, the British established a trading post in Singapore. An 1824 treaty between the Dutch and the British gave the latter control over Malacca. In 1826 the British joined the territories of Malacca, Singapore, Penang, Perai, and Dindings under a single administration called the Straits Settlement, which was initially under the jurisdiction of the British East India Company. The British allowed local sultans to manage daily administrative affairs while retaining control of the area's external affairs. However, due to competition from commercial interests in India, the Straits Settlement became a direct colony of Britain in 1867.

The Brunei Empire originally controlled most of the land on the island of Borneo including what is now East Malaysia. In 1840 James Brooke, a British adventurer, was visiting Kuching, which was then part of Brunei's domain, and successfully intervened in a revolt against the sultan of Brunei. As a reward for his efforts, the sultan made him rajah of Sarawak in 1841. By 1888, Sarawak, Brunei, and Sabah (formerly North Borneo) had become British territory.

The British developed local industries, particularly tin and rubber, and built the infrastructure to support the area's burgeoning trade. In addition to the indigenous and diverse Malay community, Malaya (as the Peninsula was then known) became home to a mix of ethnic and cultural groups, particularly Chinese and Indians, whose numbers when combined eventually outnumbered the local Malay population. The local labor shortage led the British to import labor from India, primarily from the southern regional community of Tamil, as well as from Pakistan and Sri Lanka. The Chinese came originally as laborers, but quickly moved into areas of commerce. Most of these Chinese migrated from various southern provinces of China, resulting in additional ethnic differences among the Chinese community. Aside from the ethnic divisions, the Chinese were split into two main groups, recent immigrants and Straits-born (or Baba) Chinese, those who had been born in the Straits Settlement and regarded Malaya rather than China as their homeland.

In December 1941 the Japanese started their advance on the Malay Peninsula and conquered it within three months. The Japanese invasion and quick retreat by the British shattered the myth of British invincibility and damaged their credibility in the region. All ethnic communities suffered during the Japanese occupation, although the Chinese received the harshest treatment in retaliation for their support against Japan during the latter's war with China. The Japanese exacerbated ethnic tensions by putting the Malays in charge of all administrative affairs. The Malayan People's Anti-Japanese Army (MPAJA), a communist resistance movement, had been formed after the beginning of the Sino-Japan war in 1937 and was predominantly Chinese. By 1945, the anti-Japanese war had assumed a distinct ethnic character because the Japanese forced Malay police and officials to root out members of the MPAJA. Indians were treated as foreigners and did not enjoy the same privileges as the Malays, although they fared better than the Chinese. After the defeat of Japan in August 1945, the British resumed control of Malaya.

In April 1946 the British created the Malayan Union consisting of Malacca, Penang, and the nine Malay states: Johor, Kedah, Kelantan, Negeri Sembilan, Pahang, Perak, Perlis, Selangor, and Terengganu. Singapore became the headquarters of the British Military Administration, but was not included in the Malayan Union, although they shared a common currency. In 1946 the territories of Borneo were also reorganized, and Sabah (North Borneo) and Sarawak became two separate crown colonies. Brunei remained a separate British protectorate. In 1946 the United Malays National

Organization (UMNO) was founded to organize the movement for national sovereignty; it eventually became the most important Malayan political party.

In 1948 the Union was dissolved as the result of pressure by Malaysian nationalists for establishment of an independent country. On February 1, 1948, the Malay states of the peninsula formed a federation with a British high commissioner as chief executive and a Federal Legislative Council as the legislative body. The federal government was weak, however, as most of the political power resided with the states. The new federation was torn by ethnic rivalries, primarily because the UMNO focused on reaffirming special status for Malays. A campaign of communist terrorism backed by the Chinese communists sought to destroy the British economic base and to create a countrywide revolution. While the Malays wanted independence, they had no desire to become a puppet of the Chinese government. The British government declared a state of emergency in 1948, which lasted until 1960, when terrorism was finally brought under control.

In 1955 Britain agreed to make Malaya fully independent within two years. A new constitution was adopted, which provided for a government elected by representatives of the people. In the first federal elections, held in the same year, a coalition party called the National Front (Barisan Nasional) or the MCI (Malay, Chinese, Indian) Alliance party—consisting of the UMNO, the Malayan Chinese Association (MCA), a noncommunist party, and the Malayan Indian Congress (MIC)—won an overwhelming majority of seats. The first prime minister was Tunku Abdul Rahman, who represented the National Front's dominant partner, the UMNO. He was pro-West and anti-communist, and served from 1957 to 1970.

From 1956 to 1957 the government continued talks with the British, pushing for full independence. In August 1957 the Federation of Malaya Agreement was signed and independence, Merdeka, was achieved. Talks with Great Britain as well as with Indonesia and the Philippines continued in order to determine the status of the territories of Sabah (North Borneo) and Sarawak. On September 16, 1963, Malaysia officially became an independent country consisting of the eleven states of the Federation of Malaya, Sabah (North Borneo), Sarawak, and Singapore. In 1965 Malayan fears that Singapore's Chinese majority intended to take over Malaysia led to the expulsion of Singapore from the union.

Although the Malaysian economy was stable, Malaysian politics were not, as ethnic tensions between the Malays and the Chinese remained strong. In 1969, after ethnically motivated riots against the Chinese population, the government took steps to deal with the grievances and frustrations of the economically backward Malays by adopting the New Economic Policy. Bahasa Melayu was made the national language. Further, special privileges were extended to the Malays to help them buy land, procure business licenses, receive better educational opportunities, and secure more government positions. The government created a title, *bumiputra* (sons of the soil), for the indigenous Malays, which included the aboriginals and the natives from Sarawak and Sabah. In order to create a *bumiputra* commercial and industrial community, the government announced plans to place 30 percent of the country's capital in the hands of the *bumiputra* by 1990. Despite these reforms, the Chinese continued to exercise control over business and resentment between the ethnic groups continued to mount.

In 1970 Tunku Abdul Rahman retired and was succeeded by his deputy, Tun Abdul Razak, as prime minister and as head of the UMNO. Dató Hussein bin Onn became prime minister in 1976 followed by Dató Seri Dr. Mahathir Mohamad in 1981. At times a controversial leader, Mahathir has been noted for his confrontational style of politics, internally and externally, and as a staunch advocate of *bumiputra* policies. Mahathir has also been the force behind Malaysia's impressive development and economic growth. Further, he has been a proponent of a strong Asia standing firm against Western pressures and influence. Throughout the 1980s, he promoted a "Look East" campaign, embracing Japan as an economic model and rejecting Western models. Mahathir is highly regarded by Malaysians and won reelection in 1990 for a five-year term.

The UMNO has remained the dominant force in the National Front coalition, which has ruled Malaysia since 1957, although it has been plagued by infighting and factionalism since the mid-1980s. However, opposition parties have been unable to successfully challenge the UMNO. In recent years the booming economy has focused people's attention more on material gain rather than issues concerning government accountability and corruption. However, opposition parties have focused their efforts on increasing political freedom and improving human rights. Balancing the interests and demands of the Malay Muslim fundamentalists, the moderate Malay Muslims, the Chinese, and the Indians remains a challenge for Malaysian leaders. Most older Malaysians remember the 1969 race riots and fear any group that might spark religious or communal tension. However, the younger generation is concerned that efforts to maintain racial stability will only increase government authoritarianism. Nevertheless, strong economic prospects ensure that the UMNO will remain a dominant political force.

Political Structure

Malaysia is a parliamentary democracy with a king as head of state. The country is a federation of thirteen states whose capital is Kuala Lumpur. The Federal Parliament of Malaysia has a two-house Parliament, the Senate (*Dewan Negara*) and the House of Representatives (*Dewan Rakyat*). The prime minister is appointed by the party that has a majority in the *Dewan Rakyat*. Members of the House of Representatives are elected every five years by popular vote. Some Senate members are nominated by the king and others are elected by the Legislative Assemblies of the thirteen Malaysian states. The constitution provides for a strong federal government and recent amendments have further reduced the power of the monarchy, which can no longer delay legislation and must abide by the government's advice.

At independence, the country opted to become a monarchy rather than a republic. An institution called the Council of Rulers, consisting of the nine rulers of Malaysia's states, was created. One supreme ruler is selected by its members to serve as the *Yang Di Pertuan Agung*, which means "he who is selected lord." The *Yang Di Pertuan Agung* holds the title of king for a five-year term. Technically, the king appoints the prime minister, can dissolve or maintain the Parliament, and appoints judges. However, in reality, the king functions as head of state and acts on the advice of the prime minister, who retains the real power, the Parliament.

All states have their own government and most are headed by a royal ruler, who sits on the Council of Rulers, and a chief minister (*Mentri Besar*). Four states do not have a royal ruler: Pulau Pinang, Malacca, Sabah, and Sarawak. These four states have appointed a governor, *Yang DiPertua Negeri*, as head of state.

Malaysia has an independent judiciary based on the British system and common law. The highest court is the supreme court. In some states, such as Kelantan, the Islamic *sharia* law is administered.

Economy

In 1969 the government adopted the "New Economic Policy," which was an aggressive attempt to achieve economic and social development and ethnic integration. The government plan to shift at least 30 percent of available capital to companies owned by *bumiputras* has been partially successful, reaching about 22 percent by 1991. The government then adopted its "New Development Policy," which does not have numeric quotas, but adheres to the same principles of economic distribution and social integration. Malaysia has a pool of cheap labor, but is experiencing a shortage of skilled workers and managers with technical training and higher education.

During the first half of the 1990s, the Malaysian economy continued to perform well, confirming its role as a regional economic powerhouse. Growth rates have been among the highest in the world, averaging in excess of 8 percent per year. The government has focused on promoting and developing the country's manufacturing industry. A number of free trade zones have been established throughout the country to encourage the establishment of manu-facturing enterprises with special concessions granted to export-oriented industries. The infrastructure is well-developed.

Malaysia has a mixed economy. Over the past decade the gov-ernment has succeeded in moving the economy from one that is de-pendent on agriculture to one that is export-oriented. Today only 30 percent of the population is engaged in agriculture-related jobs. The main natural resources include tin, palm oil, rubber, tropical woods, petroleum, and natural gas. Major crops include cocoa, pep-per, rice, coconuts, fruits, coffee, and tea. The country's major exports include electronic components, textiles and apparel, chem-icals, transport equipment, and wood products.

People, Values, and Social Customs

The population of Malaysia is approximately nineteen million and consists of three main ethnic groups: Malays (60 percent), Chinese (30 percent), and Indian (9 percent). There are also populations of indigenous Orang Asli and the various tribes in Sarawak and Sabah. East Malaysia has about twenty-five ethnic groups, which further complicates the ethnic balance between the two states. In many cases, the ethnic group is more of an identity determinant than the religion. Each community uses their own language among themselves and Bahasa Melayu or English when dealing with another ethnic group.

Islam is the state religion. It is the faith of almost all of the Malays and some of the Indians; about 53 percent of the population is Muslim. The constitution guarantees freedom of religion. Other religions practiced in Malaysia include Hinduism, Christianity, Buddhism, and Taoism.

The Malays, which constitute about 60 percent of the population, have had political control of the country since World War II. Since independence in 1957, the government has sought to elevate the sta-tus of the Malay population through economic policies including scholarships, tax-exemptions, and stock ownership. The government was originally concerned because the Malays lagged far behind the

Chinese and Indians in terms of economic power. After about 1982, government policy shifted more toward fairness for all three ethnic communities, but there are still many instances of race being selected over ability. Recently the Muslim movement, which is equated with being Malay, has been increasing in power. The Chinese and Indian communities have become somewhat resentful about the special status of Malays and there is little trust among the three groups.

Within the small Indian community, there are two classes, the professionals and laborers. Some individuals have been very successful, but the Indian community as a whole has not thrived. Only a few Indians hold government positions. Overall, the Indians tend to be culturally very conservative.

The Chinese community, which has been the most successful commercially, is loyal to its business interests and is often considered to have the strongest work ethic. Socially, Chinese women have been the most progressive. The Chinese have permitted the greatest degree of intermarriage between communities, followed by the Indians, and then the Malays.

In general, Malaysians tend to believe in fate, although the notion that hard work brings success is rapidly gaining ground as the work ethic becomes more widespread. Malaysians are becoming more materialistic as national wealth increases.

Seniority is always respected. In social conversation, there are specific honorific terms used for each family member depending on their age and rank within the family. Malays will often affectionately use these terms with friends and workers. Malays rarely refer to family members by just their first name, unless the family member is a child.

The older generation were influenced by the period of British rule and often are fluent in English. Malaysians under the age of forty were born in the post-colonial period and are less fluent in English. They are also more pro-Malaysia; they are less inclined to associate by race and community and have allegiance to the national identity first. Today, Malay is the primary language of instruction in the schools until college and English is the secondary language. Due to the widespread influence of international television and other media sources, the younger generation is increasingly exposed to Western values.

To get ahead in Malaysia, both connections and merit are important factors. In business, merit is more important; in government, connections and seniority are more valuable. Education is the key to economic and social advancement. Entrance into colleges is dependent on personal qualifications and sometimes on a person's connections. A person's family status and background are important in developing the "right" connections. Public colleges have quotas for Chinese and Indian students. In the early 1990s the majority of the country's political and corporate elite were alumni of Malay College, located in Kuala Kangsar; members of the Malay College Old Boys Association (MCOBA) provide each other with special access to the government, the civil service, the private sector, and academia.

Work Schedule

The days when business is not conducted vary between regions. In Selangor, Malacca, Penang, Perak, Pahang, Johor, and Negri Sembilan, there is a half-day holiday on Saturdays and a full-day holiday on Sundays. Kedah, Perlis, Terengganu, and Kelantan all retain the traditional Islamic half-day holiday on Thursday and a full-day holiday on Friday. Saturdays and Sundays are considered full workdays. This work-week schedule is gradually changing, so it is advisable to check before you arrive.

Generally, the workday begins at 8:00 or 8:30 A.M. and ends about 4:30 or 5:00 P.M., with a long two and a half hour break at noon on Friday for communal prayers at the mosques. On days other than Friday, there is a midday break from 12:45 P.M. to 2:00 P.M. Some offices are open on Saturdays from 8:00 or 8:30 A.M. to 12:30 or 1:00 P.M. Government offices are open from 8:00 or 9:00 A.M. to 4:00 P.M., Monday to Friday, and from 9:00 A.M. to 1:00 P.M. on Saturday. Banking hours are generally from 10:00 A.M. to 3:00 P.M., Monday through

Friday, and 9:30 A.M. to 11:30 A.M. on Saturday. Shops are usually open Monday to Saturday from about 9:00 A.M. to 6:00 P.M., although the department stores stay open until 9:00 P.M.

Making Contacts

Introductions are not required in Malaysia, although, as elsewhere in the world, a strong introduction will always help open doors. An introduction will also prompt your local counterpart to disclose more information about his or her company, products, and objectives. You can use introductions from former government officials, law and consulting firms, bank and corporate board members, or trade organizations.

Unsolicited letters are acceptable. The approach depends on the type and scale of your project. When approaching a private Malaysian enterprise, identify the person or division that handles your product or service. Where possible, learn about the strategic objectives of the senior executives of the company. At times, it is possible to arrange meetings once you are in Malaysia, although preplanned meetings are the best option. Do not schedule your day too tightly; leave some room for flexibility, for meetings sometimes run long by Western standards or you may want to schedule additional meetings.

Your business relationships with the people of Malaysia will depend on their education level and their exposure to the world outside Malaysia. If possible, learn abut the background of your local counterpart before your visit or early in the meeting. Ethnic differences are an underlying factor that permeates all types of business issues. Even in the private sector, ethnic differences continue to affect hiring decisions as well as the selection of outside consultants, lawyers, accountants, bankers, and the like. Therefore, it is more helpful to have a local Malay partner than a Chinese or Indian partner in light of the current environment. Firms that are interested in bidding on government contracts must have local

Malaysian partners; *bumiputra* agents will often get preferential treatment.

The government continues to exercise extensive influence and control on the private sector. The Malaysian Industrial Development Board (MIDA) oversees the promotion and coordination of all industrial activities. The Coordination Center for Investment (CCI) was established by the MIDA to be a one-stop resource agency to assist foreigners in establishing businesses in Malaysia.

Meeting People

Malaysians expect others to be punctual, although at times they themselves may not be punctual. Malaysians greet one another with a handshake, a warm smile, and a hello. Since many are Muslims, Malaysians often bring their hands back to touch their chest to symbolize that the greeting came from the heart. A foreigner is not expected to do the same, but the gesture is always appreciated. When interacting with a Malaysian woman, wait until a hand is offered before you try to shake hands. Due to the conservative nature of the culture, a slight bow of the head is often more appropriate when meeting a woman. Indian Malays may greet you in a more traditional style called the *namaste*, which involves placing both palms together as in prayer at chest level and slightly bowing the head.

Titles and protocol in Malaysia are very important and can be confusing, particularly because the same titles are often spelled differently. Men with titles should be addressed as *Datuk*, also spelled *Dato*, followed by their given (first) name. For their wives use, *Datin*. Common in Indonesia as well, these titles are used for older and senior people and indicate respect.

All members of Parliament are called by the honorific *Yang Berhormat*, sometimes abbreviated as "Y.B." in writing, which is the English equivalent of "The Honorable." When writing or speaking to a member of Parliament or State Assemblyman, never use the pronoun "you"; always use *Yang Berhormat.* When meeting with royalty, never ask to be excused or leave until the royal member indicates that you may do so. If you are pressed for time, indicate so discreetly ahead of time to your Malaysian colleague or to a royal aide. Elegant gifts from your home country are appropriate for royalty and should be given to their aides.

In normal business encounters, it is best to address a person as "Mr.," "Mrs.," or "Miss." The Malaysians use their given names (first names), while the Chinese use their family names. For Malays, use *Encik* in place of "Mr." and their given name for men. Women are usually addressed by the prefix *Cik* in place of "Miss" or the prefix *Puan* in place of "Mrs." and the given name. As noted earlier, Malaysians also use other formal titles such as *Datuk* and *Datin.* If someone is introduced to you with this title, use it rather than *Encik* or *Cik.* Chinese names usually start with the family name, for example, "Lee Chee" should be called "Mr. Lee." If you are unsure how to address someone, politely ask them or their associate. As part of the Muslim culture, Malaysian names use *bin,* which means "son of," and *binti,* which means "daughter of." You do not need to use the entire name in a letter or conversation. For example, "Ahmad bin Ali" would be addressed in a letter as "Dear Encik Ahmad." For Chinese and Indian names as well as any others with family names, use the traditional Western salutations. It is necessary, however, to use the full name on an envelope.

Business cards are always exchanged and should be given and received with both hands. In any encounter, never give or take with just the left hand, which is considered the "unclean hand." Read the card before storing it as a sign of respect. Your business card should list your company's name, your title, and even your major functional responsibility, as these all reflect status.

There are increasing numbers of women in the workforce on a full-time and part-time basis. Traditionally women have held the support and administrative positions, but this is gradually changing as more female professionals enter management positions. Women have always been well represented in the fields of medicine and teaching. There are a number of female professionals, so it is best not to make any assumptions about a woman's position until you learn her title.

On most formal occasions, and particularly if meeting with royalty, it is considered very rude to cross your legs. Keep both of your feet flat on the floor and do not rest your foot on your knee; showing the sole of your foot or your shoes is considered disrespectful and rude. Never touch someone's head, for the head is considered the spiritual part of the body. Standing with your hands on your hips implies anger. Pointing at inanimate objects should never be done with a finger, but rather with the whole hand with the thumb over the fist. Beckoning should be done using the entire right hand with the palm facing down and the fingers pointing away from you, but moving toward you in a scratching motion. Never make a fist and hit it against your open or cupped hand, for this is considered an obscene gesture. Smoking is banned in most public places.

Although Malaysians are fairly conservative, they are aware of Western customs and are tolerant of foreigners and their ways. Simple and courteous behavior is the best approach. Always show deference to senior business people. Due to ethnic differences, humor and smiling can differ among various groups. Many Malaysians smile only when they are happy.

Always begin the meeting with casual talk, more so at the first meeting than at subsequent ones. Appropriate topics include the positive aspects of your visit to Malaysia, your travels, and the weather. Do not talk about democracy-related issues, human rights, or religion, for all three are sensitive topics. It is not necessary to give a gift at a first meeting but it is acceptable to offer something with the corporate logo or a sample product. Large and expensive gifts would be considered inappropriate.

Corporate Structure

In the private sector, corporate titles and responsibilities differ between companies. Usually, the senior person is the chairman of the board. Day-to-day responsibilities are managed by the president, vice-president, and managers. In most Chinese firms, senior managers are usually family members and retain most of the decision-making authority.

In the typical ministry structure, the minister is the highest level and has a private secretary who manages his office. This person can be instrumental in arranging meetings. The next level is the deputy minister, followed by the parliamentary secretary, and then by the secretary general. Beneath the secretary general are usually two deputy secretary generals, followed by two to three undersecretaries. Below that level are two to three principal assistant secretaries and beneath that two to three assistant secretaries. Government bodies other than ministries, such as the Electricity Board, are usually headed by a chairman with a board of directors.

Negotiation

Do not expect to receive quick decisions or to finalize transactions on the first trip. You should anticipate at least two to three visits before business considerations will become serious. This will depend on the ethnic group with whom you are doing business as well as with the name recognition of your company. Large, well-established international companies will have a slightly easier time establishing credibility. Winning trust, however, will take longer for unknown companies. Many Malaysian businesspeople develop informal relationships and initiate business dealings on the golf course.

Attention and deep thought are given to issues. The Confucian ethic and the Muslim religion affect many aspects of Malaysian business. In most situations, companies are very hierarchical, with only a few decision-makers at the top. Malaysians tend to be very detail-oriented and use a lot of research in their analysis. Decisions are formulated slowly and in a very calculated manner.

Overall, Malaysians tend to be risk-averse, with Malays and Indians more so than the Chinese. Malaysians can be cautious and even reluctant to make difficult decisions, although it often depends on their exposure to and involvement in international business. Malaysians are fatalistic and believe that if a deal is meant to happen, then it will happen.

Always remain polite and courteous throughout the negotiation process. Do not raise your voice or embarrass your Malaysian counterpart, for maintaining face is a critical part of relationship building. Malaysians are not likely to say "No" directly, so you may need to ask questions indirectly. Culturally, an Indian or Malay businessperson will generally admit that he or she made a mistake. The Chinese pride themselves on being astute businesspeople and are less likely to admit to or to take responsibility for a mistake.

In business, legal contracts are honored, but verbal agreements are not. Malaysians view contracts as a flexible tool in a business relationship. Trust and honor are integral to building a strong foundation. At times, Malaysians may be offended by detailed contracts because such detail implies a lack of trust between the parties. However, smaller Malaysian businesses are more likely to suggest detailed contracts because they may be concerned about their ability to control events.

Conducting Business in a Social Setting

Dining and Drinking

Business meetings often take place over lunch and dinner, but rarely over breakfast. If you have scheduled a dinner or after-hours meeting, your Malaysian counterpart may bring his spouse or an associate. Meals are sometimes served in large bowls or dishes, with everyone putting small portions on their plate. Do not drink or eat until your Malaysian host invites you to do so. Alcohol is rarely consumed in restaurants due to the religious influence. Muslims do not eat pork or drink alcohol, while Hindus do not eat beef. When among the Malays and Indians, do not pass food or drinks with your left hand, for it is considered unclean.

Foreign businesswomen will be asked to participate in business lunches and dinners, but probably not in other social events, such as golf outings, unless her male company colleagues are present. Golf is a very important venue for building business relationships in Malaysia.

Visiting a Home

Malaysians do not usually invite business associates to their homes. However, when they do, Malaysians treat them as honored guests. Shoes should be removed before entering. Malaysians hosts will not insist on shoe removal, but are very appreciative of the gesture. (If visiting a mosque or Indian temple, you should always take off your shoes before entering. Chinese temples are usually more informal, but it is best to follow these general customs.)

When visiting a home, bring a small gift, such as fruit, sweets, or cakes, and a token of your home country or firm. Malaysians will not open gifts in front of the giver. Do not give alcohol to a Malay, particularly Muslims, unless you know them well and know that they drink.

Gift Giving

While graft does exist in Malaysia, it is not always obvious to foreigners. Formulate a global policy and adhere to it. It is best to leave such sensitive matters to your local representative or partner.

As a result of Malaysia's various religious beliefs and ethnic groups, normal gift giving can be difficult. Always give and receive gifts with both hands. For the Chinese, clocks, watches, knives, and white flowers all have negative connotations. Gifts should be given in even amounts for the Chinese. You may receive an expensive and elaborate gift from your Chinese associate. It is appropriate to accept it and then to decide at a later date whether to reciprocate. Liquor or pork items must never be given to a Muslim. Chocolates are suitable, but should not contain liquor or gelatins made from unspecified animals fats. Be careful not to give an item that could be considered offensive, such as a calendar with a picture of a woman. It is sometimes better not to give a gift rather than risk offending your counterpart. A company pen or some other gift with the logo is appropriate. For Indian businesspeople, items in odd numbers and usually ending in 1 are considered lucky. Gifts should not be opened in front of the giver.

Dress Code

The standard business attire is a suit and tie for men, and a suit, dress, or blouse and skirt for women. At casual occasions and during the evenings, a short-sleeve shirt and slacks are appropriate except for the most upscale restaurants. Long-sleeved shirts made from native batik material are appropriate for men, but it is best to wait until after the first meeting to wear non-Western attire. On social occasions or in meetings with people you already know, safari suits are acceptable, usually in brown or gray. Women can wear slacks for casual situations. Women should avoid the color yellow (printed patterns are acceptable) on formal occasions because this is the color reserved for royalty. White is reserved for death and mourning.

Useful Phrases

The official language is Bahasa Melayu (Malay). When speaking with royalty, Malaysians use more honorific versions of common words. The official second language is English, which is spoken throughout the country by members of different ethnic and linguistic groups. Various Chinese dialects and Tamil, a language from southern India, are widely spoken in their respective communities. The following list contains some key phrases in Malay with a guide to their pronunciation. For Cantonese and Tamil phrases, please refer to Chapters 4 and 14 on Hong Kong and Sri Lanka, respectively.

Hello	Hello (when using telephone) or *Ah-pah kah-bar*
Good morning	*S'lah-maht pah-ghee*
Good afternoon	*S'lah-maht see-yahng*
Good night	*S'lah-maht p'tahng*
How are you?	Same as Good morning/ afternoon/ evening
Please	*Meen-tah* (as in a request)
Thank you	*T'ree-mah kah-sih*
You are welcome	*Sah-mah, Sah-mah*
Excuse me	*Mah-ahf*
I am sorry	*Sah-yah meen-tah mah-afh*
My name is ———	*Nah-mah sah-yah*
I work for Company ———	*Sah-yah P'gah-why—*
Here is my business card	*Boh-lay-kah say-yah b'ree-kahn kahd nah-mah*
I am pleased to meet you	*Say-yah b'rah-sah gum-bee-rah car-nah burr-joom-pah dehng-ahn too-ahn* (male) / *poo-ahn* (female)
Please accept this small gift	*Boh-lay sah-yah b'ree-kahn hah-dee-yah k'cheel ee-nee k'pah-dah too-ahn* (male) / *poo-ahn* (female)
I look forward to developing a good relationship with you / your firm	*Sah-yah burr-hah-rahp kee-tah boh-lay mum-bee-nah curr-jah-sah-mah yahng bike*
I understand	*Sah-yah fah-hahm*
No, I do not understand	*Say-yah b'loom fah-hahm*
Please wait a minute	*See-lah toong-goo s'ben-tahr*
Where is the bathroom?	*Toh-long, dee-mah-nah-kah bee-lick ah-yer?*
Good-bye	*S'lah-maht jah-lahn* (to the one leaving)
	S'lah-maht teeng-gahl (to the one remaining behind)
Cheers	No equivalent*

*Malays are Muslim and accordingly do not drink.

Major Holidays:

Malaysia has a public holiday nearly every month.

January 1	New Year's Day
February 1	City Day (in Kuala Lumpur)
January/February*	Chinese New Year
February/March*	Ramadan
March*	Hari Raya Puasa
May 1	Labor Day
May 6	Wesak Day
June*	Hari Raya Haji
June 5	King's Birthday
June 21	Awal Muharram
August/September*	The Prophet Muhammad's Birthday
August 31	National Day
early November*	Deepavali
December 25	Christmas

*These holidays are based on the lunar calendar and accordingly the date changes annually.

General Facts

Climate: Malaysia is hot and humid throughout most of the year, experiencing relatively constant temperatures and weather conditions. Temperatures range from 70F (21C) to 90F (32C). The monsoon season is from mid-September to mid-December and is characterized by heavy rains and slightly lower temperatures. On most days throughout the rest of the year, there is usually one daily downpour. The sun is very strong, so be sure to take precautions and drink plenty of fluids.

Currency: The *ringgit* or the Malaysian dollar (abbreviated M$), which is divided into 100 *sen*.

Dates: Dates are written day, month, year. For example, August 21, 1995 would be written 21/8/95.

Electricity: The Malaysian current is 220 volts, 50 cycles. Many first-class hotels can supply adapters for 100 volts, 60 cycles.

Entry Requirements: American, French, and German citizens are required to have valid passports, but do not need visas for stays under three months. British and Canadians require passports, but do not need visas for stays less than six months. Businesses visas are not required if you are attending to private business matters.

Time: Malaysia has one time zone, which is eight hours ahead of Greenwich Mean Time and thirteen hours ahead of U.S. Eastern Standard Time (twelve hours during Daylight Savings Time).

Tipping: Tipping is not very common; it is not encouraged by the government. If a service charge, usually 10 percent, is already added to a bill, it is appropriate to leave only small change in addition. For porters and doormen, 1 M$ per bag is acceptable. Leave 1 M$ or small change for restaurant waiters and cab drivers.

Transportation: Within cities, taxis remain a cheap and convenient mode of transportation. Taxis are the best transportation to and from the airport. To avoid being overcharged, buy a prepaid taxi coupon from a booth outside the arrival area. On other occasions, be sure that the meter is turned on when you first get into a taxi, otherwise you could easily be charged double the fare. Early in the morning or late at night taxi drivers are reluctant to use the meter and often prefer to set a slightly arbitrary rate, which can be bargained lower. If you are using a taxi for several hours, it is easier and sometimes more economical to negotiate a day rate with the taxi driver. There is a 50 percent surcharge between midnight and 6:00 A.M. There is often a 30 percent surcharge for air-conditioning regardless of whether or not you request it. There are no meters in taxis on East Malaysia (Sabah and Sarawak) and fares must be negotiated. Most taxi drivers in the major cities speak some English.

Driving is on the left side of the street and seat belts are required, as is an international drivers' license. In Kuala Lumpur, it is not advisable to drive because accurate road maps are difficult to obtain, street names change frequently, and driving conditions can be congested and hazardous. The best way to travel in and between towns is by hiring a car and driver. All major car rental agencies offer cars and drivers for hire.

City buses are economical and convenient, although they are generally crowded and without air-conditioning. On occasion, visitors to Malaysia will still see trishaws, which are bicycles with a side carriage. These are not efficient, but serve as a good way to sightsee and experience the local flavor. Between cities, planes, trains, and buses are available. Private taxis can also be rented for travel between cities and are cheap and convenient.

Helpful Telephone Numbers

There are three types of telephones: coin phones, card phones using prepaid cards, and card phones using credit cards. Public telephones are orange and are located in orange shelters. After the dial tone is obtained, insert a 10, 20, or 50 *sen* coin and wait until the light goes off and then dial. Warning beeps usually indicate that only ten seconds of time is left unless additional coins are inserted. It is not uncommon for the public telephones to fail. In such circumstances, use telephones in coffee shops and hotels. Card phones (Kadfon), which accept prepaid cards and credit cards, are common throughout Malaysia at designated areas. Prepaid cards can be bought at Kedai Telekom and various retail agents. The country code is (60). The following are the area codes for major cities: Kuala Lumpur (03); Ipoh and Taiping (05); Johor Bahru (07); Kota Bharu, Kuala Terengganu, and Kuantan (09); Kuching (082); Malacca and Seremban (06); and Penang and Sungai Petani (04). Omit the zero when calling from outside of the country. For international calls, dial 108 to "book the call." This is the equivalent of making a reservation to place the call once a line is available.

Hospitals:

Kuala Lumpur General Hospital
Jalan Pahang
Kuala Lumpur
Tel.: (3) 292-1044

Subang Jaya Medical Center
1 Jalan Subs. 12H1a. Subang Jaya
Selangor
Tel.: (3) 734-1212

Police and Emergency Services:
Dial 999; in Kuala, Lumpur dial 241-5522

Fire: Dial 994.

Operator: Dial 102 for trunk call inquiries.

Useful Addresses

In Malaysia:

American Chamber of Commerce in Malaysia
Amoda 22, 15th Floor
Room 1501
Jalan Imbi
55100 Kuala Lumpur
Tel.: (3) 248-2407 / 2540

French Commercial Office
Technip Geoproduction
See Hoy Chan Plaza, 19th Floor
Jalan Raja Chulan
P.O. Box 12041

50766 Kuala Lumpur
Tel.: (3) 230-2369

Kuala Lumpur Visitors Centre
3 Jalan Sultan Hishamuddin
50050 Kuala Lumpur
Tel.: (3) 230-1369

Malaysian Chamber of Commerce and Industry
Plaza Pekeliling, 17th Floor
2 Jalan Tun Razak
50400 Kuala Lumpur
Tel.: (3) 441-8522

Malaysian–German Chamber of Commerce and Industry
P.O. Box 11683
50754 Kuala Lumpur
Tel.: (3) 238-3561

Malaysian Industrial Development Authority (MIDA)
Tingkat, Wisma Damansara
6th Floor
Jalan Semantan
P.O. Box 10618
50720 Kuala Lumpur
Tel.: (3) 255-3633

Malaysian Industrial Development Finance Behad (MIDF)
195a Jalan Tun Razak
Peti Surat 12110
50939 Kuala Lumpur
Tel.: (3) 261-1166

Malaysian International Chamber of Commerce and Industry
Wisma Damansara, 10th Floor
Jalan Semantan
P.O. Box 10192
50706 Kuala Lumpur
Tel.: (3) 254-1690 / 2677

Ministry of International Trade and Industry
Block 10, Kompleks Pejabat-pejabat Kerajaan
Jalan Duta
50622 Kuala Lumpur
Tel.: (3) 254-0033

Malaysia PITO
7.02, 7th Floor Bangunan Yee Seng
15 Jalan Raja Chulan
50200 Kuala Lumpur
Tel.: (3) 238-9491

Tourist Office, Headquarters
Menara Dato'Onn
Putra World Trade Centre
17th, 24th–27th Floors
45, Jalan Tun Ismail
50480 Kuala Lumpur
Tel.: (3) 293-5188

Embassies:

American Embassy
376 Jalan Tun Razak
50400 Kuala Lumpur
Tel.: (3) 248-9011

British High Commission
185 Jalan Ampang
Kuala Lumpur
Tel.: (3) 248-2122

Canadian Embassy
Plaza MBI, 7th Floor
172 Jalan Ampang
50450 Kuala Lumpur
Tel.: (3) 261-2000

French Embassy
196 Jalan Ampang
50540 Kuala Lumpur
Tel.: (3) 242-9444

German Embassy
3 Jalan U Thant
55000 Kuala Lumpur
Tel.: (3) 242-9666

In Canada:

Malaysia High Commission
60 Boteler Street
Ottawa, Ontario K1N 8Y7
Tel.: (613) 237-5182

Consulate of Malaysia (Trade)
80 Richmond Street West
Suite 905
Toronto, Ontario M5H 2A4
Tel.: (416) 869-3886

1900-925 West Georgia Street
Vancouver, B.C. V6C 3L2
Tel.: (604) 685-9550

Malaysia Tourist Information Center
830 Burrard Street
Vancouver, B.C. V6Z 2K4
Tel.: (604) 689-8899

In France:

Embassy of Malaysia
2 Bis Rue Benouville
75116 Paris
Tel.: (1) 4553-1185

Malaysian Investment Center
42 Avenue Kleber
75016 Paris
Tel.: (1) 4727-6696 / 3698

Malaysia Tourist Information Center
29 Rue des Pyramides
75001 Paris
Tel.: (1) 4297-4171

In Germany:

Embassy of Malaysia
Mittelstrasse 43
5300 Bonn 2
Tel.: (228) 376803-06

Consulates of Malaysia
Kagr. 2
2000 Hamburg 11
Tel.: (40) 372-172

Nymphenburger Strasse 134-1
8000 Munchen 19
Tel.: (89) 123-2718

Genthiner Strasse 41
D 1000 Berlin 30
Tel.: (30) 269-211

Malaysian Trade Commission
Rolex Haus, 6th Floor
Domprobst—Ketzer Str. 1-9

5000 Koln 1
Tel.: (221) 124-007 / 008

Tourist Development Corporation of Malaysia
Rossmarkt 11
60311 Frankfurt Am Main
Tel.: (69) 283-782

In the United Kingdom:

Malaysian High Commission
45–46 Belgrave Square
London SW1X 8QR
Tel.: (71) 235-8033

Malaysian Industrial Development Authority
17 Curzon Street
London W1Y 7FE
Tel.: (71) 493-0616

Tourist Development Corporation of Malaysia
57 Trafalgar Square
London WC2N 5DU
Tel.: (71) 930-7932

Malaysian Trade Commission
17 Curzon Street
London W1Y 7FE
Tel.: (71) 499-7388

In the United States:

Embassy of Malaysia
2401 Massachusetts Avenue, N.W.
Washington, DC 20008
Tel.: (202) 328-2700

Consulates of Malaysia
140 East 45th Street, 43d Floor
New York, NY 10017
Tel.: (212) 490-2722

World Trade Center Building,
Suite 3400
350 S. Figueroa Street
Los Angeles, CA 90071
Tel.: (213) 621-2911
(Commercial Section, 617-
1000)

**Consulates of Malaysia,
Commercial Section / Trade
Commission**
630 Third Avenue, 11th Floor
New York, NY 10017
Tel.: (212) 682-0232

2 Embarcadero Center
San Francisco, CA 94111
Tel.: (415) 421-6570

**Malaysian Industrial Develop-
ment Authority (MIDA)**
630 Third Avenue, 11th Floor
New York, NY 10017
Tel.: (212) 687-2491

875 N. Michigan Avenue
Suite 3350
Chicago, IL 60611
Tel.: (312) 787-4532

350 S. Figueroa Street
Los Angeles, CA 90071
Tel.: (213) 621-2661

**Malaysia Tourist Promotion
Board**
595 Madison Avenue
Suite 1800
New York, NY 10022
Tel.: (212) 754-1113

818 West Seventh Street
Los Angeles, CA 90017
Tel.: (213) 689-9702

**Permanent Mission of Malaysia
to the United Nations**
140 East 45th Street, 43d Floor
New York, NY 10017
Tel.: (212) 986-6310

U.S. Department of Commerce
International Trade
Administration
Malaysia Desk, Room 2036
14th & Constitution Avenue,
N.W.
Washington, DC 20230
Tel.: (202) 482-4958

Philippines

National Capital

● City

0   500 kilometers

0   500 miles

Thailand
Bangkok ☆

Songkhla

Andaman
Sea

Medan   Malaysia
☆ Kuala Lumpur
Singapore

Padang

Telukbetung

Jakarta ☆

Indian
Ocean

Ternate

South China
Sea

Brunei

Malaysia
● Sibu

Pontianak ●
Balikpapan ●
Banjarmasin

Majene ●
Ujingpandang ●

I n d o n e s i a.

Manila ☆

Iloilo ●
Cebu ●

Davao ●

Manado ●

PHILIPPINES

Philippine
Sea

Bula ●   Kaimana ●

Kupang ●

Geography

The Philippines is an archipelago of 7,100 islands located off the coast of Southeast Asia. Most of the islands are mountainous, prone to earthquakes, and have both dormant and active volcanoes. About 95 percent of the population resides on eleven of the largest islands. The main islands are Luzon, Mindanao, Cebu, and Palawan. The total land area of the Philippines is approximately 115,830 square miles (300,000 square kilometers). The capital, Manila, is located on the island of Luzon. Other major cities include Cebu, Iloilo, Davao, Iligan, and Cagayan de Oro.

History

The oldest human remains found in the Philippines date back 22,000 years. Relatively little is known about the prehistoric Philippines. Trade with China began in the ninth century A.D., initiating a long history of mutual interaction between the Filipinos and the Chinese. Islam came to the region in the fourteenth century, brought by traders and clergy from the Indonesian islands.

In 1521 Ferdinand Magellan became the first European to visit the Philippines. He landed on Cebu, claimed the land for King Charles I of Spain, but was killed by a local chief one month later. Over the next few decades, the Spanish sent additional exploratory expeditions to the archipelago and finally established a permanent settlement in 1565. The Spanish named the country the Philippines in honor of their king, Philip II.

One of Spain's goals was to convert the Filipinos to Christianity and then use the Philippines as a base for carrying Christianity to China and Japan. Spain was so successful in converting the Filipinos that Christianity remains the main religion in the modern Philippines. Indeed, the Philippines is the only Asian country with Christianity as the dominant faith. The Christian religious orders heavily influenced all aspects of education, social life, culture, art, and architecture in the Philippines.

Many of the problems facing the Philippines today stem from its colonial past. The huge gaps in income and power between the upper socioeconomic groups and the impoverished, low-income masses are rooted in the structure established under early Spanish rule. Roman Catholic friars, acting on behalf of the Spanish government, organized the Philippines into administrative entities. Over time the Catholic religious orders acquired huge landed estates and became wealthy. By the eighteenth century, the religious orders had become the largest landholders. The friars ran their great holdings indirectly, using the local Filipino leaders, who thus held on to their traditional power and prestige and also grew rich. In time, the church's estates were bought by wealthy Filipinos, called *principales*, and by Chinese mestizos, a change that permanently altered Philippine culture. The offspring of these new landlords were provided with educational opportunities, at home and overseas, not available to the masses, thereby forming a new social, economic, and cultural elite called the *ilustrados*, which literally means "enlightened ones." This native Philippine elite from the Spanish colonial period retained their power long after Spanish rule ended. Even in modern times, many of the country's political leaders come from these same elite families.

Although Spain accomplished the religious goal of converting the Filipinos to Catholicism, it did not succeed in the economic goal of exploiting the Philippines' natural resources and profiting from trade with its colony. Part of the problem was that Spain did not rule the Philippines directly but via Mexico.

While the Spanish failed economically, the Chinese succeeded. The possibilities for trade attracted growing numbers of Chinese to Manila. By the early seventeenth century, these Chinese, who by then played the key role in local and intra-Asia trade, had economically surpassed the Spanish. From 1603 to 1762, there were periodic riots and massacres of the Chinese as the Spanish tried to control them through restrictions and threats of violence.

In 1762 Spain joined France in the Seven Years War (1756–1763) against Britain. During the final stages of the war, the British captured the Philippines. The islands were returned to Spain in 1764, but the British victory had a significant effect on the Filipinos by damaging Spanish prestige locally and changing the old order. By 1834, foreign traders from Britain and the United States were operating in the Philippines.

In the early to mid-nineteenth century, Chinese immigrants from Fujian Province in China settled in increasing numbers in the Philippines. The Chinese established themselves as retailers, lenders, and farmers, gaining a central position in the cash-crop economy at the local and provincial levels. Chinese mestizos, who spoke Spanish, had a higher status than other Chinese due to their proficiency in the Spanish language. In general, the Spanish were racist in their attitudes towards both Filipinos and Chinese.

Throughout the mid- to later nineteenth century, the desire for independence from Spain's rule grew, particularly among the Filipino elite who had spent some time in Europe. Filipino nationalists advocated equality for Filipinos and representation in Spain, as well as the basic freedoms of speech and association. The most well-known early nationalist was José Rizal, whose writings gained wide readership among Filipinos, particularly the *ilustrados*, who were receptive to his democratic and liberal ideas. These efforts inspired an uprising in the Philippines in 1896 by Filipino nationalists. Rizal was executed by the Spanish for his alleged involvement in the uprisings. Nevertheless, resistance continued under Emilio Aguinaldo and other rebel leaders.

In 1898 the United States and Spain went to war, primarily over Cuba, another Spanish colony. The Filipinos and the Americans joined forces to defeat the Spanish. Although many Filipinos hoped their country would become independent, they were disappointed. They had thrown out the Spanish masters, but now had American ones. War broke out between the Filipinos and the Americans in 1898 and lasted formally until 1901 when Aguinaldo surrendered to the United States.

The economic effects of colonialism were devastating. However, under American rule there were improvements in education and health that enhanced the quality of life of most Filipinos. Nevertheless, major Filipino landlords still controlled most of the land and pocketed most of the wealth it generated. A small elite held most of the wealth and power, while the great mass of Filipino people lived in poverty. The disparity between rich and poor fueled unrest, prompted sporadic rural uprisings, and served to increase the popularity of Socialist and Communist groups.

Under U.S. rule, a new political structure, based on the American model, was introduced. From the outset, the Americans defined their mission as preparing the Filipinos for eventual independence. The wealthy *ilustrados* sought to cooperate with the Americans in achieving gradual independence. In 1935 the United States established the Commonwealth of the Philippines.

On December 8, 1941, Japan launched a surprise attack on the Philippines, just ten hours after they bombed Pearl Harbor. On January 2, 1942, Manila was occupied by the Japanese. The combined United States–Philippine military forces finally surrendered to the Japanese in April 1942. Philippine resistance to the Japanese, fueled by their harsh rule, strengthened and spread throughout the country as the war progressed. The Japanese surrendered the Philippines on September 2, 1945. By that time, an estimated one million Filipinos had been killed and many major cities, particularly Manila, had been severely damaged. The Filipinos wanted independence and the United States granted it. Independence was declared on July 4, 1946. Manuel Roxas became the first president. The United States retained military base rights, which eventually became a source of contention and remained so until Clark Air Force Base and Subic Bay Naval Base were closed in 1991 and 1992 repectively.

During the war, rural areas were the scene of guerilla fighting, which drove wealthy landlords to the cities for safety. Upon independence, the landlords returned to the countryside. Their demands for backrent and other landlord–tenant conflicts fueled peasant unrest and eventually uprisings, the most notable of which was the Huk Rebellion, which lasted from 1946 to 1954.

In 1965 Ferdinand E. Marcos became president. He won reelection in 1969, but declared martial law in 1972 and thereafter ruled as dictator until his ouster in 1986. Initially, Marcos authorized massive public spending programs to rebuild the infrastructure and to promote education. Talented technocrats were appointed to key economic positions. Under his early rule, the Philippines became a founding member of ASEAN (Association of Southeast Asian Nations), although disputes with Malaysia continued over control of the province of Sabah on the island of Borneo. However, after his reelection, the quality of life began to deteriorate as crime rates spiraled, corruption grew, and economic growth slowed. On September 21, 1972, in response to a supposed attack on the defense minister, Marcos declared martial law which lasted until 1981. He detained students and other activists as well as opposition leaders, of whom Benigno Aquino was the most prominent. In order to appease the Americans, Marcos justified this oppression by claiming that a network of communists were operating throughout the countryside.

During the years of martial law, corruption increased as Marcos' wife, Imelda, and her close group of associates used their influence to grant favors in return for money. Cronyism became an integral part of life in the Philippines. Government positions and state-run companies were placed under the control of well-connected rather than capable managers. Even large privately held companies were nationalized, broken up, and placed in the hands of Marcos'cronies. As a result, the economy was undermined as the Marcos government had to subsidize huge unprofitable enterprises. Distribution and marketing monopolies were also controlled by Marcos' cronies. They used their illegitimate profits to indulge themselves, to buy luxury items such as art, jewelry, and antiques, to invest in real estate, and to establish secret Swiss bank accounts.

On January 17, 1981, Marcos formally ended martial law, but most controls remained in place and Marcos' cronies continued to dominate all areas of government, the military, and commerce. Marcos won the 1981 presidential election because the main opposition groups boycotted the fixed elections. In 1980 Benigno Aquino was released from jail and permitted to go to the United States for medical treatment. On August 21, 1983, on the day of his return to the Philippines, Aquino was killed as he was escorted off an airplane by military personnel. Marcos, his wife, and their cronies were held responsible for the murder. As a result, Aquino became a martyr. Marcos was finally ousted on February 25, 1986, by the People's Power movement, consisting of the Roman Catholic hierarchy, the business elite, and factions of the armed forces, as well as millions of Filipinos who were sympathetic to Corazon Aquino, the murdered politician's widow. Corazon Aquino emerged as the leader of the movement and a bloodless revolution swept her into power.

In 1986, when Corazon Aquino became president, she was expected to rectify all of the wrongs in the political structure and society. Aquino is credited with restoring the democratic process to the Philippines with the 1987 constitution, which provided for a democratic and progressive system and received widespread popular support. However, threats of coups plagued her administration and she was less successful in attacking the widespread problems of corruption, human rights abuses, and inequitable distribution of wealth and power.

Fidel Ramos, an Aquino-backed candidate, won the 1992 elections in a peaceful and democratic transfer of power. Ramos has proven to be a strong and effective leader whose government is focused on maintaining democratic stability and promoting economic growth through reforms as part of the ongoing liberalization and internationalization of the Philippine economy.

Political Structure

Historically, power in the Philippines had been shared by a small and wealthy oligarchy characterized by powerful landed gentry and extended families. This oligarchy has lost some power since the fall of Marcos. The most recent constitution, written in 1987, was modeled after the U.S. Constitution and returned the country to a constitutional democracy with a presidential form of government. The constitution provides for checks and balances between three branches of government, executive, legislative, and judicial. The president and vice-president are elected separately by popular vote. The president, limited to serving one six-year term, heads the executive branch and appoints a cabinet.

There is a bicameral legislature consisting of the Senate and the House of Representatives. Senators are elected on a nationwide basis and serve for a maximum of two consecutive six-year terms. Representatives are elected from two hundred districts and are limited to three consecutive three-year terms. The Philippines is grouped into three geographic regions, Luzon, the Visayas, and Mindanao, and fifteen administrative regions.

The main political parties include PDP-LABAN, Lakas-NUCD, the Nacionalista party, and the Liberal party. The political structure is very bureaucratic. After Marcos's rule, the number of political parties grew rapidly, reaching approximately 105 by the 1990s. The Roman Catholic church exerts a great deal of political influence on the elections as well as governments.

The judicial system is heavily influenced by Spanish and Anglo-American law, as well as by indigenous Philippine customs. The independent court system is headed by the Supreme Court. The civil code is derived from American law in the early twentieth century.

Economy

President Ramos has successfully introduced new reforms to promote economic growth, encourage foreign investment and international trade, privatize more public entities, and streamline the bureaucracy. By 1994, the economy showed signs of improvement and inflation had been brought under control. Under Marcos, government intervention in the economy created significant inefficiencies. Now, the Philippines has mainly private enterprises, many still family managed, with some public sector entities. The Philippines remains a predominantly rural society with about half the workforce employed in agriculture-related areas.

Major exports include clothing, electronic components, nickel, coconut products, sugar, pineapples, and bananas. The country is rich in natural resources, including rice, coconuts, sugarcane, pineapples, bananas, timber, as well as the minerals copper, nickel, chromium, and gold. The major manufacturing industries include food processing, petroleum and coal, chemicals, footwear, garments, textiles, beverages, electrical machinery, electronics, furniture, other wood products, metal products, ceramics, gifts, and housewares. The service industry is becoming a major element in the economy.

Problems with the infrastructure, mainly in the power sector, continue to plague the country. The Ramos government is addressing the country's lack of electricity by encouraging the rapid development of new power projects. Other infrastructure projects focusing on transportation and communication have also been a priority. The country must also contend with periodical natural disasters, including droughts, earthquakes, and typhoons, that negatively affect the economy. A major resource is the educated, relatively inexpensive, English-speaking workforce.

People, Values, and Social Customs

The population of the Philippines is about 66.6 million. Approximately 96 percent of the population is Malay, 1 percent is Chinese, and the remaining 3 percent are mainly upland tribal groups. There are approximately 111 cultural and linguistic groups. Different Filipino groups have historical, regional, linguistic, and ethnic rivalries that continue to affect modern life. But a shared religion and the Filipino national heritage serve to keep these rivalries in check. More than 91 percent of the population are Christian, with the majority being Roman Catholic. About 5 percent of the population is Muslim; the remainder are Buddhist, Taoist, and tribal animists.

Muslims are concentrated in the southern part of the Philippines, particularly on the island of Mindanao and in the Sulu Archipelago. The Muslim community, although racially the same as other Filipinos, remains outside the mainstream of national life, due to religious, linguistic, and regional differences. Over the years, economic grievances, general government neglect, and religious prejudice have prompted the Muslims to demand a separate nation. These demands have been largely ignored, but the four provinces, Tawi-Tawi, Sulu, Lanao del Sur, and Maguindanao, on the island of Mindanao do have an autonomous regional government.

Filipinos are a racial blend of Negrito, Malay, Chinese, Spanish, American, and others who over the centuries have come to the islands and intermarried. There are four main cultural groups: lowland Christian groups (also known as Christian Malays), Muslims, upland tribal groups, and the Chinese. Philippine national identity emerged when lowland Christians, called *indios* by the Spaniards, began to refer to themselves as Filipinos. The term "Filipino" did not refer to the Chinese, Muslims, or upland tribal groups who had not been assimilated by intermarriage. *Mestizo* are the offspring of Filipino and non-Filipino marriages. Spanish *mestizos* have Spanish–Filipino parentage, and Chinese *mestizos* have Chinese–Filipino parentage. The Chinese have traditionally dominated certain commercial sectors and have periodically suffered from Filipino discrimination.

As a result of four hundred years of Spanish colonization, Spain was considered the superior culture. People with a Spanish or Western heritage are still considered superior. Spanish-sounding surnames were adopted by most Filipinos in the mid-nineteenth century, so they do not necessarily indicate Spanish heritage. At one time, Spanish was widely spoken and was taught in the schools. The Spanish language is no longer mandatory in the schools, so it is no longer widely used.

It is also important to remember that Spain did not rule the Philippines directly, but through another colony, Mexico. Visitors to the Philippines will find the culture more similar to Mexico or Latin America than to other Asian countries.

The family is the central unit in Philippine culture. Specific names for each family member indicate respect. The basic community unit is the *barrio*, or village. Sociocultural differences are evident between some regions and between rural and urban areas, but maintaining social harmony is very important. In general, Filipinos respect authority, whether the authority of age, of wealth, or of power. Filipinos are very sensitive and strive to maintain self-esteem and honor. Filipinos are tolerant, particularly of foreigners. The Filipinos, though typically deeply religious, are also fatalistic. A favorite phrase is *Bahala na*, which means "God will take care of everything."

Due to the close relationships associated with the extended family, Filipinos feel a sense of obligation to assist one another in all matters. Loyalty is first extended to the immediate family, then to the extended family, and finally to friends and clan/community members. These personal alliance relationships include real kinship, ritual kinship, patron–client ties, friendship, *utang na loob* relationships, and *suki* relationships. Although more common in traditional Philippine culture, *utang na loob* refers to a bond between people that creates a sense of obligation and interdependency as well as a need to repay debts of gratitude. *Suki* relationships are market-exchange partnerships in commercial as well as social contexts. In *suki*, personal bonds are created because of favorable business interactions. There are other values that affect interpersonal interactions. *Hiya* (shame or a loss of self-esteem) occurs when someone is unable to live up to expectations. Accordingly, most people will refrain from showing anger or displeasure and will seek to control their emotions and maintain a sense of social propriety. *Amor-propio* is the equivalent of self-respect and pride and actually reinforces the concept of *hiya*. The Filipinos also differentiate between inner self, *loob*, and outer self, *mukha*, also known as "face."

Education is valued as the main method for achieving upward economic and social mobility. The literacy rate in the Philippines is about 90 percent. The long U.S. influence has ensured that Filipinos have been exposed to Western ideas and Western goods. Further, numerous Filipinos have migrated to the United States, as well as to other countries, thereby increasing their general exposure to different cultures. Filipinos tend to be materialistic, although culturally they claim not to be, and have respect for visible wealth such as expensive watches and cars.

The Filipino culture values machismo. Nonetheless, women are considered equal to men in most situations. Filipino women, called

Filipinas, hold prominent positions in the government and the private sector. Women are employed in professional occupations as well as in factories. Women are still the primary caregivers in the home. Since the Spanish period, women have retained control of family finances. Mistresses remain a common part of the culture.

Filipinos tend to smile often in a wide variety of situations. A smile is used in several emotional circumstances, including to cover up discomfort, sadness, or nervousness. Smiles are a very important part of the culture and should be used liberally by foreigners. Filipinos rarely frown. Filipinos enjoy telling jokes and appreciate a good sense of humor. Filipinos will often make jokes at each other's expense, and everyone accepts being the target of such jokes from time to time. Foreigners should, of course, avoid such personal jabs, and concentrate on telling more neutral and objective jokes. It is also best to stay away from political and religious jokes.

Work Schedule

Most businesses and government offices are open from 9:00 A.M. to 5:00 P.M., Monday through Friday, with a break for lunch between noon and 2:00 P.M. Some private offices are open on Saturdays from 9:00 A.M. to noon, while others are open longer during the weekdays. Small businesses are often open from 9:00 or 9:30 A.M. to 7:00 or 8:00 P.M. Banks are open Monday through Friday from 9:00 A.M. to 4:00 P.M. Department stores are usually open from 9:00 or 9:30 A.M. to 7:00 or 8:00 P.M. daily. One night a week most stores are open until 10:00 P.M.; some stores close earlier on Sunday.

Making Contacts

Filipinos are less formal and more flexible than other Asians. In general, Filipinos are accustomed to interacting with Westerners, particularly Americans, making the country a relatively easy place for Westerners to conduct business. Nevertheless, introductions remain an important part of doing business. Unless you represent a large, well-known multinational firm, it is best to get an introduction from someone, such as a local partner, representative, lawyer, consultant, accountant, or banker. Filipinos are very impressed by titles and respect protocol. When selecting a local partner or representative, it is important to verify his or her credibility by ensuring that he or she has the "correct" political connections and by researching his or her existing clients and track record.

The American Chamber of Commerce (AmCham) of the Philippines with three locations in the Philippines, and the Philippine American Chamber of Commerce in New York are good resources. These offices have been operating since 1902 and 1920, respectively, and have years of extensive experience promoting trade, investment, and general business relations between the two countries. The U.S. Foreign Commercial Service (FCS) can provide market analyses as well as help you to identify agents and distributors (for a fee). The AmCham and the FCS publish a *Guide for U.S. Business* that contains addresses and general resources. The American Desk at the Philippine Board of Investments assists in promoting and facilitating U.S. investment in the Philippines. The Makati Business Club, formed in the early 1980s, supports growth and opportunities for Philippine companies. It also can aid foreigners in developing business relationships, provide firms with statistical information, and function as a forum for organizing business opinions.

To encourage foreign trade, the Philippine government has established ten industrial estates and parks (IE/Ps), four export processing zones (EPZ), and five special development programs (SDPs) throughout the Philippines. Each center provides a variety of incentives, including tax credits, foreign investment guarantees, and simplified procedures. The industrial parks are located at First Cavite and Gateway Business in Cavite; Carmelray, Laguna Technopark, Laguna International Industrial, and Light Industry and Science in the Laguna Province; Luisita Industrial in Tarlac; First Bulacan in Bulacan; Tabangao in Batangas City; and Leyte in

Isabel. The EPZs are located in Bataan, Cavite, Baguio City, and Mactan. The SDPs are the CALABARZON project, Samar Island SDP, Panay-Negros Agro-Industrial, South Cotabato–General Santos City Area, and Iligan-Cagayan de Oro.

Meeting People

Appointments should be made ahead of your arrival in the Philippines. Punctuality by foreigners is appreciated, although Filipinos are traditionally late for every appointment, business and personal. It is becoming less common to be late, particularly for business appointments with senior professionals. Nevertheless, the common Asian excuse of traffic will be accepted. Meetings should generally be scheduled in the morning, as Filipinos tend to go out for long lunches and often lapse into lethargy in the afternoons due to the weather. The first meeting should be viewed as a courtesy visit.

People greet each other with a handshake and a big warm smile. Business cards are exchanged during the first meeting. Filipinos respect authority and will be impressed by titles and positions. Filipinos will make every attempt to match people by title and responsibility level. People are referred to by their occupation, for example, "Dr. Santos" or "Attorney Santos." In other situations where the title is unknown or not applicable, use of "Mr." "Ms.," or "Mrs." is appropriate. In the initial meetings, use a formal title and a surname. Filipinos commonly use first names, but you should wait until you have been invited to do so.

Most secretaries are women. Note that secretaries for executive staff can be well informed about office politics and power situations. Further, they often screen telephone calls. Always be very courteous when dealing with secretaries, but do not shower them with excess attention. There are also a number of women in professional positions. Refrain from making an assumption about a woman's role in her company.

There is a variety of body language in the Filipino culture. Filipinos often greet each other with slightly raised eyebrows or a small nod of the head as if to signal recognition. If this body language is accompanied by a smile, it is a friendly hello. A frown would signify a challenge. Filipinos consider staring rude. Standing with your hands on your hips is interpreted as anger or a challenge. Do not point at someone or beckon with just your index finger. Use your whole hand with your palm facing down and fingers pointing away, but moving toward you in a scratching motion. Filipinos also point by shifting their eyes in the relevant direction or by pouting their mouth in the indicated direction. In comparison to people in other Asian cultures, the Filipinos tend to be more physical and may extend a pat on the back. It is best not to initiate such gestures. Physical contact in public may exist between people of the same sex, but never with someone of the opposite sex.

Meetings are always preceded by small talk in an effort to build a relationship. Refrain from discussing any controversial subjects. Many Filipinos have traveled to the United States to visit relatives and friends and often enjoying chatting about their experiences. Early on in the meeting, you should generally state your objectives for interacting with the company. Be careful not to appear demanding. Filipinos will want to know why you are there and your overall purpose. Wherever possible, identify the benefits your company can offer to the Filipino firm. Gifts are customarily presented at the first meeting. It is acceptable to offer a small gift with your corporate logo, such as a nice pen, or a sample product.

Corporate Structure

Many Filipino companies are run by members of a few key ruling families. The corporate structure is usually similar to the American corporate system. The most senior person is usually the president. After that in descending order is the executive vice-president, the senior vice-president, the first vice-president, the vice-president, the assistant vice-president, the senior manager, the manager, and the assistant manager. Foreigners should target at least the group or division heads, who are usually senior vice-presidents or vice-presidents, and who usually have decision-making authority. Titles can be misleading; only the senior-most people have authority and responsibility. Junior staff people usually work longer hours than their superiors, taking fewer breaks and shorter lunches, although most leave the office by 6 P.M.

The relationship values described earlier also apply in the business context. For example, a person who repeatedly utilizes the personal network relationships of another colleague to accomplish work or to find employment has obligated himself, creating *utang na loob*, or inner debt, and is obligated to repay the debt at some point, although not necessarily immediately. Many people in Western cultures also feel obligated to repay favors, but not with the Filipino's degree of concern for keeping the scale of obligation in balance over the long term. *Suki* relationships are commonly established when a buyer, over time, patronizes the same supplier in exchange for special treatment, such as reduced prices or better credit terms.

Negotiation

Developing trust takes time. Filipinos are more likely to trust you early on if you come with a favorable and credible introduction. But they are also willing to spend a great deal of time in developing personal relationships. The Filipino expression *pakikisama*, loosely translated as smooth interpersonal relations, is both a value and a goal. Getting along with someone requires time and effort, and achieving *pakikisama* may even take precedence over accomplishing a specific task.

Overall, time in the Philippines is very relaxed. The Spanish-influenced *manana*, which means "tomorrow," culture pervades all public- and private-sector businesses, regardless of size. *Manana* must be built into every aspect of doing business in the Philippines, from initiating contacts and developing relationships to negotiating terms and implementing schedules. Within reason, most Filipinos will meet their deadlines, although their work schedule more closely reflects the *manana* concept. For example, if a project deadline is two weeks away, most Filipinos will begin work two to three days before the end of the deadline. Foreigners should build this *manana* approach to life into their time schedules when dealing with Filipinos. Never disclose the actual deadline that you must have. Instead, set earlier and mini-deadlines, to allow for several lapses.

Decision-making tends to be concentrated in the hands of one or more key senior people and can occur quickly or slowly depending on the level of your counterpart and the size of the deal. Be sure that you are dealing with the correct level for decision-making because prominent-sounding titles are abundant and can be misleading. Group decision-making and consensus building are not always widespread, particularly in family-run enterprises, although these are gradually developing. If a decision process appears to be moving slowly, you may want to consider asking a mutual acquaintance to intervene. In many instances, decisions are reviewed and discussed by key people in informal surroundings or over a meal, so that there are no surprises in a formal negotiation. Filipinos want to know all of the details about relevant issues, as well as which individuals support specific positions, before negotiations begin. The "who" can be a critical part of the decision-making. Many Filipinos believe in fate and hold to the idea that "if a deal is meant to be, then it will." This concept of *Bahala na*, letting God take of it, can also be used as a way to avoid making hard decisions.

The Filipino "Yes" can mean a variety of things, including "Yes, I understand," "Yes, I agree," "If you say so," and even, "Yes, I hope I am unenthusiastic enough for you to understand that I really mean no." You should confirm a response several times.

Once a decision is made, implementation often takes a long time. After a senior person makes a decision, the subsequent documentation process is a rubber-stamp process. However, the bureaucracy is slow and inefficient, particularly in the public sector, as numerous signatures and documented approvals are required after a decision has been made.

Filipinos are nonconfrontational, although not so reticent as the Japanese. Common examples of ways that Filipinos say "No" are "I would like to, but I can't," "I would like to, but it is very difficult," and "I will try, and will let you know." In the last case, Filipinos will probably not let you know in the hopes that the issue will just fade away. Filipinos do not like to deliver bad news and will often just simply say nothing. Maintaining honor and face are important to Filipinos. The earlier mentioned concepts of *hiya* and *amor-propio* affect business; Filipinos may not ask questions even if they do not understand for fear of shaming themselves and losing respect. Intermediaries may be used to bring up matters that a Filipino may be embarrassed (*hiya*) to address. Junior-level Filipinos may wait for explicit directions from senior people before undertaking a task to ensure that they are performing the job correctly and to avoid making mistakes and losing face.

Filipinos will rarely admit when they have made a mistake and will rarely take blame; they dislike admitting failure. Filipinos are often quick to blame someone else. However, if something goes well, everyone will attempt to take credit. This is important to recognize when evaluating companies' and people's credentials. Filipinos will often overstate their position, authority, and responsibility level.

Never visibly show your anger or cause embarrassment to your counterpart. Use your local representative or partner to monitor progress and problems. If you must criticize, do so gently and indirectly, and do not make it personal. Shouting at a subordinate will reflect poorly on you. If possible, be sure to end with some statement of concern for the person's family and well-being. Saving face is important.

Filipinos are patient negotiators and enjoy making flowery arguments. They tend to make greater concessions as time passes. Try not to accept the first offer. Legal contracts in the Philippines are detailed and are honored by businesspeople.

Conducting Business in a Social Setting

Dining and Drinking

Filipinos enjoy developing relationships. Business socializing is very important to them. Business breakfasts are common and often take place in hotel coffee shops. Some regulars actually have established tables and "hold court" by receiving business visitors. These are power breakfasts where strong alliances are developed and business deals can be cemented. The breakfast meeting usually begins with gossip and light banter. Politicians also engage in similar "breakfast gatherings."

Business lunches are considered casual business meetings. Business dinners or cocktails are considered more intimate and are reserved for a more mature stage in a developing relationship. It is common to have a drink at the bar before sitting at the dinner table. Be careful not to drink excessively because you will cause everyone embarrassment. A dinner invitation is only accepted by a Filipino if he or she feels comfortable with you. On the social side, Filipinos continue to view it as socially acceptable to be late for dinner appointments. A guest who is punctual is considered overeager. Foreigners should try to be about twenty or thirty minutes late if they are the guest, but should be punctual if they are the host. If possible, ask your local associate for the appropriate time delay. Singalong bars are becoming popular in the Philippines; your singing skill is less important than your willing participation. Whoever extends an invitation pays for the meal.

Visiting a Home

You are doing well if a Filipino invites you to his or her home; this usually indicates acceptance. However, Filipinos will not extend an invitation unless they are comfortable with their living conditions. Punctuality can be considered rude. Arrive at least fifteen minutes after the designated time. Filipinos are very generous hosts and will go to great lengths to extend their hospitality.

It is appropriate to take flowers, a cake, a bottle of wine or scotch, or whatever your counterpart likes to drink. A hearty appetite is viewed as a compliment to the cook. Your willingness to try new foods will gain you instant acceptance, although you should feel comfortable declining something if you really do not want to try it. You should leave a small portion of food on your plate to indicate that you are finished.

Gift Giving

Although bribery, called *lagay* locally, is technically illegal, it is a normal part of many business interactions, particularly those with the government; bribery is rampant in local and regional governments. In many situations, kickbacks are already built into the contract price, often representing 5–10 percent of the value of the contract. Never give cash; this is considered an insult. Further, do not try to manage this aspect of business yourself. Ask your local partner or representative to deal with the bribery problem. Fortunately, graft is decreasing in the Philippines.

In normal business interactions, it is appropriate to give something before and after the signing of a contract; the after-signing gift should be more expensive. For example, if you invited someone to lunch during negotiations, a dinner invitation to an expensive restaurant or club after closing the deal is appropriate. Other appropriate gifts would be crystal or an item from an upscale internationally recognized store. Be sure that the item has significance, quality, and value. This is not considered a *lagay*, as described above. Prior to the signing, appropriate gestures could include nice lunches, dinners, or a local weekend vacation disguised as a working trip. In order to avoid entering into a unwanted obligation, most Philippine companies will not accept a gesture of this magnitude unless they are comfortable with you and feel that the deal will be completed.

On a personal level, it is appropriate to present gifts at Christmas to colleagues and employees as well as to people with whom you have regular dealings. Small gifts such as company products or calendars are acceptable. Gifts are never opened in front of the giver or in public. To open a gift in public indicates a materialistic nature and may cause embarrassment to all parties.

Dress Code

For men, suits are appropriate for many business situations. Most Filipino men wear the traditional open-necked shirt called a *barong tagalog*, which is heavily embroidered and made of pineapple fiber, *jusi*. An expensive *barong tagalog* is standard business attire for locals. In fact, Western ambassadors often wear the shirt when meeting with the Philippine president. Open-necked white shirts or business shirts with ties are also acceptable. If you decide to dress with local flair, a *barong tagalog* can be purchased in the Philippines. Be sure to purchase one that is heavily embroidered and expensive. The *barong tagalog* is even suitable for formal dinner occasions in place of a suit and tie.

Businesswomen tend to be more fashionably dressed. Suits and dresses in bright colors are more appropriate than dark somber colors. Women do not wear trousers for business appointments. Modesty is always expected and appreciated.

Useful Phrases

The official languages are Filipino, which is based on Tagalog and is used more widely, and English. Most people refer to Filipino as Tagalog. About eighty-seven languages and dialects are spoken throughout the islands. Eight of the languages belong to the Malay-Polynesian language family. Most Filipinos are fluent in English, so there is little need for translation in normal business and social encounters. Many people speak Taglish, a mixture of Tagalog and English. Spanish and Chinese are spoken in parts of the country. The most important Tagalog phrase is *Mabuhay*, which means "welcome" or "greetings," and can be used as a toast. The following list includes phrases and indications of their pronunciation.

Hello	*Kha-moose-tah*
Good morning	*Ma-gan-dang oo-maga, po*
Good afternoon	*Ma-gan-dang hap-pon, po*
Good evening	*Ma-gan-dang ga-bee, po*
How are you?	*Kha-moose-tah kha-yo*
Please do this	*Pa-kee-gawa nyo lang ito*
Thank you	*Sah-la-mat ho*
You are welcome	*Welcome, or Wala pong anuman*
Excuse me	*Excuse me, or Mah-kee-ra-an po* (Excuse me, may I pass)
I am sorry	I am sorry, or *Pa-sen-see-ya na po kha-yo*
My name is ———	*Ang pang-a-lan ko I* ———
I work for ———	*A-ko I sa* ———
Here is my business card	*Ee-toh ang tar-he-ta* (or business card) *ko.*
I am pleased to meet you	*Ee-kin-a-gaga-lak kong ma-kee-lala kha-yo*
Please accept this small gift	*Tang-gapin nyo po ee-toh*
May we prosper together	*Sa-nigh ma-ging ma-un-lad ta-yong par-ray-ho*
I understand	*Na-ee-in-teen-dee-han ko*
No, I do not understand	*Hin-dee ko na-ee-in-teen-dee-han*
Please wait a minute	*San-da-lee lang po*
Where is the bathroom?	*Na-san ang toy-let?*
Good-bye	*Pa-a-lam or adios*
Cheers	*Ma-boo-hi*

Major National Holidays

January 1	New Year's Day (Bagong Taon)
Thursday before Easter	Maundy Thursday (Huwebes Santo)
April*	Good Friday (Viyernes Santo)
April*	Easter (Pasko ng Pagkabuhay)
April 9	Bataan and Corregidor Day (also known as Heroism Day)
May 1	Labor Day
June 12	Independence Day

Last Sunday in August	National Heroes Day
November 1	All Saints' Day (Todo los Santos)
November 30	Bonifacio Day
December 25	Christmas (Pasko)
December 30	Rizal Day

*These holidays are observed on the first Friday and first Sunday after the paschal full moon and change from year to year.

General Facts

Climate: The tropical climate is hot and humid throughout the year. The dry cool season begins in December and lasts until February, with temperatures ranging from 70F (21C) to 88F (31C). March through May is the hot summer period, when the temperatures range from 72F (22C) to 93F (34C). The heavy monsoon and typhoon season begins in June and lasts until November, with temperatures ranging from 75F (24C) to 91F (33C).

Currency: The Philippine currency is the *peso* (abbreviated P), and is divided into 100 *centavos*.

Dates: Dates are written in the order of month, day, and year. For example, August 21, 1995, will be 8/21/95.

Electricity: The voltage is 220, 60 (Hz) cycles.

Entry Requirements: For American, British, Canadian, French, and German citizens, a valid passport is required; for stays over seven days a visa is also required.

Time: The Philippines has one time zone, which is eight hours ahead of Greenwich Mean Time and thirteen hours ahead of U.S. Eastern Standard Time (twelve hours in Daylight Savings Time).

Tipping: Due to the extensive U.S. influence, tipping is common and expected throughout the Philippines. In moderately priced restaurants a small tip is expected even if a service charge is included. In more expensive restaurants, a tip of 15 percent of the total bill is appropriate. In the nicer restaurants, singers who come by

your table should get about P 20 and twice as much if they stay
at your request. Hotel concierges expect at least P 20 to P 30.
Doormen and porters usually receive about P 10 to P 20. Taxi drivers usually receive about 10 percent or a fare amount rounded to
the nearest P 5 or P 10.

Transportation: Various modes of transportation to and from the airport are available, including taxis, hotel minibuses, and limousines.
Always allow for additional travel time, especially during rush-hour
traffic. At the Manila airport, taxis are not allowed in the arrival
area. The most reliable system is to locate the NAIA Limousine
Service booth, which charges a high rate for service to Manila. You
can also go to the departure level and pick up a yellow cab that is
depositing passengers. Taxi drivers may be reluctant if they identify
patrolmen. In general, taxis can be hailed at any street corner or at
hotels. Whenever using a taxi in the Philippines, always insist on
using the meter or agreeing to a fixed price prior to entering a taxi.
Air-conditioned taxis are at least 50 percent more expensive. For
hotel minibuses and shuttles, arrange for a pickup when you reserve
a room prior to arrival. Hotels will usually charge a premium on your
hotel bill for this convenience.

It is not advisable to drive in Manila due to the heavy traffic.
First-time visitors to the Philippines are advised to rent a car and
driver. Hotels can assist you with this upon arrival. The subway,
known as the Metro Rail or Light Rail Transit, is an easy, efficient,
and cheap form of transportation within Manila. Maps are available
at tourist offices and stations. Buses and "jeepneys" (minibuses) are
available, but less practical due to traffic. The jeepneys are a variation of the military jeeps left over after the war.

Helpful Telephone Numbers

Pay telephones are available throughout the Philippines. Connections can be weak or have crossed lines. Local calls usually require
three 25-*centavo* coins. Wait for the dialtone before dialing. Hotel

telephones are more expensive and only a few have international dialing capabilities. It is usually cheaper to use a calling or credit card than to go through the hotel operator. Philippine telephone numbers can have either six or seven digits. The country code for the Philippines is (63). The major city codes are: Manila (2); Cebu (32); and Davao (35).

Hospitals, Doctors, and Dentists:

Makati Medical Center
2 Amorsolo Street
Makati, Metro Manila
Tel.: (2) 815-9911

Manila Medical Center
1122 General Luna Street
Ermita, Manila
Tel.: (2) 591-661

Manila Doctors Hospital
667 U.N. Avenue
Ermita, Manila
Tel.: (2) 503-011

SOS Manila
Adamson Centre, 6th Floor
121 Alfaro Street
Salcedo Village
Makati, Metro Manila 1200

United Dental Services
United Doctors Medical Center
Welcome Rotonda Espana
Quezon City
Tel.: (2) 712-3655

In Manila, some major hotels have doctors and dentists on the premises:

Century Park Sheraton
Tel.: (2) 522-1011
Manila Midtown
Tel.: (2) 573-911
Manila Peninsula
Tel.: (2) 819-3456
Westin Philippine Plaza
Tel.: (2) 832-0701

Police: Dial (2) 599-011 or 594-344; for the Public Information Desk, dial (2) 702-593.

Useful Addresses

In the Philippines:

American Chamber of Commerce of the Philippines, Inc.
Corinthian Plaza, 2d Floor
Paseo de Roxas
Makati, Metro Manila 1299
Tel.: (2) 818-7911 / 6955

Cebu Chapter
WDC Building, Room 104
Osmena Blvd.
Cebu City 6000
Tel.: (32) 99-312 / 70-469

Davao Chapter
Aldevinco Building, Room 507
C. M. Recto Street
Davao City 8000
Tel.: (82) 79-365

Asian Development Bank
6 ADB Avenue
1501 Mandaluyong
(P.O. Box 789) Manila
Tel.: (2) 632-4444

Canadian Chamber of
Commerce
Interbank Building
Ground Floor
Paseo de Roxas
Makati, Metro Manila
Tel.: (2) 812-8568

Cebu Chamber of Commerce
and Industry
WDC Building, Room 104
Osmena Blvd.
Cebu City 6000
Tel.: (32) 99-312 / 99-689 / 312

Department of Trade
and Industry
4/F Board of Investments
Building
385 Sen. Gil J. Puyat Avenue
Makati, Metro Manila
Tel.: (2) 818-4561

WDC Building, Room 204
Osmena Blvd.
Cebu City 6000
Tel.: (32) 224-395

Department of Trade and
Industry, Board of
Investments, American Desk
385 Sen. Gil J. Puyat Avenue
Makati, Metro Manila
Tel.: (2) 818-1831 / 867-895 /
868-403

Department of Trade and
Industry, Board of Investments,
Investment and Marketing
Department
385 Sen. Gil J. Puyat Avenue
Makati, Metro Manila
Tel.: (2) 868-403 / 867-895 /
875-602

European Chamber of
Commerce of the Philippines
King's Court II Building
5th Floor
2129 Pasong Tamo Street, 1200
Makati, Metro Manila
Tel.: (2) 854-747 / 871-763

Makati Business Club
Princess Building, 2d Floor
104 Esteban Street,
Legaspi Village
Makati, Metro Manila
Tel.: (2) 816-2658 / 2660

Philippine Chamber of
Commerce and Industry
Secretariat Building, East Wing
Ground Floor
CCP Complex
Roxas Blvd.
Manila
Tel.: (2) 832-0309

Philippine–U.S. Business Council
Corner Pasig Blvd.
5 E. Rodriguez Jr. Avenue
Pasig, Metro Manila
Tel.: (2) 693-8576

U.S.–ASEAN Council
Thomas Jefferson Building
395 Sen. Gil J. Puyat Avenue
(Buendia Avenue Extension)
Makati, Metro Manila
Tel.: (2) 818-4336

Embassies and Consulates

American Embassy
1201 Roxas Blvd.
Ermita, Manila 1000
Tel.: (2) 521-7116

American Consulate
PCI Bank Building, 3d Floor
Gorordo Avenue
Lahug, Cebu City 6000
Tel.: (32) 311-261

British Embassy
LV Locsin Building
15th–17th Floors
6752 Ayala Avenue
Makati, Metro Manila
Tel.: (2) 816-7116

Canadian Embassy
Allied Bank Center
9th Floor
6754 Ayala Avenue
Makati, Metro Manila
Tel.: (2) 810-8861

French Embassy
Salustiana Dee Ty Tower
7th Floor
Corner Perea Street
104 Pasco de Roxas
Makati, Metro Manila
Tel.: (2) 810-7651

German Embassy
Solidbank Building
777 Paseo de Roxas
Makati, Metro Manila
Tel.: (2) 864-900

In Canada:

Embassy of the Philippines
130 Albert Street, Suite 606
Ottawa, Ontario K1P 564
Tel.: (613) 233-1121

Philippine Consulate
Rogers Building, Suite 301–308
470 Granville Street
Vancouver, B.C. V6C 1V5
Tel.: (604) 685-7645

Philippines Trade Office of the Consulate
60 Bloor Street, West, Suite 409
Toronto, Ontario M4W 3B8
Tel.: (416) 967-1788

In France:

Embassy of the Philippines
4 Hameau de Boullainvilliers
75016 Paris
Tel.: (1) 4414-5700

In Germany:

Embassy of the Philippines
Argelanderstrasse 1
53115 Bonn
Tel.: (228) 267-990

In the United Kingdom:

Embassy of the Philippines
9A Palace Green
London W8 4QE
Tel.: (71) 937-1609

Office of the Commercial Counsellor
1A Cumberland House
Kensington Court
London W85 NXE
Tel.: (71) 937-1898

In the United States:

Embassy of the Philippines
1600 Massachusetts Ave., N.W.
Washington, DC 20036
Tel.: (202) 467-9300
Trade Office: 467-9419

Philippine Consulates
556 Fifth Avenue
New York, NY 10036
Tel.: (212) 764-1330
Trade Office: 575-7925

30 North Michigan Avenue
Suite 2100
Chicago, IL 60602
Tel.: (312) 332-6458

3660 Wilshire Blvd., Suite 900
Los Angeles, CA 90010
Tel.: (213) 387-5321
Trade Office: 383-9475

445 Sutter Street, 6th Floor
San Francisco, CA 94108
Tel.: (415) 433-6666

2433 Pali Highway
Honolulu, HI 96817
Tel.: (808) 595-6316

Filipino Chamber of Commerce of Hawaii
735 Bishop Street, Suite 301
Honolulu, HI 96813
Tel.: (808) 533-0322

Philippine American Chamber of Commerce, Inc.
711 Third Avenue, Suite 1702
New York, NY 10017
Tel.: (212) 972-9326

Philippine American Chamber of Commerce
742 North Vine Street
Los Angeles, CA 90038
Tel.: (213) 962-8590

U.S. Department of Commerce
International Trade
Administration
Philippines Desk, Room 2036
14th & Constitution Avenues, N.W.
Washington, DC 20230
Tel.: (202) 482-4958

10   Singapore ———

Geography

Singapore is located at the southern tip of the Malaysian Peninsula and is linked to Malaysia by a causeway over the Johor Strait. Singapore, a city-state, consists of one main island and about fifty-nine islets. The main island of Singapore is about twenty-six miles (forty-two kilometers) long and fourteen miles (twenty-three kilometers) wide and is smaller than New York City. The topography is varied. There are small hills in the center of the island, the west has low

300

but steep ridges, and the east is generally flat with streams flowing
into the sea.

History

Traders became familiar with the island of Singapore in the third
century A.D. because they passed it on the shortest route between
India and China. By the seventh century, the Sumatran-based Srivijaya Empire had established the first maritime state in the
Malaysian archipelago. This empire ruled Sumatra, Java, and the
Malay Peninsula including Singapore, which was the site of a mi-
nor port. As a result of commerce involving Chinese, Indian, Arab,
Thai, Malay, and Javanese traders, the Malay archipelago became a
mix of cultures and languages. In 1299 a trading city was founded
on Singapore and named Singapura, which means "Lion City," by
a ruler after he sighted a strange beast that he assumed to be a lion.
Over the next three centuries Singapura was controlled by various
Asian rulers. In 1511 the Portuguese captured Malacca, forcing the
Malaccan ruler to flee south and form a new sultanate in Johore, of
which Singapura became a part. In 1613 the Portuguese burned
down the trading post at Singapura and the island was largely abandoned for the next two centuries. Sumatra became the major trading post in the area.

   In 1818 a Malay official from the Johore sultanate settled on the
island with his followers. This group shared the island with indigenous tribes and Chinese planters. A year later Sir Thomas Stamford
Raffles, a young British official of the East India Company, secured
permission from the Malay rulers to establish a trading post on the
island. He named the island after its ancient name of Singapura.
Soon, traders, merchants, and settlers from Asia, the Middle East,
and Europe were frequenting the island to profit from lucrative opportunities there, eventually making Singapore one of the most important trading centers in Asia. As a result of the mix of ethnic
groups, the island society was plagued by frequent conflicts. Never-

theless, the combination of ethnicities created a cosmopolitan environment. Many of the men who settled in Singapore to pursue their fortunes were unmarried. Accordingly, a significant number of mixed marriages occurred over the decades, resulting in an even more heterogeneous mix.

Singapore attracted numerous Chinese males, who often married the local Malay women, creating as offspring the Straits-born Chinese, also known as Baba Chinese. By the 1820s, the most numerous of Singapore's ethnic groups were the Chinese. Some had come from neighboring Malacca, others from the Chinese provinces of Guangdong and Fujian, and others from elsewhere. As a result, the Chinese community itself consisted of diverse groups with different languages and cultures.

By 1860, Indians replaced the Malays as the second largest ethnic group in Singapore. Most came as traders and merchants hoping to make their fortunes and some were very successful. Others were brought by the British as prisoners when Singapore served as a major detention center. After finishing their sentences, many prisoners remained in Singapore. Despite their individual successes, the Singaporean Indian community never became as well organized as the Chinese community, commercially or politically.

In 1826 the British incorporated the Straight Settlements, the trading ports along the Straits of Malacca and Johor including Singapore, Penang, and Malacca, as well as some smaller trading posts, into an administrative unit. In 1867 the British made the Straights Settlements a crown colony. In 1869, after the Suez Canal was opened, the Straight of Malacca became the preferred shipping route to east Asia. This event, combined with the expansion of colonialism and the continuing influence of the British in the Malay Peninsula, enhanced Singapore's position as a premier trading center. In order to support the burgeoning trade business, the island's infrastructure, banking, and communications were improved.

In the 1920s Singapore's Chinese community was wooed by China's rulers to invest heavily in China and to support mainland China. Further, at the instigation of China's ruler, Mandarin became the language taught in all Singaporean Chinese schools. Throughout the 1930s Chinese nationalism and anti-Japanese sentiment spread throughout Singapore, due in large part to the war between China and Japan.

In December 1941 the Japanese began to bomb Singapore. Local Chinese and members of other ethnic communities volunteered to help the British as rumors regarding Japanese harsh treatment of Malay Chinese spread throughout Singapore. On February 15, 1942, Singapore surrendered to the Japanese. It remained in Japanese hands until the end of the war in 1945. The Japanese renamed Singapore *Shonan*, which means "Light of the South." Indians and Malays were pressured to join the Japanese army. The Singaporean Chinese population suffered greatly during the occupation because the Japanese singled them out for retribution because of the support they had provided China in its efforts against Japan. The economy and social life were severely disrupted as the Japanese attempted to spread Japanese culture and language throughout Singapore. After the war, Singaporeans openly welcomed the return of the British to the island.

In September 1945 Singapore became the headquarters of the British Military Administration for Southeast Asia. Within a few years, the British were successful in restoring much of the infrastructure, trade, and social services that characterized Singapore before the war. The British did not include Singapore in the Malayan Union which was created in 1946 and incorporated all of the Malay states, Penang, and Malacca. However, Singapore and the Malayan Union continued to share a common currency and a basic infrastructure. Opposition by locals to the separation of Malaya (as the Peninsula was then known) and Singapore sparked the formation of Singapore's first indigenous political party, the Malayan Democratic Union, which advocated the inclusion of Singapore in an independent Malaya within the Commonwealth of Nations. Over the next few years, several political parties ranging from conservative to communist continued to support combining Singapore with the Malayan Union.

The People's Action party (PAP) was formed in 1954 in Singapore by a group of middle-class, British-educated Chinese. It sought to gain a following among the poor and non-English-speaking masses. Its mission was to promote a merger with the Malayan Union and to end colonialism. Beginning in 1956 and lasting until 1958, talks were held in London to discuss the future of Singapore. As a result of these talks, Singapore was granted internal self-government. The British retained control of the island's defense and foreign affairs. PAP was elected to power in the 1959 elections by a wide margin and Lee Kuan Yew became prime minister. On September 16, 1963, Singapore merged with Malaya and the former British Borneo territories of Sabah and Sarawak to form an independent Malaysia. However, Malaysian leaders were suspicious that ethnic Chinese, including members of PAP, intended to gradually take control of Malaysia. As a result, the Malaysian parliament unanimously voted to separate from Singapore. After two years of political tension and violence, as well as external pressure from Indonesia, Singapore was forced to separate from Malaysia and became an independent nation on August 9, 1965.

The government of Singapore turned its attention to building a strong and independent state. The government focused on building a multiracial and multilingual society that was united by a "Singaporean identity." Malay, Chinese, English, and Tamil remained the official languages. Further, the government sought to attract foreign capital by providing incentives for export industries, improving labor laws, and providing tax relief. As a result, foreign investment increased substantially, eventually making Singapore the regional center for global companies. PAP's general policies have focused on economic development as well as government management of the economy and society. Relations with Indonesia and Malaysia improved by the early 1980s and trade now provides a vital link between all three countries.

PAP has won every election since 1959, receiving all or almost all the seats in parliament. Lee Kuan Yew was prime minister from

1959 to 1990, providing Singapore with political stability and policy continuity. While elections have been honest, critics charge that the government has stifled the formation of effective opposition parties. The PAP has generally been intolerant of criticism and has jailed many dissidents.

In 1990 Lee stepped down and his deputy Goh Chok Tong, also from PAP, was sworn in as the nation's second prime minister since independence. Lee, however, remains in the cabinet as a senior minister and continues to exercise control over policy. The younger generation has demanded greater participation in the political process. The 1991 and 1992 elections were an attempt by Goh to introduce more openness in government. Still, the PAP won overwhelming majorities, reconfirming their dominance of Singaporean politics.

Political Structure

Singapore has a parliamentary system of government with a constitution based on the British model. The legislative body is a unicameral parliament with eighty-one members who are elected by the public for a five-year term and represent various territorial constituencies and six members nominated by the president for a two-year term, on the recommendation of a special parliamentary committee. A recent 1992 amendment strengthened the presidency. The president, elected directly by the electorate, has broad powers, including custodial powers over the country's reserves and the right to make key appointments in the judiciary and civil service. The president is assisted by a five-member advisory council consisting of two members appointed by the president, two appointed by the prime minister, and one appointed by the Public Service Commission.

The president also appoints a member of the majority party in parliament to be prime minister. Similar to the British style of government, the prime minister runs the government and effectively functions as chief executive. The prime minister selects a cabinet from the majority party in parliament. Singapore has only one level of government that serves as both the national and the local government. The judicial system has been influenced by the British system as well. The highest court is the Supreme Court. The judiciary is legally independent of the executive branch of government.

The government has been very successful in creating and maintaining an effective administration that focuses on economic policies. In general, the government since independence has been authoritarian, with a limited tolerance for opposition or dissent. This has allowed the government to focus on long-term goals and to make necessary, albeit unpopular, decisions. Over the years, the government has endorsed campaigns for improving various aspects of social life.

Economy

A premier regional financial and business services center, Singapore has an export-oriented economy that has enjoyed phenomenal success over the past three decades. Singapore is a major entrepôt for the Asia Pacific region, re-exporting more than 31 percent of total imports. A regional growth triangle is developing between Singapore, the Riau Islands of Indonesia (mainly Batam and Bintan), and the Malaysian state of Johor. Although the stages of economic development may differ, the three are expected to compliment one another.

Singapore is becoming the hub of commerce and finance for Southeast Asia. Many companies have located their regional headquarters there due to favorable tax and investment conditions, as well as the availability of an English-speaking, white-collar workforce. Singapore is currently experiencing a tight labor market with shortages at all skill and education levels.

Singapore has also become a major manufacturing center with extensive port and warehouse facilities. Major industries include electronics, petroleum refining, machinery, and shipbuilding and repairing. Singapore is focused on maintaining its strengths in high-tech and research and development as well as in banking and finance. Singapore has a well-developed infrastructure including modern communications, transportation, and utilities. Its deep-water harbor and strategic geographic location are the country's only natural resources.

People, Values, and Social Customs

The population of Singapore is about three million. Approximately 78 percent of the population are Chinese, 14 percent are Malay, 7 percent are Indian, while the remaining 1 percent are of varying ethnicities. Singapore has four official languages: Malay, English, Mandarin Chinese, and Tamil. Malay is the national language, but English is the language of administration, education, and commerce. The government has a policy requiring all citizens to be bilingual in English and one Asian tongue, preferably one of the three official languages. The English language is one of the most important unifying factors because of its neutrality as well as its being the major international language. The government strives to ensure that its people's ethnic heritage will not be lost in the process of modernization by mandating a second language. The government has also promoted Mandarin as the main Chinese language over the other Chinese dialects.

Singapore is a secular state with no state religion. The major religions are Buddhism (28 percent), Christianity (19 percent), Islam (16 percent), Taoism (13 percent), and Hinduism (5 percent), with the remainder (19 percent) following a variety of other religions. There are also small communities of Sikhs, Jains, Parsis, and Jews. The Chinese community believes in *feng shui*, which focuses on orienting houses, buildings, and anything material to repel *chi*, which is negative energy.

Singapore has been multi-racial and multi-ethnic since its second founding in the early 1800s. Between 1945 and 1965, most immigrants came from Malaysia, as there was free movement from Malaysia to Singapore during the period of British rule. Since 1965, the government of Singapore has been strict about immigration, accepting on a temporary basis only those individuals whose skills are critical to the economy. These temporary immigrants have been mainly either unskilled, low-paid workers or professionals employed by multinational corporations.

It is important to recognize that among the three main ethnic groups—Chinese, Malay, and Indian—are a variety of subgroups. Within the Chinese population, there are more than five subgroups with different dialects and different cultures. The Chinese subgroups include immigrants from China, Taiwan, and Hong Kong, as well as immigrants from other Chinese communities throughout Southeast Asia. The Straits-born Chinese, also known today as Peranakans, are descendants of early Chinese settlers and the indigenous Malay population, many of whom moved to Singapore from Malacca in the nineteenth century. Although they later intermarried with Chinese immigrants, many continue to identify more with Singapore and Malaya than with China. Some Straits-born Chinese speak English as their first language. In general, the Chinese community tends to have a high degree of social mobility and their status is determined by education and linguistic capabilities in English and Mandarin. This community has many wealthy business families.

The Malays trace their ancestors to various islands in the Indonesian archipelago and to the Malaysian Peninsula. Most Malays are Muslims. Many Malays receive minimal education and occupy the lower levels of the economic and social hierarchy. In contrast to neighboring Malaysia, where the Malay population has been targeted for special treatment, the government of Singapore has done little to help its Malay citizens move up the economic and social ladders.

The Indian groups hail from the modern states of India,

Bangladesh, Pakistan, Sri Lanka, and Myanmar (Burma), and as a consequence have widely differing physical traits, speak different languages, practice different religions, and have different cultural beliefs. More then two-thirds of the Indian immigrants are Tamil from India or from Sri Lanka. The Indian community has members in all economic and social strata.

Although Singapore is a relatively modern nation, these ethnic differences affect daily life and value systems. Nevertheless, the government has focused on creating a "Singaporean identity" through policies and educational campaigns that balance traditional and modern views. The goal is not the creation of a homogeneous population, but rather the nurturing of a multi-ethnic, multi-lingual society that shares a common sense of citizenship. The government wants to create a modernized, but not necessarily Westernized, society.

The government sponsors a variety of ethnic festivals and events. Most Singaporeans maintain their ethnic link by joining ethnically and/or religiously exclusive organizations. For example, some Chinese trade organizations are reserved for those who speak a specific Chinese dialect. Further, within the Chinese population, certain communities tend to be concentrated in specific professions and trades. It is important as you interact with Singaporeans to be conscious of their individual ethnic affiliations and how they interact with other Singaporeans. It is also important to recognize that hierarchies exist within each ethnic community based on ancestry and religion.

British colonial influence is evident in many parts of Singaporean society. Traditionally, foreigners were perceived as *gweilo*, or "foreign devils." Today it is possible for foreigners to become accepted as part of Singaporean society.

Families remain the most important aspect of social life. Singaporeans tend to live as small nuclear families. Limited housing combined with increasing family incomes have decreased the need and the desire for extended family living situations. However, family needs and obligations—whether those of the nuclear or of the extended family—come ahead of personal issues. The Chinese and Indian families tend to be more focused on long-term family obligation and loyalty than the Malays. But all people are expected to respect and obey elders.

The education system in Singapore is based on the British school system. Children spend six years at primary school, followed by four years at secondary school. Approximately one-quarter of the population continues on to a two-year junior college, and a smaller percentage goes on to university. The system stresses merit and competition. The education system embodies the spirit of the Singaporean identity; all races and language groups come together to compete for scholastic success and eventually professional opportunities.

Singaporeans place a heavy emphasis on excellence, hard work, and honesty, and consider education the tool for mobility. Education and wealth have always been a key to leadership roles and social standing in Singapore. The country is in transition from a society that focuses on traditional Asian values, particularly group well-being, to one that stresses individual success. The concept of *kiasu*, which implies being afraid of losing out or not getting the best in any situation, is also prevalent.

Singapore has the highest standard of living in Southeast Asia and one of the highest throughout all of Asia. The top level of society is occupied by elite, high-level civil servants, foreign multinational corporate managers, Singaporean professionals, and wealthy Chinese businessmen. The first two categories speak fluent English and are usually educated abroad. Chinese businessmen tend to be entrepreneurs who are less educated and operate exclusively in a Chinese setting. Their sons, however, are usually well educated, often abroad.

The role of women has gradually improved, although it varies by ethnic and religious groups. Today many more women work, even after marriage and the birth of their children. There are an increasing number of women in professional and managerial positions.

As a result of the variety of ethnic groups, it is difficult to generalize about smiling and humor. People will generally smile when they are happy, as well as when they are sad or nervous. Smiles are intended to hide the true emotion. Humor tends to be subdued. Avoid telling jokes to people you do not know. Refrain from making sexual jokes and comments, as Singaporeans believe that only inferior people engage in such talk.

Singapore has very strict laws regulating public behavior such as littering, jay-walking, smoking, spitting, and chewing gum. Failing to flush a public toilet is considered an offense, so most toilets now flush automatically. There are also strict laws forbidding drug trafficking; laws regulating gambling, weapons, and fireworks; laws monitoring pets and cruelty to animals; and laws preventing the sale of counterfeit goods. These laws are highly respected, as the punishment and fines can be severe. When in doubt about an activity, do not engage in it.

Work Schedule

Businesses are generally open on weekdays from 9:00 A.M. to 1:00 P.M. and from 2:00 P.M. to 5:00 or 5:30 P.M. Some are also open on Saturdays from 9:00 A.M. to 1:00 P.M. Government offices are open from 8:00 A.M. to 5:00 P.M. and are closed for one hour at 1:00 P.M. Government offices are open on Saturdays from 8:00 A.M. to 1:00 P.M. Banks are open from 10:00 A.M. to 3:00 P.M. on weekdays and from 9:30 to 11:30 A.M. on Saturdays. Most shops are open from 10:30 A.M. to 9:30 or 10:00 P.M. everyday.

Making Contacts

Foreign businesspeople can contact Singaporean firms directly, although introductions and referrals always add credibility. Depending on the nature of your business interests, it is possible to set up appointments within a few days of your arrival. This method is best for export and trade-related transactions, but less effective for establishing joint ventures and larger projects. In the Chinese business community, *guanxi*, or connections, remain very important.

Once you have made a commitment to doing business in Singapore, it is important to have a local representative or partner. Your country's embassy, the chamber of commerce, or the Singapore Office of Registry of Companies and Businesses can assist you in locating a local agent.

Meeting People

Punctuality by foreigners is expected, but may not always be reciprocated. Avoid scheduling meetings between noon and 2:00 P.M. because long lunches are normal. Offices or hotels are appropriate places for meetings. Singaporeans often prefer to conduct business over lunch rather than dinner. Business breakfasts are rare, although urgent meetings can be held at an upscale hotel's coffee shop. Most Singaporeans are aware of Western business practices and will be accommodating. Most of all, be polite.

Singaporeans are culturally conservative. It is best to call people by their title or "Mr." or "Mrs." and the family name. Refrain from using first names unless invited to do so. If you prefer, after establishing a good relationship with someone, you may invite him or her to use your first name. As a result of the island's many ethnic groups, names can be very confusing. In Chinese, the first word is the surname, and can be followed by one or two more names. Some Chinese adopt Western practices and switch the order of their name. Many Chinese women retain their maiden family name. The Malays do not use surnames and add *bin*, which means "son of," and *binti*, which means "daughter of," after the first name and add their father's first name at the end. Accordingly, Malay women usually keep their maiden name after marriage. Malays also use *Encik* in place of "Mr." and *Cik* for "Miss" or *Puan* for "Mrs." Many Indians in Singapore do not use their family names. They use their father's initial before their own name. Some Indians use "Mr." or "Mrs." and others may add "son of"(s/o) or "daughter of"(d/o) after their first name and before a family name. Business cards are not always reliable indicators of how a person prefers to be addressed, so it is acceptable to ask.

People greet one another with a handshake, often a light one, and a warm smile and say "Hello." This is accompanied by a slight nod of the head for older people. Singaporeans may not make direct eye contact with the person they are meeting, as it is considered a sign of disrespect. Westerners should not assume that this implies any type of dishonesty. Formal verbal greetings are exchanged, usually in English. When introducing people, say the name and title of the senior person first. In general, show respect and deference to elders.

Muslims, particularly Malay men, will bring their hands back to touch their chests after shaking hands to symbolize that the greeting comes from the heart. They are pleased when a foreigner returns the gesture. Women are not expected to follow suit. Some women do have professional and managerial positions, so be careful before you make any assumptions about a woman's role. Although not common, Indians may greet you in a traditional manner called a *namaste*, which requires placing both hands in a prayerlike position at chest level with a slight nod of the head.

Business cards are exchanged at the beginning of a meeting. Cards should be given and received using both hands. Examine your counterpart's card carefully to show respect. Never use the left hand only, as it is considered the "dirty hand." Given the high percentage of Chinese in the population, you may want to have your cards printed in Chinese on the reverse side.

In general, most Singaporeans are very polite. There are a few social rules worth noting. Do not rest your foot on your knee; showing the sole of your foot or shoes is considered disrespectful and rude. It is best not to cross your legs unless you are seated behind a desk or table. Beckoning should be done using the whole right hand with the palm facing the ground and the fingers pointing away from you, but moving toward you in a scratching motion. Avoid pointing with one finger; either point with your knuckle or use your whole hand. Refrain from physically touching anyone The head is considered the spiritual part of the body and should not be touched. Excessive compliments on a person's appearance, particularly a woman, is not appropriate.

You should engage in a few minutes of casual conversation on your first visit. Suitable topics include your trip to Singapore, your counterpart's experiences overseas, and positive remarks about the country. Refrain from mentioning political and religious topics. You may be asked questions about topics such as age, weight, and money, which you may feel are too personal. If you are uncomfortable answering, be polite and vague. Singaporeans believe that people who disclose too much personal, family, and emotional information lack self-control. You will find that most Singaporeans are anxious to discuss business quickly; the business environment and attitude is straightforward.

Corporate Structure

Most Singaporean businesspeople tend to be well-educated and articulate. The traditional firm has a managing director at the top followed by other directors and managers. In family-owned businesses, the senior person is usually the eldest male family member. Promotions are based more on merit than on connections.

There are numerous state and quasi-state companies that have been created by Singapore's ministries to provide a range of goods and services. The Economic Development Board, created in 1961, focuses on attracting investments in manufacturing and other value-added services. The Singapore Trade Development Board assists companies, local and foreign, in utilizing Singapore as a trading base primarily for warehousing and distribution.

Negotiation

Singaporeans value strong personal relationships, but this takes time to develop. In general, harmony is valued and is expected to be preserved. Loud voices and public displays of anger are frowned upon. People focus on cooperative behavior and teamwork. Although individual competition does exist, it is not at the expense of the group. This concept of public harmony requires that no one lose face during an interaction.

The Singaporeans, particularly the Chinese businesspeople, tend to be tough negotiators. Negotiations can proceed fairly rapidly. It is not uncommon for Singaporeans to try to pressure you into making concessions. Do not assume that Singaporeans who are Western-dressed, Western-educated, and speak English are completely Western in attitude. Singaporeans are conservative and take a long-term perspective.

Decision-making is usually carried out by a few key senior people. Older people may rely on their intuition, but intellectual analysis and rational decision-making is highly valued. All of the research information that you are willing to provide will be utilized.

Singaporeans do not say "No," as it is considered disrespectful, especially when dealing with superiors. Common expressions to avoid saying "No" include, "It is difficult . . ." or "I would like to, but. . . ." In addition, many Singaporeans may say a "Yes" that does not mean "Yes, I agree," but rather, "Yes, I understand." A "Yes" response accompanied by details is usually an affirmative response. Watch for signs, especially a sucking-in-air or hissing sound, which indicate discomfort or difficulty in giving a favorable response. People may say "Yes" with their mouth, but indicate their true feeling with their body language. There may be short periods of silence; these indicate serious thought, not lack of interest. Indians often indicate acknowledgment or agreement with a slight bob of the head from side to side.

Further, many people use the phrase "Isn't it," meaning "Isn't it right?" at the end of sentences. Culturally, this helps to build consensus at various stages. It also provides the Singaporean with the opportunity to state his or her opinion. Use such expressions to monitor progress and verify agreement. Singaporeans may not ask questions or indicate when they are uncertain, out of fear of losing face. Ask indirect questions to make sure everyone understands and is in agreement. Refrain from asking closed-ended yes or no questions.

Never criticize or disagree publicly with anyone, for it will cause your counterpart to lose face. Indicate your concerns discreetly, indirectly, and very politely. Do not direct your criticism at a person, as it will be considered personal. On the flip side, refrain from excessive compliments, for you may be perceived as insincere. Singaporeans tend to be modest and humble and are offended by boastful behavior.

It is important that all parties should appear to benefit from a transaction or negotiation. Contracts are detailed and are considered binding. Verbal agreements are not utilized. However, flexibility is considered instrumental in developing a successful, long-term relationship.

Conducting Business in a Social Setting

Dining and Drinking

Business lunches or dinners are common and usually occur in restaurants. It is appropriate to invite private-sector individuals to dine after a couple of interactions. When eating with Indians and Malays, use only your right hand to eat because the left hand is considered unclean. Leave a small amount on your plate or in your glass, or your host will assume that you want more and serve you accordingly. Business is often discussed over the meal. Follow your counterpart's lead.

Chinese banquets are important. For information on this and other Chinese dining practices, please refer to Chapter 3 on China.

Visiting a Home

Singaporeans rarely entertain at home for business. If you are invited to a home, be punctual. It is acceptable, but not expected, to bring a small gift. In Chinese homes, leave some food on your plate to indicate when you have had enough to eat. In traditional Muslim homes, the hostess may not join you, as women keep a low profile. Remove your shoes before entering most homes, particularly those of Malays and Indians (also remove your shoes when entering mosques and temples).

Gift Giving

There is no corruption in Singapore; the government is very strict on this issue. Never give money to government officials, even at New Year's. Only people such as servants, grocers, and deliverymen should receive the traditional red envelope with money at the Chinese New Year.

Gift giving, even in a moderate sense, is not common in business situations. Instead of giving an expensive gift to an individual, which may be misinterpreted as a bribe, it is better to present a group gift to the office. This could be either one gift that can be shared by everyone or a series of similar gifts for each individual. Token gifts, such as pens or items with a company logo, are appropriate, provided that they are not expensive. The recipient is obligated to reciprocate at a later date, so it is important to keep the value reasonable. If a gift is intended for only one person, present it in private so as to not embarrass anyone. Most Singaporeans will accept gifts reluctantly to indicate humility. You should gently insist that he or she accept your gift, adding that you are pleased or honored to present the gift. Further, they will not open a gift immediately in the presence of the giver or others to avoid appearing greedy. Gifts should be given with the right hand or with both hands, but never with just the left hand.

When giving gifts, it is important to take into account your intended recipient's ethnicity. Never give clocks or white flowers to Chinese because they are associated with death. For the Chinese, red, yellow, and pink are auspicious and happy colors. Never give a Chinese a knife, scissors, and other cutting instruments because these things symbolize the severing of a friendship. Suitable items for Chinese homes include sweets and cakes. Say that you brought them for the children. This is done to indicate that you recognize that the receiver is not greedy, allowing him or her to take the gift without losing face. Bring items in even numbers, for these are equated with good luck. However, avoid the number four which has a very negative connotation. Flowers are rarely given among the Chinese.

Malays enjoy receiving gifts and will usually reciprocate. Suitable gifts for Malay and Indian homes include sweets, fine chocolates, and souvenirs from your home country. For Malays, do not give gifts containing pork or alcohol. Refrain from gifts related to unclothed people or dogs, even as statues or in calendars. For Indians, avoid the colors white and black. Indians tend to prefer brighter colors such as red, yellow, and green. Money gifts can be given for weddings and should be in odd amounts, particularly ending in 1, such as 51 and 101. Never give frangipani, a white flower used in funerals.

For additional information, please refer to the chapters on China, Taiwan, Hong Kong, Malaysia, India, and Sri Lanka.

Dress Code

Due to the hot weather, business dress tends to be informal. Men usually wear a shirt and tie without a suit jacket. For women, a jacket and skirt or professional dress is most appropriate for daytime appointments. In the evenings, men often wear short-sleeved shirts and slacks, which are appropriate almost everywhere except in the most expensive restaurants. In these restaurants, long-sleeve shirts and ties are appropriate. On some occasions, jackets may be required for cocktail parties. Safari suits are rarely acceptable. Women should wear slacks only on casual occasions. Do not wear black, white, or navy blue to a party or wedding because these are traditional funeral colors.

Useful Phrases

There are four official languages: English, Mandarin Chinese, Malay, and Tamil. English is the most widely used language in business. Children are required to learn English as well as their native ethnic language. In most cases, you should speak in English, especially if your counterpart is doing so. Keep in mind that pronunciations will probably differ due to the influence of a person's mother tongue on English. Speak slowly and clearly. For Mandarin phrases, please refer to Chapter 3 on China; for Malay phrases, please refer to Chapter 8 on Malaysia; and for Tamil phrases, please refer to Chapter 14 on Sri Lanka.

Major Holidays

January 1	New Year's Day
January / February*	Chinese New Year
March /April*	Hari Raya Puasa
April**	Good Friday
May 1	Labor Day
May*	Vesak Day
June/July*	Hari Raya Haji
August 9	National Day
October / November*	Diwali
December 25	Christmas Day

*These holidays are based on the lunar calendar and change annually.
**This holiday is observed on the first Friday after the paschal full moon and changes from year to year.

General Facts

Climate: Singapore is located just north of the equator. As a result, the weather is hot and humid throughout the year, though sea breezes slightly offset the heat. The city-state has a tropical downpour every day or two throughout the year except in July. The heavy rainy season begins in mid-November and ends in mid-January. December and January are slightly cooler due to the rains, with temperatures ranging from 75F (25C) to 82F (28C). Temperatures in the other months range from 81F (27C) to 88F (31C).

Currency: The currency is the *Singapore dollar* (abbreviated as S$), which consists of 100 *cents*.

Dates: Dates are written in the British style of day, month, year. For example, June 16, 1995, would be abbreviated 16/6/95.

Electricity: The voltage is 230 (50 cycles). Most hotels have transformers for 110–120 volts (60 cycles).

Entry Requirements: American and Canadian citizens need only a valid passport for tourist entry. No visa is required for stays of fewer than fourteen days. For visits longer than 14 days, people should go to the immigration office in Singapore for a stamp of approval. Passports must be valid for a period of six months beginning on the *departure* date. European Community and Commonwealth citizens do not need visas, provided that they can show adequate funds and an onward ticket.

Time: Singapore has one time zone, which is eight hours ahead of Greenwich Mean Time and thirteen hours ahead of U.S. Eastern Standard Time (twelve hours in Daylight Savings Time).

Tipping: The government actively discourages tipping. In fact, local Singaporeans are frustrated when they see foreigners tip, as they feel it makes it more difficult for locals to get good service and attention. Nevertheless, the locals do tip doormen, porters, and room service waiters. In general, tipping occurs in tourist and foreign business areas. Waiters and taxi drivers are not tipped. Concierges generally receive S$2; doormen and porters receive S$2 to S$3; room service waiters receive S$1 to S$2.

Transportation: In general, the best way to get around Singapore is by taxi and public transportation. Taxis are cheap and readily available at taxi-cab stands or on any street. There is a restricted zone covering select parts of the business district. Taxis and cars are required to purchase a license to enter the restricted zone and pay a surcharge for leaving the zone on weekdays between 4:00 p.m. and 7:00 p.m. and on Saturdays between noon and 3:00 p.m. Some taxis may already have a license displayed. Licenses can be purchased at a kiosk near the zone.

The best way to get to and from the airport is by taxi. Many hotels also provide airport minibus or limousine service. There is bus service to travel into downtown, but it is slow and uncomfortable. Within the city, the subway—Mass Rapid Transit (MRT)—is efficient and safe. Buses are also an easy and safe mode of transportation, although they are often crowded at peak rush hours. Some buses are air-conditioned and accordingly more expensive. Exact change is required upon entering a bus with fares ranging from S$.30 to about S$.90. Car ownership and use is expensive. If you rent a car, there are specific rules for driving and wearing seatbelts.

Helpful Telephone Numbers

Public telephones are available throughout the city. To use a telephone, insert money or the Telecoms phone card after you hear a dial tone. After three minutes a buzzer will ring to indicate that another coin should be inserted. A Telecoms phone card can be used for both local and long distance calls. These cards are available in denominations of S$10, S$20, and S$50. The cost of each call is deducted from the value of the card, eventually reaching S$0. Phone cards can be purchased from Telecoms Customer Services outlets or post offices. The country/city code is (65).

Hospitals:

The following hospitals have twenty-four-hour emergency and accident departments and are accustomed to treating foreigners.

Singapore General Hospital
Outram Road
Tel.: 222-3322

Private Mount Elizabeth Hospital
3 Mount Elizabeth
Tel.: 737-2666

Gleneagles Hospital
4/6 Napier Road
Tel.: 473-7222

The American Hospital of Singapore
321 Joo Chiat Place
Tel.: 344-7588 / 345-1516

Doctors and Dentists

Ming Clinic
Tanglin Shopping Center,
No. 12-02
19 Tanglin Road
Tel.: 235-8166 or 535-8833

International Plaza Dental Surgeons
International Plaza, No. 02-39
10 Anson Road
Tel.: 220-6230 or 535-8833

Claymore Dental Surgeons
Orchard Towers, No. 05-11B

400 Orchard Road
Tel.: 737-5226 or 533-0088

SOS Singapore
International Plaza, No. 06-123/13
10 Anson Road
Singapore 0207
Tel.: 226-3936

Ambulance: Dial 995.

Police: Dial 999.

Operator Assistance: Dial 103; for international calls, dial 104.

Useful Addresses:

In Singapore:

American Chamber of Commerce in Singapore
Shaw Center, No. 16-07
1 Scotts Road
Singapore 0922
Tel.: (65) 235-0077

British Business Association
Inchcape House, 3d Floor
450–452 Alexandra Road
Singapore 0511
Tel.: (65) 475-4192

41 Duxton Road
Singapore 0208
Tel.: (65) 227-7861

Canada-ASEAN Center
80 Anson Road, No. 15-02
Singapore 0207
Tel.: (65) 225-7346

Canada Singapore Business
Association
30 Orange Grove Road, No. 07-00
Singapore
Tel.: (65) 738-9232

Economic Development Board
(EDB)
Raffles City Tower
250 North Bridge Road, No. 24-
00
Singapore 0617
Tel.: (65) 336-2288

French Business Association
4 Draycott Park
Singapore 1025
Tel.: (65) 235-8211

Registry of Companies and
Business
International Plaza, No. 05-
01/15
10 Anson Road
Singapore 0207
Tel.: (65) 227-8551

Singapore Federation of Cham-
bers of Commerce and Industry
Singapore Chinese Chamber of
Commerce and Industry
Building, No. 03-01
47 Hill Street
Singapore 0617
Tel.: (65) 338-9761

Singapore International
Chamber of Commerce
Shell Tower, No. 03-02
50 Raffles Place
Singapore 0104
Tel.: (65) 224-1255

Singapore Tourist
Promotion Board
Raffles City Tower, No. 36-04
250 North Bridge Road
Singapore 0617
Tel.: (65) 339-6633

Singapore Trade Development
Board (TDB)
World Trade Center, No. 10-40
1 Maritime Square
Telok Blangah Road
Singapore 0409
Tel.: (65) 271-9388

Trade Ministry
Treasury Building, 48th Floor
8 Shenton Way
Singapore 0207
Tel.: (65) 225-9911

U.S.-ASEAN Council
1 Colombo Court, No. 07-08
Singapore 0617
Tel.: (65) 339-8885

Embassies:

American Embassy
30 Hill Street
Singapore 0617
Tel.: (65) 338-0251

British High Commission
Tanglin Road
Singapore 1024
Tel.: (65) 473-9333

Canadian High Commission
IBM Towers,
14th and 15th Floors
80 Anson Road

Singapore 0207
Tel.: (65) 225-6363

French Embassy
Odeon Towers, No. 18-03/06
331 North Bridge Road
Singapore 0718
Tel.: (65) 339-9710

German Embassy
Far East Shopping Centre, No. 14-01
545 Orchard Road
Singapore 0923
Tel.: (65) 737-1355

In Canada:

Singapore Consulate
999 West Hastings Street
Suite 1305
Vancouver, B.C. V6C 2W2
Tel.: (604) 669-5115

Singapore Tourist Promotion Board
North Tower, Suite 1112
175 Bloor Street E.
Toronto, Ontario M4W 3R8
Tel.: (416) 323-9139

In France:

Embassy of Singapore
12 Square de l'Avenue Foch
75116 Paris
Tel.: (1) 4500-3361

Singapore Economic Development Board (EDB)
22 Avenue Victor Hugo

75116 Paris
Tel.: (1) 4500-1183

Singapore Tourist Promotion Board
Centre d'Affaires le Louvre
2 Place du Palais-Royal
75044 Paris
Tel.: (1) 4297-1616

Singapore Trade Development Board (TDB)
20 Bis Avenue Bourgain
92130 Issy Les Moulineaux
Tel.: (1) 4638-2424

In Germany:

Embassy of Singapore
Substrasse 133
5300 Bonn 2
Tel.: (228) 951-0314

Singapore Economic Development Board (EDB)
Untermainanlage 7
6000 Frankfurt am Main 1
Tel.: (69) 233838

Singapore Tourist Promotion Board
Hochstrasse 35–37, 6th Floor
60313 Frankfurt am Main 1
Tel.: (69) 297-8825

Singapore Trade Development Board (TDB)
Goethestrasse 5
6000 Frankfurt am Main 1
Tel.: (69) 281743

c/o Internationales
Schiffahrtskontor (ISKON)
Kaiserstrasse 42
D-4000 Dusseldorf 30
Tel.: (211) 499-261

In the United Kingdom:

Singapore High Commission
9 Wilton Crescent
London SW1X 8SA
Tel.: (71) 235-8315 / 5441

**Singapore Economic
Development Board**
30 Charles II Street
London SW1Y 4AE
Tel.: (71) 839-6688

**Singapore Trade Development
Board (TDB)**
Westminister Palace Gardens,
Suite 30
1–7 Artillery Row
London SW1P 1RJ
Tel.: (71) 222-0770

**Singapore Tourist
Promotion Board**
Carrington House, 1st Floor
126–130 Regent Street
London, W1R 5FE
Tel.: (71) 437-0033

In the United States:

Singapore Embassy
3501 International Place, N.W.
Washington, DC 20008
Tel.: (202) 537-3100

Singapore Consulate
2424 Southeast Bristol
Suite 320
Santa Ana Heights, CA 92707
Tel.: (714) 476-2330

c/o Hillstrom, Bale Anderson
Young (Honorary Consulate)
Polstein & Pearson
607 Marquette Avenue
Suite 400
Minneapolis, MN 55402
Tel.: (612) 332-8063

**Singapore Mission to the
United Nations**
2 U.N. Plaza, 25th Floor
New York, NY 10017
Tel.: (212) 826-0840

**Singapore Economic
Development Board (EDB)**
55 East 59th Street
New York, NY 10022
Tel.: (212) 421-2200

2049 Century Park East
Suite 400
Los Angeles, CA 90067
Tel.: (310) 553-0199

One International Place
8th Floor
Boston, MA 02110
Tel.: (617) 261-9981

Two Prudential Plaza, Suite 970
180 North Stetson Avenue
Chicago, IL 60601
Tel.: (312) 565-1100

210 Twin Dolphin Drive
Redwood City, CA 94065
Tel.: (415) 591-9102

1350 Connecticut Avenue,
N.W., Suite 504
Washington, DC 20036
Tel.: (202) 223-2571

**Singapore Trade Development
Board (STDB)**
745 Fifth Avenue, Suite 1601
New York, NY 10151
Tel.: (212) 421-2207

Los Angeles World Trade
Center, Suite 909
350 Figueroa Street
Los Angeles, CA 90071
Tel.: (213) 617-7358 / 9

**Singapore Tourist
Promotion Board**
590 Fifth Avenue, 12th Floor
New York, NY 10036
Tel.: (212) 302-4861

2 Prudential Plaza, Suite 1450
180 Stetson Avenue
Chicago, IL 60601
Tel.: (312) 938-1888

8484 Wilshire Blvd., Suite 510
Beverly Hills, CA 90211
Tel.: (213) 852-1901

U.S. Department of Commerce
International Trade
Administration
Singapore Desk, Room 2036
14th & Constitution Avenues,
N.W.
Washington, DC 20230
Tel.: (202) 482-4958

11 Thailand

Geography

The kingdom of Thailand, once known as the kingdom of Siam, is located in Southeast Asia, extends downward into the Malaysian Peninsula, and shares its southern border with Malaysia. To the northeast lies Laos, to the east Cambodia, and to the northwest Myanmar (Burma). With a total land area of 198,455 square miles (514,000 square kilometers), Thailand is about the same size as France. The country is characterized by tropical rain forests in the southern peninsular region, mountains in the north, and plains in the central region. The capital of Thailand is Bangkok (also known as Krung Thep), which is located in about the middle of the country, on the Gulf of Thailand, and is the country's largest city. Chiang Mai, Thailand's second largest city, is located inland in the northern part of the country.

History

Archaeological evidence indicates that Thailand has been occupied by humans for several thousand years. When the ancestors of the modern Thai people began migrating into the region from Southern China around A.D. 700, they found the area already populated by the Mons, whose settlements stretched from Thailand, through Myanmar, to India, and the Khmers, the ancestors of the modern Cambodians. The Mons were Buddhist and the Khmers Hindu; both religions had an effect on the Thai belief system.

The history of modern Thailand began in the thirteenth century with the emergence of two principal Thai states: Sukhothai, founded in 1220, and Chiang Mai, founded in 1296. The Thai rebellion against the Khmers resulted in the creation of Sukhothai, which is regarded as the first historical Thai Kingdom. Little is known of Sukhothai until its third Thai king, Ramkhamhaeng, who ruled from 1278 through 1318. He is still revered as the "Father of Thailand," who made a significant contribution to Thai society by fusing the Mon and Khmer traditions. He also revised and adapted the Khmer alphabet to the Thai language. Ramkhamhaeng's kingdom began to decline in the mid-fourteenth century and was eventually absorbed by the kingdom of Ayutthaya in 1378. During the same period, other Thai peoples migrated to present-day Laos and the Shan states of Burma.

The Ayutthaya kingdom, begun in 1350, lasted until 1768. It was ruled by thirty-three successive kings. During this Ayutthaya period the concept of the king as a god was introduced and elaborate royal rituals were adopted. Ramathibodi, the founder of the Ayutthaya line of kings, invited Ceylonese monks to purify the Khmer-corrupted religion of Theravada Buddhism. The resulting

Thai form of Buddhism is still in practice today. In the fourteenth century, the Ayutthaya kingdom extended its range into parts of Cambodia, eventually occupying its capital of Angkor. By the end of the fourteenth century, the Ayutthaya kingdom was the strongest power in Southeast Asia, but it lacked the manpower to maintain control over the region.

In 1569 the Burmese overran Ayutthaya, although they were eventually displaced by the Thai king Naresuan, who restored independence to the kingdom by 1600. During the following period, Ayutthaya enjoyed a golden age of arts and architecture. The Burmese attacked Ayutthaya again in 1765. After almost two years of resistance by the Thais, the Burmese captured the capital city, slaughtered most of the population, plundered the treasures, and completely burned the royal city, thereby destroying the architectural heritage of Ayutthaya. The Thais were devastated and still have animosity toward the Burmese because of this outrage.

In 1767 the Thais regrouped under the guidance of a half-Chinese general named Phraya Taksin, who rallied the nation and established a new capital in Thonburi near modern-day Bangkok. Within ten years, Taksin drove the Burmese out of Thailand. Further, Taksin brought large areas of Laos under Thai influence. General Chao Phraya Chakri became the first king of the Chakkri dynasty and was crowned as Rama I in 1782. This period, known as Rattanakosin, continues to the present day. Rama I initiated a new period of Thai expansionism. In the early nineteenth century the Thais seized provinces in Cambodia, resulting in tension with Vietnam. This was resolved by both countries agreeing to establish a joint protectorate over Cambodia.

During the nineteenth century Thai kings were successful in using diplomacy to keep out the British and the French. Thailand's continued independence was finally secured in the mid- to late-nineteenth century by ceding to the British a little of what is now Malaysia and to the French a little of what is now Cambodia and Laos.

One of the more successful Thai kings, noted for his ability to use diplomacy to keep foreigners out of the country, was King Mongkut (Rama IV), who ruled from 1851 to 1868. King Mongkut was an enlightened and well-educated ruler who understood that the only way to maintain political independence was through the introduction of Western-style reforms. (Many Westerners are familiar with King Mongkut as he is the monarch in the story, *The King and I*.) He and his son, Chulalongkorn (Rama V), are credited with transforming Thailand from a medieval kingdom into a modern nation. Chulalongkorn ruled from 1868 to 1910 and was successful in abolishing the slavelike status of serfs, developing the educational system, expanding professional opportunities, restructuring the administrative system, and introducing other reforms.

Rama VII, who reigned from 1925 to 1935, attempted to provide the country with a modern constitution. However, fervent royalists prevented him from instituting this reform. In 1932 a coalition of Thailand's military and a group of radical civilians committed to social, political, and economic reform, staged a bloodless coup and installed a constitutional regime with the king's acceptance. After a year of infighting among the civilian and military factions, the military coalition assumed full control.

In 1939 the country was renamed Thailand, meaning "Land of the Free." Phibun Songkhram, a Thai military leader, assumed the prime minister's office, promoted Thai nationalism, and encouraged Thai social behavior that conformed to Western standards. In 1941 the Phibun government cooperated closely with the occupying Japanese troops. The Phibun military regime was replaced in 1944 by a predominantly civilian government.

After the end of World War II, political infighting and economic hardship led to five civilian prime ministers and eight civilian cabinets within a two year period. The military once again challenged the civilian government. In 1947, Phibun's military faction backed two generals who seized power from the civilian government. In 1948 Field Marshall Phibun Songkhram assumed the office of prime minister and took full control of the government.

The king remains a focus of loyalty and cohesion and his support has always been necessary for the transfer of power either through coups or elections. Nevertheless, Thailand's generals have remained the real power brokers. The present king, H.M. Bhumibol Adulyadej, who has ruled since 1950, is known as Rama IX. Despite coups and other political upheavals, the country has managed to stay fairly focused on creating a modern economy.

For almost a decade Phibun was successful in balancing the interests of the military, the bureaucrats, and the economically powerful Chinese. In 1957, as part of a cosmetic attempt to liberalize the country, he announced elections, which were subsequently rigged. Marshal Sarit Thanarat took control of the government in 1958 after a bloodless coup. Sarit imposed an authoritarian system and abolished elections and the constitution, outlawed political parties, and closed a dozen newspapers.

During the past fifty years Thailand has often been the recipient of U.S. aid due to its strategic location and its anticommunist beliefs. U.S. involvement in Vietnam provided Sarit and Thailand with an opportunity for economic expansion. During the 1960s Thailand experienced extensive economic growth due in large part to American military expenditures. Further, the Thai government, fearful of communist attacks, aligned itself closely with the United States and permitted American forces to be stationed in Thailand.

After Sarit's death in 1963, Thanom Kittikachorn tried to reestablish the democratic process. He introduced a new constitution in 1968 that provided for a National Assembly with some elected members. However, in 1971, Thanom launched a coup against his own government and suspended the constitution and the National Assembly, thereby ending a three-year experiment with partial parliamentary democracy.

In December 1972 a new constitution called for an appointed legislative assembly, most of whom would be members of the military and police. This led to widespread student protests and violence. In October 1973 the government collapsed after the king withdrew his support and student protests escalated. A new 1974 constitution provided for democratic elections and led to several weak governments. The country was polarized between right-wing and left-wing groups with no political party able to win a majority or assemble a stable coalition. Meanwhile, the student movement became more radical which was attributed to communist influence. Most dissidents were labeled communists by the Thai military and right-wing politicians. On October 6, 1976, the military and police launched a bloody assault on student protesters, killing hundreds. Then the military seized power and ended Thailand's short experiment with true democracy. Thanin Kraivichien, a civilian, became prime minister with the support of the king and the military. A passionate anticommunist, his government was more repressive than those of previous military strongmen. A year later, General Kriangsak Chamanand replaced Thanin and became prime minister. Under Kriangsak, a new constitution was written and the press was given limited freedoms.

The deterioration of the country's economy led to Kriangsak's resignation in 1980. Prem Tinsulanond, the army commander in chief, became prime minister, thanks to the king's support. By then, refugees from neighboring Kampuchea (Cambodia) fleeing Vietnam's invasion of that country, became an issue for Thailand. Although the military continued to exercise authority, Kriangsak and Prem both introduced some democratic reforms.

After the July 1988 elections, Prem stepped down from power. A six-party coalition won the majority of seats in the National Assembly and General Chatichai Choonhavan, leader of the Chart Thai (Thai Nation) party, became the prime minister and formed a cabinet. Chatichai shifted power from the military to the business elite and pursued aggressive pro-development policies. However, in February 1991, due to extensive corruption in the government, the military overthrew Chatichai's government in a bloodless coup. Suchinda Kraprayoon, a military leader, assumed control, although not in the official role of prime minister. Anand Panyarachun was appointed interim prime minister. His policies focused on liberalizing and deregulating the economy.

Pro-democracy movements gained support and placed pressure on the military. In early 1992 new elections resulted in a government coalition of five pro-military parties, Samakkhi Tham, Chart Thai, the Social Action party, Prachakorn Thai, and Rassadorn. This coalition chose Narong Wongwan, a close aide of Suchinda, to be prime minister. However, he was an unacceptable choice, domestically and internationally, due to strong suspicions of involvement in heroin trafficking. Instead, Suchinda was appointed prime minister. Meanwhile, pro-democracy demonstrations against military manipulation of and participation in the government increased. On May 17, 1992, the government declared a national emergency and shot at demonstrators, killing at least one hundred people. Despite his attempt to retain power, Suchinda resigned one week later.

In June 1992, Anand Panyarachun was appointed as interim prime minister once again and moves were made to democratize the constitution. He quickly reestablished stability and appointed a cabinet. Eventually the four political parties siding with the pro-democracy movement formed a coalition under Chaun Leekpai and received a majority in the National Assembly in the September 1992 elections. The pro-military party, Chart Thai, came in second. The 1993 elections confirmed the role of the pro-democracy coalition. Chaun Leekpai has focused on promoting social stability and economic growth. During 1994, government efforts to reform the constitution and reduce corruption have continued, although political infighting threatens to disrupt the fragile political stability. Nevertheless, the economy continues to grow.

Political Structure

Thailand is a constitutional monarchy with a parliamentary system. The bicameral legislature consists of the Senate, whose members are appointed to six-year terms by the king upon the recommendation of the prime minister, and the National Assembly, whose members are elected to four-year terms by the people. Both the Senate

and the National Assembly elect the prime minister, who then selects his cabinet and leads the government. Since 1932 Thailand
has experienced twenty-six coups and created thirteen constitu-
tions. However, in recent years, transfer of power has been less violent and the country seems to be moving slowly toward democratic
processes. The judiciary has been influenced by the British legal
code.

The king, who functions as the head of state, provides stability
in an unstable political world. Many Thais revere and trust the
monarch as the true ruler of the country. Despite the various coups
and subsequent transfers of power, the king has remained at the
helm and is perceived as the symbol of national unity.

Economy

For about fifty years, Thailand has enjoyed periods of economic
growth characterized by increased foreign investment, followed by
periods of slowdown, often caused by a waning or withdrawal of foreign investment. Since the mid-1970s the government has encouraged foreign investment and the subsequent growth rate has been
impressive. Government intervention in the economy has concentrated on key sectors. Thailand's strong economic performance has
placed heavy demands on its marginal infrastructure. The government is now focusing on improving the country's basic infrastructure, including port facilities, roads, communications networks,
water treatment facilities, and power sources.

Traditionally the economy has been agriculture-based. Today,
manufacturing has become the primary force behind the economy,
but shortage of skilled labor remains a constraint. About 62 percent
of the population is employed in agriculture-related industries.
Many work on the large rubber and coconut plantations in the
southern peninsular region.

Thai industries include food processing, consumer products,
electronic goods, computer peripherals and components, and auto-

mobiles and auto parts. Major exports include textiles and clothing, rice, fish products, integrated circuits, rubber, tapioca, leather products, footwear, and precious stones and jewelry. Major crops include coffee, tobacco, cotton, jute, beans, sugar, maize, pineapples, and other fruits. The country has had difficulties with drug trafficking, but the government is making efforts to control and halt it. Tourism is fast becoming a major national industry; and a leading source of foreign exchange.

People, Values, and Social Customs

The population of Thailand is about fifty-eight million. Almost 82 percent of the people are ethnic Thais, making the country relatively racially homogeneous. The ethnic Thai can be divided into Central Thai, Thai Lao, and Southern Thai. There are four dialects of the Thai language, but they are somewhat mutually intelligible. Minority groups include Chinese, Malays, Mons, Khmers, Phuans, and recent refugees from Vietnam, Myanmar (Burma), Laos, and Cambodia.

The largest minority are the Chinese, constituting more than 12 percent of the population. The earliest Chinese immigrants were the Hokkiens, who came to Thailand in the eighteenth century to serve primarily as tax collectors for the royal family. The Teochews migrated to Thailand and became successful merchants. In the twentieth century, immigrants fleeing famine in China, swelled Thailand's Chinese population. The Chinese in Thailand have flourished thanks to education, hard work, and the tight Chinese community network. Many of Thailand's largest companies are owned by Thai Chinese. Unlike the Chinese minorities in other Southeast Asian countries, the Chinese in Thailand have not become the focus of ethnic rivalries, perhaps because the high rate of intermarriage has made it difficult to distinguish between Chinese and Thai families. Sino-Thais often take Thai surnames and speak Thai rather than Chinese, further reducing the differences. Many members of Thailand's ruling elite admit to having some Chinese ancestry.

The primary religion is Theravada Buddhism, practiced by about 95 percent of the population. Some two million Malays in Thailand are Muslims. The Thais also practice ancestor worship.

Thailand is unique among Southeast Asian nations because its culture developed independent of Western colonialism. Consequently, the Thais are very protective of their independence.

Thailand has the lowest secondary education enrollment ratio of any ASEAN country. Only about 40 percent of the nation's children aged twelve to seventeen attend school. The other 60 percent are already at work in factories or on farms. Accordingly, Thailand is experiencing a shortage of technical labor such as engineers. The government has plans to make education more accessible to its youth and to extend the age for compulsory education.

Thais value harmony and mutual respect. Preserving the dignity of others, as well as their own, is very important to them. Thais tend to be rather tolerant due to their Buddhist faith. A common expression is *Mai pen rai*, which means "Never mind, it does not matter." Problems and setbacks are not considered very important. Some say that this attitude helps to explain why military coups have been so prevalent in Thailand. Any displays of anger or rude behavior are frowned upon. All differences are expected to be resolved quietly and politely. Thais often judge everything by whether or not it is *sanuk*, or pleasurable.

Social ranking is determined by a combination of lineage, education, and economic status. Social ranking is made evident in the different ways a Thai will refer to himself depending on his status vis-à-vis the status of the listener. Foreigners need not be concerned about correct usage as long as they use polite speech. Royalty is the most respected group and the Thai use a special honorific vocabulary when referring to the royal family or directly addressing them. The Thais have tremendous respect for the monarchy and consider any slander of it an indictable offense. Hence, the film and play, *The King and I*, and the original book, *The English Governess at the*

Siamese Court, have been banned in Thailand due to the perception that they are condescending.

The family remains an integral part of Thai life. In some parts
of Thailand the people still live together as large extended families;
this is less common now in the major cities. Traditionally, wealth
and making money were not viewed very favorably. Protecting the
family, maintaining harmony, and providing sufficient food for
everyone were the most important goals. With the recent influx of
foreigners, Thais have become more materialistic.

Thailand has some very good con artists, who often create elaborate and believable schemes. Foreigners would be well-advised to
be careful about trusting strangers, particularly on the streets.

In general, women are considered inferior to men and do not
receive equal treatment. In many areas it is still acceptable for Thai
men to continue having an unofficial second wife. Male extramarital relations are common. It should be noted, however, that more
women are holding professional and executive positions. Most
women remain responsible for family matters and often manage the
household finances.

Thais smile often; the country is referred to as "the land of the
smiles." However, a smile can imply various things depending on
the circumstances. It is very important to smile often and in every
situation; a smile is the most useful tool in this culture. Do not assume, however, that the situation is positive simply because a Thai
smiles.

Work Schedule

Most businesses are open weekdays from 8:30 A.M. to 5:00 P.M. Government offices are open weekdays from 8:30 A.M. to 4:30 P.M., with
an hour lunch break at noon. Banks are open weekdays from 8:30
A.M. to 3:30 P.M. Department stores are open daily from 9:00 A.M.
to 6:00 P.M. and sometimes until 9:00 P.M. Other shops are open daily
from 9:00 or 10:00 A.M. to 8:00 P.M.

Making Contacts

Foreign companies may write directly to Thai companies, although introductions will always facilitate a firm's credibility and acceptance. Because English telephone conversations may be difficult to understand for the Thai, it is best to write. As a result of the *sanuk*, or the carefree way of life, spontaneity is acceptable and appreciated. Sometimes it is all right to schedule impromptu meetings. However, this is not advisable on your first visit to Thailand.

Foreign businesses would be wise to hire a local representative or agent, especially if they intend to buy from or sell to Thailand. The commercial office of your embassy or your country's chamber of commerce can help a firm to identify credible representatives and partners. Assess any local representative or partner's political relationships as the government is still very much involved in the private sector. Networking with government officials can be the key to doing business successfully, especially if your firm intends to do a major project.

The Board of Investment (BOI) is the principal Thai government agency responsible for providing incentives to attract foreign investment. The BOI also conducts promotion activities, both in Thailand and in various other countries. The BOI produces literature that is a good initial source for researching Thailand. A firm should also seek the advice of the commercial branch of its country's state department and the chambers of commerce.

Meeting People

Avoid business visits during the New Year Festivals (both the Chinese and the Thai ones). Foreigners are expected to be punctual, but do not expect Thais to be on time. Heavy traffic is the most common excuse for tardiness. Whenever possible, avoid scheduling meetings after 3:30 P.M. because locals often leave their offices early to get a head start on evening rush-hour traffic. First meetings may be held in offices, restaurants, or hotel lobbies. Men may be invited to "member clubs." Thais are often impressed if you stay at an expensive hotel; luxury suggests that you represent a very successful company.

When greeting a Thai, use the word *Khun* (pronounced coon) in place of "Mr." or "Mrs." and the person's first name, which is listed first on his or her business card. For example, a Westerner with the name "John Smith" would be called "*Khun* John." Among Thais, family names are not usually used. Most Thais refer to each other by their first names only. Never refer to yourself with the word *Khun*; simply say your first name. Thais will probably address you by using "Mr." or "Mrs." and your first name.

In order to avoid confusion, wait to see if your Thai counterpart extends a hand for a handshake. Thais are just beginning to adopt this foreign greeting. Most Thais greet someone by bowing slightly forward while bringing their hands to a praying position in front of them between the chest and forehead. The exact location of the hands depends on the level of respect being offered. However, the fingertips should never go above the head. This gesture, known as *wai*, is the traditional respectful greeting. Among Thais, the height and depth of a person's *wai* indicates social status. When you *wai* back to your counterpart, you need not worry about the exact position of your hands. Thais are very tolerant and will be pleased with your attempt to participate culturally. Do not *wai* secretaries and clerks. The *wai* can be used when greeting someone on arrival and departure, and also when saying "I am sorry" or "Thank you."

Business cards are always exchanged at the first meeting. It is important to carry a sufficient quantity; failure to offer a business card may make Thais suspicious of your position and authority. Hotels and department stores can help provide you with business cards. Be sure your card indicates your position and responsibility, as the Thais are impressed by titles.

Begin initial meetings with casual conversation on such topics as your travels, the beauties of Thailand, and your counterpart's overseas experiences. Thais may ask what Westerners perceive as very personal questions regarding income and status. If you are uncomfortable responding to such questions, politely offer a vague answer. Avoid topics relating to politics, the royal family, and religion. Be generous in your praise of the country and the Thai people and refrain from boasting about your country and yourself. Gifts are not required for early meetings. If you wish, you can present sample products from your company.

It is illegal to criticize the monarchy or the government. The Thais strictly enforce this law. Members of the royal family should always be publicly respected.

Standing over someone, especially someone older or more superior, is considered rude, as it implies social superiority. Westerners and other foreigners who are tall may find it difficult to avoid towering over smaller Thais. One possible way to deal with the problem is to slightly lower your head and/or upper body, rather than standing erect. While it may not make much of a difference physically, the gesture is usually noticed and appreciated.

Never show the sole of your foot to anyone, for example, by placing your feet up on a table or chair. Never touch someone with your feet. The Thais, like many Asians, regard feet as unclean. It is usually considered rude to cross your legs, so it is best to sit erect with both feet on the ground. Refrain from touching anyone or even the chairs that they are sitting on; both gestures are considered rude. When passing an object, never toss it to a Thai. Always hand it to him or her directly.

Pointing to someone should be done by gesturing with the head or chin, not by using a finger. While it is acceptable to point, it is best to avoid this gesture entirely. Beckoning should be done using your whole hand with the palm facing down and the fingers pointing away from you, but moving toward you in a scratching motion.

Corporate Structure

The typical business is headed by the managing director and/or general manager, whose immediate subordinates are directors and managers. In most companies, the more senior officers retain the authority and responsibility. Many of the country's largest businesses are owned and/or operated by people of Chinese or Sino-Thai heritage. As in most Asian countries, family links remain an important part of the business culture. Many Thai firms are centralized and have a hands-on style of management.

Over the years, many of Thailand's senior military leaders have gained control of private companies. Technically, other family members may "own" the company, but they are fronts for their relative in the military, who makes all the important decisions.

Negotiation

In general, doing business is a lengthy, drawn-out process because the concept of time in Thailand is very elastic. Do not expect quick decisions and do not expect to finalize transactions with dispatch. You may need to visit Thailand two to three times before your proposal will be seriously considered. Different Thai ethnic groups conduct business differently; often the education level and degree of international exposure of your counterparts will affect their attitudes and styles.

The Thais are focused on hierarchies and respect all forms of authority. Thai society lives by the unspoken rule never to directly oppose or to embarrass anyone. Decisions are usually made by senior management, although who makes decisions can depend on the type and size of the transaction.

Thais place a great importance on appearances, politeness, and maintaining a calm professional composure or *jai yen* (cool heart). Never lose your temper publicly for both you and your counterpart will lose face. If you do have an outburst, use a smile to mitigate the effects of any negative situation. Maintaining group harmony and avoiding conflict are critical to the Thais. Never criticize anyone or his or her ideas publicly; this would be viewed as a personal attack. Since Thais rarely criticize, it can be very difficult to obtain honest feedback about your business ideas, proposals, and products. Further, Thais, in an effort to maintain harmony, may not give you negative news or alert you to problems. To counter this problem, ask indirect questions, particularly those that can be answered affirmatively, but have a negative meaning.

The Thais' favorite saying, *Mai pen rai*, which means "Never mind, it doesn't matter," often applies to business issues. Accordingly, Thais tend to be less concerned about meeting deadlines and general productivity than most Westerners. In relation to the concept of *sanuk*, Thais enjoy spontaneity and do not care for excessive planning. Thai unwillingness to focus on accountability, tasks, and responsibilities can make it difficult to document working relationships and to keep business moving forward. This casual attitude also encourages lower-level workers to be careless in their approach to details.

It is important to use your local representative or agent to keep Thai attention focused on your transaction on a regular basis. The cliché "Out-of-sight, out-of-mind" is very valid in Thailand. Further, it is not uncommon for a Thai to say that he will be in touch and then not follow up. You should make efforts to maintain ongoing communication.

The Thais view contracts merely as an early step in developing a relationship. Therefore, they may be offended by an extensively detailed contract; this would imply that the Thai's honor is questionable. Be sensitive to such issues when you draw up agreements. In any case, you should focus on your business objectives and include the appropriate level of details in order to avoid problems in the case of a dispute. Outline how disagreements should be handled. Contracts are usually written in Thai as well as English.

Conducting Business in a Social Setting

Dining and Drinking

Thais enjoy combining business and pleasure. Business breakfasts are not very common. If you schedule a breakfast meeting, the better hotels are appropriate settings. Business lunches and dinners are more common. As a general rule, whoever extends the invitation pays for the meal and the entertainment. Thais call splitting a bill "American share," and rarely engage in it. If it is unclear who has extended the invitation, then the oldest member of the group usually accepts "the honor" of paying. If you are the only foreigner at the table, it might be a good diplomatic gesture to offer to pay; generosity is always respected and appreciated. It is not uncommon for Thais to bring liquor with them to a restaurant. Wait until your Thai counterpart mentions business before discussing it over a meal.

Thais use chopsticks only for Chinese dishes. In all other situations they use a fork and spoon. The fork is used to push the food onto the spoon. When you are finished, place your fork and spoon together at the lower right side of the plate; otherwise, it will be assumed that you want more. Never pass food with just the left hand as it is considered unclean.

While there are laws against prostitution in Thailand, the government has been lax in enforcing them. Most Thais are tolerant of prostitution and consider extramarital relations for men an integral part of life. Foreign men should feel comfortable about turning down the offer of a female "escort," a visit to a "massage parlor," and related activities. Despite the relaxed private attitudes about sex, refrain from public displays of affection between adults. Discretion is viewed as a sign of maturity. The Thais enjoy gambling and related activities.

Visiting a Home

Invitations to homes for just one or two people are rare. The Thais tend to invite groups of people to their homes, usually for an informal buffet meal. If you are invited to a Thai home, remove your shoes before entering (also remove shoes before entering a temple). Some Thais are tolerant of Western habits. Follow your host's lead. Avoid stepping on the doorsill of a home (or temple), for the Thais believe that souls reside in doorsills. It is customary to bring a small gift when visiting a home, although it is not required. Suitable gifts include souvenirs and handicrafts from your home country, sweets, and chocolates. Always wrap your gifts in brightly colored paper; the Thais enjoy bright colors. In some traditional homes, people sit on the floor. Women tuck their legs to one side and men sit cross-legged. Never stretch your legs out in front of you. Be careful not to praise a specific object or your host may feel obliged to present it to you. Rather, compliment the home overall or the children. Thais are generally very hospitable and warm.

Buddhist shrines and religious objects are sacred, so refrain from using them as a backdrop for your photographs. Women are not permitted to touch a Buddhist monk. The head is considered the most sacred part of the body and should never be touched due to the belief that the spirit, *khwan*, resides in the head.

Gift Giving

Corruption is widespread, particularly among the military and government officials, many of whom abuse their powers to enrich themselves. Most of the coups have been prompted in part by the corruption of the governments then in power. Develop a global policy concerning demands for graft and adhere to it. Avoid direct engagement in any questionable activity. The Thais prefer discretion and few will speak openly about the bribes or "commissions" they require to accomplish tasks. Your local representative or agent is much better suited to managing the subtle nuances of such issues.

In normal interactions, it is appropriate to present a small gift as the relationship develops. Thais usually focus on the thought behind the gift and less on the gift itself. Appropriate gifts are home country souvenirs, liquor, or sweets. Flowers are only given at funerals. Gifts should not be opened in the presence of the giver.

Dress Code

For men, business suits and ties are expected. Short-sleeve shirts are acceptable in the summer, when jackets and ties can often be removed. Follow your counterparts' lead. Men may also wear safari suits, usually gray or khaki, but not at a first meeting. For women, simple suits or professional dresses are appropriate. Casual wear is not suitable for Thailand's better restaurants. Loose, neat comfortable clothing is appropriate for casual settings. Avoid wearing solid purple as the color is associated with the royal family.

If you will be traveling to Thailand often, have a suit or a safari suit made by a reputable local tailor. The regional fabrics and styles are distinctive. Thais will appreciate your efforts to dress like the locals, winning you additional goodwill.

Useful Phrases

The official language is Thai, which is monosyllabic and tonal. Using the proper tone is important; the same word may have different meanings depending on the tone. Of the many Thai dialects, Central Thai is the official dialect of the government and business. It is important to note that there are different phrases when referring to men rather than women. Additionally, Thai men and women use different versions of phrases when speaking. For example, women end greetings or questions with *kha* instead of *khrap*. English is widely spoken in business. The script is written from left to right with no spaces between the words. The transliteration of Thai script into roman characters will vary depending on the translator because spelling is not standardized. The following list includes some useful phrases written as they would be pronounced.

Hello	*Sa-wat-dee khrap* (used by males); *Sa-wat-dee kha* (used by females) In general, use *khrap* after a phrase for men, and *kha* for women.
Good morning	Same as hello or *Aroon sa-wat*
Good afternoon	Same as hello
Good evening/night	Same as hello or *Ra-tree sa-wat*
How are you?	*Sa-baay dee rer kha* (used by females); *Sa-baay dee rer khap* (used by males)
Please	*Ka-roo-na* (with a request)
Thank you	*Khawp khoon*
You are welcome	*Mai pen rai*
Excuse me	*Khaw thoat*
I am sorry	(as in I am saddened) *Phom siyeh chye* (used by males); *Di-chan siyeh chye* (used by females)
My name is ——	*Phom cher* —— (used by males); *Di-chan cher* —— (used by females)
I work for ——	*Phom tham ngaan yoo thee* (used by males); *Di-chan tham ngaan yoo thee* (used by females)
Here is my business card	*An nee kher bat naam khawng phom* (used by males); *An nee kher bat naam khawng di-chan* (used by females)
I am pleased to meet you	*Phom yin-dee thee dye phop kap khoon khrap* (used by males); *Di-chan yin-dee thee dye phop kap khoon kha* (used by females)
Please accept this small gift	*Phom khaw mawp khawng khwan lek-lek noy-noy khrap* (used by males); *Di-chan khaw mawp khawng khwan lek-lek noy-noy kha* (used by females)

I look forward to developing a good relationship with you / your firm	*Phom mee khwaam wang thee cha sang sam-phan-tha-phap thee dee kap than / baw-ri-sat khawng than khrap* (used by males); *Di-chan mee khwaam wang thee cha saang sam-phan tha \ phaap thee dee kap than / baw-ri-sat khawng thaan kha* (used by females)
I understand	*Phom khao chye khrap* (used by males); *Di-chan khao chye kha* (used by females)
No, I do not understand	*Mye, phom mye khao chye khrap* (used by males); *Mye, di-chan mye khao chye kha* (used by females)
Please wait a minute	*Proat raw sak khroo*
Where is the bathroom?	*Hawng nam yoo thee nye?*
Good-bye	*Di-chan khaw laa kha* (used by females); *phom khaw laa khrap* (used by males)
Cheers	*Khaw uay phawn* (rarely used)

Major Holidays

January 1	New Year's Day
January/February*	Chinese New Year
February/March*	Makhabucha Day
April 6	Chakri Day
mid-April	Songkhran Day (Thai New Year)
May*	Ploughing Ceremony
May 1	Labor Day
May 5	Coronation Day
May/June*	Visakhabucha Day
July/August*	Asalahabucha Day
July/August*	Rains Retreat
August 12	Queen Sirikit's Birthday
October*	Ok Pansa
October 23	Chulalongkorn Day
December 5	King Bhumiphol's Birthday
December 10	Constitution Day
December 31	New Year's Eve

* These are lunar-based holidays and change from year to year.

General Facts

Climate: Thailand experiences three seasons with only minor differences in temperature. The cooler season occurs from October to February, when temperatures range from 68F (20C) to 91F (33C). Summer occurs from March to June, when temperatures range from 75F (24C) to 95F (35C). The hot and rainy season occurs from July to September, when temperatures range from 75F (24C) to 89F (32C). Summer months are hot and humid, while the cooler season is sunny and dry. During the rainy months showers occur once a day in the late afternoon.

Currency: The basic currency unit is the *baht*, which is divided into 100 *satang*.

Dates: Dates are written as day, month, and year. For example, August 6, 1995, is abbreviated as 6/8/95.

Electricity: The voltage is 220v, 50 cycles.

Entry Requirements: For American Canadian, British, French, and German citizens, a passport and a departure ticket are required. For stays longer than fifteen days, a transit visa is required. Visitors should note that after a stay of ninety days in one calendar year, they are subject to tax and must provide tax clearance documents before leaving the country. Consult your tax and legal representatives.

Time: Thailand has one time zone, which is seven hours ahead of Greenwich Mean Time and twelve hours ahead of U.S. Eastern Standard Time (eleven hours in Daylight Savings Time).

Tipping: Taxi drivers are rarely tipped. Usually, they have already added a tip in the fare. Hotel bellboys and room-service waiters should get between 10 and 50 baht. Concierges normally receive between 50 and 100 baht. Restaurants include a 10 percent service charge. It is appropriate, although not necessary, to leave an extra 10 to 20 baht on the table. Carry loose change for tipping; however, never leave only 1 baht as that would be considered an insult.

Transportation: Plane travel to and within Thailand is convenient and safe. Trains and luxury buses are also reliable and provide a good alternative, although they tend to be slow. There are plane, train, and bus services to major cities within Thailand and between Thailand and neighboring countries.

In Bangkok, the Thai use the word *soi* and a *soi* number when giving addresses. *Soi* and a number refers to a secondary street that runs off a main road. The *soi* can have a number and a name. In identifying a building on a main road, Thais usually refer to its closest *soi* and number/name. For example, "Sukhumvit, Soi 12," "Soi 12 Sukhumvit," and "Soi 12, Sukhumvit Road" all refer to the same location, Soi 12, which is a secondary street off the main road, Sukhumvit. This method can make getting around Bangkok confusing. Thais are generally quite friendly and will assist you when you are lost if you ask politely and with a smile.

It usually takes about one hour to travel from the Don Muang Airport to Bangkok, but in the rainy season, this trip can take from one to two and a half hours. There are several ways to get into Bangkok from the airport including taxi, airport limousines, and hotel buses. For taxis, use the taxi reservations counter outside of the customs areas; otherwise you are liable to be charged significantly more than the normal cost of the trip. Negotiate the price with the driver before getting into the taxi, for many cabs lack meters. Thai Airways has a minibus that runs from the airport to all major hotels. There is also train service from the airport to the central station in Bangkok which takes only forty minutes. Inquire at the airport tourist office for details.

In Bangkok, rush hour seems to last all day. The alternative to taxis is to rent a car and driver. The cost is about the same for a rental car, although self-driving is not recommended due to traffic and driving conditions. If you prefer to drive, an international driver's license is required. Call a major car rental agency prior to arriving in Bangkok or from your hotel and a car will be delivered to you. A word of caution: if a foreigner is in a traffic accident, he or

she will be judged at fault, not the Thai. Adjust your schedule to include traffic delays.

Taxis are available through hotels or by waving one down on
a street. There are plenty of taxis available, but select ones with
signs or licenses posted visibly. Whenever possible, ask a local before using a taxi for the appropriate price for the distance you expect to travel. Many drivers do not speak or understand English and
use their fingers to state a price. One finger means 10 baht, two fingers means 20 baht, and so on. Drivers usually inflate the fare 30–35
percent. Offer to pay 75 percent of the first stated price. Hotel taxis
are usually more expensive, but the drivers often speak some English.

In Bangkok, you will also find the *tuk-tuk*, a three-wheel motorcycle. While they can be faster and cheaper than taxis, the *tuk-
tuk* drivers rarely speak English and often cannot understand where
you want to go. Buses are efficient, but very crowded, and there are
some air-conditioned buses and minibuses. The fare ranges from 5
baht to 13 baht. English bus maps are available at hotels and tourist
offices.

Helpful Telephone Numbers

Public telephones are located throughout Thailand, which accept
either a 1 baht or a 5 baht coin, and sometimes both. There are
several sizes of the 1 baht coin. Accordingly, some telephones will
only take the small newer version, while others will take the old
medium-size coin. No public telephones will accept the oldest
and largest 1 baht coin. Hotel public telephones are often more
expensive. International calls can be made from some hotels, major
post offices, and private offices. Long-distance calls can only be
made on telephones that accept both coins. The country code for
Thailand is (66). Within Thailand, area codes for major cities
are: Bangkok (2), Chiang Mai (53), Hua Hin (32), Pattaya (38),
and Phuket (76).

Hospitals, Doctors, and Dentists:

Bangkok Christian Hospital
124 Silom Road
Bangkok
Tel.: (2) 233-6981 / 9

Bangkok Nursing Home
9 Convent Road
Bangkok
Tel.: (2) 233-2610 / 9

Bangkok Seventh Day Adventist Hospital
430 Pitsanulok Road
Bangkok
Tel.: (2) 281-1422

Chulalongkorn Hospital
Rama 1 Road
Bangkok
Tel.: (2) 252-8181

Dental Clinic
7 South Sathorn Road
Bangkok
Tel.: (2) 287-1036

Dental Poly Clinic
2111–2113 New Petchburi Road
Bangkok
Tel.: (2) 314-5070

Lanna Hospital
103 Superhighway
Chiang Mai
Tel.: (53) 211-037

Ambulance: Dial 246-0199

Police: Dial 191, 195, or 123 for emergency assistance. Dial 199 for a fire emergency.

Tourist Police: They are specially trained to assist foreigners and usually speak some English.
509 Vorachak Road
Bangkok
Tel.: (2) 221-6206 or 221-6209

105/1 Chiang Mai-Lamphun Road
Chiang Mai
Tel.: (53) 248-974

Operator Assistance:
Bangkok in English 13
Assistance with overseas calls:
(100) 233-2771
Local telephone inquiries:
(100) 183

Useful Addresses

In Thailand:

American Chamber of Commerce
Kian Gwan Building, 3d Floor
140 Wireless Road
Bangkok
Tel.: (2) 251-1605

Board of Trade of Thailand
150 Rajbopit Road
Bangkok 10200
Tel.: (2) 221-0555

British Chamber of Commerce
Bangkok Insurance Building
Room 206
302 Silom Road

Bangkok
Tel.: (2) 255-8866

**Department of Commercial
Registration (DCR), Ministry
of Commerce**
Thanon Maharat
Bangkok 10200
Tel.: (2) 222-9851 / 2870;
221-9889 / 4754

**Department of Export Promo-
tion, Ministry of Commerce**
22/77 Thanon Ratchadapisek Road
Bangkok 10900
Tel.: (2) 511-5066 to 77 /
512-0093 to 104

**German–Thailand Chamber of
Commerce**
G.P.O. Box 1728
699 Silom Road
Bangkok 10500
Tel.: (2) 236-2396

**Ministry of Commerce,
Department of Foreign Trade**
Sanamchai Road
Bangkok 10200
Tel.: (2) 225-1315 / 39
or 223-1481 / 5

Ministry of Industry
Thanon Rama VI
Bangkok 10400
Tel.: (2) 246-1137-43

**Office of the Board
of Investment**
555 Vipavadeé-Rangsit Road
Chatuchak
Bangkok
Tel.: (2) 537-8150

Thai Chamber of Commerce
150 Rajbolit Road
Bangkok 10200
Tel.: (2) 225-0086 or 225-4900 / 12

Thai-PITO
BB Building, 19th Floor
54 Asoke Road, Sukhumvit 21
Bangkok, 10110
Tel.: (2) 260-7310

Tourist Authority of Thailand
4 Ratchadamneon Nok Avenue
Bangkok 10100
Tel.: (2) 282-1143 / Tourist assistance: 281-3072

Embassies and Consulates:

American Embassy
95 Wireless Road
Bangkok 10330
Tel.: (2) 252-5040

American Consulates
387 Vidhayanond Road
Chiang Mai
Tel.: (53)252-629

35/6 Supakitjanya Road
Udorn
Tel.: (42) 244-270

British Embassy
1031 Wireless Road
Bangkok 10330
Tel.: (2) 253-0191 / 9

Canadian Embassy
Boonmitr Building, 11th Floor
138 Silom Road
Bangkok 10500
Tel.: (2) 237-4125

French Embassy
Charn Issara Tower,
25th Floor
942/170-171 Rama IV Road
Bangkok
Tel.: (2) 233-9522 / 3

German Embassy
9 South Sathorn Road
Bangkok 10120
Tel.: (2) 213-2331

In Canada:

Royal Thai Embassy
180 Island Park Drive
Ottawa, Ontario K1Y 0A2
Tel.: (613) 722-4444

Thai Trade Center
888 Dunsmuir Street
Suite 1180
Vancouver, B.C. V6C 3K4
Tel.: (604) 687-6400

In France:

Royal Thai Embassy
8 Rue Greuze
75116 Paris
Tel.: (1) 4727-8079 / 4704-3222

**Thailand Board of Investment
(Bureau du Conseiller
Economique)**
World Trade Center—CNIT
2 Place de la Defense, B.P. 487
92053 Paris
Tel.: (1) 4692-2740 / 1

Thai Tourist Office
90 Champs Elysees
75008 Paris
Tel.: (1) 4562-8656

In Germany:

Royal Thai Embassy
Ubierstrasse 65
5300 Bonn 2
Tel.: (228) 355065 / 8

Thai Tourist Office
58 Bethmannstrasse
D-6000 Frankfurt
Tel.: (69) 295704

**Thai Trade and Investment
Center**
Bethman Strasse 58
60311 Frankfurt am Main
Tel.: (69) 281091 / 2

Thai Trade Center
Internationales Handelszentrum
21 Postfach 170 Friedrichstr. 95
1086 Berlin
Tel.: (30) 2643-4350 / 1 / 2

Jungfernstig 1
2000 Hamburg 1
Tel.: (40) 322207

In the United Kingdom:

Royal Thai Embassy
30 Queens Gate
London SW7 5JB
Tel.: (71) 589-0173 / 2944

Thailand Information Service
28 Princes Gate
London SW7
Tel.: (71) 584-5421

Thai Trade Center
Elizabeth House, 3d Floor
St. Peter's Square

Manchester M2 3DF
Tel.: (61) 236-0445

Tourist Authority of Thailand
49 Albemarle Street
London W1X 3FE
Tel.: (71) 499-7679 / 70

In the United States:

Royal Thai Embassy
1024 Wisconsin Avenue, N.W.
Washington, DC 20007
Tel.: (202) 944-3600

Royal Thai Consulates
351 East 52d Street
New York, NY 10022
Tel.: (212) 754-1770

35 East Wacker Drive
Suite 1834
Chicago, IL 60601
Tel.: (312) 236-2447

801 N. La Brea Avenue
Los Angeles, CA 90038
Tel.: (213) 937-1894

**Office of the Economic Coun-
selor and Thai Trade Center**
5 World Trade Center
Suite 3443
New York, NY 10048
Tel.: (212) 466-1745 / 6

Thai Trade Center
5 World Trade Center
Suite 3443
New York, NY 10048
Tel.: (212) 466-1777

401 N. Michigan Avenue
Suite 544
Chicago, IL 60611
Tel.: (312) 467-0044 / 5

3660 Wilshire Blvd., Suite 230
Los Angeles, CA 90010
Tel.: (213) 380-5943

245 Peachtree Center Avenue,
N.E., Suite 2104
Atlanta, GA 30303
Tel.: (404) 659-0178

Tourist Authority of Thailand
5 World Trade Center
Suite 3443
New York, NY 10048
Tel.: (212) 432-0433

303 East Wacker Drive
Suite 400
Chicago, IL 60601
Tel.: (312) 819-3990

3440 Wilshire Blvd., Suite 1100
Los Angeles, CA 90010
Tel.: (213) 382-2353

U.S. Department of Commerce
International Trade
Administration
Thailand Desk, Room 2032
14th & Constitution
Avenues, N.W.
Washington, DC 20230
Tel.: (202) 482-4958

12 India ———————

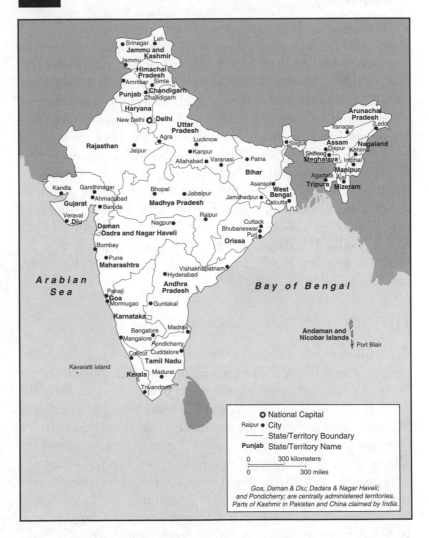

Srinagar • Leh
Jammu and Kashmir
Jammu •
Himachal Pradesh
Amritsar • • Simla
Punjab •**Chandigarh**
Chandigarh
Haryana
New Delhi ⊕ **Delhi**
Uttar Pradesh
• Agra • Lucknow

Arunachal Pradesh
Itanagar • • Ledo

Rajasthan • Jaipur
• Kanpur
Allahabad • • Varanasi • Patna
Bihar
Siliguri • • **Assam** **Nagaland**
Dispur • Kohima
Shillong • Imphal
Meghalaya **Manipur**
Agartala • Aijal
Tripura **Mizeram**

Kandla • Gandhinagar •
• Bhopal • Jabalpur Asansol • **West Bengal**
Gujarat • Ahmadabad Jamshedpur • Calcutta •
Veraval • • Baroda **Madhya Pradesh**
• **Diu**
Daman • Nagpur • Raipur
Dadra and Nagar Haveli Cuttack •
Bhubaneswar •
Bombay • **Orissa** Puri •

• Pune
Maharashtra
Vishakhapatnam •
• Hyderabad
Andhra Pradesh

Arabian Sea
Bay of Bengal

Panaji •
Goa
Mormugao • • Guntakal
Karnataka •
Bangalore • Madras •
Mangalore • **Pondicherry**
Calicut • Cuddalore •
Kavaratti Island **Tamil Nadu**
Kerala • Madurai
• Trivandrum

Andaman and Nicobar Islands
• Port Blair

⊕ National Capital
Raipur • City
——— State/Territory Boundary
Punjab State/Territory Name
0 ————— 300 kilometers
0 ————— 300 miles

Goa, Daman & Diu; Dadara & Nagar Haveli;
and Pondicherry; are centrally administered territories.
Parts of Kashmir in Pakistan and China claimed by India.

Geography

India is the seventh largest country in the world, with a total land area of 1.267 million square miles (3.28 million square kilometers); it is about one-third the size of the United States. India shares borders in the northwest with Pakistan, in the north with China, Bhutan, and Nepal, and in the east with Bangladesh and Myanmar (Burma). Indian territory also extends to the Andaman and Nicobar Islands in the Bay of Bengal as well as to the Lakshawdweep Islands in the Arabian Sea. The mainland of India consists of four main regions: the mountains in the north, including the Himalayas; the Indo-Gangetic plains in the north; a desert region in parts of the west; and a southern region, known as the Deccan, comprised of high plateaus, mountains, and coastal strips. The capital of India is New Delhi. The six largest cities in terms of population in descending order are Bombay, Calcutta, Delhi, Madras, Hyderabad, and Bangalore.

History

The earliest traces of human activity in the area date back several hundred thousand years. The first organized state in India came into being around 3000 B.C. along the Indus River Valley in the north in what is now Pakistan. Centered around the twin capitals of Mohenjo-daro and Harappa, the Indus civilization flourished for over one thousand years. It is believed that these early native Indian inhabitants were proto-Dravidians, spoke a language that was a precursor of modern Tamil, and were ruled by a king who was worshipped as a god. Very little evidence regarding this Indus culture has survived. Mohenjo-daro and Harappa were destroyed around 1600 B.C. by natural disasters, either floods or an earthquake, forcing the survivors to flee south. As a result of the collapse of the Indus civilization, Aryan invaders encountered minimal resistance around 1500 B.C. when they arrived from central Asia. The Aryans eventually conquered all of northern India, but never penetrated the south.

The Indo-Aryans were the easternmost wing of a related group of Indo-European tribes who, around 2000 B.C., began to migrate from an area between the Caspian and Black Seas to Europe, the Middle East, and India. The Aryans brought their religious beliefs and practices, called Arya-Dharma, to India, but they also adopted many indigenous beliefs and practices to create a highly eclectic mixed religion. The term "Hindu," the modern name for the resulting religion, was coined a thousand years later by Muslim invaders, who referred to the residents of the land as "Indus." The religion's holy scriptures, called the Vedas, are believed to have been written down between 1500 and 1200 B.C. The Aryan socioreligious system was based on a complex system of castes and was designed to preserve the supreme position of the highest level, the Brahmins or priest class. The second level was the Kshatriyas or warrior class. The third level was the Vaishyas or common class. The Aryans assigned the non-Aryan, indigenous people to a fourth major class, the lowest level Shudras. This social order was maintained by very strict rules that touched all aspects of life, including social obligations, marriage, diet, and travel. These rules have been preserved relatively intact to this day. Members of each caste observed its strict rules or risked becoming an outcast.

The formal Jain religion began around 700 B.C., although there is evidence of Jain philosophies prior to that time, with Buddhism emerging in India around 600 B.C. Both developed as a response against the Vedas, the caste system, and the rigorous rituals promoted by Hinduism. (Please refer to chapter on Religions.)

By the end of the sixth century B.C., there were at least a dozen princely states in northern India fighting over territory and control of trade. During the period of Aryan rule, India narrowly missed conquest by two other invaders from the West. The first was launched by the Persian King, Darius (521–486 B.C.) who conquered only the northern areas of Sind and Punjab. In 326 B.C.,

Alexander the Great reached India, but advanced no further than the Beas River. Alexander made a significant impact on India through the development of Gandharan art which represented a mixture of Grecian ideals and Buddhism.

Chandragupta, the founder of the Mauryan Empire, came to power in 321 B.C. Eventually controlling most of India, the Mauryan empire had a well-organized and efficient bureaucracy. The Mauryan emperor Ashoka is one of the great figures of Indian history. Art, philosophy, and Buddhism flourished during his rule. Ashoka made Buddhism the official state religion and was responsible for promoting its spread to Sri Lanka. Under Ashoka, the Mauryan Empire controlled more of India than any subsequent rulers except the Moghuls and the British. Hindu discontent with the extent of Buddhist influence encouraged a Brahmin general to initiate a coup that led to the collapse of the Mauryan Empire in 184 B.C. India then entered a period of political fragmentation that lasted for about five hundred years and which was characterized by the rise and fall of numerous regional kingdoms.

After the fall of the Mauryan Empire, the area that is now Pakistan was ruled until about 130 B.C. by the Bactrians, who also controlled northern Afghanistan and Parthia in Persia. The Kushans, a central Asian tribe, created an empire across Pakistan that lasted for about two centuries until about the early third century A.D.

One constant throughout Indian history is that events taking place in one part of India did not always affect other parts of the country. Kingdoms that rose, flourished, and fell in one region had little impact on life in other regions. Despite periods in which a ruler or succession of rulers unified the country, Indian history is marked by political fragmentation and regional fiefdoms that nourished wide linguistic, cultural, and religious differences.

Major southern empires included the Cholas, Pandyas, Cheras, Chalukyas, and Pallavas. Beginning with the first Chola king as early as 100 A.D., foreign trade with the southern areas of Tamil expanded, bringing wealth and material prosperity. The Chalukyas

ruled in parts of central India and extended their power north from
550 to 753 A.D., then fell to the Rashtrakutas. The Chalukyas rose
once again in 972 A.D. and ruled until 1190 A.D. Further south, the
powerful Pallavas rule began in the sixth century and lasted for two
hundred years, carrying Indian culture to Indonesia, Thailand, and
Cambodia. In 850 A.D. the Pallavas were replaced by the second
group of Cholas, who continued to move overseas and eventually
controlled the entire southern part of India, Sri Lanka, parts of the
Malay Peninsula, and the Sumatran-based Srivijaya kingdom.

Meanwhile, in the early third century A.D., the western region
that is Pakistan today fell to the Persian Sassanians. In 319 A.D. in
the eastern part of India, Chandragupta II founded the Gupta Empire, beginning the first phase of the imperial Gupta period that
lasted until 606 A.D. During this period, the arts, literature, and religion (Buddhism and Jainism) flourished, although towards the end
both religions declined in popularity as Hinduism slowly underwent
a revival lasting from the third century until the ninth century. At
the end of the Gupta period, northern India broke into several
Hindu kingdoms and was not unified again until the Muslims entered India.

By the early eighth century Muslims began to have an effect on
northern India, with Arab traders bringing Islam to the region. By
1206, Muslims had cemented their interests in India and established
a sultanate at Delhi, which lasted for some three hundred years. By
1226, the entire Ganges basin was under Muslim control; however,
the Delhi sultanate was unable to expand much farther because regional Hindu kingdoms maintained a strong defense. The Hindu
kingdom of Vijayanagar, founded in 1336, was located in southern
India and was probably the strongest Hindu kingdom during this
period.

Although Islam has been a constant in India for more than a
thousand years, the Muslims were successful in converting only
about 25 percent of India's population. During their rule, Muslims
were forced to bring Hindus into the bureaucracy because they were

unable to rule without Hindu assistance. As a consequence, the language of Urdu, which is a combination of Persian vocabulary and Hindi grammar written in a Perso-Arabic script, was developed.

The Delhi sultanate was successful in protecting the Indian subcontinent from the Mongols. But in the early sixteenth century the Delhi sultanate was replaced by another Muslim force, the Moghuls, who had the greatest influence on India of all its Muslim rulers. Six great Moghul emperors ruled for a relatively short time period: Babur (1527–1530); Humayun (1530–1556); Akbar (1556–1605); Jehangir (1605–1627); Shah Jehan (1627–1658); and Aurangzeb (1658–1707). Because of their passion for architecture, art, literature, and grandeur, the Moghuls had a significant impact on the cultural landscape of India.

Akbar, noted for being the greatest Moghul emperor, was a strong military commander as well as a fair, cultured, wise, and religiously tolerant man. Akbar is noted for recognizing that the number of Hindus in India was too great to simply subjugate them. He instead integrated the Hindus into the bureaucracy of his empire and pursued a policy of peaceful coexistence. None of the other Moghul emperors were as religiously tolerant as Akbar. Shah Jehan is credited with building the Taj Mahal in honor of his dead wife. During Jehangir and Shah Jehan's reigns, the British were granted several trading posts, which ultimately became bases for the gradual takeover of the entire country. Aurangzeb was the last of the powerful Moghul emperors. He attempted to extend the boundaries of his empire, but was brought down by internal policies and religious zealotry. His belief in Islamic fundamentalism led him to destroy many Hindu temples and erect mosques on their sites. This alienated his Hindu bureaucracy, which eventually revolted. The destruction of temples and the erection of mosques more than 350 years ago continues to fuel anger between Hindus and Muslims in India today.

The primary reason for the downfall of the Moghuls was this narrow-minded Islamic orthodoxy which alienated the Hindu Indian masses. Infighting and threats from other rulers, particularly the Marathas and the Rajputs, also contributed. Despite Muslim domination of the north, there were still some pockets of Hindu power, controlled primarily by the Rajputs. Based in Rajasthan, the Rajputs were a warrior caste with an almost fanatical devotion to bravery in battle. Their role in Indian history is similar to that of the knights in medieval Europe. For a time, they successfully opposed all foreign incursions, but they were unable to effectively unite and eventually spent more energy battling each other than their common foreign enemies.

The Marathas, based in what today is the state of Maharashtra, first rose to power under the leadership of Shivaji, who between 1646 and 1680 performed acts of military strength and heroism across central India. He continues to be idolized by many rural Indians today, especially in the state of Maharashtra. Shivaji is particularly admired because he came from a lower Hindu caste, thus proving that great leaders did not have to be Kshatriyas, members of the warrior caste. Shivaji's son and grandson were unable to maintain his legacy and the Maratha Empire dwindled. In 1761 the Marathas were defeated at Panipat by Ahmad Shah Durani from Afghanistan and the last remnants of the Maratha Empire in central India ended with the domination by the British.

The first Europeans to settle in parts of India were the Portuguese, who under the leadership of Vasco de Gama landed in 1498 on the coast of modern-day Kerala in the south in 1498. In 1510 the Portuguese captured Goa, which they controlled until 1961. In 1600 Queen Elizabeth I granted a charter to a British trading company, giving them a monopoly on British trade with India. For the next 250 years, British affairs in India were not handled by the British government, but by the British East India Trading Company. In 1612 the British made their first permanent settlement at Surat in the state of Gujarat, subsequently adding trading posts at Bombay, Madras, and Calcutta. The Dutch and the French also established trading posts.

When the Moghul Empire disintegrated in the seventeenth century, India fragmented due to a lack of strong centralized leadership. The British took advantage of India's political rivalries, waging and winning one war after another against India's many rulers. The British focused on profitable trade and were not particularly interested in converting the Indians to Christianity. This gave them an advantage over the Portuguese, who openly sought to do so. For almost a century, the French and British competed for control of Indian trade, often playing local rulers against one another and manipulating relationships between royal family members within the same kingdom. Both parties hired and trained Indian *sepoys*, local police, to guard their forts and serve in their armies. The French, led by Joseph Francois Dupleix, pursued a partially successful policy of buying the favor of India's rulers in the south, but this strategy became too expensive and was eventually abandoned.

In 1757 the British, under Robert Clive, the governor of the British East India Company in India, defeated the Indian ruler Siraj-ud-daula and his French supporters in Calcutta, thereby cementing the power of the East India Trading Company and reducing French influence. Although the French maintained an enclave at Pondicherry until 1954, India's future was now in Great Britain's hands. In 1803 the British finally defeated the Marathas. In 1849 Punjab, the last state under local rule, was conquered by the British. It was also during this period that the British conquered Nepal. However, the British found the area difficult to govern and chose instead to exercise indirect influence through trade. Further, British respect for the military prowess of the Gurkhas, soldiers from the Gorkha region of Nepal, led them to recruit and maintain separate Gurkha regiments. (See Chapter 16, on Nepal, for more information on Nepal's history.)

The British profited immensely from Indian trade, but in returned developed and implemented a strong, well-organized bureaucracy as well as an extensive railway network, roads and bridges, irrigation systems, and other infrastructure projects.

The British East India Trading Company focused primarily on commerce and did not interfere with Indian culture, beliefs, or religions. The British controlled India through a combination of direct rule in certain provinces and indirect rule in others; in the latter case, the British allowed Indian rulers to remain on their thrones, but retained control of trade policy and all other important issues. The British followed the guiding principle of divide and conquer, making India's native rulers dependent on British goodwill and playing off one faction against another. By the middle of the nineteenth century, the British East Indian Trading Company had recruited, armed, and trained more than three hundred thousand Indians, forming an army that was used to fight and subdue other Indians.

In the north in 1799, Ranjit Singh, a Sikh, became governor of Lahore and eventually controlled major areas in modern Pakistan, including Punjab, Kashmir, and the Peshwar Valley. The British eventually annexed this small empire and incorporated the Sikh soldiers into their army. Despite several efforts, the British were unsuccessful in conquering what is now the Northwest Frontier Province in modern Pakistan. In 1901 a separate and autonomous Northwest Frontier Province (NWFP), the northern-most province in modern Pakistan, was created by the British in order to satisfy the Pathans who lived there, and who had made it clear that they would never accept foreign rule.

In 1857 Indian battalions of the Bengal Army stationed near Delhi revolted against British control. Their mutiny sparked similar revolts against the British throughout northern India. Because the rebellion was fragmented and because no one leader emerged to coordinate it, it died out within a year. After this incident, the British government assumed direct control over India. Thereafter the Indian subcontinent, which included today's India, Pakistan, and Bangladesh, became the keystone in Britain's global empire, providing it with profits and prestige.

After the 1857 Mutiny, the British reorganized its Indian armies, mixing units by race, caste, and region to ensure that individual ethnic groups would be less likely to unite and rise in mutiny again. The Indians and their leaders, devastated by their impotency against British firepower, adopted an interim stance of complacency, realizing that they would have to transform themselves and unite before they could successfully challenge British rule again.

The sons of India's upper classes were often sent to Great Britain to receive a Western-style education. A small but steady flow of Indians went off to Europe, were exposed to modern, liberal ideas, and brought those ideas home to India. A nationalist movement, with two schools of thought, began to form. The radical group wanted to rid India of the British as soon as possible. The moderate group believed that before India could accept the responsibilities of self-rule, all Indians had to learn to treat each other more humanely and engage in social reform.

By the turn of the century, Indian opposition to British rule began to intensify. The Indian National Congress, which had been created in 1885 to promote more self-rule for Indians, assumed the leadership role in the struggle for independence. Gradually the Indians were given more opportunities for participation in India's administration. In 1906 the All-India Muslim League was founded in Dacca as a counterbalance to the Indian National Congress, for many Muslims feared Hindu domination. During this same period, Hinduism began another era of revival and adjustment, having lost much of its mass appeal during the Moghul and early British period. This became a unifying point within India's population.

In 1915 Mohandas Gandhi, who was later given the honorific title "Mahatma," meaning "Great Soul," returned from South Africa, where as a lawyer he had devoted himself to fighting racial discrimination. Upon his return to India, he became involved in the struggle for independence, particularly after the Amritsar massacre in 1919 during which British soldiers fired upon an unarmed crowd of protesters. Gandhi was successful in expanding the independence struggle from a concern of the small middle and upper classes to one involving India's great peasant masses. He led boycotts against British textiles and the salt tax. He was often jailed, as were other leaders, but his policy of *satyagraha*, passive resistance and noncooperation, gained him global recognition and increasing sympathy. He was also a fervent advocate of equality and tolerance and worked to rid the Hindu religion of discrimination in its caste system. Gandhi's idea of self-reliance and his policy of "home-grown," that encouraged Indians to purchase Indian-made products and reduce their reliance on foreign products, laid the foundation for an attitude that would permeate most of India's future political and economic policies.

By the end of World War II, it was apparent that independence was inevitable. The war had destroyed the myth of European superiority and Britain no longer had the financial resources to support a far-reaching global empire. However, not all Indians supported Gandhi's methods and policies as he spearheaded the drive for independence. The Muslim minority realized that an independent India would be Hindu-dominated, and that the Muslim minority would lose its British protectors. As a result, there was an alarming and sometimes violent growth of communalism. Mohammed Ali Jinnah, leader of the Muslim League, vowed to divide India into two nations. The Congress party, led by Jawaharlal Nehru, spearheaded efforts to maintain a united India. The British, under Lord Mountbatten, tried unsuccessfully to reconcile the two sides as the Congress party's fight for an independent greater India and Jinnah's egotistical bid for power over a separate nation brought India closer to armed conflict. However, the decision to divide India was made. The resulting countries were called India and Pakistan. India's independence was declared on August 15, 1947. The decision to divide, however, resulted in violent and widespread communal unrest.

The division of India remains a sore spot for many Indians, who view it as a betrayal of their nation by independence leaders from all sides as well as the British. Gandhi opposed the division, but always advocated peace as the primary objective. He was murdered on January 30, 1948, by a fanatical Hindu member of the right-wing Rashtriya Swayamsevak Sangh (the RSS) group, which advocated

Hindu supremacy through force. In his efforts to promote communal harmony and mutual respect, Gandhi often read from both Hindu and Islamic scriptures and was thus accused by fanatical Hindus of being a Muslim-lover and traitor to his own religion. To this day, some Indians, mainly Hindus, blame Gandhi for "the Partition," as it is commonly known in India, and his legacy has become bitter-sweet.

Dividing India proved difficult, because Muslim areas were scattered throughout the country, particularly in the north. The two main Muslim "islands" were on opposite sides of the country. These two regions became East and West Pakistan, separated by one thousand miles of Indian territory. A war twenty-five years later brought independence to the eastern "island," now known as Bangladesh.

Upon partition, many of India's Muslims fled their home region for refuge in Pakistan, while many Hindus and Sikhs in the new nation of Pakistan fled in the opposite direction. With almost ten million people changing sides, it is believed to have been the greatest exodus in human history. Violence broke out as Hindu-Sikh and Muslim mobs preyed upon each other and at least one million people were killed in the resulting hostilities. What should have been a time of national rejoicing became a period of chaos, death, and despair.

Partition was not the only problem to greet the newly, independent India. Throughout British rule, many princely states had been allowed to remain in existence. At the time of independence, there were still three such states that had not made a decision as to which country to join. The most well-known is Kashmir, which was predominately Muslim but had a Hindu maharaja (king). In 1948 a Pathan (Pakistani) army crossed the border into Kashmir and moved toward the capital, Srinagar. Their intent was to annex Kashmir quickly so as to avoid a military confrontation with the Indian army. However, the Pathan army stopped to plunder villages along the way, enabling the Indian army to reinforce the capital. Eventually, the indecisive Kashmiri maharaja chose to align the region with India. This became the first of several bitter conflicts between India and Pakistan over Kashmir. A 1949 United Nations cease-fire gave Pakistan control over one-third of the state in the west and northwest, while India retained control over the remaining two-thirds. The disagreement continues today as Kashmir's Muslim majority have been inclined at times to support Pakistan.

India and Pakistan fought wars again in 1965 and 1971. The 1965 war over Kashmir allowed India, the victor, to retain control of its portion of Kashmir. In 1971 India came to the aid of East Pakistan's independence efforts and fought against Pakistani forces, defeating them and thereby enabling East Pakistan to become the free nation of Bangladesh.

At independence, India's administrative system was comparatively more efficient and less corrupt than that of most other former colonial countries. Since independence, India, unlike so many former colonies, has managed to nourish its democratic institutions and policies. Nehru, the country's first prime minister, promoted a policy of global nonalignment and, along with Tito (of Yugoslavia) and Sukarno (of Indonesia), he was internationally recognized as one of the founders of the "Nonaligned Movement." Geopolitical issues forced India to gradually align itself with the former Soviet Union in response to the regional threat posed by China and U.S. support for Pakistan. The United States had determined that Pakistan had strategic value to the West because of its location next to Afghanistan and near the former Soviet Union. In 1962 India and China fought a war over a border dispute, leaving India humiliated and shaken by the Chinese aggression. India has continued to dispute sovereignty over some areas that were taken by the Chinese. In general, India and China remain wary of each other.

Nehru died in 1964 and was succeeded briefly by Lal Bahadur Shastri, who died in January 1966. Nehru's daughter, Indira Gandhi, was appointed prime minister in the same month by the Congress party chiefs who incorrectly assumed that she would be easy to manipulate. Mrs. Gandhi, no relation to Mahatma Gandhi, had two sons, Sanjay and Rajiv. A shrewd, calculating, and very capable politician, Mrs. Gandhi became one of India's strongest leaders and is often referred to as "Mother India." She held power for more than sixteen years. Maintaining the vision of her father, Mrs. Gandhi was successful in her efforts to preserve India's role as the leader of the Nonaligned Movement and third world countries.

Meanwhile, India was plagued with domestic problems, many related to its overpopulation crisis. The energy crisis of the early 1970s combined with droughts drained the economy, fueling strikes throughout the country. Facing an adverse court ruling in a voting law case and serious political opposition, Mrs. Gandhi declared a state of emergency in 1975, suspended basic rights, and jailed her opponents. This move was a blot on an otherwise predominately positive record and cost her the election in 1977. During the state of emergency, Sanjay Gandhi, her oldest and very ambitious son, gained more power and attempted to implement a forced sterilization program throughout the country. He was killed in an air accident in 1980.

The 1977 election was a testimony to the strength of India's commitment to democracy. Morarji Desai, the leader of the opposition Janata Dal, became prime minister. He only ruled for a brief three-year period, for the Janata party was disorganized and the economy suffered immensely. Mrs. Gandhi won reelection in 1980 by an overwhelming majority. With Sanjay dead, the younger son, Rajiv, became the heir apparent. The early 1980s were characterized by communal unrest, the most notable of which was the Sikh struggle, in which radical Sikhs demanded that an independent Sikh state of Khalistan be carved out of the Indian state of Punjab. In 1983 Mrs. Gandhi sent the Indian Army into the Golden Temple, the holiest temple for Sikhs, in Amritsar to flush out heavily armed radicals. This led to widespread riots and violence and eventually to Mrs. Gandhi's own assassination by a Sikh bodyguard in October 1984. The Sikh terrorists continued their sporadically violent campaign for independence throughout the rest of the decade. Stability in the northern state of Punjab remains fragile to this day.

Rajiv Gandhi, her son, was swept into power as the result of a huge sympathy vote. Unaccustomed to power, he brought a fresh, pragmatic and youthful vigor to the office. His drive for modernization, begun by Mrs. Gandhi, primed India's economic overhaul by easing import restrictions, encouraging modern technologies, and creating new industries and businesses. These initiatives came to a halt as Rajiv Gandhi's administration became plagued by accusations of bribery and corruption, particularly the Bofors scandal, in which it was alleged that a Swedish arms manufacturer had paid bribes to various prominent Indians, most of whom were close friends of the prime minister.

Rajiv Gandhi was forced out of power in 1989. He was succeeded by V. P. Singh as prime minister. Less than one year later, Singh was succeeded by Chandra Shekar, who also held office for just a year. During the 1991 elections, while on a campaign stop in the state of Tamil Nadu, Rajiv Gandhi was assassinated by a suicide bomber from the Tamil Tigers, the radical Tamil group demanding a separate Tamil state in Sri Lanka. (See Chapter 14, on Sri Lanka.)

Ironically, for a devoutly democratic country, recent succession to power in India has come as often by the bullet as by the ballot box. One of India's political problems is the development of personality cults centering on its leaders, particularly members of the Nehru family, which has provided three of India's seven prime ministers.

After Rajiv Gandhi's death, Narasimha Rao assumed leadership of the Congress party and led it to victory in 1991. The new government initiated widespread economic reforms, including reducing export and import barriers, dismantling some of the swollen bureaucracy, making the currency partially convertible, and eliminating the black market for foreign currency and gold. Efforts were also made to privatize or increase the efficiencies of unprofitable state companies. Finance Minister Manmohan Singh has been successful in beginning to dismantle the "license raj," an intricate system of government control of the economy through permits and quotas.

Kashmir became a major issue again in the early 1990s as

Pakistan-backed secessionist militants rose against the Indian army, accusing the army of over-zealous activities, including human rights abuses against the militants and protesters in the region. A near-war in early 1992 was avoided by diplomacy. Kashmiri militants remain strong, ensuring that the Kashmir issue will not be easily resolved.

Other internal problems continue to plague India, although none are severe enough to jeopardize its sovereignty. In order to gain power, Hindu–Muslim rivalries have been exploited by some political parties, primarily the BJP (Bharatiya Janata party, a staunch Hindu revivalist organization). In December 1992 the BJP led Hindu mobs to destroy a mosque in Ayodhya, a small town in central Uttar Pradesh. Because of its identity as the birthplace of the god Rama, Hindus declared their intention to rebuild a temple on the same site. Centuries before, Moghul emperors were believed to have razed several temples and built mosques in this area. The destruction of the mosque led to national riots between Hindus and Muslims. The BJP along with its paramilitary organization, the RSS (Rashtriya Swayamsevak Sangh), promotes nonsecular policies that would elevate the position of Hindus at the expense of Muslims and other minorities.

The BJP's fervent call for a pro-Hindu state was overwhelmingly rebuffed by the Indian voters in the December 1993 election. While religious tensions will not easily dissipate, their modern source is rooted more in economics and opportunities for material gain than in any specific religious differences. Even among Hindu castes, rivalries for material gain have provoked unrest and are forcing the country to address its long-standing policies (since independence) of reserving spaces in colleges and government jobs for lower caste Hindus, Muslims, and other minorities. As more Indians vie for limited education slots and government jobs, the issue of minority quotas will continue to be a major policy dispute.

Despite its internal social tensions and external border disputes, India is moving forward economically. Foreign investment has poured steadily into the country and Indian companies are rising to the challenge of competing in global markets. These economic gains have provided improved standards of living for all communities in India. Rao has been successful in retaining power despite several no-confidence votes, primarily because his economic policies have brought visible benefits to the country and have been popular with the people. However, India's annual population growth of 2.1 percent ensures that its population will surpass China's within the next decade and remains a significant problem for the government as limited resources threaten the distribution of the benefits of economic reform.

Political Structure

India has a parliamentary form of government similar to the British system. The country's twenty-six states and six union territories each has its own government. There is universal suffrage for all adults over the age of eighteen. The government consists of three separate branches: the executive, the legislative, and the judiciary. The executive branch is technically led by the president, the constitutional head of government, and the vice-president, both of whom are elected indirectly for five-year terms by the two national assemblies and selected state assemblies. Similar to the monarch in the United Kingdom, the president invites the leader of the majority party or coalition of parties to form a council of ministers, headed by the prime minister, who holds the real power.

India's bicameral legislature, called the Parliament, consists of the Lok Sabha (House of the People) and the Rajya Sabha (Council of States). The council of ministers is technically accountable to the Lok Sabha. The normal term for the Lok Sabha is five years, although elections may be called sooner by the prime minister. Rajya Sabha elections are held indirectly. The Lok Sabha is the more powerful of the two houses, although both are required to consent to all legislation.

State governments are structured similar to the federal system. A governor, appointed by the president, functions as the head of the state. The state council of ministers, headed by a chief minister, has the real power in each state, with some states exercising more national power on various issues. Some of the state legislatures are bicameral.

India has an independent judicial system, with the highest level being the Supreme Court. Indian law is based on government statutes, customary law, and case law. The legal system is well-developed in comparison with those of many other Asian countries, due in large part to the contributions by the British who developed the legal infrastructure. While India is technically a secular country, ethnic and religious differences have influenced the development of certain laws, particularly in the area of personal law. For example, Muslim men in India are permitted to marry up to four wives because this is allowed in Islamic law; however, non-Muslim men are permitted to marry only one wife at a time.

Economy

Over the past few years, India has embarked on an economic liberalization scheme that has proven to be beneficial to the country. Prior to the mid-1980s, the country pursued a policy of socialism with the state planning and controlling many sectors of the economy. Foreign investment had been discouraged except in the area of technology transfers. Prime Minister Rao's new policies provide a larger role for the private sector and encourage foreign investment. Central government intervention, licensing, and regulation have decreased, as have bureaucratic inefficiencies. India boasts a sophisticated industrial and manufacturing base, a huge pool of skilled, low-to-moderate-cost workers including professional managers, and an established free-market system.

The country is rich in natural resources such as rubber, timber, chromium, coal, iron, manganese, bauxite, mica salt, and gypsum. India has reserves of coal, gas, and oil, but remains a net importer of crude oil as domestic generation is insufficient to meet demand. Agriculture remains an important economic sector, contributing roughly 33 percent of the country's gross domestic product and employing almost 70 percent of the workforce. Major crops include rice, wheat, pulses, sugar cane, cotton, jute, oilseeds, tea, coffee, and tobacco.

The growth of Indian industry has resulted in widespread improvements and diversity in the country's manufacturing base. The major manufacturing industries include cotton and jute textiles; iron, steel, and other basic metals; petrochemicals; electrical machinery and appliances; transport equipment; chemicals; cement; fertilizers; medicines and pharmaceuticals; and food products. The power, electronics, food-processing, and telecommunications industries are developing rapidly. The financial sector, including banking and insurance, is well-developed, although efforts to modernize it are underway.

State-run entities continue to control some areas of telecommunications, banking, insurance, public utilities, and defense, as well as the production of minerals, steel, other metals, coal, natural gas, and petroleum. There have been some steps taken to shift more control to the private sector, although on a gradual and closely monitored scale.

People, Values, and Social Customs

The population of India is about 898 million, making it the second-most populous country after China. India has three major racial groups: the Indo-Aryans (72 percent), Dravidians (25 percent), and the Mongolian (3 percent), each of which has various subgroups which are easily distinguished by physical attributes. The Mongolians are concentrated in the northeastern states. People with Aryan features tend to reside in the northern areas and those with Dravidian characteristics tend to be concentrated in the south.

It is difficult to generalize about India as people's attitudes in the north can vary significantly from those in the south. There are wide differences in values, language, food, dress, and other cultural elements between each state and region as well as within religious, economic, and social classes. Each state has its own ethnic culture and often its own language. Indians are fiercely loyal to their regions as well as to their ethnic and religious communities, which has on occasion led to conflict and violence. This has also resulted in a fragmented heritage in which national identity usually comes after regional, religious and often linguistic identities.

More than 82 percent of the country's population is Hindu; about 11 percent are Muslims. The remainder of the population are Christians, Sikhs, Buddhists, Zoroastrians, Jains, or followers of various tribal religions. Despite partition and the loss of most of its Muslim population, India is home to the third largest Muslim population in the world, after Indonesia and Pakistan; it has far more Muslims than any single Arab Middle East nation. Historically, Hinduism provided a broad sense of social unity, but it was never strong enough to create a political and economic unity.

The Hindu caste system is one of the more complicated aspects of modern Indian life. It was originally developed almost three thousand years ago by the priest class, or Brahmins, in order to make their superior position in society more permanent. Eventually the system became formalized with four distinct classes, each with a prescribed set of rules for conduct and behavior. Mahatma Gandhi attempted to uplift the lowest group in society and termed them Harijans, meaning children of God. In modern times, the lowest caste are also called Dalits, which means oppressed, downtrodden, or "untouchables." In traditional settings such as rural areas or in religious ceremonies or weddings, Dalits are forbidden from serving food to higher caste Hindus, drinking from the same well, or performing certain rituals at temples. Many of them continue to work in jobs that few people in Indian society will perform, such as cleaning streets and drains and caring for cremation grounds. (Refer to the appendix on Religions.)

Caste is no longer used to determine occupation, but most affluent Indians tend to be from one of the higher castes. It should be noted that each caste has many subdivisions based on such factors as region. Historically, the oppressed had little or no opportunity for education and advancement, thus ensuring that lower caste people would be unable to break free from their social level. Government programs have sought to rectify this imbalance by providing special quotas for the Scheduled Caste (untouchables), but this has provoked widespread backlashes.

Despite India's modernization efforts, rural India, which accounts for 70 percent of the population, remains traditional and provincial with strict beliefs and practices that have changed very little throughout the centuries. Even the most educated rural people cling to their traditional beliefs. Marriages continue to be arranged within castes and regional communities, ensuring a level of social and economic homogeneity. Rural women continue to be restricted by traditional guidelines for social behavior, although the treatment of women tends to differ in proportion to an area's level of educational and economic advancement. However, it should be noted that the treatment of women does not necessarily improve with the wealth, status, and education of family members. Marriage dowries, although technically illegal, are still socially required in many communities. Greed for additional dowries has fueled the practice of bride-burning, an illegal but hard-to-prove murder, by husbands and parents-in-law who hope to receive more material wealth, including cash, cars, and appliances, from subsequent marriages.

Indians have a great deal of respect for family and elders. All of the Indian languages have specific respectful terms for each older family member. Members of the younger generation will call older Indians "Uncle" or "Auntie" whether or not they are related. This shows the younger person's respect and affection for their elders. Indians are relatively quick to accept outsiders into their family, particularly friends of their children or adults with whom they share common interests.

India is home to almost 50 percent of the world total of people who live in democratic societies. As members of the world's largest democracy, Indians take great pride in their freedom. The modern mind-set of India as a nation has been shaped in large part by its colonial experience and the resulting independence efforts and related *swadeshi* movement, which promoted economic self-reliance, particularly in science and technology.

Most Indians, particularly the less educated ones, tend to be easily aroused by social and political issues. Almost fifty years after the partition, the suspicion of Pakistan and Muslims continues to plague most non-Muslim Indians of all generations and economic backgrounds.

The introduction of satellite television throughout India and its portrayal of Western affluence has awakened India's people to their country's economic backwardness. New ideas, concepts, lifestyles and products are routinely presented by the media. Modernization and Western pop culture now permeate many aspects of Indian life. As a result, the Indian people are now eager to catch up materially, although Western cultural influence has contributed to confusion about cultural values and roots.

Until recently, most Indians viewed money, profit, and commercial activities as "dirty." It was widely assumed that a person had to be unscrupulous in order to succeed financially. This attitude was evident by the fact that the commercial caste was the third level in Hinduism and the more philosophical priest caste at the very top. In modern times this attitude has been hypocritical as most Indians place a value on material wealth and have sought to obtain it through marriage and dowry. As a result, the aversion to wealth as "dirty" stems more from frustration or inability to achieve material gains. Due to the changes in government policy and the belief that everyone can participate in the "Indian Dream," this attitude is slowly changing.

Indians tend to operate as "islands" and perceive their own particular community as the center of the world. They are very parochial, which leads them to be very critical and negative, rather than supportive of one another. Indians have always viewed foreigners, particularly Westerners, as more superior. In India fair skin and Aryan features are highly prized physical attributes. The public perception is that "white" skin is associated with the upper class, dark skin with the lower class. Many Indians feel that Western products and ideas are better than Indian ones. Therefore, the average Indian is very welcoming to foreigners. Ironically, Indians can be more accepting of foreigners, particularly Westerners, than of other Indians as a result of the nation's widespread regional, religious, and caste differences.

The literacy rate in India is about 53 percent, with male literacy rates significantly higher than female literacy rates. Generally, literacy and average level of education differ from state to state, ranging from the southern state of Kerala with the highest literacy rate at 91 percent to the northern state of Uttar Pradesh with only 42 percent literacy. Education is very important in India; it has long been viewed as the best method for achieving social and economic advancement. Certain professions, including medicine and engineering, have very high status because they are perceived as guaranteed paths to economic stability. After the tenth grade (standard) students take highly competitive national exams to determine their eligibility to study the "arts" or "sciences." Once a student enters the arts or sciences line, they cannot switch to the other. Exams after the twelfth grade determine eligibility into medical, engineering or other professional colleges. To enable them to compete more effectively on the annual standardized exams, young children are routinely tutored outside of school.

Compared with workers in many Western and some Eastern societies, Indians work fewer hours. Due to the Hindu influence, Indians have a strong belief in fate. Many Indians believe that one's whole life is determined at birth. Thus they believe that there is a limit to what a person can do to change his or her life. In practice, the power of fate is used when it is appropriate and discarded casually when not convenient.

Women remain responsible for the home and children. Traditionally, Indian women were not treated as equals by men. In modern times, many women have benefited from access to higher education and have achieved distinction in various fields, including medicine, engineering, and teaching. With the new economic reforms, more women are finding lucrative opportunities in business-related fields. On occasion, Indian women have achieved success in male-dominated areas such as politics. The status of women differs by class with middle-class women more likely to be treated as equals by their husbands because they have so many responsibilities inside and outside of the home. Nevertheless, in a general sense, women are still perceived to be inferior to men.

Work Schedule

India has a five-day workweek, although this differs by industry and region. Most businesses, banks, and government offices are open from 10:00 A.M. to 5:30 P.M., Monday to Friday, but city offices may be open from 8:00 A.M. to 6:00 P.M. Some businesses are open for a half day, others for a full day, on Saturdays. There is a one-hour lunch break on all days. Office workers usually work forty hours per week, while factory and industrial workers work a forty-eight-hour week. Due to inadequate power supplies, factories often have staggered schedules with each factory in a district closing on a different day of the week. Shops are usually open daily from 10:00 A.M. to 7:00 P.M. and are also closed one day per week, although the day differs between regions and within cities.

Making Contacts

You can write a letter to a new contact in India without first securing a formal introduction, but referrals and introductions may give you more credibility and result in a faster response. However, you should feel comfortable sending a "cold" letter to introduce your company and state your intentions. Well-known international companies will receive better responses than smaller unknown entities. You may follow the letter with a telephone call. Indians may seem unreceptive on a first call, but this is more because they do not know you yet rather than due to a lack of interest. If possible, make an in-person visit. If you use an introduction or referral, be sure not to make the Indian feel obligated or pressured to work with you. Indians do not respond well to outside pressure or obligation.

Once in India, you can schedule impromptu meetings, most Indians will be willing to meet with you provided their schedules permit the time. Direct your first communication to the seniormost person possible. Indians are very status-conscious and will seek to match you with a person of equal status from their organization.

It is advisable to maintain a local presence either by assigning someone from your company to serve in India or by hiring a local representative or agent. This person should be able to manage local administrative tasks and business relationships. A joint-venture collaboration or a technical transfer with a small minority equity stake are frequently the most effective approaches. Indians tend to be proud and boastful. Name-dropping is a common practice and people compete to list their "supposed" contacts. When evaluating local representative firms, be wary of the person who tells you he or she has very extensive connections. Check his or her references thoroughly. The desire to be more "Western," that is "better," makes many Indians compete against one another rather than assist each other.

Meeting People

In general, foreign businesspeople should avoid trying to do business close to India's major holiday periods, such as Diwali. Further, be sensitive to the religious and regional holidays that your Indian counterpart may observe.

Some executives arrive at the office late in the morning, but they also tend to stay late at the end of the day. Do not schedule any appointments earlier than 10:00 A.M. Also avoid the lunch hours between noon and 2:00 P.M. Indians are habitually late to appointments and do not mind if foreigners show up as much as fifteen minutes late. First meetings should be held at an office or in your hotel lobby.

Be careful not to make assumptions about a person's role based on his or her sex; there are senior female managers and both men and women work as secretaries. Male secretaries tend to predominate in the public sector, female secretaries in the private sector. Most secretaries or assistants often function as gate-keepers. They should be cultivated for advice about the bureaucratic processes. Foreign businesswomen will have an easier time establishing credibility if they represent larger firms or have senior titles.

In general, Indian surnames usually indicate the part of the country where a person originated. Unless you know someone well, always use a title, such as "Dr.," "Mr.," "Mrs.," or "Miss." and the surname when addressing a person. Wait until invited to use first names. You should always use formal titles and family names with senior government officials regardless of how long you have known them. Superiors are often called "Sir" or "Madam" by Indians, although foreigners are not expected to follow this practice.

Most Indian businesspeople greet each other with a handshake or the *namaste*, which is a traditional greeting carried out by placing both palms together as in a prayer at chest level and accompanied by a slight nod of the head. Foreigners should feel comfortable shaking hands. When greeting senior government officials, a *namaste* is more appropriate and will be appreciated by all Indians. In larger cities, shake hands with men and women. In smaller towns and rural areas, a *namaste* is more appropriate.

Business cards are exchanged at the first meeting, although not necessarily at the beginning of the meeting. Begin each meeting with small talk on topics such as your travels, the weather, and positive impressions of India. Indians enjoy talking and will quickly share their overseas experiences with you. It is best to refrain from talking about sensitive topics such as politics or religion. Indians usually believe that they are better informed about the West than the reverse. Western ignorance of things Indian is often perceived as an insult by Indians, who are unable to comprehend why India has not been a major focus for Westerners. Indians have always perceived themselves as a global power and are often miffed when others do not. Be sensitive to these types of issues and display an interest in India and its culture. Building relationships is important and will require more than one meeting.

You can begin to discuss business after about five minutes. Most executives are busy and value their time, although not necessarily yours. Business meetings should always be conducted with a business purpose. If you are only interested in general fact-finding and relationship building, make sure your Indian counterpart knows this in advance. Early meetings should maintain a formal tone. Indians are eager to ensure that they are perceived as serious business contenders. You may find that your Indian counterpart wants to discuss business immediately without any casual conversation. Follow your counterpart's lead. Gifts are not required, although small gestures such as sample products may be appreciated.

In the first few encounters, do not physically touch your Indian counterpart or pat him on the back. Some Indian men will touch you when discussing or explaining a point. *Never* touch a woman, other than to shake hands.

The feet are considered the dirtiest part of a person. Do not place your feet on a chair or table as this is considered disrespectful. Do not point with one finger, but instead use your whole palm. Beckoning should be done using the whole hand with the palm facing down and the fingers pointing away from you, but moving toward you in a scratching motion. In general, well-educated and affluent Indians follow European etiquette rules.

Most Indians are good-natured and smile often, although only in happy situations. They smile less than the people of some other

East Asian nations. Indians can be serious when the situation warrants it. You will be able to "see" their emotions. Indians enjoy telling jokes, often at the expense of another individual or group. However, jokes are not common in the business environment.

Corporate Structure

Most businesses in India are privately owned and highly centralized entities. Government-controlled corporations operate only in specific industries. Many of India's private companies are family owned. The key decision-maker is usually a male family member, who must approve all decisions. The typical business hierarchy consists of a chairman, a managing director/president, a general manager/vice-president, deputy general managers, managers, officers, and so on. In the private sector, titles often tend to imply more authority than actually exists.

The senior-most person in the firm is usually the chairman of board, although he has very little operational responsibility. In some family-run businesses the chairman may be the original founder; in such a case, he retains full and final authority. Usually the managing director has day-to-day authority, while those at the vice-president level and below have negligible power. Senior executives tend to work the longest hours.

Indians enjoy displaying their power and authority. There is a distinct class structure at the office. Superiors will not engage in any work, particularly physical work, perceived to be below their "level." Accordingly, subordinates are usually not considered as equals and are often treated in a condescending manner.

There are differences in attitude between the generations. Older businesspeople tend to value loyalty more than younger people do; indeed, young people have little company loyalty and switch jobs easily. In the private sector, promotions are now based more on ability than on loyalty and connections. However, family background and social status remain important criteria for moving up the ladder. The younger generation places more value on professionalism and competence.

The principal regulatory agencies in India are the Foreign Investment Promotion Board, in the Office of the Prime Minister; the Secretariat for Industrial Approvals, in the Ministry of Industry, which reviews all foreign collaboration applications; the Reserve Bank of India (RBI), which regulates all foreign investment and currency transfers; the Company Law Board; the Securities and Exchange Board of India; and the Stock Exchange Authorities of India. The country has numerous export zones and industrial parks that offer tax and regulatory incentives to promote export-oriented industries and technology transfers.

India continues to be known as the "license raj" where bureaucratic processes are time-consuming and inefficient. In recent years, the government has made serious efforts to reduce the paperwork and approval process. However, lower-level government officials remain inefficient and bureaucratic in attitude. Any large project requires the approval of many government offices and the process can take several months, if not more than a year.

Negotiation

Indians tend to trust each other only when it is convenient. Sometimes regional and religious biases can interfere with trust, but this is less common in larger companies. Over time, it is relatively easy for a foreigner to become accepted and trusted, assuming that he or she does not do anything unscrupulous. Foreigners should get to know their Indian counterpart and his family on a social basis. Bringing your own spouse and children to India on subsequent visits, and introducing them to your Indian counterpart will help cement a strong long-term relationship. If they like you, Indians will usually go out of their way to entertain and take care of your family. Most Indian professionals still perceive it as an "honor" to conduct business with foreigners. On occasion, Indians have been known to enter into discussions with foreign businesspeople to garner the prestige of dealing with foreigners even though they have no interest in making a deal.

Indians rarely take responsibility for mistakes. Errors and problems are either blamed on subordinates or simply passed over. Further, Indians are not usually timely or efficient in accomplishing tasks or meeting deadlines. Accountability is weak and procrastination is evident, especially in the public sector. It should be noted that this will differ by industry and the relative age of the senior staff. Businesspeople in Bombay, the country's commercial center, tend to be more efficient and punctual. Younger managers with advanced management training tend to have a direct, no-nonsense approach to business issues. You should maintain close contact with your Indian operations and be sensitive to the different types of local managers. Build extra time into your timetable for unexpected, but common, delays.

Decisions are made as the result of a mix of extensive research and intuition, usually by one person at the top. The decision-maker will often rely on his or her own intuition after subordinates have completed the appropriate research. Younger managers will undertake more research. Developing group consensus is not a priority. Decision-making is accomplished at a moderate pace; decisions can be made rather quickly in comparison to some other Asian countries. However, Indians tend to be very process-oriented and less results-oriented. Fate, the notion that a person has done what is required and now whatever is meant to happen will happen, influences various aspects of business. Indians will expect foreigners to have all the technical answers and may seem frustrated if you do not. Indians have a national impatience to catch up with the developed economies. Generally, Indians will take calculated risks and tend to be flexible in their approach.

Depending on their experience, age, and exposure to Western ways, Indians will not always say "No" directly. They may make negative hints, delay, or simply ignore an issue in the hopes that it will fade away. Ask probing questions in non-accusatory ways and watch for delay tactics. Explain your position and role very clearly.

Be patient, firm, and politely direct. Indians appreciate soft-spoken, polite, and non-overbearing personalities.

Indians can be very good at telling you what they think you want to hear. Their reluctance to deliver negative news will result in information being hidden or avoided. However, the younger generation is more willing to be forthright and to say "No" directly. Some Indians will grasp both ears to indicate repentance. Indians often indicate acceptance or understanding by tilting or wobbling their head from side to side. This can mean a variety of things including "Yes, I agree," "Yes, I hear you," and "OK." Ask indirect questions to verify the exact meaning. Do not automatically assume that a head tilt means approval.

Some form of government approval is required for most types of transactions. Thanks to the recent economic reforms, there is less red tape to endure. Many processes that once took several years have been shortened to a year or less. Your Indian counterpart or local representative should be able to manage this aspect of doing business for you. Patience is still critical to success.

Do not underestimate an Indian businessperson. Indians are shrewd and tough negotiators and have been raised since childhood to bargain in every aspect of daily life. Do not assume that Western-educated Indians are completely Western in attitudes and practices. Such Indians tend to combine Eastern and Western characteristics. Graduates of Indian business schools are knowledgeable about Western business concepts and buzzwords, and use this knowledge and terminology when conducting business.

Written contracts are widely used and are very detailed. Verbal agreements are not considered binding and should be supported with a written contract. Memorandums of understandings (MOU) are common tools used to document initial interest, but are not usually formally binding. Most Indians view legal contracts as merely the beginning of a business relationship.

It is not uncommon for an Indian business executive to negotiate and review legal contracts presented by foreign companies.

Lawyers have a shady reputation and, therefore, are not always used in contract negotiations. Foreigners will find that Indian business-people are usually capable of addressing all types of legal and business issues with most Indian executives being generalists rather than specialists. Senior businesspeople can legally commit a firm. Wherever possible, strive to receive payment up-front or at the closing of a transaction as Indian companies have been known to delay or ignore payment processes.

Conducting Business in a Social Setting

Dining and Drinking

Although business dining etiquette can differ by region, dinners are the preferred meal for business socializing. Business lunches are acceptable, but breakfasts are not common. Indians tend to be flexible and will strive to accommodate your schedule. You may schedule a dinner after the first office meeting. Appropriate places to dine are expensive restaurants and major hotels. Dinners are considered good opportunities to get to know one another socially, but business is also often discussed. Foreign women can invite Indian men to a business social event, but they should entertain groups of people rather than just one man. Whoever extends the invitation is expected to pay. In many instances, the Indian businessperson will offer to pay for the dinner several times as a courtesy; however, if you issued the invitation, insist that it is your "honor" or obligation to pay.

Indian food is traditionally eaten with the fingers of the right hand. Never use the left hand, which is considered unclean, to pass or accept food. Hindus do not eat beef, for cows are considered sacred. Muslims do not eat pork or drink liquor.

Alcohol is not served during meals. Most Indian businessmen drink a hard liquor, usually scotch, although some drink beer. Indian women are less likely to drink but this is changing.

Visiting a Home

Indians are very hospitable toward strangers and outsiders. They warmly welcome foreigners and will go out of their way to assist them. If they know you well enough, they will invite you to their home or to a family social event. When an Indian's child marries, he or she usually invites large numbers of family members, friends, and business acquaintances. Depending on the girl's family's finances, marriages can be large gatherings where guest lists can exceed a thousand people.

Those who live comfortably and lavishly will usually take great pride in showing off their home to you. Further, Indians can be very generous once they know you. It is the custom in many homes to remove shoes before entering. If you are invited to a home, take a small gift such as a souvenir from your native country or sweets for the children. It is not uncommon for men and women to break into separate groups at a social event. Foreigners are not expected to follow these patterns of segregation.

Gift Giving

Graft is widespread in India. Locally known as "speed money" (traditionally known as *baksheesh*), bribes must often be made at each level of the bureaucratic process. Foreigners should be wary of engaging in bribery, which is ubiquitous but illegal. Develop a global company policy for graft and adhere to it. Entrust your local counterpart to manage this aspect of doing business in India. Never directly offer money to a businessperson or government official. Further, when dealing with your home office in another country, do not fax or write about graft and related issues. It is advisable to either speak on the telephone or wait for a face-to-face meeting to discuss this issue.

While it is not necessary, you can give your business counterpart a sample product from your company or something with the corporate logo at the first meeting. Unique gifts are more appreciated than standard pens or calendars, particularly by people who travel internationally and are able to purchase most standard items. After a deal is closed, it is acceptable to exchange more expensive gifts, such as vases, expensive liquor, or fine items from your home country.

Gift giving can be tricky. Some Indian businesspeople may be offended by expensive gifts, perceiving them to be bribes. But others may actually *expect* expensive gifts as they believe it is their right. Attitudes can differ depending on characteristics such as age, industry, international exposure, and personality. Wherever possible, use your local associate to guide you on this issue.

Money gifts are given for some social events, such as marriages. Money gifts for social events are never given in even amounts such as Rs.100 or Rs.1000; always add 1 to make the amount an odd number, such as Rs.101 or Rs.1001. Ask your local counterpart about the appropriate amount to give; too little can be perceived as an insult, too much as a bribe.

Dress Code

For men, a suit and tie is appropriate for the first meeting. Thereafter, follow the lead of your local counterparts. In many instances, particularly in the warmer months, a shirt and tie is acceptable. For women, suits, dresses, or skirts and blouses are appropriate. Indians are relatively tolerant of foreigners, but be sensitive to your local surroundings and any conservative practices. Indians tend to prefer bright colors. Most Indian women wear traditional Indian outfits. For social events, Indians are often pleased when foreigners, male and female, wear traditional Indians outfits, such as a silk Nehru jacket or sari. If you choose to dress native, your hotel should be able to assist you in having something made for a moderate price.

Many Indians wear a dot, or *tika*, in the middle of their forehead. It is a symbol of blessings from the gods. Traditionally, a *tika* on a woman's forehead symbolized marriage. However, in modern times, the *tika* has become part of women's fashion and is worn in various colors and shapes.

Useful Phrases

The official languages of India include Hindi and English; the latter is widely used, especially in the courts, education, and business. In addition to Hindi and English, both of which have national status, the constitution recognizes fourteen other major languages, often with distinct alphabets and written script. There are believed to be several hundred minor languages and dialects. Most English-speaking foreigners will find that it is relatively easy to get around because most Indians speak at least some English. The following list includes some useful Hindi phrases and a guide to their pronunciation.

Hello	*Na-mas-tay*
Good morning / afternoon / evening	*Na-mas-tay*
How are you?	*Aap kaisay hain?*
Please	*Kripaya*
Thank you	*Dhanyawad*
You are welcome	*Swagat* (rarely used)
Excuse me	*Kripaya maaf keejiyeh*
I am sorry	*Maaf keejiyeh*
My name is ———	*Mera naam* ——— *hai.*
I work for ———	*Main* ——— *may kam ker-ta-hoon*
Here is my business card	*Yeh mera business card hai*
I am pleased to meet you	*Aapse milkar mujhe bahoot Khushi hui*
Please accept this small gift	*Kripaya aapyeh chhota uphaar sveekar karen*
I look forward to developing a good relationship with you / your firm.	*Main aapki company se achhay sambandh rakhana cha-ha-ta* (male) / *cha-ha-tee* (female) *hun.*
I understand	*Main samajh raha* (male) / *rahee* (female) *hun*
No, I do not understand	*Nahin main nahi samajh paaya* (male) / *paayee* (female)
Please wait a minute	*Zara, ek minute rukyeh*

Where is the bathroom?	*Bathroom kahaan hai?*
Good-bye	*Na-mas-tay*
Cheers	Cheers

Major Holidays

Avoid business visits during major holiday periods, such as Diwali. Each state or region has local holidays not listed here. Check before you travel, as many businesses close for all holidays.

January 1	New Year's Day
January 26	Republic Day
February/March*	Ramadan
February/March*	Eid-ul-Fitr (end of Ramadan celebrations)
March*	Holi
April 1	Annual closing of bank accounts
April**	Easter and Good Friday
May/June*	Eid-ul-Azha (Feast of Sacrifice)
July/August*	Muharram
August/September*	Prophet Muhammad's Birthday
August 15	Independence Day
September 30	Half year closing of bank accounts
September/October*	Durga Puja Dussera
October 2	Mahatma Gandhi's Birthday
October/November*	Diwali (Festival of Lights)
November/December*	Guru Nanak's Birthday
December 25	Christmas Day

*These holidays are based on the lunar calendar and differ from year to year.
**These holidays are observed on the first Friday and first Sunday after the paschal full moon and change from year to year.

General Facts

Climate: Temperatures and climate vary widely throughout the country due to its size with terrain that varies from rain forest to desert to mountains. Generally, there are three main seasons: the cool season from October to February; the hot season from March to June; and the monsoon season from July to September. The hot months can be unbearable, with temperatures reaching more than 113F (45C) even in the northern areas. Check with your travel agent for seasonal temperatures in specific regions. Generally the southern region will be warmer in any season, although temperature changes with the elevation.

Currency: The currency is the Indian *rupee* (abbreviated as Rs.), which is divided into 100 *paisas*. In terms of numbers, one *lakh* equals a 100,000 of anything and one *crore* equals 10,000,000 of anything.

Dates: Dates are written day, month, and year. For example, August 17, 1995, is written 17/8/95.

Electricity: The voltage is 220, 50 (Hz) cycles. It is advisable to bring a converter with a two-pin, round-headed plug.

Entry Requirements: All foreigners are required to have a valid passport and a visa for entry into India. It is advisable to get your visa in your home country; the Indian bureaucracy can make it difficult and time-consuming to obtain visas from embassies and consulates other than those in your country of citizenship and/or residency.

Time: India has one time zone, which is five and a half hours ahead of Greenwich Mean Time and ten and a half hours ahead of U.S. Eastern Standard Time (nine and half during Daylight Savings Time).

Tipping: Most major hotels and expensive restaurants add a 10 percent service charge to the bill; if they do not, leave that amount. In moderate restaurants, Rs. 40 or Rs. 30 is acceptable rather than a percentage of the total bill. For porters and taxi drivers, Rs. 5 per bag or per ride is appropriate. Private car drivers should be given more, ranging from Rs. 25 for a half day to Rs. 50 for a full day. In general, Indian workers will happily accept a tip and it will usually earn you a bit of goodwill.

Transportation: It is not advisable for first-time visitors to drive; the traffic and driving conditions in most Indian cities can be overwhelming. Further, street names and addresses are not always clearly marked. Taxis are convenient and cheap. It is also relatively inexpensive to hire a car and driver, a convenient and comfortable alternative. Your hotel can assist you in making arrangements. Many taxi and car drivers speak at least some English and most will understand the name of a destination. If you decide to drive in India, rental cars are available in the major cities. Driving is on the left and an international driver's license is required. "Marg" is the equivalent of "street."

Use taxis for travel from the airports to cites and hotels. At major airports, there are usually prepaid taxi booths, where you can buy a fixed-price taxi ticket with the value based on your final destination. Ask a policeman for assistance as you will invariably find many questionable characters attempting to "assist" you. If notified in advance, some hotels will make arrangements to have you met at the airport. Check with your travel agent. When using taxis, make sure the meter is turned on or that the fare is predetermined; Indian taxidrivers often try to take advantage of foreigners.

Travel between cities is relatively convenient and inexpensive, as most cities and towns are accessible by air. The national railway network is very extensive and provides a suitable alternative to air travel. Buses are not always comfortable and should be used as a last resort. Private cars can be hired to travel into remote areas.

Helpful Telephone Numbers

International telephone calls can be made efficiently from most hotels and offices. There are also private STD/ISD (long distance networks) calling booths in every city and even in many villages. The country code for India is (91). Major city codes are: Delhi (11); Bombay (22); Bangalore (80); Calcutta (33); and Madras (44).

Hospitals and Doctors:

Breach Candy Hospital
60 AB Desai Road
Bombay 400026
Tel.: (22) 362-6194 / 361-7611

All India Institute of Medial Sciences
Ansari Nagar
New Delhi 110029
Tel.: (11) 661123

Batra Hospital and Medical
Research Centre
1 Tughlakabad Instal Area
Mehrauli-Bdr Road
New Delhi 110062
Tel.: (11) 644-3747

Escorts Heart Institute and
Research Centre
Okhla Road
New Delhi 110025
Tel.: (11) 684-4820

Ambulance: For Bombay,
Delhi, and Madras, dial 102;
for Calcutta, dial 244-0102.

Fire: For Bombay, Delhi, and
Madras dial 101; for Calcutta,
dial 244-0101.

Police/Emergency: For Bombay,
Delhi, and Madras, dial 100;
for Calcutta, dial 220-0100.

Useful Addresses

In India:

American Business Council of
India
U-50 Hotel Hyatt Regency
New Delhi 110066
Tel.: (11) 688-5443

Associated Chambers of
Commerce
Allahabad Bank Building
17 Parliament Street
New Delhi 110001
Tel.: (11) 310-749

Chief Controller of Imports
and Exports
Ministry of Commerce
Udyog Bhawan
Maulana Azad Road
New Delhi 110001
Tel.: (11) 301-1938 / 301-1275
(Deputy Chief Controller) /
331-8857 (Licensing)

Confederation of Indian
Industries
23, 26 Institutional Area
Lodhi Road
New Delhi 110003
Tel.: (11) 462-9994

Export-Import Bank of India
Centre One, Floor 21
World Trade Centre
Cuffe Parade
Bombay 400005
Tel.: (22) 218-5272 / 218-6801

Foreign Investment Promotion
Board
Prime Minster's Secretariat
South Block
New Delhi 110011
Tel.: (11) 301-7839 / 3040

India Investment Centre
Jeevan Vihar Building
Sansad Marg
New Delhi 110001
Tel.: (11) 312-622

Indo-German Chamber of
Commerce
Maker Tower E, 1st Floor
Cuffe Parade
Bombay 400005
Tel.: (22) 218-6131

86 FG Himalaya House
23 Kasturba Gandhi Marg
New Delhi 110001
Tel.: (11) 331-4151

5 Kasturi Ranga Road
Madras 600018
Tel.: (44) 452370

Shah Sultan
Cunningham Road
Bangalore 560052
Tel.: (80) 265650

30 A/B Jawaharlal Nehru Road
Calcutta 700016
Tel.: (33) 299944

**Industrial Credit and
Investment Corporation of
India**
163 Backbay Reclamation
Bombay 400020
Tel.: (22) 2022535;
in Delhi, (11) 331-9611 / 12

**Indo-U.S. Joint Business
Council**
c/o Federation of Indian
Chambers of Commerce and
Industry
Federation House
Tansen Marg
New Delhi 110001
Tel.: (11) 331-9251

Ministry of Commerce
Udyog Bhawan
New Delhi 110011
Tel.: (11) 301-0261

**Ministry of Finance
(Economic Affairs)**
North Block
New Delhi 110001
Tel.: (11) 301-4452 (Joint
Secretary for Investments) /
301-2883 (Director)

Ministry of Industry
Udyog Bhavan
New Delhi 110001
Tel.: (11) 301-1487 (Protocol) /
301-0261 (Export Promotion) /
301-4005 / 1983 (Investment
Promotion and Project
Monitoring)

Reserve Bank of India (RBI)
New Central Office Building
Fort, Bombay 400023
Tel.: (22) 266-5726 /
286-1602 (Approvals)

**Secretariat for Industrial
Approvals, Ministry of
Industry**
Udyog Bhavan
New Delhi 110001
Tel.: (11) 301-0221 / 1983

Embassies and Consulates:

American Embassy
Shantipath
Chanakyapuri
New Delhi 110021
Tel.: (11) 600651

American Consulates
Lincoln House
78 Bhulabhai Desai Road
Bombay 400026
Tel.: (22) 363-3611

5/1 Ho Chi Minh Sarani
Calcutta 700071
Tel.: (33) 242-3611

220 Mount Road
Madras 600006
Tel.: (44) 827-3040

British High Commission
Chanakyapuri
New Delhi 110021
Tel.: (11) 601371

Canadian High Commission
7/8 Shanti Path
Chanakyapuri
New Delhi 110021
Tel.: (11) 687-6500

Canadian Consulate
41/42 Maker Chambers VI
Jamnalal Bajaj Marg
Nariman Point
Bombay 400021
Tel.: (22) 287-6027

French Embassy
2/50E Shanti Path
Chanakyapuri
New Delhi 110021
Tel.: (11) 604300

French Consulate
Bacon, 7th Floor
Madame Cama Road
Bombay 400021
Tel.: (22) 202-1217

German Embassy
6/50G Shanti Path
Chanakyapuri
New Delhi 110021
Tel.: (11) 604861

German Consulates
Hoechst House, 10th Floor
Nariman Point
193 Backbay Reclamation
Bombay 400021
Tel.: (22) 232422

1 Hastings Park Road
Alipore
Calcutta
Tel.: (33) 711141

22 Commander-in-Chief Road
Madras
Tel.: (44) 471747

In Canada:

Indian High Commission
10 Springfield Road
Ottawa, Ontario K1M 1C9
Tel.: (613) 744-3751

Indian Consulates
2 Bloor Street, Suite 500
West Cumberland
Toronto, Ontario M4W 3E2
Tel.: (416) 960-0751

325 Howe Street
Vancouver, B.C. V6C 1Z7
Tel.: (604) 662-8811

Indian Government Tourist Office
60 Bloor Street, West
Suite 1003
Toronto, Ontario M4W 3B8
Tel.: (416) 962-6279

Canada–India Business Council, Canadian Chamber of Commerce
55 Metcalfe Street, No. 1160
Ottawa, Ontario K1P 6N4
Tel.: (613) 238-4000

In France:

Embassy of India
15 Rue Alfred Dehodencq
75016 Paris
Tel.: (1) 4520-3930

Indian Tourist Office
8 Blvd. de la Madeleine
75009 Paris
Tel.: (1) 4265-8386

In Germany:

Embassy of India
Adenauerallee 262
5300 Bonn
Tel.: (228) 54-050

Indian Consulate
Mittelweg 49
60318 Frankfurt am Main 1
Tel.: (69) 153-0050

Indian Tourist Office
Kaiserstrasse 77-III
D-6000 Frankfurt am Main 1
Tel.: (69) 23-5423

German–Indian Chamber of Commerce
Oststrasse 84/11
4000 Dusseldorf 1
Tel.: (211) 360597

In the United Kingdom:

Indian High Commission
India House
Aldwych
London WC2B 4NA
Tel.: (71) 836-8484

82 New Street
Birmingham B2 4BA
Tel.: (21) 643-0366

Indian Government Tourist Office
7 Cork Street
London W1X 1PB
Tel.: (71) 437-3677

In the United States:

Embassy of India
2107 Massachusetts Avenue, N.W.
Washington, DC 20008
Tel.: (202) 939-7000

Indian Consulates
3 East 64th Street
New York, NY 10021
Tel: (212) 879-7800

150 North Michigan Avenue
Suite 1100
Chicago, IL 60601
Tel.: (312) 781-6280

540 Arguello Blvd.
San Francisco, CA 94118
Tel: (415) 668-0662

Indian Government Tourist
Office
30 Rockefeller Plaza
New York, NY 10112
Tel.: (212) 586-4901

3550 Wilshire Blvd., Suite 204
Los Angeles, CA 90010
Tel.: (213) 380-8855

U.S. India Business Council
1615 H Street, N.W.
Washington, DC 20062-2000
Tel.: (202) 463-5492

India American Chamber of
Commerce
P.O. Box 873
Grand Central Station
New York, NY 10063
Tel.: (212) 755-7181

U.S. Trade Department of
Commerce
International Trade
Administration
India Desk, Room 2308
14th & Constitution
Avenues, N.W.
Washington DC 20230
Tel.: (202) 482-2954

13 Pakistan ————

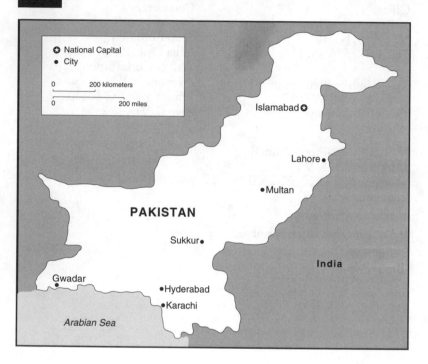

Geography

Pakistan, formally the Islamic Republic of Pakistan, shares its borders with four countries: India on the eastern border, China to the northeast, Afghanistan to the northwest, and Iran on the west. To the south of Pakistan lies the Arabian Sea. The country's total land area is 307,372 square miles (796,095 square kilometers). It is divided into four provinces: Punjab, Sindh, Baluchistan, and the Northwest Frontier Province (Peshawar). Pakistan also controls a portion of the Indian state of Jammu and Kashmir. There are six main geographical regions: the northern mountains, including portions of the Himalayan Range; the northern plateau;

the western mountains; the Baluchistan Plateau; the southeast desert; and the Indus Plain. The capital of Pakistan is Islamabad. Other major cities include Karachi, the commercial center, and Lahore.

History

Although the area's history dates back to about 3000 B.C., Pakistan has only existed as a separate political unit since the 1947 partition of British India when it became the homeland for India's Muslims. (Please refer to Chapter 12 on India for the area's history prior to 1947.)

The movement for an independent homeland for India's Muslims was the first inspired by Allama Iqbal in the 1930s. Mohammed Ali Jinnah, a British-educated lawyer and an independence movement activist, furthered this objective during India's campaign to win its independence from Great Britain. India's independence became a fact in August 1947. Independence involved the partition of British India into two separate states. The areas that were predominantly Muslim became Pakistan, while the Hindu areas became India. Pakistan resulted from the Muslim fears that, as a minority, they would be lost in a sea of Indian Hindus and the British efforts to calm these fears. Unfortunately, the new nation was an illogical entity from its inception. British India's Muslims were concentrated in the northwest, in the provinces of Punjab, Sindh, Baluchistan, and the Northwest Frontier, and in the east, in East Bengal. The former area became West Pakistan, the latter East Pakistan. The two parts of Pakistan were separated by a thousand miles of Indian territory and their populations shared little except for a common faith in Islam.

One of the more difficult provinces to divide was Kashmir, which was predominantly Muslim but had a Hindu king, who eventually chose to align with India. A 1949 United Nations cease-fire gave Pakistan control over one-third of the area in the west and northwest, with India retaining control over the remaining two-thirds.

The partition period was a bitter, violent time for both Pakistan and India, during which Hindus massacred Muslims and vice versa. Ten million people migrated from one country to the other. As a result of the partition, Pakistan ended up with few natural resources and very little manufacturing capabilities. The new country also lacked administrative workers, as few Muslims had ever served in the colonial bureaucracy. This left the country with a weak administrative infrastructure.

The most significant problem, however, was the great distance between the two Pakistans and the hostile Indian nation in between. Further separating the two parts of Pakistan were different languages (Bengali, Punjabi, Sindhi, and Urdu), different cultures, and different ways of life. Western Pakistan was the basis of the Indus Valley civilization, and had experienced numerous invasions by nomadic tribes from the west. As a result numerous cultures had been introduced, as is evident by the Persian influence. East Pakistan, on the other hand, had experienced far fewer historical invasions and, as a result, more peaceful circumstances had allowed their Bengali cultural heritage to strengthen. There were also physical differences between the two populations. Bengalis, for example, tend to be shorter in stature than most West Pakistanis, particularly Punjabis.

Upon independence in 1947, Muhammed Ali Jinnah, the key proponent of an independent Muslim state, became Pakistan's first governor-general, or head of state, and Liaquat Ali Khan became prime minister. Both Jinnah and Liaquat Ali Khan believed that Pakistan should be a secular state, a policy that was at odds with the country's Muslim religious leaders. Jinnah died in 1948, leaving his countryman in a state of shock. Liaquat Ali Khan was assassinated in 1951. The country fell into chaos as successive governor-generals and prime ministers vied for power. In March 1956, Pakistan finally created a constitution and officially became the Islamic Republic of Pakistan with a parliamentary form of secular government. Since independence, Pakistani politics has been overwhelmingly characterized by bickering, opportunism, and factionalism.

In 1958, after losing patience with the chaos and the growing autonomy movement in East Pakistan, President Iskander Mirza declared martial law and abolished all political parties. Martial law has been in force almost continuously ever since, despite repeated pledges to lift it permanently. In October 1958 Ayub Khan, the army commander-in-chief, forced Mirza to resign and made himself president while retaining control of the army. In March 1962 Ayub created a new constitution providing for a powerful president, a National Assembly, and provincial assemblies. During his rule the economy rebounded and general conditions improved, although the people enjoyed few political freedoms.

After the 1962 war between China and India (see Chapter 12 on India), Pakistan forged a relationship with China as a military and political counter to India. The first war between Pakistan and India originated in April 1965 with a border dispute. This escalated by August into a war over Kashmir. Lasting less than a month, the skirmish ended with a United Nations–imposed cease-fire with India retaining control over the majority of Kashmir. Pakistan suffered immensely in this short war and its peoples' national pride was wounded. India and Pakistan fought again in 1971 and have been on the brink of war several more times over the years. Traditionally, the former Soviet Union politically backed India in these conflicts, and China and the United States, although for different reasons, backed Pakistan.

In March 1969 an ailing Ayub handed power over to General Yahya Khan, who once again imposed martial law and named himself president. In January 1970 political activities resumed and elections were held in December. Zulfikar Ali Bhutto and his Pakistan People's party (PPP) won a majority of West Pakistan's seats in the legislature. However, the Awami party, which advocated an independent East Pakistan, won nearly all of East Pakistan's seats, giving it an overall majority. Bhutto refused to allow the Awami party, led by Sheikh Mujibur-Rahman (Sheikh Mujib), to form a government and Yahya suspended the assembly. When Sheikh Mujib was arrested in early March 1971, East Pakistan declared independence and civil war broke out between the two Pakistans. By November, India had come to the aid of East Pakistan and helped to defeat the West Pakistani troops within weeks. In December, East Pakistan, now known as Bangladesh, finally obtained independence. Pakistan finally recognized Bangladesh in 1974. (See Chapter 15 on Bangladesh)

Zulfikar Ali Bhutto became the leader of Pakistan in December 1971. He was faced with rebuilding a demoralized and economically impoverished country. As prime minister, Bhutto, a Sindhi landowner, began to align himself closely with the industrialists and landowners, despite his populist rhetoric. Bhutto's PPP won the 1977 elections, but the public, upset by rumors of fraud and corruption, publicly protested the elections as fraudulent. On July 5, 1977, his army chief, General Zia ul-Haq, staged a coup and returned Pakistan to martial law. Bhutto was arrested in 1977 and assassinated in 1979 by people loyal to General Zia ul-Haq.

General Zia made himself president, seized control of the government, postponed elections indefinitely, abolished political parties, suspended civil rights, and declared the Islamic law of *Shariah* as the basis of all law. Zia was able to hold onto power for the next seven years, primarily because of the huge military assistance from the United States, which was in response to the Soviet military invasion of Afghanistan. The United States used Zia in its efforts to support the Afghan *mujahideen* (rebel freedom fighters), who set up bases in Pakistan. Despite a ban on political parties, Bhutto's wife, Nusrat, and his daughter, Benazir, were elected to head the PPP. The two were eventually forced into exile after civil disobedience failed to unseat Zia. Under domestic and international pressure, Zia permitted token nonparty elections in 1985 and later allowed political parties to organize. Benazir Bhutto returned in 1986 and attempted to rally support, but was quickly jailed.

In August 1988 Zia died in a plane crash. Acting president Ghulam Ishaq Khan insisted on strict adherence to the constitution and declared that elections would be held. In the ensuing free elections, Bhutto's daughter, Benazir, became prime minister and the first female leader of an Islamic state in modern times. The job proved to be too overwhelming for an inexperienced politician and she was quickly dominated by the more powerful and influential army, in both domestic and international affairs. Although the last Soviet troops had officially left Afghanistan in February 1989, the United States continued to arm the Afghan guerrillas in their war against the Soviet-backed Kabul government.

President Ghulam Ishaq Khan dismissed the Bhutto government because of widespread charges of corruption in 1990, forcing national elections, which Bhutto lost. Nawaz Sharif, head of the Islamic Democratic Alliance (IDA), became prime minister in 1990.

In 1991 the United States and the former Soviet Union agreed to halt all funding of the Afghan government and the *mujahideen*. That marked the official end of Pakistan's role as a valued American strategic ally. However, leftover stockpiles of weapons from the war against Afghanistan, including Stinger missiles valued at about $8 billion, were put on the market by the guerrillas and posed major security threats to Western interests and India, which feared the results of the weapons systems falling into the wrong hands. U.S. attempts to repurchase the weapons systems have driven up the price of the weapons, threatening the success of its buy-back efforts.

Sharif was an ineffective leader who attempted to liberalize the economy and attract foreign investment while placating Muslim fundamentalists who called for more stringent adherence to Islamic law. In 1993, after being unable to provide clean government and bring law and order to such areas as the Sindh province, particularly the city of Karachi, Sharif was replaced temporarily by Moeen Qureshi. He was effective in introducing more economic liberalization policies during his short two-month interim government. Benazir Bhutto and the PPP regained power in 1993 after winning the national elections. She has been only marginally effective in managing the country's political, social, and economic affairs. Bhutto and Sharif, both vying for power, remain intent upon destroying each other. Corruption by Bhutto's family and loyalists remains unchecked. Further, internal family feuds threaten her political base. Bhutto's brother, Mir Murtaza, who recently returned to Pakistan after sixteen years in exile, and her mother have announced that he, not Benazir, inherited their father's mantle of leadership.

In recent years Pakistan's relations with India have deteriorated, as conflicts over Kashmir continue to resurface. In an effort to win support, Pakistan has sought to internationalize the Kashmir conflict and has mounted a campaign against Indian human rights abuses in the state. The current tension in Kashmir has escalated since Pakistan introduced Afghan and other foreign mercenaries into the area to support Pakistan-backed secessionist militants. The open militancy by both nations remains a major source of tension. Further, in a separate issue, the two countries' nuclear capabilities have become a concern to each other, as well as to the major Western powers, who have sought to diffuse the tension in the region.

Political Structure

Since independence, Pakistan has vacillated between parliamentary, presidential, and martial law forms of government. Currently, the country is an Islamic republic and has a parliamentary form of government, with both a president and prime minister who form the executive branch. The president, who must be a Muslim, is the head of state and is elected jointly by the Senate and National Assembly for a five-year term. The president has the power to dismiss the prime minister and the National Assembly, and also to appoint governors for each province, who in turn appoint chief ministers. The current president is Farooq Leghari.

The prime minister, who forms the cabinet, is elected by the parliament, which in turn is elected by public vote. The current prime minister is Benazir Bhutto. The parliament has two houses, the Senate and National Assembly, which are elected for six and five years, respectively. The National Assembly holds most of the power.

Pakistan's Supreme Court is the highest court in the country. In 1980 a Federal Shariat Court was established by Zia to ensure that national laws were consistent with Islamic law and in 1988 *Shariah*, Islamic law, was installed as the highest law of the land. The Shariat Court's decisions are still subject to the secular Supreme Court. The possibility that Pakistan's constitution could be changed, under pressure from the Islamic fundamentalists, and made subject to the Koran, is very real and poses a threat to the flow of foreign investment.

Economy

Pakistan has built a strong manufacturing base since the country's independence in 1947. It has become an international manufacturer of textiles, carpets, clothes, and leather and sporting goods. Pakistan's other important industries include cement, fertilizers, and steel. Tourism is a growing industry.

Pakistan remains primarily an agriculture-based economy. The main agricultural exports are rice, cotton, wheat, sugar cane, fruits, and vegetables. Natural gas is the country's most important natural resource. Pakistan is dependent on imports of oil, machinery, chemicals, and equipment.

The country underwent significant economic expansion throughout the 1980s, but has suffered financially in recent years, due to the cutoff of huge amounts of aid by the United States. This policy change resulted in part from the end of the Soviet occupation of Afghanistan and in part from United States' efforts to discourage Pakistan from further attempts to develop nuclear weapons. Further, the invasion of Kuwait by Iraq curtailed the flow of remittances sent home by Pakistani "guest workers," one of the country's major "exports" in the Persian Gulf. Almost half of the country's resources go to the armed forces.

The 1990 international failure of the Bank of Commerce and Credit (BCCI) had a negative effect on the country's banking sector as the Pakistani government was implicated in the scandal. The government continues to focus on liberalizing the economy, including relaxation of import polices and controls and the reduction of bureaucratic procedures and formalities. Plans have also been announced to privatize some state-owned industries. The government encourages foreign investment in the power and other infrastructure industries, all of which remain inadequate to service the country's expanding needs, by offering various incentives and partially privatizing the existing state-owned telecommunications and power companies.

People, Values, and Social Customs

The population of Pakistan is about 123 million. Due to its location on a number of major trade routes, Pakistan throughout its history has attracted a diverse mixture of people, cultures and languages throughout its history. The Pakistani people reveal a mix of Arab, Mongol, Indian, and European features. There are five major ethnic groups in Pakistan: Punjabi, Pathan, Sindhi, Muhajir, and the Baluchi. Most of the groups are named after the province from which they originate. There are numerous smaller ethnic groups as well.

Punjabis are descendants of ancient Indo-Aryans, comprising

about 50–60 percent of the population, a clear majority. The Pashtuns (Pathans) are also descendants of the Indo-Aryans who settled in the Northwest Frontier Province. The majority of the people in Baluchistan are Pashtuns. The Sindhi live mostly in the provinces of Punjab and Sindh. The Muhajirs (which means "refugees") are Muslim Indian immigrants who migrated to Pakistan during the partition. The Baluch tribespeople are partly Pathans, speak Pashto, and trace their ancestors to southeast Iran. All of the smaller ethnic groups remain slightly suspicious of the majority Punjabis.

Besides its ethnic divisions, Pakistani society is split along tribal, caste, and economic lines, all of which impact daily life, including behavior, education, profession, and marriages. The class system is a legacy of the Hindu tradition and the Pakistanis are very class-conscious. For example, if you dropped something, most Pakistanis would not pick it up for you, for bending for others is considered servile.

Despite all of the divisions among the Pakistanis, a common religion serves to unify them. Almost 97 percent of the population is Sunni Muslim. There are a small number of Christians who are descendants of mainly low-caste Hindu converts during the colonial period. The few Hindus and Parsis (Zoroastrians) tend to live in Lahore and Karachi. Pakistan boasts over seventy Islamic sects, most of which fall under the two major groupings of Sunni and Shiite, which differ in their interpretation of the Koran, the Islamic holy scriptures. There are pockets of Sufism throughout the country. Pakistani Muslim men pray five times a day. Pakistanis believe in fate or *Kismet*, the will of God.

Economic gains have benefited the few wealthy families who control most business and the government. The major landowners have often become regional government officials, often serving as the religious and spiritual leaders for the community as well. Most Pakistanis do not seek advice or help from their elected officials. Instead they turn to their landlord (*zamindar*) or tribal chief. Certain wealthy landowners have taken advantage of their role and have become their district's elected official.

There is some social and economic mobility, particularly in urban areas, due in part to the increased opportunities and the general economic liberalization. However, competition for jobs and economic advancement in the cities has intensified ethnic rivalries.

The family and the clan are the real basis of Pakistani society. Personal, political, and social commitments are based on family relationships. Friends are also important in expanding relationships and connections. Individuality comes second to obligations to the family and the immediate community. Obedience to elders is expected and is usually given without question. The average Pakistani is straightforward, honest, very hospitable to Westerners, and tolerant of foreigners.

In the light of Benzair Bhutto's position as prime minister, many visitors may be surprised by the role of women in Pakistan, which is still heavily influenced by Islamic traditions. In fact, Bhutto, who was educated in the West, owes her power more to being her father's daughter than as a politician in her own right. The average woman is less educated than the average male. Women are considered inferior to men; the formal religious explanation for women's subservient role is that women "need" to be protected. Some women observe *purdah*, which means they are kept from the sight of all men outside of the family by living in seclusion. Others wear a veil and dress in a *burqah*, the full-length, black or white, tentlike gown designed to totally conceal the female body. But many urban, affluent, and educated women have discarded the *burqah* and, instead, cover their head with a thin scarf called a *dupatta*. The dowry system ensures that families perceive their daughters as economic burdens. However, the status of women in Pakistan is changing, particularly in the cities. The National Assembly has reserved positions for female representatives. Further, many female have excelled in professions such as medicine and education. In urban areas, there are no formal restrictions on women's activities, such as driving a car. At any given time, the position of women in Pakistani society differs inversely with the influence of the Islamic mullahs (priests).

Work Schedule

Most businesses are open from 9:00 A.M. to 5:00 P.M. and are closed for one hour for lunch at 1:00 P.M., Sunday to Thursday. Everything is closed on Fridays, the Islamic day of holy rest. Most businesses are closed on Saturday afternoon as well, opening only in the morning, if at all. Some businesses are closed for either a half or a full day on Thursday. Government offices are open from 8:00 A.M. to 2:30 or 3:00 P.M., Saturday to Thursday. Shops are open from 9:00 or 10:00 A.M. to about 6:00 or 7:00 P.M. daily except Friday. Banks are open from 9:00 A.M. to 11:30 P.M. or noon on Saturday and from 9:00 A.M. to 1:00 P.M. Sunday to Thursday. Be aware that all offices and shops observe special hours during Ramadan.

Making Contacts

Westerners are usually well received in Pakistan and treated with polite respect. Most Pakistanis perceive Westerners as honest, fair, and efficient, but prefer to do business with friends or familiar parties with whom a level of trust has already been established. Therefore, although formal introductions are not required, they may have a significant positive impact on the success of a business interaction. Unless you are a representing a large, well-known international company, it is advisable to obtain an introduction from a mutual supplier, banker, accountant, lawyer, or your embassy. Verify references if you hire a local consultant or representative. Boasting of excessive, and sometimes unreal, capabilities is not uncommon among Pakistani businesspeople. If you intend to do business in the more rural areas, be sure that your local representative knows or can interact with the local chiefs.

The Pakistani government has established the National Investment Council (NIC), which is headed by the prime minister. It is the highest economic policy forum designed to review investment issues for all industries and to develop and coordinate all policies for foreign and domestic investment. The Pakistan Investment Board (PIB), under the chairmanship of the minister for industries, encourages foreign investment by providing general assistance to foreign investors and makes policy recommendations to the government. The government produces various annual guides, including *Pakistan Economy and Foreign Trade* and *How to Export from Pakistan*, which outline the steps to investing in, establishing an industry in, or exporting from Pakistan.

The government has established fifty-seven industrial estates throughout the country to provide infrastructure facilities, including telecommunications and utilities. There are also several special industrial zones and export processing zones (EPZs) designed to facilitate the establishment of export-oriented industries. These zones enjoy various concessions including tax holidays, exemptions on import duties for machinery, and unrestricted borrowing. Five export promotion bureau display sites are located in Karachi, Lahore, Islamabad, Peshwar, and Multan to showcase local products, manufacturers, and technical capabilities.

Meeting People

The best time to schedule appointments is between 10:00 A.M. and 1:00 P.M. as many people disappear for prayers around 1:00 P.M. Avoid Saturday meetings because many people do not adhere to a normal work schedule. Confirm your appointments once you arrive in Pakistan. While Pakistanis are often late, they appreciate punctuality in foreigners. Most Pakistani men greet each other and foreigners with a handshake. When greeting a Pakistani woman, let her make the first move. Be sensitive to how traditional your counterpart may or may not be. Women in professional and management positions who are accustomed to foreigners will most likely be aware of Western business practices.

Names can be confusing in Pakistan. At times, the name at the end is not the surname, but is actually a title such as "Khan," which implies nobility. Other noble or high-ranking titles include "Nawab," "Sahibzada," and "Sardar." Sometimes the first name is a caste name, such as "Mian," and is not used in normal address. It is easiest and safest to ask someone how he or she would like to be addressed. Many urban, educated, and often foreign-exposed Pakistanis employ the traditional Western style of name, with the given name listed first followed by the surname. Never call anyone just "Mohammad," as that it is the name of the Prophet. Pakistanis respectfully call others by their family name or title followed by *sahib*, which is the equivalent of "Mr." For women, *begum* followed by the family name is the equivalent of "Mrs." For example, "Mr. Jones" would be referred to as "Jones Sahib" or "Engineer Sahib," and "Mrs. Jones" would be called "Begum Jones." You do not need to use this system, although you may be called *sabih* or *begum*. Some Pakistanis also use the suffix *-ji* to indicate respect. Never use the suffix *-ji* when referring to yourself. Use the title and surname when addressing Pakistanis. Be sure your business card states your title; Pakistanis are often impressed by titles. Always greet the more senior person first.

Foreign businesswomen should be prepared for a struggle for acceptance. While the Pakistani businessman will meet with a foreign businesswoman, if he is a strict Muslim he will have difficulty with simple things like maintaining eye contact. This is done out of "respect" in a traditional sense. Some men will have difficulty grasping the concept of a female as the representative of a foreign company. Your company should support you unequivocally, otherwise your authority and ability to conduct business will be undermined. Further, be aware that for more traditional or untraveled

Pakistani men, Western women are considered "loose," as a result of the way women are portrayed in Hollywood movies. If you are subjected to unwelcome advances, which will most likely come from an uneducated, less exposed stranger rather than from a business associate, be firm in your response. Also be prepared for the paradox: Pakistani men who have been exposed to Western value systems and who may treat you as an equal in some situations, but then flip into more "respectful" treatment in the presence of more traditional people.

Pakistanis usually display their emotions. They smile when they are happy. While they enjoy telling jokes in personal situations, they do not tell jokes in formal business environments. Pakistanis can be stern, but some ethnic groups, such as the Punjabi, tend to be more jovial. Gestures to avoid include never showing the sole of your foot or shoe to anyone at any time and never stepping in front of or interrupting someone who is praying. The thumbs-up sign is considered obscene by some Pakistanis, so it is best to refrain from using it.

After exchanging business cards, you should spend some time exchanging pleasantries. Suitable topics include your home country, your Pakistani counterpart's overseas travels, the weather, or positive remarks about Pakistan. Pakistanis believe that it is quite acceptable to ask what Westerners might consider personal and sensitive questions.

After the first meeting, it is appropriate for you to ask general questions about someone's family and children. Never ask about a person's wife unless you know him well. A good conversationalist will usually be quickly accepted. You will usually be served tea or some other drink and you should at least sip some of it to avoid appearing rude. Meetings tend to be formal. However, Pakistanis will want to get to know you personally and develop a comfort level before discussing business. Pakistanis appreciate polite, calm, and well-mannered people. At the end of every meeting, you should shake hands with your counterpart.

Corporate Structure

Most Pakistani firms are family-owned and family-operated. The oldest family member, usually the oldest male, has primary or sole decision-making authority. Most Pakistanis consider relatives the most reliable and trustworthy of business associates. The boss is in essence the "father" of all of the employees. Corruption is widespread in Pakistan and family businesses are aggressive in maintaining their monopolies. It is best not to show interest in or knowledge of such activities.

In the public sector, the structure is very hierarchical because most Pakistanis enjoy displaying their sense of power. Dealing with government officials will often involve the issue of "commissions," or bribes. Large foreign companies may have an easier time circumventing the corruption process. Most officials have male personal assistants (PAs), who can be critical doorkeepers and should be treated with respect and cultivated with the occasional material gift or monetary gesture. PAs are usually more familiar with procedures and the system than the government officials for whom they work and this can be a valuable resource. It is important for foreigners to gain the respect and trust of both the official and the PA, although few Pakistani officials would consider a PA worthy of equal treatment. Both private- and public-sector managers tend to be dismissive and condescending toward subordinates.

Negotiation

Always show respect and deference to senior counterparts. Pakistanis appreciate foreigners who are familiar with local rules and regulations and who are sensitive to the limitations imposed on business. Avoid being condescending, even though the Pakistanis themselves condescend to others ranked below them. Never show your temper. You will earn far more respect for being patient and calm even in the face of adversity.

A certain amount of research and fact-finding will be conducted, but the final decision will be dependent on the intuition of the senior person. Most negotiations are conducted privately between key people and through relationship channels. Public negotiations are often just a formality. Pakistanis will bargain hard for concessions.

Pakistanis often say "Yes" or signal approval with a bob or tilt of the head from side to side. They often use the word *ach haa*, which means "OK," "Yes, I understand," "Oh really?" and the like. Be careful not to assume that "Yes" always means "Yes, I agree."

Pakistanis will rarely say "No" to you outright. Rather, they will adopt a hopeful attitude that something will happen. They may even say that they are "confident" that something will happen. Avoid asking yes / no questions, as Pakistanis will generally say anything to avoid making a "No" reply. They tend to speak in a roundabout manner. Pakistanis will rarely inform you if there is a problem because they do not like to give negative news or assume responsibility. Problems will either be ignored or kept hidden. Maintaining personal honor is critical and allowing others to do the same is equally important.

Pakistanis have a very relaxed concept of time. In fact the Urdu word for "yesterday" and "tomorrow" are the same, *kal*. Deadlines are rarely met. The average Pakistani will wait for instructions at every step. Further, there is a general attitude "that if God wishes for something to be done, then it will be done," with no specifics as to who will do it. In many cases, it may seem that the Pakistanis are striving for minimum accomplishment in the maximum amount of time. Be very specific and detailed in developing work plans and schedules. You should constantly monitor progress.

Legal contracts are adhered to closely. Document each step and outline each side's responsibilities. If you are buying or selling, be specific in defining your specifications. Pakistan has an arbitration court, but technically, under the 1940 Pakistan Arbitration Act, parties can select another country for arbitration.

Conducting Business in a Social Setting

Dining and Drinking

Due to the Islamic influence, Pakistanis do not eat pork or drink alcohol. The left hand is considered unclean, so never touch or pass food with it. During Ramadan, Muslims are not allowed to eat or drink (not even water) during the day. You should be especially sensitive during this time; never eat or drink in public during the daytime and be careful not to eat or drink in front of a Muslim in your office, hotel room, or other interior space.

Business dinners are more common than business lunches; business breakfasts are rare. Business is usually not conducted during a meal meeting, for dinner is considered an opportunity to develop a social relationship. Women will probably be passed over in business socializing as it would place the Pakistani man in an awkward position. Western businesswomen should probably not extend an invitation, as the Pakistanis have difficulty saying "No."

Visiting a Home

Invitations to homes are not common in the early stages of business relationships. If you are invited to a Pakistani home, be sure to remove your shoes before entering. Take along a small gift such as sweets, dried fruit, or something for the children. Do not take alcohol unless you know the person well and are sure that he drinks alcohol. Pakistanis are hospitable and generous and will seek to make sure that you have plenty of food to eat. Do not be surprised in traditional homes if the host's wife does not join you, even if your wife is present, for women are meant to remain in the background.

Gift Giving

Graft and bribery are widespread at every level. Common tactics are "overinvoicing" by the recipient party or collector of "commissions." Most Pakistanis will make their wish-list clear. It is best to leave such issues to your local partner. Further, it is not uncommon for the police to stop people toward the end of Ramadan for minor offenses with the expectation of receiving some money as a bribe; they use this method to raise money to give the customary gifts at the end of Ramadan. Again, let your driver or local counterpart handle such issues.

Small gifts are always appreciated and will earn you goodwill. Pakistanis will politely refuse a gift two or three times before accepting it. Be sure that you keep insisting until he or she takes it. Likewise, you should humbly refuse a gift several times before accepting it. Suitable gifts include items with company logos or nice pens. Do not give money except for weddings and funerals.

Dress Code

This is an Islamic society and foreigners should be aware of this influence on the dress code. For men, a suit or a shirt and tie are appropriate. Dark suits are expected for formal evening events. Women should be covered adequately and wear longer, three-quarter-length dresses or skirts. Refrain from short skirts, sleeveless blouses, and any garment that accentuates your figure. Slacks are a good option, and short-sleeve blouses, preferably ones that almost reach your elbow, are acceptable. In major cities, you will see Western fashions. Overall, modesty is appreciated.

Useful Phrases

Urdu is the national language, but it is spoken by less than 8 percent of the population, mainly Muhajirs. Urdu is a combination of Persian vocabulary and Hindi grammar and uses a Perso-Arabic script. Urdu was adopted because it was the language of the Muslim Moghul Empire. For those who speak or understand Hindi,

Urdu is very similar. There are about twenty-four languages and three hundred dialects spoken in Pakistan. The other major languages include Punjabi, Sindhi, Pashto, and Baluchi. Many educated people speak English and Persian. English is commonly used in business and the government. The following list includes some useful Urdu phrases and a guide to their pronunciation.

Hello	*Assalam aleikum* (This greeting is used any time of day and literally means "Peace be with you".)
How are you?	*Kya haal heh?*
God be willing	*Inshallah*
Please	*Meherbani kar kay*
Thank you	*Shukriya*
You are welcome	*Koi baat naheen*
Excuse me	*Maaf-ki-ji-yey* (polite)
I am sorry	*Mein maafi chahta hoon* (if the speaker is male); *Mein maafi chahti hoon* (if the speaker is female)
My name is ———	*Mera naam* ——— *heh*
I work for ———	*Mein* ——— *mae kaam karta* (male) / *karti* (female) *hoon.*
Here is my business card	*Yey mera business card hai*
I am pleased to meet you	*Aap say mil kar khooshi hooi*
Please accept this small gift	*Meherbani kar kay yey toohfa qubool kee-ji-yey*
I am look forward to developing a good relationship with you / your firm	*Aap ki company sey achchey taaloqat paida karney ki umeed hai*
I understand	*Mein samajh giya* (male) / *gai-ee* (female)
No, I do not understand	*Mein nahin samjha*
Please wait a minute	*Meherbani kar key aik minute rukyey*
Where is the bathroom?	*Bathroom kahan hai?*
Good-bye	*Khuda hafiz*
Cheers	Cheers (rarely used)

Major Holidays

February/March*	Ramadan
February/March*	Eid-ul-Fitr (end of Ramadan celebrations)

March 23	Pakistan Day
April**	Good Friday/Easter
May 1	International Labor Day
May/June*	Eid-ul-Azha (Feast of Sacrifice)
June/July*	Ashura
July 1	Bank Holiday
July/August*	Muharram
August*	Eid-Milad-un-Nabi (the Prophet Mohammed's birthday)
August 14	Independence Day
September 6	Defense of Pakistan Day
September 11	Death Anniversary of Mohammed Ali Jinnah
November 9	Iqbal Day
December 25	Birthday of Mohammed Ali Jinnah
December 31	Bank Holiday

*These holidays are based on the lunar calendar and change yearly.
**This holiday is observed on the first Friday and the first Sunday after the paschal full moon and changes from year to year.

General Facts

Climate: Pakistan has very hot summers and relatively cold winters. In the summers, from March to June, temperatures can rise as high as 113F (45C). In the winter, from October to February, nighttime temperatures may fall below freezing. From July to September, the monsoon brings heavy rains and hot temperatures. Temperatures and conditions vary within the country.

Currency: The currency is the *rupee* (abbreviated Rs), and is divided into 100 *paisa*.

Dates: Dates are written day, month, year. For example, August 21, 1995, would be abbreviated 21/8/95.

Electricity: The voltage is 220 volts, 50 (Hz) cycle AC.

Entry Requirements: American, British, Canadian, French, and German citizens need a valid passport and visa for entry. For stays longer than thirty days, you must register at the Foreigner's Registration Office prior to the thirtieth day of your stay.

Time: Pakistan has one time zone, which is five hours ahead of Greenwich Mean Time and ten hours ahead of U.S. Eastern Standard Time (nine hours in Daylight Savings Time)

Tipping: Tipping is widespread in cities and appreciated. Locally referred to as baksheesh, tipping is a way of life for many Pakistanis. It is given less for a job well done than in hopes of getting a job done at all. In major hotels and restaurants, about 10 percent is expected. In rural areas, tips may be returned as the concept is counter to the Islamic obligation to be hospitable.

Transportation: The main international airport is at Karachi and has connecting flights to all other major cities. Taxis are available for transportation into the cities. It is best to telephone your hotel in advance and ask to be met at the airport. Private cars and drivers are also available for hire by the day and are highly recommended. Within cities, taxis are convenient and cheap. You may have to negotiate the fare, as meters are often "broken." Ask your hotel for assistance. Car rentals are available, but are not recommended due to traffic, poor driving conditions, and unsafe areas. Motor-rickshaws and horse-drawn tongas provide local color. Buses and trains provide a cheap but crowded alternative. On most forms of public transportation, women and men sit separately.

Helpful Telephone Numbers

All major hotels have telephone facilities for placing domestic and international calls. You can also make international calls from public call offices, although hotels are more convenient. The country code for Pakistan is (92). The major city codes are: Islamabad (51), Karachi (21), and Lahore (42).

Hospitals:

Mideast Medical Centre
Clifton Road
Karachi
Tel.: (21) 535041

Civil Hospital
M A Jinnah Road
Karachi
Tel.: (21) 729719

Police / Emergency:

**Police Station Foreigner's
Registration Office**
1,1 Chundrigar Road
Karachi
Tel.: (21) 233737

Useful Addresses

In Pakistan:

**American Business Council
of Pakistan**
NIC Building, 6th Floor
Abbasi Shaheed Road
G.P.O. Box 1322
Karachi 74400
Tel.: (21) 526436 / 520137 / 8 / 9

**Federation of Pakistan
Chamber of Commerce**
Shahrah Firdousi
Main Clifton
Karachi 6
Tel.: (21) 532179 / 532198 /
569-1191

Jinnah Avenue
P.O. Box 2927
Islamabad
Tel.: (51) 213117 / 8

Cricket House, 3d Floor
Lahore
Tel.: (42) 485252 / 487833

**Islamabad Chamber of
Commerce and Industry**
38 Khayabane Quaid-e-Azam
Jinnah Avenue
Islamabad
Tel.: (51) 810490 / 812104

Lahore Chamber of Commerce
11 Shahrah-e-Aiwan-e-Tijarat
P.O. Box 597
Lahore, Pakistan
Tel.: (42) 305538 / 39 / 40

Ministry of Commerce
Block A
Pakistan Secretariat
Islamabad
Tel.: (51) 214936

**Overseas Investors Chamber of
Commerce and Industry**
Chamber of Commerce Building
P.O. Box 4833
Talpur Road
Karachi
Tel.: (21) 222557 / 8

**Pakistan Industrial
Development Corporation**
PIDC House
Karachi
Tel.: (21) 511080

Pakistan Tourism
Development Corporation
(PTDC)—Head Office
No. 2 Street 61, F-7/4
P.O. Box 1465
Islamabad 44000
Tel.: (51) 828814 / 811001

Embassies and Consulates:

American Embassy
Ramna 5
Diplomatic Enclave
Islamabad
Tel.: (51) 826161

American Consulates
8 Abdullah Haroon Road
Karachi
Tel.: (21) 568-5170

50 Sharah-E-Bin Badees
(Empress Road)
Simla Hills
Lahore
Tel.: (42) 636-5530

11 Hospital Road
Peshwar Cantt
Tel.: (521) 279801 / 2 / 3

British High Commission
Ramna 5
Diplomatic Enclave
Islamabad
Tel.: (51) 822131 / 5

**British Deputy High
Commission**
York Place
Runnymede Lane

Clifton
Karachi
Tel.: (21) 532041

c/o ICI Pakistan Ltd.
63 Mozang Road
Lahore
Tel.: (42) 869371 / 9

**Canadian High
Commission**
Diplomatic Enclave
Sector G-5
Islamabad
Tel.: (51) 211101 / 7

Consulate of Canada
Beach Luxury Hotel
Room 120
Moulvi Tamiz Uddin
Khan Road
Karachi 0227
Tel.: (21) 551100

French Embassy
Constitution Avenue
Diplomatic Enclave 1
Islamabad
Tel.: (51) 823551

French Consulate
Zamzama Boulevard Clifton
Block G-9
Karachi
Tel.: (21) 532295

German Embassy
Ramna 5
Diplomatic Enclave
Islamabad
Tel.: (51) 822151 / 5

German Consulate
90 Clifton
Karachi
Tel.: (21) 531031 / 2

In Canada:

High Commission of Pakistan
Burnside Building, Suite 608
151 Slater Street
Ottawa, Ontario K1P 5H3
Tel.: (613) 238-7881 / 2

Consulates of Pakistan
3421 Peel Street
Montreal, Quebec H3A 1W7
Tel.: (514) 845-2297 / 8

4881 Yonge Street, Suite 810
Willowdale, Metropolitan
Toronto, Ontario M2N 5X3
Tel.: (416) 250-1255

Pakistan Tourism Development Corporation (PTDC)
2678 West Broadway, Suite 202
Vancouver, B.C. V6K 2G3
Tel.: (604) 732-4686

In France:

Embassy of Pakistan
18 Rue Lord Byron
74008 Paris
Tel.: (1) 4561-0824

Pakistan Consulate
10 Bd., Jules-Favre
96006 Lyon
Tel.: (16) 7824-6846

In Germany:

Embassy of Pakistan
Rheinllee 24
5300 Bonn 2
Tel.: (228) 352004 / 9

Pakistan Consulate
0-1080-Berlin
Otto-Grotewohl Strasse, 3A
10117 Berlin
Tel.: (30) 229-2276

Honorary Consulates of Pakistan
Boersen Strasse 14
6000 Frankfurt am Main
Tel.: (69) 287489

Koenigsallee 30
4000 Dusseldorf
Tel.: (211) 3292-6566

Nordkanalstrasse 30
2000 Hamburg
Tel.: (40) 23750

President Kennedy-Platz 1
2800 Bremen 1, Bundesgebiet
Tel.: (421) 367-8233

Ruckert Strasse 1
8000 Munchen 2
Tel.: (89) 534880

In the United Kingdom:

High Commission of Pakistan
35–36 Lowndes Square
London SW1X 9JN
Tel.: (71) 235-2044

Consulates of Pakistan
Unique House
Napier Terrace
Laisterdyke, off Leeds Road
Bradford BD3 4DD
Tel.: (274) 661114

2/26 Constitution Hill
Birmingham B19 3HL
Tel.: (21) 233-4123

137 Norfolk Street
Glasgow G5 9EA
Tel.: (41) 429-5335

Hilton House
26–28 Hilton Street
Manchester MI 2EE
Tel.: (61) 228-1349

Pakistan Tourism Development Corporation (PTDC)— Head Office
52–54 High Holborn, Suite 433
London WC1
Tel.: (71) 242-3131

In the United States:

Embassy of Pakistan
2315 Massachusetts Avenue, N.W.
Washington, DC 20008
Tel.: (202) 939-6200 / 6585

Consulates of Pakistan
12 East 65th Street
New York, NY 10021
Tel.: (212) 879-5800

10850 Wilshire Blvd., Suite 1100
Los Angeles, CA 90024
Tel.: (310) 441-5114

U.S. Department of Commerce
International Trade
Administration
Pakistan Desk, Room 2308
14th and Constitution Avenues, N.W.
Washington, DC 20230
Tel.: (202) 482-2954

14 Sri Lanka (Ceylon)

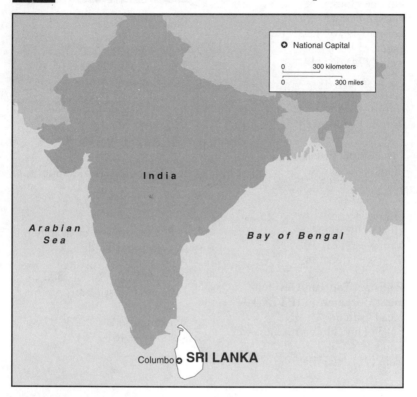

National Capital

0 — 300 kilometers
0 — 300 miles

India

Arabian
Sea

Bay of Bengal

Columbo SRI LANKA

Geography

Formerly known as Ceylon, Sri Lanka is an island located off the southern tip of India. Sri Lanka's northern-most point is only 30 miles (48 kilometers) from the Indian coast. The total land area of Sri Lanka is 24,996 miles (64,740 kilometers). The country's topography varies between scenic rolling hills and valleys, rain forests, rivers, plains, and sandy coasts. The highest peak, Pidurutalagala, is 8,281 feet (2,524 meters) high. Colombo, located on the western coast, is the capital; other major cities are Galle, Kandy, and Jaffna.

424

History

Early records indicate that man first came to the island from the Indian subcontinent several hundred thousand years ago. The Sinhalese, the island's predominant race, are believed to be of Indo-Aryan origin. Migrating from northern India around 500 B.C., the Sinhalese mixed with the island's indigenous races, the Yaksas and the Nagas. The other major ethnic group in Sri Lanka is the Tamils, who are of Dravidian origin and came from southern India around 300 B.C. (some believe that they may have arrived earlier, perhaps even before the Sinhalese).

Since its early days, Sri Lanka has been a multi-ethnic society. The Sinhalese and Tamils are believed to have coexisted in harmony until about 237 B.C., when two Tamil rulers usurped the Sinhalese throne, marking the first time Sri Lanka was ruled by Tamils. Early mixing of the two groups has rendered them almost physically indistinguishable, although cultural and religious differences do remain. Sri Lankan history is largely a chronicle of the intermittent hostility between the Indo-Aryan, Buddhist Sinhalese and the Dravidian, Hindu Tamils.

Ancient Sri Lanka was basically a feudal agricultural society. Relations between landholders and communities were also affected by the caste system, which, although less severe than India's due to the influence of Buddhism, still permeates most parts of daily life.

Buddhism came to Sri Lanka in the third century B.C. during the reign of Devanampiyatissa, a contemporary of Asoka, the last great emperor of India's Maurya dynasty. Over time, Buddhism became the state religion and influenced all aspects of society. Modern Sinhalese believe that they are the "chosen ones" destined to protect and preserve the Buddhist faith on their island, primarily from Hindu-dominated India. The early Buddhist work, the *Mahavamsa*, written in the sixth century A.D., relates the rise and fall of successive Buddhist kingdoms beginning with Vijaya, the legendary Sinhalese colonizer of Sri Lanka. Vijaya is believed to have landed on the island on the day of Buddha's entry into nirvana, his death. The *Mahavamsa* also praises early Sinhalese kings who re-pulsed attacks by Indian Hindu Tamils. Historical events relating to Buddhism give the island prestige in the Buddhist world. For ex-ample, the oral teachings of Buddha, the Tripitaka, were commit-ted to writing for the first time on Sri Lanka.

In contrast, the Hindu Tamils believe that they have their own special claim to Sri Lanka based on the evidence presented in the ancient Hindu epic *Ramayana*, which was written down about 500 B.C., but which relates stories from an oral tradition that dates back to 3000 B.C. In the legendary story, Prince Rama, an incarnation of the Hindu god Vishnu, and his perfect wife, Sita, are required to leave their palace in the northern Indian city of Ayodhya and wander thereafter in the treacherous jungles for years. Sita is even-tually abducted to the island of Lanka (now known as Sri Lanka) by its demon-king, Ravana. Prince Rama defeats Ravana, indicat-ing the final conquest of Lanka by Rama, that is, by Hinduism.

By the fifth and sixth centuries A.D., the Tamil threat to Sin-halese Buddhist kingdoms had increased due to the aggressive Hindu kingdoms in southern India, primarily the Pandya, Pallava, and Chola states. Further, Sinhalese perception of the threat in-tensified because in India, Buddhism had already receded due to competition by Hinduism. In the seventh century, Tamil influence became firmly embedded when the Sinhalese prince Manavamma seized the throne with assistance from the south Indian Pallavas. During its three centuries of rule, the Manavamma dynasty was heavily indebted to Pallava patronage. In the ninth century the Pandyans from south India invaded northern Sri Lanka, but were eventually displaced in the early eleventh century A.D. by the In-dian Chola Empire, who moved the capital from Anuradhapura to Polonnaruwa and ruled Sri Lanka directly as a province. The Chola kingdom grew so strong that it posed a threat to the Srivijaya Em-pire in what is now Malaysia and Indonesia. In 1070, however, the Sinhalese, led by King Vijayabahu, were successful in driving out the Chola dynasty. The following century of rule by Sinhalese monarchs was marked by a Buddhist renaissance and religious expansion overseas.

During the period between 1200 and 1500, a series of Sinhalese kings ruled the island. In response to threats from the Indian Chola and Pandyan empires and an expanding Tamil-ruled kingdom in northern Sri Lanka, the Sinhalese migrated toward the southern part of the island. The Tamil kingdom in the north secured control of the valuable trade area around the Jaffna Peninsula. The Sinhalese, now restricted to the southern and central part of the island, became increasingly fearful of the Tamil presence and strength in the north. However, the Tamils soon became preoccupied with resisting the advances of various southern Indian kingdoms and their threat to Sinhalese declined. Eventually, the arrival of the Portuguese prevented the island from being overrun by the Tamils.

The Portuguese, the first Europeans settlers, arrived in the early part of the sixteenth century, bringing Christianity as well as trade. The Portuguese conquered Jaffna, the Tamil capital in the north, and Kotte, which had become the nominal Sinhalese capital on the southwestern coast, and certain other ports and regions of the country. In the early seventeenth century, the Dutch arrived in search of spices and other exotic wares and named the island Ceylon. The Sri Lankans entered into an alliance with the Dutch to get rid of the Portuguese; unfortunately, this plan backfired, resulting in the replacement of one colonial ruler with another. By 1658, only the kingdom of Kandyan remained independent. Mixed marriages between Portuguese and Dutch males and Sri Lankan women led to the creation of the Burghers, a Eurasian race.

The British had the greatest and most lasting effect on Sri Lanka. In 1795–1796 the British fought the Dutch and drove them out. When the Dutch formally ceded island to the British in 1802, Sri Lanka became Britain's first crown colony. However, the Kandyan kingdom remained independent of European colonial rule until 1815, when the British finally conquered Kandyan, bringing the entire island under the control of a single power for the first time since 1197. Although the British originally perceived the island as a strategic rather than an economic asset, they eventually found the island to be a source of wealth for the empire.

Until the twentieth century, a vast forest separated the Tamil-settled north and the Sinhalese-inhabited south. During their rule, the British were generally successful in uniting the island and encouraging democratic values. British beliefs in liberalism, their emancipation of slaves, and their policy of religious toleration caused many Sri Lankans to perceive British rule as progressive compared to that by the Portuguese and the Dutch. Further, the British broadened the education system to include more of the population. They also created a Sri Lankan educated class to perform administrative and professional services.

However, the British also brought in Tamil labor from southern India to work on their plantations. These immigrant Tamils, although linguistically and religiously similar to native Sri Lankan Tamils, were perceived to be culturally inferior by native Tamils and were set off as a lower class. Moreover, the Sinhalese began to feel that the Tamils were an economically and educationally privileged group, which aroused great resentment among the Sinhalese population.

The nationalist movement remained unorganized until World War I. In 1915 the Sinhalese and the island's Muslims rioted against each other, but were put down by the British. After this incident the Sinhalese created an independence movement, using the Indian nationalist movement as their model. In 1919 they created the Ceylon National Congress. In response to Sinhalese organizations, the Tamils began to organize themselves to counter any transfer of power under Sinhalese leadership. In 1931, constitutional reforms were introduced that provided voting rights for men and women and provided the first step toward self-government. Ceylon thus became the first British colony to have universal suffrage. Voting rights opened the way for a resurgence of Buddhism and the spread of Marxism by strengthening working-class movements.

In 1942 Japan bombed the ports of the country, but Allied and

Sri Lankan forces were able to hold on to the island, thus ensuring that Japan did not gain control of the Indian Ocean. After World War II, Sri Lanka continued to negotiate with the British, finally achieving formal independence on February 4, 1948. Sri Lanka was finally free from all foreign domination, and unlike some neighboring countries, achieved independence by peaceful means. The transfer of power was smooth and the anti-British feelings did not escalate into violence until nearly a decade after independence.

The first prime minister of Ceylon was Don Stephen Senanayake, the Sinhalese head of the United National party (UNP), the island's largest political party formed as a partnership of several smaller parties. The new government continued to debate the status of the Indian Tamil immigrants who had worked on the plantations. Ethnic differences widened between the Sinahalese and Tamils, and between Sri Lankan Tamils and Indian Tamils. In 1949 a faction of the Ceylon Tamil Congress formed the Tamil Federal party under the leadership of S.J.V. Chelvanayakam. This group eventually replaced the Tamil Congress and adopted an aggressive position vis-à-vis the Sinhalese.

During the early years of the country's existence, Senanayake's efforts to diffuse tensions by keeping religion and politics separate initially met with some success. However, in July 1951 the Sri Lanka Freedom party (SLFP) was formed under the leadership of S.W.R.D. Bandaranaike and became the first major non-Marxist party to oppose the UNP, although both parties catered to the Sinhalese vote.

After Senanayake's death in 1952, the peace slowly eroded. His two successors, one of whom was his son Dudley, were unsuccessful in perpetuating his ideas. The economy faltered. At the same time, religious, cultural, and linguistic differences began to divide people. The opposition Sri Lanka Freedom party (SLFP) began to gather support, particularly from the Buddhist leadership, which had been ignored by the governing UNP. The Federal party continued to advocate an autonomous homeland for Tamils within a Sri Lankan federation. The Marxist opposition continued to be ineffective due to internal squabbling.

In 1956 the SLFP won the national elections and S. W. R. D. Bandaranaike became the prime minister. He campaigned as the defender of the besieged Sinhalese culture, rejected Western elements and the pro-Western stance of the UNP, and embraced Buddhism rather than the Hinduism practiced by the Tamils. Bandaranaike promoted a "Sinhala only" platform, declaring the Sinhalese language to be the only official language, and excluding Tamil and English as cultural imports. His overt pro-Sinhalese stance enraged the Tamils. Thereafter two completely separate, hostile political systems emerged.

In 1958 the country experienced nationwide riots between Sinhalese and Tamil groups. This was the first major episode of communal violence since independence. Bandaranaike was assassinated in 1959 by a Buddhist extremist. In March 1960 power shifted back to the UNP under Senanayake's son Dudley. However, in July of the same year, the SLFP won power back from the UNP, because the latter party had earned the reputation among the Sinhalese voters of being hostile to Sinhalese nationalist efforts. Sirimavo Ratwatte Dias (S.R.D.) Bandaranaike, the assassinated prime minister's widow, emerged as a major political force for the next twenty years. The modern world's first female prime minister, she sought to unite the country under a single national language of Sinhalese by trying to bring all of the private schools under state control. This action enraged Tamils and Catholics. She sought to use socialism as a means of tilting the balance of power toward the Sinhalese-Buddhist nationals. She nationalized numerous local and foreign companies. Sirimavo Bandaranaike reacted to Tamil resistance and civil disobedience by declaring a state of emergency and curtailing Tamil political activity.

In 1965 the SLFP lost power to the UNP due in large part to the ethnic and religious turmoil. The new government, under the leadership of Senanayake, tried to earn favor with the disaffected ethnic groups. Efforts to make Tamil an official language in Tamil-speaking regions met with violent opposition from the Sinhalese. A state of emergency was declared in 1966.

In 1968 Bandaranaike forged a coalition with two Marxist parties, the LSSP and the CPSL, creating the United Front (Samagi Peramuna), which won power in 1970. In 1971, the United Front faced a stiff threat from an ultra-left organization called the Janata Vimukti Peramuna (JVP), the People's Liberation Movement, which was supported by educated youth, the disadvantaged, and the unemployed. The JVP was an extremist Sinhalese group that favored Maoism. It attempted to overthrow the ruling regime, but was quickly put down by government forces which were led by the United Front. Nevertheless, the United Front lost credibility because of this episode. The United Front tried to reassert itself by exerting more control over the government and economy through social and economic reforms. As part of the changes, the government implemented a new constitution in 1972, which renamed the country Sri Lanka, vested legislative power in a unicameral legislature, the National State Assembly, and elevated the status of Buddhism. Provisions in this constitution angered the Tamils, who by then were calling for a separate Tamil state to be called Eelam. The socialist policies of the government did little to improve the plight of the country's poor. By February 1977, the United Front had collapsed and the UNP with Junius Richard Jayewardene as its prime minister returned to power.

In 1977 the United Front failed to win enough votes to be the main opposition party. This new role went to the Tamil United Liberation Front (TULF), led first by Chelvanayakam and then by Appapillai Amirthalingam. Jayewardene meanwhile liberalized the economy, dismantled the rigid controls imposed by the United Front, attacked inefficiency, and reduced state intervention across the board. Despite widespread distrust of foreign companies, the government sought to encourage foreign investment. Jayewardene had a pro-West, pro-American attitude, which differed from that of his predecessors. In 1978 a new constitution was approved and the role of president was expanded from ceremonial head of state to an active head of state, commander-in-chief, and chief executive. Jayewardene exchanged his title of prime minister for that of president in 1978. Tamil was also made a "national language" alongside the official language of Sinhalese.

In the mid-1970s the Tamil separatist underground movement split into six or more rival groups that were divided by ideology and caste. The strongest of the separatist groups was the Liberation Tigers of Tamil Eelam (LTTE, also known as the Tamil Tigers), which was known for its brutal acts of terrorism. In 1979 the government was forced to declare a state of emergency in the northern state of Jaffna as a result of violence between the Sinhalese majority and the Tamil minority. Other large Tamil groups, including the People's Liberation Organization of Tamil Eelam, the Tamil Eelam Liberation Army, and the Tamil Eelam Liberation Organization, began to compete with the Tamil Tigers. In the early 1980s the Tamil separatists began a guerilla war. An attack in 1983 by the Tamil Tigers on a Sinhalese army group resulted in widespread reprisals against the Tamils throughout the country. Racist mobs destroyed Tamil property and murdered Tamils. As a result, the Parliament passed a law banning any talk of separatist movements.

As a result of the ethnic link between Tamils in Sri Lanka and those in India, India had shown a keen interest in the outcome of the conflict and at times had taken positions against the Sri Lankan government, thereby fueling resentment among the Sinhalese. By the late 1970s and early 1980s, there was widespread belief in Sri Lanka that many of the Tamil separatists were operating from training camps in the southern Indian state of Tamil Nadu. In 1987, by mutual agreement between Jayewardene and Prime Minister Rajiv Gandhi of India, an Indian Peacekeeping Force (IPKF) was sent to Sri Lanka to help disarm the Tamil separatists and oversee the implementation of a cease-fire. However, the IPKF became too involved in the ethnic struggle and in 1990 they were withdrawn at the request of Ranasinghe Premdasa, the head of the UNP, who in 1989 became president. The state of emergency that had been in place for five and a half years was lifted.

The 1990 attempt at a cease-fire failed and the violence resumed. The Tamil Tigers demanded independence in the north and east. Besides efforts to halt the political crisis, the government pursued a policy of economic reform. In June 1993 President Premdasa was assassinated by a Tamil suicide bomber and Dingiri Banda Wijetunge was named president. In November 1994 Mrs. Chandrika Bandaranaike Kumaratunga, daughter of Bandaranaike and head of the People's Alliance (PA)—led by the SLFP and consisting of nine leftist parties—won the presidential election. She is expected to resume talks with the separatist Tamil rebels and continue to focus on encouraging foreign investment into the country.

Political Structure

The official name of the country is the Democratic Socialist Republic of Sri Lanka. Locally, it is also called Sri Lanka Janarajaya. The constitution is modeled upon that of France's Fifth Republic. Sri Lanka has a presidential form of government. The 1978 constitution guarantees fundamental freedom of thought, conscience, and worship. In addition, it guarantees freedom from discrimination and basic legal protections. The president is the chief of state and head of the government. He or she appoints cabinet ministers in consultation with the prime minister, who is chosen by the president with Parliament's approval. The president is elected by popular vote for a six-year term and can serve a maximum of two consecutive terms. The legislature consists of a unicameral house, the Parliament, with 225 members, who are elected by popular vote for a six-year term. They have the power to pass laws and to amend the constitution.

The judicial system is based on British common law, Roman-Dutch (Napoleonic) law, and the customary practices of the Sinhalese, Tamils, and Muslims. The president appoints judges and enjoys immunity from court action while in office. The Supreme Court is the highest court in the country.

The country has undergone numerous leadership changed since achieving independence in 1948. Racial and social divisions have frequently affected politics. Further, many leaders have taken sides in ethnic disputes, making compromise difficult to attain. The linguistic, racial, social, and regional issues that divide Sri Lanka are large and clearly definable. Despite efforts by numerous individuals, groups, and countries, it remains unclear whether the Tamil rebels and the government can reach a compromise. Efforts are underway to shift the government away from a strong presidency and back to the parliamentary system.

Economy

Since 1977, the country has shifted from a socialist to a market economy. Although the economy has performed better, income distribution is highly skewed, more as a result of corruption than any specific economic policies. Despite its relatively low per-capita income, the country has a thriving economy and a well-respected education system. Funding the struggle with separatists has been a financial drain on the government, one estimated to cost about U.S. $500 million per year.

Almost half of the population is employed in agriculture. Historically the most important crop has been rice; other important crops include coconuts, rubber, sugar cane, and tea, which has earned the country significant foreign exchange. Another source of foreign exchange comes from the numerous Sri Lankans working in the Middle East who send money back to their families. Major industrial goods include textiles and garments, and processed and packaged agricultural commodities. Tourism has recently reemerged as a major industry.

Government-controlled enterprises play a major role in the country's economy, although the government has sought to liberalize and deregulate the economy to encourage foreign investment.

People, Values, and Social Customs

The population of Sri Lanka is about 17.5 million. The four major ethnic groups are Sinhalese (74 percent), Tamil (19 percent), Moor (7 percent), and Burgher (0.3 percent). There are also small populations of Eurasians, Malays, Parsis, and Veddhas. The two main characteristics marking a person's ethnic heritage are language and religion. More than 99 percent of Sinhalese speak Sinhala and all Tamils speak Tamil; both languages are now officially recognized. People identify themselves first as members of a specific ethnic group rather than as citizens of Sri Lanka. The major religions are Theravada Buddhism (69 percent), Hinduism (15 percent), Christianity (8 percent), and Islam (7 percent). Generally, 93 percent of the Sinhalese are Buddhist; more than 80 percent of Sri Lankan and 90 percent of Indian Tamils are Hindu; all Moors are Muslim; and Burghers, Eurasians, and some Sinhalese and Tamils are Christian.

Geographical proximity between India and Sri Lanka has fostered a version of the traditional Indian caste system in Sri Lanka. It is an integral part of society, although not as rigidly held to as in India. Officially the caste system no longer exists, but each ethnic group has its own subdivisions that differentiate between people. Today, economic standing as well as physical differences contribute to the caste concept and status. Today, there are about fourteen castes that affect an individual's ritual status, marriage, and in some situations, profession. This system has resulted in a certain level of fatalism since a person's position in life is determined at birth.

The Sinhalese, who tend to be of Aryan heritage, separate themselves into the up-country (Kandyan) branch, which is considered more socially prestigious, and the low-country branch, which is a legacy from the Portuguese and the Dutch. The highest Sinhalese caste is the Goyigama, landowners and cultivators; since independence, most Sri Lankan heads of state have been a member of this group.

Among the Tamils, there is a difference between those from south India, whose ancestors were brought to Sri Lanka by the British in the 1800s to labor on their plantations, and the Sri Lankan (or Jaffna) Tamils, whose ancestors settled in Sri Lanka many centuries ago. South Indian Tamils account for about 6 percent of the population, while Jaffna Tamils account for about 13 percent. Both groups are of Dravidian stock and originate from the Indian subcontinent. The south Indian Tamils are considered economically, politically, and socially inferior to their well-established kinsfolk. Further they often represent lower castes than the elite Sri Lankan Tamils. Although language and religion serve to unite them, the two Tamil groups are really two separate ethnic communities.

The Muslims are descendants of the Arab traders who began doing business in Sri Lanka in the eighth century A.D. Most are racially intertwined with the Tamils and Sinhalese, as those Arab traders did not bring women with them and so intermarried. The Muslims are divided into three main groups: Sri Lankan Moors (93 percent), Indian Moors (2 percent), and Malays (5 percent); the latter emigrated to Sri Lanka when both Sri Lanka and Indonesia were colonies of the Dutch.

The Burghers are a small but distinct population descended from the Dutch colonialists who occupied the island from 1658 to 1796. Today, the term "Burgher" (Dutch for "town dweller") is used for any Sri Lankan who is a descendant of any European. Status ranking in the Burgher community, as in other Sri Lankan ethnic groups, is dependent on various factors, including skin color, physical stature, and life-style. In reaction to the wave of nationalism in the 1950s and 1960s and anti-Western feeling, many Burghers migrated to Europe.

The Sri Lankans are very family-oriented and respectful of elders. Living as an extended family, with grandparents, parents, children, and other family members all under one roof, is still the norm—except in the cities. To indicate respect and status, each member of the family is referred to by a specific name. Sri Lankans are very hospitable and go out of their way to entertain a visitor, due in part to their adherence to the Buddhist values of compassion and charity.

The Sri Lankans are very nationalistic and usually have very strong political views. Sri Lankans do not appreciate being confused with Indians and view themselves as culturally distinct. The elite class of Ceylonese were educated in Europe during the period of British rule. Since independence, however, the government has promoted education for all and the results have been very positive. More than 90 percent of the population is officially literate. Advanced technical and professional studies continue to be taught in English.

The average Sri Lankan is accustomed to long lines and bureaucracy, rationing, barriers, and permits. Sri Lankans tend to maintain a clear distinction between work and social life, particularly if they work for someone else. Work is perceived for the most part as a necessity for survival.

Women still occupy very traditional roles in Sri Lankan culture as caregivers and homemakers. Men dominate commerce and government. As time goes by, however, women are occupying more professional positions with responsibility.

Work Schedule

Most businesses and government offices are open from 8:30 A.M. to 4:30 P.M., Monday to Friday, with one hour for lunch. In actuality, work hours are often shorter and lunch hours longer. Some businesses are open on Saturday mornings. Banks are open from 9:00 A.M. to 1:00 P.M. on Mondays, and until 1:30 P.M. on other weekdays. Banks often close early on days before public holidays. Shops are open from 8:00 A.M. or 9:00 A.M. to 5:00 P.M., from Monday through Friday and usually on Saturday mornings as well.

Making Contacts

Foreign companies can approach Sri Lankan companies directly, although introductions help to establish credibility. There are relatively few telephone lines in Sri Lanka, so it is advisable to establish initial contact by writing. Expect letters, not faxes, in return, so allow for ample communication time. Foreign companies should hire a local representative or agent to manage their local interests and relationships. Take into account the local representative's political and ethnic affiliation, as it can be helpful or harmful. Business is closely intertwined with government and relationships should be developed in both the private and the public sectors.

If you will be on a tight schedule while in Sri Lanka, it is advisable to schedule meetings prior to your arrival. Sri Lankan businesspeople will frequently make an unscheduled call on another company, but expect to wait as much as several hours to see the intended party. Unless you have plenty of time, this approach is not recommended. However, it is worth noting that if you are already in Sri Lanka and want to visit a company, there is a fairly good chance you can arrange a meeting.

Meeting People

Many people leave their office before the official day ends at 4:30 P.M., so it is best not to schedule first meetings near the end of the day. Punctuality is expected. Most Sri Lankan businesspeople, men and women, greet one another with a handshake, though it is advisable to wait until a woman offers you her hand. The traditional greeting, used less frequently in business, is similar to the Indian *namaste*; both hands are placed together as in prayer, slightly below the chin, accompanied with a slight bow of the head. Business cards should be exchanged at first meetings.

Address people by their formal title ("Dr.," "Mr.," "Mrs."), followed by the family name. Sri Lankans are highly conscious of titles. Refrain from using first names until invited to do so. Sri Lankans will seek to match you up with someone at the same level. You should be sensitive to this system when scheduling meetings. Identify a person's title and responsibility before making any assumptions about them.

There are numerous women in the professional workplace and in the government. Women are generally treated as equals in the workplace. Foreigners, particularly women, should not smile too often, as it may be considered a form of flirtation. Sri Lankans tend to smile only when they are happy or when they wish to indicate thanks.

Buddhism has influenced various interpersonal customs. Do not touch a person's head, for it is considered the most sacred part of a person's body. Refrain from any other physical contact such as patting someone on the back. People of the same sex may hold hands as a sign of friendship. Do not point your foot or touch someone with your feet as the feet are considered the dirtiest part of the body. Pointing is rude and beckoning should be done with your arm extended in front of you and using the whole hand with the palm facing down and the fingers pointing away but moving toward you in a scratching motion.

Begin meetings with casual conversation. Sri Lankans enjoy talking and no subject is really forbidden, but it is advisable to refrain from political and religious topics since you may be unfamiliar with a person's ideology. Gifts are not expected at early meetings.

Corporate Structure

Most companies in Sri Lanka are privately run. Many are family-owned businesses that tend to be patriarchal with centralized decision-making. It can be difficult to identify the key decision-makers in most firms, as few Sri Lankans want to be publicly accountable for their actions. There is often a reluctance on the part of junior-level professionals to make decisions or to assume responsibility because these are perceived to be senior-level tasks. Fact-finding is reserved for middle-level managers so as not to waste a senior person's time. Further, most middle-level professionals are more involved with the details and may be in a better position to provide you with specifics. Concrete proposals should be presented to the most senior person possible, usually the managing director or president. Entrepreneurial spirit is widespread and Sri Lankans often run their own small businesses.

In the government sector, it is important to identify the correct ministry and official with whom you want to do business. When selecting someone from your organization to research or interact with the government, be sure to send someone who is at the same level as the official. Sri Lankans tend to deal only with people of their own rank. Officials generally have well-defined jurisdictions of authority; foreigners should familiarize themselves with the various levels required for approval on a specific transaction.

Negotiation

Sri Lankan time is generally more relaxed than Western business time. Business is conducted at a leisurely pace. You may need to visit Sri Lanka several times before you are taken seriously enough to complete a successful transaction. The speed at which your proposal is facilitated also depends on the nature and size of the deal. Do not expect quick decisions. The education level and international experience of your Sri Lankan counterpart will also be important in shaping his or her attitudes and expectations of you.

In the public sector, the decision-making process may be lengthened because people are often required to seek approvals outside their jurisdiction. The system is set up to protect any one person from having to take the responsibility for a poor decision and to save face at all times. Sri Lankans use the phrase "What to do" as a response to a wide variety of questions. It does not imply anything specific, but is simply a rhetorical device used while people look for alternative options.

To indicate "Yes," Sri Lankans, like many Indians, bob their head from side to side in a wobbly movement. When in doubt, it is best to verify any response verbally. Refrain from publicly criticizing someone; maintaining face and dignity is extremely important. Sri Lankans may not tell superiors about problems in order to protect them from losing face. Preserving harmony and having consideration for others is very much a part of the business environment. It is best not to raise your voice even if a Sri Lankan does.

The relaxed notion of time prevalent in Sri Lanka can lead to deadlines being missed or ignored. Commitment to speed and efficiency is not widespread. Tasks will be completed, but probably not in the timeframe you imagine. Build in mini-deadlines and leave ample time for delays. Often people will seek to implement a quick, but temporary solution to a problem to avoid losing face due to inaction.

The Sri Lankans believe in astrology. This may affect business interactions because they will want to determine auspicious dates for such things as signing deals or opening new buildings or factories. Contracts are detailed and adhered to closely. Verbal agreements are not widely used or considered binding.

Conducting Business in a Social Setting

Dining and Drinking

Sri Lankans use socializing as a way to get to know a potential business partner. Traditionally all food is eaten with the fingers (right hand only) although the use of utensils is becoming common in international hotels and restaurants. Never use your left hand alone for eating, presenting gifts, or touching someone as the left hand is considered dirty. Be sensitive to any religious food restrictions that your counterpart may have (Muslims do not eat pork and Hindus do not eat beef). Most socializing occurs before the meal; people leave within a half hour of the end of a meal.

Visiting a Home

In traditional homes, remove your shoes before entering. Sri Lankans are hospitable and appreciate a small gift such as wine (as long as they are not Muslim), sweets, or a souvenir from your home country. When you are finished eating, push your plate away slightly or place your hands over your plate when anyone offers you food.

Your host or hostess will urge you several times to eat more. You should decline several times, then accept if you are hungry.

Shoes and hats should be removed before entering all temples. Women are not permitted to touch Buddhist monks.

Gift Giving

Graft is pervasive in Sri Lanka and is considered a normal part of doing business. It is best to leave such matters to your local representative. Westerners should note that the government takes action against those discovered taking part in corrupt acts.

Gift giving in the normal business context is less frequent than in many other Asian countries and is not usually expected. Once a deal is closed, you may consider a tasteful gesture depending on the size of the transaction. Money is only given at New Year's and then primarily to employees or household help. Gifts should be presented with both hands to indicate respect and to show that they are given freely.

Dress Code

For men, slacks and shirts with a tie are appropriate. Local Sri Lankans often do not wear ties. For women, dresses or skirts and blouses are appropriate. Generally, the dress code is casual-conservative. White is usually reserved for death and funerals. Beige is acceptable.

Useful Phrases

The official languages are Sinhala and (since 1987) Tamil. English is spoken in commercial and administrative areas including government. Both Portuguese and Dutch words have been absorbed into the local languages. Further, many Sinhalese have adopted Portuguese names like de Silva and Fernando. The Christian religious

influences, however, are minimal. The following list of key phrases
indicates how they should be pronounced.

	Sinhala	**Tamil**
Hello	*Halo*	*Halo*
Good morning	*Ayubowan*	*Vanakkam*
Good afternoon	*Ayubowan*	*Vanakkam*
Good evening	*Ayubowan*	*Vanakkam*
How are you?	*Kohomada*	*Yeppadi irukkintrirgal*
Please	*Karunakara*	*Thayavu panni*
Thank you	*Istutiyi*	*Nandri*
You are welcome	*Upakara kirimata kamatiyi*	*Waravetkirem*
Excuse me	*Samavenna*	*Mannikkavum*
I am sorry	*Kanagotui*	*Mannikkavum*
My name is ———	*Mage nama ———*	*Yen peyar ———*
I work for ———	*Mama veda karanne ———*	*Naan velai seivathu ———*
Here is my business card	*Menna mage bisnes card eka*	*Yennudaiya business kaardu*
I am pleased to meet you	*Hamuveema gana santosai*	*Unggalai santhithathil mikka mahilchi*
Please accept this small gift	*Karunakara me podijagga piliganna*	*Intha siriya parisai pettrukkollavum / vaangkihavum*
I look forward to developing a good relationship with you / your firm	*Oba / Obe ayatanaya samaga kittuwen katayutu kirimat balaporottu venara*	*Ungaluthan nal uvavu yeivtpadhuthikulla virumbukivur*
I understand	*Mata terenava*	*Yenakku puriyavillai*
No, I do not understand	*Mata therenne nehe*	*Enakku vilanga illai*
Please wait a minute	*Uinadiyak inna*	*Oru nimisham*
Where is the bathroom?	*Bathroom eka koheda?*	*Bathroom engge ullathu*
Good-bye	Good-bye	*Vanakkam, pooi varugirein*
Cheers	Cheers	Cheers

Major Holidays

Sri Lanka has about 174 nonworking days including weekends and a generous amount of holidays, only some of which are listed below. The most common holiday is a Poya Day, which occurs about every twenty-eight days and marks the monthly full moon, a significant day for Buddhists. Each Poya Day marks a different episode in the life of Buddha or the history of Buddhism; some Poyas are more important than others. Check with the diplomatic or tourist offices before you plan your visit.

January 1	New Year's Day
January 14	Tamil Thai Pongal
February 4	Independence Commemoration Day
February / March*	Maha Sivarathri Day
March*	Eid-ul-Fitr
April**	Easter
April*	Sinhala and Tamil New Year's Day
May 1	May Day
May 22	National Heroes Day
June*	Eid-ul-Az ha
June 30	Special Bank Holiday
September*	The Prophet Mohammed's Birthday
October/November*	Diwali Festival
December 25	Christmas Day
December 31	Special Bank Holiday

*These holidays are based on the lunar calendar and differ from year to year.
**These holidays are observed on the first Friday and first Sunday after the paschal full moon and change from year to year.

General Facts

Climate: The climate is tropical and can be extremely hot in certain areas. In inland areas, the humidity can rise as high as 85 percent, although the countryside is usually more pleasant. No snow has ever been recorded on Sri Lanka's mountain peaks, although frost has been noted on occasion. There are only two main seasons, summer and the monsoons. Summer occurs from October through December, when temperatures may reach 99F (37C). There are two monsoon periods. The southwest monsoon occurs from April to July and the northeast monsoon occurs from mid-October until mid-February, overlapping with the summer months. The monsoons, which are actually seasonal winds with rain, lessen the extreme heat of the summer. Nevertheless, most days are sunny with rain in the afternoon and evening. In Colombo, the average annual temperature is 80F (27C).

Currency: The currency is the Sri Lankan *rupee* (abbreviated as Rs.). Each *rupee* is divided into 100 *cents*. One common expression is the *lakh*, which a unit measure for 100,000 of anything (money, widgets, etc.).

Dates: Dates are written day, month, year. For example, June 16, 1995, would be abbreviated 16/6/95.

Electricity: Sri Lanka uses 230–240 volts, 50 cycles. Most outlets are three-pronged, so carry an adapter.

Entry Requirements: All visitors are required to have a valid passport. American, British, Canadian, German, and French citizens may stay up to thirty days without a visa. Business visitors will need a visa regardless of length of stay. Visas may be extended at the Department of Immigration and at the Aliens Bureau for non-Commonwealth country citizens.

Time: Sri Lanka has one time zone, which is five and a half hours ahead of Greenwich Mean Time and ten and a half hours ahead of U.S. Eastern Standard Time (nine and a half hours in Daylight Savings Time).

Tipping: Tipping is common. The better restaurants will automatically add a 10 percent service charge. Most taxi drivers do not expect a tip.

Transportation: From Colombo Airport, there are three ways to get into the city. Taxis are the easiest method and are relatively inexpensive. Buses and trains are cheaper, but not as convenient. The distance is twenty-one miles (thirty-four kilometers), although it can take longer than expected due to traffic and the fact that cars share the roads with bullock carts, bicycles, and pedestrians. There is also a private air-conditioned bus that travels into Colombo.

There is a taxi stand at the airport. It is helpful to know that all vehicles—taxis, buses, and private cars—available for rent have white license plates with red numbers as opposed to yellow plates with black numbers for private cars. Within Colombo, taxis still provide the most reliable form of transportation. Taxis usually have yellow tops and are painted black. Make sure that the meter is turned on when you enter a taxi or negotiate the fare in advance. Auto-rickshaws are three-wheel scooters, which are convenient for short distances in Colombo or other major cities. Check with your hotel for transportation assistance. It is best to rent a car and driver to get around; this is relatively cheap by Western standards. Rental cars without hired drivers are not advisable because driving conditions are very difficult. Roads are narrow and few drivers observe traffic rules. Hired drivers usually speak English and can also act as guides. Ask your hotel to make arrangements for you. In Colombo, buses are stuffy and crowded. Minibuses are usually privately owned and are faster and more comfortable. Foreigners should be wary of pickpockets on all public transportation. To get around the country, there are planes, trains, and buses reaching almost every destination.

Helpful Telephone Numbers

Public telephone booths are not very common. Some stores may have a public telephone that can be used for a nominal fee, but you will have little privacy. In most cases, it is easiest to make local and international calls from hotels. The country code is (94) and the codes for major cities are: Colombo (1), Jaffna (21), and Galle (9).

Hospitals:

Hospital Durdans
3 Alfred Place
Colombo 3
Tel.: (1) 575205

Accident Service
Ward Place
Colombo 7
Tel.: (1) 693184 / 5

**Joseph Frazer Memorial
Nursing Home**
Joseph Frazer Road
Colombo 5
Tel.: (1) 588385

Central Hospital
Horton Place
Colombo 7
Tel.: (1) 596411

Ambulance: Dial 222222

Police: Dial 33333 for an
emergency; for the Tourist
Police, dial 26941 or 21111

Information:
Tourist Information Center
41 Glen Aber Place
Colombo 4

Useful Addresses

In Sri Lanka:

Aliens Bureau
New Secretariat Building
5th Floor

Colombo 1
Tel.: (1) 21111

All Ceylon Trade Chamber
212/45, 1-3 Bedhiraja Mawatha
Colombo 11
Tel.: (1) 545742

American Center
39 Sir Ernest de Silva
Mawatha
Colombo 7
Tel.: (1) 91461

**American Chamber of
Commerce in Sri Lanka**
Colombo Hilton, 3d Floor
P.O. Box 1000, Lotus Road
Colombo 1
Tel.: (1) 544644

British Council
Alfred House Terrace
off Duplication Road
Colombo 2
Tel.: (1) 437336

**Ceylon Chamber of
Commerce**
50 Navam Mawatha
P.O. Box 274
Colombo 2
Tel.: (1) 421745

Chamber of Small Industries
HPT Building
D. S. Senanayake Mawatha
Colombo 8
Tel.: (1) 91920

Department of Commerce
Rakshana Mandiraya
4th Floor
Vauxhall Street
Colombo 2
Tel.: (1) 329733

**Federation of Chambers of
Commerce and Industry**
People's Bank Building
220 Deans Road
Colombo 10
Tel.: (1) 599530

**Foreign Investment Advisory
Committee**
International Economic
Corporation Division
Ministry of Finance and
Planning
Galle Face Secretariat
3d Floor
Colombo 1
Tel.: (1) 428367

**Greater Colombo Economic
Commission**
(Has authority for Free Trade
Zone projects)
14 Sir Baron Jayatillake
Mawatha
P.O. Box 1768
Colombo 1
Tel.: (1) 434403

**National Chamber of
Commerce**
YMBA Building, 2d Floor
Main Street
Colombo 1
Tel.: (1) 541069

**National Chamber of
Industries**
Galle Face Courts 2, 1st Floor
Colombo 3
Tel.: (1) 29038

**Sri Lanka Chamber of
Commerce**
127 Lower Chatham Street
Colombo 1
Tel.: (1) 22084

**Sri Lanka Chamber of Small
Industry**
17a Dickman's Road
Colombo 5
Tel.: (1) 209788

**Sri Lanka Export Development
Board**
Ramada Renaissance Building
115 Sir Chittampalam A
Gardiner Mawatha
Colombo 2
Tel.: (1) 438513 / 5

Tourist Information Center
321 Galle Road (main office)
Colombo 3
Tel.: (1) 573175

Colombo Airport lobby
Katunayake
Tel.: (1) 0302411

**Women's Chamber of Industry
and Commerce**
10, 1/1, Sir Marcus Fernando
Mawatha
Colombo 7
Tel.: (1) 495913

Embassies:

American Embassy
210 Galle Road
Colombo 3
Tel.: (1) 448007

British High Commission
190 Galle Road, Kollupitiya
Colombo 3
Tel.: (1) 437336 / 43

Canadian Embassy
6 Gregory's Road
Cinnamon Gardens
Colombo 7
Tel.: (1) 695841 / 2 / 3

French Embassy
Villa Sarina, 34 Asoka Gardens
Colombo 4
Tel.: (1) 502320 / 1

German Embassy
40 Alfred House Avenue
Colombo 3
Tel.: (1) 580431

In Canada:

Embassy of Sri Lanka
Sandringham, Suites 102–104
85 Range Road
Ottawa, Ontario K1N 8J6
Tel.: (613) 233-8440

In France:

Embassy of Sri Lanka
15 Rue d'Astorg
75008 Paris
Tel.: (1) 4266-3501

In Germany:

Embassy of Sri Lanka
Roland Strasse 52
5300 Bonn 2
Tel.: (228) 332055

In the United Kingdom:

Embassy of Sri Lanka
13 Hyde Park Gardens
London W2 2LU
Tel.: (71) 262-1841 / 262-3996

In the United States:

Embassy of Sri Lanka
2148 Wyoming Avenue, N.W.
Washington, DC 20008
Tel.: (202) 483-4025

Sri Lanka Mission to the United Nations
630 Third Avenue, 20th Floor
New York, NY 10017
Tel.: (212) 986-7040

U.S. Department of Commerce
International Trade
Administration
Sri Lanka Desk, Room 2308
14th & Constitution Avenues,
N.W.
Washington, DC 20230
Tel.: (202) 482-2954

15 Bangladesh ———

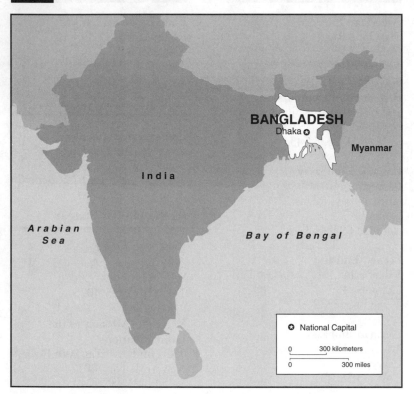

Geography

Bangladesh is located north of the Bay of Bengal with India on its western, eastern, and northern borders. Myanmar (Burma) is located to the southeast. The total size of the country is 55,126 square miles (142,776 square kilometers). The country is mostly a wide, low plain broken by low-lying hills. There are five major river systems, including the Ganges. As a result of its location and the tropical monsoon climate, Bangladesh has frequently been the victim of natural disasters including floods, cyclones, tidal waves, and droughts. The major cities include Dhaka, the capital, and Chittagong.

History

Bangladesh became a fully independent nation on December 16, 1971, although independence from Pakistan was actually declared on March 26th of that year. Historically, Bangladesh (formerly East Bengal) was part of the northern Hindu and Muslim empires in India and subsequently part of British India from the late eighteenth century onward. (For history, please refer to Chapters 12 and 13, on India and Pakistan.)

Bengal, a geographic region located in the northeastern portion of India, was home to both Hindus in the west, and Muslims in the east. Despite their different religions, the people shared a common Bengali racial stock, language, and culture. Historically, Calcutta, the major city in Bengal, was the focal point of trade, industry, transportation, and communications in the area. Under the British it had become a major trade center and the springboard for Great Britain's eventual colonial conquest of India. In 1947, when India and Pakistan divided, the eastern portion of Bengal became East Pakistan because of its Muslim majority. The western portion of Bengal, including the city of Calcutta with its Hindu majority, aligned with India. As a result, East Bengal was left with no infrastructure or industry.

West and East Pakistan coexisted uneasily, for they were not only physically separated by a thousand miles of intervening Indian territory, but also by social and cultural differences. Although it was the most populous of Pakistan's five provinces, East Pakistan believed that it was neglected in terms of economic development and political influence when compared to Pakistan's other provinces. The two Pakistans were constantly vying for political dominance of the nation, with the west as the consistent winner.

The Bangladeshi independence movement was prompted by the 1970 general election in which the Awami League in East Pakistan won enough seats to become the majority party in Pakistan's parliament. This should have elevated the party's leader, Sheikh Mujib ur-Rahman (Sheikh Mujib), to prime minister. But Pakistan's president, General Yahya Khan, did not want to transfer power to East Pakistan and instead suspended the parliament. On March 7, 1971, Sheik Mujib called on East Pakistanis to stop cooperating with West Pakistan. On March 25th the Pakistani army began a crackdown, whereupon East Pakistan declared itself independent the following day. In the resulting civil war, an estimated one million Bangladeshis were killed and another ten million fled to neighboring India. Finally, on December 3rd, the Indian army came to the aid of East Pakistan by invading the area. On December 16 victory was finally achieved and independence obtained.

In November 1972 a constitution was passed and in March 1973 elections were held. Sheikh Mujib became the new state's leader. In January 1975, however, the government declared a national state of emergency and parliament was replaced by one-party rule with Sheikh Mujib as president. On August 15th he was assassinated in a right-wing coup d'état led by a group of Islamic army officers including one of his ministers, Khandker Mustaque Ahmed, who subsequently became president. Two months later, a countercoup brought Major General Zia ur-Rahman to power. He installed A. M. Sayem, then chief justice, as president.

However, Zia took over the presidency in April 1977 and then won the 1978 elections. In late 1978 he formed the Bangladeshi Nationalist party which overwhelmingly won the elections in February of the following year. Zia was successful in bringing some stability to the country and he reintroduced civilian rule. Unfortunately, he too was assassinated during an attempted coup that took place in 1981. For a short time, his vice-president, Abdus Sattar, became president, but he was ousted in a successful 1982 coup led by Lieutenant General Ershad, the army chief of staff, who reintroduced martial law. On December 11, 1983, Ershad made himself president. His party, the Jatiya party (JP) won the May 1986 elections. However, violent antigovernment demonstrations forced Ershad to declare a state of emergency in November 1986 and dissolve parliament.

In 1988 the JP won the elections, although these were boycotted by the opposition, including the socialist Awami League. Ershad then declared Bangladesh an Islamic republic. But, like his predecessors, President Ershad was overthrown in December 1990 and has been in prison on corruption charges since then. In February of the following year new elections were held, resulting in Bangladesh's first freely elected parliament. The Bangladesh National party (BNP) came to power under the leadership of Begum Khaleda Zia, the widow of Zia ur-Rahman. In recent years women have assumed powerful leadership roles in Bangladesh, a highly unusual situation for a predominantly Muslim country. Sheikh Hasina Wajed assumed the leadership of the Awami League, her father's opposition party. Raushan Ershad took over the leadership of her husband's Jatiya party.

The government of Begum Khaleda Zia has finally brought a measure of democratic stability to the country. Nevertheless, the government faces a strong challenge from opposition parties and Muslim fundamentalists. The government has been slow to spur the economy, but has initiated new programs aimed at meeting the basic needs of the economically underprivileged people. Although Bangladesh remains one of the world's poorest countries, economic conditions are slowly improving.

Political Structure

Bangladesh currently has a parliamentary form of government with a prime minister as the executive head of government. Under this system, the prime minister has executive powers and is assisted by a cabinet, which currently consists of twenty-two ministers. The president, elected by the parliament, serves as the head of state.

Abdur Rahman Biswas has been president since October 10, 1991. The legislative branch is unicameral and is called the Jatiya Sangsad (parliament). Of its 330 members, 300 are directly elected by the people to five-year terms. Although the remaining 30 seats are reserved for women who are indirectly elected by the sitting members of parliament, women may also contest any of the 300 seats in the open elections. The parliament has the right to approve the budget, pass laws, and amend the constitution.

While the constitution technically guarantees freedom of religion, Islam has been the state religion since 1988. The judiciary consists of the Supreme Court and various lower courts. Under the present democratic system, the judiciary is technically independent from the executive and legislative branches of government. The civil code has been influenced by the British legal code.

Economy

In 1989 the government announced a major economic liberalization plan involving tax breaks, import concessions, and profit repatriation. In recent years the government has been introducing more liberal investment policies and is gradually moving toward the privatization of some industries. Inflation has been reduced and the country has amassed foreign exchange reserves of about U.S. $3 billion. However, the country remains burdened by a high foreign debt load, primarily owed to multilateral aid agencies.

The economy is primarily agrarian, with about 85 percent of the working populous employed in agriculture-related industries. Major crops include rice, wheat, jute, tea, tobacco, sugar cane, lentils, oilseeds, spices, and various fruits and vegetables. Fishing and shrimp farming are becoming viable industries.

Many of the existing industrial facilities in Bangladesh have been established to process crops. Other industries include cement, fertilizers, chemicals, jute, cotton yarn and textiles, engineering, shipbuilding, petroleum products, paints, electrical cables and lamps, and iron and steel.

People, Values, and Social Customs

With about 118 million people, Bangladesh is one of the most densely populated countries in the world. Approximately 85 percent of the population lives in rural areas. The major ethnic groups are Bengalis (98 percent) and Bihari tribesmen. Bangladesh has been influenced most strongly by Indian culture, but it has also been touched by the Burmese, Tibetan, Arab Muslim, Persian, Turk, Afghan, and Mughal cultures.

Almost 87 percent of the people are Muslims. Hindus constitute the largest religious minority at 12 percent of the population. The remainder are Buddhist, Catholic, or follow tribal and other faiths.

Due to the preponderance of rural dwellers, village life has been important in shaping the culture and life-style, with family playing a central role. In general, people tend to be warm and gentle and smile often.

The role of women in Bangladesh society is complex. Even women who have ascended to positions of power are accepted more as their husbands' wives or as their fathers' daughters than as politicians in their own right. Women have excelled in various professions, including government and business. However, the average woman remains less educated than the average male and is generally considered inferior. The formal religious explanation for this belief is that women "need" to be protected by men as a sign of respect. Some women observe *purdah*, which means to be kept from the sight of all men outside of the family by "living" behind a veil. These women dress in *burqah*, a full-length, black or white, tentlike gown, although this practice is becoming less common in major cities. Most women follow the practice of covering their head with a thin scarf called a *dupatta*. Some urban, affluent, and educated women discard the *burqah* completely and just wear the *dupatta*.

Work Schedule

Most businesses are open from 8:00 A.M. to 5:00 P.M., Saturday to Thursday. Government offices are open from 7:30 or 8:00 A.M. to 2:00 or 2:30 P.M. Friday is a holiday for offices, banks, and most shops. Banks are open from 9:00 A.M. to 1:00 P.M., Saturday to Wednesday, and from 9:00 A.M. to 11:00 A.M. on Thursday. Most shops are open from 10:00 A.M. to 8:30 P.M., Saturday to Thursday.

Making Contacts

Foreign companies can write directly to Bangladeshi firms. Government ministries can provide general assistance in identifying suitable local partners and firms. The government produces several pieces of literature; particularly recommended are *Bangladesh: A New Horizon for Investment*, which includes details on the investment procedures and other approval processes, and *Bangladesh: Towards the 21st Century*, which can be helpful in the early stages of researching Bangladesh.

Each government ministry is headed by a cabinet-level minister. Some of the larger ministries, such as industry and education, have state ministers who manage sections of the ministry and are accountable to the cabinet minister. In order to expedite the process, large multinationals should direct their first communications to the appropriate minister. Midsize and smaller firms should direct their communications to the state minister or to the most senior person they can identify.

Due to problems arising from the bureaucracy and corruption, it is advisable to hire a local contact or establish a local representative office. Your local Bangladeshi office or contact should be able to provide guidance and assistance in navigating the system.

Meeting People

Make sure to avoid scheduling a business trip on or near an Islamic holiday, particularly during the month-long holiday of Ramadan. Punctuality is always appreciated, although it is not always observed by local Bangladeshis.

Most men will greet each other with a handshake. It is best to wait until a women offers you her hand. Often a nod and a polite smile will suffice. Many Bangladeshis will perform the *namaste*, the traditional Indian greeting in which both hands are placed together at chest level as in prayer, accompanied by a small nod of the head. Business cards are exchanged at the beginning of meetings.

Due to the influx of international aid workers, Bangladeshis tend to be accustomed to and open to foreigners. You should begin your first meeting with a few minutes of casual conversation and then state your purpose for the visit. Most Bangladeshis are willing to discuss business within minutes of the start of the first meeting. Gifts are not required for the early meetings. You should, however, feel comfortable presenting samples of your products.

Corporate Structure

In the private sector, the senior-most person in a firm responsible for daily management is usually the managing director or the president. The chairman heads an organization, but generally handles strategic and long-term planning issues.

The Bangladesh Export Processing Zones Authority (BEPZA) operates free zones in various cities, including the port cities of Chittagong and Khulna and near the airport in Dhaka, where interested parties can invest and, in turn, receive special concessions. The Board of Governors, consisting of various ministries and secretaries, serves as the policymaking body of the BEPZA and is headed by the prime minister. The Board of Investment (BOI), also headed by the prime minister, consists of other ministers and secretaries, retains key powers, and facilitates foreign and local investment. Accordingly, decisions are often politically motivated. The BOI is usually the first point of contact for international businesspeople. Foreigners should direct their initial communications to the chairman or director-general at the BOI.

Negotiation

Always show respect and deference to senior counterparts. Avoid appearing condescending and never show your temper. You will earn far more respect for being patient and calm in the face of adversity. You need to judge each situation and your counterpart separately. At times, caution will be the best approach and at other times aggressive enthusiasm may serve you well.

In most companies, a certain amount of research and fact-finding will be carried out, but the final decision is usually dependent on the intuition of the senior person. Most negotiations are conducted between key people and through relationship channels.

Bangladeshis will rarely say "No" outright. Rather, they will adopt a hopeful attitude that something will happen and may even say that they are "confident or hopeful" that something will occur. Avoid asking yes/no questions.

Bangladeshis have a very relaxed concept of time and rarely meet deadlines. The average Bangladeshi will wait for instructions at every step of a process. Further, due in part to the influence of Islamic culture, there is a general attitude "that if God wishes for something to be done, then it will be done," which may cause the specifics of decision-making and implementation to be ignored. In many cases, the norm is to accomplish the minimum in the maximum amount of time. To counter this tendency, you should be very specific and detailed in developing work plans and schedules and monitor progress closely.

Bangladeshis will rarely inform you if there is a problem, as they do not like to give negative news or assume responsibility for setbacks. Problems will either be ignored or kept hidden. Maintaining personal honor is critical and allowing others to maintain theirs is equally important.

Legal contracts are utilized and observed. Document each step and outline each party's responsibilities. If you are buying or selling products, thoroughly define your specifications.

Conducting Business in a Social Setting

Dining and Drinking

Business entertaining is common and is viewed as a way to develop personal relationships. In restaurants, it is acceptable to eat either with utensils or with the right hand. The left hand is considered unclean, so never pass or touch food with it. Due to the Islamic influence, most Bangladeshis do not eat pork or drink alcohol. During Ramadan Muslims are not allowed to eat or drink (not even water) during the day. You should be religiously sensitive during this period and avoid eating or drinking in front of your counterparts or in public during the day.

Business dinners are more common than lunches and business breakfasts are rare. Formal business is usually not conducted during a dinner for this is considered an opportunity to develop a social relationship. Western women will probably not be invited to socialize because this would place the local men in an awkward position.

Visiting a Home

Once a business relationship has been established, it is common for the Bangladeshis to invite you to their home. Bangladeshis are hospitable and can be generous with friends and associates. It is appropriate to bring a gift, particularly for the children. Suitable items include local sweets and chocolates. Bangladeshis are known for having a "sweet tooth." In traditional homes, the hostess may not join you as Muslim women tend to keep low profiles and eat separately from men.

Remove your shoes before entering a home and any religious area. Before entering a temple or mosque, people often wash their feet. Do not photograph people, particularly women, without their permission. Do not perform the American "thumbs-up" gesture; it is considered obscene.

Gift Giving

Corruption involving gifts for influence is widespread. It is best to leave such matters to your local partner or agent.

Traditional gift giving is acceptable. Suitable items include tasteful souvenirs from your home country, nice pen sets, and calendars and date books. Refrain from giving gifts of alcohol or pork, particularly if your counterpart is Muslim. Do not present gifts that are extravagant, as you may make your Bangladeshi counterpart feel awkward and create a obligation.

Dress Code

For men, lightweight suits are appropriate for the early meetings while a shirt and tie may be suitable for subsequent meetings. Follow the lead of your counterpart. For women, dresses or suits are advisable. Pants are a good option because they cover the legs. Due to the Muslim and Asian influences, women should dress modestly, so do not wear short skirts or sleeveless blouses.

Useful Phrases

The official language is Bangla (Bengali). English is the second language of most professionals and students. The following list contains some helpful phrases and a guide to their pronunciation.

Hello   *Aja sunun*
Good morning   *Shupro-baht*
Good afternoon   *Shuvo-din*

Good evening	*Shuvo sondha*
How are you?	*Kemon achhen?*
Please	*Doya kore amake din*
Thank you	*Dhon-no-bad*
You are welcome	*Apo-nake swa-gotom*
Excuse me	*Khoma korben*
I am sorry	*Ami dukh-khito*
My name is ———	*Amar nam* ———
I work for ———	*Ami kaj kori* ———
Here is my business card	*Age amar card*
I am pleased to meet you	*Aponar sathe dekha kusi ho-e-chhi*
Please accept this small gift	*Onu-groho kore ei samanno upohar grohon/korun*
I look forward to developing a good relationship with you / your firm	*Aponar / Aponar farmer sathe som proko gorhe tulte agravi*
I understand	*Bhuste par-chhi*
No, I do not understand	*Na, ami bhuste parini*
Please wait a minute	*Doya-kore ek minit opek-kha korun*
Where is the bathroom?	*Bathroom-ti kotha?*
Good-bye	*Bidai*
Cheers	*Soko-ler suvo hok* (rarely used as Muslims do not drink alcohol)

Major Holidays

January*	Shab-e-Barat
February 21	National Mourning (Martyrs) Day
February/March*	Ramadan
February/March*	Eid-ul-Fitr
March 26	Independence Day
April 15	Bengali New Year
May*	Buddha Purnima
May/June*	Eid ul-Azha
September*	Eid-e-Miladunnabi (the Prophet Muhammad's Birthday)
October*	Durga Puja
October/November*	Diwali
November 7	National Solidarity Day
December 16	Victory Day
December 25	Christmas Day

*These holidays are based on the lunar calendar and change from year to year.

General Facts

Climate: Bangladesh has a tropical climate with three distinct seasons: winter (November–February), summer (March–May), and monsoon (June–October). The average annual temperatures range between 73F (23C) and 86F (30C), with summer temperatures reaching as high as 102F (39C).

Currency: The currency is the *taka*, which consists of 100 *paisa*.

Dates: Dates are written month, day, year. For example, August 6, 1995, would be abbreviated as 8/6/95.

Electricity: The voltage is 220.

Entry Requirements: All foreigners are required to have a valid passport. Tourist visas are required for stays longer than fifteen days. Business visitors are required to have visas regardless of the length of stay.

Time: Bangladesh is six hours ahead of Greenwich Mean Time and eleven hours ahead of U.S. Eastern Standard Time (ten hours in Daylight Savings Time).

Tipping: Tipping is common. In the better restaurants and hotels, 10 percent of the bill is appropriate if a service charge is not already included. For taxis, round upward to the nearest *taka*.

Transportation: Taxis are convenient and relatively inexpensive. Make sure that the meter is working or negotiate a fare beforehand. Private cars and drivers are convenient and your hotel should be able to assist you in booking a car. Women are advised to travel with a car and driver, primarily for safety reasons. Buses tend to be crowded and dirty. Street numbers and routes are not in English, making it difficult to get around. Motor rickshaws are an acceptable alternative method of transportation. Driving is on the left-hand side of the road.

    There is a Hospitality Booth (fax: 880-2-833626) at Zia International Airport in Dhaka that can assist you with a wide variety of services, including transportation during your stay. Taxis or privately hired cars are the only reliable ways of getting into the city. If you rent a car, make sure you rent from a credible agency.

Helpful Telephone Numbers

The country code is (880) and the city codes are Dhaka (2) and Chittagong (31).

Hospitals:

Dhaka Medical College
Tel.: (2) 500121 / 6

Holy Family Hospital
Tel.: (2) 831721 / 5

Sir Salimullah Medical College
Tel.: (2) 240061 / 4

Ambulance / Emergency: Dial 233333 / 254613 / 408897.

Police: Dial 254161-5 / 410061-70.

Fire: Dial 233333.

Operator: Dial 17 or 254222.

Useful Addresses

In Bangladesh:

Bangladeshi Chamber of Commerce and Industry (BCI)
BCI Bhaban
31 Dilkusha Commercial
Area (C/A)

Dhaka
Tel.: (2) 252081 / 239281-90

Bangladesh Export Promotions Bureau
122–124 Motijheel
Commercial Area
Dhaka
Tel.: (2) 833167 / 23

Bangladesh Export Processing Zones Authority (BEPZA)
222 New Eskaton Road
Dhaka
Tel.: (2) 410510 / 835325 / 832553

Chief Controller of Imports and Exports (CCI&E)
9/E Motijheel Commercial Area
Dhaka
Tel.: (2) 230289

Chittagong Chamber of Commerce and Industry (CCCI)
Chamber Building
Agrabad Commercial Area
Chittagong
Tel.: (31) 502325 / 504117

**Dhaka Chamber of Commerce
and Industry (DCCI)**
Dhaka Chamber Bhaban
65–66 Motijheel
Commercial Area
Dhaka
Tel.: (2) 232693 / 232562 /
255106

**Federation of Bangladeshi
Chambers of Commerce and
Industry (FBCCI)**
Federation Bhaban
60 Motijheel Commercial Area
Dhaka
Tel.: (2) 864680 / 864760 /
2401023

**Foreign Investors Chamber of
Commerce and Industry
(FICCI)**
4 Motijheel Commercial Area
Dhaka
Tel.: (2) 881240 to 45

**Metropolitan Chamber of
Commerce and Industry
(MCCI)**
Chamber Building
122–124 Motijheel
Commercial Area
Dhaka
Tel.: (2) 230714 / 861487 / 8 / 9

Ministry of Commerce
Bangladesh Secretariat
Dhaka
Tel.: (2) 834886 / 241358

Ministry of Industries
Shilpa Bhaban
91 Motijheel Commercial Area
Dhaka 1000
Tel.: (2) 832143

Prime Minister's Office
Old Sangsad Bhaban
Tejgaon
Dhaka
Tel.: (2) 610010 to 29

**Prime Minister's Office, Board
of Investment (BOI)**
Shilpa Bhaban
91 Motijheel Commercial Area
Dhaka 1000
Tel.: (2) 861140 / 243193 / 4 / 5

**Registrar of Joint Stock
Companies and Firms**
24–25 Dilkusha
Commercial Area
Dhaka
Tel.: (2) 252226 / 236398

Tourist Information Center
Bangladesh Parjatan
Cooperation
233 Airport Road
Tajgoan, Dhaka
Tel.: (2) 325155

Embassies:

American Embassy
Diplomatic Enclave
Madani Avenue
Baridhara, Dhaka
Tel.: (2) 884700

British High Commission
United Nations Road
Baridhara, Dhaka
Tel.: (2) 882705 / 601079

Canadian High Commission
House No. 16A
Road No. 48

Gulshan, Dhaka 1212
Tel.: (2) 607071 to 77

French Embassy
House No. 18
Road No. 108
Gulshan, Dhaka
Tel.: (2) 607083 / 4

German Embassy
178 Gulshan Avenue
Dhaka 1212
Tel.: (2) 884735 to 37

In Canada:

Bangladesh High Commission
85 Range Road, Suite 402
Ottawa, Ontario KIN 8J6
Tel.: (613) 236-0138 / 9

In France:

Embassy of Bangladesh
5 Square Petrarque
75016 Paris
Tel.: (1) 4704-9435 / 4553-4120

In Germany:

Embassy of Bangladesh
Bonner Strasse 48
5300 Bonn 2
Tel.: (228) 352525 / 362940

In the United Kingdom:

Bangladesh High Commission
28 Queen's Gate
London SW7 5JA
Tel.: (71) 584-0081

Bangladesh Assistant High Commission
31–33 Guildhall Building
12 Navigation Street
Birmingham B2, 4NT
Tel.: (21) 643-2386

28–32 Princess Street
3d Floor
Manchester, M1 4LB
Tel.: (61) 236-4853

Bangladesh Commercial Centre
41 Chamberlayne Road
London NW10 3NB
Tel.: (71) 960-3852

In the United States:

Embassy of Bangladesh
2201 Wisconsin Avenue, N.W.
Suite 300
Washington, DC 20007
Tel.: (202) 342-8372

Bangladesh Consulate General
821 U.N. Plaza, 6th Floor
New York, NY 10017
Tel.: (212) 599-6767 / 867-3434
(Permanent Mission to the
United Nations)

U.S. Department of Commerce
International Trade
Administration
Bangladesh Desk, Room 2308
14th & Constitution Avenues,
N.W.
Washington, DC 20230
Tel.: (202) 482-2954

16 | Nepal

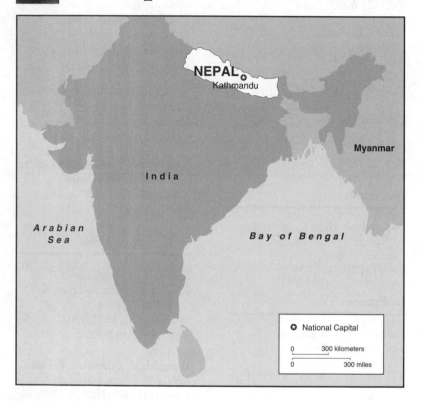

Geography

Landlocked between two global powers, the kingdom of Nepal is located between the northeast border of India and the southern border of China (Tibet). The land area of Nepal is 56,827 square miles (147,181 square kilometers). The country is very rugged with mountains, including the world's highest, Mount Everest, covering more than 80 percent of the land. The Terai, located in the southern part of Nepal, is the large flood plain of the Ganges River and has become Nepal's industrial and commercial center. The capital of Nepal, Kathmandu, is located in the central part of the country.

History

Nepal is the historic and cultural meeting point between the Caucasoid people from the plains of India to the south and the Mongoloids of Asia from the north. Early traces of civilization in the area date back to at least the eighth century B.C., when the Kirati tribe, believed to be of Mongolian origin, migrated from the east and settled in the Nepal valley. During the sixth century B.C., various groups of people, including the Khasa and the Shakya, migrated from the Aryan kingdoms already established in northern India. Prince Siddhartha Gautama, the founder of Buddhism, was a member of the Shakya clan, whose small kingdom in the foothills of the Himalayas lies in present-day Nepal. Buddhism greatly influenced the early Nepali culture. Along with the religion came an entire cultural philosophy that centered on the king as the defender of ethics, the moral code, and religious beliefs. This concept of a king as the righteous center of the political system has had a powerful impact on Nepal.

In the fourth century A.D., the Licchavis drove out the Kirati and assumed control of the area, forming the first kingdom of Nepal in the Kathmandu Valley. The Licchavis were Rajputs, a Hindu warrior caste, driven from their kingdom in north India. Hinduism reasserted itself under Licchavi rule. Hindu temples, Sanskrit literature, and the appearance of a caste system dating from this time indicate the extensive cultural and religious influence of northern India on Nepal during this era. Nepal flourished as a result of the trade between India and China and the Kathmandu Valley became the political, economic, and cultural center of Nepal.

After the decline of the Licchavi kingdom in 733 A.D., Nepal went through a transitional period during which there was no dominant ruling force. The Kathmandu Valley remained a single political unit, but various families struggled for the throne. In written language, there was a gradual movement away from Sanskrit and towards Newari, which was the language of the Newar people in the Kathmandu valley.

From about 1200 to 1482, the Khasa Malla kings were forced out of India and took over western and central Nepal, eventually uniting the kingdom. In neighboring India, the Muslim Turks gained control. In response, parts of Nepal went through a period of increased militarization. Outside the Kathmandu Valley, other areas began to emerge and small towns became established. Yakshamalla ruled from 1428 to 1482; his reign was the high point of the Malla empire in Nepal.

In 1482, a critical date in Nepal's history, the kingdom became divided. Initially, Yakshamalla's six sons tried unsuccessfully to rule together. The three kingdoms that arose as a result of their rivalry, Bhaktapur, Kathmandu, and Patan, lasted until the mid-eighteenth century. The language of the Khasa, the basis for modern Nepali, began to be spoken throughout Nepal.

In neighboring India, Muslim Moghuls ruled from 1526 to 1707. Although the Moghuls never reached Nepal, they had an indirect influence on the latter, for many of India's princes fled to the hill country on the border of Nepal and created small Rajput principalities. These princes brought Moghul military technology, techniques, and equipment, which they exchanged for land.

In the north, China intervened in an internal struggle in Tibet during the 1720s and installed the sixth Dalai Lama. As China established a military presence in Lhasa to monitor events, Nepal found itself squeezed between two powerful countries who were becoming larger and more centralized.

The first Europeans to arrive in Nepal were the Portuguese in 1628, but they had little local impact. It was the growing British presence in India, particularly in Bengal just southeast of Nepal, that was more strongly felt. Interested in trading opportunities, the British sought to exploit the divisions between the three Nepali kingdoms.

In 1559 Dravya Shah, of Indian Rajput ancestry, established a small kingdom at Gorkha, a principality west of Kathmandu. During the seventeenth and eighteenth centuries, the Gorkha kingdom slowly exploited the tensions between the three kingdoms. Prithvi

Narayan Shah assumed the Gorkha throne in 1743 and subsequently embarked on a campaign of expansion. In 1767 the British East India Company sent an expeditionary force to aid the local Nepalese kings against the Gorkhas, but withdrew when most of their force became ill. Between 1768 and 1790 Gorkha armies conquered Kathmandu, Patan, western Sikkim, and most of the rest of Nepal.

In the 1780s the Gorkhas tried to move toward Tibet, but were rebuffed by the Chinese in 1792. The victorious Chinese forced the Nepalis to sign away their trading rights in Tibet. In 1814 Nepal and the British, now moving north from India, went to war. As a result of the strength of the Gorkhas, the British were forced to bring in additional troops. They eventually conquered Nepal in February 1816, taking land to the east and west of Nepal's modern borders as well as parts of the Terai. However, the British found the Terai difficult to govern and returned the land to Nepal. The British were so impressed with the strength, courage, and fighting skill of the Gorkhas that they recruited entire Gorkha regiments to serve the British Crown. The word "Gurkha" is the British version of "Gorkha" and was originally applied to soldiers from the region.

The 1816 treaty also provided for a British resident to be stationed in Kathmandu, a stipulation that was often the precursor to outright British colonial conquest. However, the early British residents had little influence on Nepal. The kingdom was able to remain independent, although the British exercised influence through trade and close cooperation. In 1923 a friendship treaty confirmed Nepal's independence and its special relationship with British India.

In 1846 an army officer named Jang Bahadur Rana took advantage of a crisis in the court and massacred everyone except the king at a meeting in the Kot, the palace armory. The Shah king was allowed to retain nominal power, but Rana assumed the title of commander-in-chief and prime minister and ensured that his heirs would rule as prime ministers, essentially creating a second royal family. Rana is often blamed for isolating the country and establishing the dictatorship that repressed Nepal for over one hundred years. But he is also credited with eliminating factionalism and modernizing the political bureaucracy. The Ranas received support from the British throughout their rule.

Early opposition to the Ranas began in the 1920s. By the mid-1940s, Nepali opposition groups had organized themselves in Benares and Calcutta in India. In 1951 supporters of Shah King Tribhuvan overthrew the Ranas and established the Shahs as constitutional monarchs of Nepal. The Nepali Congress party (NCP), which had been created in exile in Benares, formed a cabinet. For ten years various prime ministers and cabinets ruled under the kings, but none were effective.

In 1960, convinced that Western-style democracy would not work, King Mahendra (son of King Tribhuvan) assumed direct rule, dismissed the cabinet, and wrote a new constitution. The king instituted the Panchayat system based on the traditional Hindu model of the five (panch)-member village council. The partyless Panchayat system provided for locally elected representation. The king appointed a council of ministers who made decisions that were ratified by the National Panchayat Assembly.

In 1972 King Mahendra died and was replaced by his son, King Birendra. After riots and demonstrations in the late 1970s, he held elections in 1980. The mandate was to democratically reform the Panchayat system. The most important reform was the decentralization of administrative authority down to the village or town Panchayat level. However, local patronage and corruption, encouraged by the Panchayat system, increased.

Several prime ministers were removed from office after losing no confidence votes. However, the power of the constitutional monarch did not diminish. In August 1985 ongoing civil disobedience resulted in over one thousand arrests. King Birendra's government continued its sometimes violent campaign to halt public criticism of the regime and pro-democracy demonstrations. Nevertheless, the pro-democracy movement gained momentum and eventually forced radical changes in the government.

In 1990 a new constitution established Nepal as a British-style constitutional monarchy, reducing the power of the king and dismantling the Panchayat system. The ban on political parties was also lifted. On May 12, 1991, the Nepali Congress party won the first democratic elections held in more than thirty years. Girija Prasad Koirala became prime minister. The communists also performed well. The government introduced unpopular economic reforms in 1991, leading to sharp increases in food and electricity prices. Nepal's democracy is still in its early stages and the reforms have sparked continued anti-government sentiment.

In November 1994, the Nepal Communist Party (United Marxist-Leninist or UML) gained power in the mid-term elections. The UML did not receive an absolute majority of the votes, but after two weeks King Birendra appointed Manmohan Adhikari as prime minister. Although Adhikari is Nepal's first communist prime minister, he has pledged that his government will pursue open-market economic policies and encourage foreign investment.

Political Structure

Nepal is the world's only official Hindu state. The government is a British-style constitutional monarchy with multi-party democracy. Executive power rests with the prime minister and a Council of Ministers. There are two houses in the legislature, the House of Representatives (Pratinidhi Sabha) whose 205 members are elected by popular vote for five-year terms, and the National Council (Rashtriya Sabha), whose 60 members have a six-year term with one-third retiring every two years. Of the 60 members, 35 are elected by proportional representation, 15 by local government representatives, and 10 are nominated by the king. The prime minister is the leader of the political party with a majority in the Pratinidhi Sabha.

The judicial system is based on a blend of Hindu and Western legal traditions. The new system established in 1990 provides for a Supreme Court which has final authority over all of the lower courts.

Economy

The economy is heavily dependent on trade with India. Its lack of direct access to seaports combined with the rugged mountain terrain remains an economic challenge for Nepal. Approximately 92 percent of Nepalis are economically dependent on agriculture. Major crops include rice, corn, wheat, millet, potatoes, oilseed, sugar cane, jute, and tobacco. Tourism remains an important part of the economy, providing critical foreign exchange. Nepal's Gurkha soldiers have served at home and overseas in the British, Indian, Singaporean, and Bruneian armies, and their remittances to Nepal have also been an important source of foreign exchange for the country. However, the number of Gurkhas serving overseas is rapidly diminishing, decreasing financial help from this source.

There is limited industrial activity, much of which is concentrated in cottage industries. Large manufacturing facilities exist for the following industries: grain milling, vegetable and animal oils production, sugar, textiles and garments, jute, cigarette, carpets, wood products, printing, leather, bricks and tiles, cement, and metal products. The most important mineral resources include limestone, garnet, magnesite, and talc. There is very little infrastructure; the highway, communication, and transportation systems are all very primitive. New economic reforms introduced in 1992 encourage foreign investment, permit foreign investors to own up to 100 percent equity in certain industries, and promote the expansion of the local private sector. Nepal continues to be a recipient of international aid earmarked primarily for infrastructure projects.

People, Values, and Social Customs

Nepal, with a population of 19.6 million, is one of the least urbanized countries in the world. More than 90 percent of the population lives in rural areas. The three main ethnic groups are Indo-Nepalis, Tibeto-Nepalis, and indigenous Nepalis, each of which consists of various subgroups. Each ethnic group inhabits specific altitudes.

Nepal is essentially an immigrant country, with the population divided into different races, religions, languages, and cultures. While Nepalese society is very tolerant, there has been little assimilation because each group has preserved and maintained its own culture and traditions. Marriage between the castes or between ethnic groups is uncommon.

About 89.5 percent of the population is Hindu, 5.3 percent are Buddhist, 2.7 percent are Muslim, with the remainder being Christian or various other religions. In practice, Hindu and Buddhist beliefs have intermingled and common values of physical purity, spiritual refinement, and modesty are respected. Most Nepalis believe in fate or *karma*, which is the consequences of past deeds.

Nepali society is basically feudal with strict social hierarchies. Due to Hindu influence, the rigid caste system is widespread despite being officially abolished. Hindu culture dictates that people are born into a specific level or position and remain there for life. A person's name functions almost like an identity card revealing his or her social rank and often his or her profession.

Within the Nepali society is another self-contained society, called Newari, an ethnic group predominant in the Kathmandu valley. The Newari society tends to be urban, consists of both Hindus and Buddhists, and prescribes to a complete caste system and traditions. Foreigners are likely to come into contact with people from both the larger Nepali and the smaller Newari societies. However, the most important determinant of social rank is caste, followed by ethnic and regional identity. People from the same castes create informal networks to support each another professionally and socially.

The hill tribes are divided into various clans, also known as *jaats* or *thars*, but caste differences are still more distinct than clan differences. Most hill tribes follow a combination of Buddhism and animism with some Hindu influence.

The extended family remains the central unifying factor in Nepali society. People usually share property, food, and other resources within the extended family. The village also provides a network of kinship and obligation. Class consciousness, based on religious caste and family, is widespread and different classes refer to one another through specific speech. Western popular culture in the form of movies and television has permeated even rural Nepali society. Today social status is often determined by economic standing. As a result, government officials, landowners, and merchants enjoy a relatively high social status. The military, particularly the Gurkha soldiers, are revered according to the principle of *iijat*, which values honor and self-respect.

Status in Nepal is also determined by sex; women occupy lower social positions than men of the same religion from the same ethnic group. This is particularly true among Hindus. However, in each family unit, the senior woman controls the resources and makes daily financial decisions.

Many men and women can be seen wearing a dot, or *tika*, in the middle of their forehead. It is a symbol of blessings from the gods. Traditionally, a tika on a woman's forehead indicated that she was married. However, in modern times the tika has become part of fashion, comes in various colors and even shapes, and is worn by both married and unmarried women.

Work Schedule

Most businesses are open Sunday to Friday from 10:00 A.M. to 5:00 P.M. Some international companies are closed on Sundays. Government offices are open six days a week with Saturday off. Government offices open at 10:00 A.M. and close daily at 5:00 P.M. except on Friday when they close at 3:00 P.M. In reality, few Nepalese begin work before 10:30 A.M. and they usually leave before 5:00 P.M. In winter, all government offices close one hour earlier at 4:00 P.M. Banks are open from 10:00 A.M. to 3:00 P.M. (2:30 P.M. in winter), Sunday to Thursday, and from 10:00 A.M. to 1:00 P.M. on Fridays. Most shops are open from about 10:00 A.M. to 7:00 or 8:00 P.M., Sunday to Friday. As with all offices, shops are usually closed on Saturday, the day of rest in Nepal.

Making Contacts

Foreign businesspeople, especially those from large, internationally recognized companies, can communicate directly with Nepali businesses. Although introductions can add credibility, they must be made among peers of similar rank. Personal relationships are very important and much of what gets done in Nepal is a result of good connections. Status is a very important part of society; thus you should try to meet with the most senior person possible.

The Nepalis are very class-conscious, but consider all foreigners technically outside the class system. Rules of interaction can differ widely, although when dealing with the orthodox, it is best to observe their cultural and religious practices. Status differs in each social encounter, for a person's status depends on that of the other person. One person is usually higher and one lower, and this is made evident through the type of language used. In addition to the traditional criteria of caste, religion, and family lineage, class is now also determined by wealth, education, and profession. Most Westerners will find that they are usually the "higher" person when dealing with office workers and Nepali suppliers. In contrast, when interacting with government officials or Nepali buyers, most Westerners will either be an outsider at the same level or be the "lower" person.

The Foreign Investment Promotion Division (FIPD), which is part of the Ministry of Industry, is responsible for providing information on investment opportunities, assisting foreign investors in identifying local partners, and generally helping foreign investors obtain necessary clearances and approvals. The FIPD is designed to be the primary contact for foreigners. Nepal has designated eleven industrial districts as sites where essential infrastructure is provided for industrial development. These are located in Balaju, Patan, Bhaktapur, Hetauda, Pokhara, Dharan, Butwal, Nepalgunj, Birendranagar, Rajbiraj, and Dhankuta. To promote export industries, an "export processing zone" has been established near the Tribhuvan International Airport in Kathmandu.

Meeting People

The Nepal calendar begins in mid-April with the New Year. When scheduling a trip, avoid the Nepali New Year and other major holidays. The Nepali fiscal year begins on July 16 and ends on July 15 of the following year.

The best time to schedule meetings is between 11:00 A.M. and about 1:00 P.M., when a tea break begins, but is often extended. Punctuality, while appreciated, is not strictly expected or practiced. It is acceptable to be a few minutes late. Due to the hierarchical nature of the society, punctuality is often determined by a person's status. Senior or superior people will feel no guilt in keeping a junior person waiting, subordinates are somewhat obliged to be punctual.

To the Nepalis, smiling is important in developing relationships. Handshakes are not common in Nepal, but businesspeople usually follow Western tradition and may shake hands. Wait until a hand is offered. The traditional greeting, called the *namaste*, is done by placing both palms together at chest level as if praying, accompanied by a slight nod of the head. The verbal greeting is *Namaste* or *Namaskar* when speaking to someone older or senior. This is similar to traditional greetings in India.

The Nepalis use formal titles such as "Dr.," "Mr.," and "Mrs.," plus the family name, when referring to one another. Refrain from using first names until invited to do so. As mentioned earlier, names are very important because they indicate a person's social class and often his or her profession. Traditional Nepalis refer to each other by adding the respectful suffix *-ji* to the end of their first name. Never add the suffix *-ji* to the end of your own name. There are specific honorific words to use when addressing superiors, but foreigners need not worry about these words.

There are various physical gestures that should be avoided. It is considered rude to point. Beckoning should be done with the whole hand, with the palm facing the ground and the fingers pointing away from you, but moving toward you in a scratching motion. Refrain from physically touching someone, especially their head. Never show the bottom of your foot to someone or touch someone with your feet. If your foot accidentally touches someone else, apologize immediately. Winking, especially at the opposite sex, is considered rude and vulgar.

Most meetings will begin with casual conversation. Suitable topics include your travels or positive impressions about the country. Nepalis will be impressed if you are familiar with the country and its culture. You will probably be served refreshments and you should sample them to avoid appearing rude. Meetings do not always have to be goal-oriented, for relationship building is important. Long silences are not unusual and do not indicate boredom. As a formality, Nepalis will ask permission of others before departing. Gifts are not required nor given at early meetings, although you may present sample products.

Corporate Structure

Most of the large firms are in the public sector and are protected or subsidized by the government. Connections here can matter more than ability. Local authorities may have responsibility for the implementation of policy, but do not have decision-making authority. The hierarchy generally has a managing director at the top, followed by a general manager and managers. Subordinates are not considered equals and are usually treated in a condescending manner.

The majority of foreigners tend to interact with Nepali government offices or international aid agencies. Often, projects must be coordinated between people from different organizations, government agencies, and local administrative offices. As a result, identifying the decision-makers can be difficult.

Negotiation

Many Nepalis transfer the concept of fate to business and believe that if a transaction is meant to occur, it will. The concept of time is much slower in Nepal than in Western countries. People will often use the phrase *bholi-parsi,* which literally means "tomorrow" or "the day after tomorrow," in response to a question about time. The concept of punctuality in a business sense is still relatively new.

Nepalis view foreigners, particularly Westerners, as having unlimited financial and technical resources and may have predetermined expectations. Nepalis are proud that their country was never a colony. Accordingly, they can be sensitive to foreigners coming in and telling them how to do things better. Be sensitive and refrain from belittling the country's lack of development.

Authority is very centralized and decision-making is primarily conducted at the senior levels. Even small issues need to be decided by senior people. The decision of a senior person is never questioned publicly by those in the junior levels. Research is usually done merely as a formality.

Nepalis are not likely to inform you if there are problems or errors. Refrain from public criticism or displays of anger. Nepalis avoid face-to-face public confrontations. If you need to point out an error, do so privately and in an indirect manner. Nepalis do not like to say "No" and may give you an incorrect answer to avoid saying "No." Ask indirect questions that will allow your counterpart to avoid saying "No," if appropriate. Maintaining public harmony is very important.

Efficiency and accountability are generally weak, particularly at the lower levels. It is not uncommon for transactions to be delayed due to bureaucratic procedures. Most government officials view their job as their own personal kingdom. For example, if the government officer is unavailable to perform a task, something as simple as stamping a document, no one else will do it for him. There is little individual initiative and few Nepalese want to be held accountable for errors. It is important to closely monitor developments and keep attention focused on your projects.

Legal documents are treated with a combination of respect and suspicion. All documents and stamps must be in order or the Nepali may refuse to recognize them. In the event of a dispute, Nepali law provides for arbitration held in accordance with the prevailing rules as established by the United Nations Commission for International Trade Law (UNCITRAL). Arbitrations are held in Kathmandu. If appropriate to your transaction, you may want to designate another country for arbitration in your original agreement.

Conducting Business in a Social Setting

Dining and Drinking

Nepalis, usually government officials, often use early morning meetings as a way to discuss issues without being disturbed. Because they do not observe the same separation between home and business as Westerners, do not be surprised if they drop by your hotel without warning, to socialize or discuss business. Business dinners are more common than business lunches. Typically, the person with the higher income pays; bills are never split. Do not serve or eat with your left hand, as it is considered unclean. It is appropriate to politely decline food or drink one or two times before actually tasting it. Your counterpart will do the same, so be sure to invite him or her to eat or drink several times. Food is not shared from the same plate or utensils due to religious concerns about impurity.

The cow is considered sacred, so Nepalis do not eat beef. Most traditional Brahmins and Chhetris (the Nepali equivalent of Kshatriyas in Hinduism) do not drink alcohol and they also observe various other dietary restrictions. However, many Nepalis who have traveled overseas do drink alcohol. At formal social events, it is not uncommon to adorn the guest of honor, including foreigners, with a garland of flowers (called a *mala*).

Visiting a Home

Nepalis may be reluctant to invite foreigners into their home, unless they are comfortable with their standard of living. If invited to a home, it is acceptable (although not expected) to take a gift. Suitable items include sweets, chocolates, and souvenirs from your home country. Remove your shoes before entering a home (or a holy place). In many social settings, people will naturally segregate into small groups according to their gender. Foreigners are not expected to follow these same patterns.

Gift Giving

Graft is widespread, partly as a result of the large amounts of development aid money that has been channeled into the country. *Baksheesh* is the small payment given for some service rendered. It is best to leave the problem of handling graft to your local agent.

Gifts presented outside of the normal gift-giving occasions can make the Nepali uncomfortable, for they may wonder about the motive. Giving bribes is viewed as a necessary nuisance and not as a reflection of the giver's, but rather the recipient's, moral deficiency.

Dress Code

For men, a suit or a shirt and tie are acceptable. For women, suits, dresses, or skirts and blouses are appropriate. Modesty is always appreciated.

Useful Phrases

The official language is Nepali and it is written in the Devanagari script. It is spoken by about 60 percent of the population. There are twelve other languages, many with subdialects that are spoken in specific ethnic areas. English is spoken in some urban areas, in commerce, and in tourist spots. The following list includes some key phrases and a guide to their pronunciation.

Hello / Good morning / Good afternoon / Good evening	*Namaste / Namaskar* (to superiors)
How are you?	*Hajurlai kasto chha?*
Please	*Kripayaa*
Thank you	*Dhanyabaad*
You are welcome	*Hajurlai swagat chha*
Excuse me	*Maaph garnuhos*
I am sorry	*Ma dukhit chhu, maaph paun*
My name is ———	*Mero naam ——— ho*
I work for ———	*Ma ——— nimitta kaam gardachhn*
Here is my business card	*Yo mero business card ho*
I am pleased to meet you	*Hajurlai bhetdaa khusi lagyo*
Please accept this small gift	*Kripayaa yo saano upahaar grahan garnuhos*
I look forward to developing a good relationship with you / your firm	*Ma tapain tathaa tapainko kampani sanga ramro sambhanda bikaas garne aashaa raakhda chhu*
I understand	*Malai lagdachha*
No, I do not understand	*Hoina, malai bujhina*
Please wait a minute	*Kripayaa ek minute parkhanu hos*
Where is the bathroom?	*Bathroom kaahan chha?*
Good-bye	*Namaste*
Cheers	Cheers

Major Holidays

January 11	Prithivi Jayanti
January 30	Martyrs' Day
February*	Basanta Panchami
February 19	Democracy Day
March*	Shiva Ratri
March*	Fagu
April*	Ghode Jatra
April*	Chaitra Dashami
April*	Ram Navami
mid-April*	New Year's Day
May*	Buddha Jayanti
August*	Janai Purnima
August*	Gai Jatra
August/September*	Krishnaastami
September*	Indra Jatra

September/October*   Dasain (seven days)
October/November*   Tihar
November 8   Constitution Day
December 29   Birthday of His Majesty the King

*These holidays are based on the lunar calendar and therefore change dates from year to year. The government announces the exact date for certain holidays at the beginning of each Nepali year.

General Facts

Climate: Due to Nepal's varied terrain, temperatures can differ significantly from one place to another. In Kathmandu, there are two main seasons based on the monsoon cycle. The rainy season is from June to September, with the dry season occurring in the remaining months. Kathmandu tends to be hot, with summer temperatures reaching as high as 97F (36C); even in the winter daytime temperatures average 68F (20C).

Currency: The currency is the Nepali *rupee* (abbreviated NR), often shortened to *rupee* (R). One *rupee* is made up of 100 *paisa*. Foreign exchange is often preferred as payment for hotel and restaurant bills.

Dates: Dates are written day, month, year. For example, October 20, 1995, would be abbreviated 20/10/95.

Electricity: The electricity is 220 volt, 50 (Hz) cycles.

Entry Requirements: All foreign visitors except for Indian citizens are required to have a valid passport and visa.

Time: Nepal is five hours and forty-five minutes ahead of Greenwich Mean Time and ten hours and forty-five minutes ahead of U.S. Eastern Standard Time (nine hours and forty-five minutes in Daylight Savings Time).

Tipping: Tipping is expected at the larger hotels and restaurants. About 10 percent is appropriate. If you go trekking, tip your guides more. Taxi drivers do not need to be tipped, but do appreciate a 10 percent tip. For porters and doormen, NR 1 or NR 2 is acceptable.

Transportation: Within Nepal, there are flights to various key areas but no trains. In major cities, taxis are inexpensive and reliable. Make sure their meter is working or negotiate a rate in advance. Auto-rickshaws are also available in Kathmandu. Taxis are available for transportation between cities and airports. Private cars and drivers are suitable for hire within cities, but are more expensive than flying when traveling between cities.

Helpful Telephone Numbers

International calls can be made from most hotels. The post office also has facilities for international calls. The country code is (977) and the city code for Kathmandu is (1).

Hospitals:

The medical facilities in Nepal are marginal. If possible, fly to Bangkok.

CIWEC Clinic (staffed by American doctors)
Baluwatar
Tel.: (1) 410983

Patan Hospital
Kathmandu
Tel.: (1) 521034 / 522266

Nepal International Clinic
Kathmandu
Tel.: (1) 412842

Red Cross Ambulance: Dial 215094 / 228094.

Police: Dial 216999 / 226999.

Operator: Dial 186.

Useful Addresses

In Nepal:

Department of Tourism
Tripureswar
Kathmandu
Tel.: (1) 211293 / 216779

Federation of Nepali Chambers of Commerce
Tripureswar
P.O. Box 269
Kathmandu
Tel.: (1) 212096 / 215920

Ministry of Industry, Foreign Investment Promotion Division (FIPD)
Singha Durbar
Kathmandu
Tel.: (1) 216692

Nepal–German Chamber of Commerce and Industry
Meerahome, Kitchchapokhari
Kathmandu
Tel.: (1) 228788

Nepal Chamber of Commerce
Chamber Bhavan
P.O. Box 198
Kantipath, Kathmandu
Tel.: (1) 212005 / 213318

Nepal Foreign Trade Association
P.O. Box 541
Kathmandu
Tel.: (1) 223784

Office of the Prime Minister
Singh Durbar
Kathmandu
Tel.: (1) 228555 / 227296

Trade Promotion Center
Pulchowk
Lalitpur
Tel.: (1) 524771

Embassies:

American Embassy
Pani Pokhari
Kathmandu
Tel.: (1) 411179

British Embassy
Lainchaur
P.O. Box 106
Kathmandu
Tel.: (1) 410583

Canadian High Commission
c/o Canadian High Commission
in India
7/8 Shantipath
Chanakyapuri
New Delhi 110021, India
Tel.: (91-11) 687-6500

French Embassy
c/o Embassy of France in India
2/50 E Shantipath
Chanakyapuri
New Delhi 110021, India
Tel.: (91-11) 604300

German Embassy
Kingsway
Kathmandu
Tel.: (1) 221730

In Canada:

Consulate of Nepal
Royal Bank Plaza
P. O. Box 33
Toronto, Ontario M5J 2J9
Tel.: (416) 865-0210

In France:

Embassy of Nepal
45 bis Rue des Acacias
75017 Paris
Tel.: (1) 4622-4867

Consulate of Nepal
7 bis Allee des Soupirs
31000 Toulouse
Tel.: (61) 329122

In Germany:

Embassy of Nepal
Im Hag 15
D-5300 Bonn 2
Tel.: (228) 343097 / 343099

Consulates of Nepal
Flinschstrasse 63
P.O. Box 600880
6000 Frankfurt am Main 60
Tel.: (69) 40871

Landsberger Strasse 191
D-8000 Munchen 21
Tel.: (89) 570-4406

7012 Fellbach
Stuttgart, Schineder Weg 7
Tel.: (711) 957912

Uhlandstrasse 171/172
1000 Berlin 15
Tel.: (30) 881-4049

In the United Kingdom:

Embassy of Nepal
12A Kensington
Palace Gardens
London W8 4QU
Tel.: (71) 229-1594 / 6231

In the United States:

Embassy of Nepal
2131 Leroy Place, N.W.
Washington, DC 20008
Tel.: (202) 667-4550 / 1

Consulates of Nepal
820 Second Avenue, Suite 202
New York, NY 10017
Tel.: (212) 370-4188

1500 Lake Shore Drive
Chicago, IL 60610
Tel.: (312) 787-9199

Heidelberg College
Tiffin, OH 44883
Tel.: (419) 448-2202

909 Montgomery Street
Suite 400
San Francisco, CA 94133
Tel.: (415) 434-1111

16250 Dallas Parkway
Suite 110
Dallas, TX 75248
Tel.: (214) 931-1212

212 15th Street, N.E.
Atlanta, GA 30309
Tel.: (404) 892-8152

11661 San Vincente Blvd.
Suite 510
Los Angeles, CA 90049
Tel.: (310) 420-4099

U.S. Department of Commerce
International Trade
Administration
Nepal Desk, Room 2308
14th & Constitution
Avenues, N.W.
Washington, DC 20230
Tel.: (202) 482-2954

Vietnam

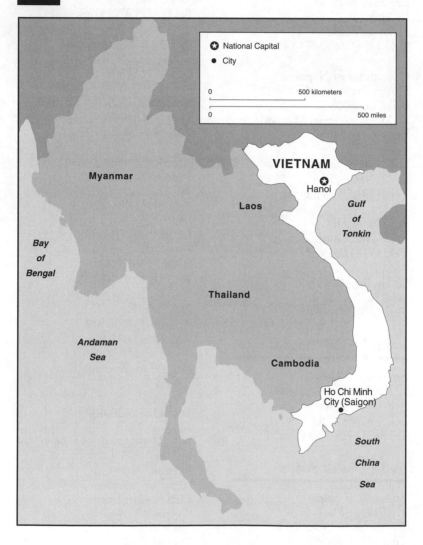

National Capital

City

0   500 kilometers

0   500 miles

Myanmar

VIETNAM

Hanoi

Laos

Gulf
of
Tonkin

Bay
of
Bengal

Thailand

Andaman
Sea

Cambodia

Ho Chi Minh
City (Saigon)

South

China

Sea

Geography

Vietnam is located on the eastern side of the Indochinese peninsula on the Gulf of Thailand and the South China Sea. It has a total land area of about 128,065 square miles (331,688 square kilometers). A long and narrow country, it has about 2,021 miles (3,260 km) of coastline and claims sovereignty over numerous islands in the Gulf of Thailand and the South China Sea. It shares borders with China, Laos, and Cambodia, and is home to the Mekong River, one of the twelve great rivers in the world. Vietnam is divided into three main regions: the mountainous region and Red River Delta in the north; the central highlands in the center; and the coastal lowlands and Mekong River Delta in the south. The capital city is Hanoi; Ho Chi Minh City, formerly Saigon, is the commercial center and largest city in Vietnam.

History

The earliest known inhabitants of Vietnam lived in the north about 500,000 years ago. Mesolithic and Neolithic cultures existed in Vietnam starting about 10,000 years ago. In the thirteenth century B.C., the Bronze Age Dong Son culture began to appear. The earliest known ancestors of the modern Vietnamese people lived in the Red River Delta from about 500–200 B.C. They were a mix of Australoid, Austronesian, and Mongoloid peoples. Throughout its history, Vietnam has been a crossroads for migrations of ethnic groups.

The southern part of modern Vietnam was ruled by various kingdoms centered in neighboring Cambodia until the seventeenth century A.D. During the period from the first to the sixth century A.D., this southern part was ruled by the Indianized Hindu kingdom of Funan. In the second century, the kingdom of Champa, also Hindu, ruled Danang. These Indian kingdoms influenced the art and architecture of southern Vietnam. By the eighth century, the Champa kingdom had expanded south and was in a constant state of war with the Vietnamese to the north and the Khmers to the west. In the seventeenth century, Cambodian kings relinquished control over the southern portion of present-day Vietnam (then referred to as Lower Cambodia) in exchange for Vietnamese military protection from Western colonial powers. (Please refer to Chapter 19 on Cambodia for further details.)

When the Chinese Qin (Chin) dynasty fell in 206 B.C. and was replaced by the Han dynasty, Trieu Da, a Chinese military commander, revolted against the new dynasty. He combined the territories under his control in southern China with territory in northern Vietnam in the Red River Delta and established the kingdom of Nam Viet (meaning "Southern Viet") in 207 B.C. The Vietnamese regard Trieu Da as the heroic defender of their homeland against the expanding Han dynasty. However, in 111 B.C. the Chinese Han armies defeated the successors of Trieu Da and incorporated Nam Viet into the Han empire, thus inaugurating a millennium of Chinese rule and influence.

Prior to this period of Chinese rule, Vietnam had been a feudal society based on hunting, fishing, and agriculture. Over the next few centuries Chinese settlers and traders moved to the Red River Delta, tried to create a centralized state, and imposed Chinese ways on all aspects of Vietnamese life and culture. Since that time, the Vietnamese have fiercely fought outsiders to maintain their political and cultural independence. The Trung Sisters' rebellion of A.D. 40, in which two sisters rallied tribal chieftains in an uprising against the local Chinese governor, is one of the most famous early acts of resistance against the Chinese. Although the Chinese counterattacked three years later and defeated the Vietnamese, the Trung Sisters are admired to this day for their courage and spirit. The long Vietnamese history of resisting Chinese rule played an important role in shaping the Vietnamese mind-set and identity.

In spite of Vietnamese resistance, the Chinese influenced many aspects of Vietnamese life, including agriculture, infrastructure, government, art, literature, religion, and philosophy. The Chinese brought Confucianism, Taoism, and Mahayana Buddhism to Vietnam. The Indians, meanwhile, introduced Theravada (Hinayana) Buddhism to the region. Buddhists monks brought the medical and scientific knowledge of both the Chinese and Indian cultures to Vietnam. Chinese dominance though thorough, did not affect the common people, who retained their pre-Han culture and language.

Vietnam finally achieved independence from Chinese rule in the early part of the tenth century A.D. For most of the next nine hundred years, various Vietnamese dynasties ruled parts of Vietnam or the whole country.

From 1407 to 1428 the Chinese Ming dynasty reasserted control over Vietnam and administered the country. The influence of Chinese traditions and values on the Vietnamese elite during this short period was extensive. During the Vietnamese Le dynasty (1428–1524), attempts were made to break away from the cultural domination of the Chinese and develop an independent Vietnamese culture. Vietnamese scholars began to use the Vietnamese language more in their writing rather than Chinese, which had long been the language of choice for the educated and elite.

While the first Europeans to make contact with Vietnam came from Rome in A.D. 166, it was not until 1516 that the next European visitors were recorded, when Portuguese sailors landed in Danang. Dominican missionaries arrived in 1527. In 1580 French missionaries from the Philippines settled in central Vietnam. Jesuits who had been expelled from Japan arrived in 1615. The most well-known Jesuit missionary was a Frenchman, Alexandre de Rhodes, who is credited with perfecting a romanized system of writing for the Vietnamese language, quoc ngu, between 1627 and 1630. In 1637 the Vietnamese permitted the Dutch to establish trading posts, but by the end of the seventeenth century most of the European merchants had left because trade was not profitable. European missionaries, however, remained and found strong support, particularly in the north. By the eighteenth century, French missionaries were lobbying their government for greater French political and military influence in Vietnam.

By the mid-1700s, the peasants' economic condition had worsened substantially due to the heavy tax burden imposed on them by Vietnamese ruling families used to finance court life and various military adventures. Peasant revolts increased. One of the most noteworthy incidents was the Tay Son Rebellion (1771–1802), led by three brothers who intended to redistribute wealth from the rich to the poor. By 1773, the Tay Son rebels controlled the whole of central Vietnam and by 1783 they had conquered the southern portion as well. In the north, the Tay Son rebels overthrew the Trinh lords, and in 1789 they defeated the Chinese who had come to the aid of the Le dynasty emperor. The Tay Son rebels were finally defeated by a combination of Vietnamese and French forces in 1802. The Nguyen dynasty (1802–1945) then came to power with the support of the French.

In the 1830s French missionaries and Vietnamese Catholics were murdered as the ruling dynasty became increasingly hostile to foreign influences. The French ultimately responded with an attack in 1858. By 1867, Vietnam, renamed Cochinchina by the French, became a direct French colony. Vietnamese resistance to being colonized was initially weak and sporadic. Indeed, certain Vietnamese communities began to promote cooperation with the French as a means to obtain technical and economic development. In 1887 the French united Cochinchina, Annam, Tonkin, Cambodia, Laos, and the port of Kwangchowan in China into a single colony, the Indochinese Union. French rule was generally politically repressive and economically exploitative. The French did little to develop the country's infrastructure. The only Vietnamese who benefited were members of the elite; in return for their cooperation—manifested by conversion to Catholicism, the adoption of French ways, and the use of the French language—they were allowed to maintain their privileged way of life.

The Vietnamese people continued to have a desire for national independence, however. This desire grew stronger as French commercial policies and management proved to be economically disastrous for the rural citizens. Some Vietnamese who rejected French rule turned to Japan and China for guidance, as these two countries had successfully pursued similar nationalistic, anti-colonial policies.

Over time, the most successful anti-colonialists were the communists, whose support was drawn predominantly from the rural communities. The first Vietnamese communist group, called the Vietnam Revolutionary Youth League, was organized by Ho Chi Minh (1890–1969) in Canton, China, in 1925. In February 1930 the Vietnamese Communist party (VCP), a union of three communist groups, was founded. That October the VCP became the Indochinese Communist party, but a failed revolt in the same year forced the party to spend much of the next decade rebuilding the movement.

In 1941 Ho Chi Minh established the communist-dominated League for the Independence of Vietnam, also known as the Viet Minh. When Nazi Germany took control of France in 1941, Indochina fell under the control of Japanese troops, who allowed the French government to continue running the daily affairs of the country. The Viet Minh, which was partially funded by the United States and Chinese, provided the only real resistance to the Japanese. In March 1945, as the war in the Pacific drew to a close, the Japanese overthrew the French-led government in Vietnam and replaced it with a puppet regime. By this time, however, the Viet Minh had grown significantly and was controlling large parts of north and central Vietnam. On September 2, 1945, after the Japanese surrendered, Ho Chi Minh declared Vietnam independent.

At the Potsdam Conference just before the end of World War II, the Allies decided to temporarily split Vietnam into two zones. Chinese forces were to occupy the north and accept Japanese surrender there, and British forces would occupy the south. Due to the chaos that ensued between enraged French settlers and various Vietnamese ethnic groups, however, the British asked the Japanese to step in to help restore order. The French arrived in Vietnam in late September 1945 to reclaim their former colony and quickly replaced the British, who were anxious to leave, and the Chinese. A period of guerrilla activity against the French began. In 1946 the Franco-Viet Minh war broke out, and lasted until 1954 when the French were finally defeated and forced out of Vietnam. The Geneva Accords, which ended the war, allowed for the temporary division of Vietnam and scheduled elections for 1956, but they never took place.

After the war, the south was ruled by a United States-backed government and the north was ruled by a communist government led by Ho Chi Minh. Although the division of Vietnam was intended to be temporary, the south resisted attempts to rejoin with the north. The first president of the southern Republic of Vietnam was Ngo Dinh Diem, who was fiercely anti-communist. Although his government had some accomplishments in the early years, it eventually became more and more corrupt. Unrest broke out in the early 1960s and Diem was assassinated in 1963. He was succeeded by various military and civilian rulers. General Nguyen Van Thieu finally took control and remained in power until 1975.

Meanwhile, in the north, the National Liberation Front (NFL) was formed to lead the drive for a reunited Vietnam under communist rule. Northern guerillas, known as Vietcong (VCs) in the south, began to infiltrate the south and establish control in isolated regions. The United States, which had become more and more involved in Vietnamese affairs since 1950, committed 16,300 military advisers and other personnel to defense of the south between 1961 and 1963.

In 1964, in response to supposed North Vietnamese aggression against two American destroyers, the U.S. Congress passed the Gulf of Tonkin Resolution, which permitted the U.S. president, Lyndon Johnson, to take "all necessary measures" to prevent further communist insurgency. In 1965 the United States committed its first combat troops to aid in the defense of South Vietnam and by December 1967 almost 500,000 American soldiers were serving in Vietnam. Meanwhile, despite massive U.S. aid, the South Vietnamese army was suffering from morale problems, desertions, and corruption.

The Tet Offensive, launched by the Viet Cong in 1968 against one hundred cities and towns in South Vietnam, was a major turning point in the war. The South Vietnamese and Americans counterattacked with intensity and force. Nevertheless, popular sentiment in the United States began to shift against the war as the American people realized that a stalemate existed. In 1969 the United States began secretly bombing Vietnamese communist areas and supply routes in neighboring Cambodia. The following year, the United States led an invasion of Cambodia to destroy the communist bases there. These efforts achieved short-term gains, but destroyed the Cambodian countryside and killed thousands of civilians. A cease-fire was finally achieved between South Vietnam, North Vietnam, the Viet Cong, and the United States on January 27, 1973.

In January 1975 the North Vietnamese launched an attack on South Vietnam, in violation of the 1973 cease-fire agreement. The weak South Vietnamese government was unable to put up much resistance. The United States, unwilling to continue an unpopular war and the accompanying financial drain, refused to send aid. By April, after the turnover of two presidents, South Vietnam surrendered to North Vietnam. As the south collapsed, many Vietnamese sought to leave the country and over the next five years more than half a million Vietnamese fled. Many of these residents left by sea, thus earning the name "boat people."

Formal reunification of the country, under the new name the Socialist Republic of Vietnam, took place in July 1976. The Communist party sent its representatives to the south to manage the reunification and the transition to socialism. However, the north was unprepared to integrate and govern the country, and there was widespread repression of the South Vietnamese. This political, economic, and social purge prompted even more Vietnamese to flee the country.

In 1978 the North Vietnamese launched a campaign against "commercial opportunists." This campaign particularly affected the ethnic Chinese (Hoa) community, for many of them had been businessmen. Many believe that the real motivation for the campaign was the long-standing hatred of the Chinese by the Vietnamese. In 1978 Vietnam signed a Friendship Treaty with the former Soviet Union and joined the Soviet-led Council for Mutual Economic Assistance (Comecom). These provided Vietnam with support in the event it was threatened by a third-party, particularly

China or Cambodia. In retaliation, China cut off all aid to Vietnam and launched a month-long "self-defense attack" on North Vietnam in February 1979.

The 1978 treaties also guaranteed Vietnam military equipment, which Vietnam used later that year to invade Cambodia, forcing the Khmer Rouge from power and installing a pro-Hanoi government. Vietnamese troops technically left Cambodia in 1989, although many remained for several years thereafter.

By 1979, Vietnamese leaders recognized that the economic goals set forth in the government's First Five-Year Plan and its Second Five-Year Plan had been unrealistic. In March 1982 the Party Congress approved the Third Five-Year Plan (1981–1985) which reversed the policy of socialization of the south and instead promoted the temporary shift to free enterprise activities in order to spur the economy. In 1986 a campaign of economic renewal, *doi moi*, was launched by Nguyen Van Linh, a reformer elected to party leadership. Linh faced strong opposition from conservatives who favored following a strict communist ideology and initially blocked many of his attempted reforms. After internal struggles, the party began to support *doi moi* and the development of an economy that was less controlled by the government and more subject to market rules and basic business accountability.

Its withdrawal from Cambodia in 1989 was intended to help Vietnam regain membership in the world community and specifically to improve relations with the United States. In February 1994, after several years of negotiations, the United States reopened trade with Vietnam after a nineteen-year embargo established in 1975 against Hanoi. Full diplomatic relations are expected to resume in the near future, with liaison offices expected to open in Washington and Hanoi.

Political Structure

The official name of the country is the Socialist Republic of Vietnam (SRV). Many of the country's political institutions were inspired by Soviet and Chinese models, and modified to suit Vietnamese circumstances.

Vietnam has a unicameral National Assembly as its highest governing body. The most recent constitution, ratified in 1992, provides for a more influential National Assembly, a shift from its previous role as a rubber stamp of the Politburo. National Assembly members are technically elected by the voters and serve for five-year terms. In the new constitution, the Council of State has been replaced by a president, currently Le Duc Anh, who is elected by the National Assembly. The Council of Ministers manages the government and is nominally elected by the National Assembly, which in turn is controlled by the Vietnamese Communist party. Prime Minister Vo Van Kiet heads the Council of Ministers, which also consists of deputy premiers, a secretary-general, various ministers, and the directors of the State Bank and the Government Inspectorate.

The political system is dominated by the Vietnamese Communist party (VCP or Viet Nam Cong San Dang), of which the current general secretary is Do Muoi. All political power has been in the hands of the Communist party since the country was unified in 1976. The party influences every aspect of political and social life, although it is more decentralized than its Soviet and Chinese models. The primary reason being that in the early days of its existence, communication was difficult, and as a result, local party members had more authority to act on their own. Party members fill almost all of the government positions, particularly ones with authority. The party is led by the National Party Congress, which elects the Central Committee, which in turn elects the Political Bureau (Politburo), the party's highest policymaking body. The Politburo establishes all policy; the National Party Congress, which meets only once every five years or on special occasions, functions mainly as a rubber stamp. The Politburo's seventeen members hold the majority of political power in the country. The Politburo manages the day-to-day affairs of the party and has the authority to issue directives to the government. The judicial system is supervised by the People's Supreme Court, the highest tribunal in Vietnam.

The National Assembly, meanwhile, nominally elects the pro-
curator general, who heads the People's Supreme Organ of Control,
which functions as a watchdog of the state, exercising extraordinary
powers of surveillance over government agencies at every level, including the courts and law enforcement. The current legal system
is incomplete, provides very little protection for foreign commercial interests, and is constantly changing.

Economy

Since reunification in 1975, Vietnam's economy has been plagued
by difficulties and inefficiencies in production and distribution, im-
balances in supply and demand, soaring inflation rates, and debt
problems. Despite having had the third largest communist economy
after those of China and the former Soviet Union during the 1980s,
Vietnam remains a poor country. Further, the collapse of the former
Soviet Union ended subsidized trade with that country which had
a negative effect on the economy.

The *doi moi* (renewal) policy, however, has begun to liberalize
the economy. Foreign investors, other than Americans, have been
pursuing business opportunities in Vietnam for several years. Nevertheless, the U.S. trade embargo had a significantly negative impact
on Vietnam's economy. The ending of the American embargo in
1994 helped to channel more private investment, more trade, and
more multilateral aid into the country. The government has succeeded in reducing inflation and industrial production has increased.
State-owned enterprises have been given more managerial autonomy and restrictions on private companies have been reduced. The
government is now focusing on additional reforms, particularly in
the legal and banking systems. A lack of skilled managers continues
to be a major economic weakness. Inadequate infrastructure, particularly in the areas of power, communications, and transportation, is
a significant impediment to the country's growth prospects.

The country is predominantly rural, with more than 70 percent
of its workforce employed in agriculture-related jobs. The major ex-

ports include crude oil, rice, rubber, marine products, coffee, coal, wood products, agricultural products, textiles, garments, machinery, and handicrafts. The country has a relatively abundant supply of natural resources, primarily coal, metals, and minerals, including iron ore, tin, copper, lead, zinc, nickel, manganese, titanium, chromite, tungsten, bauxite, apatite, graphite, mica, silica sand, and limestone. Vietnam is also focusing on the exploration and production of crude oil and natural gas. Illegal border trading and smuggling, primarily into China and through Cambodia to Thailand, is a growing problem for the government. Corruption and black markets are characteristic of the economy.

People, Values, and Social Customs

With over seventy-two million people, Vietnam is densely populated. Ethnic Vietnamese account for about 87 percent of the population. The remaining 13 percent consist of fifty-three minority ethnic groups including the Hoa (ethnic Chinese), the largest, and other smaller groups who speak more than a dozen different languages and dialects. The majority of the population resides in the north and almost 80 percent live in rural areas. The various minorities are usually geographically localized. Montagnards are one group of minorities who live in the mountainous regions and are often condescendingly referred to as *moi*, which means "savage," by the Vietnamese. Some of the minority groups are descendants of migrants from China, Cambodia, Laos, and other neighboring regions.

The ethnic Vietnamese are lowlanders, usually known as Viet or Kinh. They tend to be a homogeneous group and largely control political and social life. The power elite—party, government, and military officials—are predominantly ethnic Vietnamese.

The Hoa, the largest minority group, tend to reside in urban areas, primarily Ho Chi Minh City, and have retained a distinct Chinese cultural identity. As a result of their historical economic successes, this group has inspired the wrath of ruling governments. In the late 1970s, many fled to China as a result of Vietnam's external tensions with Cambodia and China. Those who remained have been the driving force behind much of the economic growth in Vietnam. The Chinese have excelled in commerce and dominate certain economic sectors. Further, they have created a tight community by adhering to strict internal discipline and creating a network based on blood relations.

The primary religion is Buddhism. However, over the centuries, Buddhism, Taoism, and Confucianism have fused with popular Chinese beliefs and animism to form what is referred to as the "triple religion," or *Tam Giao*. Confucianism has had a strong influence on Vietnam and has resulted in a hierarchical, paternal, and authoritarian society. The Vietnamese revere ancestors regardless of their base religion. Ancestors die, but remain close to the living and are available to help or hurt the living. About 10 percent of the population is Roman Catholic.

The Vietnamese have a deep sense of national pride as a result of their long and difficult struggle for independence from the Chinese, the French, and the Americans. They also have a strong sense of ethnic identity stemming from a common language and cultural heritage. The Vietnamese are fiercely protective of their independence and sovereignty, but this independence has been tempered with a willingness to adopt and adapt foreign ideas.

The people are resilient and focus primarily on the future. As a result, most Vietnamese do not understand why Americans have remained so preoccupied with the Vietnam War for so long, particularly since Vietnam has fought wars with Cambodia and China since then. From the Vietnamese perspective, the struggle against the Americans was relatively short. Further, to the Vietnamese the war with America was simply an extension of the struggle against the French and colonial rule.

The Vietnam War had a devastating effect on families, for many suffered the death of loved ones and long years of separation. Despite the recent war, the Vietnamese are usually friendly to Western visitors, including Americans, as they have traditionally been open to foreigners who come as guests, not as conquerors. Despite the trade embargo over the past two decades, Vietnamese place a high value on American goods. Today the Vietnamese are becoming much more aware of the rest of the world, particularly in terms of living standards. They are intent on achieving parity particularly with their neighbors, in terms of material wealth and luxury. They are very brand-conscious, placing a high value on premium product names, and they are also fashion-conscious.

In Saigon and Hanoi, millionaires (measured in U.S. dollars) are emerging, fueling widespread Vietnamese desire for success. The Vietnamese tend to be very entrepreneurial and hard-working; many hold two jobs. However, having two jobs often means that state employees focus more on their lucrative private interests, rather than on their official jobs. Some observers claim that those living in the north are more industrious than those in the south. One explanation is that the south has been the recipient of the bulk of foreign investment, enabling people to obtain wealth faster and relatively easier. In any case, an element of north–south rivalry remains a factor in business as everyone competes for investment resources.

The Vietnamese place an emphasis on education, learning, respect to elders, tradition, and politeness. Despite the efforts to make the Communist party the center of life, the Vietnamese remain very family-oriented and place a high value on loyalty and honor. The system of Confucian familial obligation still thrives. The extended family in Vietnam has traditionally been very important both financially and socially. Rural families still live as large extended units, but in urban areas the nuclear family is now becoming more common. For the past two decades the government has promoted family planning and smaller family sizes to control population, a tactic that has met with only marginal success.

Historically, women have been considered strong and resilient, often taking on a significant amount of agricultural work.

From the time of the Trung Sisters, Vietnamese women have enjoyed respect and opportunity. There are numerous women in management and professional jobs, although women tend to be concentrated in the lower-paying agricultural and light industry jobs.

Work Schedule

Most businesses are open Monday through Saturday from 7:30 A.M. to 4:30 P.M. Banks are open Monday to Friday from 8:00 A.M. to 4:30 P.M. and on Saturdays from 8:00 A.M. to 1:00 P.M. Lunchtime is usually between 11:30 A.M. to 1:30 P.M.; many businesses, shops, and all government offices are closed during this lunch period. Shops are open from about 7:30 A.M. to 7:00 P.M., with some open longer. Most Vietnamese are early risers, so businesses and shops open early.

Making Contacts

Connections and introductions are an important part of doing business in Vietnam. A written introduction or a meeting arranged by a go-between will produce the best results. Large, internationally recognized companies will usually receive a better response to cold letters than smaller, lesser-known entities. You should write to your Vietnamese party before you attempt to call for a visit. Explain the purpose of your visit and details about your company. When you send a letter, do not expect a fax or telephone response. Both services are expensive, so the Vietnamese are more likely to answer you by letter. Allow several weeks for a response. It is imperative that you conduct research while still in your home country, learn about the country, the marketplace, and identify local representatives. For any business to be consummated, you must make a long-term commitment to the country and visit it.

The Vietnamese market opened to Americans in early 1994. However, Europeans and Asians have been conducting business and actively investing in the country for the past five years and, as a result, Americans are considered behind in both time and attitude, although in some sectors more than others. With perseverance and proper diligence, the Americans can catch up to their international business peers. It should be noted that the Vietnamese are eager for Americans to participate in their economy and balance the interests expressed by Europeans, Japanese, and other Asians. In the United States, further general information on Vietnam can be obtained by fax through the PacRim Hotline (Tel. 202-482-3875), which provides trade and economic statistics as well as summaries of other issues.

Finding a reliable and credible local representative can be tricky There are some well-established consulting firms that are intimately familiar with the Vietnamese market, but companies should be wary of foreign and Vietnamese consultants who claim to have connections and to know the market. Be sure to ask for references and verify the quality and extent of the firm's previous work in Vietnam. Take care not to rely on your local partner so much that you fail to develop your own relationships with government officials. Local firms and individuals can fall out of favor and take you with them. Foreign firms may also consider selling their products and services or transacting business with Vietnam through experienced firms, agents, and consultants based in regional countries such Singapore or Hong Kong.

Large international companies may opt to base an employee in Vietnam, but representative offices are only allowed to perform research or support services. Moreover, the application process to established a local office can be time-consuming, taking up to eighteen months. Companies that are not ready to establish a permanent base in Vietnam should consider hiring a local representative to open new doors as well as to monitor any ongoing negotiation processes. The cliché "out-of-sight, out-of-mind" can be very appropriate in Vietnam. Potential local representatives include consultants, accounting firms, and law firms. Referrals and suggestions are available from the embassies and chamber of commerce offices in your home country. Review a prospective representative's client list and referrals as well the extent of their connections because a Vietnamese firm's contacts are important. There are some Vietnamese government consultant firms, but these are often unreliable and do not always have the foreign companies' best interests in mind. The Vietcochamber, the Chamber of Commerce and Industry, assists foreign companies and can facilitate introductions and meetings. It publishes *Vietnam Foreign Trade* and *The Trade Directory* and can help with obtaining and extending business visas.

Generally, business is most efficiently conducted in Ho Chi Minh City (Saigon). However, due to the backload of projects for this southern city, which has made its authorities more selective, many foreign investors are finding that Hanoi is emerging as an easier place to do business. Hanoi often has lower capital requirements and the officials are more eager to please. Throughout the country, corruption as a standard business practice is increasing, although it is still not as extensive as in some neighboring Asian countries.

Meeting People

The best times to schedule an appointment are between 9:00 A.M. and 11:00 A.M. and from 3:00 P.M. to 5:00 P.M. Most managers work longer hours than their staffs on a daily basis; however, staff can be found in the office after hours if they have work to do. Saturday afternoons are not good times for meetings, although Saturday mornings are considered acceptable for conducting business.

Confirm your appointments in advance. Business cards are always exchanged at the first meeting. The Vietnamese often use both hands to receive and give cards and also slightly bow their head to indicate respect. Never write on someone's business card, as this is a sign of disrespect. The Vietnamese shake hands with both men and women at both the beginning and the end of a meeting. If a

Vietnamese does not extend his or her hand for a handshake, a slight bow of the head will suffice. This is particularly common in the more rural areas and in interactions with women.

The order for a Vietnamese name is family name, middle name, and given name. Most Vietnamese use their given names in interactions. When referring to someone, use his or her given name with the appropriate title, such as "Mr.," "Madame," "Mrs.," or "Dr." For example, "Vu Van Khai" should be addressed as "Madame Khai."

You may hear people who know each other referring to each other by the name of the relationship. For example, older brothers and sisters have specific titles that they are called by their siblings along with their first name. This is to indicate respect. These titles are also gender-specific. A very common greeting is to use the appropriate title, the given name of the person, and the words *xin chao* (pronounced seen chow), which is a very polite hello and good-bye. Vietnamese are very appreciative when foreigners try to speak phrases in their language. Respect for age is a very important aspect of a business relationship and is integrated into the language.

Secretaries, most of whom are women, and assistants, some of whom are men, are often knowledgeable about office politics. As noted earlier, there are women in management positions who often have powerful roles. However, Vietnamese men may feel uncomfortable socializing with foreign women.

All meetings should begin with a few minutes of casual conversation. Suitable topics include your travels, the number of visits you have made to Vietnam, the weather, and your interests. You should be humble and state that you are very appreciative of your counterpart's busy schedule and that you do not want to make demands on his or her time. You should express gratitude for the opportunity to meet him or her. The Vietnamese smile often, are generally very friendly, and enjoy telling jokes. Foreigners should be wary of telling jokes, however, and be sensitive to cultural differences in humor. You will usually be served tea and something to eat. Be sure to sample everything you are served. Failure to taste or drink a small amount of anything is considered impolite. At the end of a first or even subsequent meeting, it is appropriate, although not required, to present a small gift.

Before meeting with Vietnamese, do some research. Before meeting with a senior minister, it is advisable to meet with middle-level officials to do some fact-finding and conduct additional research. Then when you meet with senior officials, you will be well prepared to conduct business and perhaps conclude a preliminary understanding and/or agreement. Arrange meetings with senior officials only when you have a specific proposal to discuss. If a Vietnamese perceives that you have nothing to offer, you may not be invited back for future meetings. Whenever possible, have written materials translated into Vietnamese.

When dealing with senior ministers and officials, begin discussing business within a few minutes, for there may be few opportunities to meet with the senior person. With middle- and junior-level people, you should not discuss much business during the first meeting but should attend to relationship building. It is appropriate to state your company's general objectives in the country. The senior Vietnamese tend to mean what they say. Accordingly, a "No" response is politely but directly stated, which is not the case in many other Asian countries.

Most foreigners will need to use translators. Make sure you hire your own translator and do not rely on your counterpart's translator, who will be inclined to tilt toward his or her boss. It is important to recognize that the audio level of a Vietnamese conversation is lower than that of a Western conversation. If your interpreter is speaking softly, that is perfectly normal. Do not ask him or her to speak louder.

Be careful about what you say when you are in Vietnam. It is not unusual for the government to monitor telephone and fax lines. Be sure not to fax any sensitive business information. The government continues to monitor foreign businesspeople in hotels, taxis and cars, and meeting rooms. Vietnamese individuals such as maids, drivers, assistants, and even translators may be passing on information about you to the government. This is done for reasons of both security and business competitiveness. Be sure not to say anything derogatory about individuals, Vietnamese businesspeople, or the government and its policies. When dealing with people either on the streets or within organizations, be polite and maintain your composure. While it is very unlikely that you would get into any kind of trouble, your business reputation could become tainted if you appear to be loud, rude, and generally negative as this type of information is often shared between ministries and senior officials. Americans who were in Vietnam during the war can mention their familiarity with the country, but should keep their comments neutral.

Do not touch a person's head, for the head is considered the spiritual center of the person. Use both hands to pass things from one person to the next. Do not point to someone. To beckon a person, use your whole hand with the palm facing down and your fingers pointing away from you but waving toward you. Do not show the sole of your foot, as it is rude and disrespectful. It is best not to cross your legs in a meeting. Do not be surprised if your business counterpart of the same sex tries to hold your hand as you are walking. This action has no sexual connotations, but is common between same-sex individuals in Vietnam. A Vietnamese will usually not do this unless he or she feels very comfortable with you.

Corporate Structure

The influence of Confucianism has resulted in a hierarchical and authoritative culture. The dominant group is the ruling party officials and the new elite in society are the high-ranking party members. However, entrepreneurs and businesspeople are quickly becoming part of the economic elite.

There are public- and private-sector organizations, although most of the big companies are state-owned, state-run companies. There are three types of companies: those owned and operated by the central government; those owned and operated by the local people's committees in the fifty-four Vietnamese provinces; and privately owned and operated companies. The centrally owned and operated companies are usually large businesses and can vary in the quality of their management. The companies run by people's committees tend to have a lower quality level of management. The privately owned and operated companies are relatively new, entrepreneurial and generally well-managed. These companies were established during the last eight years and are reasonably efficient and profitable. As family-owned businesses, they tend to be patriarchal with centralized decision-making.

In a ministry, the minister is usually a political appointee, while the deputy minister is a technocrat. Each ministry has an international relations director. All contacts and approvals must go through this department unless otherwise authorized by the minister or other senior official. If you have contacts in other ministries, however, you can use them to bypass the international relations department. It can be very helpful to cultivate ministry contacts, as they may be able to help you deal with any obstacles in other ministries.

Most foreign businesses will have to interact with the local People's Committee, which oversees local city and district investments and projects. The State Committee for Cooperation and Investment is responsible for attracting foreign investment and must issue the final approval for any transaction. However, it can be difficult to determine who really makes the decisions as there has been tension between the central and local governments on this score. The different ministries are not yet accustomed to the idea of sharing information and usually act independently, which can make obtaining approvals even more time-consuming. Approvals can take between one to three years, depending on the size of the project. Your local representative should be able to manage this business aspect for you.

Negotiation

In negotiating, be advised that the Vietnamese will try to judge your long-term commitment to their country. As they review your proposal, they will evaluate standard business issues as well as the extent of technology transfer and employee training. This last issue can often be a critical factor, for few Vietnamese have specialized training for manufacturing or management functions.

The Vietnamese are practical, flexible, and tend to take calculated risks. Foreigners need to be committed and to maintain a long-term outlook. Patience and flexibility are key, particularly when dealing with the bureaucracy. When dealing with government agencies, be prepared for confusion and changes. The Vietnamese can be tough and demanding negotiators.

Officials at senior levels have the authority to make decisions and will often do so quickly. When dealing with middle and junior officials, be prepared for a longer decision-making period, as these individuals will need to obtain approval from the senior person. Research is not generally conducted, for Vietnamese have few resources available to them. They will, however, be happy to utilize whatever information you provide. Consensus building is the key aspect of decision-making, and the process remains very bureaucratic, with most decisions made by committee. Keep in mind that many capitalistic concepts are still relatively new to the Vietnamese, although they are very quick and eager learners.

Although senior officials may politely say "No," the average Vietnamese is unlikely to say "No," and will go to great lengths to maintain harmony. The word "*da*" actually means "I understand" rather than "Yes." Be careful not to make erroneous assumptions. Ask indirect questions. If there is a problem, the Vietnamese will probably not tell you until it becomes severe. You must utilize your local partner and make frequent visits to monitor any new or ongoing transactions. On the other hand, the Vietnamese will also often solve problems themselves without telling you. Never raise your voice or visibly display your anger. Do not be too forthright in your opinion if you feel it may offend someone. While they can be frank and open, the Vietnamese are always modest and polite, and never aggressive. Many Vietnamese may not look at you directly as they try to avoid appearing too bold or rude. Foreigners, particularly

Westerners, should be careful not to assume this means that a local person is dishonest.

Communicating with other countries via telephone calls and faxes is very expensive for the Vietnamese. For this reason, you may feel that your Vietnamese counterpart is not keeping in touch with you. One solution is to offer to reimburse your counterpart for his or her communication expenses. State that you are very interested in developing a strong relationship and that you would be pleased to pay for all documented telephone and fax communications for a stated period so that he or she can communicate with you as often as necessary. Further, faxes may be a better mode of communication than the telephone as local Vietnamese may not be as conversant in English and will be better able to understand the written word.

Vietnam does not have a commercial court system. However, an arbitration system is being developed. Verbal agreements are usually honored if a relationship is already strong, but in a new relationship a verbal agreement carries little weight. The Vietnamese usually honor written contracts. Whenever possible, incorporate a foreign jurisdiction into your legal documents and clearly explain how disputes will be resolved.

Conducting Business in a Social Setting

Dining and Drinking

Business lunches and dinners are a common and enjoyable part of Vietnamese business culture. Foreigners should always try to pay the bill because entertaining can be expensive. When eating at a large traditional buffet or banquet, never pick up a dish. Everyone eats off the same plates together, sampling portions of each dish. Accordingly, be careful not to eat too much of any one dish, for you will be expected to share it with others. Eat slowly and follow your counterpart's sense of proportion. Put some food into your rice bowl and hold it close to your mouth as you eat. The spoon is held in the left hand regardless of which hand you normally use.

Because Vietnamese do not drink much, business drinking is not as important as in some other Asian countries.

Foreign men can further cement a growing business relationship by engaging in eating dog in the north or cobra in the south with their Vietnamese counterparts. This is a very traditional male concept and is by no means required of any foreign businessperson. Eating exotic delicacies and drinking together can be one of many ways to solidify relationships.

Visiting a Home

The Vietnamese are very hospitable and enjoy entertaining visitors. However, they are very concerned about being well-prepared for guests, so never go to a home unannounced. Although gifts are not required, they are always appreciated. Suitable gifts include flowers, tea, or a small token from your native country for the adults and/or the children.

Gift Giving

Corruption and bribery is fairly common at the local levels. Foreign businesspeople should develop a global company policy and adhere to it. Further, refrain from directly giving money.

Gifts are often presented at the end of meetings and upon signing a deal. Such gift giving is not considered a bribe. Suitable items include corporate logo gifts, gifts (such as pictorial calendars) from your home country or city, expensive pens for senior officials, moderately priced pens for middle-level officers, and expensive chocolates. All gifts should be nicely wrapped. Your counterpart will not open a gift in your presence as that is considered rude. Likewise, if you receive a gift, do not open it in the presence of the giver. Carry extra gifts with you when you go to Vietnam. Do not give expensive gifts early in a relationship; these should be reserved for more important events, such as when a transaction is signed, and for more developed relationships.

Dress Code

The dress code is fairly informal. Business suits or shirts and ties are suitable for men. For factory and site tours, men should wear shirts and slacks. For women, dresses or suits are appropriate.

Useful Phrases

The official language is Vietnamese, but each region has its own dialect. The written language, *quoc ngu*, is based on a Latinate phonetic alphabet. The Vietnamese language is based on syllables, with accent marks used to denote tone. Older Vietnamese, especially those from the elite, often speak some French. Many people also speak English, Russian, as well as several Chinese dialects particularly in the major cities.

The Vietnamese tend to add "Mr.," "Mrs.," or "Miss" to every sentence to enhance formality and respect. For example, instead of saying "I am sorry," the Vietnamese say "I am sorry to you." The following list includes useful phrases and a guide to how they should be pronounced.

Hello	*Chao* is pronounced as chow
	chow on—when saying hello or good-bye to an older man
	chow ba—when saying hello or good-bye to an older woman
	chow ko—when saying hello or good-bye to someone (female) the same age; use *chao anh* for a male.
	chow em—when saying hello or good-bye to a younger girl or boy
Good morning / Good afternoon / Good evening	Same as hello.
How are you?	*An / Ba / Ko man yo e?*
Please	*Lam on*
Thank you	*Kam on*
You are welcome	*Kon ko chee*

Excuse me	*Sin loi*
I am sorry	*Sin loi*
My name is ——	*Ten-toi-lae* ——
I work for ——	*Toi lam cho* ——
Here is my business card	*Da-lae the yo-au thep-kur-toi.*
I am pleased to meet you	*Han-han da-gap-on*
Please accept this small gift	*Sin-nyan man wo-nyo-na*
I look forward to developing	*Tai-man ran mot soo won he tot se ko*
a good relationship with you /	*yo ae chun tae*
your firm	
I understand	*Toi-heu*
No, I do not understand	*Kon, tai-kon hu*
Please wait a minute	*Sin-cho mot-foot*
Where is the bathroom?	*Fan ve sinh dao?* or *Toilet a dao?*
Good-bye	Same as hello
Cheers	*Kan-lee*

Major Holidays

January 1	New Year's Day (*Tet Duong Lich*)
February 3	Founding of the Communist Party of Vietnam
January / February*	Vietnamese Lunar New Year (*Tet*)
April 30	Liberation of Saigon / Victory of North Vietnam in 1975
May 1	Labor Day / International's Workers' Day
May 19	Ho Chi Minh's Birthday
June*	Buddha's Birthday (Dan Sinh)
September 2	National Day of the Socialist Republic of Vietnam
December 25	Christmas

*These holidays are lunar-based and differ from year to year.

General Facts

Climate: Vietnam has a tropical monsoon climate with relatively high humidity all year. Due to the country's variable topography, temperatures and weather conditions often differ from region to region. The winter season usually lasts from November to April, with temperatures ranging from 41F (5C) in December to 99F (37C) in April, which is the hottest month. The heavy monsoon season is from May to October, with temperatures varying only slightly between 70F (21C) and 82F (28C).

Currency: The currency is the *dong*. Many hotels, restaurants, and other service providers prefer U.S. dollars, so you should carry lots of small bills for convenience. Major hotels and restaurants will accept credit cards.

Dates: Dates are written day, month, year. For example, June 16, 1995, would be abbreviated as 16/6/95.

Electricity: In most cities and towns, the voltage is 220, 50 (Hz) cycles. In some rural areas, you may find 110 volts. It is advisable to bring a multiplug adapter because outlet types can vary, as well as a power surge protector, particularly for computers and electronic equipment.

Entry Requirements: All visitors are required to have a valid passport and visa, which should be obtained prior to arrival in the country. For business visas, you need a sponsor's letter from an organization with whom you will be conducting meetings. If you enter Vietnam for both tourism and business purposes, you must have a business visa.

Time: Vietnam has one time zone, which is seven hours ahead of Greenwich Mean Time and twelve hours ahead of U.S. Eastern Standard Time (eleven hours in Daylight Savings Time).

Tipping: Tipping is becoming more widespread with the influx of foreigners. Although not always expected, it is widely appreciated. In hotels and restaurants, 10 percent is appropriate and is usually already added into the bill. U.S. $0.50 (5,000 dong) is acceptable for taxi drivers. A nonmonetary tip that is often appreciated is a foreign pack of cigarettes.

Transportation: Of the country's more than 65,700 total miles (105,777 kilometers) of war-damaged and neglected roads, only 10 percent are paved. In early 1994 the first six-lane expressway in the north opened to traffic. The road is only about 9.3 miles (15 kilometers) long, but links Hanoi with Noi Bai International Airport, making travel more efficient. Driving is on the right-hand side of the road, driving conditions are poor, and the traffic is congested.

Within cities, hiring a car and driver is easy and inexpensive. Road and traffic conditions make self-driving dangerous. Taxis are available in Ho Chi Minh City and Hanoi in front of major hotels or by booking with an agency. Your hotel can assist you in arranging for a private car or taxi. Buses are not recommended as they tend to be crowded and slow. For shorter distances in cities, cyclos, also known as pedicabs, or *xe lam*, tiny three-wheeled trucks, are alternatives to cars. Some car, taxi, cyclo, and *xe lam* drivers speak a little English. Always carry a map and your destination and hotel name written in Vietnamese. Taxis are available to and from airports, but in Ho Chi Minh City you need to negotiate the fare with the driver. In Hanoi, taxis are metered.

Helpful Telephone Numbers

Telephone, fax, cable, and telegraph service is available in all urban areas and in more than 20 percent of the villages. International service remains very expensive, so it may be cheaper to make collect calls. Telephone cards, called UniphoneKad, are an inexpensive and simple way to make international direct-dial calls. They can be used only at special telephones, which are sometimes found in major hotel lobbies. The simplest and cheapest way to make international calls is to go to the local post office. Find out the hotel rate schedule before you phone or fax because many hotels overbill. Further, because the telephone system is being updated, telephone numbers may be out of date. The country code for Vietnam is (84).

There are five calling codes for the different provinces. Specific city codes are: Ho Chi Minh City (8) and Hanoi (4).

Hospitals:

There are no Western-standard hospitals in Vietnam. After receiving primary care locally, you should go to Hong Kong or Singapore for more extensive treatment if you can. If possible, avoid receiving blood transfusions or any injections in Vietnam. (Also, check with your embassy and/or consulate, as some have medical staff attached to their offices.)

Cho Ray Hospital (English-speaking doctors available; foreigners' section on the 10th floor)
201B Nguyen Chi Than,
District 5
Ho Chi Minh City
Tel.: (8) 254137

Nhi Dong 2 Hospital (Grall Hospital)
Ly Tu Trong Street, opposite Franco-Vietnamese Cultural Centre
Ho Chi Minh City

Thong Nhat Hospital
Corner of Ly Thuong Kiet Blvd. and Cach Mang Thang Tam Street (in the Tan Binh district)
Ho Chi Minh City

SOS Ho Chi Minh City
151, Vo Thi Sau
District 3
Ho Chi Minh City

SOS Hanoi
60 Nguyen Du
Suite 208
Hanoi

Vietnam–German Friendship Hospital (Viet Duc)
40 Trang Thi Street
Hanoi
Tel.: (4) 253531

Ambulance: For Ho Chi Minh City and Hanoi, dial 15.

Emergency: For Ho Chi Minh City, dial 296485.

Police: For Ho Chi Minh City and Hanoi, dial 13.

Fire: For Ho Chi Minh City and Hanoi, dial 14.

Operator / Information: In Ho Chi Minh City, dial 16 for directory inquiries, and 108 for directory information. You will need a translator as operators do not speak English.

Useful Addresses

In Vietnam:

**External Affairs Office of
the Foreign Ministry**
6 Thai Van Lung Street
District 1
Ho Chi Minh City
Tel.: (8) 224127

**Foreign Trade and Investment
Development Center
(FTDC)**
92-96 Nguyen Hue Blvd.
District 1
Ho Chi Minh City
Tel.: (8) 230072 / 222982 /
222912

**Ho Chi Minh City Foreign
Economic Relations Office**
1 Nam-Ky Khoi-Nghia
District 1
Ho Chi Minh City
Tel.: (8) 299541 / 296983 /
292991

**International Relations
Department of the Ministry
of Information**
58 Quan Su Street
Hanoi
Tel.: (4) 253152

Ministry of Foreign Affairs
1 Ton That Dam Street
Hanoi
Tel.: (4) 257279 / 258201,
ext. 314 or 312

**Ministry of Trade Office
Number Two**
35-37 Ben Chuong Duong
District 1
Ho Chi Minh City
Tel.: (8) 295269

**People's Committee of
Ho Chi Minh City**
86 Le Thanh Ton
District 1
Ho Chi Minh City
Tel.: (8) 290739

**State Committee for
Cooperation and Investment
(SCCI)**
178 Nguyen Dinh Chieu Street
District 3
Ho Chi Minh City
Tel.: (8) 294674 / 230339

**Vietcochamber (Chamber
of Commerce and
Industry)**
33 Ba Trieu Street
Hanoi
Tel.: (4) 252961 / 253023

69 Dong Khoi Street
District 1
Ho Chi Minh City
Tel.: (8) 294-4472

**Vietnam Trade Information
Centre**
46 Ngo Quyen Street
Hanoi
Tel.: (4) 263183 / 262319
(Head Office)

35-37 Ben Chuong Duong
District 1
Ho Chi Minh City
Tel.: (8) 294388

Embassies and Consulates:

Vietnam Liaison Office
7 Lang Ha Road
Hanoi
Tel.: (4) 350445

British Embassy
16 Pho Ly Thuong Kiet Street
Hanoi
Tel.: (4) 252349 / 252510 /
256510

Canadian Embassy
39 Nguyen Dinh Chieu Street
Hanoi
Tel.: (4) 265840 / 265845

French Embassy
198 Tran Quang Khai Street
Hanoi
Tel.: (4) 258506

French Consulate
75 Tran Quoc Thao Street
District 3
Ho Chi Minh City
Tel.: (8) 222942 / 299328
(Commercial Section)

German Embassy
25 Phan Boi Chau Street
Hanoi
Tel.: (4) 253663

German Consulate
126 Nguyen Dinh
Chieu Street
District 3
Ho Chi Minh City
Tel.: (8) 291967 / 224385

In Canada:

Embassy of Vietnam
25B Davidson Drive
Gloucester
Ottawa, Ontario K1J 6L7
Tel.: (613) 744-4963

In France:

Embassy of Vietnam
62 Rue de Boileau
75016 Paris
Tel.: (1) 4524-5063

Vietnamese Tourism-France
54 Rue Sainte Anne /
4 Rue Cherubini
75002 Paris
Tel.: (1) 4286-8637

In Germany:

Embassy of Vietnam
Konstantinstrasse 37
5200 Bonn
Tel.: (228) 357-0201

Saigon Tourist Office
Fremdenverkehrsamt Der Sr
Vietnam
Hamburger Strasse 132
200 Hamburg 76
Tel.: (40) 295245

In the United Kingdom:

Embassy of Vietnam
12–14 Victoria Road
London W8 5RD
Tel.: (71) 937-1912

In the United States:

Vietnam Liaison Office
1233 Twentieth Street, N.W.
Suite 501
Wsahington, DC 20036
Tel.: (202) 861-0737

U.S.–Vietnam Trade Council
The International Center
731 Eighth Street, S.E.
Washington, DC 20003
Tel.: (202) 547-3800

**U.S. Chamber of Commerce /
Asia-Pacific Affairs /
International Division**
1615 H Street, N.W.
Washington, DC 20062
Tel.: (202) 463-5668

The Indochina Project
2001 S Street, N.W., Suite 740
Washington, DC 20009
Tel.: (202) 483-9222

**Vietnamese Mission to the
United Nations**
20 Waterside Plaza
New York, NY 10010
Tel.: (212) 725-4680

**Vietnam–American Chamber
of Commerce, Inc.**
15 E. 26th Street, Suite 921
New York, NY 10010-1579
Tel.: (212) 532-6042

U.S. Department of Commerce
International Trade
Administration
Vietnam Desk
14th & Constitution Avenues,
N.W.
Washington, DC 20230
Tel.: (202) 482-3877

The PacRim Hotline
Tel.: (202) 482-3875

18 Myanmar (Burma)

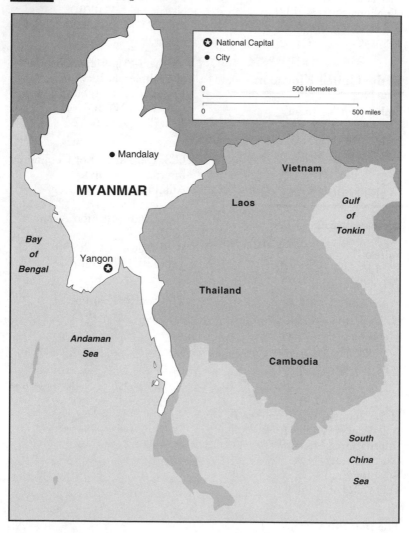

Geography

The Union of Myanmar (pronounced Mee-an-ma), formerly known as Burma, is situated on the eastern side of the Bay of Bengal. The country shares borders with Thailand and Laos to the east, China to the northeast, and Bangladesh and India to the northwest. In the south and southwest, the country faces the Bay of Bengal and the Andaman Sea along an extensive coastline. The country can be divided into several topographical areas: mountain ranges in the north and west; the Shan plateau in the east; the central belt; the Irrawaddy River delta in the south; the Rakhine coastal region; and the long Tenasserim strip in the south wedged between Thailand and the Bay of Bengal. About half of Burma's land area of 261,226 square miles (676,577 square kilometers) is covered with tropical forests. Lower Burma, the lower one-third of the country, is noted for being the wet-rice region and includes the Tenasserim coastal region, the areas around Moulmein and Pegu, and the islands stretching south toward Malaysia. The capital of Burma is Rangoon, or Yangon as it is officially called in Burmese.

History

Early historical records are vague, but seem to indicate that the Mon people, believed to have migrated from the area that is modern Thailand, settled in lower Burma almost five thousand years ago. Starting in the third century B.C., the Mons are believed to have been influenced by Indian civilization, particularly Hinduism and Buddhism. Around the same period, a second group of migrants arrived from the Tibetan plateau and settled in the Irrawaddy River region, gradually gaining supremacy over the Mon. Modern Burmese trace their ancestry to this second group of early Tibeto-Burmans; the Pyus, Kanyans, and Theks. The Pyus, who were of Mongolian stock, were the only group to leave traces of well-established civilization.

The Burmans, a people closely related to the Pyus, established settlements at Pagan, now called Bagan, as early as the second century A.D., and had created a kingdom by A.D. 849. This kingdom was destroyed in the ninth century by raiders from southern China, leaving only a loose confederation of small villages. King Anawrahta, the Burman founder of the Pagan dynasty, ruled from 1044 to 1077 and was the first ruler to unite Lower and Upper Burma as a single state. He also promoted the spread of Theravada Buddhism in his kingdom. Throughout the history of Buddhism, kings and monks have had a symbiotic relationship whereby the monks gave the kings spiritual legitimacy in return for material support.

In 1287 the Mongols, invading from China, conquered the area and destroyed the empire created by Anawrahta. Myanmar split into a number of smaller states and was not reunified until the sixteenth century. The Mongol Yuan dynasty and the Ming and Qing dynasties that followed, established a military and administrative base in Yunnan in southern China, from which they exerted a strong influence over Myanmar for several centuries. Also during this time, waves of Thai people migrated to Myanmar to escape the expanding Mongol empire, leading to a history characterized by long periods of struggle between Burman, Shan (Thai) and Mon ethnic groups.

In the early sixteenth century, King Tabinshwehti established a second Burmese empire, ruled by the Toungoo dynasty. In 1551 his brother-in-law, Bayinnaung, became king. In 1555, King Bayinnaung united Upper and Lower Burma. He conquered the Shan principalities in eastern Burma and entered Siam (modern Thailand) and Laos. In 1569 he conquered the Siamese capital of Ayutthaya, but the Siamese reasserted their independence shortly thereafter.

By 1546, the capital of Burma had been moved to Pegu, located on the coast in Lower Burma, which became a successful international trading center. A century later, the capital was moved to Ava, which was located inland in the center of the country. This change symbolized the withdrawal of effective Burman power from Lower Burma and led to the relative isolation of Burmese kings from outside influences brought by sea. Ava was eventually captured in 1752 by the Mons with French assistance.

The Mons tried to conquer the entire country, but were finally defeated by King Alaungpaya after eight years of warfare. Alaungpaya formed the third united Burmese empire, ruled by the Konbaung dynasty, the last dynasty to rule Burma before British colonial rule. His successor, Hsinbyushin, invaded Siam and completely destroyed the Siamese capital of Ayutthaya in 1767. As a result of this conquest Siamese art and literature began to influence Burmese culture.

The Burmese successfully defended themselves against several Chinese expeditions into Southeast Asia. A peace treaty that laid the foundation for good relations between Burma and China was signed in 1770. The treaty represented a victory against the Chinese and greatly boosted the pride and confidence of the Burmese people.

British traders first entered Myanmar in the early seventeenth century and thereafter vied with the French for influence in Lower Burma. The expansionist policies of the Konbaung dynasty threatened India and alarmed the British. The Burmese annexation of Assam in northeastern India led to two Anglo-Burmese Wars (1824–1826 and 1852), during which the British regained control of Assam and seized the Burmese provinces of Arakan, Tenasserim, and Pegu. Instability within the Burmese leadership made the response to British encroachment very weak. Finally, after the third Anglo-Burmese War (1885), all of Myanmar fell into British hands. The British named the conquered country "Burma" and made it a province of India.

Under British colonial rule, a Western-style commercial base was established in Burma. Unfortunately, the wealth generated there ended up in the pockets of British merchants, plantation owners, civil servants, and moneylenders from the Indian Chettier group. Most of the indigenous population remained in poverty. The British encouraged the immigration of Indian laborers into Burma to work on the plantations. Most of these immigrants came from the Indian states of Bengal and Madras. Burmese resentment developed as the British appointed immigrant Indians to government positions. By the early 1930s, some six hundred thousand immigrant Indians accounted for almost 10 percent of the population in Lower Burma and held more than 50 percent of the government jobs. The British also angered the Burmese people by terminating a long-standing Burmese government policy of subsidizing the Buddhist faith.

By the turn of the century, a Burmese brand of nationalism mixed with support of Buddhism emerged. In 1902 the Young Men's Buddhist Association (YMBA) was founded on the model of the YMCA (Young Men's Christian Association) and rapidly became a strong pro-independence organization. In 1923 the British granted Burma a limited amount of independence, allowing the Burmese to independently manage the country's administrative affairs, although the British viceroy in India retained authority over most major issues. A peasant uprising in Burma in 1931 pushed the British to make another major change in Burma's status and in 1937 Burma was separated from its unnatural union with India.

One of the early Burmese nationalist leaders was Aung San, who started his political career in the early twentieth century while at Rangoon University. In 1935 he led the Thakin movement, *thakin* meaning "master." By calling other Burmese "thakin," the leaders broke the code of courtesy as the term had been reserved for use by the Burmese when politely and respectfully referring to the British. Other leaders of this movement included U Nu and Ne Win. Thakin's leaders espoused a variety of political philosophies, including socialism and fascism, but they were united in their demand for complete independence. Like many other Asian nationalists in the 1930s, the Thakin leaders looked to Japan for support of their movement.

In December 1941 the Japanese invaded Burma and quickly defeated the British. Though the Japanese were initially welcomed as liberators, the Burmese soon realized that they had replaced one colonial ruler with another, for the Japanese occupation proved to be harsh. Aung San, commander of the new Burma National Army (BNA), helped to defeat the Japanese in 1945 and quickly assumed control of Burma by eliminating all of his domestic rivals. However, he was assassinated in 1947 by a right-wing gunman. The British bowed to the inevitable and granted Burma independence. This was finally achieved on January 4, 1948, amid chaos and unrest, for the new nation was deeply divided among ethnic enclaves.

The Burmese government had appointed U Nu (prior to 1951 known as Thakin Nu) to succeed Aung San as prime minister. The country faced political and economic collapse. Warfare between various ethnic groups and political groups erupted. The Communists, who had supported Aung San, and the Karens, an ethnic minority with the Chinese origins that had converted to Christianity, waged war against the newly formed Burmese government. The Communists hoped to establish a socialist state The Karens, who had been persecuted by Burma's Buddhist kings, resented the departure of the British. Various ethnic groups pressed for independence. The protests and general unrest has continued into the present.

U Nu's commitment to Buddhism and rejection of Marxist socialism shaped his domestic and foreign policies. In an effort to appease the ethnic interests, U Nu established separate states for the various minorities, but the fighting continued. For a brief period between 1958 and 1960, General Ne Win was appointed prime minister of a caretaker government. U Nu returned to power in 1960.

In 1962 General Ne Win led a coup d'état against U Nu's democratic government and established the Revolutionary Council. Burma has been under military rule ever since. Ne Win was able to restore stability, but at great cost to Burma's young democracy. The constitution was suspended, the government assumed control of the media and education, and student protests were banned. All industries were nationalized and an economic policy based on isolationism and self-sufficiency was set forth. Economic disaster followed.

By 1964, all other political parties had been banned. In 1969 a new constitution was drafted promising a transition to a democratic society. In reality, however, the country moved toward socialism. As leader of the Burmese Socialist Programme party (BSPP), created in

1962 by the military, Ne Win retained power and became president
of the new Socialist Republic of the Union of Burma. In 1974 a second new constitution was adopted and the government confirmed its
commitment to the policy of the "Burmese Way to Socialism," based
on self-reliance, state control, isolation, and strict neutrality.

During the mid-1970s the economy remained slake. Many party
officials were purged by Ne Win, who preferred to believe that faulty
implementation of policy, not the policy itself, was to blame for
Burma's collapsing economy. The purges produced more discontent.
Coups were planned and insurgency spread through the ranks of the
military. In 1981, Ne Win was succeeded by U San Yu as president.
Ne Win remained leader of the BSPP.

In March 1988 a student protest, fueled by the demonetization
of the currency in 1985 and 1987, sparked nationwide pro-
democracy demonstrations, which were brutally suppressed by the
military. The military State Law and Order Restoration Council
(SLORC) then assumed control and formed a government. The
country's name was changed to the Union of Myanmar and all signs
were changed to Burmese. Rangoon became Yangon. General Ne
Win resigned as party leader, although there was some speculation
that he had organized the coup and continues to exercise influence.
General Saw Maung, a Western-educated lawyer and close friend
of Ne Win, eventually became the leader of the SLORC. Although
he promised limited reforms, his government has been repressive
and has been accused of widespread human rights abuses. The government has silenced the democracy movement through the sys-
tematic use of terror and torture. Many observers believe that the
internal situation is slowly improving today. Nevertheless, Western
business interests have withheld their investments primarily due to
the lack of political freedom and the jailing of political dissidents,
of whom Daw Aung San Suu Kyi, the daughter of Aung San, is most
well known.

By 1989 more than two hundred political parties had formed.
The largest was the National League for Democracy (NLD) which

was headed by Aung San Suu Kyi. In the elections of that year, the NLD overwhelmingly won, but the military, under the SLORC, disregarded the elections, imprisoned many opposition leaders, and retained control of the government. Prior to the election, in 1989, Aung San Suu Kyi was placed under house arrest, where she remains today, preferring house arrest to exile. In 1991 she was awarded the Nobel Peace Prize for her nonviolent struggle for democracy and human rights. In 1992 General Than Shwe, known for being a moderate and an advocate of economic reform, replaced General Saw Maung as chairman of the SLORC. However, General Khin Nyunt, the head of the military intelligence, is believed to be the true leader. In 1993 the government promised to draft a new constitution and institute reforms.

In September 1994 General Than Shwe met for the first time with Aung San Suu Kyi, primarily in response to international concern over the country's human rights situation, which has resulted in blocking millions of dollars in international development aid for Myanmar. The government recognizes that Aung San Suu Kyi's release from house arrest is a key to solving many of the nation's political and economic problems.

The government of Myanmar today controls most of the country, but rebels, mainly ethnic insurgents and warlord gangs, hold many of the mountainous regions on Myanmar's borders. Many of these groups support themselves by trafficking in opium. The SLORC has recently begun to negotiatie cease-fires, offering regional autonomy to these groups, and even permitting them to continue the drug trade. The purpose in forging compromises and alliances with them is to obtain some form of peace.

Political Structure

Myanmar is a single-party socialist government headed by a prime minister and a nine-person cabinet. The political power lies with the National Unity party (NUP) and the State Law and Order

Restoration Council (SLORC), the ruling military junta. The SLORC has twenty-one members, all of whom are generals. Some of the SLORC's members also hold ministerial positions.

The government stated that a new constitution was being written in 1994, but nothing has been made public. It is believed that the new constitution is being drafted in order to prevent reformer Aung San Suu Kyi from running for office. The Myanmar government is using Indonesia as its model for its shift from tight military control to a slightly looser controls. However, the new constitution is expected to reassert the power of the military, making any change nominal at best.

The legal infrastructure is virtually nonexistent. Most laws are in the form of directives and orders from the government and change frequently. In November 1988 the SLORC passed the Investment Law of Myanmar, which allowed foreign investments and removed the restrictions on private-sector participation in the economy, both domestic and international.

Economy

Burma's economy has suffered for three decades due to a policy of isolation and an unsuccessful attempt at self-sufficiency. In 1988 the SLORC started to reverse some of these BSPP policies, adopting some market reforms and seeking to increase tourism, which had previously been controlled and limited by the government. Inflation has remained high, but exports of raw materials have earned the country much-needed foreign exchange. Foreign investment, primarily from other Asian countries rather than the West, has been trickling into Myanmar.

Myanmar is a major exporter of hardwood products, having about 80 percent of the world's teak reserves as well as large supplies of other hardwood trees. The country is also rich in mineral resources, including silver, lead, tungsten, and marble; precious gems such as rubies, sapphires, and jade; and oil and gas.

About 40 percent of the country's economy comes from agriculture-related industries. The major crops include rice, cotton, tobacco, jute, sugar cane, tea, rubber, coconut, and the edible seeds from various peas, beans, and lentils. Fish and shrimp are also abundant and are becoming viable industries. At one time the country was also a major exporter of rice, but this has declined recently. Myanmar is a major player in the international drug trade as a producer of opium. While Myanmar is generously endowed with natural resources, the country has basically no infrastructure and the country's communication, transportation, and power services are inadequate.

One of the unique aspects of Myanmar's economy is the demonetization of its currency. Every few years the government recalls its printed money. The two recalls in 1985 and 1987 led to the 1988 student protests. While the government's intention has been to stamp out the black market and reduce the profits of Chinese entrepreneurs who thrive in Myanmar, the poor suffer the most because their money is no longer legal tender and their paper currency becomes worthless.

People, Values, and Social Customs

The population of Myanmar is about forty-three million. There are three main racial groups: Mon-Khmers (Mon), Tibeto-Burmans (Burmans), and Thai-Shans (Thai). Approximately two-thirds of the population are Tibeto-Burmans. The seven main minority groups are the Shan (Thai), Karen, Kayah, Kachin, Chin, Mon, and Arakanese (Rakhine), each name referring to the specific areas in which they live. There are also a number of Indians and Chinese in Burma. The term "Burman" refers specifically to a member of the Tibeto-Burman ethnic group; "Burmese" refers to all of the people living within the national boundaries of Burma. Despite the change in the name of the country from "Burma" to "Myanmar," its citizens are still called Burmese.

The Burmans tend to hold most of the country's political and economic power, a situation that fuels the animosity of other ethnic groups. A three-tiered citizenship law now limits the political power of non-Burmans, further aggravating the situation. The Burmese are proud of their culture and respect those who live by its values and spirit. Burmese having Westernized attitudes are looked down upon. The Burmese also consider themselves to be superior to Indians, Chinese, and Eurasians.

Indians once represented a substantial portion of Burma's population. At the turn of the century, Rangoon was predominantly Indian as businessmen followed the laborers there. Indian moneylenders from the Chettiars, a merchant group, found substantial success there. However, the Burmese government reversed the British government's pro-Indian policy after independence, and all Indian-held land was nationalized. By the 1990s, the Indian population had dropped by more than 80 percent to less than 100,000.

Historically, Burmese society was not as hierarchically rigid as that of neighboring India. The king and the royal family were firmly positioned at the very top, but other Burmese could advance to prominent positions through education and ability.

Families are at the center of Burmese society. Elders are respected because they are the senior family members, and even bosses are perceived as father or mother figures. Family members are referred to by specific names that indicate status and respect. Extended family and other social relationships are very important and all attempts are made to maintain harmonious and smooth relations. These relationships serve as a model for other interactions. For example, the recipient of a favor is under an obligation to do a favor in return. To many Burmese, excessive talk of money is regarded as tasteless.

The Burmese have traditionally respected astrology and related sciences. Monks must be consulted to determine auspicious dates for major events, such as weddings and the opening of a business. Accordingly, the Burmese can be very superstitious.

The Burmese enjoy ceremonies and have numerous rituals for

happy occasions, called *tha yei,* and sad ones, called *na yei. Ah-nar-de* or *ah-nar-hmu* is a concept that involves consideration for another person. It is important to avoid imposing on someone, causing trouble for them, or doing something that could result in their loss of face. The Burmese will try to avoid appearing overly eager. People are expected to be considerate of one another and to empathize in difficult times. Once insulted or rejected, the Burmese can develop grudges, but in general most Burmese tend to be carefree and easy-going.

The Burmese smile often when they are happy, as well as in negative or embarrassing situations. People will smile to cover up their discomfort in dealing with foreigners; few Burmese have experience interacting with outsiders. Foreigners, therefore, need to differentiate between the various smiles and related emotions. Burmese humor is often based on puns. Storytelling is a common part of the culture.

Women in Myanmar have historically enjoyed more freedom and equality than elsewhere in Asia, although they still keep a low public profile. Women are educated and enjoy full property rights. Traditionally, Burmese women have run small family businesses. Many women are able to select their own marriage partners, a practice that contrasts sharply with practices in many other Asian countries. They often retain their maiden names after marriage. Women usually manage the family finances as well as all household responsibilities. One of the few areas in Burmese society where women are forced to accept an inferior role is in Buddhist religious practices.

Buddhism is the primary religion and has had a tremendous influence on Burmese society and its values. About 85 percent of Burmese are Buddhist. Most Burmese believe in the Buddhist concept of *kan or karma,* in which intentions are as important as deeds and future lives are determined by present actions. The Burmese have a strong belief in the power of fate. Other religions practiced in Myanmar include Christianity, Hinduism, and Islam. Be sure to remove your shoes before entering temples or religious areas. Women should never touch a Buddhist monk.

Work Schedule

In general most businesses and government offices are open from
9:00 A.M. to 4:30 P.M., Monday to Friday. Some private enterprises
may stay open later. Banks are open on weekdays from 10:00 A.M.
to 2:00 P.M. Most shops and restaurants are open for longer hours
and on weekends.

Making Contacts

Introductions are critical, as Burmese business culture is based on
networks. Connections are required for almost every aspect of social
and business life. Just as in the social arena, business favors received
are expected to be returned. For example, if you receive an
introduction from someone, you are obligated to perform a favor for
that person. This attitude is one of the primary reasons that corruption has become so widespread in Myanmar; favors received
are often reciprocated as gifts, that is, as graft. Your embassy in
Myanmar as well as consulting firms, lawyers, and bankers may be
able to assist you in developing introductions.

Once you have decided to operate in Myanmar, it is advisable
to hire a local representative, agent, or partner, for a local is better
suited to handling the nuances of the system and managing local
staff. When selecting a local representative or partner, be aware that
due to the new economic policies, there are many new entrepreneurs, some of whom will try to oversell their capabilities. Choose
a partner who has established high-level connections. Junior or
middle-level connections will have little value. When scheduling
appointments, try to meet with the most senior person possible.

The government has established joint venture corporations
(JVC) to team up with foreign investors. The Union of Myanmar
Economic Holdings Limited, a holding company established by active and veteran members of Myanmar's army, is another option as
a local partner. These enterprises are better suited to be partners
rather than your local representatives, as their loyalties are to state

business. Foreigners can enter into business relationships with these or other state enterprises, cooperative societies, and local private business partners. Foreigners can also operate businesses as independent owners. As a result of government involvement in business, patronage is widespread. The ruling elite and their families and friends are benefiting the most from the recent economic reforms.

Business is generally conducted face-to-face. Most Burmese will not conduct business with someone they have not met, so you will need to travel to Burma if you wish to do business there. Due to the country's isolation, many Burmese unrealistically expect foreigners to have unlimited resources and knowledge.

It is important to remember that Myanmar has been politically and economically isolated for about three decades. As a socialist economy, production targets were established for every product and service. The bureaucracy created to manage the economy grew larger and larger, and as inefficiency spread, so too did pilferage, waste, and corruption. During those three decades, shortages of all types of goods became commonplace and the black market thrived. Furthermore, as a result of government rationing, everything, including paper, equipment, cars, and even such items as clothes and shoes, was recycled. This attitude continues to affect business today, so that most Burmese believe that everything can be repaired and used more than once.

Meeting People

Punctuality is expected of foreigners, but is not usually practiced by the Burmese. "Rubber time" is common, for people have a very relaxed attitude toward time. Senior officers and ministers may keep visitors, who are expected to be punctual, waiting for hours. Most Burmese do not shake hands, but some may adopt Western practices in business interactions. In general, one should wait until a hand is offered, particularly with women, before offering yours. A simple nod of the head and a smile is often appropriate. Be sensitive to the Burmese preference for social hierarchy. One should be most attentive to the senior person, as defined by age and rank within the company. Most business is conducted in English. However, you may wish to retain a translator for social purposes. (Refer to the Introduction for hints on utilizing translators.) Business cards should be presented at the first meeting.

Burmese names come from various sources including astrologers and the day of the week on which a person was born. The Burmese do not have a system of family names and most women retain their complete names after marriage. Due to the colonial influence, some Burmese have Western names. It is always appreciated when foreigners extend traditional Burmese courtesies such as using the honorifics that indicate status and respect. The prefix *U* (pronounced oo) is used as an honorific "Mr." when addressing senior men. *Maung* is the prefix for younger men and it is associated with humility. *Ma* is used to refer to all females until they reach adulthood in their twenties. *Daw* is used to address all adult women regardless of their age, although it is rarely used for children. Burmese should be addressed using the appropriate prefix and their full name. However, Burmese names can be confusing and it is advisable to ask a person which form of address he or she prefers. The Burmese will most likely use formal titles, "Mr.," "Mrs.," "Dr.," and so on, when referring to you. Wait until invited to use first names.

In general, most people are open about their willingness to conduct business. Most government officials are direct and relatively frank. The first meeting is often used to learn more about each participant. It is best to present the overall perspective of your company and strategic plans rather than specific detailed proposals at first meetings. The first part of a meeting should be spent chatting about casual topics such as your travels and positive impressions of Myanmar. Refrain from discussing politics or religion. Citizens are forbidden to discuss politics with foreigners. The Burmese may ask questions that Westerners would perceive as being personal. Be polite and somewhat vague if you feel uncomfortable answering in great detail. Keep in mind that raised voices are frowned upon. A small, but tasteful gift should be presented at the first meeting. Suitable items include nice pens, liquor, sample products, or items with corporate logos.

Do not physically touch anyone, particularly someone of the opposite sex. Never show or point your feet at someone, as the feet are considered the dirtiest part of a person. Refrain from placing your feet on a chair or table, for this is considered disrespectful. Because the head is considered the most spiritual part of the body, touching someone's head is considered disrespectful.

Corporate Culture

Most foreigners will conduct business with the government through the SLORC-controlled holding company. Ministries representing different fields and industries are divided into directorates that provide services and manage the government-owned corporations.

The most senior people in the ministerial corporations are managing directors and director generals, followed by general managers. One should always meet with the senior-most person possible. Most of the ministers are micromanagers and oversee every aspect of business. Government officials are very concerned with maintaining power. The Foreign Investment Commission, headed by the deputy prime minister and the minister for national planning and economic development, must approve all investments. There are fourteen ministers in the commission.

Under the socialist system, party membership and standing were more important than experience and expertise in determining promotions. As a consequence, managers were often inexperienced and incompetent. Many of the enterprises that had been operating fairly smoothly prior to 1962 were run into the ground. Accountability was practically nonexistent and attempts by the government in the 1970s to hold individuals responsible were unsuccessful. In order to accomplish things, businesspeople should maintain relationships with junior- as well as senior-level people. In general, management tends to be inefficient, but things are changing and capability is slowly becoming as important as connections, particularly in private enterprises.

Since the government began to open the economy in 1988, many Burmese have embarked on entrepreneurial activities. However, the government has retained control of key industries, such as timber and oil. Existing family businesses have been able to expand. However, lack of exposure to international business practices and trends has limited the success of the private sector.

Negotiation

Throughout Myanmar, there is a general mistrust of foreigners, in part due to Myanmar's history and in part due to the recent political climate. Accordingly, it can take a great deal of effort and time to develop the trust and confidence of local counterparts. Foreigners must make an effort to show common interests. It is also very important to develop social relationships outside of the business arena, as they are often valued more than business relationships, at times outweighing the merits of the business transaction.

Decision-making is done by the most senior people and is usually based more on intuition than on research, which is conducted as a formality, if at all. The Burmese tend to be cautious and risk-averse and often rely on group consensus. The decision-making and the implementation processes can be very slow and drawn out due to the bureaucracy. Graft has become a common method for speeding up these processes.

The Burmese do not like to say "No" because it causes loss of face; they will often avoid situations in which they must be negative. If a person is unable to answer in the affirmative, he or she is more likely to say, "I would like to, but. . . ." The Burmese will often say "Yes," but will actually mean "I understand" or "OK," not "Yes, I agree." Be careful not to assume that a "Yes" is a positive or affirmative response.

The foreigner may encounter initial difficulty when doing business in Myanmar. Individual initiative and accountability are weak, for the Burmese have had little incentive to perform well. Procrastination is common, as the concept of time differs from the West. To succeed, it is important to have a local partner who can maintain close contact and monitor the progress on any transaction. If there is a problem, the Burmese will rarely tell you and will either try to cover it up or ignore it in the hopes that it will go away. Further, the Burmese will probably not ask questions or inform you if they do not understand something, out of fear of losing face. Refrain from public criticism and never raise your voice. Maintaining face and dignity for all parties is vital. Criticism is usually considered a personal insult. Be sure to ask non-judgmental questions.

The Burmese view contracts as the basis for building relationships. Written agreements are detailed and adhered to closely. If possible, have your contracts name a foreign jurisdiction in which to settle disputes.

Conducting Business in a Social Setting

Dining and Drinking

Developing personal and social relationships is critical to doing business in Myanmar. Most business entertaining is formal and occurs in hotels and restaurants. Business dinners are common, but business breakfasts and lunches are relatively uncommon. Chinese cuisine is usually considered the most luxurious. Western cuisine is served in the larger hotels. You should select an upscale restaurant if you are inviting a Burmese to a meal. If you are invited to a dinner, you can—although it is not expected—bring a small gift such as a souvenir from your home country or a bottle of fine wine. It is not uncommon for the Burmese to decline second portions of food several times before taking it. Most Burmese avoid eating pork and beef. Pork is not eaten by those who worship spirits; devout Buddhists do not eat beef. During the Buddhist Lent, some Buddhists become vegetarians. The Burmese consume little alcohol.

Visiting a Home

The Burmese rarely invite foreigners to their homes because the government frequently monitors foreign visitors' activities. If you are invited to a home, you should take a small gift, such as chocolates, sweets, fruits, or a souvenir from your home country. Gifts for the children are appreciated. Remove your shoes before entering a home.

Gift Giving

Corruption is widespread; almost everyone tries to profit from the inefficiencies that emerged back in the 1970s when there were shortages of most consumer goods. As a result, "survival" justified everything from accepting bribes to stealing. Due to low income levels, this attitude remains widespread. Develop a global policy for your company and adhere to it. Your local counterpart is best equipped to manage such issues.

Generally, the Burmese appreciate gifts of cigarettes and liquor; these are not considered graft. Other appropriate gifts include nice pens, diaries, calendars, and golf balls if your counterpart plays the sport. Most Burmese will politely decline a gift initially, saying something to the effect of "You should not have gone to so much trouble." Continue to insist that he or she take it and note "that it was your privilege or honor to present it." Gifts should not be opened in front of the giver so as to avoid any awkwardness as well as to avoid appearing overly eager or greedy. The Burmese may not appear to be appreciative of your gift. The concept of *ah-nar-de* creates a dilemma. To be very appreciative would indicate greed and the Burmese are concerned about appearing rude.

Money is sometimes given at weddings, primarily when the wedding couple appears to need it. It should be given in multiples of 100, as that is considered a symbol of long life. However, it is usually best to give a tangible gift, such as a tasteful household item or souvenir from your home country. Refrain from gifts of knives and scissors and any other cutting instruments. The color black should be avoided at happy events as it is considered a somber color. Money, in any denomination, is given at funerals, but only if the family appears to need it. Your local representative can help you determine the appropriate amount.

Dress Code

A suit or a shirt and tie are appropriate dress for men. Burmese men wear a *tike-pon*, which is an overcoat, to the office and to meetings. Dresses, suits, skirts and blouses, or pant suits (not for first meetings) are suitable for women. Short-sleeve blouses should be reserved for more casual situations. Dress appropriately for the weather. The traditional dress for both men and women is a *longhi*, also known as a sarong.

Useful Phrases

The official language of Myanmar is Burmese and is spoken by most of the people. The Burmese language is tonal, making it difficult to speak. The script is derived from the Pali script of southern India. Non-Burmans usually speak their own language in addition to Burmese; there are some eighty languages spoken throughout Myanmar. English is understood by many, particularly elderly people who remember it from the days of the British Raj. However, use of English was forbidden under General Ne Win, so younger people are less likely to speak the language. The following list includes some useful phrases and a guide to their pronunciation.

Hello	*Nae cong de la*
Good morning	*Ming glaba* (not commonly used and never used on sad occasions)
Good afternoon	Use English "bye" or "good-bye" when leaving
Good evening	Use English "bye" or "good-bye" when leaving
How are you?	*Nae cong de la*

Please	*Jae su bue yu eh*
Thank you	*Jae su din ba de* (not used every time a service is received)
You are welcome	*Gae sa ma she bu*
Excuse me	*Jae su bue yu eh*
I am sorry	Say in English
My name is ———	*Gin dou na mae* ——— (used by males); *Gin mar na mae* ——— (used by females)
I work for ———	*Gin dou a lowd joung* ———
Here is my business card	*Gin dou a load gup ya*
I am pleased to meet you	*Dui ya da wan da ba de*
Please accept this small gift	*Jae su bue be gin dou lae song daen ta bah*
I understand	*Gin dou na lae ba de*
No, I do not understand	*Gin dou na ma lae bu*
Please wait a minute	*Jae su beu be ka na som ba*
Where is the bathroom?	*Now bae kan ka bae ma lae?*
No problem	*Ya ba de*
Good-bye	Say in English
Cheers	Say in English

Major Holidays

January 4	Independence Day
February 12	Union Day
March 2	Peasants Day (anniversary of the 1962 coup d'état)
March 27	Tatmadaw (Armed Forces Day)
April*	Water Festival
May 1	Labor Day
May*	Kasone Banyan (Water Festival)
July*	Beginning of Buddhist Lent
July 19	Martyr's Day
October*	End of Buddhist Lent
November*	Tazaungdaing
December*	National Day
December*	Karen New Year
December 25	Christmas Day

*These holidays are based on the lunar calendar and therefore change from year to year. The Burmese have a festival almost every month based on the lunar calendar. Check with your embassy or trade office before you plan your trip.

General Facts

Climate: In general, the climate is hot and tropical, with three seasons. In the dry season, from March to June, the temperature averages between 86F (30C) and 96F (36C). During the monsoon, which lasts from July to October, the temperature usually falls between 84F (29C) and 88F (31C). The cool season occurs from November to February, with temperatures ranging from 88F (31C) to 92F (33). Temperatures can differ depending on the region, with the river valleys and delta reaching temperatures as high as 104F (40C), going even higher in the dry zone.

Currency: The official currency is the *kyat* (pronounced chat, and abbreviated as K). Until 1994, the two most common large denominations of the currency were 45 and 90 because General Ne Win, the former leader, believed (as do many Burmese) that 9 and its multiples are lucky. However, the government now issues denominations of 20, 50, 100, and 500 *kyat*. All foreigners must use Foreign Exchange Certificates (FEC) for transactions at designated areas only, including hotels and some restaurants. The government prohibits use of FECs outside of these designated locations, which can be inconvenient. This practice has also fueled a widespread black market offering steep premiums for foreign currencies. Do not cooperate with the freelance money changers.

Similar to India, 100,000 *kyat* is called a *lakh* or *theinn* in Burmese; K10,000,000 is called *crore* in the Indian context and *gaday* in Burmese.

Dates: Dates are written day, month, year. For example, May 25, 1995, would be abbreviated as 25/5/95.

Electricity: The voltage is 220.

Entry Requirements: All foreigners are required to have a valid passport, a tourist or business visa, and a departure ticket.

Time: Myanmar has one time zone, which is six and a half hours ahead of Greenwich Mean Time and eleven and a half hours ahead of U.S. Eastern Standard Time (ten and a half hours in Daylight Savings Time).

Tipping: Although there is no tradition of tipping, the gesture is widespread, but more with the intention of getting something done than as acknowledgement for a job well done.

Transportation: The only way into Myanmar is by airplane. The government has restrictions on how and where foreigners may enter the country and travel. New visitors to the country are advised to remain in the major cities for a variety of reasons, including a shortage of reliable transportation options.

Within Myanmar, planes, trains, and buses provide options for transport. Trains and buses are crowded and slow. The best way to travel is by private car and driver. Ask for assistance because drivers may try to overcharge you. There are few public taxis so it is advisable to retain the one you find at the airport. Taxis are generally also available outside the better hotels.

Helpful Telephone Numbers

Because the communications system is currently inadequate, it is best to go to the Yangon central telegraph office (located at Pansodan and Mahabandoola Street) to make overseas telephone calls. The country code is (95) and the city code for Yangon is (1).

Hospitals:

It is advisable to go to Thailand or India for medical care.

Diplomatic Hospital
Kyaikkasan Road, near Royal Lake
Yangon
Tel.: (1) 50149

Useful Addresses

In Myanmar:

**Myanmar Travel and Tours
(Tourist Burma)**
77 Sule Pagoda Road
Yangon

**Union of Myanmar Foreign
Investment Commission**
653–691 Merchant Street
P.O. Box 346
Yangon
Tel.: (1) 82946

Embassies:

There are no British or French
diplomatic offices in Myanmar.

American Embassy
581 Merchant Street
Yangon
Tel.: (1) 82055 / 82182

Canadian Embassy
c/o P.O. Box 2090
Bangkok 10500, Thailand

German Embassy
32 Nat Mauk Street
Yangon
Tel.: (1) 50477 / 50603

In Canada:

Embassy of Myanmar
The Sandringham
Suite 901–902
85 Range Road
Ottawa, Ontario K1N 8/6
Tel.: (613) 232-6434

In France:

Embassy of Myanmar
60 Rue de Courcelles
3d Floor
75008 Paris
Tel.: (1) 4225-5695

In Germany:

Embassy of Myanmar
Schumann Strasse 112
5300 Bonn 1
Tel.: (228) 210091

In the United Kingdom:

Embassy of Myanmar
19A Charles Street
London WIX 8ER
Tel.: (71) 499-8841 /
629-4486

In the United States:

Embassy of Myanmar
2300 S Street, N.W.
Washington, DC 20008
Tel.: (202) 332-9044

**Permanent Mission to the
United Nations**
10 East 77th Street
New York, NY 10021
Tel.: (212) 535-1310

U.S. Department of Commerce
International Trade
Administration
Burma (Myanmar) Desk
Room 2032
14th & Constitution Avenues,
N.W.
Washington, DC 20230
Tel.: (202) 482-3894

19 Cambodia ────

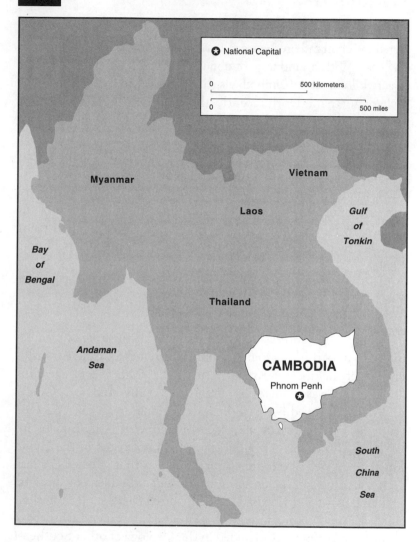

Geography

Cambodia is located just north of the Gulf of Thailand and is bordered by Thailand on the west, Laos on the north, and Vietnam on the east. With a land area of about 69,898 square miles (181,035 square kilometers), Cambodia is slightly larger than half the size of Italy or Vietnam. Until recently, the country had been known by visitors as the "gentle land of smiling people." Cambodia has two important bodies of water, the Mekong River and the Tonle Sap (Great Lake). The northern border is characterized by dense forests and high plateaus. In the center of the country is a low-lying plain; this is where the majority of Cambodians reside. The southern coast is a strip of heavily forested lowlands isolated from the rest of the country by mountains, with the highest peak Phnom Aoral rising to 5,948 feet (1813 meters). The capital of Cambodia is Phnom Penh.

History

For the first six centuries A.D., the present-day territory of Cambodia was part of the kingdom of Funan, which is the Chinese transliteration of the ancient Khmer form of the word *phnom*, meaning "hill." Funan was an important trade link between India and China, and was influenced by both of those nations. India exercised the strongest external influence on early Southeast Asia. Indians introduced Hinduism and Buddhism, which coexisted in the Funan kingdom, as well as other cultural influences that affected the language, art, and society. From India also came the idea of a despotic god-king (*devaraja*) who had to be supported by his subjects as their link with supernatural forces. This later became a central aspect of Khmer society and was included in the ideology of other Southeast Asian countries.

In the sixth century the Kambujas who lived in the middle Mekong region, north of modern-day Cambodia, conquered the Funan kingdom and established a new state called Chenla, which split into two divisions in the late seventh century. Land Chenla in the north was stable during the next century. In contrast, Water Chenla in the south along the Gulf of Thailand was fragmented by various dynastic rivalries. Java invaded and controlled this part of the country during the eighth century.

Modern Cambodia is the successor-state of the mighty Khmer empire that ruled much of present-day Vietnam, Laos, and Thailand from the ninth to the fourteenth centuries. Khmer rule in Cambodia began in the early ninth century. Around A.D. 800, Jayavarman II, a prince who had been distantly related to earlier dynasties, returned from Java. He established a new state religion in which the Khmer ruler would be the god-king and whose destiny became synonymous with the destiny of the country.

Jayavarman and his descendants ruled the country until the beginning of the thirteenth century. By the tenth century, Khmer rule extended from Cambodia to modern-day Vietnam, Thailand and Laos. During the eleventh and twelfth centuries, the Khmers fought a series of wars with the Vietnamese, the Burmese, and the Chams, an empire in southern Vietnam, resulting in chaos and destruction.

Jayavarman VII restored order and rebuilt the Khmer empire. This highly advanced, Indianized Khmer civilization had a significant influence on the region's cultural and artistic development. Angkor Wat, the world's largest religious building, was built in the twelfth century to honor the Hindu god Vishnu. The decline of the great city of Angkor began in the early thirteenth century. Over the next century, Hinduism was rejected as a major religion and the people shifted to embrace Theravada (also known as Hinayana) Buddhism. By the early fourteenth century, Sanskrit was replaced by the Pali language.

By the fourteenth century, Thailand (Siam) began to annex parts of Cambodia, eventually occupying Angkor in the middle of the fifteenth century. For the next one hundred and fifty years, there was warfare between the Khmers and the Thais. Dynastic rivalries further increased the confusion in the region. The Thais captured the new Khmer capital of Phnom Penh in 1594. The Cambodian king, Satha, asked the Spanish to assist in reinstalling Khmer rule. but by the time the Spaniards arrived, King Satha had been deposed. The Spaniards then installed one of Satha's sons as king. However the Spanish stay in Cambodia was short-lived; the Spanish garrison at Phnom Penh was massacred in 1599 after locals became resentful of the extent of Spanish power. Satha's brother became king in 1600 with the assistance of the Thais who were interested in maintaining influence over Cambodia.

The next two and a half centuries were characterized by weak Cambodian kings who often sought the assistance and protection of either Thailand or Vietnam. In the seventeenth century the Vietnamese ruler demanded that, in exchange for protection, the Vietnamese be permitted to settle in the southern part of Cambodia, in what was known as Lower Cambodia. The Cambodian king agreed and thereby lost what has since become southern Vietnam. The Thais gradually took control of the western provinces of Cambodia and late eighteenth century the Thais controlled the Cambodian royal family.

In 1863 an extension of their interests in Vietnam, the French pressed Cambodia into signing a treaty that gave France jurisdiction. Early French control was less interventionist than that exerted by other colonial powers, mainly because French attention was focused on Vietnam. However, the presence of the French helped dissuade Cambodia's neighbors from taking any more territory. By 1884, France had pushed the Cambodian rulers into signing another treaty that made Cambodia a colony of France. This ignited a two-year rebellion, the only major anticolonial movement in the country for more than sixty years. During the next two decades, the French provided the Cambodian king, Norodom, and his court with extravagances, which served to increase the symbolic position of the monarchy. In contrast to the people of Vietnam and other neighboring colonies, the Cambodians did not promote any meaningful nationalistic movements.

Cambodian kings ruled, but the French controlled Cambodia, exploiting its people and resources. This situation lasted until 1941, when the Japanese invaded and occupied all of Southeast Asia. The French named eighteen-year-old Prince Norodom Sihanouk as the new king of Cambodia in absentia. The French assumed that Prince Sihanouk would be easily manipulated, but they were wrong. After World War II ended, the French returned to Cambodia and sought to make it an autonomous state within the French Union. From 1945 to 1953, the country was in a state of uncertainty and political turmoil. France was not able to restore the prewar status quo, in large part because it was fighting—and losing—a war with the communist-led nationalists in Vietnam. (See Chapter 17, on Vietnam.)

In January 1953, King Sihanouk began what was referred to as a "Royal Crusade." He dissolved the parliament and declared martial law. He declared Cambodia's independence on November 9, 1953. However, internal strife continued between the King and his domestic opponents. In March 1955, Sihanouk abdicated the throne in favor of his father, Norodom Suramarit, and established a new political party, the People's Socialist Community. His party won every seat in Parliament in the 1955 elections. Sihanouk dominated the Cambodian political scene for the next fifteen years while serving as prime minister. In 1960, after the death of his father, he became chief of state.

Although he feared the North Vietnamese communists, Sihanouk perceived South Vietnam and Thailand, both allies of the United States, as the greatest security threats to Cambodia. In 1965 Sihanouk broke off diplomatic relations with the United States after being convinced that the United States was plotting against him and his family. Sihanouk thereafter tilted toward North Vietnam and China and allowed North Vietnam to use Cambodian territory in its war against South Vietnam and the United States. As a result, right-wing elements in Cambodia, including the officer corps of the army and the urban elite, became disillusioned with Sihanouk. In addition, left-wing Cambodians were resentful of Sihanouk's internal policies, which forbade political dissent. The masses were also fed up with widespread corruption in the government. In 1967 a rural-based rebellion broke out and Sihanouk concluded that the greatest threat to his power came from the left. With additional pressure from the army, he launched a policy of harsh repression against the left.

Sihanouk's position greatly deteriorated as the conflict between the army and the leftist rebels intensified. In 1970, while he was out of the country on an overseas trip, Sihanouk was deposed. General Lon Nol and Sihanouk's cousin, Prince Sisowath Matak, usually known as Sirik Matak, took over. Sihanouk relocated to Beijing, where he set up a government in exile with nominal control of the Khmer Rouge, an indigenous Cambodian revolutionary movement. In 1969 the United States had begun secret bombings of suspected communist military camps in the country. In 1970 the United States and South Vietnam intensified these bombings in an effort to destroy the Viet Cong and North Vietnamese troops based in Cambodia. Continuing into 1973, these bombings killed thousands of innocent Cambodian civilians.

The Lon Nol government was very unpopular due to the widespread corruption and greed of its officials. Savage internal fighting spread throughout the country, and between 1970 and 1975 hundreds of thousands of civilians were killed. During the early 1970s, the Khmer Rouge, led by Pol Pot, a Paris-educated political leader, focused its efforts on overthrowing the Lon Nol regime. Despite massive U.S. military and economic aid, Lon Nol was unable to successfully destroy the Khmer Rouge. On April 17, 1975, the Khmer Rouge defeated the Lon Nol government and Cambodia fell under Khmer Rouge control.

The Khmer Rouge, a staunch communist group, implemented an extremely harsh restructuring of Cambodia in its attempt to make the country a Maoist, peasant-dominated cooperative. The entire population was forced to do manual labor. All relations with the outside world were cut off, except for limited contact with China. From 1975 to about 1979, almost one and a half million Cambodians were directly killed by or died due to policies of the Khmer Rouge as they embarked on a campaign of terror and mass genocide. Intellectuals and educated professionals were murdered. Anyone who wore eyeglasses or spoke a foreign language was also killed. All forms of religious expression were prohibited; temples were closed and monks murdered. Sihanouk, who had returned to Cambodia in 1975 to head the Khmer Rouge government, resigned after three months and was placed under house arrest. It is believed that he was kept alive mainly at the request of the Chinese, who considered him useful. In January 1979 he was transferred to Beijing due to the Vietnamese invasion of Cambodia.

Between 1975 and 1978, Pol Pot's Khmer Rouge instigated clashes on and within the borders of Vietnam, killing hundreds of Vietnamese. The Khmer Rouge tried to lay claim to the southern part of Vietnam, which had been part of Cambodia until the seventeenth century. In December 1978 the Vietnamese launched an invasion of Cambodia and overthrew the Pol Pot regime. In 1979 the Vietnamese assumed de facto control of Cambodia and installed a new government led by two former Khmer Rouge officers, Hun Sen and Heng Samrin, both of whom had defected to Vietnam earlier. The official account, however, is that the new government of Hun Sen and Heng Samrin came to power through a revolutionary uprising in Cambodia against the Pol Pot regime. Hun Sen served as foreign minister from 1979 to 1984 and as prime minister from 1985 to 1993, while Heng Samrin served as president of the Council of State from 1979 to 1993. The Vietnamese invasion resulted in widespread destruction of rice crops, which led to famine. The United Nations launched a famine-relief effort in 1979.

In June 1982 Sihanouk agreed to head a military and political group opposed to the Hun Sen and Heng Samrin government and its Vietnamese backers. This opposition group consisted of a coalition of three main groups: the FUNCINPEC (the French acronym for the Cambodian National Front for an Independent, Neutral, Peaceful, and Cooperative Cambodia), which was a royalist group loyal to Sihanouk; the Khmer People's National Liberation Front, a noncommunist group; and the Khmer Rouge (also known as the

Party of Democratic Kampuchea), which was the most powerful of the three. Together these three opposing factions, led by the Khmer Rouge, engaged in guerrilla warfare in order to destabilize the government of Hun Sen and Heng Samrin, called the State of Cambodia (SOC). The political arm of the SOC is the Cambodian People's Party (CPP).

In 1985 Vietnamese forces attacked all the major rebel forces in Cambodia. As a result, the Khmer Rouge and its allies were forced to retreat to Thailand. Since then the Khmer Rouge has bombed villages, planted thousands of mines throughout Cambodia, destroyed roads and infrastructure, and kidnapped and murdered Cambodian local officials. For much of the 1980s, Thailand supported the Khmer Rouge, for the Thai government saw the guerrillas as a counterweight to Vietnamese power in the region. The Khmer Rouge also received smaller levels of assistance from Malaysia, Singapore, and indirectly, the United States. This aid enabled them to become, over time, a strong military force. U.S. support was directed toward the noncommunist factions of the opposition coalition mentioned above, but this coalition is dominated by the Khmer Rouge, allowing them control over the resources.

In 1989 Vietnam announced that it would withdraw its troops from Cambodia in response to international political and economic pressures. Nevertheless, some Vietnamese soldiers disguised as Cambodians remained for another year. The Khmer Rouge viewed this withdrawal as an opportunity to regain control and increased their attacks on their fellow Cambodians. In 1990 the Phnom Penh government and the three factions of the opposition accepted a United Nations Security Council plan that established a Supreme National Council comprised of six government officials and six opposition representatives, all under the leadership of Sihanouk. The council was intended to ensure the sovereignty of Cambodia. In turn, the council permitted a United Nations–transition government to manage key areas of foreign affairs, defense, internal security, finance, and administration. The plan was implemented in late 1991 and U.N. personnel arrived in 1992. The general aim of the plan has been to monitor a cease-fire and to repatriate hundreds of thousands of Cambodian refugees living in camps in Thailand. Free elections were conducted in May 1993. For Cambodians, the U.N. presence and elections were believed to be the only way to rid the country of the Khmer Rouge. However, the Khmer Rouge forces have continued to wreak sporadic havoc on the country.

As the winners of the May 1993 election, FUNCINPEC (the royalist party) headed by Prince Norodom Ranariddh, the son of Prince Norodom Sihanouk, attempted to create a coalition with the SOC government under Hun Sen. This temporary coalition ended in September 1993 when the two major political parties, the FUNCINPEC and the People's party, agreed that Prince Norodom Ranariddh would become the civilian leader as first prime minister and that his father, Prince Sihanouk, would once again become king, with Hun Sen of the SOC serving as second prime minister. Even now the SOC, with the CPP as their political arm, wields a great deal of influence over the military, ensuring that the role of Hun Sen will continue to be important.

In July 1994 a failed coup attempt by Prince Norodom Chakrapong and former interior minister Sin Song had no significant impact on the economic stability of the country. Several days later the Cambodian Parliament voted to outlaw the Khmer Rouge. Nevertheless, the Khmer Rouge and its powerful military force remain a significant threat. Reports in the late 1980s and early 1990s indicated that Thailand continues to support the Khmer Rouge. Public disclosure of this information forced the Thai government to reduce military support for the Khmer Rouge. Even after the 1993 election, the Khmer Rouge continued to wage guerrilla warfare in the countryside. There is periodic evidence of collaboration between the Khmer Rouge and the Cambodian military, which remains engaged in widespread banditry and mafia-like enterprises. Despite the chaotic environment, business interests between Cambodia and its neighbors are expected to help solidify international support for the government.

Since at least the sixteenth century Cambodia was called Kampuchea (also Kambuja) by the Khmers. "Cambodia" is the English version of the Portuguese word, *Camboxa*, and the French word, *Cambodge*, both of which are adaptations of "Kambuja." Since independence in 1953, the country has had six different names in English: the Kingdom of Cambodia (1953–1970), the Khmer Republic (1970–1975), Democratic Kampuchea (1975–1979), the People's Republic of Kampuchea (1979–1989), the State of Cambodia (1989–1993), and the Kingdom of Cambodia (1993 to the present). The Khmer Rouge insists that foreigners refer to the country as "Kampuchea." The decision to change the name back to Cambodia was an effort by the government to distance itself from the unpopular and brutal legacy of the Khmer Rouge.

Political Structure

Until 1993, the Cambodian political system was based on traditional communist systems. The new liberal constitution, written in late 1993, provides for a constitutional monarchy, but is plagued with contradictions and may not survive the test of time. The constitution provides for a liberal democratic system in which there are three separate, but not equal, branches of government: executive, legislative, and judicial. Technically, there is a dual structure, with a constitutional monarchy similar to that in Sweden or Belgium, and a legislature based on the American system.

The government has retained aspects of the previous communist system in which power is decentralized by province and the local leader has total authority. This is now combined with an executive and legislative rule, but primarily only in the capital, Phnom Penh. According to the constitution, the legislature has the ultimate power and is responsible for passing laws. The executive office and its ministries are responsible for drafting laws, which are then submitted to the legislature for approval. However, the true power rests with the powerbrokers of the coalition parties.

The Committee of the Throne, headed by Chea Sim, a communist hardliner, is responsible for selecting the king. In Cambodian history, there have been two principal lineages of the royal family, Norodom and Sisowath. For the past fifty years, the Norodom line has dominated the royal family.

The judicial system is still under development and remains nonfunctional. Foreign aid programs have set the judicial system as a priority.

Economy

Cambodia's economy is in shambles as a result of decades of war and widespread destruction. Further, much of the educated population was murdered by the Khmer Rouge under Pol Pot, providing few native human resources for the rebuilding efforts.

In the late 1980s private enterprise and free-market concepts were promoted over socialist principles. It has been suggested that today more than 70 percent of Cambodia's businesses are in private hands again. There is less state intervention in the economy than in some neighboring countries. However, the decentralized system has fueled massive corruption and inhibited the government's ability to monitor development projects.

The United Nations presence has had a significant inflationary effect on the economy because U.N. wages far exceeded local wage levels. U.N. aid has focused on rebuilding basic infrastructure and services. Nevertheless, the country is still faced with inadequate roads, water supply systems, power, and telecommunications. Until recently, most of the government's financial resources were dedicated to defense. The government elected in 1993 has been relatively successful in curbing inflation, increasing tax revenues, and stabilizing the currency. Its goals are to rebuild and improve the country's infrastructure, open the economy, spur growth, and eliminate corruption. In August 1994 the government passed more liberal investment laws designed to encourage foreign investment. However, without political stability, Cambodia is unlikely to attract significant foreign business interests.

Removal of the land mines will remain a major issue for the rebuilding of the country's economy since many are planted in rich agricultural areas. The cost of removing the mines is prohibitively high, resulting in government inaction.

Cambodia's major exports include fish, pepper, gems, forest products, and rubber. The country is self-sufficient in rice production. The gems are found primarily in Khmer Rouge–controlled territory, and accordingly their sale mainly benefits the rebels. More than 80 percent of the population is employed in agriculture.

People, Values, and Social Customs

The population of Cambodia is approximately eight or nine million. About 90 percent of the population is ethnic Khmer, with the remainder split between ethnic Vietnamese, Chinese, and Chams. The Khmers are indigenous to Cambodia and have inhabited the land for almost two thousand years. The concept of Cambodian citizenship is equated with ethnic Khmer identity. Other ethnic groups, including Vietnamese, Chinese, and Burmese, are not entitled to the full rights of Cambodian citizenship even though their families may have lived in Cambodia for several generations. The Khmers generally have a feeling of cultural superiority.

Cambodian culture is heavily influenced by Indian culture, particularly in the areas of social classes, religious rituals, art, and literature. During the centuries of Indian influence, the society was divided into three classes: royalty, scholar-officials, and peasants. To some extent these distinctions remain, with the urban elite now taking the place formerly held by the scholar-official class.

The Vietnamese and the Chinese are often viewed suspiciously by Cambodians, due to years of aggression by both countries. Anti-Vietnamese feeling has dropped because many have returned to

Vietnam to pursue economic opportunity there. As a result of centuries of interaction, there has been significant cultural give and take between Thailand and Cambodia. This is in contrast to Vietnam, with which Cambodia has little in common. For centuries, Vietnam looked to China for political, religious, and cultural influences, but Cambodia was first oriented first toward India and later toward Thailand. Cambodian attitudes toward the United States tend to be positive. However, members of the Khmer Rouge perceive the United States as their archenemy.

The major religions are Buddhism, Hinduism, and Islam. Between 1975 and 1979, a majority of the country's Buddhist monks were murdered by the Khmer Rouge. By the late 1980s, however, Buddhism was reinstalled as the state religion. Hinduism was a major religion in the country from the first to the fourteenth century. The Cham Muslims are descendants of the Cham population who migrated from Vietnam after the final defeat of the Champa kingdom by the Vietnamese in 1471.

The national religion is Thervada Buddhism, which stresses passivity and provides the foundation for the social fabric of the country. In rural areas Buddhism has merged over the centuries with animistic practices and Hindu beliefs and rituals. As a result, Cambodia's brand of Buddhism does not promote collective social responsibility. Instead, it teaches that individuals are responsible for their own lives and actions. The Hindu belief in a predestined fate has provided Cambodians with little incentive to take action to improve their economic and social position. Decades of communist policy have also contributed to the general lack of initiative among the people today.

During the centuries of Hindu influence, god-kings were the source of all political and moral authority and held absolute power. Historically, the Buddhist concept of political authority was also based on the premise that given human imperfection, kings were needed to maintain social order. As a result, the relationship between kings and Buddhism was reciprocal with each legitimizing the other's power, creating an integrated religious-political state. In modern times, Buddhism has been used by every ruler including Pol Pot to legitimize their political control. Accordingly, loyalty to the Cambodian nation has come to be equated with loyalty to the government in power.

Cambodians are still shocked by their country's recent history and the extent of the widespread destruction and suffering. Fear and suspicion often affect interactions. Nevertheless, they are generally warm, welcoming, and tolerant. Cambodians remain friendly and will go out of their way to help if you ask for assistance. Be sensitive in the topics you discuss with Cambodians. Historically, Cambodians have often turned to external powers to rescue them from their troubles. As a result, Cambodians have initially welcomed foreigners, but then become deeply disillusioned when these foreigners exploit them. The next "rescuers" are assumed to be international business interests. This pattern is already becoming evident in the country's relations with Thailand. There is a small backlash developing against Thailand's aggressive investment program, which has focused mainly on national resource extraction and tourism and not on developing Cambodia's infrastructure. However, Cambodians believe that the presence of Western visitors symbolizes that life is getting better. Most Cambodians consider themselves special survivors of the country's recent history and are resilient in attitude. Endurance and perseverance are valued.

Cambodians can also be hard workers. They tend to view time and life in terms of seasons. While Cambodian society has high standards for moral behavior, it imposes few consequences for deviant behavior. Group harmony is highly valued. Maintaining personal and family honor is very important to Cambodians, even in their interactions with foreigners. As in most agrarian societies, family is at the center of all relationships. Respect is always given to elders and superiors, although this is changing slowly. Cambodian society remains very male-dominated. Women often manage the household budgets in addition to their childrearing and family responsibilities.

Cambodians smile in both positive and negative situations. A smile is often used to hide inner feelings and functions as both a means of self-defense and an expression of respect for others. Cambodians enjoy telling jokes and exchanging humorous anecdotes.

Work Schedule

Government offices are officially open Monday to Saturday from 7:00 or 7:30 A.M. to 5:30 P.M. However, few Cambodians work that early or that late. Most people leave their workplace by 4:00 or 4:30 P.M. The lunchbreak and siesta are from 11:00 or 11:30 A.M. to about 2:00 or 2:30 P.M. Private businesses and shops generally follow the same schedule, although some shops may remain open longer.

Making Contacts

Connections are an important aspect of Cambodian life. You should try to find someone to introduce you before attempting to make contact with the government or a company. Begin with the diplomatic and trade missions in your home country, if there are any. Another option is to locate former Cambodians who have emigrated, but may still be connected to their home country, professionally and personally. Well-known foreign companies are less likely to need introductions. Once you establish a presence in Cambodia, local representatives or partners are needed to keep your business interests alive and conduct business on your behalf. In general, Cambodians welcome foreign businesspeople. They are eager to become part of the regional economic boom. Most of the current business interests in the country tend to be large consortiums dominated by Southeast Asian enterprises focusing on infrastructure projects.

Communicating with people in Cambodia is frustrating because postal services are slow. Fax services are uncommon and are so prohibitively expensive that you may not receive responses. Be patient and sensitive in your interactions. It might be advisable to diplomatically offer to pay the fax and other communications expenses of your contacts and local counterpart or agent in order to increase communication frequency. When you are in Cambodia, you will need to hire an interpreter who can also function as your guide.

Only the senior officials have authority. As a result, you should try to meet with the senior-most person possible. If your project is a large one, it is advisable to meet with the government minister first, who will then direct you to those people positioned to carry out the mechanics of the deal. If you are dealing with senior-level officials who are Western-educated, their attitudes and responses may be somewhat more predictable and familiar.

Meeting People

Cambodians traditionally greet each other by placing their hands with the palms facing together in front of their chests and bowing slightly. For those familiar with India, this is similar to the *namaste*. In modern times, men usually shake hands, although women exchange the traditional greeting. Foreigners should shake hands with both men and women, but should wait until the woman offers her hand before extending their own.

In both business and social settings certain physical gestures are considered impolite. It is impolite to show the soles of your feet or to point a finger at someone. To beckon someone always use your whole hand with the palm facing downward and the fingers pointing away, but motioning toward you. Do not beckon with just your index finger or with your palm facing upward; these gestures are sexually suggestive. Do not pat anyone on the head, including children, for the head is considered sacred and spiritual.

In formal situations, you may address people by *Lok* ("Mr.") or *Lok Srey* ("Mrs.") and the family name. This greeting conveys respect and formality. It is also appropriate to use "Mr." or "Mrs." and the first name. Royalty should be addressed as "Your Highness" or "Your Majesty." You will note that Cambodians, in informal situations, will refer to an older man as *Bang* and to an older woman is *Bang Srey*. These terms indicate the privileged position of a senior person over a junior person.

Begin meetings with some casual conversation on topics such as your travels or your positive impressions of the country. Be careful about what you say and to whom you say it. Private citizens often act as informants. However, if you served in the Vietnam War or were stationed in the area, it may be to your benefit to mention your experience in the region. There is currently a significant U.S. military contingent in Cambodia to train the royal army. Always be polite in your social and professional interactions. Gifts are not required for initial meetings. If you prefer, present some samples of your products or an inexpensive but tasteful item with your corporate logo. If you are meeting with a member of the royal family, a gift is appropriate. Elegant handicrafts or souvenirs are suitable. Consult your local partner or representative for guidance.

Corporate Structure

Historically, Cambodians have not been very business-oriented or entrepreneurial. In traditional Asian society, merchants and businesspeople were not considered valuable members of society. Most modern Cambodian businesses are public entities, but usually operate like private concerns. Each province is governed by a local political leader who functions as a economic warlord. Patronage for family and friends is almost a requirement in order to remain in power. As a result, bribery is a way of life for Cambodians. Corruption is widespread, particularly in the public sector.

The private sector has been influenced by French corporate structures. The management hierarchy is usually headed by the director general, followed by the general manager, and the managers. On occasion, a president ranks at the top above the director general.

Traditionally, before a foreign entity was able to launch any enterprise, it was necessary to obtain the king's permission. However, as of the time of writing this book, the king was dying and it is difficult to predict the extent of power of the next king.

As a consequence of the Khmer Rouge's regime, there are virtually no older Cambodians with advanced training in the fields of business, medicine, law, engineering, or education. Members of Cambodia's educated class were either killed off or fled the country during the Khmer Rouge rule.

There are virtually no women with responsible roles in the government. However, most small businesses and individual proprietorships are staffed by women. The NGO (nongovernmental organizations) community is providing more women with increasing responsibilities.

Negotiation

Cambodians residing in the cities are less willing to trust each other. In the villages, family histories result in a network of trusting relationships. Recent history has made people more suspicious of one another. However, once they trust you, Cambodians tend to be loyal and valuable friends. As is the case in most developing countries, foreigners who show an interest in developing long-term relationships will fare the best. Incorporating a training element for local employees into any contract will be popular because the government is focused on developing the skills of its labor force.

Decision-making is concentrated at the very top, with only one or two real decision-makers. In general, Cambodians tend to be reluctant to make decisions and defer to their superiors. Cambodians tend to rely on intuition rather than extensive research when making decisions. Research-gathering efforts are often just a formality. At times, decisions will be made relatively quickly if the Cambodians perceive that a delay will lead to a loss of opportunity. Cambodians are not risk-oriented and may express concern about deviating from their perceived norms. They are not efficient or timely in their work.

There is very little accountability; few people will assume individual responsibility for their actions. More powerful individuals are relied upon to make decisions and resolve conflicts. If a situation cannot be resolved easily, the Cambodian often withdraws completely. In all interactions saving face is critical for all parties involved. Cambodians are reluctant to say "No" outright, as it is considered impolite. They may say things like, "I would like to, but. . . ." A "Yes" can mean either "Yes, I am listening," or "Yes, I understand," or "Yes, it is acceptable."

Showing anger is also considered impolite and will reflect poorly on you. Excessive emotions indicate a lack of self-control. Maintaining harmony and self-discipline are important characteristics. Indicate your feelings or intentions indirectly, for example, through a tone of voice. Foreigners should refrain from being pushy or too forward.

Cambodia has no real body of corporate law. Leftover French laws and accounting systems further complicate business dealings. Foreign companies should try to use a foreign court or arbitration system as the governing basis for any agreement. Cambodians view contracts as flexible; they are considered the starting point of a relationship and may need to be fine-tuned as circumstances change.

Conducting Business in a Social Setting

Dining and Drinking

Cambodians enjoy food and dining. Business lunches are becoming popular as a way to develop relationships. Hotel restaurants and bars are appropriate for business meals.

Visiting a Home

Cambodians are traditionally very hospitable. Most people remove their shoes when entering a home (or a holy place). In traditional homes, Cambodians sit on mats on the floor when eating. Men sit in the lotus position and women sit with their feet to one side. Western-educated Cambodians may be more European in style and attitude. A gift should be taken when visiting a home.

Gift Giving

Graft and corruption, in the form of monetary bribes, has long been an integral part of Cambodian life but the government is making attempts to curtail the corruption. Set a global policy and adhere to it. International companies do not need to engage in graft to succeed in doing business in Cambodia.

In a normal business context, small gifts are always appreciated. Suitable gifts include items with corporate logos, fine chocolates, handicrafts, souvenirs from your home country, liquors, and nice pens. Gifts do not need to be expensive, just tasteful. Do not give cash. In many companies, gifts are given to employees at New Years.

Dress Code

For both men and women, conservative clothing and colors are best. Western clothes are common, particularly in the cities. For men, shirts and ties are acceptable. For women, conservative dresses, suits, or skirts and blouses are suitable. In private homes, men and women wear sarongs. White is the funeral or death color.

Useful Phrases

The official language is Khmer. In recent history, many educated Cambodians spoke French, which is still spoken by the older generations and those in government. English is gaining widespread popularity. Khmer can be a difficult and confusing language. There are thirty-three consonants and twenty-six vowels. The pronunciation of a vowel depends on the type of consonant preceding it.

Consonants at the end of words are barely pronounced and are almost dropped. The final "r" often written at the end of words is silent. For example, Angkor is pronounced "Angkoh."

The French have been aggressive in their attempts to revive their connection in Cambodia. French is taught in the schools and businesspeople are beginning to use the language more often. The younger generation is determined, however, to learn English. The following list includes useful phrases, and indicates how they would be pronounced in Khmer:

Hello	*Sua sday*
Good morning	*Agrum sua sday*
Good afternoon	*Sayoan sua sday*
Good evening	*Riatray sua sday*
How are you?	*Naq sok sapbaay cia tee?*
Please	*Soom*
Thank you	*Ar kun*
You are welcome	*Soom svaakum*
Excuse me	*Soom tooh*
I am sorry	*Knom soom a'phey tooh*
My name is ———	*Knom cmaah*
I work for ———	*Knom tvaa kaa daambay*
Here is my business card	*Nih qaa ban kaanie rabah knom*
I am pleased to meet you	*Knom riik riey dael baan cuab naq*
Please accept this small gift	*Soom tatual voattho anuhsaavarii daa tooc nih*
I look forward to developing a good relationship with you / your firm	*Knom sankhim thaa nin paanriin tumnaq tunman cia muay naq*
I understand	*Knom yaal*
No, I do not understand	*Tee knom min yaal tee*
Please wait a minute	*Soom run caam bantac*
Where is the bathroom?	*Taa bantub tak niv eae na?*
Good-bye	*Laa haay*
Cheers	*Aba saa to*

Major Holidays

January 7	National Day (commemorating the Vietnamese overthrow of Pol Pot)

January/February*	Tet (Vietnamese and Chinese New Year)
February 18	Anniversary of Friendship Treaty between Cambodia and Vietnam
April*	Cambodian New Year (three days)
April 17	Victory Day (Revolution Day)
April*	Visak Bauchea (birth of Buddha)
May 1	May Day
May*	Chrat Prea Angkal (ceremonial beginning of sowing season)
May 9	Genocide Day (memorial for Khmer Rouge atrocities)
June 19	Anniversary of founding of Revolutionary Forces of Kampuchea
June 28	Anniversary of founding of People's Revolutionary Party of Cambodia
September*	Prachum Ben (offerings to spirits of ancestors)
October/November*	Festival of the Reversing Current (Water Festival)
December 2	Anniversary of founding of the Front for National Reconstruction

General Facts

Climate: There are two major monsoon periods in Cambodia. The heavy rains occur between May and October. A dry monsoon, which occurs between November and March, is characterized by light rains and winds. The rain usually appears in the afternoons. April is the hottest month, with temperatures reaching as high as 110F (43C). January is the coolest month, with the average temperature around 81F (27C).

Currency: The currency of Cambodia is the *riel* (abbreviated as r and written after the amount). Travelers are not allowed to take *riels* into and out of the country. Further, a black market exists with a higher exchange rate. Gold is sometimes used for larger transactions. When

---

*These holidays are based on the lunar calendar and vary from year to year.

the Khmer Rouge came into power in 1975, they abolished the currency and destroyed the National Bank building. New *riel* notes were issued in 1980. U.S. dollars and Thai *baht* are widely accepted; travelers checks issued by American Express, Barclays, Citicorp, Thomas Cook, and Visa can be exchanged. Credit cards are not widely used. It is best to carry cash, as you will often be charged tourist prices quoted in U.S. dollars for accommodations and basic services.

Dates: Dates are abbreviated in the order of the day, month, and year. For example, April 25, 1995, would be written 25/4/95.

Electricity: The voltage is 220, 50 hertz, throughout most of the country. In many towns, electricity is only available during the evening hours. It is advisable to travel with a flashlight because power outages occur often.

Entry Requirements: A valid passport and visa is required for entry. Cambodia has diplomatic and consular relations with about twenty countries. Visas for Cambodia may be obtained in Bangkok, Hanoi, Saigon, Vientiane, Paris, and Moscow. Visas are often easily obtained upon arrival at Pochentong Airport in Phnom Penh. Some travel agencies in Bangkok, Hong Kong, and Singapore also provide visas for a premium price. If you will be in Vietnam or Laos prior to your trip to Cambodia, the consular offices in these countries will be able to give you a visa. Visa extensions may be obtained from the Foreign Ministry in Cambodia.

In Laos, the embassy is located at Thanon Saphan Thong Neua in Vientiane (Tel.: 2750 / 4527). The embassy in Vietnam is located in Hanoi at 71 Tran Hung Dao Street (Tel.: 253788 / 9). The Consulate office in Vietnam is in Saigon and is located at 41 Phung Khac Khoan Street (Tel.: 292751 / 2)

Time: Cambodia has one time zone, which is seven hours ahead of Greenwich Mean Time and twelve hours ahead of U.S. Eastern Standard Time (eleven hours in Daylight Savings Time).

Tipping: Tipping is not expected, but is appreciated as most Cambodians have a limited income. Sometimes a 10 percent service charge is already added to a hotel or restaurant bill.

Transportation: Direct flights into Phnom Penh originate in only a few foreign cities, including Bangkok, Singapore, Kuala Lumpur, Jakarta, Saigon, Hanoi, Vientiane, and Moscow, and often occur only on select days. Visitors may also enter Cambodia by bus or car from Vietnam or Thailand. Trains operate only within Cambodia. However, for security reasons, it is not advisable to travel by bus, train, or car. Travel within Cambodia can be treacherous due to the numerous land mines planted throughout the countryside by the Khmer Rouge and government forces over the years of fighting. Further, in addition to the damages caused by war, the road network is relatively poor and does not extend into many parts of the country.

In Phnom Penh, you will need to hire a car and driver to get around as taxis are nonexistent. Cyclos, called *samlors*, are also a convenient and inexpensive method of getting around Phnom Penh. However, a car and driver is the most advisable method.

Helpful Telephone Numbers

The telephone system is relatively poor, although it is rapidly improving. Telephone calls can be expensive, particularly international calls. The country code for Cambodia is (855) and the city code for Phnom Penh is (23).

Hospitals: The medical facilities in Cambodia are not sterile and there are shortages of medicines and equipment. Further, many of the country's doctors were killed by the Khmer Rouge. Prior to your arrival, make contingency plans to transport you to a nearby country, such as Singapore, Thailand, or even Vietnam, in the event of a medical emergency. Carry basic medical supplies and medicines with you at all times. If you need emergency assistance, seek out a foreign aid office or worker. Ambulances and emergency services are uncommon. The best advice is to have major medical insurance with provisions for evacuation in a medical emergency. Khmer-Soviet Hospital is considered the best hospital in Phnom Penh. The Revolution Hospital is located on Achar Mean at 80 Street in Phnom Penh.

Useful Addresses

In Cambodia:

Foreign Ministry
240 Street (on the western side of Quai Karl Marx)
Phnom Penh
Tel.: (23) 24641 / 23241 / 24441

Ministry of Information and Culture
180 Street (opposite 395 Achar Mean Blvd.)
Phnom Penh
Tel.: (23) 24769

Ministry of Tourism
232 Street (across from 447 Achar Mean Blvd.)
Phnom Penh
Tel.: (23) 22107

Phnom Penh Tourism Office
313 Quai Karl Marx
Phnom Penh
Tel.: (23) 23949 / 25349 / 24059

Embassies:

American Embassy
27 EO Street 240
Phnom Penh
Tel.: (23) 26436

British Mission
29 Street 75
Phnom Penh
Tel.: (23) 27124

Canadian Embassy
c/o The Australian Embassy
Villa II, Street 254
Chartaumuk, Daun Penh District
Phnom Penh
Tel.: (23) 26000 / 1

French Embassy
3 Rue 57 Bang Keng Kang 1
Phnom Penh
Tel.: (23) 27110

German Embassy
Sangkat, Boeung Pralit, Khan 7 Janvier
Phnom Penh
Tel.: (23) 26381

In Canada:

There are no Cambodian diplomatic offices in Canada.

In France:

Embassy of the Kingdom of Cambodia
11 Avenue Charles Floquet
75007 Paris
Tel.: (1) 4065-0470

In Germany:

There are no Cambodian diplomatic offices in Germany, although one is expected to open in 1995.

In the United Kingdom:

There are no Cambodian diplomatic offices in the United Kingdom, although one is expected to open in 1995.

In the United States:

There are no Cambodian diplomatic offices in the United States, although one is expected to open in 1995.

Cambodian Mission to the United Nations
866 U.N. Plaza, Suite 420
New York, NY 10017
Tel.: (212) 421-7626

U.S. Department of Commerce
International Trade Administration
Cambodia Desk, Room 2036
14th & Constitution Avenues, N.W.
Washington, DC 20230
Tel.: (202) 482-4958

The Cambodia Campaign
(more formally known as the Campaign to Oppose the Return of the Khmer Rouge [CORKR]) in Washington, DC, is a valuable resource. The Cambodia Campaign, an international network of nonprofit organizations working together to promote a better future for the Cambodian people, has extensive information about political, economic, and social issues. You can contact the CORKR at 100

Maryland Avenue, N. E.
Suite 303
Washington, DC 20002
Tel.:(202) 544-8446

20 Laos _____

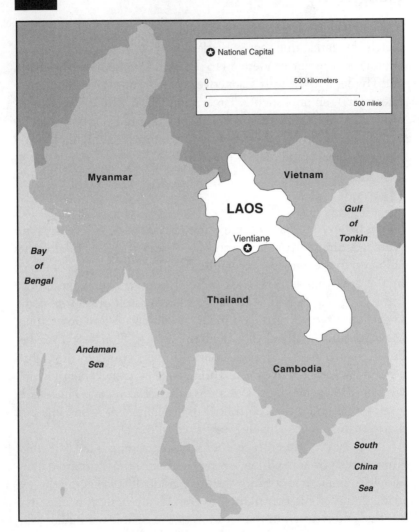

National Capital

0   500 kilometers

0   500 miles

Myanmar

Vietnam

LAOS

Vientiane

Gulf
of
Tonkin

Bay
of
Bengal

Thailand

Andaman
Sea

Cambodia

South

China

Sea

Geography

The Lao People's Democratic Republic, or Laos, is surrounded completely by land and shares borders with China and Myanmar (Burma) to the north, Vietnam to the east, Cambodia to the south, and Thailand to the west. Laos covers 91,430 miles (236,800 square kilometers), an area slightly larger than Great Britain. The country's two main features are its rivers and mountains. More than 70 percent of the land is covered with mountain ranges, highlands, and plateaus. The capital of Laos is Vientiane.

History

Laos is believed to have been inhabited as far back as ten thousand years ago. Similar to Vietnam and Cambodia, the early inhabitants belonged to the Austro-Thai family. The Thai-Kadai, predominant in the area that is now Laos, were the most significant ethnolinguistic group in Southeast Asia and, as a result of their periodic migrations, settled parts of India, Myanmar, Vietnam, China, Malaysia, and Thailand. The modern Lao and Thai people are believed to have migrated south from China beginning in the eighth century A.D. and to have formed principalities, called *muang*, which were headed by hereditary chieftains called *chao muang*. These early groups were under the control of either Khmers or Mons, the two major ethnic groups already established in the region.

In the mid-thirteenth century A.D., the Mongols led by Kublai Khan seized power in China, a dynastic change that prompted more people to migrate south into the area, gradually displacing the existing groups. This contributed to the Thai rebellion against the Khmers and resulted in the creation of the Sukhothai kingdom in what is today northern Thailand. The Thai king and chieftains loyal to him formed the Lan Na Thai (Million Thai Rice Fields) kingdom, also known as Lanna, which extended across north-central Thailand. In the fourteenth century Fa Ngum conquered most of northeastern Thailand and named the territories Lan Xang (Million Elephants).

Originally created as a Khmer empire, Lan Xang is considered by many to be the foundation of the Laotian nation. Buddhism became the state religion and the Pha Bang, a large gold Buddha image, became a talismanic symbol for the sovereignty of the Lao kingdom. Although Lan Xang was a large and powerful kingdom and a thriving regional trading center, it was unable to conquer the highland mountain tribes. Phaya Samsenthai, who succeeded Fa Ngum in 1373, had a significant influence on the country. He is credited with reorganizing the royal administration, building temples and schools, and developing the economy.

In 1571 the monarch, King Settathirath, disappeared and the kingdom began to decline until it was revived by King Suliya Vongsa in 1637. The next sixty years are considered a "golden age" because this king ruled longer than any other monarch and expanded the country's frontiers. Upon his death in 1694, a three-way struggle for the throne ensued, eventually leading to the fragmentation of Lan Xang into three separate kingdoms. This separation lasted almost eighty years until the kingdom of Siam began to exert influence over the area. By the end of the 1800s, Siam controlled the entire region. In the mid-1800s the French, who were active in neighboring Vietnam, persuaded the king of Luang Phabang, a northern province, to accept French protection against the Siamese and Chinese Ho bandits. Through a succession of treaties, the Siamese relinquished control of their territory east of the Mekong River, but kept the area west of it.

The French united all the remaining Lao principalities into one nation and named it Laos, which is the French plural for "Lao." For the French, Laos served primarily as a buffer between French-controlled Vietnam, British-controlled Burma, and British-influenced Thailand. The French did not build any infrastructure, such as schools, roads, or railroads, in their colony. Further, the French installed a Vietnamese-staffed, French-led civil service in

Laos, which stifled development and modernization, and whose influence is still evident in the modern Laotian government bureaucracy.

In 1941 the Japanese occupied all of French Indochina. There was little resistance from the people of Laos; they actually enjoyed more autonomy under Japanese than under French rule. Near the end of the war, the Japanese convinced King Sisavang Vong, who had been installed by and who was loyal to France, to declare independence from France. Prince Phetsarat, the prime minister, skeptical of the king's commitment to throwing off the French yoke, created a resistance movement called Lao Issara (Free Lao) to ensure that France would not regain control of the country. The French tried to reestablish their control in 1945 and declared Laos to be a French protectorate. However, Prince Phetsarat's party drafted a new constitution and proclaimed the country independent on October 12, 1945. When the king refused to sign the new document, he was deposed by the National Assembly, but was reinstated in April 1946 when he made his peace with the Lao Issara movement.

The French then invaded Laos with the aid of local Lao guerrilla forces, who called themselves "Free French," and thoroughly defeated the Lao Issara forces. Many of the independence movement's leaders fled to Thailand, where they established a government in exile. The period of renewed French rule was short; by 1949, Laos was declared an independent associate state of the French Union. Although recognized by the United Nations as a separate country, Laos was not given the status of a truly independent nation. During the negotiations with the French, the Lao Issara split into three factions. One faction, led by Prince Souphanouvong, joined forces with the Indochinese Communist party (ICP), which was headed by Ho Chi Minh in Vietnam. Together the two groups formed an anti-colonial resistance force, later known as the Pathet Lao (Lao People's Party), in the northeast part of Laos. Kaysone Phomvihane also became active on behalf of the ICP in the eastern mountain districts.

In 1953 France, preoccupied with holding on to Vietnam, sought to reduce its colonial burden and granted full sovereignty to Laos. From 1953 to 1954, Laos was a constitutional monarchy whose government was controlled by a French-educated elite. However, the Pathet Lao fought the new government in hopes of achieving communist liberation. Aided by Viet Minh forces from Vietnam, the Pathet Lao increased their efforts in the countryside and eventually established control over the northeastern provinces of Hua Phan and Phong Sali, effectively dividing the country. At that point, the United States began to fund the Lao government out of fear of the influence of the Viet Minh communists on Southeast Asia.

In 1957 the Lao Patriotic Front (LPF), the political arm of the Pathet Lao, reached a settlement with the royal Lao government and agreed to take part in a coalition government called the Government of National Union. In 1958 the LPF won thirteen of the twenty-one seats in the National Assembly elections, a victory that indicated widespread support for the communists. A right-wing reaction, fueled in part by the U.S. decision to withdraw all aid to Laos, led to the arrests of LPF ministers and deputies and to the fall of the Government of National Union. Phoui Sananikone was installed as prime minister by the government of Wieng Chan, which was effectively under the control of the Committee for the Defense of National Interests (CDNI), a right-wing political organization. However, the French-educated elite continued to run the government. With support from the North Vietnamese, the LPF returned to the countryside to continue organizing the resistance movement. The North Vietnamese used the sparsely populated eastern side of Laos as a supply route to the southern part of Vietnam, creating the "Ho Chi Minh Trail." The United States began to fund the Laotian government again to counter the influence of the North Vietnamese.

In 1960 a military coup d'état focused superpower attention on Laos and the possibility of a communist takeover of its government. In 1962, after two years of negotiations, another attempt to form a coalition government failed. In 1964 there were a series of coup d'états and countercoups. The Pathet Lao emerged on one side, with the neutralist and right-wing factions on the opposing side. By 1965, the Pathet Lao refused to participate in any more coalition governments, for they were convinced that they would never be given a true voice in governing the country.

From 1964 to 1973 the Vietnam War intensified. The United States secretly bombed Laos, particularly those areas that were strongholds of the Pathet Lao. A CIA-trained army, consisting primarily of Hmong tribesmen, was formed with Thai assistance to counter the influence of the Pathet Lao.

In 1973 a cease-fire agreement was reached in Laos and the country was divided into eleven Pathet Lao–controlled zones and two non–Pathet Lao zones. A coalition government was formed in April 1974 with royalist, neutralist, and LPF representations. The LPF quickly increased its power, and on May 4, 1975, several non–Pathet Lao ministers and generals were forced to resign. Many of the country's political and economic elite left Laos for exile in Thailand. In December 1975 the LPF abolished the monarchy and established the Lao People's Democratic Republic with the Lao People's Revolutionary party (LPRP) as the ruling party. Kaysone Phomvihane, supported by communist North Vietnamese, was made prime minister and retained that position until his death in 1992. King Savang Vatthana, initially a figurehead in the new government, was banished in 1977.

The LPRP implemented a policy of accelerated socialization similar to that promoted by the Vietnamese. The tendency to follow the Vietnamese on various policies resulted in a rapid contraction of the private sector and a shift to agricultural cooperatives. The influence of Buddhism as a state religion was also reduced. During the first two years of LPRP rule, thousands of refugees left Laos due to the harsh political and economic policies of the LPRP. At decade's end, almost 10 percent of the population had fled the country, mostly to Thailand. As a result of this mass emigration and general unrest, the government implemented some reforms to permit a degree of free enterprise and more liberal conditions. By the mid-1980s, the exodus had stopped. By the late 1980s, the government had abolished its "re-education camps," where former royalists and government officials had been sent as punishment and to force them to embrace communism. The decline of the former Soviet Union has had an effect on Laos and the government has since sought to introduce additional liberal economic and political policies. The first national elections were held in 1989 and a new constitution was adopted in 1991.

Political Structure

The Lao People's Democratic Republic was formed on December 2, 1975, and the country has been officially communist ever since. Its institutions and actions have been modeled after and influenced by the Vietnamese Communist party.

The central ruling political body is the Lao People's Revolutionary party (LPRP), which is elected by the Party Congress, which meets only once every four or five years to elect party leaders. The main power is held by the Politburo which officially makes all governmental policy decisions. Theoretically, members of the Politburo are selected by the Party Central Committee. In practice, the secretary-general of the Politburo, the Secretariat, and the Central Committee is usually the same person, ensuring the election of his candidates.

For seventeen years, Kaysone Phomvihane held the positions of prime minister, secretary-general of the Politburo and the Central Committee, and president of the LPRP. The current prime minister and chairman of the LPRP is General Khamtay Siphandone. The head of state is Nouhak Phoumsavan.

The government consists of the prime minister, deputy prime ministers, and ministers. The National Assembly is the legislative body, which has between forty and forty-five members. About two-thirds are from the LPRP; the Lao Front for National Construction, which was created in 1979 as a political cover for the Lao People's Party; and the

Alliance of Lao Patriotic Neutralist Forces. The remaining one-third of the members come from groups that are left-leaning. The National Assembly meets twice a year and has various on-paper powers, including the right to amend the constitution and to endorse or amend laws, but primarily serves to rubber-stamp the actions of the prime minister. The president, the head of state who is also the head of the armed forces, is elected by the National Assembly for a five-year term. Laos is divided into sixteen provinces and an independent prefecture for Vientiane.

The People's Supreme Court oversees the judicial system. During the past three years, new common, penal, foreign investment, property, and labor laws have been passed.

Economy

Agriculture dominates the economy and employs almost 85 percent of the population. Much of the remainder of the workforce is employed by the army or the civil service. Fishing and forestry are key segments of the agricultural sector; two-thirds of the land is covered with forests. The main crops include rice, corn, wheat, vegetables, tobacco, and coffee. The country also has rich mineral resources, including tin, lead, coal, potash, gypsum, iron ore, zinc, petroleum, gold, silver, and precious stones, many of which have yet to be fully exploited. The country also exports electricity, derived from hydroelectric power, to Thailand, providing significant foreign currency exchange.

There are relatively few manufacturing facilities in Laos; however, the country does have factories that produce beer, cigarettes, soft drinks, cement, and garments. The shortage of an educated and trained workforce will inhibit the expansion of the manufacturing sector in the near future.

In early 1987 the government began to liberalize the economy and moved toward creating a private-sector focus through its "New Economic Mechanism," which was designed to introduce market forces and to decentralize the economy. Laos has some of the most liberal foreign investment laws in all of Asia, allowing foreign investors to own up to 100 percent of enterprises in Laos. New roads are expected to create better links with neighboring countries and provide more trade opportunities. Foreign aid continues to be the single-most important contributor to the national budget.

In April 1994 the Friendship Bridge connecting Thailand and Laos was completed. The bridge is part of a land transport corridor from Singapore to Beijing and will eventually bring benefits to the Lao economy.

People, Values, and Social Customs

The population of Laos is approximately 4.2 million. Laos has been influenced by four key cultures: Lao, Hmong-Mien, Khmer, and Thai. These cultures are evident in the country's sixty-eight ethnic groups, which today are classified into three major categories: Lao Lum (55 percent), Lao Theung (27 percent), and Lao Sung (18 percent). These three classifications follow the increase in elevation from lowlands to highlands according to the original habitat of the various groups.

The Lao Lum are ethnic lowland Lao who speak Lao. An ethnic subgroup of the Thai peoples, they migrated throughout Southeast Asia, south China, and the northeastern part of the Indian subcontinent. This group adopted Theravada Buddhism as their preferred religion in the fifth century A.D. The Lao Theung are related to the Mon-Khmer peoples and reside in midland areas of Laos. With a history of serving as indentured servants for migrating Thai, this group continues to work as laborers for the Lao Sung, tribal groups living in the highlands. The Lao Sung are the most recent immigrants. They have moved within the last century into Laos from Burma, Tibet, and southern China. The tribal Thai, a Lao Thai subgroup of the Lao Lum, also tend to be highland dwellers and have generally resisted absorption into Lao society.

There are also groups of Chinese who have migrated to Laos over the centuries as merchants and traders, dominating private businesses up through today. In the past century, more Thai have come to the cities in Laos to pursue commercial opportunities, but not settled there permanently. North Indians and Pakistanis also reside in Laotian cities, working primarily in the garment industry. In addition, there are some pockets of Burmese, Bangladeshis, and Cambodians.

Most of the country (85 percent) follows Theravada Buddhism. Minorities in the highlands also practice animism and ancestral worship. Many Laotians also practice *phii* worship, which reveres guardian spirits, even though this form of worship is officially banned. Buddha images are considered sacred and should not be touched or photographed.

Historically, the country and its people have usually been economically dependent on external powers. These entities have included Thailand, Vietnam, Burma, France, the former Soviet Union, and the United States. This history of dependency has affected people's outlook, as they assume that outside forces will improve their political and economic situation. Dependency also fosters disillusionment, for the Laotians are periodically forced to realize that their "saviors" are self-interested and not really devoted to Laotian welfare.

The Laotians place a high value on loyalty to their extended family and friends. Living together as a multi-generational family is still very common. Only about 20 percent of the population lives in urban areas, where the nuclear-family system is becoming more common. Respect for elders is very important and maintaining social harmony is critical. The Laotian people learn at an early age to defer to those who are older or more senior in position. Although they are somewhat individualistic, the Laotians value harmonious group relations above all else.

In general, people smile frequently when they are happy, but also when they are sad. Facial expressions are not a reliable guide to true emotion. Foreigners should listen to what a person is saying in order to better understand and react to a situation.

Work Schedule

Most offices are open Monday to Friday from 8:00 A.M. to 5:00 P.M., with a two-hour lunch break from 12:00 to 2:00 P.M., when most places close down. On Saturdays, offices are open from 8:00 A.M. to noon. Shops are open during the same hours and either stay open for lunch or close for only one hour. Banks are open from 8:30 A.M. to 4:00 P.M., Monday to Friday.

Making Contacts

Laos is generally open to Westerners for business and investment. The commercial section of the Lao embassy, particularly in the United States, will be helpful and relatively prompt in assisting businesspeople who want to do business in Laos. In Laos itself, the National Chamber of Commerce can assist you in identifying and developing business relationships.

Foreigners can write to Laotian business interests without an introduction, but having one will smooth the way. Do not call a company until you have written first. You should direct your first communications to the president or manager. In most instances, you will receive a response directly from that person. On occasion, your communications may be directed to a more appropriate department or level for a response. Be wary of middlemen; they are not always necessary to develop a new business relationship. Once you have established a relationship with a Laotian concern and received some kind of commitment, you may want to hire a local agent to ensure that your business interests are being looked after.

There is still a close relationship between business and government, so you should develop and maintain contacts with both spheres. To develop relationships with government officials, write to them directly or utilize the Lao embassy in your home country for an introduction. Local partners can also assist you in developing and maintaining relationships with the government. As might be expected, government officials are oriented toward promoting infrastructure and development projects, as well as projects that include training and skills development for local employees. In your initial letter to government officials, stress the local benefits your business proposal will produce.

Meeting People

The best time to schedule an appointment is between 9:00 and 11:00 A.M. Avoid the midday lunch period. Punctuality is appreciated, but it is acceptable to be five or ten minutes late.

Most Laotians greet each other by using the *nop*, a traditional greeting in which both hands are placed together as in prayer at about chest level, but not touching the body. This is accompanied by a small bow of the head to show respect. This greeting is similar to the *namaste* performed in Indian cultures. The *nop* is used as a greeting upon arrival and departure, as well as an expression of thanks. The handshake is becoming more widespread and is used in most cities. Names are listed in Western style with the given (first) name followed by the family name. Laotians should be addressed by using a title, such as "Mr." or "Mrs.," and the first name. Always smile when greeting someone as the smile is considered one of the most important expressions. As a courtesy, you should always thank someone for meeting with you.

The first few minutes of a meeting should be spent discussing general topics such as your travels, the weather, or positive impressions of Laos. In general, you will find that the Laotian businessperson is interested in what you have to offer and will want to discuss specific business proposals. A gift is not usually given at a first meeting. If you have samples of your product or a small item with a company logo, you may present it, but it is not necessary. Be sure that the gift is not too expensive or elaborate, for it might embarrass your counterpart and create an obligation for him or her.

The Laotian people are warm and friendly and will try to accommodate foreigners. Laotian people are trustworthy and will over time extend their trust to foreigners. Language is a major barrier to building relationships because few Laotians speak English. You might want to consider hiring a translator.

When sitting with people from Laos, be careful not to offend them by pointing the soles of your shoes toward them. The feet are considered the least spiritual part of the body and should be kept flat on the floor. The head is considered the most spiritual part of the body, so refrain from touching it.

Corporate Structure

The typical corporate structure consists of president, managing director, manager, and staff. The president, along with the board of directors, sets the policies for the corporation. The president usually makes all the important decisions. Senior managers and executives tend to work longer hours than subordinates.

Some women hold positions of responsibility because they are generally considered as capable as men. Women tend to work in the textile and garment industries, as well as in medicine and education.

Negotiation

The Laotians are frank and sincere, but may initially appear cautious to foreigners. In private enterprises, decisions are made by the senior person and are frequently based on intuition. In public entities, decision-making is usually dependent on the opinions of a few key senior people. Some research is conducted, but more as a formality than as a foundation for decision-making. The Laotians are generally risk-averse and conservative in their approach.

Never allow any strong emotion, including anger, disappointment, or even excessive enthusiasm, to show. The Laotians value cool and calm personality characteristics. Never criticize a person publicly, as you will both lose face. Negative criticism should be made gently and should target a project or problem, not a person.

The Laotians have a very relaxed attitude toward most issues, particularly time. The general perception is that each moment should be enjoyed, with the focus on the present not on the future. A common Lao expression, *Bo pen nyang*, which means "never mind," is used in many situations. As a result, the Laotians tend to dismiss or discount problems, as they may upset the harmony and balance. If there is a problem, Laotians will often ignore it in hopes that it will go away. The Laotians do not say "No" directly and will usually make negative hints or just ignore a proposal they do not like.

The legal system remains undeveloped when compared to other Asian countries. Due to the recent vintage of the first legal code in 1988, there is little evidence to determine Laotian consistency in the enforcement of laws and regulations. Generally, written contracts are used and adhered to in all business relationships. Memorandums of Understandings (MOU) are a common way to document new relationships in the initial planning stages. Most Laotians view contracts as merely the foundation for a business relationship and, accordingly, make changes when necessary. Specific terms may need to be adjusted as circumstances change. Be sure to detail the terms so that there is less opportunity for confusion.

Conducting Business in a Social Setting

Dining and Drinking

Lunches and dinners are more common for doing business than breakfasts. Such meals are used as an opportunity to develop a personal relationship. Business can be discussed, but usually later in the meal. It is advisable to follow your counterpart's lead. The person who extends the invitation usually pays. In some instances, it may be advisable for the foreign businessperson to offer to pay because their Laotian associates may have limited resources.

Visiting a Home

Once a Laotian feels comfortable with you, he may invite you to his home for major occasions such as weddings, family parties, or the New Year. While it is not customary to bring gifts, small gestures will be appreciated. Do not bring anything expensive as this will only embarrass your host, for he may be unable to reciprocate. In traditional homes, remove your shoes before you enter. In general, most Laotians are very hospitable.

Gift Giving

Gift giving is not widespread. Inexpensive items with company logos or souvenirs and handicrafts from your home country are appreciated and acceptable. Gifts are not required at every meeting.

Dress Code

For men, business suits, safari suits, or a shirt and tie are appropriate. Women should wear dresses, suits, or a skirt and blouse.

Useful Phrases

The official language is Lao, a monosyllabic and tonal language. Accents and vocabularies differ throughout the country. All Lao dialects are members of the Thai half of the Thai-Kadai language family; thus standard Lao is very similar to standard Thai. As a result, most Lao understand Thai. French is a secondary language and is often used in government and in business. English is spoken, but mostly among the younger generation. Russian is also understood by many people. You should note that there is no "r" sound in spoken Lao and it should be pronounced as "l" or as "h." The following list contains some useful phrases and a guide to their pronunciation.

Hello	*Sabay dee*
Good morning	same as hello or *aloon sa-wat*
Good afternoon	same as hello
Good evening	same as hello or *la-tee sa-wat*
How are you?	*Than sabay dee baw*
Please	*Kaloona* (as a request); *sern* (as an invitation to do something)
Thank you	*Khawp chye*
You are welcome	*Baw pen nyang*
Excuse me	*Khaw thoat*
I am sorry	*Khoy siye chye* (only in the sense of being saddened, not as in excuse me)
My name is ———	*Khoy ser* ———
I work for ———	*Khoy het viek yoo*
Here is my business card	*An nee men bat nam khawng khoy*
I am pleased to meet you	*Khoy nyin dee thee dye phop kap than*
Please accept this small gift	*Khoy khaw mawp khawn khwan lek-lek noy-noy*
I look forward to developing a good relationship with you / your firm	*Khoy wang va cha dye sang sam-phan-tha-phap thee dee nam than / bawlisat khawng than*
I understand	*Khoy khao chye*
No, I do not understand	*Baw khoy baw khao chye*
Please wait a minute	*Kaloona tha sak noy nung*
Where is the bathroom?	*Hawng nam yoo sye*
Good-bye	*Khoy khaw la kawn*
Cheers	*Khaw uay sye*

Major Holidays

January 1	New Year's Day
January / February*	Chinese New Year / Tet
April 13–15	Lao New Year
May 1	Labor Day
December 2	National Day

*This holiday is based on the lunar calendar and accordingly the date changes annually.

General Facts

Climate: There are essentially three seasons, with variations throughout the country. The hot season is between February and May, with temperatures reaching 100F (38C). The heavy monsoon season lasts from June to October, with temperatures averaging 82F (28C). The cool season is from November to January, during which time temperatures can drop to 59F (15C) and below 32F (0C) in the mountains.

Currency: The currency is the *kip*. The U.S. dollar and the Thai *baht* are also widely used, particularly at hotels, restaurants, and shops in the cities.

Dates: Dates are abbreviated in the order of day, month, year. For example, August 21, 1995, would be written 21/8/95.

Electricity: The voltage is 220.

Entry Requirements: All foreigners are required to have a valid passport and a visa. Business visas are valid for one entry within three months from the date of issuance. Visas are usually issued for a one-month period and can be extended for another month.

Time: Laos has one time zone, which is seven hours ahead of Greenwich Mean Time and twelve hours ahead of U.S. Eastern Standard Time (eleven hours in Daylight Savings Time).

Tipping: Tipping is not customary, although small and kind gestures, such as a pack of cigarettes, will always be appreciated.

Transportation: The best way to get into Laos is by air into Wattay Airport in Vientiane. A few taxis are available at the airport for the short ten-minute drive into the city. In Vientiane, taxis are also available in front of major hotels. It is advisable and cheap to hire a private car and driver for the day. Your hotel can assist you. Three-wheeled motorcycle taxis, called *samlors*, are common in the cities. The bicycle *samlor* is common in large and small towns. When traveling between cities in Laos, it is best to go by air; roads are only marginally adequate and relatively undeveloped. The word, *thanon*, is the Lao equivalent of street, avenue and route.

Helpful Telephone Numbers

Telephones are available and international calls can be placed from hotels or from the International Telephone Office, which is always open. You can make all locals calls from your hotel. The country code is (856). The city code for Vientiane is (21).

Hospitals and Health Clinics: Whenever possible, you should go to Bangkok, Thailand, or another major city in the region for medical treatment as facilities in Laos are very poor.

Police: Dial 213901. Located on Thanon Setthathirat.

Fire: Dial 212708.

Operator / Telephone Office: Dial 178 or 179, for information, and 159 for the overseas operator.

Useful Addresses

In Laos:

Committee for Planning and Cooperation, Permanent Office for Foreign Investment
Luang Prabang Road
Vientiane
Tel.:(21) 217020 / 19

Lao National Chamber of Commerce and Industry
Phon Xay Road
P.O. Box 1163
Vientiane
Tel.:(21) 412392

Ministry of Industry and Handicrafts
Nong Bone Road
Vientiane
Tel.:(21) 413008 / 9 / 1

Ministry of Trade
Phon Xay Road
Vientiane
Tel.:(21) 412006 / 7

Embassies:

American Embassy
Thanon Bartolini
Vientiane
Tel.:(21) 212581 / 2 / 5

British Embassy (resident in Bangkok, Thailand)
Wireless Road
Bangkok, Thailand
Tel.:(66-2) 253-0191

Canadian Embassy (resident in Bangkok, Thailand)
Boonmitr Building
11th Floor
138 Silom Road
Bangkok 10500, Thailand
Tel.:(66-2) 237-4125

French Embassy
Setthathirath Street
Vientiane
Tel.:(21) 215259 / 215264

German Embassy
26 Sokpaluang Road
Vientiane
Tel.:(21) 314322 / 312110 / 312111

In Canada:

Chamber of Commerce of Laos
6420 Rue Victoria, No. 2
Montreal PQ H3W 2S7

In France:

Embassy of Laos
74 Avenue Raymond Poincarre
75016 Paris
Tel.:(1) 533-0298 / 704-2254

In Germany:

Embassy of Laos
1100 Berlin Esplanade 17
Berlin

In the United Kingdom:

There are no diplomatic or trade offices in the United Kingdom.

In the United States:

Embassy of Laos
2222 South Street, N.W.
Washington, DC 20008
Tel.:(202) 667-0088 / 332-6416

U.S. Department of Commerce
International Trade Administration
Laos Desk, Room 2036
14th & Constitution Avenues, N.W.
Washington, DC 20230
Tel.:(202) 482-4958

Appendix: Major Asian Religions

The following overview of the major religions discussed in this book will provide some insight as to their history and practice. In keeping with the book's focus on the social and business culture of each country, certain aspects of these religions are not discussed. Many of the Asian religions have numerous sects and divisions, as well as regional variations. The general summary offered here is not intended to be comprehensive and should be supplemented by to other sources.

Ancestor Worship

While ancestor worship differs in practice among countries and regions, there are some generalities about the Asian concept of ancestor worship. Ancestor worship is based on the premise that the natural and supernatural are connected as part of the same whole. This religious practice is based on the assumptions that people's souls live on and protect their descendants and that these descendants can communicate with their ancestors. The family, by worshipping the spirits of their ancestors, can expect to be repaid by the good fortune created by the activities of their ancestors in the afterworld.

People believe that upon death a person becomes a spirit, who still has the same needs as people on earth, including a home, clothing, food, and money. For all of these needs, the spirit relies on the still-living family. Therefore, when someone dies, the family will burn money and miniature paper houses. In modern times, more luxurious items have been added. The intention is to keep the spirits happy so that they do not wander around and cause harm. Further, it is believed that a soul with no descendants is doomed to eternal wandering because it will not receive the appropriate homage. Many homes have built-in wall shelves to house the ancestral tablets on which each ancestor's name and title is inscribed. Special periodic rituals are performed in the home and near the grave to honor the spirits. Ancestor's souls are believed to remain near their grave site and need to be acknowledged with regular rituals and offerings of food, currency, and other appropriate items.

Buddhism

There are three essential components or key jewels (*triratna*) that constitute the core of Buddhism: the Buddha, his teachings, and the Buddhist community. As a formal act of becoming a Buddhist, every Buddhist vows to take refuge in these three jewels and to engage in contemplation.

Buddhism, which preaches nonviolence and spiritual harmony, is said to have been founded by Siddhartha Gautama, a prince who lived in the sixth and fifth centuries B.C. in what is today northern India and southern Nepal. His followers referred to him as *Shakyamuni*, which means "sage of the Shakya clan." Shakyamuni was born a Hindu, a Kshatriya caste prince, but rejected the formal structured religion prescribed by the Hindu priest caste, the Brahmins. Gautama was frustrated by the misery in the world and Hinduism's inability to overcome it. Despite a luxury-filled upbringing, he abandoned palace life and the pleasures of the material world at the age of twenty-nine to search for an end to man's suffering. He became a homeless wanderer who sought the guidance of various ascetic teachers. Dissatisfied that he had not been able to attain spiritual liberation, he rejected the ascetic way and turned to meditation to seek salvation on his own. While meditating under a bodhi-tree at the age of thirty-five, he achieved illumination and discovered the path to complete enlightenment. *Buddha* is a title that means "enlightened one," hence Buddhism is considered to be the religion of the "enlightened one." Initially, the Buddha remained silent because he could not verbally convey his experience of enlightenment. However, at the request of others, he finally began to preach. He founded an order of monks and for the next forty-five years communicated his ideas. He died in 486 or 483 B.C. at the age of eighty.

Aspects of Buddhist philosophy had long been present in ancient Indian society, but were not formalized into a religion until Gautama, who is not believed to be the first or only Buddha. Sources differ on how many Buddhas existed before him; there may have been either four or six, as well as several other legendary Buddhas who are only noted in stories with no evidence of their existence. In any event, Shakyamuni is not expected to be the last Buddha.

Shakyamuni Buddha discovered four noble truths regarding the cycle of existence (*samsara*) and the possibility of being removed from this cycle, which was the main query of Indian philosophy at the time. "Removal" refers to achieving an inner peace and enlightened living, not necessarily a physical removal such as death.

The first truth was that all life is inherently imperfect, full of sorrow and suffering, and that true happiness can be achieved only by overcoming this suffering. The second truth is that the suffering-ridden quality of existence is caused by craving, desire, and ignorance. The third truth states that life's suffering and sorrow will cease once earthly desires are eliminated. The fourth truth states that the way to overcome suffering and earthly desires is by following an eightfold path of training, disciplined morality, and contemplation of *nirvana*, a condition beyond the limits of the mind and free of all material and earthly desires. Nirvana can be achieved only by those who overcome desire, hatred, and delusion.

However, unlike other Indian philosophies of the time, Buddhism did not advocate a life of strict abstinence. Buddha believed that there were two extremes to life. One extreme was an indulgent life given over to the pursuit of material pleasures and lusts; this kind of life was degrading, vulgar, unworthy, and useless. The other extreme was asceticism, a life given over to self-torture, which was painful, unworthy, and useless. Buddha guided followers to the

"Middle Path," which led to insight, wisdom, serenity, knowledge, enlightenment, and eventually to nirvana.

There is no central god figure in Buddhism. Instead, Buddhists believe that the ability to find spiritual enlightenment already lies within all people. They need to follow the Middle Path in order to achieve it. There are two kinds of Buddhas and both have achieved enlightenment; one chooses to teach others and the other does not.

Within one hundred years of Buddha's death, different Buddhist sects emerged. While they shared certain core beliefs, each sect had varying interpretations of the Buddha's teachings. Today, there are two major schools of Buddhism, Hinayana and Mahayana. Hinayana, also known as the Theravada school or the Indian version, has been in existence since the beginnings of Buddhism. It is considered closest to the original form of Buddhism as preached by Gautama. Emerging between the death of Buddha and the first century B.C., Hinayana is often called the southern school because it spread through Southeast Asia. Mahayana, which arose in the first century A.D., is also known as the northern school because it took hold in the north, mainly Nepal, Tibet, China, Korea, Mongolia, Vietnam, and Japan. There are several philosophical differences between the two sects.

The Theravada or Hinayana school believes that Gautama was the great teacher and the one-and-only enlightened one, but that he was not divine. In contrast, the Mahayana school believes that Gautama was only one of many mortal "enlightened ones" and that there are countless transcendent Buddhas. Because the Mahayana school built upon earlier teachings and expanded the doctrine to include more laypeople, while the Theravada school strictly preserves the principles outlined in the early Buddhist teachings, the Mahayana Buddhists adopted the name "Greater Vehicle," while derogatorily giving Theravada the name, "Lesser Vehicle." The Mahayana school believes that any layperson can achieve nirvana or enlightenment, whereas the Theravada school believes that only ordained monks and nuns can do so. Mahayana Buddhism preaches that the ideal Buddhist is the person who strives to perfect himself or herself by cultivating the necessary virtues—generosity, morality, patience, vigor, concentration, and wisdom—and who, after achieving perfection, chooses to remain in the world to help others in their search for perfection. The Theravada school believes that the ideal person strives to become a perfected saint ready for nirvana. In essence, the goal of Hinayana Buddhism is personal liberation, while the goal of Mahayana Buddhism is to seek liberation for all people. Both sects believe that only men can become Buddhas; women must be reborn as men before being able to become a Buddha.

By the third century, Buddhism had spread outside of India, adapting itself to local conditions within each country. Today, Mahayana Buddhism is primarily practiced in China, Tibet, Japan, Vietnam, and Korea. Hinayana Buddhism has taken hold in Cambodia, Laos, Myanmar (Burma), Sri Lanka, India, Nepal, and Thailand. Both sects of Buddhism are practiced in Malaysia, Philippines, and Singapore. A major feature of Buddhism is that the religion does not preclude belief in other faiths. As a result, in countries like China, Hong Kong, and Taiwan, people practice mixtures of religions combining elements of Buddhism with their indigenous faiths.

Zen Buddhism took its early forms in China from the fourth to the ninth centuries under the name of *Chan*, which means "meditative." It eventually was transmitted to Japan where it became known as Zen. Zen is a sect of Mahayana Buddhism that practices silent meditation in order to achieve serenity of the mind and the higher state of being. Zen rejects theology and written texts.

Confucianism

Named after the ancient Chinese philosopher Confucius, Confucianism esteems rationality and a natural sense of order. With very few rituals and no concept of a deity, Confucianism is more a moral philosophy than a religion. It preaches a social order based on strict ethical principles; promotes a polity led by educated, ethical, and wise men; and stresses "right living." Confucianism espouses strong interpersonal relationships and loyalties, ancestor worship, education, and hard work.

The name Confucius is the latinized form of the Chinese K'ung-tzu or "Master Kung." Confucius was born in 551 B.C. in the Shandung Province in China. He is believed to be the first person in Chinese history to develop a code of ethics. He and his disciples developed the Confucian philosophy in the sixth century B.C. Further development of the doctrine was influenced by Mencius (372–289 B.C.) and Hsun-tzu (313–238 B.C.). Focusing on man and society rather than God and nature, Confucian philosophy rejected all supernaturalism.

Because of the importance of duty and hierarchy in Confucianism, Confucius created a code of ethics to guide the individual in all types of social interactions. The code defined a person's specific obligations to family, society, and the state. Confucianism taught that virtue could only be attained through learning. As a result, education rather than birthright was the means for social and economic mobility. However, historically, only the wealthy could afford the required education, thus creating an indirect birthright.

Confucianism was adopted by China's scholar-official class and became the basis of political unity in China. It gradually spread to other neighboring countries. Due to its tolerance for other faiths, Confucianism thrived alongside existing religions and was influenced by the teachings of other philosophical schools, mainly Taoism and Buddhism.

In Confucianism, emperors were, determined by birth and education, with the "Mandate of Heaven" to rule their people, who in turn owed the emperor complete allegiance. The emperor was responsible for the prosperity of his people and the maintenance of justice and order throughout the realm. Natural disasters were sometimes interpreted as a sign that the Mandate from Heaven had been withdrawn.

Today, Confucianism continues to have a significant influence on society in China, Hong Kong, Japan, Korea, Taiwan, and Vietnam, as well as on a small population in Indonesia.

Hinduism

The roots of Hinduism can be traced back to the civilization that grew along the Indus River Valley in what is now modern-day Pakistan around 1500 B.C. Aryan invaders introduced their religious beliefs and practices, called Arya-Dharma, which included a caste hierarchy, to the area. But they also absorbed a number of indigenous values and beliefs. The resulting mix of Aryan and native Indian beliefs is Hinduism. As a religion based on mythology, Hinduism does not have a human founder.

Hindus believe that there is one divine principal, with many gods representing various aspects of that supreme principle. The one omnipresent god has three main physical representations: Brahma, the creator; Vishnu, the preserver or manager of the universe; and Shiva, the destroyer. Hindu statues and stories depict various gods or goddesses responsible for different characteristics such as knowledge, wealth, and good luck. Shiva, the destroyer, is probably the most powerful and often the most worshipped of Hindu gods, for the Hindus believe that out of destruction comes creation.

There are several ancient Hindu texts that articulate the philosophies of the faith. The Vedas, the oldest of Hindu sacred writings, are collections of prayers, hymns, rituals, and mythological and philosophical commentaries. There are also numerous epic stories about gods, heroes, and saints. The *Mahabharata* depicts the story of a great battle believed to have occurred in northern India. The *Mahabharata* includes the *Bhagavad Gita*, which is a poem in which the soldier / philosopher Krishna explains the duties of a true warrior to Prince Arjuna. The *Ramayana*, tells of Prince Rama's exile in the forests and his subsequent expedition to rescue his wife, Sita, from the demon-king Rawana.

Hinduism centers around the belief that all human beings go

through a series of reincarnations. Achieving freedom from this cycle depends on your fate or "karma," which is the consequence of all your thoughts and physical actions. Bad actions or thoughts result in bad karma and a lower level of reincarnation. In contrast, good deeds and thoughts will result in good karma and the eventual release from the cycle of life and ascendance to a higher form of spiritual being. Thus, one's present actions will determine one's future existence. One basic concept is that of *dharma*, "natural law," and the social and religious obligations that it imposes. Individuals are expected to play their proper role in society as determined by their dharma.

The Hindu caste system is one of the most confusing aspects of modern life, for even the most educated people appear to cling to belief in castes. The caste system was originally developed in the early stages of Hinduism by the priest class, or Brahmins, in order to make their superior position in society more permanent. Eventually the system became formalized with four distinct classes determined by birth, each with a prescribed set of rules of conduct. The Brahmins, the highest caste, are responsible for determining moral issues as well as caste rules. Brahmins are believed to be the final judges of ritual purity, which is a vital element in Hindu life. The Kshatriyas or warrior caste, the next level, are the soldier and administrator class. In most cases India's nobles were members of the Kshatriya caste. The third level are the Vaishyas, the caste that includes farmers, artisans, and people who are in business. The fourth level is the Shudras, who are the peasant and craftsman class. There is a fifth level below these four castes, the level of "the untouchables." This group, also called "the Scheduled Castes," literally have no caste and perform the most menial and degrading jobs in Indian society. Mahatma Gandhi attempted to uplift this group in society and termed them *Harijans*, meaning "children of God." In modern times, untouchables are called *Dalits*, which means oppressed or downtrodden people. Traditionally, an untouchable was literally just that, untouchable. Anyone from a higher caste who had the misfortune to have been touched by one would have to go through a series of cleansing rituals. Untouchables were not allowed near kitchens or food, temples, or other sacred places. In traditional communities, these beliefs persist.

Generally, rituals must be performed by Brahmins, although others are allowed to conduct the more simple rituals. There are rituals for all types of passage-of-life events, including birth, special birthdays, marriage, and death. There are also rituals to bless initiations and beginnings, including the opening of a new factory or office. Brahmins preside over most temples and religious organizations.

Hinduism spread to Indonesia and eventually to Bali, although the Hinduism practiced today in Bali is distinctly different from that practiced on the Indian subcontinent. Hinduism is also practiced in Bangladesh, Cambodia, Hong Kong, India, Nepal, Malaysia, Myanmar (Burma), Indonesia, Singapore, and Sri Lanka.

Islam

Islam was founded in A.D. 622 by the Arab prophet Muhammad (also spelled Mohammed) who transmitted the word of God, Allah, to his people. The followers of Islam are called Muslims. In A.D. 612 the Prophet Muhammad, born in A.D. 570, began to preach a new religious philosophy based on revelations from God. These teachings were eventually compiled into the Koran (also Qur'an), the sacred holy book of Islam. The relgion of Islam believes that Muhammad was the last, but not the only, prophet of God. The religion recognizes the previous historical messengers of God, including Abraham, Ishmael, Isaac, David, Moses, and Jesus. Muhammad's teachings were heavily influenced by Judaism and Christianity. In theory, Muslims do not believe that Muhammad founded the religion of Islam, but only restored it during the final stages of its evolution. God is believed to be the true founder of the religion.

It is believed that Muhammad's early revelations were made in response to the materialistic greed and selfish attitudes prevalent in Meccan society. After being persecuted in the city of Mecca, Muhammad relocated in A.D. 622 with his followers to the city of Yathrib, which was renamed Medina. This population of this pagan Arab city gradually converted to Islam. It was here that Muhammad was able to create a new social order. In essence, Mecca was the birthplace of Islam as a religion and Medina became the religion's birthplace as a state and a way of life.

The word *Islam*, derived from Arabic, means submission to the will of God and complete obedience to his law. According to Islam, there is one all-powerful, all-pervading God called Allah. The religion considers it a sin to believe in any god other than Allah. People are believed to be God's highest creation, although they are misled and tempted to commit sins by Satan, an evil spirit. By following the teachings of Muhammad, people can be guided to the truth. Islam believes in a heaven (Paradise) and a hell.

The Koran is believed to be the exact word of God. It dictates behavioral codes concerning the social, economic, and political aspects of life. The Koran emphasizes moral responsibility, autonomy, and the dignity of the individual. Further, it dictates strict social rules and specific courses of behavior for various social events, including marriage, divorce, death, and inheritance. In certain instances, particularly with regard to the treatment of women, what the Koran prescribes, respect and equality, and what Muslim tradition and practice have encouraged, submission and inequality, appear to be at odds. Much of the legal discrimination against women began two to three centuries after the founding of Islam when the interpretation of the faith was in the hands of extremely conservative male scholars. Because the Koran was not a complete guide, these religious scholars developed a complex set of guidelines for Muslims, known as *Shariah*, as a supplement to the Koran. The Shariah became the basis of Muslim legal and social codes and provides guidelines for every type of decision. Accordingly, the state, society, and religion became one unit.

Most Muslims perceive their religion as the foundation of all ethics, morality, and family life. Religion is intertwined with daily life and is not confined to specific times and places. Therefore, regardless of the traditional distinctions of family, lineage, class, ethnicity, and wealth, all Muslims are considered equal to one another. The focus is on a divinely guided community whose religion is expressed in ethics and justice, not personal enlightenment or salvation.

The overall aim of every Muslim is to prepare for the Day of Judgment by pursuing a just and righteous life. In practice, every Muslim has five fundamental obligations that make up the "pillars" of the religion. These five pillars of faith are: declare allegiance to Islam; pray five times daily; give a defined portion of wealth and material goods to charity; make at least one pilgrimage (*hajj*) in a lifetime to Mecca; and fast during the month of Ramadan. During Ramadan Muslims will not eat or drink from sunup to sundown, only in the early morning hours before sunrise and at night after sunset. As evidence of the practical nature of the religion, Islam exempts the very young, the old, the sick, and travelers from fasting. During one of the last three nights of Ramadan, generally believed to be the twenty-seventh day, the *Koran* was supposedly revealed to Muhammad for the first time. The end of Ramadan is followed by Id-ul-fitr, the feast of breaking the fast.

One concept of Islam that has been subject to interpretation and controversy is the notion of *jihad*, holy war. The basis of jihad is that the extension of their faith is a holy duty and struggle for all Muslims.

During his life, Muhammad concentrated on the teachings of the word of God and individual obligation. He made no provisions for his successor. As a result, a power struggle ensued in the century following his death. Various caliphs, representatives of the Prophet, emerged. The conflicting demands of political unity and religious purity, apparent in early Islamic history, caused Islam to split into two major sects, Sunni and Shiite (also known as Shia.). Both sects believe in the same basic elements of Islam, but they differ on the issue of succession. The Sunnis, the sect to which a majority of modern-day Muslims belong, believe that loyalty to the established order of Umma, the divinely inspired community, is most important and should transcend any other dissension. The Shiite believe that only a divinely inspired political leadership is worthy of a Muslim's loyalty. Most Shiites believe that only a few people have been worthy of being divine guides. They are historically loyal to Ali, the Prophet's cousin and son-in-law. The Shiite sect eventually split further over differing interpretations of succession. Sufism, often referred to as Islamic mysticism, is largely a Sunni phenomena.

Of the twenty Asian countries profiled in this book, Islam is practiced primarily in Bangladesh, Brunei, Cambodia, China, India, Indonesia, Malaysia, Myanmar (Burma), Nepal, Pakistan, the Philippines, Singapore, Sri Lanka, and Thailand.

Jainism

Although the historical origins of Jainism are poorly documented, Jain philosophy was crafted in India before the eighth century B.C., with the major developments occurring between 800 and 500 B.C. Jainism recognizes twenty-four *Tirthankaras*, or masters, who have conveyed the religion's principles. Mahavira, the twenty-fourth Tirthankara, is believed to have been a contemporary of Buddha (Siddhartha Gautama) and lived in the sixth century B.C. Little is known about the first twenty-three, but the last Tirthankara, Mahavira, "the teacher of the present age," formally founded Jainism as a religious community when he and eleven of his disciples became one of the first groups to turn against the Hindu Brahmins and the sacrificial rituals of Hinduism.

While the religion does not technically recognize any god or supreme creator, most followers of Jainism worship Mahavira and the other Tirthankaras as deities. Elaborate daily and periodic rituals are performed to honor Mahavira and his achievement of *moksha*, ultimate enlightenment. In theory, this religion preaches that divinity lives within each person and attainment of perfection can be achieved through the right belief, right knowledge, and right action. The basis of Jainism is the liberation of the soul from the bondage of earthly desires and karmic matter through human effort and purification. The Jains believe that the ultimate state of enlightenment, *moksha*, can be achieved even by ordinary people by ridding themselves of negative earthly desires such as hate, jealously, and greed.

According to Jainism, the universe is a vast organism full of life. Souls wandering the universe take forms as humans, animals, plants, or other entities. Although trapped in material things, these souls are pure and capable of omniscient knowledge and thus, all are capable of liberation. Unless a soul is liberated, the endless cycle of birth, death and related suffering will continue. Every act, physical and mental, is believed to attract karmic matter, defiling the purity and limiting the knowledge of the soul. Acts and thoughts that are prompted by desire, hate, or violence are the worst kind. Hence, Jainism preaches nonviolence to all living things, whether human, animal, or plant. Jainism believes that each present moment is "earned" by a person's actions in a former life. Further, a person's present actions will determine his or her next life. Poor conduct causes a person to be reborn as a less capable person, an animal, or even as a plant. The ultimate goal is to free oneself from the cycle of "human bondage" and discover the perfection inherent in the soul.

Jains believe that liberation is achieved through several steps: faith in the teachings of Jainism, avoiding actions that are based on desires that could harm others, ascetic practices designed to minimize the influences of karmic matter, and the ultimate cessation of all activities through meditation. Through insight and knowledge combined with the right moral conduct and actions, the soul can free itself from the cycle of births and deaths and life's related suffering and rise to the very top of the universe in a state of absolute bliss.

The Angas are a compilation of Mahavir's teachings and constitutes the core of the Jain Scriptures. There are also numerous philosophical writings compiled over the course of fifteen hundred years beginning in the fifth century B.C. There are two main sects of Jainism, Digambar and Svetambar. The Digambar sect insists on total nudity for their male ascetics, for wearing even the slightest of clothing is a form of earthly attachment. The Svetambar sect believes that clothing is insignificant and, accordingly, that nudity is an option, not a requirement. The Digambaras believe that women can only become Tirthankaras after rebirth as men, while Svetambaras believe that women can become Tirthankaras and thus should be allowed to live the monastic life. Today, Jainism is practiced primarily in India, although there is a small community in Singapore.

Shintoism

Shinto, which literally means "way of the gods," was the original religion of Japan. In its early form it was a primitive nature religion consisting of a system of beliefs and rites connected to the worship of nature deities. All forms of nature, including rivers and mountains, are associated with a deity, or *kami*. The most important deities are Father Heaven and Mother Earth, who created the Japanese islands and the rest of the deities. According to Shinto belief, Amaterasu Omikami, the Heaven-Radiant Great Divinity, was the most important of their creations. Legend holds that she was sent into the sky to become ruler over the sun. She sent her grandson down to earth, who laid hold of the islands that comprise Japan and founded an eternal dynasty. This mythological representation of the founding of Japan and the imperial lineage is a central part of Shinto beliefs.

In the fifth and sixth centuries A.D., Shintoism was heavily influenced by Confucianism, from which it adopted ancestor worship, and Buddhism, from which it borrowed various philosophical ideas and rites. In 1868 Shinto became Japan's state religion; thereafter the emperor was worshipped as a god. However, during the American Occupation of Japan after its defeat in World War II, the emperor renounced all claim to divinity. Japan is the only country that follows Shintoism.

Shintoism is polytheistic and, therefore, is tolerant of other religions and gods. The focus of the religion is on maintaining ritual purity and a high respect for nature. The various deities are worshipped through offerings, prayers, and festivals.

Sikhism

Guru Nanak (1469–1539), the founder of the Sikh religion, was born a Hindu, but became dissatisfied with the religion while he was still a teenager. He then explored Islam, but found that faith unsatisfactory as well. After experiencing enlightenment, Guru Nanak announced that God was neither Hindu nor Muslim and created a synthesis of the religious teachings of the Hindus and the invading Muslims in historical India. Sikh beliefs derive from the words of wisdom of the true Divine Guru (spiritual teacher), God, as preached by Guru Nanak and the nine gurus who followed him. The tenth Guru, Gobind Singh (1675–1708), declared that he would be the last guru and that in the future the Sikh Scriptures, called the Guru Granth or Sacred Book, would be the guru.

Guru Nanak rejected a society divided by caste or religion and substituted his belief in a humanitarian and egalitarian society. Men and women would have equal status and everyone was eligible to become a priest. Sikhs believe that God created the world and human beings to inhabit it, but that people have become too attached to the pleasures and concerns of the world and separated from God. As a consequence, people are too self-centered, which in turn leads to human suffering, including the endless cycle of death and rebirth. Sikhs believe that rituals, ceremonies, and extreme asceticism, are useless; they hold that the ultimate union of love with God can only be achieved through purification of the heart and meditation.

As a result of Islamic persecution, Sikhism became politicized. To protect the faith from the Muslim conquerors in India, Guru Gobind Singh militarized the religion and created the Pure Order

(*Khalsa*) of Men, mostly Hindus of any caste, who pledged their loyalty to the faith. To symbolize their struggle against the Muslim invaders and as a public sign of their loyalty to Sikhism, men were required to wear the five K's: uncut hair (later distinguished by a turban), comb, sword or dagger, wrist guard, and short pants. He declared a code of discipline for all Sikhs: tobacco, the eating of meat slaughtered by Muslim rituals, and sex with Muslims were all forbidden. Henceforth, all Sikh men took the name "Singh" (lion), which was traditionally an Indian name for kings, as a second name; all Sikh women, took the name of "Kaur" (princess). In India, not everyone with the name "Singh" is Sikh, but all Sikhs use the name "Singh" as either a second or family name. Sikhism is practiced primarily in India, but also in Hong Kong and Indian communities throughout Asia.

Taoism

Taoism (also spelled Daoism) arose from the philosophy of Lao Tzu (Laotse), who was born in China around 604 B.C., some fifty years before Confucius. Lao Tzu's philosophy is summarized in a book written in the third century B.C., the *Tao Te Ching* (*The Way and Its Power*). Chang Ling has been credited with formally establishing the religion in 143 B.C. By the fifth century A.D., Taoism had adopted many features of Mahayana Buddhism; for example, the organization of the priesthood and Tao rituals imitated Buddhism. The original pictogram for Tao is the "way" as well as "teaching," and the term has been used in the sense of human behavior and moral laws.

The main doctrine of Taoism is focused on the Tao, which is understood as emptiness and basis of all being. From this arose the cosmos and *yin-yang*, which in turn produced the five elements, known as *wu-hsing*, and the "ten thousand things," known as *wan-wu* which means "the all." The concept of *yin-yang* is based on opposing manifestations of the supreme ultimate, earth and heaven. The underlying premise is that all things are locked in a cyclical process. As everything reaches its extreme stage, it transforms into its opposite. Accordingly the energies of *yin* and *yang* must always be balanced. The five elements are water, fire, wood, metal, and earth. These elements refer to abstract forces and are symbols for the basic characteristics of matter.

The aim of Taoism is to preserve and increase a person's vital force by rendering the body invulnerable. Taoists use meditation as a means of preventing the deities already inhabiting the human body from leaving it, a process known as *yang-sheng*. To live a full life, a person must avoid wasting vital energy and rediscover the perfect simplicity of living naturally. The Taoist seeks to conform to the natural rhythms of universal life. Taoism teaches that people should live in obscurity and not seek glory. Those who are preoccupied with the pursuit of fame or fortune are wasting their vital forces, and thus denying themselves all hope of achieving true holiness. The aim of the Taoist is to achieve a sense of unity, simplicity, and emptiness. Taoists believe that to seek knowledge means to acquire; in contrast, to seek the Tao means to let go.

There are wide differences between the Taoist religion and the Taoist philosophy. The followers of philosophical Taoism, *Tao-chia*, strive to achieve a mystical union with the Tao through meditation and by following the nature of the Tao in thought and action. Unlike religious Taoists, the philosophical Taoists are uninterested in achieving immortality. A central feature of philosophical Taoism is spontaneous and unmotivated action.

In contrast, the Taoist religion, *tao-chiao*, focuses on the mystical side of human nature and promises physical immortality in return for faith. Taoists employ breathing techniques, alchemy, dietary rules, special sexual practices, and follow a general code of conduct in the hopes of achieving immortality. The most important ceremonies include communal fasts, collective confessions, healing sessions, and other rituals.

Today, Taoism is practiced in China, Korea, Malaysia, the Philippines, Singapore, Taiwan, and Vietnam.

Bibliography

Abegglen, James C. *Sea Change*. New York: Free Press, 1994.

Acuff, Frank L. *How to Negotiate Anything with Anyone Anywhere Around the World*. New York: AMACOM, 1993.

Ali, Abdullah. *Malaysian Protocol and Correct Forms of Address*. Singapore: Times Books International, 1988.

Asia Pacific Business Travel Guide. San Francisco: Pacific Asia Travel Association, 1993.

Axtell, Roger, ed. *Dos and Taboos around the World*. New York: John Wiley & Sons, 1993.

Axtell, Roger, ed. *Gestures*. New York: John Wiley & Sons, 1991.

Bit, Seanglim. *The Warrior Heritage: A Psychological Perspective of Cambodian Trauma*. El Cerrito, Calif.: Author, 1991.

Borthwick, Mark. *Pacific Century: Emergence of Modern Pacific Asia*. Boulder, Colo.: Westview Press, 1992.

Bunge, Frederica M. *Burma: A Country Study*. Washington, D.C.: Department of the Army, Federal Research Division, 1983.

Bunge, Frederica M. *Indonesia: A Country Study*. Washington, D.C.: Department of the Army, Federal Research Division, 1983.

Bunge, Frederica M. *Malaysia: A Country Study*. Washington, D.C.: Department of the Army, Federal Research Division, 1985.

Burbank, Jon. *Culture Shock: Nepal*. Portland, Oregon: Graphic Arts Center Publishing Company, 1992.

Choegyal, Lisa, ed. *Insight Guides: Nepal*. Hong Kong: APA Publications, 1992.

Cima, Ronald J. *Vietnam: A Country Study*. Washington, D.C.: Department of the Army, Federal Research Division, 1989.

Cooper, Robert and Nanthapa Cooper. *Culture Shock: Thailand*. Portland, Oregon: Graphic Arts Center Publishing Company, 1990.

Cragg, Claudia. *Hunting with the Tigers*. San Diego, California: Pfeiffer & Company, 1993.

Craig, Joann Meriwether. *Culture Shock: Singapore*. Portland, Oregon: Graphic Arts Center Publishing Company, 1993.

Devine, Elizabeth and Nancy L. Braganti. *The Travelers' Guide to Asian Customs and Manners*. New York: St. Martin's Press, 1986.

Doing Business in India. New York: Price Waterhouse, 1993.

Doing Business in Indonesia. New York: Price Waterhouse, 1993.

Doing Business in Korea. New York: Price Waterhouse, 1992.

Doing Business in Malaysia. New York: Price Waterhouse, 1992.

Doing Business in Taiwan. New York: Price Waterhouse, 1991.

Doing Business with Taiwan, R.O.C. Taipei, Taiwan: China External Trade Development Council, 1993.

Dolan, Ronald E. *Philippines: A Country Study*. Washington, D.C.: Department of the Army, Federal Research Division, 1993.

Encyclopedia of Eastern Philosophy and Religion. Boston: Shambhala Publications, 1994.

Eu, Geoffrey. *Insight Guides: Malaysia*. Hong Kong: APA Publications, 1992.

Finlay, Hugh, Geoff Crowther, Bryn Thomas, and Tony Wheeler. *India: A Travel Survival Kit*. Hawthorn, Australia: Lonely Planet Publications, 1993.

Fodor's India. New York: Fodor's Travel Publications, 1993.

Fodor's Southeast Asia. New York: Fodor's Travel Publications, 1993.

Fodor's Thailand. New York: Fodor's Travel Publications, 1991.

Gochenour, Theodore. *Considering Filipinos*. Yarmouth, Maine: Intercultural Press, 1990.

How to Trade with Korea: A Guide to Trade and Investment. Seoul: Korea Trade Promotion Corporation, 1993.

Keuneman, Herbert. *Sri Lanka*. 5th ed. Hong Kong: APA Publications, 1987.

Kolanad, Gitanjali. *Culture Shock: India*. Portland, Oregon: Graphic Arts Center Publishing Company, 1994.

Koller, John M. *The Indian Way*. New York: Macmillan, 1982.

LePoer, Barbara Leitch. *Singapore: A Country Study*. Washington, D.C.: Department of the Army, Federal Research Division, 1991.

Mann, Richard I. *Business in Indonesia*. Toronto: Gateway Books, 1990.

Mittman, Karin, and Zafar Ihsan. *Culture Shock: Pakistan*. Portland, Oregon: Graphic Arts Center Publishing Company, 1991.

Mooney, Paul. *Taiwan: Treasure Island*. Lincolnwood, Illinois: Passport Books, 1993.

Rearwin, David. *The Asia Business Book*. Yarmouth, Maine: Intercultural Press, 1991.

Reichschauer, Edwin O. *The Japanese*. Tokyo: Charles E. Tuttle Company, 1980.

Rigg, Jonathan. *Southeast Asia: A Region in Transition*. London: Unwin Hyman, 1991.

Robinson, Daniel and Joe Cummings. *Vietnam, Laos, and Cambodia: A Travel Survival Kit*. Berkeley, California: Lonely Planet Publications, 1991.

Roces, Alfredo and Grace Roces. *Culture Shock: Philippines*. Portland, Oregon: Graphic Arts Center Publishing Company, 1992.

Ross, Russell R. and Andrea Matles Savada. *Sri Lanka: A Country Study*. Washington, D.C.: Department of the Army, Federal Research Division, 1990.

Rowland, Diana. *Japanese Business Etiquette*. New York: Warner Books, 1985.

Rutledge, Len. *Maverick Guide to Vietnam, Laos, and Cambodia*. Gretna, Louisiana: Pelican Publishing Company, 1993.

Salacuse, Jeswald. *Making Global Deals: What Every Executive Should Know about Negotiating Abroad*. New York: Times Books, 1991.

SarDesai, D. R. *Southeast Asia: Past and Present*. Boulder, Colorado: Westview Press, 1989.

Savada, Andrea Matles *Nepal and Bhutan: A Country Study*, Washington, D.C.: Department of the Army, Federal Research Division, 1993.

Savada, Andrea Matles, and William Shaw. *South Korea: A Country Study*. Washington, D.C.: Department of the Army, Federal Research Division, 1992.

Sinclair, Kevin with Iris Wong Po-yee. *Culture Shock: China*. Portland, Oregon: Graphic Arts Center Publishing Company, 1994.

Skabelund, Grant P., ed. *Culturegrams for the 90's*. Provo, Utah: Brigham Young University, David M. Kennedy Center for International Studies, 1991.

Storey, Robert. *Vietnam: A Travel Survival Kit*. Berkeley, California: Lonely Planet Publications, 1993.

Summerfield, John. *Fodor's China*. New York: Fodor's Travel Publications, 1992.

The Wall Street Journal Guides to Business Travel: Pacific Rim. New York: Fodor's Travel Publications, 1991.

Worden, Robert L., Andrea Matles Savada, and Ronald E. Dolan. *China: A Country Study*. Washington, D.C.: Department of the Army, Federal Research Division, 1988.

Wilson, A. Jeyaratnam. *The Break-Up of Sri Lanka: The Sinhalese-Tamil Conflict*. Honolulu: University of Hawaii Press, 1988.

Wolpert, Stanley. *India*. Berkeley and Los Angeles: University of California Press, 1991.

Yin, Saw Myat. *Culture Shock: Burma*. Portland, Oregon: Graphic Arts Center Publishing Company, 1994.

Index

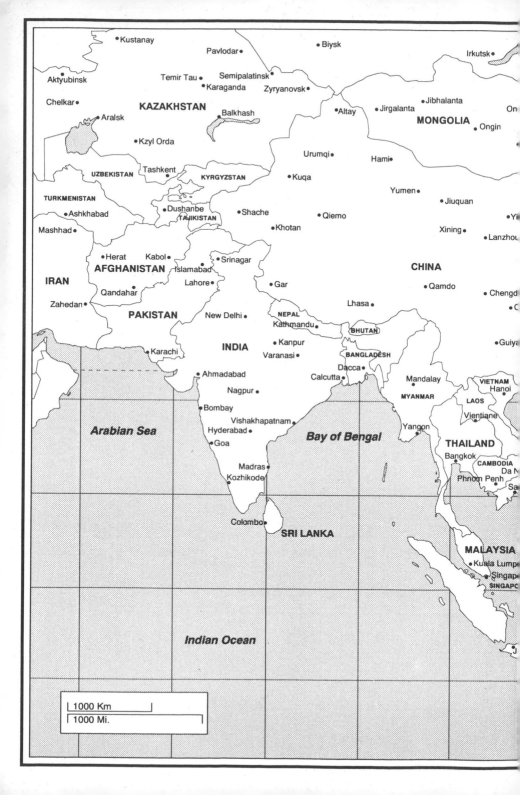